The Wiley Blackwell Reader in Practical Theology

The Wiley Blackwell Reader in Practical Theology

Edited by Bonnie J. Miller-McLemore

WILEY Blackwell

This edition first published 2019
© 2019 John Wiley & Sons Ltd.

Registered Offices
John Wiley & Sons, Inc., 111 River Street, Hoboken, NJ 07030, USA
John Wiley & Sons Ltd, The Atrium, Southern Gate, Chichester, West Sussex, PO19 8SQ, UK

Editorial Office
The Atrium, Southern Gate, Chichester, West Sussex, PO19 8SQ, UK

For details of our global editorial offices, customer services, and more information about Wiley products visit us at www.wiley.com.

Wiley also publishes its books in a variety of electronic formats and by print-on-demand. Some content that appears in standard print versions of this book may not be available in other formats.

Library of Congress Cataloging-in-Publication Data

Name: Miller-McLemore, Bonnie J., editor.
Title: The Wiley Blackwell reader in practical theology / edited by Bonnie J.
    Miller-McLemore.
Description: First Edition. | Hoboken : Wiley, 2019. | Includes index. |
    Identifiers: LCCN 2019005876 (print) | LCCN 2019021459 (ebook) | ISBN
    9781119408475 (Adobe PDF) | ISBN 9781119408499 (ePub) | ISBN 9781119408468
    (pbk)
Subjects: LCSH: Theology, Practical.
Classification: LCC BV3 (ebook) | LCC BV3 .W535 2019 (print) | DDC 230–dc23 LC record
    available at https://lccn.loc.gov/2019005876

Cover Design: Wiley
Cover Images: © HelloRF Zcool/Shutterstock, © Piyawan Tantibankul/Shutterstock

Set in 10/12pt Warnock by SPi Global, Pondicherry, India
Printed and bound in Singapore by Markono Print Media Pte Ltd

10   9   8   7   6   5   4   3   2   1

Contents

Preface and Acknowledgments

Bonnie J. Miller-McLemore

Most books, I would wager, begin with a serious underestimation of the work involved. This *Reader* was no exception. Picking classic essays for a collection seemed on first blush like an especially straightforward book project compared to most others. I honestly did not anticipate the hazards, including the risk of "epistemic violence" explored by Courtney T. Goto in an important essay in this collection. Indian feminist Gayatri Spivak uses the phrase *epistemic violence* to capture the marginalization and even obliteration of the realities of the already minoritized. Most of us commit the act of oversight in our scholarship regardless of how conscientious we are. But omission is especially egregious when it comes to a reader, even though, somewhat ironically, a reader is by definition a selection of scholarship and, consequently, inevitably exclusive.

Right upfront, therefore, I need to recognize the challenge of selection, what liberationists have dubbed the granting of "epistemological privilege" to certain voices. You will not find in this volume all that is needed to grasp contemporary practical theology. Which is, when you think about it, a good problem to have, since it suggests that the discipline of practical theology is thriving. Instead, what you will find, I hope, is a rich and fruitful basis on which to begin or to continue your hunt for what you need to know about theology as it happens up close and on the ground.

I am also sure that I made the project more difficult than necessary (a unique personality flaw). I experimented, for example, with doing individual introductions for each chapter and then, once underway, felt obliged to keep going with this plan, even as I discovered that situating the major contributions of twenty-eight authors (two of which were later eliminated to save space) felt a bit like preparing for doctoral exams. I also sought a kind of cohesiveness for the volume that is perhaps senseless and impossible in a sprawling, even purposively imprecise field like practical theology. Perhaps most time-consuming: I cut words to shorten essays, dangerously toying with other people's prized prose (an act I will avoid from here on out) in a painstaking effort to gain space for additional chapters and make chapters more readable.

In the General Introduction that follows, I describe in greater detail more substantive challenges that run beyond these personal proclivities. For now, let me say briefly how the initial enticement to compile this *Reader* arose on my way to acknowledging those to whom I am in debt.

Four years ago, shortly after the publication of *The Wiley Blackwell Companion to Practical Theology* in 2012, Rebecca Harkin, an editor at Wiley Blackwell, approached me with the idea of doing a volume that would replace *The Blackwell Reader in Pastoral and Practical Theology* published in 2000. It would not be as much work as the *Companion*, she encouraged. Since a reader would only contain previously published works, "you won't have to chase down late-running contributors." That was, indeed, an upside of this project, even if not quite the benefit that she imagined, and I remain grateful for her invitation. She has since accepted a new role within the publishing company, but her vision for what is needed in theology has been astute, and I am glad to have been a beneficiary of her knowledge and foresight. Catriona King assumed editorial responsibilities in summer 2017 and has done a superb job seeing the project through to completion. I also thank the editorial staff at Wiley Blackwell more generally, especially freelance permissions editor Beth Dufour and project editor Manish Luthra, for managing with grace and efficiency the many complicated particulars that surround a volume such as this (e.g., seeking copyright permission, overseeing abridgments).

For guidance as the *Reader* evolved, I have many people to thank. Three anonymous reviewers, solicited by the press, provided important feedback and correctives, including Jaco Dreyer who was also gracious enough to disclose his identity when I approached him for advice. I am especially grateful for my most immediate colleague at Vanderbilt, Phillis Isabella Sheppard. She is unflagging in her collegial friendship and offered incisive counsel at several crucial moments as I moved out from under a more conventional (and white) approach to the field. I also treasure the contributions of another valuable Vanderbilt colleague, the late Dale Andrews. From our first conversations on the Executive Committee of the Association of Practical Theology in 2002 to our co-teaching a seminar in practical theology in 2012 and 2016 and our final conversation in spring 2017, he taught me a great deal. He exemplified an incredible commitment to the discipline, a prophetic comfort with racial politics, and a refreshing collegial humor. I can almost hear his booming laughter in response to my quibbles and quandaries about this book ("my, my, my," as he would say). As I hope is evident in the General Introduction, I learned a lot as I went along, mostly about my oversights. Phillis and Dale helped me avoid potholes at strategic points and offered solace when I hit them.

As this suggests, Vanderbilt is a wonderful environment in which to learn, and it served as a fertile place for this work in other ways. The contributions of doctoral student and research assistant Arelis Benítez were crucial. She provided hours of support that included perceptive insights into the larger theoretical framework, potential authors, and all manner of detail such as titles and subtitles as well as an extensive facility with technology and an ability to see tasks before I suggested them. I also thank Vanderbilt University, Dean Emilie Townes, and my faculty colleagues in the Divinity School for a spring 2018 research leave and a University Research Scholar Grant that funded travel, consultation, research materials, and related assistance. It would have taken me at least another year to complete this project without this support.

Beyond school and publisher, the colleagues with whom I wrote *Christian Practical Wisdom*, Dorothy Bass, Kathleen Cahalan, James Nieman, and Christian Scharen, remain an invaluable sounding board and circle of friendship. They spoke up at several turning points, helping me discern whether to take up this work at all and then weighing in on drafts of the content and argument. Like Phillis, Dorothy and Chris suggested that the only way to move through the overwhelming decisions about what to include was a clear rationale. Kathleen's observation that internet availability makes a reader unnecessary led me to consider ways to make this volume worth its cost, such as introductory material, essays abridged for easier reading, and an overarching thread that holds the volume together and advances the discipline. I also thank Tone Strangeland Kaufman and the Norwegian School of Theology for the invitation to share my research-in-progress with a day-long doctoral seminar in Oslo in April 2017. She, along with Pete Ward and others in attendance, provided a helpful perspective from outside the United States. Several other people may not know about their influence but merit appreciation for their friendship and wisdom: Courtney Goto, Sam Lee, Carmen Nanko-Fernández, Eric Stoddart, Valburga Schmiedt Streck, Júlio Cézar Adam, Heather Walton, Claire Wolfteich, Joyce Ann Mercer, Katherine Turpin, Tom Beaudoin, Yolanda Dreyer, Lee Butler, Ryan LaMothe, Mindy McGarrah Sharp, Laine Walters Young, and Kishundra King. All the authors in the volume have had their impact, but their contributions will become obvious as you continue to read.

After thirty-eight years of marriage, I risk repeating earlier acknowledgments of my husband Mark Miller-McLemore. The major difference in my gratitude today is that, as our kids have grown and left our immediate household, he had to listen to a lot more equivocating than he probably wanted to hear, even if I still did not ask him to read anything. So, Mark, if you do read this eventually, you will know what readers far and wide have learned – that my love and appreciation for you abound.

General Introduction

Bonnie J. Miller-McLemore

Aim and Definition

The *Wiley Blackwell Reader in Practical Theology* offers a collection of landmark and pioneering essays from practical theology's renaissance as an academic discipline in the twentieth- and twenty-first century. It hopes to provide ready access to previously published resources that represent major milestones, important growing edges, and useful classificatory rubrics. In short, the *Reader* serves as a handy primer to classic scholarship in the contemporary discipline of practical theology.

The volume not only offers a bird's-eye-view of the discipline, however. The collection also shows how practical theologians have advanced a steady *epistemological insurgency* in the last several years, unsettling conventional boundaries that define where theology is located and how it is done. Unsatisfied with theology as an abstract cognitive exercise performed by an elite cadre of thinkers in academy and ecclesia, practical theologians have gradually resituated the study and practice of theology more immediately within bodies, time, action, and community. Efforts to understand "theology-in-the-midst-of-practice" gained initial momentum in the discipline in the 1950s and the 1980s, following a more general "quotidian turn" in religious studies.[1] But especially innovative contributions have emerged in the last decade as diverse scholars offer fresh approaches to the field.

The *Reader* intentionally reflects this growing diversity. Not surprisingly, therefore, many selections highlight race and racism as critical subthemes. There are additional reasons for this emphasis, however. Intolerance, xenophobia, chauvinism, ultranationalism, and coloniality remain prevailing problems of our time. In fact, in the United States and in some other countries, white supremacy and misogyny have gained an alarming level of public and political acceptability. Several essays, therefore, address residual and relentless bigotries, not only of racism but also of other oppressions and biases surrounding human difference.

Race, gender, and other differences receive attention in the *Reader* for a third and final reason directly related to the focus on theological knowledge: advances in the last few decades in critical theory, liberation theologies, and postcolonial and decolonial studies have only deepened and extended the epistemological protest already nascent in and endemic to the field's origins. In the 1950s, Latin American liberation theologians had already pointed out the limitations of Western epistemology, claiming the wisdom of grassroots movements and analyzing the pervasive impact of interest, location, material resources, and power on the construction of knowledge. Similar efforts continue today in postcolonial, decolonial, and migration studies.[2] These developments have had an ongoing influence on practical theologians, especially in recent years. In other words, this volume contains essays in practical theology that emphasize race, gender, and other differences as a result of the *Reader*'s interest in scholarly diversity, its commitment to resisting political hegemonies, and its recognition of important epistemological trends.

In this respect, it is worth noting that the *Reader* reflects in its very construction the dedication of practical theology to specific issues on the ground in the present moment. Practical theology is by definition dedicated to particularities, not comprehensiveness, which means that certain materials get privileged, and other contributions in practical theology's larger corpus get left out. A *Reader* from another historical and cultural time and place under different leadership and influence would necessarily look quite different. This observation is both an admission of limitation and an apt and honest description of practical theology's reality. A comparable collection in another discipline might expect orderly coverage; such an attempt in practical theology would defy the discipline's own definition.

In general, readers will discover in this collection an unsystematic but innovative and ever-evolving exploration of theology as more than doctrine, abstract theory about God, or critical thinking about faith; instead, these essays investigate theology as a living, breathing reality that emerges within and is powerfully shaped by what people do, feel, and say in everyday life and practice. In fact, one way to define the discipline of practical theology is by seeing it as that area of religious and theological study invested in grasping the theological meaning and relevance of the quotidian, what we might label a *hermeneutics of lived theology*.[3]

Background and Further Reflection on Definition

In the most immediate sense, the new *Reader* offers a successor to the first *Blackwell Reader in Pastoral and Practical Theology*, published in 2000, now nearly two decades old. Edited by two British Anglican authors, James Woodward and Stephen Pattison, the *Blackwell Reader*'s mix of eight reprinted and fifteen newly solicited essays successfully advanced the discipline of practical theology on the heels of its renaissance in the 1980s and 1990s. The publication marked practical theology's twentieth-century transformation, transpiring internationally, from a ministerial area devoted to preparation for ordained ministry to an intellectual enterprise embracing broader contextual concerns within congregations and society at large. Pastoral and practical theology should no longer be narrowly restricted, the editors argued, to "training for ministry in the skills… needed for practical tasks," merely the application of knowledge learned in biblical, historical, and systematic studies to ministry – a linear theory-to-practice model that presumed that the discipline has no substantive theological content of its own.[4] The book redefined pastoral and practical theology around the intersection of beliefs and practices, or to use Woodward and Pattison's words, "as a prime place where contemporary experience and the resources of the religious tradition meet in a critical dialogue."

They concluded their introduction with a sizeable list of disciplinary attributes – unsystematic, flexible, provisional, contextual, dialectical, committed, transformational, experiential, and so forth – that juxtapose the discipline to other areas and implicitly suggest the disruptive epistemological undercurrent that this *Reader* lifts up.

The current *Reader* follows but also provides a needed corrective to the original. The nearly all white, mostly male, and predominantly Protestant UK and US cast reflected the restricted origins of the discipline's 1980s renewal and fails to represent the increasing diversity among students, scholars, and professionals. Only one entry, an excerpt from Seward Hiltner's *Preface to Pastoral Theology*, appears in both *Reader*s, and Hiltner's inclusion as the sole historical figure in the first *Reader* reveals its liberal Protestant slant. The original *Reader* also blurred disciplinary boundaries between pastoral and practical theologies, defining them as interchangeable, characteristic of the 1990s and the British location of its editors, but less adequate today in Britain and elsewhere. Its commissioned chapters have become period pieces that no longer illustrate the state-of-the-art in the discipline or pivotal accomplishments for the contributors. In essence, a great deal has transpired in the last two decades, making it time for a new *Reader* with greater authorial diversity and increased clarity about practical theology's definition, parameters, and contributions. Practical theology is no longer the "diffuse and fragmented subject area" that the editors of the early *Reader* once described.[5]

The new *Reader* profits more directly from a complementary volume, *The Wiley Blackwell Companion to Practical Theology*, published in 2012. The *Companion* offers a comprehensive introduction to practical theology through fifty-six targeted essays by internationally distinguished scholars.[6] Its introduction describes intellectual and institutional developments, distinguishes practical from pastoral theology, and develops a fourfold schema for sorting through the multivalent ways in which one term, *practical theology*, gets used in different settings for distinct purposes.

Recapping historical developments that have shaped the field would duplicate material in the *Companion*, but it may be helpful to reiterate briefly definitions that are explored in more detail there. Both practical theology and pastoral theology now include more than the study of what pastors do in congregations, although both terms still get used to refer to congregational ministry and leadership. *Practical theology* is the more encompassing of the two, indicating an integrative pursuit that bridges subdisciplines and the study of lived theology in wider society more generally. It functions not only as a discipline but also as an umbrella field, just as the medical field includes a range of subspecialties. It refers to an *activity* practiced by all believers within religious communities and ordinary life; a *method* used by scholars, students, clergy, clinicians, and activists to study theology in the midst of practice; a *curricular area* in theological studies focused on the ministerial arts (e.g., care, education, worship, preaching, and so forth); and a specialized *scholarly discipline* in its own right interested in overseeing developments in all four arenas.

This fourfold definition attempts to capture the varying ways people commonly employ the term and allay confusion when the same term gets used for equally valuable but different purposes. In contrast with the mid-to-late twentieth-century era represented by the original *Reader*, practical theology today means more than the "bland shorthand mantras" that describe the discipline as interested simply in the "relationship between beliefs and practices."[7] Instead, as argued in the *Companion*, "Practical theology is a general way of doing theology concerned with the embodiment of religious belief in the day-to-day lives of individuals and communities." As such,

> Practical theology is seldom a systematic enterprise, aimed at the ordering of beliefs about God, the church, or classic texts. More often it is an open-ended, contingent, unfinished grasp or analysis of faith in action. It focuses on the tangible, the local, the concrete, and the embodied.... Its subject matter is often described through generic words that suggest movement in time and space, such as *action, practice, praxis, experience, situation, event,* and *performance....*It depends on knowledge and experience of people outside narrow areas of expertise and specialization.[8]

Finally, "in its focus on concrete instances of religious life, its objective is both to understand and to influence religious wisdom or faith in action in congregations and public life more generally."[9] In the end, as this *Reader* hopes to demonstrate, practical theology fundamentally "redefines what constitutes theological knowledge or wisdom."[10]

Rationale Behind the *Reader*

Given the wealth of resources now available in practical theology, a clear rationale to determine what to include in a *Reader* was requisite. As I've already suggested, the basic criterion for selection was *epistemological provocation*: Do an essay and scholar encourage people to reframe their presuppositions about theological knowledge, challenging theology's conventional boundaries and exploring in new ways how people know the "divine" or "transcendent" and live out their convictions?

A major epistemological reorientation appeared in the field in 1958 when Seward Hiltner, now heralded as a key forerunner by scholars in both pastoral and practical theology, insisted that the "proper study of practice would illuminate theological understanding itself." Study of practice, he argued in his *Preface to Pastoral Theology*, "leads to a body of knowledge and not merely skill or technique."[11] A couple of decades later, Rodney Hunter acknowledged his debt to Hiltner but expressed frustration that so few people grasped the radicalism of Hiltner's proposal. Hunter lamented that Hiltner himself had failed to develop the "full epistemological import" of his claim.[12] Hunter identified the effort to elucidate theology as practical knowledge as its most distinctive contribution, but he admitted that scholars in the discipline remain "in some quandary" about the "distinctive character of practical knowledge in relation to other kinds."[13] Exactly how scholars or other interested parties gain theological knowledge through practice remained unclear, and this matter has continued to elude academics and laypeople alike.

A few years ago, a coauthored book, *Christian Practical Wisdom: What It Is, Why It Matters*, refocused this discussion, beginning with a fundamental question: "Why is the very kind of knowledge that people need to live well – what we call *practical wisdom* – the least understood, the hardest to learn, and often the most devalued kind of knowledge?"[14] The book explores reasons behind practical wisdom's subjugation by abstract theoretical knowledge and ways to ameliorate and rebalance the disjuncture. A key chapter in *Christian Practical Wisdom* traces the history of how practical knowledge has evolved within the theological academy in the last half century and argues that an "important epistemological reorientation stands at the core" of practical theology's twentieth-century revival "even though this has received little notice or analysis."[15] Although the chapter is by no means an exhaustive overview, it tells a powerful story, providing a fresh account of the discipline and making a case for the epistemological insurgency that organizes this *Reader*.[16]

In a word, this *Reader* asks: What does it mean to study theology in practice? In what way do "living documents" – the primary "texts" or sources in the pastoral and practical disciplines – provide knowledge and what are the limits? How does practical knowledge compare and relate to other forms of knowledge? Is there any such thing as practical *theological* knowledge? And how does one generate "theological knowledge that does *not* surrender its practical character," as Hunter asked almost forty years ago?[17] Between 1980 and today, people have explored these questions in divergent ways.

Refinements in the Selection Principle

Ironically, the intellectual, religious, and racial bonds between authors that made possible the argument in *Christian Practical Wisdom* also restricted it. Political and scholarly developments that coincided with the publication of the book in 2016 revealed limitations triggered by the homogeneity of its authors. These same political and intellectual developments have also influenced the contents of this *Reader*.

On the wider political front, in the year after *Christian Practical Wisdom* went to press in late 2015, the United States witnessed repeated assaults and homicides of unarmed African American men, women, and children by police and vigilantes; the acquittal of those charged, especially white police; and, the 2016 presidential election. The blatant racial violence and the impediments to justice echoed centuries of abuse in a new virulent key (e.g., the 1991 Los Angeles beating of Rodney King, the 1955 beating and mutilation of Emmett Till, the US lynchings of the late nineteenth and early twentieth century, and three centuries of US enslavement). The election seemed like an endorsement of lying, violating white male bravado in its extreme. It represented a national psychic and political backlash against people of color, women, immigrants, and non-Christian foreigners that erupted out of wounded white male narcissism, lying just below the surface throughout Obama's presidential tenure but running back through the civil war, slavery, and colonial history. These developments exposed white supremacy's resiliency, raising serious questions about white responsibility for its perpetuation. Although to a certain extent these problems are unique to the United States, white nationalism and supremacist movements in the United States have had parallels in other so-called developed countries and in countries where turbulent movements for democracy struggle against brutal regimes. In short, since 2016 we have witnessed intense racial and religious schisms and antipathies around the globe.

Meanwhile, on the intellectual scene, when Willie Jennings responded to *Christian Practical Wisdom* for a book panel at the American Academy of Religion (AAR) on the heels of the 2016 election, he wondered whether there is a "form of anti-wisdom," a "white practical wisdom" that unwittingly sustains racism. Is there, in his words, a "cultivated ability to constantly refresh a sense of white racial belonging and to find ingenious ways to subvert and void every attempt to form identity that should be more determinative than whiteness"? Or, are practical theologians capable of cultivating an "antiracial aesthetic sensibility," a Christian practical wisdom that undoes the false and destructive practices of distorted racial belonging?[18] His pondering raised important questions that demanded a reorientation in the aim of the *Reader* itself: how plural are our epistemological narratives, and do they address and undo some of the more disturbing distortions in our knowing?

In the brief two years between *Christian Practical Wisdom* and this volume, other practical theologians have spoken out about the virulence of white racism and imperialism within our own discipline. "Practical theology rarely considers the perspective of those who are not white," Phillis Sheppard argues in a chapter in *Conundrums in Practical Theology*, also published in 2016, "and even more rarely allows such persons to speak for themselves." Our citation practices exemplify the problem. "We rarely include the work of people of color. Instead, we cite certain field-defining scholars and mentors over and over again. The result is that we reproduce particular perspectives" and reinforce racism in the discipline and racial injustice in society.[19]

Sheppard is not alone in her observations. In another chapter in *Conundrums*, Courtney Goto traces pervasive patterns that perpetuate subtle hierarchies and subjugations. In anthologies portraying prominent approaches to the field, such as *Opening the Field of Practical Theology*, white people do the generic chapters on primary themes (e.g., the main chapters on empirical, hermeneutical, Protestant, and Catholic practical theology), while people from non-white ethnic groups get assigned race-specific chapters. Among other problems with this distribution of labor, it puts Goto (and others similarly positioned) in the double-bind of "coercive mimeticism" in which she must either play the role of the "good" Asian American reducing racial complexity and fitting into predefined white categories or remain voiceless and unseen, furthering racial marginalization. The minoritized are expected to display their race consciousness, whereas "confessing for white theorists is neither required, nor common, nor encouraged." White theologians "rarely write confessionally in terms of whiteness," she observes, "and are not expected to articulate how their whiteness…affects their thinking, research, and writing."[20] She develops these ideas more extensively in an important field-redefining book that came out as the *Reader* went to press, *Taking on Practical Theology.*[21]

In essence, as Anthony Reddie observed during a session at the International Academy of Practical Theology in 2017, whiteness creates an "invisible, unthematized, epistemological hegemony" in practical theology.[22] Practical theologians thereby risk "becoming another face of imperializing theologizing that colonizes and homogenizes," as Carmen Nanko-Fernández had already warned five years earlier.[23] Even though most scholars in Latin@ communities see the exploration of everyday practices as essential to doing theology, white practical theologians have remained sadly oblivious of a potentially rich partnership. The obsession with method among white scholars, Nanko-Fernández ventures, has served as barrier to full participation by forcing creative thought into preconceived and limited categories and by denying "local and indigenous epistemologies."[24]

We might extend observations that Melinda McGarrah Sharp has made about cultural breaches or blunders in pastoral relationships to white scholars in the discipline of practical theology itself. All too often, she observes, when pastoral caregivers encounter another culture or context, they assume that they know what is "right."[25] But their assumptions are often grossly distorted. "Dehumanizing representations impede recognition" of other cultures and peoples in two ways, she claims – by perpetuating habits that prevent recognition of personhood and by masking the violence of imposed categories as a form of "cultural caretaking" or as "good" for others or as "good" for the discipline in practical theology's case.[26]

Notably, back in 2014, at the urging of Goto and other contributors to *Opening the Field of Practical Theology*, Tom Beaudoin and Kathryn Turpin agreed to write an unplanned but important chapter on "white practical theology" for the book. "White practical theologians have not often had to give an account of our own cultural norms and dominance," they observed. They trace how a white "proprietary spirit," ignorant of the narrowness and racialized nature of its own assumptions, has determined the categories that organize the field.[27] Of most immediate relevance for this *Reader*: Understanding this history calls for an "active rereading of 'classics'" in the discipline.[28]

Reconsidering the Classics

What essays and which scholars do we recognize as "classics"? How has the term not just preserved valuable work, but also perpetuated exclusion and discrimination? These are crucial questions to ask when compiling a *Reader*. They become even more important when investigating practical theology's epistemological contributions.

Jennings's own account of modern theology's downfall in *The Christian Imagination* shows how the dominance of scientific theory and abstract reasoning in the modern Enlightenment went hand-in-hand with Western enslavement, imperialism, and the forging of color codes around a white hegemony endorsed by Christian theology. In particular, modern theology's artificial separation of historical and systematic theology from missiology – and its ignorance about how practical theology functions on the ground, I would add – has hidden from view the interconnections between doctrinal claims and the European slave trade and expansionism.

In a powerful example that Jennings expounds, "one would be hard-pressed to find even a small treatment of Acosta in standard systematic or historical theological texts."[29] Who is José de Acosta, otherwise theologically astute readers might ask, and why does he matter? He is the Spanish Jesuit priest who brought to Lima, Peru in 1572 a Christianity indelibly mixed with white racist classification and subjugation of non-white peoples. He epitomizes the modern blending of theological categories about God with racial metaphor that displaced peoples from their homelands and then replaced previous identities of place with a hierarchical ranking by color, discounting indigenous religious knowledge and ordering intelligence by skin coloration. So, in Acosta, Jennings says, the "Augustinian-Anselmic dictum *faith seeking understanding* mutates into *faith judging intelligence.*"[30]

The modern abstraction of theology from practice – what Jennings describes as theology done at "commanding heights" – has functioned throughout modernity as a convenient device for *not seeing* lived realities, whether of race, gender, bodies, or land and animals, and this aloofness obscures "the imperialist matrix" out of which modern Christianity has grown.[31] The "immorality here lies in the loss of historical consciousness," he observes.[32] In short, Acosta "marks an epistemological crisis in the history of Christian theology" that modern theologians have willingly forgotten.[33] But, "without understanding the legacy" of Acosta, we cannot begin to understand the appearance of Peruvian Gustavo Gutiérrez's *A Theology of Liberation*, and all that it entails, three hundred and seventy-seven years after Acosta's return to Spain from Peru.[34]

So where to from here? Sheppard and others offer compelling suggestions on next steps, suggestions that this *Reader* attempts to embody. To begin, endless debates about epistemology can hide or distract us from the ethical issues that lie within and beneath them and that call for an ethical turn in our work. "Rather than pursue the epistemological question" – what do we know through our bodies, for example, or "how do actual physical bodies shape religious and theological knowledge" – scholars need to consider a more overtly ethical question: "what do raced bodies require *of* us as individuals and communities?"[35] Practical theologians have a moral mandate to tell the "truth about white racist supremacy," she says, citing M. Shawn Copeland.[36] Our complicity with silence sustains the reproduction of oppressive images and practices. In other words, to what ethical actions does our research and teaching call us? Whom do we harm and whom do we help by our scholarship?

In another chapter in *Conundrums in Practical Theology* but from a different race and global location, Jaco Dreyer moves from epistemology to ontology. Questions about epistemology require, he says, a turn to basic questions of ontology and personhood: who are we as beings in relationship to other beings?[37] This question arises from his own global and local context. He began his career in practical theology as a scientist, concerned with obtaining "objective" knowledge untainted by personal values or hidden ethical or religious assumptions. But now the problem of researcher "objectivity" has become ever more complex, raising far more radical quandaries about racism, coloniality, and the "knowledge system itself."[38] How might he, as a white Afrikaner male, address the biases that shape and distort his research in religion as a member of the "group of 'white settlers' who colonized South African and who are held responsible for [a] colonial heritage" that continues to perpetuate "vast disparities in economic power between the different racial groups"?[39] He admits his own complicity "in the marginalization of epistemologies, ontologies, and methodologies that differ from my (Western-centered) research paradigm and the ongoing racism that this entails."[40] Ultimately, given human temptation to hide from iniquity, practical theologians must consider what philosopher Paul Ricoeur labels *attestation* – a searching of our "heart of hearts" for guidance, daring to act while admitting our faults and fragility.[41]

At another AAR book panel in the shadow of the 2016 election – this one on *Conundrums in Practical Theology* – Christian Scharen makes clear the mandate that he hears from Goto, Dreyer, Sheppard, and his own conscience: "as the culture shifts from *assumed* to *conscious* white racial identity,…white practical theology must be done as a protest against white racial identity," taking seriously the violence endemic to racism and responding critically to "its own history of racialized discourse."[42] Where are we committing what Nanko-Fernández calls "racism of omission," borrowing a phrase from her colleague Gilberto Cavazos-González to describe an erasure of Latino/a theologians in practical theology?[43] And what are we and our constituencies doing about it?

As it turns out, practical theologians have distinct gifts to offer here. Scholars in practical theology have spent the last several decades developing skills of self-reflectivity and social interpretation; we have learned and practiced what it means to embody "evenly hovering attention" (Sigmund Freud's term) to ourselves and to living contexts, attending, listening, describing, and conversing at micro and macro levels; we have seldom shied away from the ethical and the normative in our research and teaching; and many of us have sustained commitment to social change and political justice as essential components of good theology.

The manner in which the contributors to *Opening the Field of Practical Theology* broached the racial conflict that emerged in their midst demonstrates the facility of practical theologians to rise to the occasion. Rather than shutting down discussion, the group found a way forward that did not resolve the problem in the volume entirely but began to address it. To the credit of the book's editors and participants, the group heard Goto's concern and searched for a response. The overall plan for the book could not be altered at the late date, but a chapter on whiteness and white practical theology could be added, a partial but nonetheless meaningful solution. That the group met face-to-face in the same setting that shaped the writing of *Christian Practical Wisdom* – on the campus of a Benedictine monastery and university where the religious order and its preservation of nature and spiritual rhythms set a crucial context for reflection and engagement – is not coincidental to this occurrence. As the authors of *Christian Practical Wisdom* attest, scholars need to find different ways of doing our research than conventional patterns of isolated individual library research. As claimed in the opening and closing chapters of *Christian Practical Wisdom*, writing together as friends in conversation and community over a longer period of time in an environment attuned to deeper transcendent meaning was itself an exercise in practical wisdom that mattered as much as the book's content.

Authorship and Organization

What are the concrete implications for authorship and voice in the *Reader*? The volume retains a place for so-called "classics," but it also invites readers to reflect on the term itself. Some of the earlier works may merit the label in their effort to make a case for practical theology's viability as an area of study for church and academy. But they also reflect the predominantly white male origins of the twentieth-century revival of the discipline, even though these same authors questioned dominant theological discourse and often found themselves at a disadvantage in academic institutions that dismissed or derided their "practical" orientation. The *Reader* also purposively highlights essays that have been overlooked or suppressed in the privileging of certain perspectives (e.g., white, male, middle class, Western etc.), but on closer look, were also definitive.

In short, the book makes two types of essays more readily accessible to a wider audience: publications that people regularly cite or recommend as representative of the discipline's rejuvenation and development; and fresh perspectives, perhaps less familiar and less frequently cited, that deepen the discipline's priorities or plow new ground. In doing so, the volume hopes to bridge two worlds that may not be entirely possible to bridge. That is, the *Reader* provides a book where people of diverse backgrounds can see themselves despite the troubled history out of which we all continue to work, while also reaching out to those in dominant but changing contexts who may not completely understand or even appreciate the diversity or the general direction that the volume heads.

Consequently, the *Reader* contains selections from the last half-century, but to honor diverse voices the majority of essays come from the last twenty years. The table of contents intentionally includes as many women as men and more people of color than white.

Although the book features US and English-language scholarship and, therefore, does not benefit from important research in other languages, the book capitalizes on the diversity of the US context itself and reflects international influences on the English-language discussion. Several authors are first- and second-generation US immigrants from other continents, and over a third of the authors come from outside the United States.

Of course, divisions and binaries of race, gender, sexuality, nationality, and so forth reflect artificial and oppressive classifications that do not adequately encompass the complexity of human subjectivity, much less the developments in practical theology. These constructions sometimes merely reify and reinforce prejudice. The United States itself is a precarious and even haunted experiment in ethnic, racial, and immigrant diversity. Indeed, *all* the US contributors are essentially immigrants even if sometimes several generations removed, some with ancestors who cruelly colonized, others with forebears brought against their will, and many with parents and grandparents who came to US shores with dreams of safety and security. However, for now at least, despite their problems and limitations, these categories of difference do some work for the volume by providing a means to mark and evaluate the distribution of power and the implementation of justice in the creation of theological knowledge,

The *Reader* is divided into two parts with the start of the twenty-first century as a turning point. The book begins in Part I with twenty-first rather than twentieth-century materials. By postponing twentieth-century readings until Part Two, the book hopes to evade two problems. A volume organized from the earliest to the most recent literature would put heavily theoretical material ahead of lively engagement with grounded practice and feature white European and European American men up front. Leading with readings from the twenty-first century allows for a more immediate encounter with diverse voices in the field. As important, the *Reader* foregrounds the heightened attention in the twenty-first century to practices and materiality – place, bodies, stuff, knowhow, and so forth. Following the precedent of *The Wiley Blackwell Companion to Practical Theology*, the *Reader* also assumes that "constitutive activities of daily life" are basic to practical theology. Practical theology "either has relevance for everyday faith and life or it has little meaning at all."[44] That said, readers who wish to understand ideas as they evolved historically may find it useful to begin with Part II.

Chapters in Part I are organized into three parts around three foci, depending on their primary emphasis: place, body, or practical know-how. This is only a rough division, however; most essays in Part I contain reflection on more than one of these themes. Chapters in each subsection of Part I and chapters in Part II as a whole are ordered chronologically by date of publication, and publication dates are retained next to titles in the table of contents and chapter headings. Knowing when an essay is published, especially with the earlier material, should help orient readers, revealing what ideas emerged in which contexts and tracing patterns in intellectual development.

Brief editorial introductions precede each entry, providing background and lifting up key contributions. These introductions list two or three additional bibliographical sources – in most cases an important publication by the author of the essay and an additional reference or two to major figures in practical theology or closely related disciplines who have significantly influenced the author and the field. These references are an important way to flag valuable scholarship that may not appear in the *Reader* but has played a pivotal role in the discipline. The references also recognize contributors who have flown under the radar as a result of biases in the discipline.

Few essays appear in their entirety. To reduce book price, allow for a few more entries, and aid in comprehension, most essays have been abridged. There are real personal and political risks in tampering with other people's scholarship. Authors treasure the words we write, and words matter greatly in voice and articulation of arguments. The abbreviations were done with as much care as possible, trying hard to retain the original flow and force of an argument. But, no doubt, vital ideas, metaphors, and stories were lost for the sake of other causes. Curious readers may wish to return to the original source to learn from the unabridged version.

Limitations

I have already noted some of the *Reader*'s limitations. The selection principle used to build the *Reader* is only one of several possible approaches. In this regard, the book represents "a" rather than "the" *Reader*, a temporary placeholder in a rich and ongoing enterprise. I am more aware now than when I edited the *Companion* in 2012 that organizing a major reference work for a discipline is a slippery slope.[45] Such works not only describe a discipline; they create and produce it, shaping prescriptive and normative expectations about definition and parameters. They may even inadvertently "solidify" rather than alleviate certain patterns of dominance, as Eric Stoddart points out in his review of the *Companion*.[46] Telling a discipline's history is always part "myth and mystery," as Friedrich Schweitzer remarks in his own attempt to recount how the first international society in practical theology began.[47] To put together a *Reader* supports and sustains a discipline, but it is also an act of political construction with all the benefits and hazards that this involves. Selecting entries is itself a privileging of voices, a playing with complicated questions of power, knowledge, and its production, influenced by all sorts of biases, from economic to systemic and personal prejudice.

Nonetheless, even though the *Reader* adopts a rationale for its selection and organization, it hopes to "open up" rather than close off the field, to borrow a phrase others have used. Disagreements with the approach chosen here should be greeted, as Dreyer recommends, not as a "stumbling block" or a reality to be "passively tolerated," but as an opportunity for valuable interchange in a naturally "dialogic pluralist" discipline.[48] Acknowledging that a volume of twenty-some chapters does not represent all that has transpired in the discipline will not solve the limitations, but it at least recognizes the provisional status of this work.[49] It needs to be read alongside other important overview texts that have redefined the discipline in recent years.[50] Each essay's citations as well as the editorial introductions and suggested reading offer a path to other valuable reading.

Three further limitations represent matters that cannot be resolved within these pages and, hence, growing edges for future scholarship: Western/northern hegemony; progressive Christian biases; and Christian-centrism. First, the book does not include important non-English-language scholarship – not just from Europe, Asia, and North America, but also from the global south, including developments that critique Western practical theology from a postcolonial and decolonial perspective. English has become the lingua franca for market and academy, but it has this honor, we need to remember, because of colonial and capitalist imperialism. The lack of classic texts from the southern hemisphere is partially due to difficulties scholars face in getting published without support and capital from Western and northern institutions and colleagues who inhabit more advantageous economic positions. This situation reflects a problematic underside of neoliberal capitalism and its inequities that has received initial exploration by US pastoral theologians and needs further redress.[51]

Second, the *Reader* retains an unapologetic preference for a progressive Christianity that values tolerance, inclusivity, and social justice. Greater inclusion of minoritized groups indirectly brings greater representation of other Christian traditions and approaches, including Catholic and evangelical, but it does not fully counter the omission of more conservative perspectives. Fortunately, there are now anthologies available, published in the last few years, especially in Catholic practical theology. These books provide excellent sources for tracing practical theology's earlier sources in sacramental, spiritual, liturgical, and social justice literature.[52] There are no similar collections of evangelical practical theology, but single-author publications have begun to address the vacuum.[53] Readers are encouraged, once again, to follow the footnotes to contributions beyond the *Reader.* Of further note in this regard, in 2015 the late Dale Andrews and Robert Smith published the first anthology of *Black Practical Theology*, compiled around a unique approach of inviting three groups – pastoral leaders, practical theologians, and scholars from other theological disciplines – to talk with each other about prominent issues for black churches.[54]

Practical theology may have gained intra-Christian plurality as a discipline, but the *Reader* does not address a third growing edge – the Christian-centric biases of the discipline and the need to attend to non-Christian religions and their interests related to practical theology (with the exception of Chapter 14 by Michel Andraos). Beaudoin is right when he argues that "practical theology (in the USA) has been too untroubled in its Christian confidence," excluding both the "religious other" and "nonaffiliated/ secular persons" in its reclamation of religious practices as a source of knowledge.[55] Some of the more exciting explorations in practical theology are happening around interreligious engagement.[56] But religious pluralism and diversity have languished "in the background," causing Kathleen Greider to urge practical theologians, in her entry in *The Companion* over five years ago, to broaden the religious parameters of the discipline.[57] The *Reader* is, in actuality, a *Reader* in *Christian* practical theology. When more scholarship with religiously diverse representation appears in practical theology, it will be a sign that the current *Reader* has outgrown its shelf life.

It is precisely practical theology's interest in location and place that makes these oversights disconcerting and urges us toward a fuller international, intra-Christian, and interreligious participation. By the very nature of the discipline, practical theology is committed to the non-elite and the underrepresented when it comes to practical theological knowledge. Indeed, practical theologians are deeply interested in the material "conditions for the production of practical theological scholarship: who gets to do it and how," as Beaudoin notes.[58] Thus, omission of non-Christian perspectives, diversity within Christianity, and voices from the southern hemisphere or other parts of the world bothers us more than it might scholars in other disciplines.

Practical theology is an odd discipline whose own disciplinary principles render it precarious: it critiques the academy of which it strives to remain a part; it undermines its own efforts to systematize its definitions and parameters by stressing the indefinable and elusive nature of its subject matter; it defines its discipline by insisting that only interdisciplinary research can address the subjects that it tackles; it demands intense descriptive attention to grounded realities but argues for normative action; it studies religious faith but recognizes that the fulsome nature of faith eludes objective academic measures and standards; and it locates theological reality indelibly in the present and the local, making every contribution immediately outdated and surpassed by the next development, the new context. The list could go on.

The *Reader* as a whole, therefore, largely reflects what Brazilian scholar Júlio Adams aptly calls "moving theology." Different than a "rational, formal, closed theology" based on "paradigms such as interpretation and textuality," moving theology "puts us in touch with that which pulsates in the life of a human being," "life in its rawness, fragmentariness."[59] Or, to borrow Heather Walton's words, practical theologians often attempt "to speak about what is deeply sensed but not easily articulated," about "'things' about which direct speech seems currently not possible." We turn to alternative "forms of expression" – poetic, artistic, aesthetic, fictive, elegiac, passionate, liturgical, prayerful, and so forth – because these forms seem "more able to bear the weight that theology does not seem able to carry at the current time."[60]

What you have in your hands, in other words, is a fluid and necessarily limited period piece; it is where time stopped in 2017 – the date at which the *Reader* was compiled. Nonetheless, the *Reader* hopes to serve, for a limited stint at least, as a valuable resource in practical theology and in related cognate disciplines. In one way or another, each essay seeks fresh ways of grappling with theology-in-practice, challenging the status quo in theology by reimagining practical theological knowing in fresh ways. By bringing together and reprinting groundbreaking essays in practical theology, the *Reader* creates a one-volume resource that marks the discipline's accomplishments and makes key materials available to interested parties in university, seminary, and ministerial contexts. As such, it hopes to support new learners and advanced scholars who desire a basic orientation to fundamental and cutting-edge resources in the discipline, while also creating space for new voices in the century ahead.

Notes

1 See Thomas A. Tween, "After the Quotidian Turn: Interpretive Categories and Scholarly Trajectories in the Study of Religion Since the 1960s," *The Journal of Religion* 95, no. 3 (2015), 361–385.
2 See, for example, Chapters 19 and 21 in this volume as well as books such as Clodovis Boff, *Theology and Praxis: Epistemological Foundations* (Maryknoll, NY: Orbis, 1987); Walter D. Mignolo, *Local Histories/Global Designs: Coloniality, Subaltern Knowledges, and Border Thinking* (Princeton, NJ: Princeton University Press, 2000); Ada María Isasi-Díaz, "Lo Cotidiano: A Key Element of Mujerista Theology," *Journal of Hispanic/Latino Theology* 10, no. 1 (2002), 5–17; Manuel A. Vásquez, *More than Belief: A Materialist Theory of Religion* (New York: Oxford University Press, 2011); and Ada María Isasi-Díaz and Eduardo Mendieta, eds., *Decolonizing Epistemologies: Latina/o Theology and Philosophy* (New York: Fordham, 2012). See also Thomas Groome's brief analysis of the epistemological influence of critical theory and liberation theology in *Christian Religious Education: Sharing Our Story and Vision* (San Francisco: Jossey-Bass, 1980), 165–177 and *Sharing Faith: A Comprehensive Approach to Religious Education and Pastoral Ministry* (New York: HarperCollins, 1991), pp. 72–84.

3 To define and underscore the discipline's hermeneutical focus on *theology*, this phrase modifies words used by some international scholars, *hermeneutics of lived religion.* See for example R. Ruard Ganzevoort, "Forks in the Road when Tracing the Sacred: Practical Theology as Hermeneutics of Lived Religion," Presidential address delivered at the International Academy of Practical Theology, Chicago, March 8, 2009, http://citeseerx.ist.psu.edu/viewdoc/summary?doi=10.1.1.489.9830, accessed July 3, 2017; Wilhelm Gräb, "Practical Theology as a Religious and Cultural Hermeneutics of Christian Practice," *International Journal of Practical Theology* 16, no. 1 (2012), 79–92.

4 James Woodward and Stephen Pattison, "Preface," in Woodard and Pattison, eds., *The Blackwell Reader in Pastoral and Practical Theology* (Oxford: Blackwell Publishers, 2000), xiii. This definition appears throughout Pattison's work and reflects the influence of a pivotal 1972 essay by Scottish Presbyterian pastoral theologian Alastair Campbell, "Is Practical Theology Possible?" *Scottish Journal of Theology* 25, no. 2 (1972), 217–227, also reprinted in Woodward and Pattison, *Blackwell Reader*, 77–88; and David Tracy's correlational method. See Tracy, "A Correlational Model of Practical Theology Revisited," in Edward Foley, ed., *Religion, Diversity, and Conflict* (Berlin: Lit Verlag, 2011), 49–61.

5 Woodward and Pattison, "Preface," xiv; Pattison and Woodward, "An Introduction," 4; see also 6, 13.

6 Bonnie J. Miller-McLemore, ed., *The Wiley Blackwell Companion to Practical Theology* (Malden, MA: Wiley Blackwell, 2012). For an overview, see especially Miller-McLemore, "Introduction: The Contributions of Practical Theology," 1–20.

7 Miller-McLemore, "Contributions," 17.

8 Miller-McLemore, "Contributions," 14, emphasis in the original.

9 Miller-McLemore, "Contributions," 14.

10 Miller-McLemore, "Contributions," 17.

11 Seward Hiltner, *Preface to Pastoral Theology* (Nashville: Abingdon, 1958), 47, 218. See Chapter 17 in this volume.

12 Rodney J. Hunter, "A Perspectival View of Pastoral Theology: A Critique of Hiltner's Theory," *Journal of Pastoral Care* 4, no. 4 (1985), 20.

13 Rodney J. Hunter, "The Future of Pastoral Theology," *Pastoral Psychology* 29, no. 1 (1980), 65. See Chapter 20 in this volume.

14 Dorothy C. Bass, Kathleen A, Cahalan, Bonnie J. Miller-McLemore, James R. Nieman, and Christian B. Scharen, *Christian Practical Wisdom: What It Is, Why It Matters* (Grand Rapids, Eerdmans, 2016).

15 Bonnie J. Miller-McLemore, "Disciplining: Academic Theology and Practical Knowledge," in Dorothy C. Bass et al., *Christian Practical Wisdom: What It Is, Why It Matters* (Grand Rapids, Eerdmans, 2016), 176.

16 This chapter initially served as a lead essay for the *Reader* but was cut to save space.

17 Hunter, "Perspectival View," 31, 32, emphasis in text.

18 Willie Jennings, unpublished remarks, panel on *Christian Practical Wisdom*, American Academy of Religion, November 22, 2016.

19 Phillis Sheppard, "Raced Bodies: Portraying Bodies, Reifying Racism," in Joyce Ann Mercer and Bonnie J. Miller-McLemore, eds., *Conundrums in Practical Theology* (Leiden: Brill, 2016), 222. See Chapter 10 in this volume.

20 Courtney T. Goto, "The Racialized 'Zoo,'" in Joyce Ann Mercer and Bonnie J. Miller-McLemore, eds., *Conundrums in Practical Theology* (Leiden: Brill, 2016), 129.

21 See Courtney T. Goto, *Taking on Practical Theology: The Idolization of Context and the Hope of Community* (Leiden: Brill, 2018). See also Chapter 16 in this volume.

22 Anthony Reddie, "The Invisible Spectre of Whiteness: Disembodied White Human Subjectivity and Epistemological Hegemony," unpublished conference paper, International Academy of Practical Theology, Oslo, Norway, April 24, 2017. See also Anthony G. Reddie, ed., *Black Theology, Slavery, and Contemporary Christianity* (New York: Routledge, 2016).

23 Carmen Nanko-Fernández, "Held Hostage by Method?: Interrupting Pedagogical Assumptions – Latinamente." *Theological Education* 48, no. 1 (2013), 36. See also Chapter 5 in this volume.

24 Nanko-Fernández, "Held Hostage by Method?," 39.

25 Melinda McGarrah Sharp, *Misunderstanding Stories: Toward a Postcolonial Pastoral Theology* (Eugene, Oregon: Pickwick, 2013).

26 Sharp, *Misunderstanding Stories*, 93.

27 Tom Beaudoin and Katherine Turpin, "White Practical Theology," in Kathleen A. Cahalan and Gordon S. Mikoski, eds., *Opening the Field of Practical Theology: An Introduction* (New York: Rowman and Littlefield, 2014), 251, 254.

28 Beaudoin and Turpin, "White Practical Theology," 268.

29 Willie James Jennings, *The Christian Imagination: Theology and the Origins of Race* (New Haven: Yale University Press, 2017), 115.

30 Jennings, *Christian Imagination*, 108.

31 Jennings, *Christian Imagination*, 7.

32 Jennings, *Christian Imagination*, 115.

33 Jennings, *Christian Imagination*, 70.

34 Jennings, *Christian Imagination*, 115.

35 Sheppard, "Raced Bodies," 244–5, her emphasis.

36 M. Shawn Copeland, "Racism and the Vocation of the Christian Theologian," *Spiritus* 2 (2002): 21, cited by Sheppard, "Raced Bodies," 245.

37 Jaco S. Dreyer, "Knowledge, Subjectivity, (De)Coloniaity, and the Conundrum of Reflexivity," in Joyce Ann Mercer and Bonnie J. Miller-McLemore, eds., *Conundrums in Practical Theology* (Leiden: Brill, 2016), 103.

38 Dreyer, "Conundrum of Reflexivity," 98.

39 Dreyer, "Conundrum of Reflexivity," 96.

40 Dreyer, "Conundrum of Reflexivity," 97.

41 Dreyer, "Conundrum of Reflexivity," 106 citing Paul Ricoeur, *Philosophical Anthropology: Writings and Lectures,* Volume 3, eds. Johann Michel and Jérôme Porée, trans. David Pellauer (Cambridge: Polity Press, 2016), 267.

42 Scharen, unpublished response to a panel on *Conundrums in Practical Theology,* American Academy of Religion, November 19, 2016, his emphasis.

43 Carmen Nanko-Fernández, *Theologizing en Espanglish: Context, Community, and Ministry* (Maryknoll, NY: Orbis, 2010), 21–22. See Gilberto Cavazos-González, "Racism of Omission," March 4, 2011, *Spiritualitas: On the Study of Christian Spirituality* – sobre el estudio de la espiritualidad cristiana, http://spiritualitas. edublogs.org, accessed March 15, 2018.

44 Miller-McLemore, "Contributions," 7.

45 See Bonnie J. Miller-McLemore, "The Hubris and Folly of Defining a Discipline: Reflections on the Evolution of *The Wiley Blackwell Companion to Practical Theology,*" *Toronto Journal of Theology* 29, no. 1 (2013): 143–174.

46 Eric Stoddart, *Advancing Practical Theology: Critical Discipleship for Disturbing Times* (London: SCM Press, 2014), 109–110.

47 See Friedrich Schweitzer, "The Beginnings of the International Academy of Practical Theology," on the International Academy of Practical Theology website, http://www.ia-practicaltheology.org/history/, accessed June 19, 2017. See also Bonnie J. Miller-McLemore, "A Tale of Two Cities: The Evolution of the International Academy of Practical Theology," *HTS Teologiese Studies/Theological Studies* 73, no. 4 (October 2017).

48 Jaco Dreyer, "Practical Theology and Intradisciplinary Diversity: A Response to Miller-McLemore's Five Misunderstandings about Practical Theology," *International Journal of Practical Theology* 16, no. 1 (2012), 49.

49 As an example of an omission that deserves noting, see Pamela Couture's book, *We are Not All Victims: Local Peacebuilding in the Democratic Republic of Congo* (Zürich: Lit Verlag, 2016). Couture's book contains a fascinating chapter on her epistemological meditations as she recounts the peacemaking activities in the Congo (pp. 1–22). That she was so careful about ways of knowing exemplifies the argument of the *Reader* that many practical theologians remain sensitive to questions of the construction of knowledge in theology.

50 See, for example, *The Wiley Blackwell Companion to Practical Theology*, *Opening the Field of Practical Theology*, and sources cited below in notes 51, 52, and 53.

51 Several scholars in US pastoral theology have taken up this task. See, for example, Cedric C. Johnson, *Race, Religion, and Resilience in the Neoliberal Age* (New York: Palgrave Macmillan, 2016); Bruce Rogers-Vaughn, *Caring for Souls in a Neoliberal Age* (New York: Palgrave Macmillan, 2016); and Ryan Lamoth, *Care of Souls, Care of Polis: Toward a Political Pastoral Theology* (Eugene, Oregon: Cascade, 2017). See also Stoddart, *Advancing Practical Theology*.

52 See, for example, James Sweeney, Gema Simmonds, and David Lonsdale, eds., *Keeping the Faith in Practice: Aspects of Catholic Pastoral Theology* (London: SCM, 2010); Claire E. Wolfteich, ed., *Invitation to Practical Theology: Catholic Voices and Visions* (New York: Paulist, 2014); and Claire E. Wolfteich and Annemie Dillen, eds., *Catholic Approaches in Practical Theology: International and Interdisciplinary Perspectives* (Leuven: Peeters, 2016).

53 See, for example, Mark J. Cartledge, *Practical Theology: Charismatic and Empirical Approaches* (Eugene, OR: Wipf and Stock, 2012) and *Meditations of the Spirit: Interventions in Practical Theology* (Grand Rapids: Eerdmans, 2015); Andrew Root, *Christopraxis: A Practical Theology of the Cross* (Minneapolis: Fortress, 2014); and Pete Ward, *Introducing Practical Theology: Mission, Ministry, and the Life of the Church* (Grand Rapids: Baker, 2017).

54 Dale P. Andrews and Robert London Smith, Jr, eds., *Black Practical Theology* (Waco: Baylor University Press, 2015). See also Chapter 1 in this volume.

55 Tom Beaudoin, "Why Does Practice Matter Theologically," in Joyce Ann Mercer and Bonnie J. Miller-McLemore, eds., *Conundrums in Practical Theology* (Leiden: Brill, 2016), 12.

56 See, for example, Edward Foley, *Theological Reflection Across Religious Tradition: The Turn to Reflective Believing* (Lanham, Maryland: Rowman & Littlefield, 2015); and Pamela Couture, Pamela McCarroll, and Nevin Reda, "Reforming Spaces for a Postcolonial Inter-religious Practical Theology: Pedagogical Reflections," paper presented at the International Academy of Practical Theology, Oslo, Norway, April 24, 2017. There is also literature in more specialized spheres of ministry, especially in spiritual care, such as Daniel S. Schipani, ed., *Multifaith Views in Spiritual Care* (New York: Pandora, 2013) and John R. Mabry, *Spiritual Guidance Across Religions: A Sourcebook for Spiritual Directors and other Professionals Providing Counsel to People of Differing Faith Traditions* (Woodstock, Vermont: Skylight Paths, 2014).

57 Kathleen J. Greider, "Religious Pluralism and Christian-Centricism," in Bonnie J. Miller-McLemore, ed., *The Wiley Blackwell Companion to Practical Theology* (Malden, MA: Wiley Blackwell, 2012), 454.

58 Tom Beaudoin, Response to *The Wiley Blackwell Companion to Practical Theology*, America Academy of Religion, San Francisco, November 13, 2011. See also his *Consuming Faith: Integrating Who We Are with What We Buy* (Lanham, MD: Sheed & Ward, 2003).

59 Júlio Cézar Adams, "Moving Theology: Perspectives of Practical Theology as Hermeneutics of Lived Religion in Brazil," paper posted for the International Academy of Practical Theology, Oslo, Norway, April 20–4, 2017, 8. Now available through the Conference Series, *Reforming Theology: The Politics of Body and Space*, eds., Auli Vähäkangas, Sivert Angel, and Kirstine Helboe Johansen, https://iapt-cs.org/ojs/index. php/iaptcs/article/view/57, accessed May 13, 2019.

60 Heather Walton, *Writing Methods in Theological Reflection* (London: SCM Press, 2014), xii, 161. See also Chapter 8 in this volume.

Part I

Twenty-First Century Practical Theology: Places, Bodies, Know-How

Section I

Places

1

Bridging Black Theology and Folk Religion (2002)*

Dale Andrews

Introduction

The *Reader* honors the contribution of the late Dale Andrews by putting his essay in a prime position. Distinguished Professor of Homiletics, Social Justice, and Practical Theology at Vanderbilt University, he died in his mid-fifties as the *Reader* was coming to fruition, leaving a rich legacy of research on prophetic and pastoral preaching and apprenticeship pedagogy for others to cultivate.

If the *Reader* were organized chronologically, this entry would appear in the middle on the heels of "classics" from the twentieth century that contributed to the discipline's rebirth. In some ways, this excerpt from the penultimate chapter of Andrews's 2002 book, *Practical Theology for Black Churches: Bridging Black Theology and African American Folk Religion*, fits well in that context. He is one of the first African Americans to locate his work squarely within the discipline. Practical theology defined the nature of his work as a churchman in the African Methodist Episcopal Zion Church and a scholar with a unique interdisciplinary doctorate in homiletics and pastoral theology with David Buttrick and Liston Mills at Vanderbilt University. He found in practical theology the ideal means by which to explain the wider *telos* of his scholarship, which reached across several practically oriented disciplines. His monograph grew out of his dissertation, completed in the late 1990s, and Don Browning is one of the sources in practical theology that he cites in a chapter otherwise devoted to Old Testament scholarship on covenant and prophecy. A few years later, however, during a panel at the American Academy of Religion, Andrews observes that Browning is too ensconced in the "Western cultural mainstream" to fit Andrews's orientation. Indeed, Andrews's demand that practical theology attend to "black religious folk life" marks this entry as definitive.

Hence, even as Andrews's essay belongs with twentieth-century classics, it also has an essential place in Part I. Encouraged by a third Vanderbilt faculty, black studies scholar and ethicist Victor Anderson, who questioned the monolithic characterization of "the black church" by theologians such as James Cone, Andrews offers his own incisive critique of black academic theology from a practical theological perspective. He negotiates

---

*Original publication details: Dale P. Andrews, "Prophetic Black Theology in Covenant," pp. 106–28 from *Practical Theology for Black Churches: Bridging Black Theology and African American Folk Religion* (Louisville: WJK, 2002).

The Wiley Blackwell Reader in Practical Theology, First Edition. Edited by Bonnie J. Miller-McLemore.
© 2019 John Wiley & Sons Ltd. Published 2019 by John Wiley & Sons Ltd.

this challenge with characteristic wisdom and finesse marked by his notorious humor. While pointing out the perverted ideology of white racism, he also laments colleagues who denigrate black spirituality as provincial, otherworldly, and too focused on internal needs. He wants to "reground" black liberation theology, done primarily in academic settings, in a prophetic framework that is "more convergent with religious folk life in African American churches." In contrast to those who use the term *folk life* pejoratively, he reclaims it as a crucial way to get at "ways of knowing" ignored by black scholars. The full nature of liberation cannot be comprehended outside its covenantal place within the spiritual setting of the church. In fact, liberation and social justice are "acts of worship" that only reach their full potential alongside ecclesiastical practices like confession, repentance, and forgiveness. In short, Andrews demands an "alternative consciousness" that refuses to separate worship from intellectual debates.

In this essay and throughout his work, Andrews is an inveterate model of integrative thinking and action, standing passionately at the juncture of preaching and pastoral care, prophetic and pastoral ministry, personal faith and social justice, and even between black and white communities in his own orientation and relationships. In all these spaces and places, he strove to serve as the ultimate mediator and bridge across difference, debate, and discrimination and, in doing so, met his vocation.

Suggested Further Reading

- Dale P. Andrews and Robert London Smith, Jr, eds., *Black Practical Theology* (Waco: Baylor University Press, 2015).
- Edward P. Wimberly and Anne Streaty Wimberly, *Liberation and Human Wholeness: The Conversion Experiences of Black People in Slavery and Freedom* (Nashville: Abingdon Press, 1986).

***

Black theology stands in the biblical prophetic traditions. The accent on liberation characterizes its prophetic voice. Black theologians contend that black churches have forgotten this historical interpretation of the gospel message. Rejecting the predominance of the refuge function of black churches, black theologians appeal to the immediate responsibility of socioeconomic and political freedom for African Americans. They contend that the refuge function has become antithetical to the practical drive for liberation. In the revolutionary language of the Black Power Movement, black theology makes liberation the principal agenda for black church ministry. The central ideas behind the campaign of black theology have been black identity and sociopolitical liberation by any means deemed necessary. Black churches have embraced these principles but largely remain opposed to the conditions or means set by black theology. This rift between black churches and black theology has grown due to the pervasive disparagement of the refuge image of the Church. Black theology pitches its prophetic voice in this derision of black religious life and the ideal of liberation ethics.

Both black theologians and black church leaders profess to fill the prophetic office. Yet they find little common ground beyond shared visions of wholeness and freedom. What follows is a review of just how black theology and black churches respectively operate within the prophetic traditions. The first task is to understand and evaluate black theology's appeal to the classical use of prophetic consciousness. The second task is to review black churches' appeals to a covenantal theology of prophetic inspiration. Each appeal appears to suffer from myopic and polarized attention to the functional relationship between religious life and social justice. Though each critique offers redress of the respective prophetic traditions utilized by black theology and black churches, a third task is to build a bridge for developing a common prophetic office between them. Reader-response criticism offers a method for developing the prophetic office, which accents the experiences of religious life in encountering and interpreting biblical traditions. My ultimate goal is to reground the liberation ethics of black theology in a prophetic role more convergent with religious folk life in African American churches.

Prophetic Consciousness and Black Theology

When speaking of prophetic consciousness, a person may easily assume that one is dealing with a special mind-set that originated with the Hebrew prophets. Such an argument, however, risks too many generalities. Instead, prophetic consciousness places particular emphasis on the guiding images and sacred mission of the classical prophets within the religious folk traditions. The biblical prophets did not receive their call to prophetic ministry outside of a religious culture. In fact, the religious culture among the Israelites was central to the prophetic ministry. Therefore, it seems necessary to begin with the prophets' own orientation toward the religious life of the Israelites.

Walter Brueggemann suggests that the task of prophetic ministry was to proclaim and nurture an "alternative consciousness" oriented toward a "newness" in relating to God, the religious community, and humanity.[1] This "newness" was usually seen as a corrective to the consciousness of the dominant culture. Immediately, however, questions should arise regarding how one identifies the dominant culture. Certainly, prophetic communities had been part of the dominant culture as well as marginalized by the dominant culture. The relationship between the prophetic community and the dominant culture throughout the history of the Israelites was a complex one. The classical prophets of the Hebrew Bible extended across the preexilic, exilic, and postexilic periods of Hebrew history.[2] Each age was characterized by a distinctive social consciousness balanced between identification with the dominant culture and subjugation under another dominant culture. Even in the ages of subjugation, prophetic consciousness also addressed the principal disposition of their own religious subculture. In either situation, a prophetic or alternative consciousness critiqued the contemporary social order and directed it toward socioreligious reform.[3]

Prophetic black theology acknowledges this twofold responsibility in presenting a "newness" in the consciousness of black religious life. First, black theology addresses the needs and concerns of a people who live under an oppressively dominating culture. Yet black theology also directs its voice toward the dominating culture. The latter address frequently becomes the primary focus of its prophetic voice, simply because of the priority given to sociopolitical interests. In either case, however, black theology calls for social accountability. In this vein, it points to an alternative consciousness within the black community. The distinction lies in religious meaning, which informs both macro and micro levels of social relationships.

A prophetic alternative consciousness is not an independent ideology. By independent ideology I refer to an isolation of the secular order of life from a religious worldview.

Religious life in the prophetic tradition does not isolate secular matters. Actually, the religious culture of the Israelites was all encompassing.[4] Yahweh was therefore involved in all aspects of the world. Humanity not only had a stake in this divine activity but shared in it as well.[5] How persons conducted themselves in public and private matters could not be detached from their religious understanding of human relationships and their relationship with Yahweh.[6] Prophetic consciousness rooted self-identity in this relationship to Yahweh. Similarly, a prophetic black theology cannot isolate black public life from the context of black religious consciousness.

The idea that prophetic alternative consciousness involved the interrelatedness of private and public life raises important implications for the prophetic office. The central context of the prophetic traditions was Israel's or Judah's relationship to Yahweh, and therefore human relationships as well. What actually constituted the content of prophecy is more difficult to pin down. Modern culture commonly reduces prophecy to predictions of the future. The directive of alternative consciousness, however, dictated the contemporary historical period as the focus of prophecy. Future prophecy was best understood within the contemporary historical interpretation of religious and public life.[7]

Another common reduction of the prophetic traditions occurs in the area of social action. Any narrow identification of prophetic concern should raise some misgivings. One should resist a simplistic coupling of prophetic consciousness and social action. Brueggemann is careful to equate social action with more normative understandings of pastoral ministry and acts of worship. He contends that prophetic alternative consciousness is a far more "radical" notion than a social action agenda implies.[8] From within the earliest biblical prophetic traditions, however, Brueggemann concedes that the claims upon human justice and liberation are given radical viability when held by an oppressed "intentional community" of faith.[9] The religious life of that community also becomes a foundation and point of address in prophetic social concern.

Black theology suggests that God's will for freedom is the primary bearing for marginalized people. A dominating oppressive culture will obviously find other qualities of biblical religion most germane. The conflict between central interpretations of prophetic consciousness then becomes a difficult platform for black theology. Social justice significantly predominates in prophetic communication to the oppressive culture as well as the marginalized community. Black theology must also unmask oppression or domination within its own tradition as well. The challenge for black theology lies in conditions of mutuality between social action and religious piety. Prophetic consciousness does not treat religious piety aside from social consciousness per se, but rather insists upon their mutuality.[10] Therefore, the newness called for by an alternative prophetic consciousness does not create a new religion. Newness envisions alternative realities for the deceptions of the dominating culture.[11]

Neither alternative consciousness nor its prophetic newness is an independent enterprise. The prophet does not communicate secular notions of social morality, but rather speaks from divine conversation between the religious community and its historical or social context.[12] Hence, prophetic intention abides in the discernment and declaration of God's desires within the human situation. The prophet engages the human situation with the divine perspective.[13]

Abraham Heschel points out that interpretations highlighting the passion for social justice among the prophets often identify the tradition as a religion of morality.[14] Black theology's disparagement of contemporary black spirituality indicates a similar under-standing of the prophetic. To the contrary, however, the prophetic traditions place justice within an intimate affair between God and humanity. In this relationship God is ultimately defined by neither social justice nor liberation alone. Justice and liberation stand in reflexive relationships with such other defining religious principles as repentance, mercy, grace, and forgiveness. Consequently, Heschel places the prophetic traditions under the discernment of divine pathos.[15] I believe that within the divine pathos of the prophetic, black theology may begin to discern just how black churches view their own spirituality. This is not to say that the churches do not require a prophetic corrective from black theology. My desire is to reposition black theology within the religious life of black churches, where black theology can develop a mutual understanding of revelation for its prophetic message.

Prophecy indicates God's communication or revelation.[16] God is the initiator. The prophetic experience is God's communication not only to the prophet, but to the life of an intentional faith community. It is not human correction. In what he calls *anthro-potropism,* Heschel describes the prophetic experience as "a sense of being pursued."[17] Anthropotropic experiences by their very nature are not sustained as isolated events. They occur in some relation to humanity turning to God. Heschel identifies these turning events in our worship practices as *theotropism.*[18] Though Heschel characterizes theotropism in priestly or pastoral ministry, the strength of his argument lies in the dialogical relationship between anthropotropic and theotropic experiences. Both experiences sustain the prophetic tradition. He explains:

> Anthropotropism finds its supreme expression in prophecy; theotropism, in psalmody. Characteristic of the former is the election or the call that comes to a prophet from above; characteristic of the latter is repentance and conversion. One must not assume, however, that both types are mutually exclusive. The existence of the prophet, for example, is sustained by both kinds of events. And conversion, the stmcture of which is theotropic, is often accompanied by an anthropotropic experience.[19]

The gulf stretching between black theology and black churches betrays the necessary relationship between anthropotropic and theotropic experiences. Black theology disparages the predominance of the refuge function in black churches. The refuge image of black ecclesiology, it is charged, abdicates its social responsibility as defined by the liberation ethics of black theology. In contrast, black churches view the refuge function within the convergence of anthropotropic and theotropic experiences in religious life. This perspective is best illustrated by the central roles that conversion experiences, personal salvation, and religious piety have assumed in black religious life and church ministries. Though black theology correctly challenges the churches' neglect of social responsibilities in prophetic ministry, its critical assessment of the refuge function lacks attention to anthropotropic-theotropic interpretations of black religious piety.

In making a political ideology of liberation its primary point of departure, or making it a priori to spiritual or emotional liberation, black theology has made an unsuccessful attempt at redefining black religious life. I have argued that a neglected evaluation of the impact of American individualism in religious folk life has been a major factor in this failure. Black theology has focused on anthropotropic condemnation of religious folk life in black churches. Though this move is not without precedence, black theology's recourse completely subordinates theotropic religious life to the interests of anthropotropic judgment. *The chasm exists because the relationship between prophetic judgment and religious life becomes intentionally ordinal. In effect, the broken continuity that black theology seeks to correct in black churches actually remains, though in the platform of black theology it is inverted.*

Black churches also have been blind to the disruption that American individualism causes in the convergence of anthropotropism and theotropism. As a response to social powerlessness, black churches adopted theotropic campaigns of spiritual salvation, moral purity, and institutionalism in trying to overcome the perverted ideology at the core of racist practices. Black churches perceive such efforts within the convergence of liberation and refuge, or anthropotropism and theotropism, respectively. However, I maintain that the evolution of American individualism in black religious culture disrupts the social efficacy of their ecclesial praxis. Theotropic events have indeed marked the predominance of the refuge function within black churches. Therefore, for the prophetic office, this juncture remains a critical point of exploration in assessing the inefficacy of the Church as refuge and the loss of its prophetic liberation ethics. A covenant model of ecclesiology would facilitate this exploration.

Covenantal Theology, Prophetic Inspiration, and Black Churches

The biblical traditions of prophecy did not seek to introduce unprecedented doctrines about God. The prophetic traditions were rooted in the covenantal relationship between Yahweh and the Israelites.[20] Yet religious life under the covenants was not limited to personal worship. Social justice was integral to covenantal theology. Both the community's and the individual's relationship to Yahweh held direct implications for social and interpersonal relationships among the Israelites. The prophets relied heavily on the mutuality between religious life and Yahweh's moral law. The authority or justification of moral life was not independent of God's will and sovereignty.[21] A similar mutuality was found between personal piety and communal worship. Community worship maintained the importance of individual devotion but certainly could not neglect the socioethical demands of the covenants.[22] Therefore, the basis of social ethics was grounded in the religious cult of the covenants.

The prophets redressed the breach of covenantal law in the lives of the Israelites. The foundation of social morality rested in the ethics of covenantal law. The prophets urged adherence to covenantal law. However, the prophets did not function as legal reformers.[23] Their concerns are best viewed in the context of the religious culture. The prophets did not permit the Israelites to stratify or to separate personal religious piety and social ethics. Each required the other. Obedience to the covenants, and therefore to Yahweh, required both.

Understanding the relationship between personal piety and social ethics holds significant implications for black theology and black churches. It obliges black theology to recognize the appropriate infrastructure for its prophetic judgment upon black churches. Liberation, itself, does not singularly constitute the covenant relationship with God. Liberation and the religious worship of Yahweh are mutually dependent.

Covenantal theology ties these together so intricately that liberation and social justice themselves must be considered acts of worship.[24] The prophetic task, then, of black theology is in reestablishing its liberation ethics within the pastoral praxis of black churches. The personal spirituality common to contemporary black religious life is not rejected by the biblical covenant traditions. A spirituality that lacks attention to social justice is the point of redress. Therefore, the covenant traditions present an important biblical source of prophetic inspiration in black theology and black churches.

Relating the prophetic office of black theology to the biblical covenant tradition immediately presents a dilemma. Just which biblical covenant should serve as the referential authority for black ecclesiology? The traditional covenant model of black ecclesiology, of course, will be the focus of prophetic inspiration. Here, however, the difficulty is in determining the biblical covenant most apropos for guiding black theology in this venture. The two most prevalent choices in prophetic biblical literature are the Mosaic (Sinai) covenant and the Davidic (Zion) covenant.

Not surprisingly, many churches regard these covenants in a fluid progression of Israelite history. Little attention is given to the geographic and historical divisions of the northern and southern kingdoms of Israel and Judah. Biblical scholarship, however, holds the two covenants as distinctive traditions.[25] The Mosaic covenant reflects a tradition of protest within the social and theological development of intentional communities of faith. The Davidic covenant emerges out of a tradition of triumphant political consolidation substantiated by a theological vision.[26]

The allure of bilateral theological interpretations is understandable. Strong relationships between the two covenant traditions do exist. Biblical scholar Jon Levenson suggests that the Sinaitic tradition of covenant renewal and the Zionistic tradition of royal dynasty do coexist theologically in biblical literature.[27] He convincingly argues that Sinai covenant traditions were, in part, assumed into the Zionistic traditions.[28] This argument, however, does not advance a common interpretation of the two covenant traditions. Even where there exists good evidence of the influence of the Sinai covenant during the times of the exilic and postexilic prophets, the royal tradition of the Davidic covenant endured as the immediate authority. The royal tradition emphasized Yahweh's unwavering commitment to the nation through the Davidic lineage. Although the Davidic covenant marks a major transition in prophetic literature, there is no suggestion by the prophets that it actually replaces the Sinaitic covenant.[29] Levenson asserts that nothing exempts the Davidic dynasty from adherence to the Sinaitic covenant.[30] In fact, when the classical prophets address the monarchical dynasty, they refer to the neglect of covenantal (Mosaic) law.[31]

The proclamation of the Sinai covenant is given in Exodus 19:3–8. Based on what Yahweh did in the liberation of the Israelites from Egypt, a special covenant relationship was formed.[32] The focus of the Sinai covenant lies within the moral character of the relationship between Yahweh and the Israelites. The authority of the covenant is Yahweh's sovereignty as evidenced by divine acts in the Exodus event, which include the Sinai experiences. Both parties of the covenant, Yahweh and the Israelites, accepted certain responsibilities. However, the relationship was not a partnership between equals.[33] The Israelites accepted conditions of obedience to Yahweh under compliance to the terms of the covenant. The Decalogue in Exodus 20:2–17 and Book of the Covenant in Exodus 20:22–23:33 provide the basic contents or stipulations. These covenant stipulations became commandments and laws.

Adherence and defiance held consequences in the blessings and curses of Yahweh, respectively. Prophetic traditions constructed a theology of Israelite history based upon interpretations of adherence or defiance of the covenant.[34] Due to the moral emphasis within covenantal law, one begins to perceive the reasoning behind prophetic inspiration. Prophecy was riveted upon the moral sensibilities of the Israelites. According to Levenson, "Israel was able to develop a coherent correlation between experience and morals, especially public morals, the relationship between [a person] and [his or her] neighbor."[35] The covenant was not limited to codes of ceremonial or personal worship. As mentioned above, personal and social morality were held in the same regard as ceremonial acts of worship. The covenant decreed these ethical social obligations to be integral to religious life or, more accurately, worship.[36]

The moral agency of the Sinai covenant community was tied to its Exodus liturgy. The Sinai covenant forged an alternative community whose ideology was based upon liberation from oppression.[37] This community would be unlike the sociopolitical systems of their former oppressors in Egypt, as well as distinctive from the Canaanite order of society. It would be insufficient to argue that the alternative consciousness of this community was simply the monotheistic worship of Yahweh. The covenantal worship of Yahweh made moral claims upon Israel's faith identity. The correlation, then, between covenant and morality weighed directly upon prophetic inspiration.

Directly associated with the moral accountability of the covenant community, prophecy's liberation ethics plays a prominent role. The Sinai tradition itself, along with the covenant's stipulations for its recitation,[38] relies upon the Exodus event of liberation. The Exodus story not only marks God's relation to these oppressed people, but also unifies previously fragmented family clans and tribes into a community of Israelites.[39] Since the covenant is grounded in the liberation of the Israelites, their new alternative community is evidenced by the liberation ethics present in their own social interactions.[40]

Despite the formation of covenant communities out of liberation experiences shaping religious life, the question still remains, Is liberation the ultimate character of the Sinai covenant? Brueggemann argues that covenant theology models a different relationship to God as well as mediating social life. It serves as a guide in repudiating social exploitation in the cause of social justice.[41] Herein lies the substance of liberation. Liberation directs the community's own social practices and even social reorganization. Liberation is not limited to Israel's emancipation. The Exodus event and the covenant require the social practices of a liberating justice as well. Covenantal liberation therefore engages in repentance and social reform.[42] Liberation is an appropriate voice of prophetic inspiration. However, it must serve as an impetus for social morality dictated by a unique relationship to God. Within this understanding, liberation is misunderstood when lifted to the ultimate expression of God's covenant with humanity. Liberation is indispensable and even primary. Yet it must operate within, and not above, the greater ends of God's will for human relationships. Repentance and reform become the integral visions of liberation. [...]

Therefore, prophetic inspiration actually placed social justice within a covenantal understanding of religious life.

[...]

A pivotal phenomenon in the Israelites' historical self-awareness is the liberating activity of Yahweh in the Exodus event. Liberation alone, however, did not constitute ultimate knowledge of Yahweh. [...] Freedom in itself was not the goal. [...] The Sinai covenant defined the responsibilities of freedom in religious and social life. [...]

Covenantal theology developed as the prophets related the responsibilities of freedom within an intentional alternative community molded by Yahweh.[43] [...] In fact, the covenant and the relationship with Yahweh precluded "autonomous freedom."[44] Biblical liberation invoked covenant in social ethics and the worship life of the community.[45] [...] Hence, within Israelite historical self-awareness, and therefore covenantal theology, liberation was more accurately understood within an integral relationship with repentance and social reform, inseparable from the religious folk life of worship.

[...]

The Davidic covenant would ultimately supplant the predominance of the Sinai covenant, but it could not ignore it. [...]

Although much earlier than the exilic period, the Solomonic reign is most illustrative of the problems produced by the Davidic dynasty confronting covenantal theology. Solomon's grand achievements spawned oppressive social conditions. Solomon's kingdom had lost much of the "alternative consciousness" raised by the prophetic voice of the Mosaic covenant.[46] Solomon was primarily concerned with the solidification of kingship under the Davidic dynasty. Even the completion of the Jerusalem temple would serve such ends. Solomon achieved excessive wealth with an oppressive social system. Oppressive social policies were able to endure due to the wealth of the controlling class. The concurrent control of religious leadership and social class granted divine authority to the role and will of the king."[47] Thus the actual freedom and voice of God became part of the king's reign itself. The traditional role of the prophet was effectually undermined. And the king, his court, and the controlling class monopolized interpretations of well-being, justice, and religious sanction.[48]

Prophetic discernment realigned from a Mosaic "alternative consciousness" to this royal consciousness of the Davidic dynasty. The Davidic covenant became the embodiment of social and religious order endowed with a far more centralized power of interpretation.[49] Monarchical solidification displaced religious leadership.[50] Prophetic concern, therefore, intensified over the myopic perception of the monarchy, the imposed conditions of injustice, and the subjugation of covenant obligations. Prophetic judgment against the monarchy pronounced the violation of God's will and sovereignty. With the centralization of political, religious, and ethical power in the monarchy, prophetic judgment declared social righteousness as the divine will for the state. The static shape of institutional religious leadership had become an earmark of the royal dynasty and led to its ultimate rebuke under prophetic inspiration.[51]

[...]

[...] Prophetic inspiration still carried over the repentance and reform message from the Sinai tradition. However, covenantal theology centered repentance and reform within God's will and activity on behalf of reconciliation. [...]

This consciousness in prophetic inspiration cannot be adequately defined by liberation per se. Rather, liberation functionally remains an initial scope of prophetic inspiration, but does not consume its field of view or its ultimate vision. In short, *prophetic inspiration moves liberation from its historical metanarrative (the Exodus event) into a covenantal theology that disallows the preemption of, or detachment from, repentance, reform, and reconciliation.* It reorients the relationship between the historical metanarrative and its meaning in an intentional alternate community. *Prophetic inspiration, thereby, operates under the objective of practical theology, interpreting revelation for; but also from within, the life of the faith community.* This sense of the prophetic office has characterized the reticence of black churches to accept fully the critical judgment of black theology.

The covenant model explores the historical development of black ecclesiology in ways quite helpful to the prophetic consciousness of black theology. Black churches have developed the prophetic inspiration of repentance and reconciliation but relegate reform predominately to individual, spiritual inspiration. Unfortunately, black theology's answer commits the reverse offense. Covenantal theology and the covenant model of black ecclesiology may still prove helpful in developing the prophetic office between black theology and black churches. The final task is to root this prophetic office within contemporary religious life of African American churches.

Prophetic Practical Theology

Practical theology is particularly concerned with praxis in Christian ministry. It is not merely an application in systematic or constructive theology. Instead, practical theology defines the theological grounds and methods for the church's mission, presence, and practice of ministry.[52] The liberation ethics of black theology does offer an important hermeneutic for prophetic inspiration. However, the oppositional dialectic method of black theology does not meet the functional demands of practical theology. While a dialectic methodology may prove useful to argue one's theology, it does not provide the necessary tools for a praxis-oriented enterprise. A methodology suited to the development of black practical theology is critically absent from black theology. Such a methodology is necessary for black theology to become the prophetic voice it seeks to be for black churches.

For black theology, prophetic consciousness has focused on the content of judgment and liberation. Attempts to root itself within the antebellum traditions of black churches have been unsuccessful in identifying with contemporary African American folk religion. Black churches, in turn, have also failed to establish a prophetic office that reforms religious praxis to respond to the challenges of black theology. A covenant model of black ecclesiology offers a source of accountability for prophetic inspiration as a corrective for the often costly predominance of refuge spirituality in religious praxis.

The covenant traditions do suggest a heuristic methodology well suited to the tasks of practical theology. That methodology is observable in reader response criticism. Reader response criticism heightens the significance of the reader in the encounter with biblical texts. The effects of a biblical text on the reader become part of the process of interpretation, rather than simply the results of it. Meaning cannot be established apart from the text's life in the reader.[53] Instead, meaning develops in the process or interaction between the text and the reader.[54] Within reader response criticism, the reader creates meaning out of this interaction. Many connections and breaches are possible between the text, the traditions of interpretation, and the reader. The point is that the reader creates meaning from the encounter with the text. Reader response criticism is, therefore, an ongoing process.[55]

The development of the covenant traditions constructed and reinterpreted both the historical conditions and biblical criteria in the formation of faith identity, mission, and ministry. The prophetic office accented the voices of revelation and interpretation. Prophetic interpretation worked within the religious life of the faith community to reinterpret covenant traditions within the changing historical context. Similarly, prophetic practical theology moves beyond initial interpretations to explore the reevaluation and redefinition of praxis within the churches' biblical traditions. A covenant model of black ecclesiology is particularly helpful insofar as it encompasses the same biblical traditions through which black theology makes its prophetic claims. The prophetic office of black theology, however, must work with the faith identity of black churches in their encounter with the biblical traditions and historical interpretation. This type of process features the significant events of reader response criticism.

There is biblical precedence for a similar process of reader response criticism.
[...]
[...] The Davidic covenant could not simply ignore the authority of the Sinai tradition. In fact, prophetic inspiration held the Davidic dynasty directly responsible to Mosaic law as God's new covenantal vassal. However, in the reconciliation of the surviving remnant, the prophetic tradition transferred the promises and responsibilities of the Davidic covenant directly to the people themselves.[56]

What I find particularly helpful in reader response criticism is the emphasis on "meaning as a function"[57] in the interpretation of biblical revelation. The role of the reader, the effects of a text, and the receiving-responding activities that can occur in a community of faith move the process toward reform.[58] Interpretation can be driven by social experiences and folk wisdom.[59] What is received in a tradition or heard in response to a text becomes a strong, deep factor in meaning making within a community of faith. I call this process "hearer-response criticism."[60]

In hearer-response criticism, oral culture or folk traditions communicate meaning in their historical contexts as part of an ongoing process. The notion may be easier to perceive if we recall that the prophetic office originally produced oracles to be heard and received in religious folk communities. The participation of the community is evident in the meaning-making process among those who inherited these oral folk traditions. I believe this participation in meaning making reflects the role of the community in black ecclesiology and African American religious folk traditions. [...] Oral traditions in African American churches function to interpret religious experience as well as accommodate new interpretations and new experiences into the ongoing life of the community. Similarly, the dynamic potential of hearer-response criticism may be seen in the historical shaping of prophetic traditions in relation to folk wisdom traditions.
[...]
One of the better examples of hearer-response criticism and the prophetic office is the work of Womanist theology, wherein the deconstruction of theological and ideological traditions is part of a larger process of creating new modes and methods of inquiry and religious praxis.[61] Hearer-response criticism offers a mode and method of prophetic redress already familiar to African American religious communities, even in the stark reality of its neglect.

Black theology must recognize there are social forces that produce prophets[62] and ecclesial praxis as well. In fact, the prophetic outcry of the early black theology project was as much a product of the social forces of a revolutionary age as it was the response to racism or any neglectful response among black churches. Hearer-response criticism capitalizes on the reader-response process by pressing us beyond the notion that biblical revelation is a matter of location and extraction of content or truth.[63] Of course, the risk comes in forms of subjectivism or relativism. Yet the desire is to consider the actions and context, which include time and place, that are involved in responding to a text.[64] These considerations undergird the "continuing" interpretations of any religious community.[65] The effort to overcome the risks of relativism lie in the pursuit of coherence among the multiple potential readings or hearings.[66]

Covenantal theology can function as a practical theology standing in the biblical prophetic traditions. The Sinai and Davidic covenants were two principal covenants for the biblical prophets. In them, prophecy claims its referential authority. The covenants serve as points of reference in understanding God's will for Israel. Obedience, judgment, grace, and salvation converge to comprise a practical theological interpretation of history and divine revelation. The immediate implications for God's covenant people are liberation, repentance, reform, and reconciliation. To isolate any one component as the preemptive indication of the prophetic tradition disrupts the full revelation of God's will for humanity. For black theology, the theme of liberation alone can neither adequately characterize God's self-revelation in the prophetic agency of the Hebrew Bible, nor sufficiently comprise a practical theology for African American religious praxis. The prophetic voice of black theology has neglected the relationship of liberation ethics to the folk life of black churches. The covenantal theology of the biblical prophetic traditions cultivates interdependence among liberation, repentance, reform, and reconciliation. I contend that hearer-response criticism of a covenant model of black ecclesiology offers a constructive framework for black theology to establish a truly prophetic voice within black churches. Liberation ethics can make prophetic demands upon black religious folk life. But within a covenantal practical theology the prophetic tradition places liberation ethics in mutual interaction with repentance, reform, and reconciliation.

When liberation is held in this context, it functions prophetically from within the religious community. Appeals to heroic history, common in black theology, limit the prophetic to the authority of the tradition. A prophetic practical theology speaks from the tradition but struggles from within the dynamics of faith operating in religious folk life to reorient the Church toward its calling as an "intentional alternative community."

Notes

1 Walter Brueggemann, *The Prophetic Imagination* (Philadelphia: Fortress Press, 1978), 13.
2 Brevard S. Childs, *Biblical Theology of the Old and New Testaments* (Minneapolis: Fortress Press, 1992), 158, 161–4, 171.
3 Brueggemann, *The Prophetic Imagination*, 13–14.
4 Gerhard von Rad, *Old Testament Theology: The Theology of Israel's Historical Traditions*, trans. D.M.G. Stalker (London: Oliver & Boyd, 1962), l:152–3.
5 Ibid.
6 Ronald E. Clements, *Prophecy and Covenant, Studies in Biblical Theology* (Naperville, IL: Alec R. Allenson, 1965), 16–17.
7 von Rad explains that even when the prophets refer to the future they are, in fact, deeply concerned with the past. The prophets viewed themselves, in their present ages, as standing in pivotal turning points in Israelite history. See von Rad, *Old Testament Theology: The Theology of Israel's Prophetic Traditions*, trans. D.M.G. Stalker (London: Oliver & Boyd, 1965), 2:299
8 Brueggemann, *The Prophetic Imagination,* 28.
9 Ibid., 29.

10 Yehezkel Kaufmann, *The Religion of Israel: From Its Beginnings to the Babylonian Exile*, trans. Moshe Greenberg (New York: Schocken Books, 1972), 158–60, 345. Kaufmann emphasizes that the treatment of moral and religious sin together uniquely distinguishes the classical prophets from the historical books of the Hebrew Bible. The historical books view Israel's sin primarily as idolatry, marked frequently by a preoccupation with ancient Eastern customs. Although Kaufmann's work in Jewish theology has been criticized as reductionistic, his position on the mutuality between religious piety and social justice in prophetic consciousness is substantiated by other biblical scholars. Brueggemann posits two major trajectories emerging from the covenant traditions that extend into prophetic consciousness. These trajectories are social justice and religious purity. [...] See Walter Brueggemann, *Theology of the Old Testament: Testimony, Dispute, Advocacy* (Minneapolis: Fortress Press, 1997), 187–93, 677–9.

11 Brueggemann, *The Prophetic Imagination*, 49.

12 Abraham J. Heschel, *The Prophets* (New York: Harper & Row, 1962), 1:x.

13 Ibid., 1:24. 14.

14 Ibid., 1:218.

15 Heschel, *The Prophets*, 1:217–19.

16 Ibid., 2:216–17.

17 Ibid., 2:220.

18 Ibid.

19 Ibid., 2:222.

20 Clements, *Prophecy and Covenant*, 16.

21 Gerhard von Rad, *God at Work in Israel*, trans. John H. Marks (Nashville: Abingdon Press, 1980), 185–6.

22 Clements, *Prophecy and Covenant*, 86, 99.

23 Ibid., 79–80.

24 Ibid., 99–101.

25 Walter Brueggemann, *A Social Reading of the Old Testament: Prophetic Approaches to Israel's Communal Life*, ed. Patrick D. Miller (Minneapolis: Fortress Press, 1994), 13–14.

26 Ibid.

27 Jon D. Levenson, *Sinai and Zion: An Entry into the Jewish Bible* (New York: HarperCollins, 1985), 187–217.

28 Ibid., 199, 206.

29 Ibid., 99.

30 Ibid.

31 Brueggemann, *Theology of the Old Testament*, 197.

32 Levenson, *Sinai and Zion*, 24–6.

33 Ibid., 26–30.

34 Ibid., 55.

35 Ibid.

36 Clements, *Prophecy and Covenant*, 75.

37 Brueggemann, *A Social Reading of the Old Testament*, 267.

38 Levenson, *Sinai and Zion*, 29.

39 Brueggemann, *A Social Reading of the Old Testament*, 268.

40 Ibid., 64.

41 Ibid., 61.

42 Ibid., 61–4.

43 John J. Collins, "The Exodus and Biblical Theology," *Biblical Theology Bulletin* 24(1995): 156.

44 Brueggemann, *Theology of the Old Testament,* 200.

45 Kathleen S. Nash, "Let Justice Surge," *The Bible Today* 31 (Sept. 1993): 266.

46 Brueggemann, *Prophetic Imagination,* 30–32.

47 Ibid., 34.

48 Ibid., 36–37.

49 Ibid., 39.

50 Walther Eichrodt, *Theology of the Old Testament*, trans. J.A. Baker (Philadelphia: Westminster Press, 1961), 451.

51 Ibid., 454–6.

52 Edward Farley, "Practical Theology, Protestant," in *Dictionary of Pastoral Care and Counseling,* 934. See also Don S. Browning, *A Fundamental Practical Theology Descriptive and Strategic Proposals* (Minneapolis: Fortress Press, 1991), 8–9, 55–7. Browning argues that all theology properly conceived is fundamentally practical theology. He distinguishes specific theological attention to Church praxis as strategic practical theology, which involves a practice-theory-practice methodology.

53 Jane P. Tompkins, ed., *Reader-Response Criticism: From Formalism to Post Structuralism* (Baltimore: John Hopkins University Press, 1980), ix.

54 Wolfgang Iser, "Interaction between Text and Reader," in *The Reader in the Text: Essays on Audience and Interpretation*, ed. Susan R. Suleiman and Inge Crosman (Princeton: Princeton University Press, 1980), 109.

55 See Wolfgang Iser, "The Reading Process: A Phenomenological Approach," in *Reader-Response Criticism,* ed. Tompkins; also, Stanley E. Fish, "Literature in the Reader: Affective Styles," in *Reader-Response Criticism,* ed. Tompkins.

56 von Rad, *The Message of the Prophets,* 239–40.

57 Carl R. Holladay, "Contemporary Methods of Reading the Bible," in *The New Interpreter's Bible* (Nashville: Abingdon Press, 1994), 1:144.

58 Ibid., 143–44.

59 James Earl Massey, "Reading the Bible as African Americans," in *The New Interpreter's Bible,* 1:157–8. Here Massey relies heavily on Vincent L. Wimbush, "The Bible and African Americans: An Outline of an Interpretative History," in *Stony the Road We Trod: African American Biblical Interpretation,* ed. Cain Hope Felder (Minneapolis: Fortress Press, 1991).

60 This term emerged from critical dialogue with biblical scholar and colleague Eugene March. The notion of hearer-response criticism attempts to draw critical correlation between the reader-response process and oral culture

61 Katie Geneva Cannon, *Katie's Canon: Womanism and the Soul of the Black Community* (New York: Continuum Publishing Co., 1996), l37f.

62 Ferdinand E. Deist, "The Prophets: Are We Heading for a Paradigm Switch?" in *The Place Is Too Small for Us,* ed. Gordon, 596.

63 Edgar V. McKnight, "Reader-Response Criticism," in *To Each Its Own Meaning: An Introduction to Biblical Criticisms and Their Application*, ed. Steven L. McKenzie and Stephen R. Haynes (Louisville, Ky.: Westminster John Knox Press, 1999), 230.

64 Ibid., 232–3.

65 Ibid., 235.

66 Edgar V. McKnight, *Post-Modern Use of the Bible: The Emergence of Reader Oriented Criticism* (Nashville: Abingdon Press, 1988), 234.

2

Mapping Latino/a Practical Theology (2004)*

Allan Figueroa Deck

Introduction

This chapter showcases one of the first comprehensive overviews of developments in practical theology in the Catholic Latino/a context. The essay first appeared in a 2004 issue of *Theological Studies* alongside five other articles on Latino/a ministry. Distinct from the other contributors, however, Allan Figueroa Deck, a Jesuit priest who studied Latin American Studies and missiology at St. Louis University and Gregorian University, situates his remarks squarely within practical theology.

This entry is also distinct from others in the *Reader* in defining practical theology primarily in terms of the church. *Place* in this essay is the church broadly defined and, more specifically, the growing presence of Latinos/as in the Catholic Church, what Deck calls the "second wave" in his 1989 book. He adopts a correlational and liberation-ist approach, turning to the pastoral circle of see-judge-act articulated by Joe Holland and Peter Henriot in 1983 and widely used among Catholic educators. But he considers these ideas within a new place, the context of Latino/a faith and ministry. So, on one hand, he challenges the "clerical paradigm" that locates all authority in the ordained leaders (often "not Hispanic") and argues for greater recognition of lay responsibility. But, on the other hand, he raises an important criticism of practical theology, sug-gesting that its bent toward correlation and liberation has obscured the necessary grounding in a "more explicit…Christian vision" directly connected to a "nuanced con-cept of evangelization." The latter does not refer to Christian conversion, however; it entails three moves – infiltrating the cultural and secular world (inculturation), seeking economic and political justice (liberation), and reaching out to other Christians and religions (ecumenical and interreligious dialogue).

Deck's Catholic commitments lead him to perceive the growth of Latino/a Evangelicals and Pentecostals as a problem rather than an opportunity. However, his essay offers at least four corrections to theological knowledge that are important for the *Reader*: First, he insists that scholars in the discipline of practical theology grapple with the growing Latino/a presence in the church and academy. Second, he argues that doctrinal

Original publication details: Allan Figueroa Deck, "A Latino Practical Theology: Mapping the Road Ahead," pp. 275–97 from *Theological Studies* 65:2 (2004).

proclamations about justice and interreligious dialogue are insufficient when they do not make their way into practice. Third, he underscores the value of emotive expression and the love of mystery and ritual within popular religion and challenges definitions of religion that make the "serene, orderly, rationalistic" religion of the middle class the standard bearer. Finally, he laments the superficiality of claims about multiculturalism among church officials who still fail to honor "each and every culture." As he concludes, "Latino/a Catholicism offers some fascinating possibilities" precisely because of its strong orientation toward "an affective, symbolic, and ritual search for meaning rather than a dry, rational-cognitive, or fundamentalist one."

Suggested Further Reading

- Allan Figueroa Deck, *The Second Wave: Hispanic Ministry and the Evangelization of Cultures* (Mahwah, NJ: Paulist, 1989).
- Joe Holland and Peter Henriot, *Social Analysis: Linking Faith and Justice* (Maryknoll, NY: Orbis, 1983).
- Casiano Floristán, *Teología Práctica: Teoría y Praxis de la Acción Pastoral*, 5th ed. (Salmanca, España: Ediciones Sígueme, 2002).

***

The transformation of US Catholicism from a community of predominantly European ancestry to one of Latin American origin is now well underway. Essayist Gregory Rodríguez has written about the "Mexicanization" of American Catholicism.[1] In many US church quarters today just as in civil society at large, there is more awareness and even acceptance of this ecclesial and societal sea change brought about by immigration in general and by Latin American immigration in particular. The US Census for 2000 confirmed the predictions of an earlier decade to the effect that Latinos/as would become the largest US minority. That census also confirmed what observers had been noting throughout the decade of the 1990s, namely, the significant presence of Latinos/as in virtually every part of the United States. That presence is no longer a merely regional matter, but a relentless, national trend dramatically affecting such unlikely places as North Carolina, Iowa, and Alaska.

There are several other relatively new and significant trends as well. The Latino/a population, for instance, is more diverse than ever before in terms of national origin, level of assimilation, English-Spanish language proficiency, and, most important of all, generation.[2] Latinos/as no longer live predominantly in barrios, inner cities, and urban centers. Slightly more than half live in suburbs.[3] The majority are no longer immigrants but rather native US born, and they are younger than ever before. Some Latinos/as at least have experienced upward mobility. They have more small businesses, more professionals, CEOs, and even millionaires than ever before. The political importance of Latinos/as is now taken for granted: Latino/a voters can decide the outcome of elections in several major states such as California, Texas, Florida, and New York.

[...]

As a practical theologian, I began to look at the unfolding Latino/a drama several years ago in *The Second Wave*. Things were different, perhaps easier, back then. In that work I used a simple pastoral-theological tool, the "see-judge-act" method also called the pastoral circle, that goes back to the pioneering work of Cardinal Joseph Cardijn and the Young Catholic Workers of the early decades of the 20th century.[4] That methodology is reflected in the stress given to scrutinizing the "signs of the times" in the thought of Vatican II as well as in contemporary Catholic social teaching. For the Vatican II generation of Catholics like myself, the spirit of that method is evoked by the oft quoted opening lines of *Gaudium et spes:* "The joys and hopes, the grief and anguish of the people of our time, especially of those who are poor or afflicted, are the joys and hopes, the grief and anguish of the followers of Christ as well."[5]

Joe Holland and Peter Henriot summarized the key elements of social analysis as a pastoral methodology in what they call the pastoral circle. Its key elements are historical, structural, value laden, non-dogmatic, and action oriented. Particularly in Latin America, this method stressed the importance of the analysis of reality and pastoral planning and was supported by liberation theologians as well as by many bishops. A whole generation of Latino/a Catholic leaders adapted the "see-judge-act" method for the process of national *encuentros,* gatherings of Latino/a Catholic leadership, that ran from 1972 to 1986. These events were sponsored by the US bishops and produced the most authoritative church teaching on US Latino/a Catholicism of those decades. Today those findings and orientations require considerable revision in light of many changes as reflected in the bishops' latest instruction titled *Encuentro and Mission.*[6]

Revisiting *The Second Wave*

In view of these developments, I wish to revisit my earlier project of providing a practical theological framework for Hispanic ministry.[7] I then highlight key issues that affect that ministry in light of ongoing needs and new developments. In *The Second Wave* I tried to give an overview of the Hispanic reality of California, then and now the place with the largest Hispanic population. [...]

The concept of evangelization, as I use it, is understood to be an implicit methodology by which the practical theological task can be approached. This means, on the one hand, taking very seriously the Church's turn toward the gospel message of Christ and its encounter with culture in the anthropological sense. On the other hand, this means linking faith to the promotion of justice, transformative action, as Catholic social teaching and liberation theology stress. [...]

[...]

In my estimation, the most serious flaw in pastoral theological method in the spirit of Vatican II has been a certain arbitrariness in regard to the norms and elements of the Catholic tradition actually invoked for the purpose of assessing or "judging" the reality at hand. There has been a lack of a clear and compelling vision. Perhaps a source of this attitude is found in the admission by Holland and Henriot that the approach they take to the pastoral method as social analysis is "non-dogmatic, i.e. drawing upon a variety of perspectives and 'schools' of analysis."[8] Today more than two decades later, one can see the limitations of such a "non-dogmatic" approach. It was fashionable, for instance, to apply biblically based themes, even central ones such as the Exodus theme of liberation, to specific situations such as the oppression and structural violence typical of Latino/a contexts in the US and elsewhere. Despite the good intentions of the proponents, the biblical focus on liberation was used to sanction all types of practical pastoral activities, particularly "conscientization," community organizing, and other forms of empowering the marginal and encouraging them to become subjects rather than objects of history.

This practical theological task, however, was often pursued in an undifferentiated, diffuse way that made it difficult to distinguish a Christian vision of Church and society from secular ones. In the post-Vatican II period of liberation theology Christian responses to the reality of oppression in or outside the Church seemed more informed, on the one hand, by a soft leftist ideology or, on the other, a crusty restorationism. More importantly, the lack of a sufficiently grounded and refined appeal to Christian sources, whether biblical, traditional, or magisterial, led to the production of pastoral plans and actions that remained too general, overarching or repetitive and not sufficiently targeted and specific. For theologically inspired pastoral action to be adequate what is required is attention to reality at the micro level of persons, family, community, and locality as well as the macro level of nation, continent, or "developing world." It also requires a more explicit grounding in a Christian vision of things, lest pastoral practice lose its distinctive faith dimension and relevance to real people.[9] Paul Lakeland, for instance, pleads for a constructive postmodern theological apologetics as a pressing theological need.[10] Somewhat along the same lines liberation theologian José Comblin critiques liberation theology:

> The greatest reproach that can be made against liberation theology is that it has not devoted enough attention to the true drama of human persons, to their destiny, their vocation, and consequently to the ground of the issue of freedom.... It does not come out clearly enough in their writings. This lack has made it possible for their followers or hasty activists to spread a superficial notion of Christianity that reduces it to a strategy of political or social struggle.[11]

Then and Now

In reflecting on the soundness of the relatively simple methodology pursued in *The Second Wave* I still believe it has much in its favor. It seems that pastoral ministry still continues to lack a clear and convincing focus. One learns in establishing a business and pursuing strategic planning that a clear mission statement makes all the difference. From the mission flow goals and objectives. So, in pastoral theology, a clear statement of the mission is fundamental. It seemed to me that the rich, nuanced concept of evangelization as expressed in *Evangelii nuntiandi* constitutes just such a foundation. So evangelization became the lens by which the pastoral reality in my book was assessed. Paul VI's approach and subsequently that of John Paul II – the "new evangelization" – are still arguably the most ecclesially sanctioned, illuminating and practical visions at hand for what is supposed to be happening in the life of Christian communities today. The rich concept of evangelization provides good criteria for assessing how to respond practically and pastorally to the ongoing challenges and opportunities facing the People of God, not only with regard to the US Hispanic presence, but across the board. The stress on evangelization provides a foundation based on the doctrine of the incarnation which informs a great deal of missiology today. Pastoral theology similarly requires today a more explicit theological foundation and evangelization provides one.

Timothy Matovina has noted a fundamental gap between what interests Latino/a Catholics and what interests the mainstream US Catholics. Euroamerican Catholics tend to look inwardly at issues like clericalism, dissent from church teaching, matters revolving around sexual orientation, accountability, the exercise of episcopal authority, celibacy, and women's ordination issues. These matters are regularly viewed from the angle of liberal/conservative polarizations. Hispanics are somewhere else. They are concerned with the nitty-gritty realities of jobs, making ends meet, raising children, and avoiding violence in our society. They are concerned about the credibility of the Church's leadership in pressing social, economic, and public policy areas such as the living wage, unionization drives, immigration, access to education, and the human development of their huge numbers of young people. These are different agendas indeed.[12]

[...]

The Acids of Postmodernity?

[...] The postmodern rhetoric of diversity and multiculturalism has simply captured the thought and imagination of many people in both the academy and the Church over the past two decades. Sociologist of religion John A. Coleman in a perceptive piece published in *Origins* has reminded us about the inadequacy of the discourse on multiculturalism in many Catholic pastoral contexts today. Coleman refers to this as "sentimental inclusive rhetorics which in fact do not honor cultural difference."[13] Coleman echoes something that missiologist Robert Schreiter noted about the reality of worldwide migrations for which societies have not yet devised any clear plans or policies regarding how such diverse groups might live together. Francis Mannion, in an earlier critique, laid out some of the pitfalls in what he calls the soft multiculturalism that pastoral agents and thinkers have sometimes adopted uncritically.[14] While the Church can certainly find in the prevailing trends and ideologies of secular culture many helpful, even necessary lessons, there is no substitute for a vision of the present informed by a theological understanding of Christian identity. That is what the Church's contemporary approach to evangelization provides. That has been what I argue is lacking in the formulation of a practical theological vision for the challenges of Latino/a ministry today.[15]

What is Evangelization?

The most basic sources for understanding the central role played by the Church's contemporary view of evangelization are three: *Gaudium et spes* (nos. 56 ff.), Paul VI's *Evangelii nuntiandi,* and John Paul II's *Ecclesia in America.* These documents define evangelization as an ongoing process by which the gospel of Jesus Christ is proclaimed. But it hardly ends there. The conversion process stands on three legs: inculturation, liberation, and ecumenical/interreligious dialogue. Elsewhere, I have argued that the Church's teaching on evangelization has simply not been received, that lip service is given to it but ultimately church leaders including the laity are not exactly united behind this vision.[16]

Inculturation

Inculturation refers to the appeal that the gospel message makes to the core values and meaning at the heart of a person's and an entire people's way of life.[17] This process often begins in the hearts of individuals but must eventually include broader circles of family, community, and ultimately the culture itself. The target of evangelization, in other words, is not just individuals but entire cultures. Faith has not become deep and authentic until it penetrates the many levels of value and meaning, the symbols, rituals, and metanarratives of a people. Inculturation, moreover, is not a one-way street: cultures shed light upon, bring new perspectives to, and make palatable the truths of the gospel.[18] This ability to find truth in what is other, as well as this openness and receptivity, are at the heart of Catholic tradition. In history this occurs in the way Christianity, particularly in its Western and Eastern Orthodox expressions, negotiates, absorbs, and/or substitutes for the most sacred symbols of the people it encounters along the way.[19]

Liberation

Liberation is a constitutive dimension of evangelization, that is, of the Church's mission because authentic conversion undergone by persons and entire cultures has tangible results in the personal call to freedom as well as in culture and in the attainment of social, economic, and political justice. The linkage between evangelization and transformative action is boldly asserted in *Justice in the World* (the 1971 statement of the International Synod of Bishops) and in *Evangelii nuntiandi*.[20] This means that the conversion began in and through the encounter with Jesus Christ has broad repercussions in the public domain. Political participation is not an optional activity for committed Christians, since to abstain from participating according to one's ability is to fail in love of neighbor and to deny in practice a fundamental gospel imperative. Matters of public policy such as access to food, shelter, medical attention, education, human and civil rights profoundly affect the well-being of one's neighbor. To manifest true charity for all is not enough. To fight for justice, especially for the poor and marginal of the earth, is also a gospel imperative and a matter of prophetic identity for Catholics.

Catholic social teaching's failure to reach the laity in the pew has much to do with the failure to make explicit the link between faith and justice. This is a major challenge for practical theology. Catholic social teaching, as many have said before, is a "well-kept secret" precisely because the connection between faith and justice, evangelization and liberation, has largely been denied *in practice,* often ignored or benignly neglected in preaching, in catechesis, and in Catholic education and theological discourse itself.

Ecumenical and Interreligious Dialogue

The third leg on which the Church's understanding of evangelization stands is ecumenical and interreligious dialogue. The realization that ecumenism and interreligious dialogue is an essential component of Christian identity today is arguably even less appreciated in practice than is action on behalf of justice. Dialogue in the thought of Vatican II considered that Christians in their dealing with "others" presume that meaning and truth can be found in the heart and discourse of all people of good will. Consequently, an essential quality of Christian life is a genuine desire to share in the religious experience of others. The challenge of pluralism today revolves around how that sharing can take place in such a way that everyone's identity in the dialogue process is truly respected.[21] The Church in its magisterial teaching on evangelization uses the term "interreligious dialogue." Behind the phrase is a struggle to find a way for committed Christians to deal respectfully with otherness in a world characterized by growing pluralism in the form of multilingualism, multiculturalism, and the free market of religions. This matter is crucial for Hispanics, too, even though they are not often seen as participants in this dialogue. Yet, they too are deeply affected by the anomie that comes from migration and the double dose of Paul Ricoeur's famous acids. Latino/a immigrants and their young families are plunged into the heart of modernity even as that world transmutes into postmodernity.

The New Americans According to Three Scholars

First, the pioneering social science analyses of medical sociologist David Hayes-Bautista are quite illuminating and suggestive. They provide input from social science that any creative pastoral outreach to Latinos/as today must take into account. In his latest study the UCLA researcher describes *la nueva California* that is the homeland of the nation's largest Latino/a population. His research focuses on California which accounts for almost one-third of the nation's Latino/a population. Hayes-Bautista's research over the past 15 years has been inspired by his conviction that fellow researchers, academics, social activists, and politicians have repeatedly reinforced the portrayal of Latinos/as as victims. For various reasons it has been politically correct to stress the underclass analogy: poverty, lack of educational attainment, lack of medical attention, and so forth. Dwelling on these realities can become counterproductive, encouraging a victim's complex that disempowers people. Hayes-Bautista does not deny that Latinos/as suffer serious social, economic, and political marginality. What concerns him, however, is the failure to find and highlight the positive strengths of Latinos/as, their gifts and distinctiveness.

Hayes-Bautista focuses on three fundamental social indicators: health, work, and family formation. As a medical sociologist he applied the concept of "epidemiological paradox" to his remarkable research findings: Latinos/as live at least four years longer than the average middle-class Euroamerican. The birth weight of Hispanic babies is almost the same as that for middle-class Euroamericans despite the fact that prenatal care is much less accessible to Latinas than to the Euroamerican middle class. The infant mortality rate for Hispanics is lower than that of Whites and African Americans. Compared to Whites or African Americans, Latinos/as have lower incidences of cancer and heart disease in California.

Hispanic participation in the work force is prodigious. For as long as records have been kept in California, Hispanics have the highest levels of participation in the work force of any racial/ethnic group. This has led to the coy observation that some Americans tout the Protestant work ethic and the Hispanic Catholics put it into practice! The data on family formation is also quite revealing. As Hayes-Bautista puts it: "Latinos are more likely to form family units than any other racial/ethnic group in California when family is defined as consisting of the conventional couple with children."[22]

In an effort to understand the sources and meaning of these somewhat paradoxical findings Hayes-Bautista has developed what he calls the concept of Latino/a civil society. He describes that society as being less individualistic, more family oriented and communitarian than the prevailing Euroamerican one. He sees religion and spirituality as playing a crucial role in people's lives and believes that future study is needed to establish more clearly how Latino/a spirituality accounts for at least some of the paradoxes his research has uncovered. He suggests that the coming Latino/a majority in California will create a *nueva California.* Insofar as this trend is also a national one, he suggests that the Hispanic presence may also presage a *nuevo Estados Unidos,* with "new Americans."

A second scholar, Virgilio Elizondo, has captured the spirit of the Hispanic contribution to US culture in much of his writing and public speaking. He struggled to articulate the nature of the process that has been unfolding in the Hispanic homelands of the Southwest, Texas and California, and now throughout the nation:

> This new synthesis is easy to talk about, but it never takes place easily. There is first a deep and profound loneliness, the loneliness of not even being able to conceptualize and verbalize the reasons for the social alienation... The inner self will be suppressed into an almost total silence. Finally, through struggle and suffering a new identity will begin to emerge and the self will be able to shout out, "I am." This new identity does not eliminate either the original culture of the parents or the culture of the new country. On the contrary, it enriches both by opening up each to the possibilities of the other.[23]

Third, Richard Rodríguez, a most evocative essayist, using the tools of a true person of letters, contemplates the emerging demographic profile of the United States. He focuses on the dual dynamics of the Americanization of Hispanics and the Hispanicization of the Americans. He deftly applies the metaphor of color poetically to evoke the nature and import of this new reality: Latinos/as are coloring the identity of Americans who have traditionally preferred to describe themselves in terms of black and white. Brown is now the color on the ascendancy. Rodríguez uses this to talk about dramatic and subtle changes in the very quality of life, values, pursuits, and way of being in the crucible of US society and Church today.[24]

One might ask whether the same observations, a fortiori, could not be made regarding the churches, especially the Roman Catholic Church, in the United States. The "new Catholics" are and increasingly will be Hispanic. Taking the suggestions and intuitions of these writers and researchers seriously, and keeping in mind the many findings about the Latino/a presence noted thus far, what are the critical pastoral issues facing the Church?

Key Issues for Practical Theology

Lay Ecclesial Leadership and Ministry

While the lack of adequate numbers of ecclesial ministers of any kind – priests, deacons, religious men and women, and laity – is a serious matter for the entire US Church, it is particularly acute in the case of Hispanics. Even at this late date there persists in some quarters the attitude, sometimes explicit but often implicit, that the current situation is an aberration that temporarily requires laity to assume roles of ecclesial leadership. The ideal is to return to "the good old days" when Father assumed all the important leadership roles. Such a view flies in the face of John Paul II's observation: "The renewal of the Church in America will not be possible without the active presence of the laity. Therefore they are largely responsible for the future of the Church."[25]

In dioceses and parishes with large Hispanic populations the majority of ministers in positions of leadership such as priests and ministry directors are not Hispanic. Diocesan, parish, or university based lay formation/leadership programs of any kind for Latinos/as are growing but still woefully inadequate. One might ask in this connection what resources are applied to lay ministry formation. It would be a fascinating [...] to determine how much money is devoted to the formation of lay ministers, coworkers, and partners. This would be one meaningful way to discover how focused these institutions really are on evangelization, the Church's mission and identity.

Underlying this serious ministerial inadequacy is the persistence of a vertical, priest and religious centered vision of ecclesial leadership. The ministerial structure that results from this clerical paradigm is simply unable as a practical matter to respond to the real population, the huge numbers of baptized Hispanics, whose faith will never develop without the benefit of a vibrant local community of faith. Such a community requires leadership and service in the form of ministers of many kinds, including the priest, but by no means limited to him. Another way to say this is to observe that a Church totally on its mission and identity, that is, on evangelization, requires a much more open, differentiated, and flexible ministerial structure.

The historical and systematic theologians of Church, priesthood, and ministry can argue about the basis in Scripture and tradition for this or that approach or arrangement. The Vatican may set down the acceptable doctrinal parameters regarding these much disputed matters. But it is undeniable that our current approach leads to serious practical inadequacies. The Church is unable to truly attend to its members adequately, and, as a result: (1) ministers from other Christian denominations are filling the gap, and (2) significant numbers of Hispanic Catholics lose even their distinctive cultural Catholic values and fade away into the unchurched, secular North American milieu. In the case of Hispanics the movement away from Catholicism is now well documented.

While there is no one, simple explanation for this phenomenon, certainly common sense suggests that many Hispanics would remain in the Catholic Church if it had a ministerial structure adequate to the challenge. Currently it lacks a sufficient number of people, authorized ministers, to receive, nurture, and develop the faith of Hispanics. In an age of modernization, cultural shocks, urbanization, and so many other dramatic changes, more ministerial attention not less is demanded. From a Hispanic point of view, therefore, the reconfiguration of ministry is an especially urgent practical task.

Popular Religion

The writings of many Latino/a theologians have significantly contributed to the awareness in the academy and within pastoral contexts about the central importance for effective Hispanic ministry of the people's faith and popular religiosity.[26] Yet, it must be observed that Catholic leadership in dioceses, parishes, and schools continues to reflect the late modern sensibilities of the Vatican II generation. In the effort to dialogue with the world, which 40 years ago meant the Enlightenment world, this generation tended to buy into several of the concerns of liberal Protestantism. Langdon Gilkey, writing more than 25 years ago, correctly assessed the situation [...]:

> Related essentially to the bourgeois middle-class worlds of Europe, Britain and America, and in the last two to the "Wasp" worlds of small towns and suburbs, Protestantism seems, despite its conservative and neo-conservative theologies of transcendence, to have been so engulfed in that world *as merely to reproduce the individualistic, quantatative, moralistic, non-emotional, and in many respects naturalistic, bourgeois world in ecclesiastical form.*[27]

From a Latino/a point of view, the mainstream US Catholic Church seems not unlike the Protestant one described by Gilkey. In response to the deadening influence of this Atlantic American bourgeois modernity Gilkey suggests that Roman Catholicism has several strengths that his Protestantism does not. Some of these are the strengths that echo ones found in Latino/a Catholicism:

> Catholicism has had a continuing experience, unequaled in other forms of Western Christianity, of the presence of God and grace mediated through symbols to the entire course of human life...transcendent mystery impinging continually on human existence through a wide variety or range of symbols— material, sensuous, aesthetic, active, verbal, and intellectual... often almost magical in character and within rites and practices often openly superstitious in their forms.[28]

Gilkey expresses a fear that Roman Catholic leadership [...] may fail to appreciate the strengths of the Catholic tradition and unwittingly go down the path of liberal Protestantism. I see the discomfort with Latino/a popular religion and worship as a manifestation of what Gilkey is saying. [...] This showed itself in the impetus to proceed with renewal that took the form of post-Tridentine standardization of practices and beliefs. This trend produced priests, catechists, teachers, and theologians driven by the need to purify the faith and its practice not from heresy, but from the accretions of anomalous forms of devotion that irritated Protestants and offended a certain antiseptic middle-class bias. Even mainstream American Catholic piety came under duress, while the more exotic forms of non-Western popular Catholicism like the Hispanic became more unacceptable than ever. Vatican II reformers saw their task as purifying the Catholic faith from all the unnecessary baggage of the past, especially the multiplication of symbolic, ritual practices that emerged through a process of an untidy religious syncretism.

As if that were not enough, other influential leaders of a liberationist persuasion tended either to jettison the people's religion or drastically to redeem it from its heavily narcotic function. A strong, socially oriented Catholic renewal sought to "conscienticize" Hispanic Catholics, in order to make them aware of the sources of injustice and act to bring about real social change. The models of Hispanic ministry that prevailed in the last two or three decades of the 20th century were informed by the imperatives of renewal or liberation. These tended to be antagonistic toward popular Catholicism.

A third model, traditionalism often in a quasi national church setting, sought to replicate the old customs over and over again and in this sense was not antagonistic to the
people's religion. Nevertheless, this model showed little concern for the dynamics of the
encounter with modernization and the mainstream culture. Consequently, it was and
is inadequate for immigrant people and their children seeking help in the process of
integration.

Another factor powerfully influencing the tone and texture of pastoral practice of
recent times is the growing professionalization of ministry in the Church. This led to a
situation in which lay leaders became more educated but sometimes less conversant
with or respectful toward the people's ways. The lack of a general educational background has not allowed many Hispanics to pursue college-level (not to speak of gradu-
ate-level) theological or pastoral studies. As a result the leadership of catechetical
programs, diocesan offices, and schools of ministry are not Hispanic and often quite
removed from the life worlds of the Hispanic faithful. Training programs have curricula
that reflect Euroamerican preferences that either ignore or diminish the people's
Catholicism. A similar process sometimes occurs in seminaries. [...] This has taken its
toll on the ability of parishes, schools, and other Catholic institutions to work with the
people's faith instead of ignore or even oppose it.

Sensitivity to Hispanics requires exposure to the people, knowledge about their history and way of being. It also means that one must appreciate the role of symbol, ritual,
and narrative in their lives. The experience of a relatively rigid and highly univocal,
standardized US Catholicism must concede more than a little to the deeply expressive,
graphic, polyvalent, and anomalous religiosity of the people. This has been no small
leap for Catholics schooled in mainstream theology and pastoral studies in the decades
after Vatican II. The clash continues in the area of esthetic taste, for example, in the
liturgical norms that invoke simplicity and clarity when in fact the people prefer exuber-
ance and variety.[29]

The Flight to Other Churches

For more than 20 years the news media have been reporting the flight of Latinos/as
from the Roman Catholic Church to other Christian denominations.[30] This trend is
true for both the United States and Latin America itself. The result is that for the first
time in history one cannot presume that persons of Latin American origin are Roman
Catholic. There are critical masses of Protestant (particularly Evangelical and
Pentecostal) Hispanics virtually wherever Latin Americans can be found. While there is
no one cause for this historic development, there are, in my view, two underlying reasons. The first is simple enough and has been discussed already: the Roman Catholic
Church is not adequately structured to minister effectively to such a large population.
In the context of the dramatic movement of Hispanics from the countryside to the
urban centers, across borders of nations and from premodernity to modernity and postmodernity, the Catholic Church has continued to trust in its post-Tridentine ministerial
structure. [...] In order to serve the Hispanic Catholic populations of North and South
America there need to be more ministers. [...] We must ask why our ministerial structure is not responding.

A second source of the movement away from Catholicism is the discomfort with and
outright hostility toward popular religion among many church leaders. This, too, I have

already discussed. The religion of the popular masses in Latin America is characterized by: (1) a strong sense of God's transcendence or otherness, with a corresponding orientation toward the sacred and mysterious; (2) a generous acceptance of the reality of miracles; (3) a strong bias toward mediations of all kinds such as sacraments and sacramentals, symbols, images, rituals, and sacred stories; (4) a profoundly affective orientation, one that places a premium on the expression of emotions and passions. The serene, orderly, rationalistic religion of the middle class in the United States is simply different from the hybrid and sensuous Catholicism of Latinos/as.

Evangelical Christians and Pentecostals have ironically often shown a greater affinity for these Latino/a religious sensibilities than have mainstream US Roman Catholics. In Latin America the Roman Catholic Church has struggled to find ways to relate to the people in a way that stresses continuity between the rich if anomalous Catholicism of the people's past and the requirements of normative Catholicism in the spirit of Vatican II.

Multiculturalism

The Church's pastoral response to the challenges of Hispanic ministry has not always been well served by the ideology of multiculturalism as it has unfolded in the US over the last two decades. The documents of the Roman magisterium tend to avoid the word "multicultural." They favor the concept of inculturation and evangelization of culture which other sources render as contextualization. Of course, the word multicultural is useful to speak about the reality of the interfacing of several distinct cultures. Often, however, it is used in such a way as to obscure the serious pastoral need to relate specifically to each and every culture, not merely create some generalized atmosphere of tolerance among diverse cultural, racial, and language groups. It also bypasses the serious matter of leadership development. In many multicultural situations the outside culture does not easily achieve a role of leadership. Instead leadership remains in the hands of the insiders.[31]

[...]

John Coleman notes five basic ways in which the multicultural approach is inadequate: (1) Merging cultural/language groups with a larger congregation too soon has a negative affect on the strength of their religious commitments. (2) Successful immigrant parishes are not only places of worship but also social centers where health, social, and material needs are addressed. (3) Prayer and worship should not normally be multicultural or bilingual because a people prefer to pray in their mother tongue. (4) If church space is used by diverse cultural groups the issue of how to arrange and adorn this space are critical. Immigrant people especially need a sense of their own turf. There are elements of design and esthetics proper to each culture. A multicultural setting frustrates this need or denies it to them. (5) Leadership training is a sine qua non for effective pastoral ministries for Hispanics. A multicultural context often prescinds from this urgent need because there are other qualified non-Hispanic leaders available.[32]

Spotlight on Youth

Dean Hoge and colleagues produced an important social science analysis of Catholic young adults that draws five key conclusions about Latino/a young adults. First, as one might expect, popular devotions and spirituality in the form of prayer are more important to Latinos/as than to any other cohort in the study. Second, Latinos/as have more friends in their parish communities than any other cohort studied and they actually think more positively about their parishes than any other group. Third, Latinos/as accept the claims to truth made by the Church more readily than other groups. In this sense they continue to be rooted more in the Catholic tradition as they have known it. Fourth, they are also more convinced that social justice issues like closing the gap between the rich and the poor and caring for the environment are important to Catholics.[33] The researchers also note what Riebe-Estrella observes [...] regarding the growing preference of Latinos/as for English. But this does not mean that they are simply assimilating and can now forget their language and culture. Rather, the lesson to be learned is that English is an appropriate language for Hispanic ministry as well as Spanish.

These findings echo some of the points already made. [...] From all of this, what conclusions can be made regarding future directions for Hispanic ministry?

Practical Implications

The practical response made to the challenge of the Hispanic presence is obviously a crucial matter for the vitality of the Church in the United States. One could argue that it is *the* central issue certainly from the point of view of demographics. What is at stake here is not a part of the US Church, but its entirety. A practical theological vision must respond to the reality of the whole, not just a part. Ultimately, it is not a question about the evangelization of Hispanics; it is about the evangelization of US culture and society across the board. In what follows I will summarize the more salient points and end with a best-case scenario, a utopian vision, as it were, of where a practical theology focused on the Hispanic presence may be taking us.

As I have argued, the situation requires a credible ecclesial vision, one provided by the concept of evangelization and the new evangelization. This vision, at least in theory, has become central to the official Church's way of looking at the reality of the Church in the modern world including that of the Americas, North and South. For various reasons, church leaders have so far failed to communicate a clear sense of the mission, one that is received and put into practice. The Euroamerican Church is traumatized and paralyzed by the sexual abuse scandals, legal battles, and financial crises. Concomitantly, Hispanic Catholics continue to emerge in every section of the country. They are ripe for evangelization as the apostolic movements in the Church like the Cursillo, the Charismatic Renewal, Marriage Encounter, and the Neo-Catechumenate know very well. Other Christian denominations, moreover, have shown much creativity and spunk in responding to this *kairos* moment. Catholic parishes, nevertheless, are generally not in an evangelizing mode.[34] They reflect the suburban, middle class and establishment mind-sets that resist outreach to newcomers. Until leadership takes this malaise in hand, Hispanic ministry will continue to be characterized by a certain lack of urgency, half-measures, and holding actions. This is a sign, moreover, of a generalized apostolic mediocrity affecting the entire US Church.

At the heart of the problem, of course, is a pastoral imagination held captive too long by an outmoded clerical paradigm. This must give way to other practical ministerial structures, if the US Church is to have the mobility, diversity, and energy it needs to respond to the unique opportunity offered it by the human windfall of immigrants and their youthfulness. Interestingly enough, telltale signs of the future are already emerging. For instance, the permanent diaconate continues to grow and the Hispanic part of it is very significant. The prospect of a permanent commitment to service in the Church as a married person is very appealing to Latinos/as. In parishes all over the nation laity, especially women, are assuming roles of leadership in all aspects of the parish except those strictly limited to the priest. For the first time in the history of the Western Church laywomen and laymen are becoming the professional theological class. These are "signs of the times" that augur hopeful, future developments. One can either fight and resist them or support them in the search for a renewed, vigorous pastoral praxis. Concretely, the Church's understanding of its mission requires that emphasis be placed on training and capacity building of laity for many tasks of service *ad intra* in the Church as well as leadership *ad extra* in the world of commerce, the professions, labor, business, and the public square. This, of course, will not happen without a massive reallocation of resources, human and financial, on the part of parishes, dioceses, religious congregations, Catholic schools, and other institutions.

The polarizations in the contemporary Church, liberal and conservative, lead to an anomie that demands a response that is both vigorous and respectful of the range of sensibilities actually present among the people of God. The concept of evangelization, as I have tried to show, provides a way to bridge ideological divides. The teaching on evangelization can be seen as a synthesis of Vatican II's call for a theology of correlation that accordingly gives great importance to dialogue with cultures, including those of modernity and postmodernity. It honors ecumenism and interreligious dialogue. Yet the evangelization of cultures asserts the Christian proclamation, the gospel, with conviction and in terms of a clear mission and vision.

Hispanic Catholicism is uniquely positioned to respond to a more comprehensive, less polarized and ideologically driven Catholic imagination of the third millennium's world Church. This emergent Catholicism, caught between Canada and Mexico, as it were, is hybrid in its birth and seeks a more felicitous balance between a Mediterranean tolerance for ambiguity and a Nordic drive for coherence. Strongly oriented to an affective, symbolic, and ritual search for meaning rather than a dry, rational-cognitive, or fundamentalist one, Latino/a Catholicism offers some fascinating possibilities precisely in the context of a postmodern world characterized by a desperate search for meaning. In years to come the formation of ministers in the Church, preaching, catechesis, and Catholic education must free themselves from the straitjacket of Western bourgeois religion. This means creating many relatively small communities of faith in which prayer, ritual, and faith-sharing in community are practiced with greater ease, affect, and naturalness than in the somewhat staid, inhibited environments of Catholic parishes today. This means linking institutional religion and the visible Church with personal spirituality and community in a more intentional way, rather than allowing postmodernity's drive toward fragmentation to win the day. Latino/a Catholicism is poised for the battle.

Familiarity with more than one language and culture will be deeply prized in the Church to come. Pastoral praxis will be less univocal, more differentiated. It will value the need for ongoing analysis of reality, theological reflection and revision of programs. A one-size-fits-all mentality will give way to a healthy sense of diversity of means. Ministers will be available who match the vast range of gender, culture, social class, styles, languages, sexual orientation, and backgrounds of God's people.

The Hispanic presence also means that issues of social justice become centerstage. The churches understanding of evangelization in unison with Catholic social teaching makes action for justice an essential element in the proclamation of God's word in Jesus Christ. The strong middle-class bias of many US Catholics today with its drive toward privatization of religion and the dichotomization of faith from justice will be challenged to change. Attention to the reality of the poor and marginal people of this earth, an option for the poor, will be a natural and unavoidable consequence of true Christian discipleship. This may take the form of more Church-based community organizations. [...]

The Hispanic presence will require Catholic leaders to adopt a much more differentiated and creative approach to ministry. The parish as an instrument for evangelization will be seen as inadequate in light of the need to take the gospel to many spaces often not touched by the parish: the workplace, youth, rural areas, inner cities, the professions, science, industry, and business. Catholic schools, colleges, and universities will see the need to return once again to their original purpose which often was the education of immigrant and working-class people, not the pursuit of success in the marketplace by serving mainly the educational needs of middle-class and upper-middle-class people. Since Latinos/as continue to experience upward mobility and acculturation, an effective practical theology must focus on what it means to be middle-class and Catholic. This must be done in such a way that the Catholic and Hispanic sense of solidarity and community is not swallowed up by the relentless individualism of US culture.

Conclusion

These reflections lead to the conclusion that *cultural discernment* will become a practical theological skill more prized than ever before. While affirming the good, the true and the beautiful in each and every culture including the Euroamerican, pastoral ministry will evangelize culture by stressing gospel-based values that critique the dehumanizing tendencies of every culture including the Euroamerican and Hispanic. Practical theology will tend then to take the Church beyond the confines of this or that culturally based ministry. In the name of a Christian vision of each and every human person, the evils of materialism, consumerism, and individualism will be denounced. Other negative cultural patterns and structural sins and injustices will be identified. God's countervailing reign of justice, love, and peace will be proclaimed and enacted in the Christian community's sacramental life, prayer, and social action, that is, in deeds more than words.

Notes

1 Gregory Rodríguez, "A Church, Changing," *The Wall Street Journal*, 8 March 2002. It would be more correct to say "Hispanicization" or "Latinization" of the US Church. Fully two-thirds of US Latinos/as are of Mexican origin, but virtually all of Latin America is represented in the wider population.
2 See Sylvia A. Marotta and Jorge G. García, "Latinos in the United States in 2000," *Hispanic Journal of Behavioral Sciences* 25, no. 1 (February 2003), 13–34.

3 Fifty-four percent of all Latinos now reside in the suburbs according to Roberto Suro et al., *Latino Growth in Metropolitan America: Changing Patterns, New Lo cations* (Washington: Center on Urban and Metropolitan Policy and the Pew Hispanic Center, 2001), 7.

4 Joe Holland and Peter Henriot articulated this methodology in *Social Analysis: Linking Faith and Justice* (Maryknoll, NY: Orbis, 1983), 7–30.

5 *Gaudium et spes*, no.1. Translation from *The Documents of Vatican II*, ed. Austin Flannery, rev. inclusive language ed. (Northport, NY: Costello, 1996).

6 Perhaps the most incisive assessment of the status of Latinos in the US Catholic Church in the decade of the 1970s and 1980s is Joseph Fitzpatrick's "A Survey of Literature on Hispanic Ministry," in *Strangers and Aliens No Longer*, ed. Eugene F. Hemrick (Washington.: USCCB, 1993), 63–87.

7 See also Thomas H. Groome, *Sharing Faith: A Comprehensive Approach to Religious Education and Pastoral Ministry* (San Francisco: HarperSanFrancisco, 1991); Don S. Browning, *A Fundamental Practical Theology* (Minneapolis: Fortress, 1991); Casiano Floristán, *Teología Práctica* (Salamanca: Ediciones Sígueme, 1991); Ray S. Anderson, *The Shape of Practical Theology to Come* (Downers Grove, IL: InterVarsity, 2001).

8 Holland and Henriot, *Social Analysis: Linking Faith and Justice*, 30.

9 As I and others have noted elsewhere, during the dramatic period of liberation movements and theology in Latin America (1965–90) huge numbers of the poor in that continent voted with their feet and choose to identify with charismatic, Pentecostal or Evangelical forms of Christianity. One possible explanation for this is the clear religious identity and distinctiveness of these religious expressions, something they often did not see in socially and politically progressive Catholicism or Protestantism. See Allan Figueroa Deck, "The Challenge of Evangelical/ Pentecostal Christianity to Hispanic Catholicism," in *Hispanic Catholic Culture in the United States*, ed. Jay P. Dolan and Allan Figueroa Deck (Notre Dame: University of Notre Dame, 1994), 427–8.

10 Paul Lakeland, *Postmodernity: Christian Identity in a Fragmented Age* (Minneapolis: Fortress, 1997), 88.

11 José Comblin, *Called for Freedom: The Changing Context of Liberation Theology* (Maryknoll, NY: Orbis, 1998), 197.

12 Timothy Matovina, "A Fundamental Gap," *America* 188 (March 17, 2003), 6–8. Writing several years ago for the symposium on conservative and liberal American Catholics, I attempted to show how Latino/a Catholics do not easily fit into liberalconservative characterizations. See Allan Figueroa Deck, "A Pox on Both Your Houses: A View of Catholic Conservative-Liberal Polarities from the Hispanic Margin," in *Being Right: Conservative Catholics in America*, ed. Mary Jo Weaver and R. Scott Appleby (Bloomington: Indiana University, 1995).

13 John A. Coleman, "Pastoral Strategies for Multicultural Parishes," *Origins* 31 (January 10, 2002), 497.

14 M. Francis Mannion, "Evangelization and American Ethnicity," in *Catholicity and the New Evangelization*, ed. Anthony J. Mastroeni (Corpus Christi: Proceedings from the Seventeenth Convention of the Fellowship of Catholic Scholars, 1994). Mannion describes "soft multiculturalism" as follows: "… an approach that regards ethnic Catholicism as culturally interesting and worth preserving for the expressive variety it provides, yet has no profound stake in the spiritual values ethnic cultures bring to Catholicism. Mainstream American Catholicism assumes the general cultural-liking for

ethnicity, but at a fairly romantic level. It pays lip service to cultural diversity and, in general, only looks kindly on ethnic expressions that support a liberal, middle-class ecclesial agenda. Soft multiculturalism is prone to the celebration of ethnic diversity in the church, yet exhibits a lack of real commitment to or conviction about the crucial necessity, both for church and society, of the conservation and advancement of the cultural and religious values of ethnic communities."

15 Practical theology needs to be correlational, in continuous dialogue with its ever changing contexts. But it must be epiphanic too: inspired by a vision of the good, the true, and the beautiful that takes one beyond the confines of cultural mediations. See Joseph A. Komonchak, "Dealing with Diversity and Disagreement: Vatican II and Beyond," *Fifth Annual Lecture of the Catholic Common Ground Initiative* (New York: National Pastoral Life Center, 2003), 14.

16 See my chapter "Evangelization as Conceptual Framework for the Church's Mission: The Case of US Hispanics," in *Evangelizing America*, ed. Thomas P. Rausch (Mahwah, NJ: Paulist, 2004).

17 Michael Paul Gallagher, *Clashing Symbols: An Introduction to Faith and Culture* (New York: Paulist, 1998).

18 Gerald A. Arbuckle has written extensively about the theory and practice of inculturation. See *Earthing the Gospel: An Inculturation Handbook for the Pastoral Worker* (Maryknoll, NY: Orbis, 1990).

19 I say "absorbs" in the present because the process is really not over. This is so because inculturation means […] the […] ongoing mingling of symbols and rituals, what anthropologists call "syncretism" among the Latin American Catholics (in North and South America and the Caribbean) who account for more than a third of all Roman Catholics in the world.

20 We are familiar with the oft-quoted assertion of the 1971 International Synod of Bishops in their document titled *Justice in the World:* "Action on behalf of justice and participation in the transformation of the world fully appear to us as a constitutive dimension of the preaching of the Gospel." See David J. O'Brien and Thomas A. Shannon, *Catholic Social Thought: The Documentary Heritage* (Maryknoll, N.Y.: Orbis, 1992), 289.

21 See *Unitatis redintegratio* no. 4, and *Nostra aetate* no. 2.

22 See David Hayes-Bautista, *No Longer A Minority* (Los Angeles: UCLA Chicano Research Center Publications, 1992), 17.

23 Virgilio P. Elizondo, *The Future Is Mestizo: Life Where Cultures Meet* (Bloomington, IN: Meyer-Stone, 1988), 100.

24 Richard Rodríguez, *Brown: The Last Discovery of America* (New York: Viking, 2002)

25 Pope John Paul II, *Ecclesia in America* (Washington: USCCB, 1999) no. 44.

26 See Orlando O. Espín, *The Faith of the People: Theological Reflections on Popular Catholicism* (Maryknoll, NY: Orbis, 1997).

27 Langdon Gilkey, *Catholicism Confronts Modernity* (New York: Seabury, 1975), 14.

28 Ibid., 20.

29 Mark R. Francis and Arturo J. Pérez-Rodríguez, *Primero Dios: Hispanic Liturgical Resource* (Chicago: Liturgy Training, 1997); also *Misa, Mesa y Musa: Liturgy in the US Hispanic Church,* ed. Kenneth G. Davis (Schiller Park, IL: World Library, 1997).

30 M. D. Litonjua, "Pentecostalism in Latin America," *Journal of Hispanic/Latino Theology* 7 (May 2000), 26–48; also Edward L. Cleary and Hannah W. Stewart-Gambino, *Power,*

Politics and Pentecostals in Latin America (Boulder, CO: Westview, 1997). For an analysis of the several causes for the flight in the United States, see Allan Figueroa Deck, "The Challenge of Evangelical/Pentecostal Christianity to Hispanic Catholicism," in *Hispanic Catholic Culture in the US: Issues and Concerns*, ed. Jay P. Dolan and Allan Figueroa Deck (Notre Dame: University of Notre Dame, 1994), 409–39.

31 See William Cenkner, *The Multicultural Church: A New Landscape in US Theologies* (New York: Paulist, 1996).

32 John A. Coleman, "Pastoral Strategies for Multicultural Parishes," 498.

33 Dean R. Hoge, William D. Dinges, Mary Johnson, and Juan L. González, Jr, *Young Adult Catholics: Religion in the Culture of Choice* (Notre Dame: University of Notre Dame, 2001), 118–19.

34 Avery Dulles, "John Paul II and the New Evangelization," *America* 166 (Feb. 1, 1992), 52.

3

Immigrant Faith Communities as Interpreters (2008)*

Faustino M. Cruz

Introduction

Faustino Cruz, born and raised in Manila, a Marist priest and established leader in theological education and practical theology, now Dean of Fordham's Graduate School of Religion and Religious Education, states his argument succinctly in his opening paragraph: give immigrants voice and agency in interpreting their lives by engaging them in participatory action research.

Like Deck, Cruz writes within and for the Catholic Church, drawing as Deck does on *Evangelii Nuntiandi*, Pope Paul VI's 1975 statement on evangelization. His essay, however, is wider in scope. After a brief opening section on Catholic teaching, the essay goes far beyond the church narrowly construed to the place of immigrants in theological construction. Although the essay might not appear on first blush to tackle philosophical and epistemological questions or attend to the discipline of practical theology, it does so subtly and thoroughly through practical response to the plight of immigrants. In describing ministries of care for those who have lost their homeland, Cruz questions the "factories of knowledge" that produce elite concepts at great distance from people's lives. Christian "proclamation must unquestionably take place 'where [people] are, not where [the church] would like them to be.'" Here, practical theology's epistemological reorientation runs back to Brazilian educator Paulo Freire. Knowledge is gained through "conscientization through praxis." Its production is collectivist, located among ordinary people, especially those under duress. Cruz legitimizes the knowledge of those often excluded through participatory action research, which not only gets immigrants involved but also "dismantles the privilege that researchers (as experts) traditionally maintain over their objectified learners/data."

The essay abounds with narrative portraits of knowledge creation through the work of the people – women who provide "thick description" by taking photos of the dire circumstances under which they give birth ("photo voice") and children and adults who express the terror of state-sponsored violence through alternative modalities of "drama, movement, mask making, collages, storytelling, sound/silence, and drawing" ("creative

Original publication details: Faustino M. Cruz, "Immigrant Faith Communities as Interpreters: Educating for Participatory Action," pp. 27–37 from *New Theology Review* 21:4 (November 2008).

workshops"). Cruz writes out of his own life as an immigrant-scholar dedicated to making a difference, going beyond intellectual debate to show what good theologically oriented practice looks like.

Suggested Further Reading

- Faustino Cruz, "The Tension between Scholarship and Service," in Bonnie McLemore and Joyce Ann Mercer, eds., *Conundrums in Practical Theology* (Leiden: Brill, 2016), 60–89.
- Paulo Freire, *Pedagogy of the Oppressed*, 20th anniversary ed., trans. Myra Mergman Ramos (New York: Herder & Herder, 1994).

***

United States immigrants have gentrified neighborhoods, provided start-up capital to new entrepreneurs, organized literacy and language mentoring programs, established senior citizen and youth centers, and offered health and legal aid to other newcomers. Through their multiple belonging and affiliation with groups such as neighborhood organizations, family benevolent associations, and civic and cultural clubs, they have purposefully acted as agent-subjects of their own transformation (Cruz). Their engagement in public life – at least within their own ethnic boundaries – poses a challenge for the church. I argue that the effectiveness of immigrant ministry depends on how intentionally immigrants become interpreters of their own daily life and struggle and the extent to which the church collaborates with other sectors of society that shape the ecology of immigrant life. This pastoral vision may be achieved by educating immigrants for participatory action.

Pastoral Care of Immigrants

The pastoral care of immigrants has been, for the US Catholic Church, a particular locus of prophetic challenge and hope. It is a concrete example of evangelizing and transforming "humanity from within and making it new" (*Evangelii Nuntiandi* [EN], no. 18), acting from within a culture in a "vital way, in depth and right to...the very root" of the lives of people in relationship with one another and with God (EN, no. 20). The church has called for solidarity to carry out this mission, particularly when public policy and societal indifference further relegate the poor, minorities, and immigrants to the margins of US society (NCCB 1995, 22). "The Church...is required by the Gospel and by its long tradition to promote and defend the human rights and dignity of people on the move, to advocate social remedies to their problems and to foster opportunities for their spiritual and religious growth" (NCCB 1976). Toward this end, it engages in public discourse to influence government policy and to educate the public to respond to the Christian call (NCCB 1998, 1), "for I was a stranger and you welcomed me" (Matt 25:35).

Dioceses throughout the country have addressed the pastoral needs of immigrants by establishing hospitality centers; designing and implementing culturally accommodated educational, catechetical, and liturgical programs; and offering social and other related immigrant support services. In "Building Bridges: Profiles of Diocesan Ministry to Ethnic Groups," Father Anthony McGuire, former director of the USCCB Office for the

Pastoral Care of Migrants and Refugees, writes that dioceses throughout the United States vary in location and scope, in the intricacy of issues pertaining to specific ethnic groups, and in their pastoral strategy with new immigrants. McGuire explains: "There is no one model that serves every (arch)diocese. The only common factor for successful outreach is that there is some kind of central coordination, whether by full-time or part-time staff person or persons or by volunteer committees" (USCC 1999, 7).

De facto, ethnic ministry is segregated from the mainline functions and resources of other diocesan offices.

However, central coordination does not always assure the active participation and involvement of the whole diocese in responding to the needs of newcomers. In some dioceses, an office of ethnic ministry or migration functions as a micro-diocese. *De facto*, ethnic ministry is segregated from the mainline functions and resources of other diocesan offices, such as family life, religious education, worship, or lay ministry. Consequently, ethnic and language specific issues, challenges, and exigencies are relegated to a desk or department that must comprehensively attend to the catechetical, liturgical, educational, and other pastoral care needs of newcomers, mostly with limited staff and funding. While advancing unity and inclusion – at least in principle – such structure could inadvertently advance a culture of "separate but unequal."

Therefore, to generate accurately the fundamental themes of immigrant life, pastoral ministers must appropriately utilize indigenous and creative resources, such as autochthonous languages, signs, symbols, and rituals (EN, no. 63). Second, we must engage in problem-posing, codifying, and decodifying issues depicting daily struggle and survival in light of the Gospel. Third, our reflective practice must intentionally result in a deliberate action toward personal conversion and social transformation; otherwise, our voice of challenge and hope "loses much of its force and effectiveness" (EN, no. 63). Lastly, how we proclaim the Gospel must be contingent upon "the different circumstances of time, place and culture, and because they...present a certain challenge to our capacity for discovery and adaptation" (EN, no. 40). Therefore, our proclamation must unquestionably take place "where [people] are, not where [the church] would like them to be" (Donovan, vii). To know where persons and communities are, we must provide a "theological analysis of the total social situation in which the church finds itself" (Kinast, 874; Bergant et al.). One strategic approach is by educating for participatory action.

Participatory Action

Educating for Participatory Action (EPA) is grounded in the theory and practice of Participatory Action Research (PAR). PAR is a strategy for understanding critically social issues and bringing about systemic change through intentional, mutual action (Maguire; Fals-Borda and Rahman; Park et al.; Tandon). It integrates and engages three activities for emancipatory or transformative practice: education, research, and action (Hall, xiv).

Practitioners trace the earliest usage of the term participatory research to the 1970s in Tanzania (Tandon, 6). Adult educators in several emerging nations of Africa (and subsequently in Latin America and Asia) began to examine the root causes of societal disintegration, assess the impact of their educational efforts, and understand more fully the process of adult learning. They discovered a grave disparity between their method of research and their pedagogical creed. On one hand, the *factories of knowledge* that privileged the elite of the new nation-states determined the agenda of development and informed their method of inquiry (Park et al., xiii). The process relied heavily on the natural sciences; subscribed to the myths of neutrality, objectivity, and scientific absolutism; and advanced the paradigm of behaviorism and empiricism. It indiscriminately diminished participants into objects of manipulation and reduced their experiences into *objective data* or a problem left only for experts to solve (Tandon, 5–6).

On the other hand, the same adult educators located their learners in the center. They emphasized the learners' capacity to learn about, act within, and transform their reality by assuming control over their learning process. They grounded this approach in Paulo Freire's pedagogy of the oppressed that is essentially an instrument for promoting critical consciousness (Freire 1973).

Using pictures of and captions about their daily realities, the women have informed policymakers of what they have witnessed in their own words.

Freire's pedagogical efforts focus on the humanization of learners into subjects who know and act (capable of apprehending the reality of another), rather than objects that are known and acted upon (objective data). He explains: "If I perceive the reality as the dialectical relationship between subject and object, then I have to use methods of investigation which involve the people of the area being studied as researchers; they should take part in the investigation themselves and not serve as passive objects of the study" (Freire 1982). This liberating aspect of education is an intrinsic requirement for any proposal that promotes the inherent dignity and inalienable rights of all humans, especially those who are marginalized (Freire 1994, 31).

Freire asserts that persons learn to perceive social, political, and economic contradictions; to analyze their reality and become more aware of constraints on their lives; and to take actions to transform their human situation. They achieve this conscientization through praxis that involves the dialectical operation of critical thinking (reflection) and purposeful activity (action). Reflection and action inform each other, perform interactively, and lead to transformation (Freire 1994, 91).

Grounded in reflective action, PAR intentionally dismantles the privilege that researchers (as experts) traditionally maintain over their objectified learners/data. This paradigm shift requires the purposeful inclusion of diverse participants in the process of gaining and creating meaning. When this is carried out, educational research leads to knowledge production, as well as the development of consciousness and mobilization for action (Gaventa, 19). Knowledge construction becomes the creative and emancipatory work of the people that results in *right action*.

Therefore, PAR is fundamentally a collectivist rather than an individualistic process of inquiry (Tandon, 12; Gilligan 1992; Lyons, 124–45). It is a system of knowledge production of ordinary people, specifically those who are deprived, oppressed, or underprivileged. Knowledge is constructed for their daily struggle and survival; it is not intended to give the elite or the dominant enclave a base of power and control. PAR emphasizes a collaborative commitment to investigate a problem, relies on indigenous knowledge to understand more fully the problem, and takes individual and/or communal action to deal with the stated problem (Tandon, 7).

To achieve its goals, PAR creates a "bridging environment" (Kegan, 294) between professional researchers and marginalized groups to perform a locally determined and controlled action for radical social change (Maguire, 29). In PAR, knowledge and power, life and work are dialectically engaged for emancipation. PAR informs and forms the oppressed to acquire and sustain sufficient transformative projects, actions, and struggles. It advances sociopolitical meaning-making processes compatible with and familiar to the grassroots (Fals-Borda and Rahman, 4). Thus, it legitimizes the knowledge competently produced by persons whom decision-makers and stakeholders traditionally exclude; this knowledge is a constitutive element of *right action* (Fals-Borda and Rahman, 15).

North American educators have incorporated various aspects of the PAR method into projects designed to address social and community issues (Forester et al.; McIntyre). PAR provides an alternative strategy for illuminating complex social phenomena in the context of systemic change. It addresses the following fundamental questions: What is knowledge production for? Who participates in setting the agenda, collecting and analyzing data, and monitoring the process? How is knowledge produced, and what necessary creative and indigenous resources are utilized and legitimized? Who owns and benefits from the knowledge produced? What action will be carried out, and what are its implications for the daily life and struggle of the community? Some practitioners have utilized PAR in conjunction with related participatory strategies. Two of the most widely applied approaches are Photo Voice, a method of community photography, and Creative Workshops.

Photo Voice

Caroline Wang draws from her experience of working with sixty-two Chinese village women as community photographers and develops a methodology that fosters large-scale participation for community photography called Photo Voice (Wang et al., 1995a). Wang and a team of public health workers placed cameras in the hands of village women and have advanced this approach in the face of a "pervasive assumption that peasant women lacked the intelligence and creativity to portray their lives in a meaningful way" (Wang 1995b, 8). Using pictures of and captions about their daily realities, the women have informed policymakers of what they have witnessed *in their own words* (Wang and Burris, 172), heightening their knowledge about women in an androcentric society. Since then, children, grassroots workers, and other constituents with little access to systems that make decisions over their lives have made their knowledge public.

Rooted in Freire's pedagogy for critical consciousness and perceived through the lenses of feminism and documentary photography, Photo Voice enables persons to codify and reflect critically on their lives as "they see them" (Wang and Burris, 171). Photographs serve as one kind of code or "representation of the existential situation of the learners," borrowing Freire's expression (Freire 1970, 14). These codes reflect the community back to itself, mirroring the sociopolitical realities that affect daily life.

In Wang's project, images and words by and about women constitute the content of a curriculum for social change (Wang and Burris, 172). The caption of "Woman Postpartum," a photo taken by twenty-five-year-old Fu Qiong reads as follows:

> This woman gave birth to her baby three days ago at home. It isn't that women don't want to go to the hospital for delivery. The real reason is that many farmers who are not quite well-to-do can't afford the medical bill. Because women carry a great burden in the field and in the house, they seldom have time to go to the hospital for a physical check-up, or to treat and cure illness. In poor mountain areas, home births are common. (Wang 1995a, 69)

Guided by a process of decodification, a community of interpreters is convened to reflect critically on Fu Qiong's picture and address questions such as, What do you see in the picture? What does it mean for our lives and us? Why are things this way, and what are its consequences? What do we need to change, and how will we go about it? (Freire 1978, 54)

These questions have implications particularly for persons living under oppressive systems, who learn to view social problems as a *normal abnormality* or "terror as usual." Mick Taussig describes the ambiguity and disorientation this tragedy creates: "I am referring to a state of doubleness of social being in which one moves in bursts between somehow accepting the situation as normal, only to be thrown into a panic or shocked into disorientation by an event, a rumor, a sight, something said, or not said – something that even while it requires the normal in order to make its impact, destroys it" (Taussig, 3–20).

In many oppressive societies, racism, sexism, and other forms of prejudice and discrimination have become normal abnormalities. In effect, the reflective process facilitated by Photo Voice produces community-knowledge-for-action that enables persons who are powerless, underprivileged, and economically deprived to retrieve their *suspended stories* and confront policymakers about the dehumanizing consequences of institutionally legitimized normal abnormalities (Wang 1995b, 1, 9).

In the United States, Photo Voice can become a viable participatory action strategy for immigrant communities that are excluded from participating in making decisions that affect their lives (Wang and Burris, 171–86; Wang 1995c). It is a plausible method for expanding a collective understanding of thick descriptions seen through the eyes of youth, young adults, women, and those who are informally educated. Community photographers can identify daily practices, social issues, and societal challenges in order to generate analyses and explore solutions through interagency collaborations with university, church, school, and local neighborhoods. They can make meaning of and respond to *generative themes* such as urban violence, racial tension, and abject poverty. It is an innovative and participatory process of apprehending other people's realities – as a possibility for ourselves – for right action and transformation (Wang and Burris, 171).

Creative Workshops

Community educators and psychologists working with children and adults affected by war and state-sponsored violence in Latin America developed the theoretical framework of Creative Workshops. This framework supports an action-reflection approach of theory development. Unlike most intrapsychic approaches to psychology, creative workshops shift the focus of therapy from the effects of war on the individual to its effects on family, community, and other psychosocial contexts. For more than twenty years, M. Brinton Lykes, one of the leading proponents of this approach, has developed mental health programs with Guatemalan rural health promoters and child care providers who attend to child and youth survivors of organized, state-sponsored violence (Lykes 1994, 543–52). Her team has selectively incorporated Mayan indigenous (Kim, 143) practices and cultural resources (e.g., plants, rocks, soil); creative arts; and insights and strategies from community psychology, participatory action research, and emancipatory education. Their work has resulted in creative workshops that have taken place in various cultural contexts with children, youth, and adults.

Workshop participants work collaboratively in processes using drama, movement, mask making, collages, storytelling, sound/silence, and drawing. The team prepares participants to serve as future coordinators and facilitators of psycho-social assistance workshops with survivors of terror, violence, and other forms of institutionalized oppression (Harran). These activities have created an environment of trust and security in which participant-survivors and participant-facilitators have reflexively socialized their *silenced narratives* of war and violence.

Creative workshop participants learn to negate a hidden curriculum of normal abnormalities in which they have been socialized, to engage collectively their suspended memory. Second, they explore indigenous and creative ways to apprehend the dehumanizing consequences of terror and oppression in their lives. Using their own resources – in addition to those brought in by outside facilitators – they begin to see their reality with their eyes and articulate their words with their own voices. Third, they facilitate community rituals that allow them to unfreeze their grief and embrace forgiveness and reconciliation as a possibility for themselves – sometimes even for their perpetrators. Participatory action strategies, such as Photo Voice and Creative Workshops, impel them to renegotiate positions of power and privilege on the basis of age, gender, ordination, race, language, and so forth. These principles and practices shape the curriculum of educating for participatory action.

Educating for Participatory Action

Annabel Calilung and Cora Villaraza are among thousands of nurses recruited by US hospitals since the 1960s. Typical of immigrants from the Philippines, they regularly remit money and goods to their homeland in a gesture of solidarity and gratitude. "That is why when you see Filipinos here, they tend to work, work, and work," Annabel explains. Consumed by the daily challenges of immigrant life, many of them suffer from spiritual displacement (Rodriguez-Soto, A13).

Consequently, Annabel and Cora were inspired to gather a small group of nurses in South Florida to regularly participate in biblical reflections and prayer. While civic, regional, and professional affiliations had addressed many of their social needs, Annabel argued that "nothing really is being done about our spiritual growth." "Slowly, our faith, our traditions are set aside," she lamented (Rodriguez-Soto, A13). Cora and Annabel have deeply valued the assistance they have received from the church, but they also yearn to participate intentionally in performing right action, particularly in carrying out the church's mission to welcome the stranger.

In July 1996, members of the prayer group decided to take action: they invited me to serve as a pastoral consultant and organize a town-hall meeting that I had proposed, which was held on August 26. Prior to the gathering, local organizers "thought maybe 50 people would show." "We had 150," they proudly disclosed to a local news reporter, celebrating the fact that families "came from as far north as Boca Raton and as far south as Kendall" (Rodriguez-Soto, A13). I had designed the meeting for about thirty participants, and as I watched more and more people walking into the parish hall at Saint Bartholomew Church, I relied on flexibility, improvisation, and God's grace to facilitate a participatory process.

At the assembly, the participants collectively identified four fundamental caegories of pastoral concerns: liturgy, family life, evangelization, and community center. Each of the four concerns created a space in which Filipino immigrants could reach into the very root of their lives *in relatedness*, locating a context for effective evangelization. They envisioned culturally inclusive liturgies presided by priests fluent in Tagalog or other regional languages. They affirmed the importance of promoting popular religiosity such as devotions to San Lorenzo Ruiz (the first Filipino saint), novenas to Our Lady of Perpetual Help and the Santo Niño, and the Advent ritual of Simbang Gabi. They recognized that academic and spiritual formation was required to carry out their vision. Thus, they wished to establish a school of ministry that would provide competent training to future Filipino pastoral ministers, in partnership with the archdiocese. The participants underscored the need to serve all immigrants, regardless of their ethnicity and religious affiliation, clearly indicative of a commitment toward the common good.

Auxiliary Bishop Agustín Roman, himself an immigrant from Cuba, wrote on how the Archdiocese of Miami "reaches out to these wonderful and faith-filled people who, much on their own initiative, have been meeting in small groups to strengthen and support each other in their Catholic faith" (Roman). The phrases "small group" and "own initiative" provided vital clues for understanding the origins of Filipino Catholic ministry in South Florida. For "what began with a small prayer group of Filipino nurses grew into a first-ever archdiocesan retreat and Mass for Filipino Catholics" and laid the cornerstone for Filipino lay ministry in the archdiocese (Rodriguez-Soto, A13).

More than ten years since the first consultation, local pastoral leaders continue to utilize various creative workshop strategies such as brainstorming, dyads, creative drawing, dramatization, and storytelling. They have learned to use photographs not only to document significant events but more importantly to code vital "texts" of their lives as a community of interpreters. The various activities helped them to integrate diverse ways of knowing, advance empathic conversations, promote collaborative action, and uphold inclusion.

A pastoral approach that advances participatory action aims to affirm, challenge, and transform multiple immigrant identities and affiliations, legitimize a concrete reality that embodies their ultimate concern, and create alternative templates that foster an empathic relationship with God and the ecology of all creation. This right action must be carried out within the ecology of immigrant life (school-church-university-community) while advancing and sustaining disciple-citizenship. As a result, the church will not only utilize the gifts and talents brought by immigrants; rather, it will protect their human right to participate fully in making decisions that affect their lives, both private and public, toward the common good.

References

Bergant, Dianne, Faustino Cruz, Kathleen Dorsey-Bellow, Bernard Lee, and Maureen O'Brien. *Theological Reflection for Transformation.* Chicago: Center for the Study of Religious Life, 2004.

Cruz, Faustino. "Ministry for a Multicultural Church and Society." *Reflective Practice: Formation and Supervision in Ministry* 88 (2007) 43–60.

Donovan, Vincent. *Christianity Rediscovered.* Maryknoll, NY: Orbis Books, 1993.

Evangelii Nuntiandi (Apostolic Exhortation of His Holiness Pope Paul VI) (December 8, 1975). http://www.vatican.va/holy_father/paul_vi/apost_exhortations/documents/hf_p-vi_exh19751208_evangelii-nuntiandi_en.html (accessed January 4, 2008).

Fals-Borda, Orlando, and Mohammad Anisur Rahman. *Action and Knowledge: Breaking the Monopoly with Participatory Action Research.* New York: Apex Press, 1991.

Hall, Bud. "Introduction." In Peter Park, Mary Brydon-Miller, Bud Hall, and Ted Jackson, eds., *Voices of Change: Participatory Research in the United States and Canada.* Toronto: Ontario Institute for Studies in Education, 1993, xiv.

Forester, J., J. Pitt, and J. Welsh. *Profiles of Participatory Action Researchers.* Cornell, NY: Einaudi Center for International Studies and Department of City and Regional Planning, Cornell University, 1993.

Freire, Paulo. *Cultural Action for Freedom.* Cambridge, MA: Harvard Educational Review, 1970.

———. *Education for Critical Consciousness.* New York: Continuum, 1973.

———. *Pedagogy of the Oppressed.* Twentieth anniversary ed. Trans. Myra Mergman Ramos. New York: Herder and Herder, 1994.

———. "Creating Alternative Research Methods: Learning to Do It by Doing It." In Budd Hall, Arthur Gillette, and Rajesh Tandon, eds., *Creating Knowledge: A Monopoly.* New Delhi: Society for Participatory Research, 1982.

Gaventa, John. "Participatory Research in North America." *Convergence* 221, nos. 2–3 (1988) 9–18.

Gilligan, Carol. *In a Different Voice: Psychological Theory and Women's Development.* Cambridge, MA: Harvard University Press, 1992.

Harran, Tyler. *Grouped-based Mental Health Work with Survivors of War in El Salvador.* Chestnut Hill, MA: Boston College, 1994.

Kegan, Robert. *In Over Our Heads: The Mental Demands of Modern Life.* Cambridge, MA: Harvard University Press, 1994.

Kim, Uichol. "Indigenous Psychology." In Richard Brislin, ed., *Applied Cross-Cultural Psychology*, vol. 14. Newbury Park, CA: Sage Publications, 1990, 142–60.

Kinast, Robert L. "Pastoral Theology-Catholic." In Rodney J. Hunter, ed., *Dictionary of Pastoral Care and Counseling.* Nashville: Abingdon Press, 1996, 874.

Lykes, M. Brinton. "Terror, Silencing, and Children: International Multidisciplinary Collabo- ration with Guatemalan Maya Communities." *Social Science and Medicine* 38, no. 4 (1994) 543–52.

Lyons, Nona. "Two Perspectives on Self, Relationships, and Morality." *Harvard Educational Review* 53 (1983) 124–45.

Maguire, Patricia. *Doing Participatory Research: A Feminist Approach.* Amherst, MA: The Center for International Education, University of Amherst, 1987.

McIntyre, Alice. *Making Meaning of Whiteness: Exploring Racial Identity with White Teachers.* Albany, NY: SUNY Press, 1997.

National Conference of Catholic Bishops. *One Family Under God: A Statement of the US Bishops' Committee on Migration.* Washington, DC: United States Catholic Conference, 1995.

———. "Resolution on the Pastoral Concern of the Church for People on the Move" (November 11, 1976). From synopsis available at: http://usccb.org/mrs/synopsis.pdf (accessed June 30, 2008).

National Conference of Catholic Bishops, Migration and Refugee Services. "The Church's Mission to Immigrants, Refugees, and People on the Move." Unpublished document, 1998.

Park, Peter, Mary Brydon-Miller, Bud Hall, and Ted Jackson, eds. *Voices of Change: Participatory Research in the United States and Canada.* Toronto: Ontario Institute for Studies in Education, 1993.

Rodriguez-Soto, Ana. "Filipinos Share their Faith at First-ever Retreat, Mass." *The Florida Catholic* (October 10, 1996) A13.

Roman, Agustín. "Letter to Rev. Faustino Cruz, SM." Miami, FL: Archdiocese of Miami, July 25, 1996.

Tandon, Rajesh. "Social Transformation and Participatory Research." *Convergence* 21, nos. 2–3 (1988) 5–18.

Taussig, Mick. "Terror as Usual: Walter Benjamin's Theory of History as a State of Siege." *Sociological Text* (Fall/Winter 1989) 3–20.

United States Catholic Conference, Migration and Refugee Services Office for the Pastoral Care of Migrants and Refugees. *Building Bridges: Profiles of Diocesan Ministry to Ethnic Groups*. Washington, DC: United States Catholic Conference, September 1999.

Wang, Caroline, and Mary Ann Burris. "Empowerment through Photo Novella: Portraits of Participation." *Health Education Quarterly* 21, no. 2 (Summer 1994) 171–86.

Wang, Caroline, et al., eds. *Visual Voices: 100 Photographs of Village China by the Women of Yunnan Province*. Yunnan, China: Yunnan Publishing House, 1995a.

Wang, Caroline, Mary Ann Burris, and Xiang Yue Ping. "Chinese Village Women as Visual Anthropologists: A Participatory Approach to Reaching Policymakers." *Social Science and Medicine* (1995b) 1–10.

Wang, Caroline. *Methodology for Community Photography: Participatory Needs Assessment and the Critical Image*. Unpublished manuscript, October 1995.

4

My GPS Does Not Work in Puerto Rico (2011)*,1

Loida I. Martell

Introduction

In the last two decades, Loida I. Martell has played an invaluable role in the development of evángelica theology. A bicoastal Puerto Rican, graduate of Fordham University,
and now professor of constructive theology and Vice President of Academic Affairs at
Lexington Theological Seminary, she has made an important claim for Protestantism
in what has been a predominantly Catholic Hispanic landscape. Distinct from the
English *evangelical*, the term *evángelica* refers to a Latin and Caribbean American
Protestantism formed in progressive waves of colonization by the confluence of Iberian
Catholicism, indigenous traditions, African religions, and Protestantism. Her mentors
and peers are few but critically important – historical theologian Justo González, one
of the few Protestants in the early Latin American theology movement, and, more
recently, Elizabeth Conde-Frazier and Zaida Maldonado Pérez with whom Martell
coauthored a groundbreaking book, *Latina Evangélicas: A Theological Survey from the
Margins* (2013).

Although Martell's publications often focus on conventional loci in systematic theology, she resists constricting labels. Martell demonstrates a strong practical bent that
emerges naturally from her Latina outlook and her experiences as a licensed veterinar-
ian and an ordained American Baptist pastor who served a congregation in New York
City for fifteen years. As reflected in several footnotes in the following essay, she sustains important alliances with Conde-Frazier who deserves recognition for her significant contributions as the first Protestant Latina practical theologian with expertise in
religious education.

In this essay, Martell explores evangélica spirituality as defined by three elements –
sacred place, *presencia de Dios*, and *testimonio encarnado*. Her depiction of these
three unsettles basic philosophical motifs in Western epistemology, particularly the
constructs of space and time. In contrast to the temporal obsession of western and
northern theology, she describes a "priority of spaciality over time." This reorientation in
knowledge is palpably illustrated when she describes how assumptions built into the

*Original publication details: Loida I. Martell-Otero, "My GPS Does Not Work in Puerto Rico: An Evangélica
Spirituality," pp. 256–75 from *American Baptist Quarterly* 30:3/4 (Fall/Winter 2011).

GPS – road names, address numbers, and mileage measurements – *no tiene sentido,* do not make sense in a world where space is viewed in terms of land, people, and connections. Sacred spaces and the sacramentality of place shape memory and knowledge, not time and chronicity. This spatial reorientation demands a coinciding temporal relocation, rending phrases such as *to kill* or *waste time* incomprehensible. In an evángelica world, time is not possessed but given. To cultivate *vínculos* (connections and community) takes time and presence. Therefore, contrary to racist stereotypes about tardiness and misperception of *ahorita* or *mañana* (later) as a sign of laziness, Martell redefines the terms. To say *ahorita* is about more than an eschatological hope for a better tomorrow, as González imagines; *ahorita* protests the Western timelines and deadlines of today. It joins those working "inhumane hours for non-living wages" and insists that "only so much can or should be accomplished within a given space of time."

These claims about place, time, and human knowledge are undergirded by alternative views of how to interpret God's presence. Specifically, when evangélicas use the term *sentir* or feel, they are talking about far more than *feeling*. *Sentir* also refers to *sentido* or sense. To claim one can *sentir la presencia de Dios* is to say that "God's presence makes eminent sense, that it gives direction and purpose to our lives." From this perspective, other "epistemological tools" for discerning practical wisdom emerge, including song, short musical refrains drawn from biblical verse, story and testimony, prayer, communal discernment, and proverbial sayings. Indeed, in a oppressive world where "words have been cheapened, distorted, and used in lying and destructive ways," silence itself becomes an essential means for interpreting divine action.

Suggested Further Reading

- Loida I. Martell-Otero, Aaida Maldonado Pérez, and Elizabeth Conde-Frazier, *Latina Evangélicas: A Theological Survey from the Margins* (Eugene, OR: Cascade, 2013).
- Justo L. González, *Mañana: Christian Theology from a Hispanic Perspective* (Nashville: Abingdon, 1990).
- Elizabeth Conde-Frazier, "Hispanic Protestant Spirituality," in José D. Rodríguez and Loida I. Martell-Otero, eds., *Teología en Conjunto: A Collaborative Hispanic Protestant Theology* (Louisville: Westminster John Knox 1997), 125–45.

***

Spirituality is a familiar topic to many. There is a lengthy tradition of scholarship and practice on the subject. [...] "Spirituality" evokes the images of such mystical giants as Francis of Assisi, Bernard Clairvaux, Julian of Norwich, and Catherine of Siena. Those of us in the Spanish-speaking world are more familiar with Juan de la Cruz, [...] Teresa de Ávila, [...] and Ignacio de Loyola.

[...]

Nevertheless, my purpose is not so ambitious as to attempt to engage the topic from such an array of perspectives. [...] Rather, my goal simply is to approach spirituality from a very particular perspective and context: that of a bicoastal Puerto Rican evangélica who has grown up in the church and now ministers in the world of academia as a constructive theologian. From that perspective, I begin with the assumption that spirituality can be defined as the development of intimate relations with the perichoretic Triune God who desires for us to love one another and to love creation, of which we are an intimate part. I further assume that spirituality does not imply "immateriality" but rather is an incarnational – embodied, if you will – reality that takes place and therefore commits us to live out our vocation in holistic ways in the world and in the Church, faithful to the eschatological promise of the Reign of God. It moves us to create "sacred spaces" that are "outside the gate" where the displaced and forgotten are found. Given those assumptions, I argue that spirituality for evangélicas includes three important elements: *presencia de Dias,* sacred place, and *testimonio encarnado.* Spirituality reminds us of the grace of God's gifts and our concomitant responsibility to dream dreams and have visions. These, in turn, re-order our priorities as we live out our daily lives and seek justice in a hurting and violent world.

Evangélica Roots of Spirituality: A Brief Survey

The spirituality of evangélicas is influenced historically by four critical strains that are relevant to this discussion. Iberian Catholicism, shaped and influenced by Jewish and Moorish mystical and religious practices and beliefs, encountered those of the Taino Indians that inhabited the island. While direct information about Taino religious traditions is not available to us, Spanish documents as well as archeological finds have afforded us a general framework.[2] In light of the genocide and exploitation of the indigenous peoples by invading colonizers – whether military or religious – African slaves were later introduced to the island. The often violent and unequal encounter of these three distinctive worldviews resulted in a popular Catholic faith espoused by the majority of the island's inhabitants. It, in turn, proved influential upon the various waves of Protestants that invaded Puerto Rico (and Latin America) through the military, imperial, and religious actions of the inhabitants of the North Atlantic nations. This produced a distinctive brand of Protestantism that I denote under the rubric of "evangélica." It should not be confused with or translated to the English "evangelical" – with its concomitant theological, sociological and political connotations distinctive to the United States.[3]

Latina/o scholars have been amply exploring the Iberian Catholic influences on Latino religiosity, including the rich contribution of Spanish mystics to Puerto Rican and Latino/a general belief and practice, and to theology and spirituality in particular. Conversations with our Afro-Caribbean and African American colleagues have allowed us to also mine the richness of traditions that African beliefs contributed to our overall faith. What has been less explored, I believe, is what our indigenous roots have provided to the conversation, a critique presented by Lara Medina a year ago to Mexican American and other theologians who claimed *mestizaje* as an important epistemological tool, but who in the long run, she believed, only explored the European roots of the faith.[4] *Mestizaje* has been defined as a process in which the encounter of two or more biological or cultural groups (usually indigenous with European) creates a third distinctive group that nevertheless retains the characteristics of its parents.[5] While the terminology of *mestizaje* has been found to be problematic by some – a discussion which is beyond the scope of this paper – Medina's criticism should be taken seriously. I hope to correct that tendency and when possible, note where our indigenous legacy has contributed to our evangélica religious sensibilities.

I believe that one of those characteristics is the importance of music in evangélica worship and expressions of spirituality. For our African forebears, music was an important way to call upon the gods. In Taíno tribal life, music played a critical role in communal celebrations as well as in healing rituals. Virgilio Elizondo observes that in Mayan culture the proper way to speak of the gods was through *flor y canto/*flower and song.[6] It is not surprising then that music plays a central role for evangélica expressions of spirituality and theology. In many instances, when they are at a loss for words to express their love of God or the depth of an experience they are undergoing, they will break into song, especially *coritos* – short refrains, often based on a biblical text and put to rhythmic music autochthonous to the island.

Another important legacy derived from our African and indigenous roots is the place of storytelling, now transmuted in the form of "witnessing"/*testimonio.* In the evangélica churches, time is set aside for members to share their *testimonios* – to tell their personal stories of their encounters with God in their daily lives. More often than not, testimonios are shared by women, who use them as vehicles of empowerment and voice amid religious institutions that would otherwise exclude them from the pulpit. However, testimonios are not limited to the spaces of the institutional church. As Elizabeth Conde-Frazier and others have noted, testimonios are stories shared in a variety of contexts.[7] They provide a rich theological epistemological tool for the shared community. They often serve liberative and subversive purposes.[...]

La Presencia de Dios

In the *bohíos*/dwellings of Taíno families, one would find *cemís* – figurines that contained the spirit of a tree, a rock, or an ancestor. If a tree spoke to them, they would cut it down and carve out the figurine, believing that the cemí retained the essential spirit of its original source.[8] In this way, the gods resided in the midst of their homes. They would always be present. The later influence of African *orishas* and Iberian Catholic views about God transmuted this understanding into what Orlando O. Espín has described as a "sacramental worldview" – one that sees an inherent relationality/*vínculo* between the divine and the created world.[9] Vínculo is more than just relationality. It implies "ties that bind," and therefore intimacy in the relationship. Where there are vínculos, there is also commitment.

For evangélicas, this sense of God's presence is reflected wonderfully in the popular corito, *Dios está aquí/God is here*:

> Dios está aquí/ Tan cierto como el aire que respiro/ Tan cierto como en la mañana se levanta el sol/ Tan cierto que cuando le hablo Dios me puede oír/ Lo puedo sentir cuando está a mi lado/ Lo puedo sentir dentro de mi corazón.[10]

When an evangélica sings this song, it is not meant to be a privatistic or simply interiorized moment. It is rather the affirmation that God is present in the world. It is an acknowledgment that God's transcendence is manifested in God's immanent presence.

God is the One who is not afar but is characterized by *presencia.* As one evangélica testified, "espiritualidad es sentir que Dios es mío y yo soy de [Dios], sentir su paz, su aliento, su amor." For her, it was "experimentar la presencia de Dios," not while in isolated prayer but in the spaces of the everyday, particularly in the midst of loss and crisis.[11] When evangélicas say that they can *sentir la presencia de Dios,* it is more than just a feeling. *Sentir/*feel is also the root for *sentido/* sense. To sentir la presencia is to also say that God's presence makes eminent sense, that it gives direction and purpose to our lives. This sense that presencia brings is an "awareness of the grace of God that over-whelms" us, and energizes us to be attentive to the interconnectedness of community and the necessity of issues of justice in the world.[12]

God's presencia is embodied in the spaces of the everyday/*en lo cotidiano*. Evangélicas find it strange when they hear Euro-American theologians emphasize God's transcend-ence and mystery. It is not that they negate God's transcendence. Rather, evangélicas interpret transcendence through God's radical presence in the midst of the created spaces. Like the Incarnation, it is an "embodied transcendence." This is particularly life-giving to evangélicas in the United States – many who are poor, invisible, silenced and marginalized, who are told that they are no-bodies, and that their beliefs are no-sense. Their communities and dreams are rent apart, and they are often abandoned by social structures, including ecclesial ones, that should be life-giving. For them, God's embod-ied transcendence in the world makes eminent sense/*tiene sentido*. It is the modernist insistence of compartmentalizing the secular and the sacred – as evidenced in the con-tinuous expressions of God's "breaking into the world" as if God were a thief breaking into someone else's abode – that makes no-sense/*no tiene sentido* to them. Where there is vínculo, there cannot be "breaking in." There can only be presencia.

Our indigenous roots, in particular, have made us sensitive to God's speaking in embodied ways. Euro-centric worldviews too often have scoffed at what they have con-sidered syncretic or animistic worldviews. The Latino/a worldview in general, and I daresay, the evangélica in particular, has no problem in sensing God's Spirit incarna-tionally in and through the created world: in the blowing of the wind, the singing of the birds, the crashing of the waves, and the song of the *coqui*, as well as through the wis-dom of the extended community.[13] God also speaks in the silences. For women who have been historically silenced, and who live in a world where words have been cheap-ened, distorted, and used in lying and destructive ways, evangélicas have learned to value silence and to interpret God's voice in the midst of it. This is why prayer and communal discernment are important aspects of evangélica spirituality. Whether in the crevices of silences or in the spaces of the created world, evangélicas live in "abiding astonishment" humbly attentive to God's presence, patiently listening to learn God's will for the well-being of the world.[14] In so doing, they derive not only life and joy, but also affirmation in unexpected quarters in a world that often would deny those things to them. Perhaps this is why, even in the midst of pain and sorrow, they sing:

> Estamos de fiesta con Jesús/ Al cielo queremos ir/ y todos reunidos a la mesa/ es Cristo quien va servir/ Poderoso es nuestro Dios/[15]

Or:

> Has cambiado mi lamento en baile/ Me ceñiste de alegría/ Por eso a ti cantaré gloria mía/ Y no estaré callada/ Señor Dios mío te alabaré/ Te alabaré para siem-pre/ Porque has cambiado mi lamento en baile/ Señor Dios mío te alabaré.[16]

The Latina culture is deeply communal. It is a culture of relationality and of sharing. There are vínculos not just with God but with each other and with the created world.

It is interesting that in the Taíno language, the words "yours" or "mine" did not exist.[17] African culture reinforced this worldview. This communal spirit is often expressed in the common saying, "*Hoy por ti, mañana por mi*/Today for you, tomorrow for me," which assumes that all things belong to God and are made available to whoever needs it at a given moment. It is not surprising then that evangélicas hold a deep resonance with the God who is Community-in-Godself. The God whose presencia is acknowledged is Triune. Zaida Maldonado Pérez asserts that for evangélicas "the Trinity is the subject [of] our praise and the essence of our purpose for living" rather than the result of philosophical speculation or belief in rote formulations.[18] That is to say, evangélicas acknowledge God Creator – who has made them, their families, the places that they inhabit, who provides for them, and who above all, is Savior. *Dias está aquí* particularly through Jesús Christ. Jesús experienced what it was to be a brown *sato* like them, who was therefore marginalized, poor, and rejected.[19] This Jesús is God *presente* outside the gate of justice among those who are daily devalued and treated as *sobraja*/leftovers in the world.[20]

Particularly notable is what Maldonado Pérez calls the "pneumato logical nuance" of evangélica notions of God. Spirit does not mean "invisible" nor does it mean "immaterial." Spirit is an embodied transcendence in the world and particularly in the community. The Spirit brings life, song, and hope in the spaces of our lives where death seeks to be lord. The Spirit is Life-Giver who breathes upon, anoints, empowers, and moves us to embody God's love in the world. It is the presence, the moving, the gifts of the Spirit that prevents evangelica spirituality from becoming self-centered and deaf to the cries of "the least these." If, as Molly T. Marshall has so wonderfully articulated, the Spirit is the One who invites us to join in the perichoretic – that is to say, an intimate mutuality or interdependence – dance of God's love, then it is also the Spirit that has us go forth in what Maldonado Pérez calls the "va y ven" of the Triniarian movement to serve where there is most need in that world.[21]

[...]

Sacred Spaces of Lo Cotidiano: Visteme Despacio Que Voy de Prisa

One of the most distinctive aspects of Puerto Rican evangélica spirituality is its valuing of place over time. Place is where one *is*. Place is the space in which vínculos unfold. One discerns God's presence there, and in doing so community takes place. I suspect that this valuation of spatiality over temporality is another legacy of our indigenous forebears. Such a valuation arises from a notion that there are sacred spaces in creation that are a part of a people's history. Sacred spaces have power. They retain subversive "cultural memories" that belong to the voiceless, and which sometimes precede the historical narratives of those in power. Sacred spaces are often interpreted to be geographical locations in which the divine has been manifest in some distinct fashion. A worldview that prioritizes spatiality over temporality tends to perceive creation as an integral part of the community.[22]

This priority of spatiality over time was underscored for me last summer when I returned to Puerto Rico after a fifteen-year absence. Since I have no sense of direction, I made sure to bring along my trusty Garmin GPS unit to ensure that I would find all the places I needed to go to during my two week visit. To my dismay, the unit was unable to locate any of the places I asked of it. Google maps and MapQuest were equally useless.

In the spots where I knew there were homes, these representatives of modern technology only showed large swaths of blue, as if people and homes and places did not exist.

Added to my sense of cognitive dissonance, I had to re-remember that time and geography were measured very differently on the island. Having been away for so long, I had learned the pacing of the dominant culture of the United States, which tends to prize temporality. Time is of the essence. Time is perceived as *chronos*: measurable, discrete, and finite. Yet, as finite, it creates levels of anxiety. [...] It is within the framework of this priority of temporality over spatiality that I learned such terms as "killing time," "pressed for time," and "don't waste time." I had forgotten that when I first heard such terminology, *no tenía sentido*. How can you kill, press, or waste time? [...] We cannot waste or kill time in the same way we cannot waste or kill space. It is not ours but grace-full gifts of the divine in which we are to see God's vision for creation unfold. *Eso tiene sentido.*

I had almost forgotten how jarring it always seems to me when invited to a Euro-American church to preach that I usually first have to ask, "how much time do I have?" Euro-Americans often critique people from cultures who do not prize time. They become annoyed with their tendency to "not be on time." How different in a culture that prizes spatiality over temporality! [...] Place is where *vínculos* are cultivated. Consequently, we counter such criticisms with humor and refer to "Puerto Rican time" to remind our critics that we measure time and space differently.

The first few days of being in on the island, I had to re-adjust my priorities. My GPS did not work in Puerto Rico! It could never understand place. I, on the other hand, had to re-learn how to find places. The GPS, like the dominant culture, wanted precise coordinates: it sought measurement in miles, latitude, and longitude. It wanted addresses! I had to remember that when I ask someone in Puerto Rico for instructions, I never ask for an address. I ask for a place by inquiring about the people who reside there: "where does such and such live?" or by referring to a story that the place represents – the historical memory that resides there. I would never be told how many miles to drive, or what road to take.[...] In fact, if I inquired about road numbers, people would look at me strange. "*¿Qué?*/What?" [...] I had to remember to understand the language of directions that described rolling hills, curves on the road, don Genaro's store on the corner, and the palm tree where I had to take a right. I learned to find places. I never once got lost.

[...]

There are particular places that hold special power of holiness, of "sacramentahty" if you will. Such places are awash with "cultural memory" that is ancient. Here in Puerto Rico, *el Yunque* – which the Federal government has claimed as a national rain forest – and Guavate are two such places. Associated with the Taíno gods by Puerto Ricans, such places invite one to enter into a spirit of reverence. One can hear the voice of the Spirit in these sacred spaces. [...]

This culturally different approach to time and space is often expressed in Puerto Rico through the term *ahorita*, which means "later." Other Latino/a groups use the term *mañana* – which is the title of one of Justo L. González's books. In it, he discusses the dominant culture's disdain for the Latino/a penchant for using that word whenever they are asked to do something, interpreting it as a form of laziness. González explains that it is not laziness but rather a "radical questioning of today" because today is in the hands of those in power, while *mañana* expresses an eschatological hope "of a new reality."[23] I want to suggest, however, that for Latinas it is related to our prioritizing of place. As Latinas, we have been socialized to be incarnational: we are aware of the rhythms of our bodies and the place of our social locations, and how these impact our identities. We are aware of how we must always negotiate the spaces we inhabit and how the world around us relates to us and we towards it. We are aware of our place in the community. This awareness leads us to focus more on embodied presence than on *chronos*. That is to say, if place is the cross section of sacred *kairos* where relations are cultivated and community flourishes, then *ahorita* is an affirmation that what we are doing, who we are with, and the place where we are located are more important than someone's agenda or timelines. Those agendas can wait for *ahorita*. […] We are being *presente en lo cotidiano* because *tiene sentido. Mañana* has no substance; it has no guarantee. This is why we often end our sentences with *si Dios quiere/*if God wills – *mañana* will come only if God wills but we cannot plan definitely for it. We only have the now and what is present before us. In that present, the people we are with in a given place do have substance. They deserve our unmerited attention and love because they are the ones that God has placed in our path to bless and to be conduits of blessings. *!Presente!*

Ahorita has another connotation. Time as *chronos* is often used as a commodity for those in power. How many times have I not heard the phrase, "get more bang for the buck" as an indication of the exploitation of labor of the powerless? Latinas, particularly the poor and im/migrant workers, know this well. Their bodies have been, like the woman in the synagogue in Luke 13: 10–17, "stooped over" time, working inhumane hours for non-living wages. When Latinas say *ahorita,* they are reclaiming the belief of their indigenous forebears that only so much can or should be accomplished within a given space of time because people, not things and certainly not tasks, are important. To be present is important. To encounter God is important. *Si Dios quiere* understands time as *kairos,* as God-given grace that takes place. This is why when I am invited to a Latina church to preach, my question is not how much time do I have but who is my audience and what is the theme or topic. The concern is for the people who are attending who have worked hard all week and now gather to await a Word from God. They do not care how long they have to be there. They realize that to cultivate *vínculos* that form community, and *presencia* takes time and above all, takes place. They have to be *presente* for God to be *presente*. They are *presente* to each other, to experience God's *presencia* in their midst. These things are not to be rushed. It take place in God time in God space, *si Dios quiere*.

Towards A Holistic Spirituality of Place and Presence: Testimonio Encarnada

Most Latinas in general, and *evangélicas* in particular, have experienced seismic shifts and great loss over the course of their history, both in their native lands but especially in the context of the United States. Without going into the specifics of statistics, let me summarize by saying that they are part of a population that is mired in poverty and must face the consequences of racism, cultural discrimination, and classism on a daily basis. They live constantly under the threat of violence – whether institutional or personal. For some, the structural forces that have produced global homelessness and the migratory patterns that are part of the "new globalization" have exposed them to the dangers and horrors of what it means to live and work in border towns in *maquiladoras,* undergo the dangerous trek across those borders, and enter into hostile territory where they are treated like "strangers in a strange land."[24]

Puerto Rican women have been part of that history of violence. The contemporary expressions of globalization did not begin with the fall of the Berlin Wall as it has been claimed of late, but rather with the colonizing practices begun with such exploitive practices as the *Braceros* program in Mexico and *Operation Bootstrap* and the economic policies initiated in Puerto Rico in the mid-twentieth century. The latter was a policy, I might add, that included using childbearing age women as guinea pigs for pharmaceutical trials of contraceptives and sterilizing procedures carried out without their consent as a response to the "population control problem" fabricated by the United States.[25]

Not all Latinas are immigrants, of course. Not all are poor. Yet even those who are bona fide citizens of the United States by birth have been treated in dehumanizing ways. They are often treated as *sobrajas*/left overs; that is to say, as people with no inherent worth. They are made to feel invisible. They are laughed at, ignored, silenced, marginalized, exploited, and violated in myriad and sundry ways. Many know what it means to live in neighborhoods that are filled with danger, residing in substandard housing, with little or no opportunities for a decent quality of life. We are constantly "put in our place." Even the Church has been complicit. The history of racism in the white church has been shameful; the sexism in Spanish churches often relegates them to circumscribed roles and prevents their access to the sacred space of the pulpit. Too often Latinas, including *evangélicas*, have been told explicitly or tacitly that for them "there is no place at the inn."

In order to survive, and even to thrive under such dehumanizing conditions, *evangélicas* have shifted the notion of sacred space by creating new ones where they can experience *presencia* and *vínculos* that are life-giving for them. Conde-Frazier has described how *evangélicas* create these spaces in communal celebrations such as baby showers or even in the bathroom stalls of bathrooms as they share their *testimonios*.[26] I have witnessed women create these spaces in gatherings over meals, at the church, or as they gather to plan a project that will benefit the community. I have witnessed it when they share their *testimonios* and especially when they sing *coritos* to give voice to their laments or praise God for divine grace in their lives. It is in sharing their stories and affirming *la presencia de Dios* in the spaces that they live that they make such places holy, and receive empowerment and healing from the Spirit. [...] The world – and in particular the places that are "outside the gate" where the marginalized are relegated – is now the sacred place where they feel/*sentir* called to serve God. They have a firm conviction that the Spirit has anointed and empowered them for this reason. Through such service, they experience God's grace-full *presencia*. If God has blessed them, they must now go forth and be a blessing in the world. If Jesus promised them that God is preparing a place for them, then they are called to make spaces for those who have been displaced. Thus *evangélica* spirituality is not so much an interiorized, privatized affair that looks to the good of the individual as much as it is an embodied *testimonio*, a praxis that is both passionate and compassionate – that is to say, one that seeks justice, especially for those who are unable to fend for themselves.

When *evangélicas* speak of having visions and dreaming dreams, it is not ecstatic escapism, but an ability to see what is in around them in new ways. [...] They have resisted the racist strictures of the world and the sexist barriers of the Church with an abiding sense of call that gives them *coraje* – a word that implies both anger and courage – to go to places of rejection, darkness, despair, and death, to do what needs to be done in the name of God, whom they love more than life itself. God, then, is the source of their call. God is the reason for their being. Because they love God and recognize God as the source of all life, the very expression of that love must be in service in the world. Theirs is an embodied witness *un testimonio encarnado* of spirituality. These then are their spiritual practices: to go to the places where no one else wants to go and where by themselves they would hesitate to go, to respond to the cries of pain and suffering, loss and want, and there to bring a word of hope that they themselves receive through the blowing of God's Spirit in their midst. [...]

Some Implications to Consider

[...] I want to challenge us to an embodied spirituality, *una espiritualidad encarnada* that is very much aware of where we are and who and what is present around us, and to the discernment of the Spirit's invitation to partake of a perichoretic dance of justice, mercy, and love.

I believe that a shift from a temporal emphasis to a spatial emphasis, from attention to timelines to concern for where we are and who inhabits these spaces has implications for us all. The first is in the arena of eschatology. We have tended to compartmentalize our Christian lives into "spiritual" and "the world/the material." Consequently, we tend to think about "the last things" in this way: there is a "now," a sinful world in which we are entrapped and from which we must escape at all costs. There is a "spiritual" or "other" world to which we seek escape. This "now" world has no connection with that "utopia" world. This world is "down here," while that other world is "up there." Yet the biblical witness does not support nor sustain such a dichotomous view. Jesus's constant teaching about the Reign of God was that we were to seek it in the midst of us. [...]

What if we stopped compartmentalizing our spiritual lives and begin to live out a holistic spirituality such that this place is the spiritual arena in which God reveals God's presence, purpose, and vision in the midst of us and through us? *Parousia* is often defined as "Jesus' return" rather than its more correct definition of "presence." What a seismic shift in the conversation of everyday people if we stopped thinking of *when* Jesus is coming and who gets left behind, and rather begin to think about *where* we are and *what* God expects of us *in this place.* [...]

[...]

The second implication is for our churches. Why do we gather and for what reasons are we there? Are the places where we worship "sacred spaces?" Is it an opportunity to be pre-sente before God as well as truly presente to our communities? Are our churches [...] places of sanctuary where the hurting, forgotten, oppressed, and dehumanized can find life and hope? What would happen if our parishioners stopped looking at their watches and began looking at each other? What would happen if they stopped worrying about their agendas and took a look at the neighborhoods, indeed at the place in which they are located? What if, instead of *when,* they worried about *where* and *what* of the Spirit's empowering?

[...]

Elsewhere I have described the brokenness that is visible in our society, and especially the brokenness suffered by the Latina/o community in the United States as a "compound fracture," one that is compounded generationally, but also by the structural and personal complexities that defy any attempts at easy repairs.[27] Ephesians 4 reminds us that the Spirit has been given to "equip"/*katartismos* the saints. Katartismos was borrowed from the secular world and originally meant to "heal broken bones" or "mend torn nets." To be aware of place and presence is to be acutely aware of the "compound fracture" and fissures created by the sinful powers and principalities that have produced economic disparities, global homelessness, violation of poor women and children of two thirds of the world, ecological despoliation, and so much other damage. To begin to address such profound concerns, we must begin with a spirituality of presence that asks not *when* but where and how; that is concerned not with agendas but with what are we to do. We begin by teaching our church members new ways of measuring urgency: that church is the place where we come to form community, to begin to practice being with each other and being present to the world. [...] Can we practice being a church that brings the world's pain and despair into our homes even as the Taínos brought in their cemís, and pray over them, and seek discernment from the Lord, having the courage to say, "Here am I, Lord. Send me."? Can our churches become "sacred spaces?"

There are implications for those of us in academia, as well. We too have become so in tuned to the rhythms of time that I wonder if we have lost sight of the presencia that gives sentido to what we do and why we are doing it. If [...] our spirituality gives expression to what we value most, [...] what does the day-to-day praxis of our professional lives say about our priorities and our vision for ministry?[29] What are we modeling for our students, who in turn become the leaders, teachers, and shapers of our churches and communities? We so often live under the pressure of deadlines. I wonder sometimes if deadlines have become the gods upon which we too often sacrifice its adherents, whether they be students, faculty, administrators, or staff. If so, how are we to teach about a Life-giving Spirit and go forth with joy if we live under the continuous cloud of something which begins with the word "dead?" I am not recommending chaos. Yet when we re-prioritize place – which does honor *kairos* and both divine and created space – as sacred, that space where life is cherished and the expectation of an encounter between God, community, and the created world is honored, it seems to me that we allow breathing space to witness to God's creativity in our midst: "behold, all things are made new." We give space to be presente for our students and for the academic community that surrounds us. We also give space to hear the Spirit's convicting breath that gives *testimonio* of the people we have forgotten to welcome in those spaces.[...] We who teach ethics and about justice are called to embody it, to give *testimonio* of what we teach in the way we live out our teaching vocations in the spaces of the everyday.

Our challenge then is to live out fully the implications of a holistic spirituality of place and presencia in all aspects of our lives. In so doing, it is my hope we can experience a new Pentecost: to see new visions and dream new dreams of what God is doing and can do in our midst as we face the increasing challenges of a suffering and unjust world; that we can develop new hearing to hear the cries of those who stand outside the gates; and that we can take to heart Jesus' challenges to those who seek to follow him and go to the places where the Spirit sends us rather than looking at the time. It is my hope that we truly live out a spirituality that focuses on the where rather than the when, on the vínculos rather than the tasks. May we hear the Spirit's invitation to dance, but always make sure that no one is left in corner outside of the festivities.

Notes

1 This paper was presented at the American Baptist Churches/USA Pre-Biennial Gathering of Theologians and Theological Educators at the Seminario Evangélico de Puerto Rico, June 23, 2011. My thanks to the Wabash Center for the sabbatical grant that

supported my research. Special thanks to the Seminario Evangélico, its dean, Dr. José Irizarry, and its library staff for opening their doors to me as a visiting professor, and to Palmer Theological Seminary and its library staff for their consistent support of all my research needs, no matter how obscure or esoteric.

2 This framework has some serious drawbacks, and has been subject to colonizing interpretations that need to be critically re-examined. Even the name "Taíno" is a Spanish misnomer of the Arawak tribes the conquistadors encountered, who called themselves "taino/good." See Ricardo E Alegría, *Apuntes en Torno a la Mitología de los Indios Taínos de las Antillas Mayores y Sus Orígenes Suramericanos* (Spain: Centro de Estudios Avanzado de Puerto Rico y el Caribe, 1978), 20–21. Eugenio Fernández Méndez, *Arte y Mitología de los Indios Taínos de las Antillas Mayores* (Sanjuan, Puerto Rico: Ediciones "CEMI," 1979), 29. For a critique of these methods, see Arlene Dávila, "Local/Diasporic Taínos: Towards a Cultural Politics of Memory, Reality and Imagery," in *Taína Revival: Critical Perspectives on Puerto Rican Identity and Cultural Politics,* ed. Gabriel Haslip-Viera (Princeton, NJ: Markus Wiener Publishers, 2001).

3 For more on *evangélicas,* see Loida Martell-Otero, "Women Doing Theology: Una Perspective Evangélica," *Apuntes* 3, no. 14 (Fall 1994): 67–85 as well as Elizabeth Conde Frazier and Loida L Martell-Otero, "US Latina Evangelicas," in *Encyclopedia of Women and Religion in North America,* vol. 1, eds. Rosemary Skinner Keller and Rosemary Radford Ruether (Bloomington: Indiana University Press, 2006).

4 Lara Medina, "Response to Tink Tinker," in *Wading Through Many Voices: Toward a Theology of Public Conversation,* ed. Harold J. Recinos (Lanham, MA: Rowman and Littlefield Publishers, Inc., 2011), 275–6.

5 Virgilio Elizondo, *Galilean Journey: The Mexican-American Promise,* 2nd ed. (Maryknoll, NY: Orbis Books, 2000), 10. It should be noted that mestizaje has never been a "neutral" or "natural" event, but rather has been associated historically with conquest, rape, colonization and neo-colonization/ globalization. See Andrea Smith, "Sexual Violence and American Indian Genocide," and Traci. C. West, "Spirit-Colonizing Violations: Racism, Sexual Violence and Black American Woman," both in *Remembering Conquest: Feminist/ Womanist Perspectives on Religion, Colonization, and Sexual Violence* (New York: Hawthorne Pastoral Press, 1999). Also Julia Esquivel, "Conquered and Violated Women," in *1492–1992: The Voice of the Victims,* eds. Leonardo Boff and Virgil Elizondo (London: SCM Press, 1991).

6 Virgil Elizondo, *Guadalupe: Mother of Creation* (Maryknoll, NY: Orbis Books, 1997), 118.

7 Conde-Frazier, "Hispanic Protestant Spirituality, 139–140. Jeannette Rodríguez, *Stories We Live/ Cuentos Que Vivimos: Hispanic Women's Spirituality* (New York: Paulist Press, 1996), 59.

8 Labor Gómez Acevedo and Manuel Ballesteros Gaibrois, *Vida y Cultura Precolombinas de Puerto Rico* (Río Piedras, Puerto Rico: Editorial Cultural, Inc., 1980), 61–2.

9 Orlando O. Espín, "Pentecostalism and Popular Catholicism: The Poor and *Traditio,"* *Journal of Hispanic/ Latino Theology* 3, no. 2 (November 1995): 27.

10 "God is here/ As truly as the air that I breathe/ As truly as the sun rises in the morning/ As truly as when I speak God hears me/ I can feel God when God is at my side/ I can feel God in my heart." Translation mine.

11 "Spirituality is feeling that God is mine and that I am [God's], to feel [God's] peace, encouragement, and love," Cynthia Román to author, electronic communication, August 18, 2010. My thanks to Ms. Román and her family who I interviewed for this project.

12 Elizabeth Conde-Frazier, "Crossing Wilderness and Desert Toward Community: The Spirituality of Research and Scholarship," *Perspectivas* 3 (Princeton, NJ: Hispanic Theological Initiative, 2000), 14. Conde-Frazier, "Hispanic Protestant Spirituality," 142.

13 Coquí is the Puerto Rican tree frog that is heard ubiquitously throughout the island, especially in the evening hours.

14 Walter Brueggeman, *Abiding Astonishment: Psalms, Modernity and the Making of History* (Louisville: Westminster John Knox Press, 1991), 42.

15 "We are in celebration [partying] with Jesus/ To heaven we want to go/ And everyone is sitting at the table/ and Jesus is one who will serve/ The Lord is powerful." Translation mine.

16 Based on Psalm 30: "You have changed my lament to dance/ You have girded me with joy [happiness]/ And that is why I will sing to you, my glory, and I will not be silenced/ Lord my God I will praise you/ I will praise you forever/ Because you changed my lament to dance/ Lord my God I will praise you." Translation mine.

17 José Alcina Franch, "La Cultura Taina Como Sociedad de Transición," in *La Cultura Taína*, ed. Las Culturas de America en la Epoca de Descubrimiento (Madrid: Turner Libras, 1989), 70.

18 Zaida Maldonado Pérez, "The Trinity *Es y Son Familia*," in *Latina Evangelicas: A Theological Survey from the Margins*, eds. Loida I. Martell-Otero, Elizabeth Conde-Frazier, and Zaida Maldonado Pérez (Eugene, OR: Cascade Publishers, 2013), manuscript 8.

19 *Sato* is Puerto Rican slang for a mongrel dog but can also refer to "immoral" behavior. For my application of "sato" to Christological reflection from an evangélica perspective see Loida I. Martell-Otero, "Encuentro con el Jesús Sato: An Evangélica Soter-ology," in *Jesus in the Hispanic Community: Images of Christ from Theology to Popular Religion*, eds. Harold J. Recinos and Hugo Magallanes (Louisville: Westminster John Knox Press, 2010).

20 See Orlando E. Costas, *Christ Outside the Gate: Mission Beyond Christendom* (Maryknoll, NY: Orbis Books, 1982), "Epilogue."

21 Molly T. Marshall, *Joining the Dance: A Theology of the Spirit* (Valley Forge, PA: Judson Press, 2003), 6–7. Maldonado Pérez, manuscript 8.

22 George E. "Tink" Tinker, *American Indian Liberation: A Theology of Sovereignty* (Maryknoll, NY: Orbis Books, 2008), 9. See also Vine Deloria, Jr., *God is Red: A Native View of Religion*, 3rd ed. (Golden, CO: Fulcrum, 2003), 84–7, 120. For more about the power of place and its retention of cultural memory, see Roger Friedland and Richard D. Hecht, "The Power of Place," in *Religion, Violence, Memory and Place*, eds. Oren Baruch Stier and J. Shawn Landres (Bloomington: Indiana University Press, 2006). Also, J. Rodríguez, *Cuentos Que Vivimos*, 9–10.

23 Justo L. *Gonzalez, Mañana: Christian Theology from a Hispanic Perspective* (Nashville: Abingdon Press, 1990), 164.

24 Robert Heinlein, *Stranger in a Strange Land* (New York: Ace Books, 1961). For documentation of the impact of immigration on women and children in particular, please see Daisy L. Machado, "Voices from *Nepantla:* Latinas in US Religious History," in *Feminist Intercultural Theology: Latina Explorations for a Just World*, eds. María Pilar Aquino and María José Rosado-Nunes (Maryknoll, NY: Orbis Books, 2007). Also Miguel de la Torre, *Trails of Hope and Terror: Testimonies on Immigration* (Maryknoll, NY Orbis Books, 2009). Elizabeth Conde-Frazier, *Listen to the Children: Conversations with Immigrant Families* (Valley Forge, PA: Judson Press, 2011).

25 See Helen Rodríguez Trias, *Women and the Health Care System: Sterilization Abuse* (New York: Barnard College, 1978). Also Annette B. Ramirez de Arrellano and Conrad

Seipp, *Colonialism, Catholicism, and Contraception: A History of Birth Control in Puerto Rico* (Chapel Hill: The University of North Carolina Press, 1983). Also refer to Loida I. Martell-Otero, "Creating a Sacred Space: An *Iglesia Evangélica* Response to Global Homelessness," *Dialog* 49, no. I (2010): 9–18.

26 Elizabeth Conde-Frazier, "Latina Women and Immigration," *Journal of Latin American Theology* 3, no. 2 (2008): 67–74. See also J. Rodríguez, *Cuentos Que Vivimos*, 59.

27 Loida I. Martell-Otero, "Of Satos and Saints: Salvation from the Periphery," *Perspectivas* (Princeton, NJ: Hispanic Theological Initiative, 2001): 16–17.

5

Performative Theologies (2014)*

Carmen Nanko-Fernández

Introduction

For Carmen Nanko-Fernández, Professor of Hispanic Theology and Ministry at Catholic Theological Union, theology is "geographically bounded," tied to particular places, while also taking fresh shape through reenactment and performance. Educated at Catholic University of America with wide-ranging interests in theology and culture, she is a willing provocateur, exposing the embedded theologies of nationalism in US baseball, for example, and pointing out duplicity within conventional forms of ecclesial and academic theology more generally. An "hostilidad pastoral/pastoral hostility" rather than pastoral care is a necessary and understandable response, she suggests, to frustrating injustices and hardships.

Nanko-Fernández approaches practical theology with similar boldness. Her 2010 book, *Theologizing en Espanglish: Context, Community, and Ministry*, entertains "new ways of theologizing," "deliberatively link[ing] theology and pastoral ministry." But she refrains from identifying as a practical theologian not just because dubbing Latin@ scholarship *practical* has been an arrogant way to dismiss it, but also because the discipline itself has failed to recognize and include Latin@ scholarship. As she explains in the first footnote, she plays with language, using Spanglish as a tool and symbol to disrupt English dominance, capture the daily experience of Latin@s, and underscore the hybridity of her own hermeneutic. She also challenges the implicit racism of those who dismiss theologizing from a particular place as meaningful only to those from that particular group.

Like Andrews and Deck, the following essay affirms popular piety as an overlooked site for theological study. The essay is loaded with illustrations – celebrations of the days of the dead, the feast of Our Lady of Guadalupe, las posadas, Three Kings' Day, and Via Crucis or the Way of the Cross. Echoing Anton Boisen's reclamation of living documents, she maintains that "we have much to learn if we regard these practices as living texts, as complicated articulations of theological significance…rather than quaint artifacts or simplistic faith." But going beyond what twentieth-century pastoral and

Original publication details: Carmen Nanko-Fernández, "Performative Theologies: Ritualizing the Daily Latinamente," pp. 21–30 from *Liturgy* 29:3 (2014) [with slight updates to the original by the author].

practical theologians imagined, she moves from texts to performances and explores the theologies embedded within them as linked to older liturgical forms from medieval pre-conquest Europe, indigenous rituals, and African and Spanish interaction. She uses words like *graphic, visceral,* and *physical* to capture a liturgical wisdom-in-motion that "appeals to the senses, involves the body, invites the imagination, and calls forth investment in our daily living." As is true for many Latin@s, the place of theologizing is lo cotidiano. Although sociologists like Meredith McQuire and Nancy Ammerman study *lived religion*, Nanko-Fernandez sees in everyday religious practices a *lived theology* sparked by the "incarnational and sacramental imaginations operative in…ritualizing." Even if not analyzed or fully understood by most sociologists, theological claims are communicated through ritual. Her work insists on what Orlando Espín saw in Hispanic popular Catholicism more generally – "'arguably, and above all else, *an epistemology*,'" a distinct way of doing and knowing theology.

Suggested Further Reading

- Carmen Nanko-Fernández, *Theologizing en Espanglish: Context, Community, and Ministry* (Maryknoll, NY: Orbis, 2010).
- Orlando O. Espín, *The Faith of the People: Theological Reflections on Popular Catholocism* (Maryknoll, NY: Orbis, 1997).
- Virgilio Elizondo, *Galilean Journey: The Mexican-American Promise* (Maryknoll, NY: Orbis, 1983; revised and expanded, 2000).

***

While the thirty days from September 15 through October 15 commemorate nuestra national latinidad as Hispanic Heritage month, every month is actually Hispanic Heritage month, in a liturgical sense, with our daily collection of santos, santas, virgenes, and holy days celebrating nuestra religiosidad. So, for instance, on November 1 and 2, there is the celebration of the days of the dead; over a month later, the feast of Nuestra Señora de Guadalupe (Our Lady of Guadalupe); in Advent, there will be las posadas (the search for lodging); and, two weeks after Christmas, el Día de los Tres Reyes Magos (Three Kings' Day). These are but a few examples where popular religious practices are prominent en nuestras comunidades latinas (in Latin@ communities) in ways that can baffle pastoral ministers, who strain to comprehend how these and other practices ritualizing the daily relate to the liturgy of the Church.[1]

As a matter of disclosure, I write as a Latin@ theologian, in other words, as one who engages theological scholarship and pastoral practice in ways that appreciate vida cotidiana (daily lived experience) as source, place, and context for our theologizing. I draw on a wealth of resources arising from centuries of theologizing out of our hispanidad. I am not, nor do I pretend to be, a sacramental theologian or a liturgist. I have been, however, intrigued by the practical implications of sacramental theologies for many years.

In 1999, sociologist Thomas Bamat and historian Jean-Paul Wiest published the results of a three-year interdisciplinary project administered by the Maryknoll Center for Mission Study and Research. In *Popular Catholicism in a World Church: Seven Case Studies in Inculturation,* they investigated, with a team of scholars, seven local contexts: two in South America, one in the English-speaking Caribbean, two in Africa, and two in Asia.[2] While this book is an invaluable resource, I was struck by the fact that the studies did not include a local context from Latin@ America, by which I mean a community falling under the umbrella of Hispanic in the United States. This exclusion gives the impression that the globalized North somehow does not experience nor theologically reflect on the phenomena that Latino theologian Orlando Espín calls "the faith of the people."[3] It also ignores the impact of migrations that situate the global South in the barrios of el norte, the North.

Bamat and Wiest note tensions between "popular and official Catholicism." However they also observe that recent treatments of popular devotion in church teachings and pastoral attitudes reflect a more appreciative stance. As an example, in his 2010 pastoral letter, Benedict XVI cautions seminarians not to dismiss popular piety: "Through that piety, the faith has entered human hearts and become part of the common patrimony of sentiments and customs, shaping the life and emotions of the community. Popular piety is thus one of the Church's great treasures. The faith has taken on flesh and blood." He indicates a tendency toward "the irrational" and the "superficial" that needs to be "purified and refocused," yet he affirms popular piety is "worthy of our love and it truly makes us into the 'People of God.'"[4] While positive in its overall evaluation, discernible still in the pope's words are perceptions of popular religious expressions as superstitious and contrary to reason. Under Pope Francis a significant change occurs whereby he attests to the value of popular religious practices as sources and instances of theologizing. In *Evangeli Gaudium* he affirms what has long been a given for Latin@ theologians, namely "Expressions of popular piety have much to teach us; for those who are capable of reading them, they are a locus theologicus which demands our attention."[5]

There is no doubt that, as with all religious expression, popular religion too is subject to abuse and malpractice. Without ignoring that reality, I propose we explore the "faith of the people" in ways that illuminate the incarnational and sacramental imaginations operative in this Catholic ritualizing in church, on the streets, and in the home. From this stance, the "faith of the people" emerges as a series of ritual texts of – and, in – our daily living. Again, Espín reminds us that they are popular not because of their widespread appeal, but because of their origins in ordinary participants and in ordinary places; in other words, they are "of the people."

These popular practices, in all of their complexity, are embedded and embodied theological reflections that evoke and reflect creative, affective, sensuous, and even kinetic means of responding to the divine presence in the concrete circumstances and quotidian rhythms of human existence. These popular religious expressions are forms of traditioning, catechizing and pastoral caregiving; they do not separate strands of living or place them in contrived correlations that seek to distinguish culture from religious tradition. These manifestations of the "faith of the people" blur distinctions between secular and sacred activity, public and domestic space, official and unofficial church ritual. They are liturgical and even sacramental – yet, outside of the official liturgy.

My intent is not to romanticize popular Catholicism as lived latinamente; rather it is to propose that more is going on here than has been previously recognized, an insight consistent with the musings of other Latin@ theologians. It is to entertain the possibility that we have much to learn if we regard these practices as living texts, as complicated articulations of theological significance, as ground for our God-talk rather than quaint artifacts or simplistic faith. The texts and practices of nuestras vidas cotidianas, such as los coritos y las virgenes, descansos y altarcitos, los santos y las santas, articulated in the church, in the street, on the side of a highway, in the home, or even in museums – these are contexts of the sacred with a fresh yet more ancient provenance than many of us realize. In what follows, I focus our attention in three distinct directions:

1) Latin@ popular religious practice as part of a greater stream of liturgical diversity that is our Catholic legacy;
2) the role of place in popular religious expression; and,
3) the "faith of the people" as performed theology.

Latin@ Popular Religious Practice as Part and Parcel of the Larger Catholic Liturgical Legacy

There is a tendency to consider Hispanic popular Catholicism exclusively in cultural terms. In other words, these practices are tolerated (even, occasionally, celebrated) but only as means toward the pastoral goal of cultivating culturally relevant expressions of faith. While laudable for its cultural sensitivity, this approach unintentionally conveys a sense that such practices are exotic or alien. The focus is on "them" and how to connect "their practices" to "'our' or 'the' universal" liturgy. Instead, if we take seriously research by Latin@ scholars in liturgy and sacraments, like Jaime Lara and Raúl Gómez-Ruiz, or in popular religion, like Orlando Espín, then we may be able to appreciate that what we are experiencing are strands of older liturgical practices that have survived Tridentine reforms as well as the temptation toward iconoclasm present after Vatican II.

Lara stakes a claim that medieval liturgy found new expression in las Américas and is therefore the basis for Hispanic popular religiosity. He explains:

> What today we call "popular" or even attempt to erase in the name of good liturgy was once a part of official Church rituals and missals. They survive for many reasons. One is because they are the ancient practices of the original evangelizers
> .... Another may be because they were so similar... to some pre-conquest rituals of the old religions. Besides they are colorful and of immediate appeal.[6]

This insight shifts the paradigm in significant ways: what was thought to be alien and in need of incorporation is actually the remnant of our Catholic patrimony alive and well in las Américas.

As another example, sacramental theologian Gómez-Ruiz explores the connections between Hispanic popular Catholicism and the Mozarabic rite, a rite from seventh-century Spain. Gómez-Ruiz finds similarities in specific practices and attitudes that persist in this survivor of Roman attempts to impose ritual uniformity. He references an intersecting inclination to "bring elements of everyday life into the liturgy and transport liturgical elements into everyday life."[7]

The wealth of ritual diversity in las Américas also exists as a result of the interactions among Spaniards, indigenous peoples, and Africans. Of course, it cannot be ignored that these encounters are born of Spain's colonizing and evangelizing enterprise. These complicated relationships bear the stigma of violence, conquest, and slavery – and are often reflected in the history of popular religious practices. For example, theologian Miguel Díaz reminds contemporary readers that early narratives of Nuestra Señora de la Caridad (Our Lady of Charity) begin with her accompaniment of Africans and the indigenous Tainos who were enslaved and lived on the margins of a poor copper-mining town in Cobre de Cuba. In the early stories of her adventures, interventions, and miracles with various members of this community, Díaz points to what he calls "sacramental interactions." For Díaz:

> While these interactions suggest affirming relationships – persons care for her, abide with her, converse with her, and even disagree with some of her actions (for example, her unexplained disappearances) – the story also witnesses less affirming relationships. The vanquishment of the members of this copper-mining community and the pillaging of the land they abide in reveal the kind of oppressive relationships challenged by... *Caridad.*[8]

These intercultural encounters also disclose intersecting cosmo-visions evident in popular religious practices and useful in Christian evangelization. At the juncture of medieval and baroque Iberian Catholicism, various indigenous cosmologies and West African religions, ritualizing engaged the senses, attended to aesthetics, realized the power of the affective and freely employed performative dimensions. Espín reminds us that creedal beliefs were communicated and "expressed primarily in and through symbol and rite, through devotions and liturgical practices. The teaching of the gospel did not usually occur through the spoken, magisterial word, but through the symbolic, 'performative' word."[9] The attraction to religious pageantry in all three worldviews enhanced the catechetical value of religious theater from pastorelas to passion plays. At the same time, African, indigenous American, and Iberian cosmo-visions perceived no demarcations between sacred and secular in the way that obsesses most contemporary US Americans. The daily participates in the sacred; and the ancient practice of tending altarcitos, or home altars, continues to reflect that fluidity.

What might it mean to reframe the relationship between popular practice and liturgy in terms that recognize a long-intertwined history whereby each is rooted? What value arises from situating these practices as part of a rich intercultural legacy, as vestiges of ancient liturgies? What might we gain if we retrieve from this past wisdom, still embedded in popular Catholicism, an appreciation that good liturgy appeals to the senses, involves the body, invites the imagination, and calls forth investment in our daily living?

The Role of Place in Popular Religious Expression

In a certain sense, popular religious expressions are geographically bounded. The prevalence of devotions are tied to local and regional patrons; María under her many titles, apparitions, and milagros, as well as the naming of particular santos y santas, illustrate the point. At the same time there is portability and flexibility to popular practices; they move with their faithful and adapt to changing circumstances, resources, and needs. For those doing ministry in the United States, it is important to recognize that, while these popular expressions are rooted in Latin American and Iberian traditions, our US context shapes and reshapes them profoundly. With this reality in mind, it is worth our entertaining the following three points.

First, the role of public institutions in reigniting interest in some of these practices, and/or in generating new practices, cannot be ignored. For example, the pervasiveness in the United States of altars for the dead in domestic, public, and ecclesial spaces is attributable in a significant way to museums, to the Chicano movement, and to migratory patterns. In the 1970s, some galleries and museums in California mounted Días de los Muertos exhibits. This tradition, in turn, spread to other urban areas like Chicago that had both sizeable immigrant and established Mexican American communities and museos de la raza. Ofrendas (or, altars filled with objects of remembrance) created by artists as part of these exhibitions blurred the lines between art and sacred expression, so much so that to this day any number of museums, including the Puerto Rican Museo del Barrio in New York, sponsor exhibits as well as hands-on workshops and even spaces for visitors to post names of their dead whom they wish to memorialize. Since 1986, Chicago's National Museum of Mexican Art has been inviting visitors "to celebrate life by glimpsing death."[10] In 2007, the museum installed a powerful ofrenda remembering thirty-two students from Chicago Public Schools killed primarily by gun violence.[11] Political statement? Memorial? Art? Popular religious expression? How do we even begin to separate the strands?

The revival of carving santos de palo (or, saints of wood) in Puerto Rico owes a debt to the art museum in Ponce and sponsorship by the island's tourism industry, print media outlets, and business community, including the prominently featured Bacardi Rum Corporation. In fact, the largest single collection of these carvings belongs to the Smithsonian Institution in Washington, DC, a donation from Teodoro Vidal Santoni, a Puerto Rican collector of the island's material culture.[12] The role of the carvers in the traditioning of enculturated faith was not lost on the Archbishop of San Juan. In his pastoral letter on popular piety and Catholic identity in Puerto Rico, released on August 15, 2009, Archbishop Roberto González Nieves observes that "the carvers continue to understand their art as a gift that comes from heaven. As with the icons of the eastern church, the carving of santos calls for a mystical disposition and a special state of mind."[13] For the archbishop, this popular expression of carving and of keeping these santos in one's home "embraces cult and culture."[14] The cultural significance of such objects of faith and the processes that produce them are intricately tied to identity.

What is to be learned here? For one, it is discernible that the threads of religious impulse cannot be easily exorcised from the greater fabric of civic life. For another, popular religious symbols and practices are polyvalent and can be interpreted in ways that are not explicitly or implicitly religious.

Place impacts meaning, and popular religious expressions accrete meaning from their contexts. In the United States, las posadas have increasingly become a part of the last week of Advent. Each night the journey of the pregnant Mary and her husband Joseph are reenacted as participants knock upon their neighbors' doors in search of lodging for the family. After a series of rejections, the final stop of the nightly pilgrimage concludes with an invitation to the holy pilgrims to enter and receive modest shelter not only in the home but in the heart: "Entren, Santos Peregrinos, reciban este rincón, que aunque es pobre la morada, os la doy de corazón (Enter, holy pilgrims, receive this corner; although the dwelling is poor, I give it from the heart)." This acceptance is celebrated with a nightly fiesta at the final home where the Word made flesh finally finds lodging. This ritualized migration points to the presence of God, in the company of the neighbor/participants who herald the Holy Family's arrival, and in the home that the Incarnate Word makes among us. At the same time las posadas visibly narrate rejection, inhospitality, and struggle. This participatory experience viscerally situates incarnation in the heart of community with its attendant obligations. This theology-in-motion confronts believers with a fundamental question: will the Word made flesh find a home here, and, if so, what are the implications for one's actions and responsibilities in relation to others? Is it any surprise, then, that in parts of the United States the posada has become a strategic public ritual employed by some religious and social activists seeking comprehensive and just immigration reform?[15]

At the same time what originally were home-based neighborhood practices have increasingly shifted into the church. There are often practical reasons for this move. For example, in rural areas the distances between homes makes neighborly visits dependent upon transportation. In some urban areas, safety issues may be a concern. In the United States, large gatherings require a parade permit – a sometimes costly venture that does not reward spontaneity. Contextual realities shape popular expressions, especially those that spill into the streets.

Third, new contexts with their struggles give life to new popular expressions. Consider the devotion to Santo Toribio Romo González, a Mexican martyr of the twentieth-century Cristero War, a rebellion familiar to some from the film, *For Greater Glory*. Santo Toribio was one of twenty-five priests and laity canonized by John Paul II in 2000, primarily for fidelity to his ministry even in the face of danger and death. Before his canonization, Toribio developed a reputation for helping migrants cross the border between Mexico and the United States. The first stories appear to arise in the 1980s with tales of immigrants encountering a blue-eyed, Spanish-speaking male, sometimes dressed as a priest, other times not, often driving a truck. He offered assistance and, when asked, said he could be found in the village of Santa Ana de Guadalupe in Jalisco. Countless migrants, especially those who cross the border as "alternately documented," see him as their patron. In fact, some fifty thousand faithful were said to have viewed his statue from his home parish during a 2011 tour of California, while his home church in Mexico has become a tourist/pilgrimage site drawing upwards of three hundred thousand visitors a year.[16] Ironically, Toribio was opposed to Mexican emigration in his time, a position he articulated in a slapstick morality play he authored in 1920 entitled *Let's Go North!* Today he continues to be prominent on both sides of the border in those lives touched by the trials of migration. His great-nephew explains:

> Santo Toribio is a superstar among saints. No certified holy man has lent his name and image to as many restaurants, grocery stores, pharmacies, travel agencies and employment centers. Toribio even has a brand of designer sneakers called Brinco ($215 in boutique stores). Border Patrol agents frequently arrest undocumented border crossers carrying scapulars and key chains with the image of this ubiquitous blue-eyed miracle worker.[17]

Geography matters! Gómez-Ruiz proposes that, in the United States, the separation of church and state propels Latin@s, especially immigrants, toward activities in the local church. In Latin America, it is possible to imbibe Catholicism and retain identity from the ambience and rhythms of daily life in ways not accessible in the United States. Sustenance of religious identity in an environment that favors privatization and compartmentalization of faith to particular spheres of life may be disorienting. However, equally disorienting are experiences of church that unwittingly privilege reason and text in ways that distance the experience of church from the poetics of lived daily experience in all its struggles and sacramental complexity.

The "Faith of the People" as Performative Theology

Popular Catholicism cannot be reduced to a collection of pious devotions, home rituals, superstitious beliefs, or magical thinking that can then be retrieved, dissected, analyzed, deconstructed, and dismissed. Theologian Orlando Espín counters temptations to underestimate its power and tenacity by reminding us that Hispanic popular Catholicism is "arguably, and above all else, *an epistemology: a way of constructing and interpreting the 'real' by means that are culturally-specific*, grounded in equally culturally specific experiences of God and of the Christian message."[18] It is this theological significance that is often overlooked when popular practices are regarded from sociological perspectives; and I would suggest that it is popular religious practice as performative theologizing that drives some "to affirm only what they paternalistically perceive to be 'acceptable,' or attempt to control popular manifestations in the interest of religious orthodoxy."[19]

Roberto Goizueta once commented, "Our knowledge of who we are, as US Hispanics, and who Jesus is emerges from our interaction with him in the Holy Thursday and Good Friday processions."[20] It is an identity born in the motion of accompanying the incarnate God and his mother through one of the most devastating and humiliating events a family or individual could experience: unjust detention, abandonment, torture, and public execution. This acompañamiento is physical and concrete and takes place annually, in cities from New York to San Antonio, from Los Angeles to Chicago. Latin@ communities hit the streets during Semana Santa (Holy Week) for el Vía Crucis, the Way of the Cross. Each of these graphic reenactments of the last hours of Jesus' life situates the crucified Christ in the heart of countless barrios and at the margins of institutional power and wealth that collude in their very marginalization. These reconfigurations of public space interrupt the rhythms of daily business, challenging participants and observers alike to contemplate anew their responsibilities to justice and right relations demanded by the reign of God.

Vía Crucis, like las posadas, recovers a performative dimension of biblical texts, just as these narratives were received by their earliest audiences. These representations underscore the lived, embodied, and embedded dynamics associated with texts perceived as good news. The interactivity between "performer and audience" blurs the boundaries between neighbor and actor, and the movements among home, street, and church defy simplistic constructions of public and domestic manifestations of faith. The implications of the incarnation are actualized locally and particularly, individually and collectively – and all in the context of the complicated topography of daily living.

Another example is the popular religious expression of los Días de los Muertos as celebrated in homes, parishes, schools, and communities across the United States. Originally from southern Mexico and parts of Central America, this practice has been in a process of transformation in the United States for more than forty years now. Its journey has roots in the Chicano movement's search for identity and in its response to the suffering of its times, namely the struggle for civil rights and the war in Vietnam. Through its propagation by museums in the United States, it acquired pan-Latin@ significance, an affirmation of the value of cultural practices from communities typically portrayed as exotic and/or supplicant. Today one is hard pressed not to find an ofrenda, a Day of the Dead altar, displayed in places of public gathering, especially in multicultural communities and churches, and, of course, in museums. All of these venues invite a level of interactivity and public visibility that challenges assumptions about the lines between the sacred and the secular. Are these practices helping people make sense of death? Are they traditioning cultural identities? Are they acts of resistance against forces that strive to erase memory? Are they familiar because they represent the hybridity that is increasingly a part of the lived reality of the United States? I suspect it is all of the above and more. What is intriguing, however, is how the specter of the separation of church and state still haunts the museums – who in their explanations and teaching guides tend to focus on the indigenous religious roots while avoiding or minimizing the distinctively Spanish Catholic elements of this syncretic practice. Still, ofrendas indicate how such popular devotions perform a distinctive theology.

First, this popular expression engages our humanity in multidimensional ways. The construction of ofrendas is a creative and labor-intensive activity. They are poignant in what they include; photos of loved ones, their favorite foods, toys, and even signs of their vices – cigars, alcohol, and coffee cups often make an appearance. They are humorous, mocking death's sting, with assorted skeletons engaging in the activities of daily life. They make you laugh and they make you cry. Ofrendas blur distinctions. They include elements from Meso-American religions and from the Catholic holy days commemorating All Souls and All Saints. They reflect the roots of their ancient places and of their new contexts, and of longing for homes left in diaspora. Ofrendas also highlight the reality that death is the great social equalizer – bishop, wealthy patron, and poor campesino all end up the same way.

Second, Hispanic popular Catholicism is relational. Jesús, María, los santos y las santas, the dead and the living all participate in a network of mutual accountability that even death cannot violate. The sociocentric aspect is certainly on display in the preparation of ofrendas. Often enough, they are communal or family ventures – with plenty of disagreements over aesthetic preferences. They assume a level of intimacy that requires an ongoing commitment to accompany – a promise even death cannot disrupt. They provide means for intercultural communication. Consider the reflections from some non-Latin@ members of a local multicultural parish that I visited a few years ago. Parishioners expressed heartfelt surprise about how much they had learned about their neighbors and fellow parishioners from the ofrendas. They now better understood behaviors that had been misinterpreted – for example, one woman's aloofness was understood in a new way when it was realized through her altarcito that she had lost a child. Others spoke of points of connection across their families. Some expressed gratitude for the way the ofrendas gave them permission to mourn their own losses and remember them in a public way. Others recalled that even their own cultural inheritances had ways of dealing with death and loss that had been forgotten. Ofrendas in this parish served as a step to bring disparate members of the same body into relationship.

Third, popular religious expressions serve multiple functions; key among them is resistance. These practices resist all that demeans life, which is why, even in the face of death, many of the practices retain a spirit of celebration. The practices surrounding the days of the dead serve as resistance to US customs that sanitize death and the process of dying. Some have speculated that these practices of memorialization have become more prevalent after the trauma of September 11, 2001. In some cases, they provide permission to mourn and remember; in others, opportunity to teach about the cycle of life; and, in still others, they provide space for the healing process.

Popular religious practices have pastoral value. I would even go so far as to say that in some circumstances they are expressions of "ministry of and by the people." They emerge from attempts by the earliest mendicant evangelizers to catechize and tradition people into the faith in manners comprehensible across cultural divides. Now, they are often the purview of the laity and, in particular, women occupy leadership roles here in passing on the faith. The days of the dead also serve a pastoral care function, fostering healing, reconciliation, resilience, and liberation.

Finally, popular religious practices articulate theological claims. They image a God who accompanies through the joys and struggles of daily living; a God who can be known by the company kept, through our encounters with those who are filled with God's spirit – María, los santos y las santas. They image a God who "gets it," who understands the vulnerability of the human condition, thus the prevalence of practices surrounding the Word made flesh, especially at his most vulnerable moments of birth, passion, and death. The days of the dead are performed eschatology. They point toward a divine reign that is present and still in process, to relationships sustained beyond death, to a communion of saints.

Popular religious practices are not antithetical to liturgy; in fact, they appear to have deep roots in Catholic liturgies, even if these have been long forgotten. They are companions in the transmission of the faith, and sometimes companions that serve to remind, chide, and caution each other. Popular religious practices experienced latinamente are not quaint artifacts of simple people or means of escaping the challenges of contemporary life. Quite the opposite, they emerge as performative theologizing, means of making sense out of and navigating the joyful, the painful, and the baffling. Their appeal, I suspect, is due in part to their groundedness in the realities and expressions of daily life and in their engagement of our humanity in an organic and multidimensional way. Popular religious practices are fluid, adaptable, and relevant. They also blur boundaries.

As the Catholic Church in the United States, like the general population, moves from Latin@ minority to Latin@ plurality, we cannot afford to ignore the genuine theologizing and ritualizing performed in Latin@ homes and on the streets. The "faith of our people" and their popular devotional practices are nuestra fé tambien, part of a rich, ancient and complex network of global Catholicism that must be honored rather than marginalized, incorporated rather than ignored.

Notes

1 This article employs Spanglish as both an intentional writing strategy and as a metaphor for the hybridity constituted by the Hispanic presence in the United States. Spanglish is one of many terms used to describe the fusion of Spanish and English in daily communication. It is manifest here through the following conventions. First, words and expressions in Spanish are not italicized unless they appear as such in direct quotations; at times sentences include both languages. Second, I identify as Hispan@ or Latin@ and created @, the 'at' symbol (el arroba) with an accent mark. I borrow the use of @ as a gender inclusive suffix, which at the same time destabilizes gender polarities. I add the acute accent (@) to emphasize the role of social location and situatedness in theology done latinamente.

2 Thomas Bamat, and Jean-Paul Wiest, *Popular Catholicism in a World Church: Seven Case Studies in Inculturation* (Maryknoll, NY: Orbis Books, 1999).

3 Orlando O. Espín, *The Faith of the People: Theological Reflections on Popular Catholicism* (Maryknoll, NY: Orbis Books, 1997).

4 Pope Benedict XVI, "Letter of His Holiness Benedict XVI to Seminarians,"http://www. vatican.va/ holy_father/benedict_xvi/letters/2010/documents/hf_ben-xvi_ let_20101018_seminaristi_en.html (Oct. 18, 2010), no. 4 (accessed Feb. 8, 2014).

5 Pope Francis, *Evangeli Gaudium*, 2013, #126, http://w2.vatican.va/content/francesco/ en/apost_exhortations/documents/papa-francesco_esortazione-ap_20131124_evangelii-gaudium.html (accessed June 22, 2018).

6 Jaime Lara, "The Liturgical Roots of Hispanic Popular Religiosity," in *Misa, Mesa y Musa: Liturgy in the US Hispanic Church*, ed. Kenneth G. Davis (Schiller Park, IL: World Library Publications, 1997), 32.

7 Raúl Gómez-Ruiz, *Mozarabs, Hispanics and the Church* (Maryknoll, NY: Orbis Books, 2007), 181.

8 Miguel H. Díaz, "Dime con quién andas y te diré quién eres: We Walk-with Our Lady of Charity," in *From the Heart of Our People: Latino/a Explorations in Catholic Systematic Theology*, eds. Orlando O. Espín and Miguel H. Díaz (Maryknoll, NY: Orbis Books, 1999), 153–71.

9 Espín, *Faith of the People*, 119.

10 National Museum of Mexican Art, *Hanal Pixán: Food For the Souls*, Día de los Muertos Twenty-Sixth Annual Exhibition, 2012, http://www.nationalmuseumofmexicanart.org/ exhibits/featured/ d%C3%AD-de-los-muertos-2012 (last accessed October 2012).

11 To see a description and image of this ofrenda, go to "Mexican Museum Honors Day of the Dead," *People's World* (November 2, 2007), http://www.peoplesworld.org/ mexican-museum-honors-day-of-the-dead/ (accessed Feb. 8, 2014).

12 See, for example, National Museum of American History, "A Vision of Puerto Rico: The Teodoro Vidal Collection," http://amhistory.si.edu/vidal/about/ (accessed Feb. 4, 2014).

13 See Roberto Octavio González Nieves, OFM, "¡Bendición! Carta Pastoral sobre Identidad Catoʹlica y Piedad Popular en Puerto Rico," *El Visitante* (6–12 Septiembre 2009), paragraph #53 at http://www. elvisitante.biz/visitante-web/2009/evwebed3609/ pdf/suplemento.pdf (accessed Feb. 4, 2014).

14 Ibid.

15 Some of this material about las posadas has appeared in other venues; see, for example, Carmen Nanko-Fernández, "Buscando una posada con a God-in-Motion," *Homiletical Hot Tub* (Dec. 1, 2008) at http://www.goodpreacher.com/blog/index.php?page=177 (accessed Feb. 4, 2014).

16 See, for example, David Agren, "Cristero Martyr Now Popular Patron of Mexican Migrants Headed to US," *Catholic News Service* (May 31, 2012), at http://www. catholicnews.com/data/stories/ cns/1202255.htm (accessed Feb. 8, 2014).

17 See David Dorado Romo, "My Tío the Saint," *Texas Monthly* (Nov. 2010) at http://www. texasmonthly.com/story/my-t%C3%ADo-saint (accessed Feb. 8, 2014).

18 Orlando O. Espín, "Traditioning: Culture, Daily Life and Popular Religion, and Their Impact on Christian Tradition," in *Futuring Our Past: Explorations in the Theology of Tradition*, eds. Orlando O. Espín and Gary Macy (Maryknoll, NY: Orbis Books, 2006), 9.

19 Bamat and Wiest, *Popular Catholicism*, 13.

20 Roberto S. Goizueta, *Caminemos con Jesús: Toward a Hispanic/Latino Theology of Accompaniment* (Maryknoll, NY: Orbis Books, 1995), 158.

Section II

Bodies

6

Ecclesiology as if Bodies Mattered (2007)*

Mary McClintock Fulkerson

Introduction

In emphasizing place and bodies, this essay by Mary McClintock Fulkerson offers a nice transition from Section I to Section II. It appeared the same year as her book, *Places of Redemption: Theology for a Worldly Church*, which spells out in more detail themes introduced here.

Trained in systematic theology, Fulkerson crossed over into practical theology midway through her more than three-decade career at Duke Divinity School. Her interest in practical theology arose out of frustration with the cognitive captivity of her home discipline. But early signs of practical leanings appear in her doctoral study and first book, *Changing the Subject: Women's Discourses and Feminist Theology* (2001), which uses conversations with Presbyterian and Pentecostal women to contest limited portraits of women's religious experience in liberal feminism. About the time she was completing her doctorate at Vanderbilt in the mid-1980s, one of her mentors, Edward Farley, was contributing a key essay to an early anthology funded by the Lilly Endowment in which he redefines practical theology as a discipline whose primary task is "interpreting situations" (an essay that gets reprinted in the first *Blackwell Reader in Pastoral and Practical Theology*). He criticizes systematic theology for its failure to "thematize situationality itself" (1987, 11), effecting a "distanciation from the experientiality and activity of faith." We need a discipline, he says, that analyzes situations, not written texts (though regrettably he makes no mention of either Boisen's mandate to study living documents or Hiltner's turn to practice).

Over a decade later, Fulkerson overhauls Farley's project. To execute a theological reading of contemporary situations in her ethnographic study of a small interracial United Methodist Church, she must broaden her framework considerably from an approach that is still too intellectualist to capture realities that she witnessed – a situational "obliviousness" that outreaches what Farley named in the 1980s using the same term. To understand the disjuncture between stated commitments to racial and social

Original publication details: Mary McClintock Fulkerson, "A Place to Appear: Ecclesiology As If Bodies Mattered," pp. 159–71 from *Theology Today* 64 (2007).

justice and habituated patterns of white dominance and ableism, she needs new lenses that take bodies and "prereflective visceral responses as seriously as stated convictions." With the benefit of further developments in practical theology, cultural anthropology, critical race theory, and place theory, she moves from a view of theology as language and discourse to its enactment in the midst of practices, bodies, and place. In her words, "to frame this lived faith theologically required categories that captured not simply what these congregants believed…but their habituations as well." Claims about redemption require more than story and proclamation; they demand "places to appear" in the community itself.

As in other entries, this essay calls for attention to more than linguistic and cognitive knowledge. Theological knowledge evolves in close proximity to visceral bodily stereotypes and prereflective habits. Bodily acts are themselves the communication. Taking account of bodies requires a consideration of emotions previously bracketed or obscured – aversion, fear, anxiety, disgust, and so forth.

Suggested Further Reading

- Mary McClintock Fulkerson, *Places of Redemption: Theology for a Worldly Church* (New York: Oxford University Press, 2007).
- Edward Farley, "Interpreting Situations: An Inquiry in the Nature of Practical Theology," in Lewis S. Midge and James N. Poling, eds., *Formation and Reflection: The Promise of Practical Theology* (Philadelphia: Fortress, 1987), 1–26.
- James Nieman, "Attending Locally: Theologies in Congregations," International Journal ofPractical Theology 6, no. 2 (2002): 198–225.

***

My title suggests an image for "church" that may seem a bit thin. A "place to appear" sounds as if all one need do is make an appearance on Sunday morning at 11:00 and something called Christian community will happen – an ecclesiology of simply "showing up." As a corrective to overly intellectualist concepts of faith, I understand "a place to appear" as an antidote to obliviousness.[1] The dictionary definition of *obliviousness* is a kind of forgetfulness or "unmindfulness." It suggests a kind of experiential and geographical disregard that forms an a priori social condition of widely acknowledged forms of injustice. A "not-seeing" that indirectly supports many disparities in well-being in the United States, obliviousness is more likely to shape white, middle- and upper-middle-class churches than overt oppression of the marginalized. A "place to appear," then, is intended to suggest what might disrupt and alter such disregard.

My choice of categories results from two-and-a-half years of participant observation in a small interracial United Methodist church. Both "a place to appear" and "obliviousness" arise from reviewing my attempts to make sense out of this congregation as an amateur ethnographer/theologian in 1996–1999.

A Problem of Framing: Respecting Ordinary Lived Faith

At its most robust, Good Samaritan United Methodist Church (UMC) was one-third African American, one-third African, and one-third Anglo-American. It came into being when Dan, a white, middle-aged pastor with a vision, resurrected what had been a dying white church in an integrated working-class area of a midsized southern city.

The church's new "vision" originated in a Bible study held by a small group of the remaining white members. Led by Dan, they interpreted the story of the Ethiopian eunuch (Acts 8), in Dan's words, as a call to "go and find people who are different from us … the over-looked, the looked-over and passed-over."

Despite the problematic racial dynamics of the image, the church was remarkably successful in its newly discerned mission. By 1996 there were 146 congregants on the roll and much diversity. Within a year the community decided that the new category of "eunuchs" – or "folks who are different from us" – should include what they called "special needs" people, and their outreach extended to two nearby group homes. Once members figured out how to attract people of different races and how to adapt worship for the group-home participants, Good Samaritan's problems were how to stay afloat – the average income of members at that time was $28,334 – and how such very different people could get along. At its most basic, *my* problem as a theologian was how to frame this unusual place. What was it about Christian faith that could bring people together across such differences in race, nationality, class, and ability? The lenses with which I was most familiar, however, did not prove adequate to the task.

That may seem odd. My natural approach as a theologian would seem to make sense – namely, to find out how members articulate the "what" and the "why" of their vision. It was, after all, a vision generated by a biblical story. How appropriate it would be to determine what other biblical, theological, as well as local-cultural discourses went into the forging of this ministry. Certainly ethnographic study follows the self-understandings of members of communities. To answer such questions, I read their denominational literature, did interviews with most of the active members and ministers, and attended worship services, Bible studies, meetings, and every kind of church event.

A first challenge to my approach came from the fact that "belief and value commitments" are typically underdeveloped and "ambiguous" in the ordinary practices of faith, as Kathryn Tanner says.[2] My inquiries as to how this congregation decided to become an interracial church were not met with much theological sophistication. Communicative idioms of an oral culture were more prevalent than the long, coherent arguments of those of us who write for a living.[3] Many were not from Methodist traditions, and the denomination did not have a powerful force on their views. With a litmus of orthodoxy, they pretty much all got failing grades. Admittedly, the broadening of my lens with participant observation did allow focus on the importance of activities and rituals. In addition, models in practical theology allow for expansion beyond a narrow intellectualist/orthodox framing of faith.[4]

However, a more useful frame for mapping this community was the popular MacIntyrean concept of practice. "Practice" shifted my focus to lived faith and allowed for an evaluative lens in a way that congregational studies and cultural anthropology did not. Alasdair MacIntyre's widely used definition describes activities that can instantiate and extend the goods of a tradition.[5] A practice is

> any coherent and complex form of socially established cooperative human activity through which goods internal to that form of activity are realized in the course of trying to achieve those standards of excellence that are appropriate to, and partially definitive of, that form of activity, with the result that human powers to achieve excellence, and human conceptions of the ends and goods involved, are systematically extended. Interpreted within the frame of practices, Christian tradition can be understood as a communicative process best imagined as participatory, vision-shaped activities.

Further, the category of practice allows respect for activities that would otherwise never qualify as "theological." Skills with their own criteria of excellence can be brought into relation to the goods of the Christian tradition, in this case, to Good Samaritan's vision. Members' practices can be evaluated in terms of their capacity to advance the good of Christian welcome to the "other." Rather than asking if their worship was properly Methodist or only serving the function of ritual – as important as that question might be – with the MacIntyrean category, I asked whether worship accomplished the specific communal goods of the church's vision to welcome persons with disabilities and of different races. The MacIntyrean frame thus broadened my study of the church beyond classical ecclesiastical categories, such as sacramental and confessional practices. Ordinary life activities could qualify as extending Christian welcome insofar as their goods were consonant with Jesus' radical love and other themes favored by Good Samaritan.

With all the advantages of the category of practice, however, there were also limitations. These emerged from a second challenge in the self-understanding of the faith community.

The Challenge of Color Blindness

"We don't see color here, just Christians." This boast came from one of the longtime members of Good Samaritan. Indeed, the church's interracial makeup was no small accomplishment in a racialized society like the United States. Not seeing color, however, is a complicated issue. It represents the condensation of our deeply contradictory race history. Although most white Americans have been saying for some time that they are in favor of racial integration and equal opportunity, "what has changed in recent years," in Andrew Hacker's words, is not living patterns but only "the way people speak in public."[6] Recent studies indicate signs of increasing segregation in schools.[7] The percentage of significantly interracial Protestant churches is shockingly low: only 6 percent of evangelical churches and 2.5 percent of mainline churches are congregations in which no more than 80 percent of the membership identifies as the same race. The more highly educated US whites are, the less likely they are to be in racially mixed churches or neighborhoods.[8] Expanding this paradox of welcome and reality to the population labeled "disabled" finds similar contradictions prevailing.

The point is not simply that we are failing to act on our beliefs. It is that a prominent cultural discourse of inclusion – "not seeing" color (or disability) – is just as often the *denial* of racism and its effects as it is a boast that our common humanity can bring us together. Ellis Cose argues that in its current form, color blindness "is not a racial equalizer but a silencer – a way of quashing questions about the continuing racial stratification of the society and a way of feeling good about the fact that the world of elites remains so predominantly white."[9]

Although the refusal to see color served in the early days of the US civil rights movement to *dismantle* legal segregation, in a changed social context it has become something quite different. Legally, "constitutional color blindness" is a highly problematic philosophy that serves the retrenchment of historical racial disparities.[10] Such blindness is really avoidance, which is linked historically to the denial of injustice. Practices that pretend not to notice race and other marginalizing differences such as disability also work as (ostensible) gestures of kindness, adding real paternalism to the mix that is obliviousness.[11]

On my first visit to Good Samaritan UMC there were more Africans and African Americans in attendance than whites, and I became acutely aware of the whiteness of my skin and my unfamiliarity with the experience of being a racial minority. When I approached two of the group-home members, one with Down syndrome, the other sitting twisted in a wheelchair, I felt uncomfortable, not knowing where to put my body or how to communicate with them. Upon later reflection, I judged that my feeling of strangeness in response to the unaccustomed "blackness" of the place and the presence of people with disabilities suggested that my conscious commitments to inclusiveness were not correlated with my habituated sense of the normal. My awkward postures "confessed" a disruption of the dominant world I inhabit, signaling an implicit disconnect between my convictions and these perceptions. This tacit sense that surprised me when I became self-conscious of my whiteness and my bodiedness suggests forms of occlusion operating in my own internalized sense of the world. As evidence of a broader social "unaccustomedness" to black and disabled bodies, this discomfort has significance far beyond my own sense of disease. It is an unaccustomedness and obliviousness with widespread parallels, not only at Good Samaritan UMC but in the larger society, as I suggested earlier. It is an obliviousness that comes with dominance.

While Good Samaritan was greatly successful in becoming a diverse community, its members brought with them the habituations of the wider social reality. Some of those habituations corresponded to my reactions, what I will call a "wound" of the dominant. During the first year of its rebirth, a visiting preacher from Liberia came, and the number of blacks at the service increased. Some white members who originally had been agreeable to the inclusiveness vision complained to the minister that the church was getting "too black." The numerical fallacy of the statement does not take away from its important witness to a deeply internalized sense of a dominant group.

My awkwardness in relation to the man in the wheelchair also signifies something larger than personal idiosyncrasy. So common are reactions like mine to people with disabilities that they have been given a name – rituals of degradation.[12] Few churches know how to welcome such people as those from group homes and mental institutions. In Rosemary Garland-Thomson's terms, they are often experienced as grotesque or "freaks."[13] Not only are there problems of physical inaccessibility, but churchly conventions protecting sacred silence help reproduce the larger society's ghettoizing of these "special needs" people.[14] Group homes are most likely to be found in low-income neighborhoods due to the power of wealth and influence in the control of residential zoning. Such conditions are widespread.

The challenge of understanding Good Samaritan UMC, then, is that talk there about not seeing difference is a condensation of both obliviousness to harm as well as gestures toward redeeming it. To get at this paradox, my approach to this congregation became more complicated. From an inquiry into beliefs, my study now broadened to ask how faith intersected with a situation characterized by forms of obliviousness marked and sustained by larger social-political processes. Concerned to discover how this community was complicit in "not seeing," I had to ask also how my framing categories might be oblivious to these complexities. Not only would a frame confined to beliefs fail to register such complexities in a helpful way, but MacIntyrean practices were unlikely to as well.

Categories were needed that could display the intersection of social realities with faith but in a way that took prereflective visceral responses as seriously as stated convictions. For understanding the character of the brokenness that haunted this situation demanded attention to how it is that having "race" and "disability" evoke reactions to bodies in ways that being white or normal-bodied do not, at least in the perception of a dominant such as myself. Reminiscent of associations of bodies with femaleness and rationality with maleness, the marked character of certain bodies and not others is a sure signal of power differentials. And these associations shape even the most well intentioned Christians.

Framing Transformation: Attending to Obliviousness

This situation of differences had to be framed in a way that took the interaction of marked bodies into account. How might members' beliefs diverge from their internal sense of comfort with those perceived as different? What other sensibility than belief needed my theological attention? Such questions guided the way I portrayed Good Samaritan UMC.

The obliviousness that afflicts our tolerant nation and, inevitably, this community is not so much a cognitive problem on the part of the dominant, as, for example, in racist or able-ist beliefs. Neither is it primarily found in the malice that characterizes these "isms." The original members of the Good Samaritan congregation understood themselves to be welcoming of, not prejudiced toward, those who were marked as different. White members claimed "not to see color, just Christians." "Normal" members of all races indicated welcome for those with "special needs." Like the majority of North Americans, these "Good Samaritans" disavowed bias against those who are different.

Obliviousness is a form of not seeing that is not primarily intentional but reflexive. A kind of disregard, both experiential and geographical, it may coexist with well-meaning attitudes. However, obliviousness can signal fear and aversion as well, thereby creating the a priori condition of forms of injustice.[15] We see this in its connection to more explicit forms of human malice toward the other. Malice is founded in the power of the visceral, the "pulse of attraction and aversion" that characterizes all human interactions, says political theorist Iris Young.[16] It is this visceral register where fear, anxiety, and disgust occur, responses that can characterize human reactions to those who are different. These reactions take form as the cultural marking of bodies, identifying them as racialized, gendered, sexualized, and "normal/abnormal." Projecting all manner of anxiety and fear onto "othered" bodies, these conventions also generate rationalizations that justify marginalization, racism, sexism, and other oppressions based upon difference. In the place of knowledge of particular individuals, then, we substitute social stereotypes.[17]

I came, then, to treat Good Samaritan UMC as a complex text about difference and a variety of positionings in relation to difference – about "whiteness" as well as "color," and "normal" and "not normal." To frame this lived faith theologically required categories that captured not simply what these congregants believed, that is, their vision and their biblical and theological convictions, but their habituations as well. The "wound" of the dominant is located in our incorporative or bodily habits, as shaped by desires, fears, and visceral reactions – all of which go into what we experience as "normal." As well intentioned as members of Good Samaritan were, they were not free of these social enculturations. The wound of obliviousness for those who are white and able-bodied occurs as a continuum of experience, extending from beliefs to desire and visceral reaction to embodied others; the wounds of those victimized by obliviousness are not identical but have to do with being marked as "other."

One of the ways in which such bodily practices shaped Good Samaritan was in the form of incorporative practices of propriety. Part of a cultural tradition, incorporative practices of propriety are distinguished from written or inscribed traditions, because they are bodily activities. These habituated norms for "proper behavior" are learned and passed on by a society as part of its identity.[18] Not necessarily explicit, these norms are internalized as the respectable way to use and place one's body – from table manners, like how to hold a fork, to postures of deference or the proper ways different genders can display themselves. From the enslavement of Africans and Jim Crow laws to more recent residential, religious, and work segregation, much of US society has been habituated into racialized bodily proprieties. Such practices involve the postures and gestures that are acceptable, that is, where differently racialized persons can "properly" put their bodies.

Racialized proprieties are not separate "cultures"; those for African Americans are inextricably linked with those designated as "white." For whites this has meant habituation into being the dominant race, that is, not having race. For African Americans bodily habituation is defined with a legacy that led to what W. E. B. DuBois famously called the "twoness" of black consciousness.[19] While being black is differentiated by many enculturations (gender, class, sexuality), *to have to always be aware* of the dominant race as well as one's own is key in the production of bodily proprieties for African American communities. However many ways of being white are otherwise differentiated – and similarly inflected by gender, class, and sexuality – *to be able to be oblivious* to one's own race and to the "other" are key to bodily proprieties for those called "white." For African members of Good Samaritan UMC who need not be concerned with "being black" in their home countries, this means that they *have to* attend to it in the United States and that there is a hierarchy within blackness itself.

I propose that white members of Good Samaritan UMC were habituated into *a bodily sense of ownership of public or social space.*[20] Their bodies feel comfortable in most places outside their homes; they can travel without concern or heightened self-awareness. What is produced by this practice is appropriately called "white space," indicating the historic dominance of whites and the continued "spell" of that dominance even when legal discrimination is past. A mode of free and comfortable movement, this bodily propriety is possible wherever the majority of bodies are white or any black bodies present are somehow displaying "properly" subservient postures.

African American proprieties relative to this "white-owned space" range from the subverted gaze and submissive posture of the slave to the messages sent by the uniformed body of the janitor, housekeeper, or other marker of lower status. While Good Samaritan's African Americans cannot be described as if they were simply victims, many had likely been habituated into practices of propriety shaped by the double consciousness – a consciousness of white dominated space that calls for careful placement of their black bodies and a consciousness of their own cultures where, whatever else defined "proper," bodies are less constrained by the dominant race. This consciousness of their own cultures is a topic of enormous richness, from the proud display and adornment of bodies that came to characterize the black church, to all variety of creative proprieties.[21] The former is a residual that has been characterized for many by what bell hooks calls the "terror of whiteness."[22] If not a response to terror, as was the case in the past, these practices are still inevitably shaped by a need to be aware of the effect of their own presence in "white space."

Consciousness of vigilance is inseparably connected to the obliviousness of much white sensibility, for "white people can 'safely' imagine that they are invisible to black people," says bell hooks.[23] The idea of proper places for one's body is hardly conceivable for whites; this is a largely invisible propriety. There is, then, a linked if asymmetrical character to these racialized incorporative practices of propriety, and they are evident in two dynamics at work in Good Samaritan UMC.

When some white Good Samaritans complained that the church was getting "too black," they were not observing a literal numerical imbalance. Rather, they were displaying their (normally unconscious) bodily propriety of ownership of space. The first dynamic, then, is a discomfort connected to something like fear, whether of loss of control or aversion and guilt. The second dynamic is suggested by what caused the discomfort – the disruption of that space. At Good Samaritan black bodies became hypervisible when they increased in number, elegantly adorned for worship. The complaint by white members signaled an emerging consciousness of their racialized propriety, but it also signaled the possibility of its destabilization. Something more empowering than hypervigilance in the presence of whites was emerging for nonwhite members, perhaps assisting in the transformation of white-owned space.

In short, by broadening my frame to include the category of bodily practices and their accompanying affective responses, I saw that practices that extended the goods of welcoming the "eunuch" were not limited to the following biblical or theological mandates. Equally important were the disruptions and alterations of members' inherited bodily enculturations. Although it did not surface in public complaints, discomfort on the part of the "normal bodied" around the "special needs" folks was typical, with the exception of those with much experience with persons with disabilities – namely, a number of parents whose children had disabilities. In order to be successful, "welcoming the eunuch" had to entail more than the not seeing of race or disability. It had to create a place where wounds of obliviousness could surface and be addressed.

Practices and a Place to Appear

A place to appear cannot simply be an occasion of hypothetical inclusion or of good intentions. It requires alteration of what supports our obliviousnesses: deep, embedded habituations and their residual layered affects and fears. With regard to racialized habituations, the attainment and enhancement of capacities to welcome the "stranger" at Good Samaritan looked different for African Americans, Africans, and whites, and I cannot capture the nuances of that here. However, what seemed to best address these inherited bodily proprieties were activities where people worked together, made decisions together, and did so in situations of shared power.[24] The development of comfort levels with those deemed "other" were crucial to shifting awareness. The face-to-face "homemaking practices" of cooking and eating, cleaning the church, sharing stories, and meeting as United Methodist Women all created spaces for developing empathy among members. For the whites these practices created possibilities to recognize the agency of the blacks, for blacks the possibility to humanize whites, and for Africans to humanize African Americans and vice versa. Such "togetherness" occurred on a continuum, and outcomes were not always transparent. However, these practices were "faithful to the vision" insofar as they helped diminish proprieties of ownership of space for whites and lessen the hypervigilance of African Americans.

Habituations into discomfort around persons with disabilities were also part of the obliviousness that underlay the structural injustices against them. However, alteration of such discomfort depended a great deal on attention to forms of communication. To this end there were important alterations in the worship services, such as welcoming of noise and outbursts normally considered disruptive in sacred space. Over time the capacities of a few "normate"[25] members to attend to and be with persons with disabilities were enhanced. Despite efforts to include the persons from group homes, however, much of the biblical and creedal material was not effective. Participants simply were not able to understand these communications. Real change required the capacity to communicate with such persons, a skill often missing from typical notions of accountability in the ecclesial community. Many persons with special needs use nonsymbolic modes of communication, such as body movements, gestures, facial expressions, and touching.[26] The practices that began to create a sense of acknowledgment for group home members included music, face-to-face greeting and naming, and a great variety of kinesthetic movements.

Altered bodily proprieties and modes of communication went hand in hand, of course, with interpretive practices in enhancing these forms of mutual appearing. Shared discourses around welcoming the stranger, Jesus' life, radical dependence on God, and confession of one's blindness helped create a logic for these practices, defining their MacIntyrean ends. In the end what mattered most was not whether a practice was "biblical" or orthodox, but whether it enhanced members' capacities to "appear" to one another.

Concluding Issues

A place to appear requires alteration of consciousness and attention to modes of communication that go beyond the linguistic and the intentional. Failure to take these seriously could mean liturgies of "reconciliation" that only reconfirm the already complacent assumption of dominant groups that we believe in the equality of all God's children and that none of us are prejudiced. It easily misses the nonsymbolic communication necessary for reciprocal relations with groups of people with disabilities. Failure to attend to this continuum of experience will be accompanied, however indirectly, by a limiting of theological lenses.

I have not provided a complete theological (or ecclesiological) read of this community. Minimally that would require completing the latent anthropology in my analysis with attention to human desire, where the proper telos of desire is a sustaining relation with the eternal God. However, I am suggesting that the transformation of obliviousness and its social harms that go with our everyday lives, whether in or out of church, requires creation of its opposite: "a shared space of appearance."[27] What is needed to counter such harm is a place to be recognized by and to recognize the "other." Being seen and heard by others, being acknowledged by others of different social locations – this is essential to political life. It is also essential to a community of faith.

Of course, unless our habituations into the proprieties of dominant groups are transgressed in some way by "others," our well-meaning obliviousness and its accompanying unintended consequences will continue. Appeal to our common unity in the body of Christ can function like "color blindness" as a mechanism of avoidance. To the extent that Good Samaritan UMC was a place where people of different races and abilities "appeared" in significant ways to one another (and were not merely prayed for), it was an ecclesial – even a redemptive – community.

Notes

1 If obliviousness is a sinful deformation, a place to appear is a sign of its redemption, a case I cannot make in this essay.
2 Kathryn Tanner, "Theological Reflection and Christian Practices," in *Practicing Theology: Beliefs and Practices in Christian Life*, ed. Miroslav Volf and Dorothy C. Bass (Grand Rapids: Eerdmans, 2002), 230.
3 See Tex Sample, *Ministry in an Oral Culture: Living with Will Rogers, Uncle Remus, and Minnie Pearl* (Louisville, KY: Westminster John Knox, 1994), 9–10; and Walter J. Ong, *Orality and Literacy: The Technologizing of the World* (London: Routledge, 1982), 20–77.
4 See Don S. Browning, *A Fundamental Practical Theology: Descriptive and Strategic Proposals* (Minneapolis: Fortress, 1991); and James Nieman, "Attending Locally: Theologies in Congregations," *International Journal of Practical Theology* 6, no. 2 (Fall 2002): 198–225.
5 Alasdair MacIntyre, *After Virtue: A Study in Moral Theology*, 2nd ed. (Notre Dame, IN: University of Notre Dame Press, 1984), 222.
6 Andrew Hacker, *Two Nations: Black and White, Separate, Hostile, Unequal* (New York: Scribner, 2003), 52.
7 See "Race in American Public Schools: Rapidly Resegregating School Districts," press release, August 8, 2002, from the report of Harvard University's Civil Rights Project, "Race in American Public Schools: Rapidly Resegregating School Districts."
8 Michael Emerson and Chris Smith, *Divided by Faith: Evangelical Religion and the Problem of Race in America* (New York: Oxford University Press, 2000), 10.
9 Ellis Cose, *Color-Blind: Seeing Beyond Race in a Race-Obsessed World* (New York: HarperCollins, 1997), 210.
10 See Neil Gotanda, "A Critique of 'Our Constitution Is Color-Blind,'" in *Critical Race Theory: The Key Writings That Formed the Movement*, ed. Kimberle Crenshaw (New York: New Press, 1995).
11 For the parallel, see Cose, *Color-Blind*, 189–90.
12 Nancy L. Eiesland, *The Disabled God: Toward a Liberatory Theology of Disability* (Nashville: Abingdon, 1994), 92–3.
13 See Rosemary Garland-Thomson, ed., *Freakery: Cultural Spectacles of the Extraordinary Body* (New York: New York University Press, 1996).
14 See Nancy L. Eiesland, "Barriers and Bridges: Relating the Disability Rights Movement and Religious Organizations," in *Human Disability and the Service of God: Reassessing Religious Practice*, ed. Nancy L. Eiesland and Don E. Saliers (Nashville: Abingdon, 1998), 200–29.

15 See Kimberley Curtis, *Our Sense of the Real: Aesthetic Experience and Arendtian Politics* (Ithaca, NY: Cornell University Press, 1999).

16 Iris Marion Young, *Justice and the Politics of Difference* (Princeton, NJ: Princeton University Press, 1990), 123; see also William Connolly, *Why I Am Not a Secularist* (Minneapolis: University of Minnesota Press, 1999), 19–29.

17 Glenn C. Loury, *The Anatomy of Racial Inequality* (Cambridge, MA: Harvard University Press, 2002), 65–7.

18 See Paul Connerton, *How Societies Remember* (Cambridge: Cambridge University Press, 1989).

19 W.E.B. DuBois, *The Souls of Black Folk* (New York: Modem Library, 2003), xii, 7–9.

20 I thank William Hart for naming this practice of propriety.

21 See Anthony Pinn, *Terror and Triumph: The Nature of Black Religion* (Minneapolis: Fortress, 2003).

22 See bell hooks, "Whiteness in the Black Imagination" in *Killing Rage* (New York: Henry Holt, 1995), 31–50; and hooks, "Homeplace," in *Yearning: Race, Gender, and Cultural Politics* (Boston: South End, 1990), 41.

23 Hooks, "Whiteness in the Black Imagination," 35.

24 On the claim that a relation to a black with a higher socioeconomic status matters most to whites, see Mary R. Jackman and Marie Crane, "'Some of My Best Friends Are Black': Interracial Friendship and Whites' Racial Attitudes," *Public Opinion Quarterly* 50 (1980).

25 "Normate" is a term used to indicate the artificiality of designating some people as "normal."

26 Ellin Siegel and Amy Wetherby, "Nonsymbolic Communication," in *Instruction of Students with Severe Disabilities*, 5th ed., ed. Martha E. Snell and Fredda Brown (Upper Saddle River, NJ: Prentice-Hall, 2000), 409.

27 Curtis, *Our Sense of the Real*, 14.

7

A Hermeneutics of the Knees (2008)*

Cláudio Carvalhaes

Introduction

Whereas Fulkerson writes as one awakened from white obliviousness of racism, Brazilian Cláudio Carvalhaes writes from within the colonized body and asks how to move (literally) toward a new reconfiguration within Western Christian liturgy. What would liturgical theology (and by implication, practical theology) look like with limber knees and open legs?

Carvalhaes earned his doctorate at Union Theological Seminary in 2007 with Janet Walton and Delores Williams and has recently returned as Associate Professor of Worship. Self-described as a shoeshine boy from working class São Paulo, Brazil, and now an ordained elder in the Presbyterian Church (USA) with twenty years in the United States, he draws on his outsider position to gain perspective on Westernized Christianity, its individualism, and its ignorance about the impact of colonization on its core premises. This essay raises deeply practical theological questions about bodies and knowledge, even if he does not address the discipline directly. It first appeared in *Studies in World Christianity* alongside several articles on liturgical dance and gesture (e.g., in Tonga, Kenya, and Southern Africa). He brings expertise in liturgy, an area underrepresented in a tradition dominated by a Protestant emphasis on religious education, preaching, pastoral theology, and care, and he adopts a unique postcolonial and postmodern orientation within what Don Saliers describes as the "liberationist moral and political critiques of Christian liturgy."

In the entry, Carvalhaes provides an evocative portrait of the repression of bodily knowledge in Western Christianity, its exportation to non-Western contexts through colonization (e.g., in Brazil's carnival and samba), and its restitution through liturgical forms more accepting of bodily parts and persons previously excised and exiled. Written while Carvalhaes was a doctoral student and teaching at Louisville Presbyterian Theological Seminary, the essay does not construct so much as deconstruct, following feminist theologian Marcella Althaus-Reid and postmodernist Mark C. Taylor. He captures the problems of what he calls "liturgical proper," the Westernized, rationalized

Original publication details: Cláudio Carvalhaes, "'Gimme de Kneebone Bent': Liturgics, Dance, Resistance, and a Hermeneutics of the Knees," pp. 1–18 from *Studies in World Christianity: The Edinburgh Review of Theology and Religion* 14:1 (2008).

imposition of an immobile God and sketches the beginnings of a "hermeneutics of the knees" that stretches rather than does away with liturgical ordering as new participants redefine the range of proper practices and participants. He draws extensively on an essay by Brazilian theologian and Methodist pastor Nancy Cardoso Pereira to argue that the "movements of our knees are intrinsically related to the ways we think, create and live our worlds." Reclaiming knowledge of bodies, knees, and dance in worship is integral to de-evangelization and de-colonization.

Suggested Further Reading

- Cláudio Carvalhaes, *Eucharist and Globalization: Redrawing the Borders of Eucharistic Hospitality* (Eugene, OR: Pickwick, 2013).
- Ivone Gebara, *Out of the Depths: Women's Experience of Evil and Salvation*, trans. Ann Patrick Ware (Minneapolis: Augsburg Fortress, 2002).
- Don Saliers, *Worship as Theology: Foretaste of Glory Divine* (Nashville: Abingdon, 1994).

***

Shall we all dance to the *Lord*? But what Lord? To whose Lord shall we bend our knees in prayer, honour, dance and praise? Can our knees be naked? Can we open our legs? How much skin can we show without apologizing? Are we allowed to get the sensuous fever while dancing a tango, a salsa, or a samba? How should our knees behave in the *house of the Lord*? And whose house is God's house? Is there a proper way to dance in a worship service? What parts of our bodies can we move without distressing the proper liturgical order rooted in respect, faith, rationality, tradition and good manners?

Our knees connect liturgy with ecclesiology, theology, colonialisation, dance and bodies. I was asked to write about dance in Brazil/Latin America, perhaps because Brazil is well known for its dancing spirit, as one can see in our carnival, samba, joy and beautiful women. All of that is true. But the task for this article was more specific. I had to write about dance within Christian communities. Then, the whole aspect of dance was turned upside down in my head. In truth, we do not dance in historic Protestant churches in Brazil and in that regard we do not differ one inch from many of our brothers and sisters in Edinburgh, Rome, Geneva or the United States – at least when dance is concerned. We just do not dance. Only our Pentecostal brothers and sisters can dance. Moreover, new Pentecostal churches and the Charismatic branch of the Roman Catholic Church now have aerobics during worship services. You leave these services all wet!

However, I decided to write about some of the conditions that prevent many Brazilian Christians from dancing in their Sunday liturgies. In spite of our wonderful carnival, we do not and cannot dance in Protestant churches. God forbid we move our bodies beyond the 'please stand' and 'you may be seated' parts of the service. While worshiping, we usually do not need more than our eyes to see the altar/table and the priest/pastor, our hands to hold the bulletin and hymnal books and our mouths to sing and pray. We mostly need our ears to listen endlessly.

Let us start by saying that the problem with dancing obviously has to do with problems with our knees, which bend and move our bodies. The knees have always been a dangerous element in the Christian faith. In spite of the doctrine of the incarnation,

God's *excessive knee movement* in Christ, the Christian body in general remained a frightened space where things can easily get out of control. The knees held the possibilities for pleasure, desire and resistance, these fervent enemies of reason and control, and must be denied and/or kept under surveillance of a proper spiritual faith. Rubero Alves, a Brazilian thinker and poet, says:

> We thought of finding God where the body ends: and we made the body suffer and we turn it into a heavy load, an obedient entity, a machine of work, into an enemy to be silenced, and that way we persecuted the body to the point of praising death as the way to God, as if God preferred the smell of sepulchres to the delights of paradise. And we became cruel, violent, allowing exploration and war. For, if God can only be found beyond the body, then everything can be done to the body. (Alves 1983)

Our evangelisation in Latin America, both from Roman Catholicism and Protestantism, taught us to be careful, suspicious and even hateful of our bodies. We learned that there was a proper (read civilised) way of moving, believing, acting, singing, looking, gesturing, touching within the worshiping space and in the world. Silently, the Christian evangelisation targeted first of all, our knees. They were taken from our own control and educated by priests and pastors to behave accordingly. Put in another way, through a powerful and continuous catechesis, we were/are taught that we were/are to learn three main things: to control our knees, to internalise a proper code of behaviour and to be happy with it.

This education began when Latin America became the hosts of (well intentioned) guests and missionaries; but in no time we 'suddenly' became the guests of our once guests, now our hosts. Soon we began appealing to be accepted in our own land, to learn how to be worthy, and to become citizens of our own countries. Our hosts became so violent and they pressured our knees so intensely that one day we could not hold our knees together anymore. In 1985, when Pope John Paul II visited Peru, he received a Bible from an indigenous leader in Cusco, once the heart of the Inca empire. The Pope heard how the Bible had been used to systematically disrespect the knees and the dignity of the indigenous people since 1492.

This long, complicated and yet simple educational process made us become something else, that which we never knew we were or could have been. Now we try to know that which we can only imagine we might have been, and do that imagining through colonised eyes and a colonised imaginary (Gruzinski 2003). We became estranged from our bodies, and the shadow of shame and punishment still hovers around our bodies. As we lament all that was taken from us, we are not ungrateful for what Christianity has given to us. Latin America is a Christian continent. However, for many, our knees are still stiff and we do not remember that we can dance. We do not even ask for permission. We just cannot. To move is to stir things up, and perhaps get too much 'in' control rather that 'out of' control. To dance is to become the owners of our own bodies, to become responsible for them; but to do that we must get our knees loosened up and take action from a sexual, bodily faith.

In this article I will investigate the ways in which our liturgical *grid/order/proper* faith provided/allowed patterns for us to move accordingly within very specific limits. Second, I will analyse ways in which the liturgical proper eliminated *differences* and made us similar to our hosts-once-guests. Finally, inspired by Nancy Pereira Cardoso, one of our most creative and fascinating biblicists and theologians in Brazil, I will engage with what she calls a *de-evangelization of our knees* and propose a feminist hermeneutic of the knees as a way to help us move forward and, hopefully, to dance.

The Liturgical Proper

[...]

The historical array of liturgical possibilities within Christian churches, in general, has always been determined by historical procedures and definitions, which have been turned into official documents that control 'tradition'. These not only presuppose certain conditions of possibilities but also ordain behaviour, establish ethical demands and a proper faith, including a prescribed assortment of beliefs and practices. The range of these sets of liturgical possibilities (i.e., *lex orandi* and *lex credendi,* practices and beliefs) have historically been developed out of official canons based on theologically chosen and approved sources, all of them defined, limited and established over time according to a means of maintaining power, namely, tradition.

These liturgical Christian possibilities have always gravitated toward or drawn upon the same structure that one might call a *liturgical proper.* This *liturgical proper* entails a universal logic or code that surrounds the liturgical and the theological with a fixed, unmoved structure that, by the very condition of its fixed and immobile essence, makes it possible for the liturgical thought or practice to always be reasonable, meaningful and intelligible according to proper, acceptable, theological grounding.

This ground is specified by *onto-theo-logical* underpinnings, or *metaphysical* understandings, that define the ways in which Christian religious meanings are conceived of and consequently practised. Gordon Lathrop defines precisely the metaphysical and onto-theological underpinnings of what I am calling here the *liturgical proper* when he demarcates the worship patterns of the Christian *ordo* (from the Latin order, structure, shape, pattern):

> [...]*Ordo* here will not mean simply the written directions about what service to schedule at what time or what specific rite, scripture readings, or prayers to use, although that is one primary meaning of the word in the West, but the presuppositions active behind such scheduling. [...] To inquire into the structure of the *ordo* is to inquire about the way meaning occurs in Christian worship. The thesis operative here is this: meaning occurs through structure [...] (Lathrop 1993)

Thus, the wide spectrum of liturgical possibilities, with its own specificities defined according to each Christian denomination, and each of them established by its own liturgical procedures and theological account regarding their own tradition, rely on this metaphysical structure, on this *onto-theo-logical* pattern that regulates both being (us) and Being (God).

However, let us pause for a second and try to understand what is this metaphysical, *onto-theo-logical* structure? Mark A. Wrathall helps us:

> Since Plato, philosophers in the West have proposed various conceptions of a supreme God that was the ground of the existence and intelligibility of all that is. [...] This means that metaphysics tried to understand the being of everything that is through a simultaneous determination of its essence or most universal trait (the 'onto' in 'onto-theology'), and a determination of the ground of source of the totality of beings in some highest or divine entity (the 'theo' in onto-'theology'). (Wrathall 2003)

The Christian liturgical logic understands *being* under the overarching realm of Being. In other words, this code relies entirely on a metaphysical structure, [...] an *a priori* idea of God as the origin of everything that *is*, a totalising presence. [...] Thus, the liturgical endeavour is a way of *re-presenting* that which has always been *there* through a constant and irrefutable metaphysical presence. [...] This self-enclosed God does not have a body, much less knees, and cannot move or be moved, but instead, God moves everything. [...] Within this structure, the consequence is that theologians and liturgists become the gate-keepers of the proper.

However, what this proper does and offers are directly related to what it cannot offer and cannot do, or rather, to its improper parts. In other words, the understanding of God can only be possible because of what it excludes. For instance, the approved liturgical/theological documents in any denomination only exist at the expense of what it avoids, represses and/or denies. [...] In other words, the condition of the possibility of the existence of God, and consequently its theological and liturgical developments, depend on that which is *other*, strange, unfamiliar and impossible to *God's self*. Or, one can only talk about the knee because it has never been part of the confession of the Christian faith.

Liturgy and Alterity

Let me start by giving one definition of alterity:

> Etymologically 'alterity is the condition of otherness ... many modernists pursued alterity for its disruptive potential, but it never had a fixed location. In the wake of feminist theory and postcolonial discourse, the term has taken on a renewed valence, wherein alterity is privileged as a position of radical critique of the dominant culture – of what it cannot think or address or permit at all – more than as a place of romantic escape from it. (Foster *et al.* 2005)

How should liturgy deal with *alterity*, that which has to do with *difference*, that which alters its order, confuses its scripts, transgress its postulates, and does not resemble the very idea of the same but rather, can only be related to something akin to an intrusion, a foreigner matter, a deviant behaviour, an iconoclastic move, an improper performance? In other words, how should liturgy host a parasite, that which undoes the condition of its possibility and scatters the very element of its structure? Or, more suc-cinctly, what has this liturgical code forgotten, denied, repressed and negated?

To answer this question, it is necessary to explore the shadowed rational and not often paradoxical consequences of the logic of the modem liturgical code that is based on hierarchical dichotomies: body and soul, knee and mind, good and bad, God and Evil, safe and condemned, us and them, black and white, clean and dirty, true (proper) and false (improper), men and women. These binary structures have set aside and denied that which they cannot sense, whose appearance cannot be identified or accepted, since it disrupts and disfigures the figural status of its rationality. Nonetheless, as said before, that which the liturgical logic denies is what gives possibility to the structure of its rationality. In other words, the very identity of the Christian liturgical code can only be defined by that which it cannot identify, that is, its own *alterity*, that which is different, unknown. Mark C. Taylor states:

> The history of society and culture is, in large measure, a history of the struggle with the endlessly complex problems of difference and otherness.... A (20th) century that opened with the publication of *The Interpretation of Dreams* should have learned by now that the repressed never goes away but always returns – sometimes violently...The problem of the other; however, is not only political; it is also an issue of considerable artistic, philosophical, psychological, and theo-logical importance. (Taylor 1998)

Historically, one result of this dualism and repression within the field of liturgical studies has been the absence of women in liturgical rites and the imposition of white, patriarchal and heterosexual religious frameworks that settle the universal mode for liturgical ges-tures. The women, along with queer, black and colonised people, represented the other in the liturgical structures. As a consequence, these colonialist liturgical movements still deny, dismiss and/or bracket the presence of the *other* in the proper religious spaces where power control is always at stake. The *other* have knees, and they should be evangelised in order to behave accordingly, to the proper Christian faith. The coloniser spreads and forces its familiar rationality within the colonised as a way to move the *other* into same-ness, turning the *other* into the coloniser's self-realization. Thus, the unknown becomes knowable, safe, and open to deal with and to control. This makes Barbara Brown Taylor, a prominent and wonderful Anglican thinker and preacher, feel *at home* in the worshipful service in a 'small, tin-roofed (Anglican) church in Western Kenya'. She said:

> I did not understand a word of the service, but *I understood perfectly what we were doing* that morning. I had learned it halfway around the world in another language, including the part that begins: 'We believe in one God ...' *Essentially mysterious but entirely accessible, the sacraments are pure genius for teaching us what we need to know about our relationship with God.* (Taylor 1993, emphasis mine)

This *pure genius* of the sacraments teaches and establishes the limits of the familiar, the 'figurable', the 'representable', the controllable and the attainable. This *genius* turns the other and its unfamiliar, threatening assets into a mirror, changing the unfamiliar, what does not resemble *us,* into familiar, recognisable terms, elements, postures, rationality, behaviour, practices, gestures and so on. The universal liturgical code, based on universal understandings of being (us) in relation to Being (God), serves as a movement between us (the proper, the coloniser) and them (the improper, the colonised). This movement turns the other into itself, providing connection by establishing a safe distance through binaries (us and them), clearing up differences, edges and oppositions, and firming the ground of the *unmoved mover* (i.e., God/coloniser), as the only ground for comprehension, perception and rationality.

This strange familiarity came to Barbara Taylor with the fact that the *liturgical code* was pulsing at that small church the same way it pulses at her own denomination in the United States, giving frame, meaning, rhythm, authenticity and thus security to that moment. The *otherness* of the Kenyans was shadowed by the light shone through the structures of the inherent liturgical and theological logic that made Taylor say, 'I understood perfectly' and felt it 'entirely accessible.' In the proper performance of the sacraments, she *knew* everything she needed to know about her relationship with God, so much so that the people of Kenya, the *other*, became a joyous surplus, since they were not actually needed once the liturgical frame and theological words were already given. This surplus could come then as a native dance or an offering by Kenyans in colourful clothes, which obscures from the idea that it was a colonised, universal logic that framed, structured and imposed the whole reasoning of religion over *the other*. Moreover, in her experience, *the other* was turned into her sameness and she did not have to deal with any scary elements of a strange faith.

This overarching control of modern and colonial rationality means that anybody from Europe to the USA, Latin America to Asia, Azores Islands to Papua New Guinea, can sense some kind of familiarity with the logic of Christian liturgical representations. Outside these *meaningful ways* there are only shadows, the shadows of the *other*, of inconsistency, of moving knees, of 'unpresentability' and the absence of a proper knowledge.

As we try to move our knees, our task is to find that which is not proper within and outside of this exclusive horizon of meaning, so that the colonised, the subaltern, the *other*, might have a chance to become the owners of their knees and their own dancing relations around the world, rather than always continuing to be the same of their coloniser. In order to do that, one must *liturgise* that which might have been left *unthought*, *unliturgised*, that which does not fit into an acceptable rationality and waits to spur the imagination. In other words, one tries to capture what cannot be captured, to hear the noises of the *other* [...] According to Mark C. Taylor, to think the unthinkable is to *think not*. [...]

> To think not is to linger with a negative, which is not merely negative. The not is something like a non-negative negative that is not positive. It is virtually impossible to articulate this strange notion in terms that do not seem utterly paradoxical (unlike the structuralists who taught us to think in dualistic terms). Thinking not explores territory that is not only unmapped but it is unmappable. [...] (Taylor 2000)

The unmapped/unmappable territory of religion invites us to linger a little longer with the negative (i.e., that which cannot be named because it is so scandalous, improper, unethical, outrageous, unbalanced and scary). [...] By moving into the negative space, into the shadowed spaces rejected by the traditional proper, we can add to our liturgies some of the things we never thought we could. We should not only play but perform, sing, protest, dance and enact the negative that goes on in the world, those disastrous aspects of life. Not only the death of Jesus on the cross, but also the unspeakable pain of people in Asia after the Tsunami, or the complete abandonment by the government of the African Americans in New Orleans, USA, or the monstrous gap between the rich and poor in Brazil. To move into the negative space is to linger with questions that are not so easy to console or answer. It is to think of our liturgies as *liturgical performances*, as moveable, fluid and changeable, performative orders with different set ups of spaces, renewed wording of prayers and songs, as ways to break down the [...] *immediacies* within our society that narrow us down into the known and approved; immediacies that shrink our lives to a handful of binary oppositions, our bodies to fossilised identities, and our imaginations to economic wants.

However, moving into the shadows does not necessarily mean shedding light anymore than the establishment of something new. There is no rush into the new but rather, to complicate the already intricate relationship between shadow and light. [...] We have a huge tradition to follow and we are responsible for it and for the work of our ancestors. [...]

I do not intend to deny or dismiss the official definitions and designations of liturgy since these definitions are not going away anytime soon, but rather to think about ways to open up the field of liturgy to wrestle with unimagined movements of our knees, of our bodies, of our feelings, sensations and perceptions, wondering about and between the (ir)rationalities of God, our faith, and its (im)possible representations. Heidegger said, 'Perhaps, there is a thinking outside of the distinction of rational and irrational [...] (Taussig 1999).

The movement of our knees might be what Heidegger calls a 'clearing' (Heidegger 1993). It provides a *thinking* that does not entail only our heads but also our bodies. It may begin with our knees and the ways we might think, move, touch, kiss and praise God. It does not serve as a way out of metaphysics but offers a way of thinking our faith and liturgical space through our knees.

A Feminist Latin American Hermeneutics of the Knees

Liberation theologians forgot to pay attention to our knees as well. They did not see that it was our knees that were tied up by injustice and stiffed by death. We were taught to stay put and that 'they' would bring redemption to our lives. Especially for women, the knees were targeted in an effort to silence them and control their acts of resistance. In order to become subjects of one's own history, one has to move and take over things on our own knees. Perhaps we never heard about our knees because liberation theology had its own bodily and sexual stiffness (Althaus-Reid 2000).

[...] Our knees perform our lost identities. Between the streets of carnival and the road to church lies the ability of women to dance, and also to survive in spaces of poverty, violence and resistance. In the midst of the abuse and abandonment of men and government, poor women hold their lives and the lives of their children right at the bending part of their legs. But they are not bending their knees to accept somebody else's impositions anymore. In spite of all the catechesis and attempted rigidity, it is between the femur, the tibia, the muscles and the patella that they carry their strength and know how to hold and bend life, the world and the word of God.

The knee is not only a place to hold weight but also a place to think. Rodin's famous sculpture *the thinker* shows that the left elbow of the thinker is placed at the right leg right at the knee. This is a very unusual position for thinking. It is both uncomfortable and painful. Perhaps Rodin wanted to tell us the obvious, that to think is a painful action. However, perhaps Rodin suggests that the exercise of thinking happens at the knees.

Nancy Cardoso Pereira is a third world theologian working with poor people in Brazil and Latin America today. Working with women in poverty she realised that the knees are a powerful theological-erotic-biblical-bodily-political hermeneutical exercise to empower women. With them, she discovered how the women's knees have been domesticated, obscured, and exploited, and that for one to have freedom, one has to be in charge of one's own knees. Pereira says:

> The interior part of our knees is also the bending of our morality, and of our shame. The construction of bodies and the metabolisms of knowledge production, the domestication of objective and subjective bending of men and women. Knees are educated and evangelised in distinctive ways, with different dislocations, vertices and openings. Knees learn to control and are controlled. (Pereira 2006)

The movements of our knees are intrinsically related to the ways we think, create and live our worlds. Our knees, along with our bodies, learn what to accept and to reject, and are aware of control and subjection. Our knees know what touches are allowed, what movements they are supposed to do. [...]

The coming-to-know of her own body, without shame or apologies, the gasping for the fact that she came to discover that some *erased* parts of her body were actually there, and that what was deliberately denied, terrorised and made null, could be felt as joy, pulsation, movement, pleasure and whatever she wanted it to be; all because she started to touch her knee.

[...]

Our liturgical gesturings are usually schizophrenic. Our bodies are often disconnected from much of what happens in the worship services. It is as if our bodies must be shut down while the mouths of the preachers speak endlessly, and the ears of the people listen eternally. The knees are made to be quiet, to carry the body in appropriateness. The equation of belief and rigidity is the correlation between silence and death, and our bodies are caught up in this entanglement. Our knees are made to believe and not to move, to stand together and never, ever open the legs. Pereira powerfully establishes the following connections: 'The bodies learned to obey first the weight of violence and of the punishment that were accompanied by the catecheses and the homily. Nobody was invited to be convinced. The knees were co-opted to bend and then belief was invented' (Pereira 2006).

At first, the Christian message of love came to our hearts through the bending of our knees. Once our knees were bent appropriately, we were evangelised, converted. And we believed in this love. The symbols were so beautiful. Kneeling to God, what better expression of surrender? But then, when we tried to stand up and walk and dance, we were told that we could not do that anymore. For a long time, we forgot that we had knees and that there was dance. We were left only believing in our liturgies. Pereira continues to relate liturgy and the domestication of our knees:

> To be on our knees for the Angelus means a lot: first, this prayer represents the acceptance of the major beliefs regarding Mary: Divine Incarnation, maintenance of Virginity, Annunciation; second, the ringing of the bells mark the prayers of the Angelus, regulate the hours of the day and emphasise the dominion of the church over time. To the first ring, we begin to work, then the second ring and it is time to eat and finally the last ring and we must go back home. Thus, kneeling at the ringing of the bell at the Angelus is to accept the Church as owner of time and the sacred history as the fountain of order. (Pereira 2006)

None of our gestures in our liturgies are done without a purpose, a sense, a history, an intention and, unfortunately, they are not done only out of piety. The religious structures of power take over our hearts, minds and bodies and place us under a power that suppresses and controls our bodies according to the rules made by man. God might not have much to do with it. And everything is done there, at the liturgical space, a space that is never neutral, never untouched by politics, power or control. Pereira says:

> Seated: legs crossed. The repeated aspects of learning by generations of women: the gap within the legs avoided. The gap between the legs and its cartography... All the effort placed on the knees with the learning of yes! And the no! The knees as collective knowledge, deposited in the joint and its capacity to bend. To transit between allowed positions and through the vortices of abused movements, absorbing what centuries of culture and biology had developed for the female knees: obedience, seclusion, grace. (Pereira 2006)

To undo this abusive control over the cartography of the female knees and legs is to undo the metaphysics of patriarchalism, heterosexualism, and centuries of learning the proper that men have imposed and learned to gladly approve. Women must discover their knees again and then be able to dance and move their knees in our worship services without fear, anxiety, grace or obedience. Pereira says:

> Connected: femur, tibia, patella, cartilage and ligaments. These are my knees. I got here alone. I am not going to tremble from fear, shame, coldness or indecision. This is the best lost night of all nights. Besides, from now on, I am the owner of my knees and nobody else. (Pereira 2006)

Who controls our knees? This is a key question. What has the church done to our knees? Were our knees shadowed by the proper? At church, our knees had to bend in a sign of obedience and had to follow the places that we were told. The knees could never jump up and down, could never be shown, could never misbehave. Knees became the location in our bodies where we are put to shame. To bend our knees is never a sign of resistance but a sign of giving up, of surrender. With our knees bent we cannot go anywhere, cannot escape, cannot run, cannot affront. The bending of our knees is the controlling of our movements and finally, the usurpation of our own lives, in the name of the proper, for the sake of sameness and safety.

What would happen to our liturgies if women started to open their legs and loosen the rigidity of their knees in this sacred space? Would we *allow* them to dance that way? To let the knee dance is to open up the possibility to entertain the unknown, which could be a parasite and disturb our safe, proper and respectful ways of worshiping God. Thus, all this boils down to this one question: Who holds the control of our knees?

Conclusion

The [original] title of this article makes a clear reference to an expression found in a song sung by African slaves in United States, 'gimme de kneebone bent'. Jacqui Malone writes about its origins:

> Africans brought to North America were no doubt affirming their ancestral values when they sang a slave song that urged dancers to 'gimme de kneebone bent.' To many western and central Africans, flexed joints represented life and energy, while straightened hips, elbows, and knees epitomized rigidity and death. The bent kneebone symbolized the ability to 'get down.' (Malone 1996)

The ability to get down does not mean surrender or subservience but rather an assurance that the body had strength to move, to twist, to shake, to hold an energy that was like a belief. If the body was alive, they were alive. The knee bent was a certainty that final death was not close by, and that even the rigidity of the social system demonstrated through exploitation, violence and death could not hold back the aliveness of those bending knees. Moreover, these bending joints, these fighting knees that, along with the movements of hands, arms, hips, torso, head and foot, would bring about changes in culture and would write and change history. We must develop a new hermeneutic of our knees for our theological liturgical practices and thinking. They are signs of resistance, of political struggles, of sexual battles. Those who are in charge of their knees are perhaps more aware of their sexual lives. Against the fixation of the phallic, erected, fetishised discourse of a Christian message that makes our bodies stiff, we should shout with our bending knees and challenge the metaphysical arrogance of heterosexuality.

Liturgical performances that invoke 'Gimme de kneebone bent' and evoke a hermeneutic of the knees can, even if awkwardly, loosen up the structures of stiffened truth and develop the power of women, making uncomfortable that which seems to be safe. The metaphysics of the proper and the denial of difference have an immense influence in controlling our knees, and respectively our ability and desire to dance. Once we are able to find and practice ways to unlock the codes that keep alterity away and the theological and the liturgical proper that keep women's knees stiffened, controlled, exploited, secluded and obedient, we will be able to dance with God and create liturgical performances that will not do away with the order of our liturgies, but will expand the possibilities of its liturgical gestures and movements.

[...]

A feminist approach to the knees is just the first stop on this road to a hermeneutics of the body, an approach that should be always corrected by other knee movements and thoughts. [...] With our bones bent and our hips telling the truth, we will undo centuries of colonisation, discover our naked knees and finally learn how to dance to God as we never did before.

References

Althaus-Reid, Marcella. 2000. *Indecent Theology: Theological Perversions in Sex, Gender and Politics*. London: Routledge.

Alves, Rubem. 1983. *Creio na Ressurreição do Corpo*. Rio de Janeiro: Cedi.

Foster, Hal, Rosalind Krauss, Yve-Alain Bois, and Benjamin H.D. Buchloh. 2005. *Art Since 1900 Modernism, Antimodernism and Postmodemism*. New York: Thames and Hudson.

Gruzinski, Serge. 2003. *A Colonisação do Imaginario*, trans.B. Perrone-Moisés. Vol. Séculos XVl–XVlll, *Sociedades Indígenas e Ocidentalização México Espanhol*. Sao Paulo: Companhia das Letras.

Heidegger, Martin. 1993. "The End of Philosophy and the Task of Thinking," in *Heidegger, Basic Writings*, ed. D.F. Krell. New York: Harper and Row.

Lathrop, Gordon W. 1993. *Holy Things. A Liturgical Theology*. Minneapolis: Fortress Press.

Malone, Jacqui. 1996. *Steppin' on the Blues:* The *Visible Rhythms of African American Dance*. Chicago: University of Illinois Press.

Pereira, Nancy Cardoso. 2006. Des-Evangelização dos Joelhos. Epistemologia, Osteoporose & Aflição! (De-Evangelization of the Knees. Epistemology, Osteoporoses and Affliction). São Leopoldo, RS, Brazil: II Congresso de Gênero e Religião (Congress of Gender and Religion II).

Taussig, Michael. 1999. *Defacement, Public Secrecy and the Labor of the Negative*. Stanford: Stanford University Press.

Taylor, Barbara Brown. 1993. *The Preaching Life*. Cambridge, MA: Cowley Publications.

Taylor, Mark C. 1998. *Altarity*. London: The University of Chicago Press.

——. 2000. "Retracings" in *The Craft of Religious Studies*, ed. J.R. Stone. London: Palgrave.

Wrathall, Mark A. 2003. "Introduction: Metaphysics and Onto-theology," in *Religion After Metaphysics*, ed. M.A. Wrathall. Cambridge, MA: Cambridge University Press.

8

Desiring Things (2013)*

Heather Walton

Introduction

Interest in theology, culture, and politics drew Heather Walton to what she sees as one of the most interdisciplinary areas of theological studies – practical theology. The area also fit her demonstrable love of the church and her desire to guide those aspiring to ministry. Professor of Theology and Creative Practice at the University of Glasgow, she brings to practical theology a rich engagement with literature and considerable literary gifts and expertise.

Walton's reclamation of poetics and *poesis* as essential to theological knowledge is one of her singular contributions. *Poesis* is no longer an inferior stepsister straggling behind two older siblings in Aristotle's triumvirate on knowledge, *phronesis* and *theoria*. It holds comparable importance. In literary theory, *poetics* refers to the means by which authors create texts, but *poesis* has a more expansive connotation that includes material productivity, knowing through making, and craft knowledge. Walton advances *poesis* as a persuasive mode of knowing through both theoretical argument and creative writing, engaging previously neglected sources, such as the work of Henri LeFebvre and Michel de Certeau. She also incorporates nonconventional material into prose arguments; crafts beautifully telling portraits of theology intertwined with earthy existence, often out her own life experiences; and experiments with alternative literary genres, such as journaling, autoethonography, and life writing. Her writing merges these intellectual and literary gifts, providing at once narrative illustration, guidance for writing, and argument for the place of *poesis* in theology.

This essay was first presented at the 2011 International Academy of Practical Theology in Amsterdam and was published in its conference volume in 2013. Reprinted in *Writing Methods in Theological Reflection* (2014), it sits alongside other essays on *poesis* that appeared around this time. Although the essay does not focus on bodies per se, it appears in this section of the *Reader* because it reappraises all the material accoutrements that sustain bodily life. Is love of things a crime, she asks? And if not, what kind

Original publication details: Heather Walton, "Desiring Things: Practical Theology and the New Materialisms," pp. 131–9 from *City of Desires – A Place for God? Practical Theological Perspectives*, eds. R. Ruard Ganzevoort, Rein Brouwer, and Bonnie Miller-McLemore (Berlin: Lit Verlag, 2013).

of value lies in material things? In exploring the new materialisms and how "stuff" enhances politics and practices, she pushes back against a long history of degradation of the supposedly inert world not only in religious worldviews such as Christianity, but also in social movements such as Marxism. This essay also shows how literature and a literary approach complement and correct a practical theology grounded solely in the social sciences, ethics, and philosophy.

Here and in her work overall, Walton invites her readers to pursue "forms of expression that are more able to bear the weight that theology does not seem able to carry at the current time… 'things' about which direct speech seems currently not possible" (*Writing Methods*, 2014, p. 161). She offers a way of seeing everyday things made invisible under the reign of dominant epistemologies, things one cannot measure through number or comparison. In doing so, she engages in a kind of empirical theology but in quite a different way than conventionally understood via scientific methods of quantitative and qualitative research.

Suggested Further Reading

- Heather Walton, *Writing Methods in Theological Reflection* (London: SCM Press, 2014).
- James Hopewell, *Congregation: Stories and Structures* (London: SM Press, 1988).

***

My daughter was laying pink cheeked and sweetly asleep in bed. Her toys were abandoned on the living room floor. Blossom, the favorite doll, was sprawled face down on the carpet. Her stiff limbs outstretched and her long golden nylon hair tangled. I bent to pick her up and it was as if a current ran through me. A small but perceptible force that made me shiver slightly. This doll could not be impersonally handled but commanded respect. She was animated and something of my child's life was bounded up in her. I combed her hair with my fingers, smoothed her dress and sat her in my daughter's little chair where she could be found and loved again next morning.

It is so poignant each time I return to my parents' house. They are vividly alive but frail now. Each visit could be the last time we are all together and we anticipate in our gestures a loss that is palpable but restrained. The very objects in the house manifest this fragile state. Once they were bold and substantial things, sufficient in themselves, confidently approached, used and put away. Now they have a spectral quality – manifesting for us a past we can only touch through them. I always linger in the kitchen. I lift the blue lid from the sugar bin and breathe in the more-than-fifty-years of sweetness it has held inside. I take out the spoons shaped like cockle shells which I so loved as a little girl. The spoons are no longer used. The silver has worn off in places but they are still pretty. Like a thief of time I slip one into my bag when I leave.

My home now is a modern flat with white walls overlooking a terrace garden. There is a bright, chaotic 70s vibe blended with (or toned down by!) a contemporary minimalism. It combines awareness of current trends with an idiosyncratic style. What a guest entering would not know is that only the big grey sofa was purchased new for full price. Everything else was found on the street, bought second hand, sold cheap because it was blemished. Things have been repainted, recovered, and arranged to disguise flaws and scratches. I am good at this work and proud of my skills. The achieved whole is immensely satisfying to me because I know its secrets perhaps? It is my home. As I walk around in the evening, lighting candles, turning down the lights, opening a bottle of wine, I am content. Here we all are sheltered. Here in this place. So blessed.

On the edge of contemporary theory a new materialism is emerging. It restores to us the love of objects and the vitality of things.

When I was a child, to ascribe value to possessions was not a crime. My parents moved into a small new house when I was three years old. For two years we had no carpet in the lounge and my parents saved for a glorious purple and raspberry creation (it was the 60s!) and we invited all the neighbors round to celebrate the day it was laid down. My father was a sign writer and the house was full of witty and beautiful adverts made for display around the town. My mother wore full-skirted dresses with rose prints and scarlet lipstick. She kept her letters in a milk soft leather handbag that smelled of cologne. When Mary Quant came along, she transformed into a slim blonde goddess in black and white and wore false eyelashes that lived, like skinny centipedes, on her dressing table next to the daisy earrings. I had fashion and fun, color and beauty and in my hopeful, young, aspiring working class neighborhood none of this was a crime.

It was in the early 70s that the DJ on the Saturday morning show began to warn about pollution and the environmental crisis. I was of an age then when famine and poverty loomed large upon my personal horizon. The petty material pleasures of my parents' generation appeared as a poor substitute for passionate ideals. The beautiful head of Che Guevara hung on my bedroom wall. When I went to University, I encountered Marxism and liberation theology. I left for Africa immediately after graduation. My faith and life were given over to the struggle and the love of things had become a kind of crime.

But a fascination endured. I turned to Marx who so well describes the power of the commodity and wrote, "A commodity appears at first sight an extremely obvious, trivial thing. But its analysis brings out that it is a very strange thing, abounding in metaphysical subtleties and theological niceties" (Marx 1990, 163). Although the values the commodity represents are, for him, without substance, they have a religious power which is mysterious and compelling, phantasmagorically transforming the everyday. As T. Richards writes, those who seriously seek to comprehend commodity culture enter a "fantastic realm in which things act, speak, rise, fall, evolve" (Richards 1991, 11). Walter Benjamin became my preferred companion in this strange land, I think, because he loved rather than condemned the objects that, in his messianic materialist perspective, both bespoke and denied transcendence (see Wolin 1994). He loved the arcades and the market stalls where he rummaged for the infinite amongst the glittering trinkets and little bits of lace.

And I found other friends who helped me to move beyond the sternness of Marxist critique towards an intuition of the ways in which an engagement with things could enhance politics and practice. Gaston Bachelard, in *The Poetics of Space* (1994), restored to me the world of the house in which the soul is formed. He explores how this world of material intimacy shelters and nourishes the imagination which is the intimate of action. Entering his attic room, overlooking the fields and deeply scented with the perfume of raisins drying, blessed my own, rather less romantic, memories of childhood in a suburban home. "The House we were born in is physically inscribed in us. …We would find our way in the dark to the distant attic. …The word habit is too worn a word to describe this passionate liaison of our bodies, which do not forget, with an unforgettable house" (Bachelard 1994, 14–15).

Etty Hillesum (1985) helped me to understand that combating the ugliness of fascism was not only an effort of will but an aesthetic achievement. Resistance could be sustained through appreciation of sweet smelling soap and a lilac blouse, the scent of jasmine beneath the eves and a cyclamen carefully placed beside a reading lamp. In a less poetic but more analytical frame, a feminist hermeneutics of suspicion caused me to question why the commodity and the consumer are alike gendered female and regarded as selfish, dangerous, shallow, saturated with seduction, and inimical alike to virtue and to reason.

I have made a journey from a naive love of things, through critique to a revised appreciation of the power of things in human life. This could be seen as a journey frequently repeated as we mature. I am sure it is. However, it is also a political and spiritual journey, which is of particular significance at this point in time as we look to the challenges we face politically and environmentally. The dynamics of critique, whether from a Marxist, environmental, or indeed eco-spiritual/theological perspective, inadequately respond to the fact that things matter to people. We have not explored this issue sufficiently but have sought to maintain our innocence of the truly catastrophic consequences of inappropriate manifestations of desire through forms of analysis that crudely employ terms such as *commodity* and *consumption* without taking seriously the enchanted world in which people and objects interact. As Daniel Miller writes, "stuff is ubiquitous and problematic. But whatever our environmental fears or concerns we will not be helped by an attitude to stuff that simply opposes ourselves to it as though the more we think of things as alien the more we think ourselves pure" (Miller 2010, 5).

I have come to believe that the development of new forms of materialism that attempt a loving critique of the order of things – Jurgen Habermas describes Benjamin's materialist hermeneutics as redemptive criticism (see Habermas, Brewster and Buchner 1979) – offers the best chance we have to develop an ethical environmental practice. In order to assess the challenges this shift in perspective represents for practical theologians, I now turn to the work of two new materialists, Daniel Miller, an anthropologist at University College London (quoted above) and Jane Bennett, a philosopher at John Hopkins University. I chose these theorists because their work is engaging, polemical, and readily delivers strong ideas that are accessible even in a short chapter such as this. I also chose them because both eschew the "nature romanticism" which is, unfortunately in my opinion, the most common resource employed by theologians who think about material world.

Daniel Miller and World Making Material

As an anthropologist, Miller has spent many years exploring cultural systems from the West Indies to India as well as maintaining a recurring commitment to research in his own "backyard" of London, one of the planet's greatest and most complex cities. Looking back over these endeavors, he makes the simple point that "non-industrial societies are just as much material cultures as we are" (Miller 2010, 4), and, indeed, when resources are scarce the highest degree of social attention and energy must be devoted to the material mechanisms that sustain social interaction. In making this claim, Miller effectively challenges the romance of the primitive and the nostalgia for purer state of being in which objects were assumed to hold less significance than they do today. Clearly, forms of materialism will vary, but from an anthropological perspective, Miller argues, it is impossible to imagine human culture without the nurturing guardianship performed by things. He takes up and amplifies Pierre Bourdieu's narrative of how amongst the Kabyle a child is introduced to the order of the house and required to learn that things must be placed high or low, on the left or right. This constructed order represents a domestic induction into a wider cosmology, which maintains the pattern of existence despite the apparent diversity of experience: "This seems to me to correspond very well to what I call the humility of things. Objects don't shout at you like teachers ... but they help you gently to learn how to act appropriately ... objects make people. Before we can make things we are ourselves grown up and matured in the light of things that come to us from previous generations. ...Things, not mind you individual things, but the whole system of things with their internal order, make us the people we are." (Miller 2010, 53).

So people form webs of meaning through complex interactions with networks of people *and* things, and yet so often in our binary culture we assume that healthy relationships with people are threatened by an attention to things. This assumption is challenged by a simple but effective piece of research conducted by Miller in an ordinary London street and published as *The Comfort of Things* (2008). Miller and a colleague questioned inhabitants about the objects they lived with. They found that those who enjoyed a rich relationships with objects (commonplace things – a woman kept McDonalds "Happy Meal" toys whilst a couple made elaborate Christmas decorations) had a similarly rich relationship with people. Those whose lives were starkly bereft of beloved possessions were similarly starved of meaningful personal relationships.

But his research took Miller beyond reversing the terms of that familiar moral equation stating that there is an inverse relationship between love of people and love of things. He discovered people *not only* engage with objects as part of a holistic system of meaningful relationships but *they also* construct within domestic space micro cosmological systems that are often far more meaningful and present to them than the larger social and religious systems in which they may participate at one remove.

> The point is that household material culture may express an order which in each case seems equivalent to what *one might term* a social cosmology, *if this* was the order of things, values and relationships of a society. A very little cosmology perhaps ... and one that in only a few cases ever develops into an abstract philosophy or system of belief...Nevertheless such a cosmology is holistic rather than fragmented and ... [although] the focus is on the interior space these aesthetics are not isolated from the wider world (Miller 2008, 294).

Indeed these micro-material cosmologies sustain identity and help generate the resilience necessary to pattern life creatively and interact meaningfully with others.

Having challenged taken-for-granted assumptions about "human" and "thing" relationships by refusing a neat divide between them, Miller continues his deconstruction of our moral economy. He argues that the West accords unwarranted respect to a depth ontology: "The assumption is the *being* we truly are is located deep inside ourselves and is in direct opposition to the surface. A clothes shopper is shallow because a philosopher or saint is deep...But these are all metaphors. Deep inside ourselves is blood and bile not philosophical certainty" (Miller 2010, 16).

An analysis of how clothes function in a number of specific communities allows Miller to suggest that external (we might call them *surface)* moods, styles, choices relate to questions of real concern to people which are often negotiated at skin level with implications of greater consequence than we might have supposed. Miller is attempting to articulate concerns at play in the affective domain of contemporary life and suggest that the separation we have enforced between this world, which we used to call private though it isn't private or even personal, and the public arena is unsustainable. Barriers we may have wanted to keep in place because they protect our cherished assumptions about what is a legitimate concern have already long been breached. "In the hybrid world that is everyday life, it is often the intimate and sensual realms that are most effective in determining the acceptability and plausibility of the regimes of thought we call rationality and even ontology. Through the realm of clothes we see how, for most people, systems of thinking about the world have to feel right" (Miller 2010, 41).

We practical theologians have an attachment to "deep" metaphors for human identity and a concern to articulate our insights rationally in the public square. We may thus find it difficult to re-value the superficial and the emotive. However, I wish to emphasize that Miller is asking us to question fundamentally our hierarchy of values on the basis of the desire people have for things. What is at stake here is a spiritual, ethical, and political appreciation of life in the world that fully embraces the palpably material affective dimensions of life. Miller's Jewish faith informs his desire for a spiritual wholeness achieved by living fully immersed in the ambiguous complexities of the everyday. To wish to escape them is for him a form of hubris with catastrophic consequences. Why, he challenges, have we been active participants in the abjection of things? Perhaps because of our fear of pollution, ambiguity and corruption?

> [D]enigrating material things and pushing them down, is one of the main ways we raise ourselves up onto apparent pedestals divorced from our own materiality and the material reality of the world we live within. I am not sure about a spirituality that is obtained by ideals of purity and separation or that enlightenment is reached by a denial of the material, … everyday life and the glorious mess of contradiction and ambivalence that is found there (Miller 2010, 156).

Jane Bennett and Vital Matters

Miller's political vision is of a world in which we acknowledge the significance of materialism in order that we find better ways of living in relationship with each other and within our environments. I now turn to the work of Jane Bennett, who shares Miller's conviction that a denial of the importance of materiality has been a key factor in bringing us to the current environmental crisis: "In the context of, in particular, an American political economy, there seems to be a resonance between the idea of matter as dull stuff/passive resource and a set of gigantically wasteful production and consumption practices that foul our own nest. These practices endanger and immiserate workers, children, animals and plants here and abroad. To the extent that the figure of inert matter sustains this consumptive style another figure might disrupt it" (Bennett 2009, 98).

The first step towards disrupting this exploitative system is to acknowledge the enchanting power of the object: not nature, but the thing. From Kant to the romantic poets, from ecofeminism to environmental theology, we have crafted the resources to engage respectfully with the wonder of the natural world. Bennett's concern is that these resources have not developed in relation to the "other stuff" around us. Instead we have fallen into the habit of "parsing the world into dull matter and vibrant life" (Bennett, 2010, vii) and this figure of "dead or thoroughly instrumentalized matter feeds …our earth destroying fantasies of conquest and consumption" (Bennett 2010, viii).

A lot of Bennett's work is figured in respectful disagreement with Marxist perspectives on commodity culture. As I have argued, no one can fault Marx on his prophetic grasp of the mysterious attraction of the commodity. Interestingly, Bennett suggests that Marx's early studies in Epicurean philosophy may have influenced his perspective on the vital power that the object represents. However, Marx and his later followers were so convinced in their diagnosis of the perceptual disorder called "commodity fetishism" through which "Humans become blind to the pain and suffering embedded in the commodity […] (Bennett 2001, 113) that they could only offer the most stringent remedies for this sickness. For a cure they have offered relentless criticism: "the primary fear motivating their story is that we live in a system where the forces of domination have become resistant to all but the most relentless strains of critical reflection" (Bennett 2001, 129). But what if, asks Bennett, this "cure" serves merely to aggravate the symptoms we experience and yet brings no relief? What follows if we concede that the wonder and enchantment we experience in relation to things is because they are wonderful and enchanting, because they generate physical, emotional, and aesthetic pleasure and actively impress themselves upon us in every aspect of life? Saying yes to this pleasurable encounter is not seduction and need not imply a reckless abandonment of rational critique: "[For] Horkheimer and Adorno, to say yes to pleasure is to say no to critical thinking. Although pleasure can entail stupidity, passivity and eventually moral indifference, I contend that it can also enliven, energise and, under the right circumstances, support ethical generosity…part of the energy needed to challenge injustice comes from the reservoir of enchantment − including that derived from commodities. For without enchantment you might lack the impetus to act against the very injustices that you critically discern" (Bennett 2001, 128).

In contrast to the anxious spirit of frugality that dominates both political and theological criticisms of the way we live, Bennett advocates the cultivation of a sense of delight in material generativity, plentitude, and an affective openness to vital materiality. She ventures that these approaches may be more sustaining of impulses towards justice, sharing, and mutuality than life-denying thriftiness. This inclusive, participatory, and celebratory attitude towards life in all its fullness is only possible once we abandon our default position that human beings, and possibly other intelligent creatures like dolphins, are the only vital agents ("actants") in the moral universe and contemplate a new order of things.

> I am trying to take 'things' more seriously than political theorists had been taking them. By 'things', I mean the materialities usually figured as inanimate objects, passive utilities, occasional interruptions, or background context − figured, that is, in all ways that give the creative power to humans…Our habit of parsing the world into passive matter (it) and vibrant life (us) is what Jacques Ranciere (in another context) called a 'partition of the sensible'. In other words it limits what we are able to sense…What would the world look like and feel like were the life/ matter binary to fall into disuse, were it to be translated into differences in degree rather than kind?…What I try to do when I write is to call myself and others to a

different direction, to point to those uneven spaces where none humans are actants, where agency is always an assemblage, where matter is not inert, where man
is not lord but everything is made of the same quirky stuff...I can't predict what
politics would emerge from this. My hunch is that the grass would be greener in
a world of vital materialities. (Bennett 2009, 92)

Vital matter always tends towards a confederacy of agency, a hybridity of subjectivity, a
complexity of causality. It promises a new form of non-innocent, participatory politics.
The tendency to transform human into machine is countered by an opposing force which
anthropomorphizes the agency of matter. For Bennett, this is a religious, or at any rate a
spiritual, option. Whilst highly critical of both catholic and evangelical tendencies to place
the human at the center of creation, she is not against a theological anthropomorphism of
her own. Borrowing ideas from her friend Hent de Vries and his "political theology", she
compares vital materiality to the absolute, the stubborn, intangible, imponderable, and
recalcitrant "stuff" of existence and writes her own creed in these terms:

> I believe in one matter-energy, the maker of things seen and unseen. I believe that
> this pluriverse is traversed by heterogeneities that are constantly *doing things.*
> I believe that it is wrong to deny vitality to nonhuman bodies, forces and forms,
> and that a careful course of anthropomorphisation can help reveal that vitality,
> even though it resists full translation and exceeds my comprehensive grasp.
> I believe that encounters with lively matter can chasten my fantasies of human
> mastery, highlight the common materiality of all that is (Bennett 2010, 122).

Questions for Practical Theology

It is obvious that I find the thinking of Miller and Bennett promising and interesting,
but the question remains as to whether it is compatible with theological thinking, a
question that as a Christian theologian I must admit is troubling. Whilst we can identify
traces of a confident, material cosmology in some elements of the biblical tradition,
there are many parts of the New Testament that would conflict with this worldview:
overall, the Christian religion is largely resistant to "stuff". However, there are hints
within Franciscan and other spiritual traditions that appear to offer some resources for
creative new theological thinking in this area. For example, Franciscan Sister and theologian Ilia Delio celebrates a Christocentric reading of material world – including inani-
mate objects – developed by Franciscan theologians: "For Scotus and for Bonaventure,
the universe is the external embodiment of the inner Word of God...Bonaventure writes
that in his transfiguration Christ shares existence with all things: with the stones he
shares existence, with the plants he shares life, with animals he shares sensation... 'In his
human nature,' he stated, 'Christ embraces something of every creature in himself'"
(Delio 2003, 19).

As is well known, the poet-priest Gerard Manley Hopkins was deeply influenced by
Scotus, particularly his notion that each being and object articulates through being
itself the divine-self-in-all-things. His kingfisher poem is one of the most famous
expressions of this conviction and in this Hopkins declares that each "mortal thing"
serves God by being itself: "Crying Whát I dó is me: for that I came" (1976a, 51).

However, the turmoil of Hopkins later life and his unwilling exile in great industrial cities, produced an altered outlook in the poet. In his later work the material order, blighted by trade and mechanization, is no longer viewed as revelatory but as soiled, deceitful, and doomed. The fabric of life is "mortal trash" and "world's wildfire leaves but ash" (1976b, 65). Radical incarnational theology is abandoned in favor of a faith in that which lies beyond what exists here on earth. This move is one made by Christian theology over and over again when it discovers no way of reconciling the ambivalence of material existence with its faith in redemptive providence.

Practical theologians might be thought amongst those least likely to abandon the quest to find theological meaning in the common substance of existence and, as Bonnie Miller-McLemore (2012) suggests, there are compelling reasons for understanding practical theology as the theology of everyday life. However, there are aspects of the way the discipline has developed that currently place us in the front ranks of those who are theologically affronted by the ambivalent mess of stuff.

As Stephen Pattison argues, practical theology is [obsessively] driven by its desire to be useful and make a difference (Pattison 2007, 268). As a busy and frugal discipline with serious work to do, it has very rarely relaxed into reflection upon the affective aesthetic realm or much succumbed to the pleasures of enchantment. As theologians, our concern with the public sphere and the conventions of communicative rationality have been "complemented" by a corresponding distaste for the domestic and incoherent world of things. The powerful legacy of Don Browning has been significant here. Whilst by no means a reductive thinker, Browning tuned our impulses towards phronesis, and accompanying this has been an unthinking subordination of poesis – with its emphasis upon the material construction of meaning and things (see Walton 2012).

The new materialisms challenge us to reassess this hierarchy of values and rediscover the importance of affectivity, perception, and imagination in [the] theological realm. It will be an uncomfortable and difficult task for practical theologians to enter the ambiguous and problematic world of stuff for, as we have heard above from Miller, there is a loss of purity, a fall involved here. And yet, perhaps it will be a *felix culpa*? Personally, I think a glory awaits us in rediscovering the reality of incarnation in an iridescent world of materiality. One of my favorite writers, Elizabeth Smart, presents a vision of enchantment in the material order which I like very much and which I think speaks of a joy that might empower us in the work to which we have set our hands and our hearts:

> Something happened today.
>
> They presented themselves pathetically, pleading that they last so much longer than life. They greeted me as if we were all dust together at last.
>
> Kinship was established.
>
> This happened coming up Sloane Street, while the traffic lights flashed and black buildings strained upwards waiting to be noticed.
>
> It was a short Sunday love-affair with very little pain.
>
> Afterwards, the dresses in the shop windows leaned towards me like lusty millionaires with generous impulses.

What reward for giving love to a stone.

It was impossible to be poor that whole February day.

What do people do at 5.30 in the afternoon, when there's an early amethyst sky and happiness explodes irresponsible and irrepressible over the weary city?

What if perfections strikes loud and shocking on the Tottenham Court Road? What if even a squashed matchbox can sidle into your sympathies.

How to meet the minute except by walking down Tottenham Court Road stuffed with love?...

Now is not the time to sit alone in your room, eating plums, reading Kierkegaard, hammering at your sores (Smart 1991, 47).

References

Bachelard, G. 1994. *The Poetics of Space*. Trans. Maria Jolas. Boston: Beacon
Bennett, J. 2001. *The Enchantment of Modern life*. Princeton: Princeton University Press.
Bennett, J. 2009. "Agency, Nature and Emergent Properties. An Interview with Jane Bennett." *Contemporary Political Theory* (8), 90–105.
Bennett, J. 2010. *Vibrant Matter: A Political Ecology of Things*. Durham: Duke University Press.
Delio, I. 2003. "Revisiting the Franciscan Doctrine of Christ." *Theological Studies* 64(1), 3–23.
Habermas, J., Brewster, P., and Buchner, C. 1979. "Consciousness-Raising or Redemptive Criticism. The Contemporaneity of Walter Benjamin." *New German Critique* (17), 30–59.
Hillesum, E. 1985. *An Interrupted Life. The Diaries of Etty Hillesum 1941–43*. New York: Washington Square Press.
Hopkins, G.M. 1976a. "As kingfishers catch fire, dragonflies draw flame." In: Gardener, W.H. (ed.) *Gerard Manley Hopkins: Poems and Prose*. Exeter: Wheaton.
Hopkins, G.M. 1976b. "That Nature is a Heraclitean Fire and the Comfort of the Ressurection." In: Gardener, W.H. (ed) *Gerard Manley Hopkins: Poems and Prose*. Exeter: Wheaton.
Marx, K. 1990. *Capital: A Critique of Political Economy*, Vol. 1 [Translated by Fowkes, B.]. New York: Penguin.
Miller, D. 2008. *The Comfort of Things*. Cambridge: Polity.
Miller, D. 2010. *Stuff*. Cambridge: Polity.
Miller-McLemore, B. 2012. "Introduction. The Contributions of Practical Theology." In: Miller McLemore, B. (ed.) *The Wiley Blackwell Companion to Practical Theology*. Oxford: Wiley Blackwell.
Pattison, S. 2007. *The Challenge of Practical Theology. Selected Essays*. London: Jessica Kingsley.
Richards, T. 1991. *The Commodity Culture of Victorian England. Advertising and Spectacle, 1851–1914*. London: Verso.
Smart, E. 1991. *The Assumption of the Rogues and Rascals*. London: Paladin.
Walton, H. 2012. "Poetics." In: Miller-McLemore, B. (ed.) *The Wiley Blackwell Companion to Practical Theology*. Oxford: Wiley Blackwell.
Wolin, R. 1994. *Walter Benjamin. An Aesthetics of Redemption*. Berkeley: University of California Press.

9

The Bodies We Teach By (2014)*,1

Mai-Anh Le Tran

Introduction

Past president of the Religious Education Association, an ordained United Methodist elder, and an experienced educator, Mai-Anh Le Tran recently returned to her alma matter, Garrett-Evangelical Theological Seminary, as Associate Professor of Religious Education and Practical Theology. Expertise in congregational studies and Christian education and a strong international and postcolonial orientation shape her approach to practical theology. Claiming her vocational identity in her faculty blurb as "an academic who understands that her embodied self is a palimpsest of multiple and contradictory worlds," she does not shy away from difficult topics, including the church's silence in a world marked by violence, the central concern of her recent book, *Reset the Heart: Unlearning Violence, Relearning Hope.*

Although scholars in theological schools seldom scrutinize our own institutional behaviors, Tran turns the lens on ourselves in this essay. The practice under inspection lies at the core of the scholarly identity and epistemology – our patterns and practices of teaching. Tran does not retreat to abstractions about the teaching life. Instead, one of the powerful aspects of the essay is where she begins – with a "seemingly innocuous" bodily micro-aggression that set off reverberating visceral reactions and remembrances. Her response of "acid reflux" will move readers, whether they identify with her experience on the receiving end of racist dismissal or recognize themselves as the offending party. The essay as a whole offers instance after instance of bodily aggression, grounding her argument in thick institutional description. It appears alongside other chapters by noteworthy practical theologians such as Elizabeth Conde-Frazier, Boyung Lee, and Nancy Ramsay in a volume, *Teaching for a Culturally Diverse and Racially Just World* (2014), that benefits from the work of the Wabash Center for Teaching and Learning in Theology and Religion.

Epistemological themes, particularly in relationship to bodies, run like an undercurrent throughout the essay. How we teach says a great deal about our theory of knowledge, as religious education scholar Thomas Groome made evident in the 1980s. Schools,

Original publication details: Mai-Anh Le Tran, "When Subjects Matter: The Bodies We Teach By," pp. 31–51 from *Teaching for a Culturally Diverse and Racially Just World*, ed. Eleazar Fernandez (Eugene, OR: Cascade Books, 2014). For full citations of books and essays referenced below, see the Bibliography in Fernandez, ed., *Teaching for a Culturally Diverse and Racially Just World.*

congregations, and social institutions can at one and the same time spout policies against discrimination *and* subtly dispute, distrust, and undermine the authority of the Other, persons whose raced, classed, nationalized, and sexualized bodies do not fit dominant expectations. "Unsuspecting and repeated ejections thrust a body into existential limbo," she writes, "It is with this *impermanent body* that I teach…. each day in full anticipation of that eject button." How does one sustain claims about knowledge in such a setting? "No one taught me that in graduate school." In Tran's strategies for claiming and conveying theological knowledge, she puts everyday wisdom and action alongside broader theoretical claims about standpoint theory, positionality, intersectionality, and border pedagogy.

Suggested Further Reading

- Mai-Anh Le Tran, *Reset the Heart: Unlearning Violence, Relearning Hope* (Nashville: Abingdon, 2017).
- Marcella Althaus-Reid, *Indecent Theology: Theological Perversions in Sex, Gender, and Politics* (New York: Routledge, 2000).

***

A Political Story of Fittonias

One St Louis afternoon, my sister and I wandered into a local Lowe's to pick up some gardening tools. On the spur of the moment, Hoang-Anh went to look for some silver-veined fittonias, a garden plant of the family *Acanthaceae*, which she had once acquired back in her days in Berkeley, California. Not seeing them anywhere, my sister approached a store employee who was working in the plant section – an older woman of quiet demeanor – and asked if the store carried fittonias.

"You're looking for what … ?"

"Fittonias – particularly the silver-veined variety. Do you know if this store has them?"

"You mean pe-tu-nias?" She enunciated with deliberateness.

My antennas perked up. We are not twelve, nor hard of hearing: Why the slow speech?

"Oh, no, not petunias. I mean 'fittonias.' You know, I think they're called 'mosaic plants', cute and small, they'd be just perfect for my desk! But I haven't been able to find them anywhere …" The sister rambled on.

"Oh? Oh … I don't know … I've not heard of fittonias before…" The woman looked increasingly perplexed. Then, with hesitation, "Are they from *your* country or *my* country?"

Hoang-Anh and I looked at each other, dumbstruck. A simple question about a garden plant suddenly *ejected* us two naturalized US citizens right out of *this* country, and neither of us knew how to respond.

Visceral memories shot through my stiffened body: the "ching chong" noises made by local teens as they passed by our house when we first moved into the neighborhood … my fifth grade teacher flapping her arms in front of the class to ask if I had left Vietnam by boat or by plane … the secret shame throughout my sullen early-teens of having to eat "free lunch" at school thanks to public aid for newly settled immigrants of the "Orderly

Departure Program"[2] ... an overzealous colleague who got very close to my face, asking if I could provide examples of how the cultural rules for body contact might be interpreted differently by "my people back home" ... my first return to Vietnam after twenty years, being teased by the locals for having the body shape and accent of "a little American" .... In that instant, an inquiry about fittonias' origin created a convergence of memories: from autobiographical memories of multi-ethnic lineage (Sino-Vietnamese) and multi-religious heritage (ancestor veneration, Buddhist, Christian); to episodic memories of relatives who had dispersed by boat or into "reeducation camps" at the end of a war just about everyone loved to hate; to social memories of threats, taunts, jeers, jokes, platitudes and praises directed at racialized and sexualized subjects like me who became "naturalized"[3] US citizens after a period of "alien resident" status; to historical memories of laws and legislations that regulate the rules of belonging and the flow of bodies for labor and love; to psychosomatic memories of sounds, sights, and smells that congeal incidents of identity contestation ....There you have it, "the personal is political" in plural modalities.

I think back to that occasion frequently and wonder why it is that a seemingly innocuous question of whether fittonias came from *my* country of origin would induce such acid reflux. After all, as a White male American Facebook "friend" of my sister retorted when she recounted the episode [...] the store employee was just asking an innocent question, and was not intending to insult. Why overreact with insinuations of racial ignorance or prejudice? The commentator's rebuke rendered us silent ... but it was a torrid silence of quiet rage that cuts right to our core. If this country is *hers,* then what does that make us as inhabitants of this living space? Unsuspecting and repeated ejections thrust a body into existential limbo, for any incident that questions the legitimacy of our being *somewhere* reifies our ineligibility for rightful permanence *anywhere.* [...] As a theological educator, it is with this *impermanent body* that I teach, and despite all the confidence, gumption, and even arrogance built over the years from painstaking personal and professional discipline, I still teach each day in full anticipation of that eject button – for it has never failed to set off in moments suspecting or unsuspecting within the academic setting. No one taught me that in graduate school.

The Teaching Body

> There is a body in the room. We ignore it.... Usually, of course, we ignore the body by ignoring it – we don't speak about it, we don't look directly at it, we change the subject quickly if there's a risk of noticing it. Sometimes, however, we have to ignore it by speaking about it – by saying the right things and then carrying on with our assigned topic.[4]

Most academics never learned how to teach. We are credentialed and authorized for having demonstrated some level of mastery over a cornucopia of "subject matters," but few doctoral programs focus on preparing scholars for the discipline and a life of *teaching.* Not only that, the *subjects* that arguably matter most in academic teaching/ learning – the identities and bodies of the teachers – remain irreducibly complicated and vexing for educational research, policies, and practices.

Every academic institution recruits faculty who are *some*body – not just *any*body, and certainly not *no*body. The complications lie in determining which "body" counts in which matters. In legalistic terms, theological schools as Affirmative Action/Equal Employment Opportunity (AA/EEO) employers must, with varying degrees of explicitness, tout a policy against discrimination on account of age, race/color, sex, creed, religion, disability, and national origin. In reality, theological schools suffer from the same staggering gaps found in institutions of higher learning at large: the gaps between institutional *concepts* of anti-discrimination, diversity, inclusion, and actual institutional *practices* as experienced by their respective members.[5] The picture looks bleak: educators report feeling that they are teaching in "socially oppressive structures."[6] [...] In the process of proving that s/he is *somebody,* the teacher finds herself embroiled in professional, cultural, political and individual "identity work."[7] [...]

The trouble is, there does not exist an authoritative "faculty manual" for this process of *becoming* for the theological educator. The ignored "body in the room" in the opening quotation refers to an educator's lament over the body dilemmas of those teaching in lands ravaged by conflict and violence in Israel and Palestine. [...] Few US (theological) educators could fathom their "democratic" teaching/learning environments to be so deadly (unless one is teaching on the "wrong" side of town in parts of the country such as East Saint Louis?). However, articulators of a "critical pedagogy of place" remind us that every space of teaching/learning is an "ever-changing confluence of culture, environment, politics, and power," and the identity work of the teacher inevitably responds to the tides of their social location.[8]

Following this conviction, the ponderings about the teacher's "identity" in this chapter are both decisive and meandering. First, there is determined adherence to the Freirean premise that "since education is by nature social, historical, and political, there is no way we can talk about some universal, unchanging role [or identity] for the teacher."[9] As scholars of critical pedagogy and critical race theory point out, identity is a constructive project of "self-information," catalyzed by the frictions of personal agentive will and socio-cultural-political forces. Second, [...] there is intentional mindfulness of how teaching bodies are particularly raced, classed, nationalized, and sexualized in the academy, with a preference for thick description over against essentializing identity claims.[10] And that is why things get murky: given the uneven waters of identity work, we are held accountable to what New Testament scholar and Asian American theological educator Tat-siong Benny Liew calls "reading with *yin yang* eyes" – eyes which see "both the living and the dead," which refuse to idealize, valorize, or patronize the "sights/sites" of identity negotiations, but rather hold in tension contradictions, dissonances and paradoxes.[11] In this way, *yin yang* eyes are "queer" – they see identity *not* as fixed positive essence, but as unstable, unsettling positionality "marked" (i.e., constituted) in fluid situations and porous contexts.[12] "Thick description" of racial-ethnic "markings" of teaching bodies requires meanderings through these sorts of murky waters.

To queer identity thusly is also to denormativize prevailing sources of identity authorization, including the one preferred by many marginalized subjects: personal experience. [...] Rather, "witness bearing" of identity work done within in-between crevices (or "interstitial space"[13]) is instructive and constructive when it enriches thick description, expands the repertoires of counter-narratives, resurrects alternative standpoints and viewpoints, broadens collective consciousness, and catalyzes momentum for systemic change.[14]

[...] Four foundational questions serve as guideposts for the ensuing reflections on the racial-ethnic teacher's identity work:[15] *(1) Who is the teacher? (2) What are the sources of a teacher's authority? (3) What practices must they hone? (4) What is the telos of their teaching life?* "Who is the teacher?" grounds explorations of the teacher's identity upon vocational-professional discernment. It pushes such questions as, what kind of teacher-scholars are we? What do we aspire to be? What parts of ourselves are involved in the teaching/learning tasks, given our identity "markings"? "What authorizes the teacher?" elicits generative themes related to the political negotiations and contestations of a teacher's credibility and authenticity, particularized in how racialized, genderized, or sexualized identities are *shuttled* back and forth between centers and margins of power.[16] "What teaching techniques and practices must they hone?" invites ponderings about tactics or strategies of minoritized[17] teachers who must improvise, adapt, and innovate to gain institutional footing and remain ingenuous to their vocational aspirations. "What is the *telos* of teaching?" presses for utopian ideals, for the freedom to imagine why we theological educators do what we do apart from socio-political determinism. After all, within the theological world, teaching is considered a "charism" and "calling." [...]

Who is the Teacher? Gladiator of Ambiguity

"... [A]ll teachers worth their salt regularly ask themselves whether they have made the right career choice."[18] The declaration comes from a renowned education theorist, prodigious author, award-winning teacher, Distinguished Professor of a major university – a self-identified White male with pedigrees from the U.K. to boot. Describing the teaching practice as analogous to white-water rafting, Stephen Brookfield asserts that the "skillful teacher" is one who "muddles through" the calm waters and turbulence of teaching with "practical reasoning – or the ability to scan situations, make judgments, and respond with the best use of technical know-how. As "gladiators of ambiguity," they are prepared to expect the unexpected, and their "intuitive confidence" only grows through disciplined, persistent practice of their craft.[19]

Ambiguous an art as teaching is, who do teachers think they are? This question pivots *vocational discernment* to the center of identity exploration. Why did we go into teaching? What kind of teachers are we? What kind of teachers are we striving to *become*? This is no retreat to universal philosophical abstraction about the teaching life, for that would undermine the premise put forth earlier about the political/politicized nature of a racial-ethnic teacher's identity work. We will get to that. Rather, this is a brash attempt to force to the forefront one foundational dimension of "professional competence": How often do theological educators think about their identity, competency, and integrity *qua* "teachers"? How seriously do theological educators take their role as "reflective practitioners," maintaining disciplined critical reflection upon the *why* and *what* and *how* of their daily teaching practices? [...] How do teachers reflect upon their ethico-political responsibilities and presence in the classroom and in the academic institution ?[20]

Needless to say, this question is more complicated than it appears. "Professional competence" is *never politically neutral*,[21] and the variances of course outcomes assessment are a prime example of the politicized nature of (e)valuation. The material reality of the teaching life is defined by *body* politics: a teacher sits/stands/walks alongside learners as a "marked" body – wrestling with tensions between performance and perception, competency and credibility. The proverbial injunction "Do as I say, not as I do" may have been reversed for an emphasis on embodied pedagogy: "Do as I *do*, not as I *say*."[22] And yet, such pedagogical wisdom would only be heeded if the teacher manages to persuade others that she/he is worth being seen and heard in the first place. All "teaching bodies" are raced, classed, nationalized, and sexualized in the academy, but racial-ethnic minoritized bodies recall from (counter-dominant) history lessons that as far back as the early beginnings of the American republic, the "perfect body" and the "perfect intellect" was only reserved for the "perfect gender" of the "perfect race."[23] Teachers who find themselves continuously minoritized on account of *ex-centric*[24] identity markings have borne frequent witness to the ambiguity of their bodies being the "non-written text" in academic teaching.[25] Like it or not, their impermanent, ambiguous body becomes an "implicit curriculum" that either underscores or undermines the subject matters being taught. [...] As such, judgments about "good" or "bad" teaching become as much an evaluation of the teacher's *identity performance*[26] (and the institution's forbearance of it) as it is an assessment of their teaching competencies. There lies a quandary for minoritized teaching bodies: discerning which performance is the *real* subject of scrutiny – their competence as teachers/scholars, their (in)ability to "look the part" of a competent teacher/scholar, or a combination thereof. Working doubly hard to "pass" as knowledgeable and credible has become an all too common refrain.[27] "Passing" turns eerie when ex-centric teaching bodies realize that it takes nothing short of "death masks" to project to nostalgic audiences the recognizability of the good days of yore. Look, they plead: the old standard-bearers are still here ... look how well we can be mediums for their immortality.

"Who are you as a teacher?" may be a question of vocational discernment, but "Who do you *think* you are, anyway?" is a spin-off which, when uttered with a certain intonation, signals an interrogation of the teacher's "credit report" – the breakdown of their credibility and the sources of its authentication.[28] [...] Playing it "straight" or outwitting the script becomes the creative tension for a teacher seeking legitimation, realizing that the performing body is a *de facto* locus of struggle.

What Authorizes the Teacher? Teaching Body as Site/Sight of Struggle

It has been said that two maladies vex the life of academics: hero complex and impostorship anxiety.[29] [...] Research has shown that while the impostor syndrome may be ubiquitous, the severity of its effects has alarming correlations with the political markings of teaching bodies.[30] Savvy educator Stephen Brookfield refers to a principle articulated by English political observer Simon Hoggart: TATBTS – The Ability To Be Taken Seriously.[31] [...] The problem is, following Paulo Freire's admonishment, TATBTS is *not* a neutral quality.

Visibility, Vulnerability, Viability

In recent years, women faculty of color have broken tough ground in bearing witness to the struggle to be taken seriously within so-called majority institutions of higher learning. Anthologies such as *Still Searching for Our Mothers' Gardens*[32] invoke the rallying cry of earlier generations of feminist/womanist scholars to continue the tradition of narrating counter-stories of the multiple jeopardy of scholar-teachers whose positionality is minoritized by the intersections of race, gender, sexuality, and national-ity. With anecdotal honesty, empirical details, painstaking research, and analytic sharp-ness, these educators testify to inscrutable academic dilemmas. [...] Three generative themes illustrate this web of complexity: "visibility, vulnerability, and viability."[33]

Visibility

Visibility – being seen – already means to be judged by what one looks like. This enfleshment of teaching bodies is not freeing, but rather fear-ridden due to the knowledge that one is constantly under the shadows of scrutinizing gaze. It is a form of psycho-political exposure that turns teachers into what educator Ana Maria Freire calls "interdicted bodies" – forbidden to be," inhibited through self-monitoring.[34] At the intra-psychic level, the demands of physical, mental, and emotional health beckon pru-dent attention to care of self, but such concern is often difficult to negotiate within the *habitus* of institutional and academic life. Physiologically, sexualized female teaching bodies struggle with exposed bodily curvatures as much as menstrual flows, but who cares when the teacher is only supposed to be the disembodied "talking head" – mentally objective, emotionally persuasive, physically virulent? With biology being culturally and politically charged, we recall Audre Lorde's description of the "mythical norm" that haunts minoritized female consciousness: "white, thin, male, young, heterosexual, christian, and financially secure."[35] [...]

[...] How are they stereotypically deemed "dangerous" (angry, vixen, feminazi, terrorizing)?[36] How must they be stereotypically "nice" (compliant, "mule" exotic/tropic)? What would qualify them as "smart," "competent," or "authoritative?" [And what about ...] inappropriate body contact (head-patting, chin-touching, face-cuddling, arm-brushing); sexualized advances from students and colleagues; overt inquiries or rumor mills about marital status or dating "preferences"; being passed over ("is there a teacher in this room?"), mistaken for someone else ("I didn't know there were two Asians/Blacks/Latino/as here"), put on the spot to defend one's teaching status ("sorry, only faculty are allowed here"); being spoken for by other well-meaning sympathizers, or tasked to enlighten so-called "ignorant" interlocutors ... These are but minor anecdotal punctuations to the endless testimonials provided by teacher-scholars whose visible bodies render their credibility as teacher perpetually ambiguous.

Taking seriously the standpoint feminist concepts of *positionality* (identity work is place-based, situational and contextual) and *intersectionality* (identity is constructed and performed within a matrix of dynamic, intersecting identity statuses which are never fixed markers),[37] it is important to take account of the very particular ways in which oppressive body (stereo)types serve as identity straitjackets. [...] Sadly, visibility often functions as a source of *de*-authorization.

Vulnerability

Here lies a catch-22: is it better to be *invisible*? That is a converse dilemma for the teaching body. For in both visibility and invisibility, the marked teaching body is *vulnerable* when it comes to various levels of performance evaluations. [...] Women faculty of color [...] report higher external and self-imposed expectations when it comes to identity and performance evaluations. Entrenched within academic institutions are invisible, implicit standards by which teachers are assessed, and according to which vulnerable teachers may be found wanting. [...]

Moreover, faculty of minoritized status regularly report the stress of having to bear the extra weight of representation: they must proudly demonstrate the institution's interest in diversity; they must be available as mentors to minority students who lack structural support; they must exercise teaching authority over minority students without subjecting the latter to public shame; [...] they must ensure the development of critical competencies to address social location in their own teaching and scholarship (because it is not an "innate" capacity or knowledge base); they must fight to make context-specific perspectives and concerns central to the "mainstream" curriculum, and they must not offend. [...]

[...] "It sure is rotten to be a straight White male these days!" a student declares. The racial-ethnic minority female teacher [...] suddenly realizes the vulnerability of her teaching task: on the one hand, she desires to expose a variety of "invisible" privileges at work in the student's statement and worldview; on the other hand, she is aware of the potential risks of being dismissed wholesale for alleged political bias. [...]

Viability

One could charge that majority academic institutions operate by the principle of *unnatural* selection. It is not so much "survival of the fittest," for Darwinian natural selection assumes that species that can adapt to their immediate environment will survive. No matter how hard they try to "fit in," some teaching bodies remain vulnerable to (r)ejections from their host environments. The *viability* of the teacher as "outsider within"[38] is thus dependent upon their ability to cultivate coping mechanisms. [...]

[...] Typical dilemmas of survival – *survivre*, to out-live – include the sense of self-shame, social isolation, lack of mentoring, lack of collegial support system, and lack of institutional security.[39] Academic coding of meritocracy and colorblind racism breed self-doubting questions: by what merit was I hired, and by what merit will I continue to be valued? Alliances for solidarity are easily subject to territorialized identity politics: Why are *they* hanging together? [...] "Token hire" carries more layered meaning in these crushing economic times, in which deliberations over faculty shape and size, for meager-sized institutions, are driven as much by the economy as by institutional, curricular, or disciplinary politics. [...]

To remain viable in a constant state of insecurity, isolation, or alienation, racial-ethnic minority teachers have called for a variety of fringe practices for institutional maneuvering.[40]

Aliens Ineligible for Citizenship

It seems worthwhile for an excursus at this point on how issues of "visibility, vulnerability, and viability" play out for a racial/ethnic minority group (in)famous for their "model minority" status in higher education and the cultural mainstream, despite their marginality within (theological and religious) educational research literature: Asian Americans and Pacific Islanders (AAPI).[41] (Stereo)typically portrayed as minorities who have attained "universal and unparalleled academic and occupational success,"[42] AAPIs are often cited as exemplars of American meritocracy, in which upward mobility is attained through a perfected work ethic comprised of old world values and American (Protestant) individual self-help. Pitted against other racial/ethic minority groups (particularly African Americans and Latino/as [...]), AAPIs as an aggregated racial grouping serve as a foil for multiple sides of affirmative action debates. *The Rise of Asian Americans,* the 2012 Pew Research Center's "comprehensive" study of Asians in the US, is perhaps the most recent example of how obscured and over-simplified demographic data can serve to buttress dominant cultural anxieties about a minority population's alleged steady ascension to the top. Released in the thick of contentious national debates about immigration "reform," the report offers fodder for antagonistic delineations between "good" and "bad" immigrants/citizens.

Against this backdrop, educational researchers have begun to challenge how aggregate empirical data on educational performance and achievement have been used to obscure the actual struggles of Asian Pacific Americans in living up to the model minority trope.[43] A multiple passport-holding executive from Hong Kong, a Korean grocery shop-owner, a Filipino doctor, a Laotian refugee in middle Tennessee, a migrant from the US territory of American Samoa, and an Amerasian child of biracial heritage would all be homogenized under the "Asian or Pacific Islander" racial category.[44] Subsequently, based upon the ostensible "success" of a select few ethnic representatives, [...] *all* AAPIs are typecast in cultural discourse as the "new whites" or "almost white" by the model minority myth, in the midst of looming fears of immigrant infiltrations.[45] This misconception conveniently ignores AAPI collective and historical experiences of exclusion, prejudice, discrimination, harassment, pressure to conform, and survival struggles in mainstream America. [...] More ominously, the model minority trope and instrumental use of selective empirical data together force AAPIs into identity straitjackets.[46] [...] As inassimilable new immigrants, they must perform according to the model minority script, or risk being "re-foreignized" and ejected as "yellow perils," as has been proven throughout US history.[47]

If cognizant of the dynamics of racialization described above, an Asian American teacher – or, more specifically, a one-point-five-generation Vietnamese refugee-turned-naturalized-US citizen – would step into the classroom wary of the various holographic identity constructs being projected upon her. [...] She is acutely aware of the cultural caricatures of the Asian female: beguiling geisha, diminutive mail-ordered bride, military sex worker, conniving brothel madam, innocent village girl, submissive Confucian wife, whip-lashing tiger mom, tradition-bound matriarch, plasma-breathing martial artist, nerdy Asiatic brainiac who "stole" an American job or admissions ticket to an elite academic institution, or (given post-September 11 xenophobia) an instrument for political or religious terrorism [...] At the same time, she stands as an authoritative figure, granted a certain extent of institutional endorsement by virtue of the teaching office, her own charisma, and the body of knowledge over which she had proven acceptable mastery. This teacher does well to remember that just as identity is a performance rather than a fixed status marker, her authority as teacher is also a constant (and improvisational) performative contestation. [...]

What techniques and practices might this teacher hone for such improvisational identity work? [...]

Magico-Religious Wavering Between Worlds:[48] Teaching Practices

In a letter penned for North American educators, the late Brazilian education reformer Paulo Freire wrote: "[A] teacher must be fully cognizant of the political nature of his/her practice and assume responsibility for this rather than denying it."[49] Freire was not alone in articulating the *political* nature of teaching. It is at base persuasive, if not directive; to varying degrees, it is an intentional effort to exert influence upon knowledge (what we know), affect (what we value), behavior (how we act). As such, scholars of critical pedagogy push the recognition that "knowledge is power" toward closer scrutiny of how power is configured by the boundaries of knowledge systems, and how the boundary coordinates of such systems can be "remapped, reterritorialized, and decentered" for multiplied reference points in our "reading of the world."[50] This epistemological disposition of "border pedagogy" assumes that learners are crossers of borders that are "historically constructed and socially organized within maps of rules and regulations that limit and enable particular identities, individual capacities, and social forms."[51] Teachers, therefore, are also border-crossers who might do well if they learn and apply what sociologist Aihwa Ong describes of the contemporary global "flexible citizen": "*trans*versal," "*trans*actional," "*trans*lational," and "*trans*gressive" practices that are "incited, enabled, and regulated by the logics" of the academic landscape.[52] These figurative abstractions can be broken down into a few components of "practical wisdom" for the teacher, following the cues of those who employ critical race theory (CRT) for educational analysis.

[...]Challenging notions of race as mere ideological constructs or essentialized, objective attributes, CRT scrutinizes the function of power/differentials in race relations, especially the power of White privilege ("whitestream"). In principle, CRT posits three central tenets. First, it highlights counter-narratives of marginal, subordinated voices as a strategy to decentralize and denormalize dominant grand narratives. Second, it takes advantage of "interest convergence" as leverage for championing equity, since the majority would be more prone to accommodate minority interest if there is overlapping benefit. Third, it targets systemic, structural change (social justice), informed by interdisciplinary and multi-issue analyses.[53]

Pedagogy of Dissent

Following CRT's first tenet, the teacher as "border-crosser" could learn to wield the *trans*gressive power of counter-stories that subtly offer "oppositional" definitions of reality.[54] Their own identity work as an ex-centric teaching body is the living enactment of transversed norms: a "non-standard" subject asserting credibility and authenticity in ways that are slightly slanted, off-kilter, zigzagging, but enough to render problematic so-called normative coordinates of identity. Thus, the identity work of a Chinese-Peruvian ("Chinotino" for Chinese-Latino) teaching in the US as a "global immigrant" unsettles various racialized binary oppositions.[55] A Black Caribbean narrative adds layers to the homogenized US Black experience, calling to attention a longer history of colonial racialization and subordination of the non-White "other."[56] A queer faculty of color forces serious consideration of "intersectionality" to expose power inscribed by both race and heteronormativity.[57] The identity work of these teachers, in effect, serves as counter-normative "curriculum."[58] [...]

Oppositional narratives need not be mild, as womanist scholars have long insisted. What Audre Lorde called *symphonic anger,* "loaded with information and energy," may very well be the emotive response in the face of "exclusion... of racial distortions, of silence, ill-use, stereotyping, defensiveness, misnaming, betrayal, and co-optation."[59] Similarly, bell hooks found her confidence through risky "back talk." Preferred over silent protest, and more directive than informal women speech, "sharp-tongued" talking back is for hooks "a gesture of defiance."[60] [...]

[...] Following CRT's third tenet, the teacher as border intellectual passes over banal tolerance in favor of educational practices that examine power and privilege in the nooks and crannies of macro-structures and micro-realities. Brookfield and Holst suggest three concrete practices: 1) "ideological detoxification," or deconstruction of implicit ideological values [...]; 2) intentional disruption of privilege of all forms [...], especially those enjoyed in daily routines and institutional configurations; and 3) deep, sustained immersion in "alternative conceptions of normality," [...] that seeks opportunities for serious confrontation with difference.[61] [...]

CRT's [second] tenet regarding "interest convergence" is perhaps most elusive for the minoritized teacher, for they must seek ways to *translate* their talents and interests to institutional cultures. [...] In this act of negotiation, the teacher as "flexible citizen" knows that individual interests are more readily considered if and when they align with institutional interests. [...] Thus, viability (survival) [...] relies on forms of "horizontal comradeship"[62] forged out of affinities or strategic alliances. Perhaps most poignantly, the teacher as flexible, mobile, "nomadic subject" lives by the practical wisdom that (institutional) *home* is [...] a matrix of locations in which *belonging* is the product of imaginative collective struggle. [...]

For Those Who Dare to Teach: Telos of the Teaching Life

> What we need more than anything else is not *textbooks*, but *textpeople*. It is the personality of the teacher which is the text that the pupils read: the text that they will never forget.[63]

A Freirean teacher is reminded that education is "a form of intervention in the world," and it begins with the very presence of the "textperson" standing in the room, asking herself/himself: "Do I stand for what I teach? Do I believe what I say?"[64] [...] With discipline, courage, and the earthiness that is the root of humility (*humilis*),[65] ambiguous, impermanent, ex-centric, border-crossing, space-invading, transgressive "flexible bodies" may very well be receivers and proclaimers of "apocalyptic" (revealing, unveiling)[66] visions to propel theological/religious education into the twenty-first century.

Notes

1 Chapter title inspired by Dan P. McAdams's *The Stories We Live By*.
2 Rumbaut, "Vietnamese, Laotian, and Cambodian Americans," 179.
3 The 1952 Naturalization Act prohibited racial and gender restrictions in determining naturalization eligibility. Takaki, *Iron Cages*, 299–300.
4 Greenwood, "Education in a Culture of Violence," 351. Citing Elbaz-Luwisch, "How Is Education Possible When There's a Body in the Middle of the Room?," 9.
5 Prater, et al., "Disclose and Demystify."
6 Ibid., 16.
7 Clarke, "The Ethico-Politics of Teacher Identity," 186.

8 Greenwood, "Education in a Culture of Violence," 356.

9 Freire, "Letter to North-American Teachers," 211.

10 This hermeneutic strategy follows postcolonial feminist cues, as modeled by Mohanty, *Feminism without Borders*, 5.

11 Liew, *What Is Asian American Biblical Hermeneutics?*,13–15, 19, 25–33.

12 Loughlin, "What Is Queer? Theology after Identity," 150.

13 Kwok, "Fishing the Asia Pacific," 18.

14 Mohanty, *Feminism without Borders*, 77–8; Foss-Snowden, "Standpoint Theory and Discontinuing Denial of Racism, Sexism, and Ageism," 88.

15 Building upon Michel Foucault's notion of "ethics as self-formation," Matthew Clarke of the University of Hong Kong proffers a social constructionist framework for understanding the "ethico-political identity work" of the teacher, comprised of four axes: substance, authority-sources, techniques and practices, and *telos*. The four central questions of this chapter follow these four axes. Clarke, "The Ethico-Politics of Teacher Identity," 186.

16 Trinh, "Cotton and Iron," 330. Inter-spatial shuttling was an attempted metaphor before rediscovery of Trinh's use of it in her exquisite essay.

17 "Minoritized" is preferred over "minority" to emphasize the ideological and political processes of identity negotiations rather than fixed statuses.

18 Brookfield, *The Skillful Teacher*, 8.

19 Ibid., 6–9, 12.

20 Freire, *Pedagogy of Freedom*, 90.

21 Freire, "Letter to North-American Teachers," 212.

22 hooks, "Engaged Pedagogy."

23 Takaki, *Iron Cages*, 262–3.

24 Althaus-Reid, *Indecent Theology*, 22.

25 Pinn, "Reading the Signs: The Body as Non-Written Text," 87.

26 Zamudio, *Critical Race Theory Matters*, 51; Carbado and Gulati, "Working Identity" 1301.

27 Sealey-Ruiz, "Reading, Writing, and Racism," 46.

28 Brookfield discusses "credibility" and "authenticity" as two values which stu dents often say they most desire in teachers. *The Skillful Teacher*, 56. See chapter 4.

29 Brookfield, The *Skillful Teacher*, 76–83.

30 See, for instance, Harvey, "The Impostor Phenomenon and Achievement."

31 Brookfield, The *Skillful Teacher*, 245; Hoggart, *On the House*, 46.

32 Niles and Gordon, eds., *Still Searching for Our Mothers' Gardens*. Cf. Alice Walker's 1983 classic, *In Search of Our Mothers' Gardens*. Early respected anthologies of Asian feminist voices include *Making Waves*, ed. Asian Women United of California, and *Dragon Ladies*, ed. Sonia Shah. A more recent contribution edited by Gabriella Gutiérrez y Muhs, *Presumed Incompetent: The Intersections of Race and Class for Women in Academia*, is garnering much attention.

33 Foss-Snowden, "Standpoint Theory and Discontinuing Denial of Racism, Sexism, and Ageism," 83. Citing Mitchell, "Visible, Vulnerable, and Viable."

34 Freire, *Teachers as Cultural Workers*, 9.

35 Lorde, *Sister Outsider*, 2nd ed., 116.

36 bell hooks does not mince words: "angry mean black bitch"! In *Teaching Critical Thinking*, 99.

37 See Harding, "Gendered Ways of Knowing and the 'Epistemological Crisis' of the West."

38 Gordon, "Watching My B/lack," 47.

39 Prater, et al., "Disclose and Demystify."

40 See Gatison, "Playing the Game."

41 "Oceanic" is recently the preferred term over "Pacific Islander."

42 Museus and Kiang, "Deconstructing the Model Minority Myth," 6.

43 See, for instance, Nakanishi and Nishida, eds., *The Asian American Educational Experience.* More information may be obtained by following the research initiatives of the National Commission on Asian American and Pacific Islander Research in Education.

44 Palumbo-Liu, *Asian/American.* See esp. chapter 7.

45 Ibid., 110–13.

46 Museus and Kiang, "Deconstructing the Model Minority Myth," 6–11; Palumbo-Liu, 196; Espiritu, *Asian American Women and Men,* chapter 4.

47 Palumbo-Liu, *Asian/American,* 18, 146.

48 van Gennep, The *Rites of Passage,* 18.

49 Freire, "Letter to North-American Teachers," 211.

50 Giroux, *Pedagogy and the Politics of Hope,* 147. In his "Letter to North-American Teachers," Freire wrote that the skill to read the *word* generates the capacity to read the *world.* Also in Freire, *Teachers as Cultural Workers,* 18.

51 Giroux, *Pedagogy and the Politics of Hope,* 147.

52 Ong, *Flexible Citizenship,* 4.

53 Gillborn, "Critical Race Theory and Education," 26–7; Zamudio, *Critical Race Theory Matters,* 16, 22–3; Museus, *Conducting Research on Asian Americans,* 59; Brookfield and Holst, *Radicalizing Learning,* 193. See also Delgado, *Critical Race Theory.*

54 Zamudio, *Critical Race Theory Matters,* 16.

55 Kong, "Immigration, Racial Identity, and Adult Education."

56 Alfred, "Challenging Racism through Postcolonial Discourse."

57 Misawa, "Musings on Controversial Intersections of Positionality." Cites Kumashiro, *Troubling Intersections of Race and Sexuality.*

58 Kong, "Immigration, Racial Identity, and Adult Education," 240. Cites Pinar, "Notes on Understanding Curriculum as Racial Text."

59 Lorde, *Sister Outsider,* 2nd ed., 124.

60 hooks, *Talking Back,* 337–40.

61 Brookfield and Holst, *Radicalizing Learning,* 201–9.

62 Mohanty, *Feminism Without Borders,* 46. Citing Anderson, *Imagined Communities,* 11–16.

63 Heschel, *The Insecurity of Freedom,* 237.

64 Freire, *Pedagogy of Freedom,* 90; Heschel, *The Insecurity of Freedom,* 237.

65 Cahalan, *Introducing the Practice of Ministry,* 75.

66 Liew, *What Is Asian American Biblical Hermeneutics?* 135–6.

10

Raced Bodies (2016)*

Phillis Isabella Sheppard

Introduction

Phillis Isabella Sheppard is a widely respected scholar in womanist practical theology with expertise in psychology of religion and psychoanalysis, now teaching at Vanderbilt University. Her 2011 book, *Self, Culture and Others in Womanist Practical Theology*, was singular in its study of black women's lives, drawing on case studies and clinical work and engaging black psychoanalysis and psychoanalytic literary criticism. A measured, generous, and courageous reader of her sources, she invites white colleagues to greater engagement with race, sexuality, and social activism. At the same time, she also pushes womanist theology to attend to the psychological, black churches to amend endemic patriarchy and heterosexism, and close colleagues to proceed carefully in turning to Afrocentric traditions. Her most recent research analyzes nonconventional religious forms and practices such as outsider art and cyberspace for their meaning and implications for black religious experience.

This essay is one of the flagship chapters in the *Reader* and one of Sheppard's boldest moves thus far. Indeed, it is a pivot point for the volume, flagging new directions in practical theology around questions of bodies, race, epistemology, and ethics. She offers a wake-up call for the discipline on several levels. First, she suggests that a discipline attuned to concrete lived religion cannot ignore actual bodies. However, the written word and the very production of texts themselves – certainly what most academics do best – occludes our ability to engage lived experience, especially when it comes to racialized ways of inhabiting culture. Second, she tests other avenues for engaging bodies in her prose. Her essay includes photographs [see original publication], poetry, liturgy, and vignettes from media outlets, social media, and classroom encounters. Third, in these portraits, she asks us to see all the bodies, including previously invisible ones, the white children in particular, as integral to racialized politics. Fourth, as an essay that originally appeared in *Conundrums in Practical Theology* (2016), she grapples with a troubling dilemma – how to engage raced bodies without reifying embedded racist

Original publication details: Phillis Isabella Sheppard, "Raced Bodies: Portraying Bodies, Reifying Racism," pp. 219–49 from *Conundrums in Practical Theology*, eds. Joyce Ann Mercer and Bonnie J. Miller-McLemore (Leiden: Brill, 2016). To view the photos discussed in the section on "Malformed White Bodies," see the original publication.

ideologies. Finally and perhaps most important, she suggests that the discipline's important contribution and challenge is not simply epistemological. Alongside epistemological insurgency lie equally pressing ethical questions about what readers, students, and the wider public do with fresh insights into embedded and local knowledge. Practical theology has always retained an emphasis on practical implications and transformation. But Sheppard sharpens the agenda, asking readers to consider "what do raced bodies require of us as individuals and communities?"

Suggested Further Reading

- Phillis Isabella Sheppard, *Self, Culture, and Others in Womanist Practical Theology* (New York: Palgrave Macmillan, 2011).
- Emilie M. Townes, *Womanist Ethics and the Cultural Production of Evil* (New York: Palgrave Macmillan, 2006).
- Evelyn Parker, "Womanist Practical Theology," in Bonnie J. Miller-McLemore, ed., *The Wiley Blackwell Companion to Practical Theology*, pp. 20413 (Malden, MA: Wiley Blackwell, 2012).

***

Conundrum:
a: a question or problem having only a conjectural answer
b: an intricate and difficult problem[1]

The anthropologist Zora Neale Hurston proclaimed, "Research is formalized curiosity. It is poking and prying with a purpose." In this chapter, I poke and pry and problematize the near absence of raced bodies in practical theology. Even though race is wedged into the crevices of the United States cultural imagination and in day-to-day practices of research, actual raced bodies seldom confront us in our critical texts. The poking and prodding, however, exposes a conundrum closely connected to the problem of appropriation and reciprocity with which womanist and feminist ethicists have grappled. Womanist ethicist Emilie M. Townes admonished that there are dangers in exercising a "hegemonic control" when we take up other peoples' experiences and incorporate them "into a mundane and unnuanced analysis."[2] In the case of the hegemonic appropriation of raced bodies in research, the aims of the researcher – to publish and raise questions for the discipline – can be privileged such that the negative cultural depictions of raced bodies are reinforced. In other words, raced bodies do not exist in a vacuum. They can be appropriated but not without also giving form to the racist ideologies attached to those bodies. Herein lies the conundrum: if practical theology commits to a robust analysis of raced bodies and, in essence, critiques current discourses on bodies, it will do so with an ingrained bias that reads raced bodies through the lens of racist imaginaries. In other words, the researchers and readers alike are already predisposed to read through the lens of cultural misrepresentations.

Racist depictions of raced bodies within disciplines form the very individuals who shape those disciplines. This is just one indication of the pervasiveness of our malformation. Due to the increased numbers of previously underrepresented groups, practical theologians are discussing race in a variety of ways. Most often the literature is focused on particularity and written by people whose bodies are the sites for racing. In this chapter, I return to a longstanding concern: the place of bodies in practical theological discourse and practices. The struggle to take bodies' experience seriously, on their own terms, has been documented.[3] The problem is twofold: those doing the theorizing have tended to be those in the majority and, despite all our theorizing, scholars who are the subject of that theorizing often remain absent. They are not represented, and they are not speaking about their own bodies. It is a challenge and maybe impossible to reserve a place for the lived bodily experiences when we rely so much on text rather than embodied experience in our scholarship. This is even more problematic when we are reduced to discourse that considers "the body" as if we all experience the same bodily experiences. In the absence of non-white academic bodies doing the talking, we are left with theories of the body where race is acknowledged but quickly relegated to the footnote and reference sections, and where the text advises the reader to consult scholars of color rather than actually including their voices.

Two questions shed light on the conundrum: First, how are practical theological scholarship and practice implicated in the invisibility of lived raced bodies? Second, can practical theology prioritize the lived experience of raced bodies without exploiting or reproducing the negative cultural productions of raced experiences? All too frequently practical theology fails to theorize the experiences and therefore perpetuates the invisibility. In addition, practical theology is sometimes appropriated to reinforce negative cultural images of some raced bodies. In this chapter, I intersperse pictures [and pictorial analysis], personal narrative, and pedagogical practices with the goal of rethinking and at times undermining the ways in which raced bodies are represented, ignored, or exploited.

Race as a Social and Historical Construct

In recent years, the highly contested dialogue around race has been critiqued for its reliance on the US context of structural oppression of black people who are the descendants of enslaved Africans. The limitation of these discussions is that the complexity of the history of race as a category is lost. Also lost is the history and practice of defining and appointing racial classification onto groups of people. This specialized grouping included black Americans, Asian Americans, Native Americans, Indigenous peoples, multi-racial/ethnic categories, such as mulatto, and white Americans. In this process of categorization, each group was granted varying degrees of legal rights and opportunities based on the group's proximity to whiteness. Each group was also subject to various forms of discrimination based on proximity to blackness. The construction of social, economic, and political relations between "raced groups" in the US remains contested, as is the more recent "racing" of groups new to the US. Racing groups of people remains a social, structural, and legal process reserved for those wielding political and economic power – those claiming white as the normative designation.

Obviously critical race studies and whiteness studies have shed a small, direct light in this direction, but in practical theology we suffer even more from the lack of a robust and sustained engagement with the complexity of whiteness, race, and power as race is lived in our field. While practical theologians consider "social analysis" crucial to our work, the intersections that frame race are frequently tangential to our actual thinking.

Practical theologians are still grappling with race as a social construct. Put more bluntly, many practical theologians still act as if race is an ontological reality, something unchangeable and set in stone, rather than a social inscription and therefore eminently changeable. But the idea of race and the attributes assigned to "the races" is a part of the early DNA of the US. The effect of the idea of race cannot be ignored and is patently obvious in societally pervasive choreographed acts of racism. People in power use the category of race to define others in order to regulate and indeed diminish their access to certain cultural goods, such as education, jobs, and sexual self-determination. Race structures our relationship to each other, to our surroundings, and to language. For instance, depending on the racial identity of the speaker and listener, one may live in a suburb or "ethnic enclave" or "the ghetto."

The category of race, while often thought of as solely based on color, has a more complex history. Race is a legal category and a legal designation that has been contested in the US, and, for some groups, has changed over time.[4] In cases where groups were redefined and moved from white to non-white status, the consequences were legal, economic, and social. Thus, the category of race should be viewed in terms of its history and its effect rather than as a fixed biological reality. Racial categories evolve over time and ultimately re-produce the ideology of racial superiority, generally that of whiteness.

In addition, racial categories structure professional and relational dynamics, as we can see in practical theology. I have already mentioned that practical theology rarely considers the perspective of those who are not white, and even more rarely allows such persons to speak for themselves. In addition, we see the negative work of racial categories by looking at citation practices across the discipline: we rarely include the work of people of color. Instead, we cite certain field-defining scholars and mentors over and over again. The result is that we reproduce particular perspectives and particular selves and avoid the challenge of grounding and expanding our knowledge in the experiences of raced bodies. This leaves (the unacknowledged) white bodies in the driver's seat of practical theology as in so many other fields.

When Raced Bodies Appear

Womanist practical theologians are among those who have increasingly paid attention to black women's bodies. Evelyn Parker [...] notes that black women's bodies are the sites where the discourse on and the lived realities at the core of black life are inscribed. Even so, "the corpus of womanist practical theology on embodiment is small,"[5] and this lack of attention to black female embodiment has implications for the trajectory of womanist practical theology and beyond. For when we consider the practices and impact of racism, we need to ask ourselves what bodies we see in our texts and which ones are missing.

For those of us who appropriate psychoanalytic perspectives in our work, we often find that bodies of any color are absent in the theories we employ, and post-Freudian constructions give even Freud's emphasis on the nexus between biological (body) and psyche scant attention. Contemporary clinical theory and practice leans toward an emphasis on the intersubjective, relational, and the constructive – usually without explicitly theorizing the body's or bodies' position in theory or practice. Two noteworthy exceptions are Joyce McDougall and Janine Chasseguet-Smirgel. In their work, both reconfigure the body's place in the psyche and consider classical psychoanalytic views concerning gender and sexuality.[6] [...] These psychoanalytic perspectives are helpful in the recovery of the body, but the body they recover is generic, not only theoretically but also culturally and racially. Thus, for our purposes, the theoretical conclusions are not without problems. Though McDoughall and Chasseguet-Smirgel practiced in France and Britain, and though race as a construct has a different history and reality in those contexts, race is nonetheless a feature of social interaction in those countries too. Yet even here raced bodies are invisible.

We do, however, see a psychoanalytic concern with the relationship between race, gender, and culture in womanist practical theology. My own book as well as works by Markeva Hill and Stephanie Crumpton are evidence of this.[7] In these texts, the primary aims are to re-situate black women's experiences in practical and pastoral theology by critiquing their absence and to articulate a womanist practical theology informed by psychoanalytic theory. Some of them appropriate self psychology and object relations, revised in light of black culture and black women's experience of culture, religion, and embodiment. These authors pay particular attention to persons who have experienced bodily violations, such as sexual abuse, domestic violence, and social violence in religious, intimate, and cultural contexts. They depict black female embodiment most powerfully when they make ethnography integral. Significant effort is given to black women as readers of culture and interpreters of their own experience. These works must be read as advancing the black female body in theological and psychoanalytic discourse, and close readings also suggest that black female bodies are, to some degree, represented as black bodies in distress. I would add that despite the clear commitment to addressing black bodies, the texts often privilege theories over bodies to scaffold the work. The absence of the raced body in practical theology and its place in womanist practical theology also shines a light on the conundrum of raced bodies: black bodies can be central to theorizing and simultaneously reproduce raced social dynamics. In my own consideration of this conundrum, I make raced bodies the fulcrum and observe in vivo this dynamic of reproduction. I also expand the reading of whose bodies are raced, and, finally, I consider the ethical demand that raced bodies place on our discipline.

[...]

The psychologies and ideologies of privilege are entrenched in the scholarly production and constructive efforts of practical theology. With rare exception, the lived realities of raced bodies generally fail to materialize or to become the basis for the discussion. Thus, discussing racism and the body relies on the listeners' and the presenters' preexisting internalized images. And the conundrum arises: when racial bodies do "show up," we must ask if the words and images of raced bodies in scholarship mirror negative images and ideas that reside in the psyches of some readers. Thus, unless practical theologians engage in critical social analysis, their professional advancement will occur at the expense and exploitation of raced bodies.

Given the commitment to describing lived experience, practical theology will more thoroughly inhabit its identity and aims when it pays attention to raced bodies. This effort is not without complication as is evident in cultural historian Sandar Gilman's treatment of Saartie Baartman, a black South African woman whose body was displayed publically as part of the raced medical discourse of the early 1800s. In the medical and scientific literature of the day, Baartman is referred to as the Hottentot Venus and described as having a "hideous form" with a "horribly flattened nose," large and primitive genitalia, and protruding buttocks. Gilman notes that in addition to being on display in South Africa, she was exhibited in London and Paris. Under the guise of science and medicine, she served as an example of a primitive, different (from white European), and apelike female. Her body and the medical discourse surrounding it undergirded negative views of black female sexuality. Even after her death, Baartman was exhibited. However, in his critique of the exploitation of black women's bodies to satisfy European sexualized fantasies, Gilman perpetuates such exploitation by including in his book photos from the medical journals. Thus, Baartman was yet again displayed and discussed in the service of white scientific discourse. He sought to reveal the ways in which medical iconography expresses racial and gender ideologies. Yet, his unnecessary and unnecessarily frequent display of Baartman's naked body reproduced the sexualized content of the medical iconography he sought to challenge and, just as the medical journals of the 1800s, made the reader complicit in the process.[8] Practical theology will have to combat such practices too.

Pedagogical Mirrors: Racing White Bodies

Some years ago, in a class on "African American Spirituality and Religion," I had the class view the website www.withoutsanctuary.org created by James Allen. It is a gallery of photos turned into postcards depicting lynchings between 1882–1968 in the US. My primary aim for the class was to wrench "spirituality" out of the hegemonic grasp of white Christian western perspectives.

The class was comprised of five or six black African Americans, one woman from Puerto Rico and one from Argentina, and five white students of Swedish-American background. Prior to viewing the website, the discussions had been robust, sometimes a little loud, but deeply engaged. As the class became less vocal and after a period of silence, I asked what was happening. All of them were angry – with me. Some were angry that I had exposed this horrible past; others, mostly white students, were angry that now I had created gulf between them and black students in the class. The Latina women were angry that they "felt horrible" and no longer knew how to participate in the conversation. The visuals were too much. Bodies hanging and displayed on a large screen was too much.

As I reflected on their intense responses, and my own, I knew there was more that I needed to include in this discussion of terrorized raced bodies. Over time, I realized that for all my focus on embodiment and the black/brown body, I had theorized the black body, ignored white bodies, and presumed only adult bodies as engaged in the act of lynching. As a consequence, I was surprised by the amount of anger directed toward me. It was evident that I had internalized a message that lynching was a one-dimensional bodily production where only black bodies were to perform race.

Yet the truth is that the photos of the lynchings can be viewed from a variety of perspectives, including one that focuses on the participation of white bodies, as Allen himself suggests in his own work. In a postcard chronicling the 1935 lynching of Rubin Stacy, a young white girl of about 10 is shown among the crowd of white observers. She is smiling. Her face stands out in the crowd of whiteness: she is the only one smiling.[9]

Generally, we have focused on the black bodies being lynched and not on the entertainment-seeking white bodies. Allen, in his narration, repeatedly makes clear that lynching was a public, social, and socially acceptable ritual event for whites to attend. And, as is evident in Allen's photos, the intended audience included white children. It can be argued that these ritual events were a means of socialization designed to sustain community and power dynamics. Lynching is a ritual practice, practical theologian Emmanuel Lartey reminds us in a discussion of healing ritual: "Ritual is engaged in to effect transformation in the physical and material circumstances of the living community [...]."[10] In communal acts of lynching, the ritual was for incarnation of a cultural artifact and enactment of evil.

[...]Historian Amy Louise Woods apprehends the religious features of lynching in its linguistic justification. [...] Advocates "borrowed the language of evangelical moral crusades to justify – and sanctify" their actions. The rituals themselves "also uncannily reenacted evangelical church practices... (and) imbued lynching with the sacred meaning and even consecrated it as God's vengeance... the presence of witnesses linked individual members of the crowd to a larger community of believers."[11] Thus, lynching performed a major interior and social aspect of religion of the time; it distinguished the righteous from the unrighteous, the saved from the damned. Lynching made it clear that the base line was predicated on raced bodies.

Whereas ritual that is liturgy is sometimes defined as the work of the people of God and aimed at the transformation of the individual and community, the ritual of lynching worked to transform the (predominantly male) black body into the grotesque and subjugated. Lynching enforced conformity to racialized asymmetrical social positions: white bodies as enforcers and black bodies as the subjugated. Thus, lynching as ritual formed and socialized blacks *and* whites in relation to one another over a lifetime and across communities. Lynching was part and parcel of lived bodies' racialized and ritual experience. Pastoral theologian Lee H. Butler traces the "orchestrated" and even choreographed terroristic nature of lynchings. He sees a link between lynching and the care of souls – and I concur. Lynching as a social symbol of oppression and arbitrary and lethal violence primarily directed toward black Americans is socially and psychologically powerful. It leaves what Butler calls a "psychic imprint,"[12] what Jay-Paul Hinds metaphorically describes as "Traces on the Blackboard" and "vestiges of racism on the African American psyche."[13] Its legacy is psychological but it is also social in that it is internalized in the collective cultural identifications of black Americans as well as in white Americans. This is why a picture, an effigy, or linguistic reference to the possibility of lynching evokes rage, terror, and protest and why white Americans can still draw on it as a symbol of white power and a threat reminding black men and families of the potential for violence, retribution, and murder. These vestiges are not just imprinted on the psyches of black Americans but also on the psyches of white Americans who make use of the history to signify violent intent readily directed toward black people. Lynching then is clearly a concern for the care of souls despite the great resistance to seeing it as such.

[...]

Whereas lynching postcards primarily produced the disfigured black male body, colonialist photography and postcards of the African and African American women, often in various stages of nakedness, gained their own social capital by proliferating dehumanized and uncivilized views of black femaleness. Cultural anthropologist Christraud Geary notes that "in the heyday of postcard production before the First World War (1914–1918), postcards were akin to newspapers and covered all kinds of topics."[14] Black women's bodies, often half clothed and sometimes naked, were readily available. These postcards were touted as a form of ethnographic research and claimed to represent "Africans' daily life" while actually revealing ideologies of race, gender, and culture of "Western photographers' and consumers' imagination" – thus creating, reproducing, and sustaining a static imaginary of tribal Africa.[15] Moreover, they marketed black women's images as forms of erotica and pornography. The texts that accompanied the postcards and the notes written on the blank side fueled the colonial racialized sexual fetishes of African black life. [...] Thus, postcards of black bodies, and in this case, black women's bodies, reveal and shape western imagination and notions of the manipulability of black bodies by and for the gratification of white sexualized and racialized appetites. So, unlike the aim of lynching postcards of inscribing murderous terror and entertainment, many of these postcards inscribe a text of sexual "primitivity," availability, and exploitability at will. The black female's body is used to prove her need for civilizing influence and appropriated for the aggressive sexual gaze. Exposing the veiled perverted desires of the photographers and consumers, however, does not free us from the conundrum that runs through this essay: "the critic may become the expository agent and contribute to this legacies' continuous impact and exploitation" regardless of intent.[16] The wrestling, however, must continue in order for practical theology to take raced bodies seriously.

[...]

Like writer and activist Darnell Moore, I am interested in the ways in which religious scholars have theorized or failed to theorize the "Black body." More specifically, I am interested in the places and ways our theorizing has dislocated the actual body from our discourse. More broadly, I am interested in how some bodies – black bodies – are allowed into the discourse as more "raced" than other bodies. In other words, black bodies, it seems to me, represent race and racism. Moore is helpful because he describes a communicating body that expresses its own discreet experiences. Thus, he argues for the body's subjectivity:

> Bodies speak. And if we attentively listen, we may perceive enchanting utterances or terrible articulations: deep bewailing; faded susurrations; or divine musings. Bodies emote. Every moment when tears spill from our eyes, cold chills race across the skin, and the heart thumps with the chest cavity, we bear witness to an emotive performance. Bodies remember. They are recorders of histories: recalling life's journeys, capturing ethereal groanings, calling forth blissful memories, summoning joys and pains, the hurts and the healings, that which we choose to remember and even that which we will to forget.[17]

Thus bodies have linguistic and evocative qualities; that is, bodies communicate subjectivity and produce responses that are context-specific and ripe with meanings. As a consequence of this communicative, evocative, and meaning producing ability, bodies' subjectivities can be altered and transformed, and they in turn affect the subjectivity of surrounding communicating bodies. Thus bodies engender subjectivities.

Shortly after the Ferguson killing of Michael Brown, two doctoral students at Vanderbilt Divinity School organized an exhibit and forum, "Nightmare On ~~Elm~~ Our Street." Courtney Bryant created a "Living Memorial" that my class on womanism attended. We struggled to take in the battered black and brown bodies. We made a slow meditation walk through the memorial of large sculptures of those who had been beaten or murdered by police. The walk was disruptive. Pictures and posters filled with quotations that most of us had heard before were now jarring when paired with sculptures. Some of the quotations are listed below.

Sign 4: Nearly two times every week in the United States, a police officer killed a black civilian, 2007–2012

Sign 5: Black males aged 15 to 19 are eight times as likely as white males to be gun homicide victims, 2009

Sign 6: "The idea of calling this poor young man [Michael Brown] unarmed when he was 6′4″, 300 pounds, full of muscles, apparently, according to what I read in the New York Times, on marijuana. To call him unarmed is like calling Sonny Liston unarmed or Cassius Clay unarmed. He wasn't unarmed. He was armed with his incredibly strong, scary self." ~ Ben Stein, Aug. 27, 2014

Sign 7: What does this mean for me?

Sign 8: Police are "barometers of the society in which they operate." Hubert Williams, former police director of Newark, N.J., and Patrick V. Murphy, former commissioner of the New York City Police Department, 1990

Sign 9: Black people are almost three times more likely than white people to be subjected to force or threatened with force by the police, 2008[18]

One person noted that initially she thought the experience would be like going to a museum, but instead the memorial "invaded" the space and forced a response. In a museum, one has time to ward off despair, anger, and hopelessness. The memorial had no "trigger warning."[19] The "nightmare on our streets" requires mourning and grieving. Bodies on display surrounded by quotations and statistics disrupted our sense of *knowing.* No longer could brown and black bodies under attack be an intellectual discussion of abstract methodologies, thought, and aims. Bodies displayed in the center of academic discourse – dead – were here made visible, visceral, animated. They became speaking bodies. What do dead but speaking bodies say to us? What are their demands? [...]

[...]

Bodies Formed to Speak

In 1994 I experienced a blatant form of racially based housing discrimination. As a Sister of Providence in my third year, I moved into an apartment with another sister – a white woman – with the landlord's agreement. Though he had not met me, he liked renting to nuns. He also assumed I was white. One week after moving in, his son met me, and that evening the owner called to say he needed us to move in a week because a family member needed the apartment. As it turned out, no family member was seeking housing; he simply did not want a black person living in the apartment. My body spoke in stammering communiqué. Slowly over a three-year period, beginning with a mediation process, and finally litigation, I went completely bald. I lost all the hair on my body except my eyebrows and lashes. Truthfully, I did not *think* about *going* bald; rather, I felt pangs of loss and rage as my hair was stolen from me. My dermatologist, an expert on alopecia areata, determined, after several forms of treatment, that I would probably remain bald for the rest of my life. At one point, when I had one round mound of hair about two inches wide and long left, he suggested we "just shave it off. The rest is not coming back." I refused, not because I thought that he was wrong but because I did not want to participate in the theft. He was quite "curious" because he had not seen such a case of alopecia areata from someone not experiencing some other form of medical illness.

Psychiatrist Laurence J. Kirmayer argues that "there are two orders of experience: the order of the body and the order of the text."[20] He argues that our aching bodies remind us of this, that "if the text stands for a hard-won rational order, imposed on thought through the careful composition of writing, the body provides a structure to thought that is, in part, extra-rational and disorderly. This extra-rational dimension to thought carries important information about emotional, aesthetic, and moral value."[21] His work is both a corrective to the absence of the body (especially in psychiatric and medical illness discourse) and further problematizes the body in relation to illness and society. In locating the body's "insistence on meaning" in the realm of the extra-rational, bodies that express the experiences related to or resulting from racism, sexism, hetero-sexism, or colorism subtly become marked as irrational. This problem is, of course, an old one that specifically and more readily marks black and brown bodies, women's bodies, transgendered bodies, and all bodies that do not reflect the bodies assumed to be white/male/heterosexual/body.

[...]

Racing Transgender Bodies

I am persuaded to consider transgender experience at this point as a further example of the conundrum concerning raced bodies because I have been interested in how the news outlets have covered Bruce Jenner's transition to being a transgender woman. His expensive and highly choreographed entrance on the Hollywood stage of "reality TV," touted as a generic transition process, is obviously problematic when viewed through the lens of race, gender, class, and sexuality. His photograph on *Vanity Fair* reproduces fantasies, mostly men's, of femininity, gender, and sexuality. Caitlyn's gender non-conformity and transformation is presented in stark contrast to the narrative of most transgender women of color. Sakia Gunn, a black fifteen year-old lesbian who identified as aggressive (very male identified), was murdered in 2003 when she rejected the sexual advances of a group of black men who attempted to "pick-up" Gunn and her friends. Her murder was a hate crime that barely made the local news.

I am not suggesting that these two women – one senior-aged and one still a teenager – did not both struggle mightily with expressing their identities. I am pointing out the obvious: Sakia Gunn, a black woman, was brutally murdered on the street, yet her murder was barely reported, and Caitlyn Jenner, a white transgender woman, is glamorized, making money, and experiencing considerable fame. A young black woman is unknown to many. A very privileged white woman is photographed and reported on multiple times a day. We are told her body is what women strive for – and in her transformation, and with a lot of money and social capital, she has achieved it.

Kelly Cogswell and Ana Simo offer a reason for Sakia's murder and its minimal coverage. It is not just white racism that renders Sakia invisible and unimportant as a black lesbian who resists oppressive notions of femininity and gender; it is the deeply hostile view that both blacks and whites hold toward black queers that reproduces violence against queer bodies: "The reason why Sakia Gunn was killed, and why her murder has faded from the headlines, is that both whites and blacks wish young black queers would disappear. Until things change, they will, thanks to violence, and AIDS, and hate."[22] What is apparent is that some nonconforming gendered raced bodies, black and brown, remain targets of violence and hate while other white raced bodies with financial and social standing are given a space of public acceptance. The conundrum emerges in recognizing the racism and classism present in the public dismissal of Sakia Gunn's murder and the racial, sexist, and classist privilege afforded Caitlyn Jenner.[...]

[...]

Malformed White Bodies' Lived Experience

Contrary to the common ideation that the racing of bodies is predominantly a phenomena limited to brown and black bodies, everyone and every group is subject to racing in the US context. However, there is variation and variety in the life of the raced body. Some of the variation and variety is due to color, gender, racial classification, class, ethnicity, sexual orientation, and education. What might these bodies be telling us?

[A] photo taken by Todd Robertson in 1992 [shows a] very young child wearing KKK attire and staring at his reflection in a black state trooper's guard shield. We cannot know but are compelled to ask, what might this child experience, and how might it influence his formation as a white child to see such a reflection of himself? We might also ask, what might the black officer experience during this occasion of protecting the KKK's right to march? And finally, the child's mother, whose back is to the viewer of the photo is almost on the periphery, dressed in black. We cannot see her expression.

In [a] 1959 picture [of] the integration of the school system by the "Little Rock Nine," [we see] two Little Rock, Arkansas, white children. The angry adults and the mob festering with rage immediately draw our attention. But [if we look closer, we see] two children: a white girl to the viewer's left, with her face turned away from the crowd and their line of gaze, and the boy to the right behind the flag, his hands clasped together on top of his forehead. Unlike the adults, these children seem to be experiencing something very different from the adults. Is the girl being formed or forced to turn away from white mob behavior or to not notice or to experience her own full affective experience? How are hers, and the boy's, white bodily responses relevant or represented in the work of practical theology? How is their bodily presence integral to their formation?

In [another] photograph, [we see a] black reporter, L. Alex Wilson, who was then editor of the Memphis, Tennessee-based office of *The Defender*, cover[ing] the Little Rock story. While there, he was repeatedly attacked.[23] Will Counts, who also took many photographs we have come to associate with that crisis, took the photograph. The white crowd behind Wilson and the unnamed white man who is "riding" Wilson's back all reproduce various representations of raced bodies: Wilson is straddled like a horse and resists being ridden. The crowd, some adjacent with the bulk following have an investment in Wilson's submission. I ask of the photograph(er): what are you telling us about white and black bodies? And, are you seeking to reveal, transform, or solely represent the power dynamics between white and black raced bodies? Or is the photographer a disinterested, objective conveyor of images? While I may be employing what Ayo Abletou Coty describes as a "postcolonial response to colonial representations"[24] of white and black bodies, I must also ask: have I only reproduced raced bodies in an already culturally embedded and socially established asymmetrical power relation? These kinds of quandaries and questions about raced bodies in society and in practical theology have given me pause, and at times lead me to despair.

What then is the conundrum with which I struggle? Can we take up raced bodies in our work as practical theologians? Will these images of white racism in action, while generally invisible as a daily dynamic, reveal, transform, or reproduce stereotypes and icons of terror? Although in practical theology we are able to analyze race, gender, and sexuality, I wonder whether we are able to represent fully lived raced bodies in our scholarship – our texts – without benefiting from the underside of "images, icons, and ideologies" in the name of research. The academy demands texts but we are faced with profound limits. One limit is that the "ideology of whiteness becomes actualized and normalized to the point of invisibility by way of language, media culture, and schooling."[25] Strangely enough, it is not just whiteness that becomes actualized and normalized into invisibility: black bodily experiences are conscripted into maintaining the invisibility of whiteness. This conscription occurs through the calculated establishment of norms that reflect an unacknowledged culture of whiteness. And this culture of whiteness moves among us in bodily forms and cultural practices.

This is not a new conundrum for me: Over fifteen years ago, I wrote a dissertation entitled *Fleshing the Theory: A Critical Analysis of Select Theories of the Body in Light of Black Women's Experience.* The generally understood task of scholarship – theological and otherwise – replaces the body's experience of race and of being a raced body with text, words, and a certain distance. It is not lost on me that in most of the news stories, YouTube videos of protesters and police responses, and "on the street" interviews concerning Michael Brown and his death, so very little was said about his body, riddled with bullets bleeding lying in the street. However, after the grand jury failed to indict the officer, his mother said, "this could be your child. This could be anybody's child."[26] What as practical theologians do we hear being said to our field when we join Mrs. Brown staring at her black teenaged son riddled with bullets on a street in Ferguson, Missouri? Do we replace violated bodies with abstract theological questions and categories "appropriate" for and required by the scholarly guilds that claim our allegiance? Yes, it may be that our academic settings demand this of us. However, sometimes, it is a truth-telling act if we do not comply with that demand. The specter of raced bodies looms over practical theology – powerfully felt but unseen – and demands critical responses.

The Ethical Demands of Raced Bodies for Practical Theology

Liturgy of Terror

Liturgy: the work of the people; public work; public practices with intention[27]
The Word: Black bodies
What if we were to admit we are living in exile from God –?
What if we were to confess that violence, the wielding of guns, and bloodshed – the liturgy of terror – is sin?
What if we were to examine the liturgy of terror as is it used for sadistic pleasure,

Raced Bodies (2016) | 153

[*Why was he licking his lips?*],
psychic relief – through domination –
to escape the ethical demands of the day – and admit: It is evil?
What kind of people would we know our selves to be – living among?[28]

The metaethical: The fact of the lived experience of raced bodies demands both a meta-ethical and normative turn in practical theology. Such shifts are not easy to make. Rather than pursue the epistemological question (what can we know from the body?) or a theological one (how do actual physical bodies shape religious and theological knowledge?[29]), I am making an ethical inquiry: what do raced bodies require *of* us as individuals and communities? Bodies formed to speak surely make ethical claims. The ethical turn is to include the reality of raced bodies while not reproducing the widespread stereotypes. But this ethical demand also insists that practical theology's scholarship more fully represent and engage scholars whose experiences and scholarship is not white and situated in other dominant categories. Moral theologian and womanist M. Shawn Copeland is helpful in her discussion of "racism and the vocation of the Christian theologian." The vocation of the Christian theologian is to hold tightly

> the spirit-filled, prophetic, critical, and creative edge... our theology must stand with society's most abject, despised, and oppressed... In the twilight of American culture, telling the truth about white racist supremacy is a theological obligation, no matter how cauterizing those truths may be. To speak about theology as truth-telling is to accentuate its core responsibility..."[30]

The question for practical theologians is: what do raced bodies require of our practical theology? The struggle to take on this inquiry, and how to do it, brings to mind womanist ethicist Katie Cannon's description of her task as an ethicist: The work of the black womanist ethicist is to "debunk, unmask, and disentangle the historically conditioned value judgments and power relations that undergird the particularities of race, sex, and class oppression."[31]

Furthermore, Cannon questions "an unspoken informal code within the guild that the Black woman academician must engage in... abstract moral discourse or else she runs the risk of being misunderstood, misinterpreted, and frequently devalued."[32] A similar concern grabs my attention; that is, is there a code within practical theology that demands that we treat raced bodies as invisible and, as a consequence, as having no moral agency? Invisible raced bodies without moral agency cannot make moral demands of our discipline or of lived raced bodies. Thus, raced bodies are rendered morally neutral, lacking moral action and lacking moral value. Such a rendering of raced bodies then means they can be missed or mistreated in our scholarship in whatever way serves our disciplinary and professional purposes. Cannon is of further assistance when she notes that, "When ethical discourse provides truncated and distorted pictures of Black women, the society at large uses these oppressive stereotypes to define what it is to be Black and female in America."[33] She highlights our dilemma – a practical theology that ignores raced bodies is morally defunct and supplies society with a means to reproduce negative images that buttress oppressive structural (legal, religious, and relational) practices. Practical theology is complicit in silence and the failure to recognize moral agency of raced bodies. The other side of the conundrum is how should practical theology engage raced bodies and be accountable to their ethical demands while contending with the reality that such efforts can be exploited to reinforce racial cultural dynamics? The conundrum notwithstanding, a practical theology emerging from ethical commitments to articulating lived experience and the transformation of practices of oppression must turn to raced bodies as a central feature of our work.

The ethical turn here is very much connected to the conundrum of this chapter. The explicit question, "what do raced bodies require *of* practical theology?" is new and reiterates the conundrum. Practical theology requires an architecture that takes raced bodies seriously and makes raced bodies visible; however, in making raced bodies visible, dynamic, and powerful enough to evoke the transformation of communities, individuals, and religious and spiritual practices, it risks reproducing the very raced and racist ideologies it seeks to eradicate in the service of justice.

The resistance to recognizing the ethical demands of black bodies is significant. Most recently, for instance, resistance is evident in the linguistic culture wars between the Black Lives Matter movement and the counter messages of the All Lives Matter movement. Black Lives Matter, a movement that insists that black bodies matter and have moral value and agency, is a response to police violence against black children, men, and women. It claims that murdered black bodies should make ethical demands on society and the justice system. The shift to All Lives Matter seeks to undo the ethical demands by ignoring and erasing the larger social context that perpetuates the message that black lives do not matter and may be subjected to arbitrary and lethal violence. Thus, the All Lives Matter response actually reproduces white moral norms that are ineffectual for articulating a vision of the world where black lives really do matter. In actuality, All Lives Matter reinvigorates practices that are ultimately designed to protect white bodies by ignoring the broad social context of police brutality against black and brown bodies. The social location, and therefore the very different experiences, of lived raced bodies are rendered ethically irrelevant. If we are to turn toward the ethical task in this conundrum, we have to ask on the front end of our work what difference raced bodies make for/in practical theology, certainly in the scholarship on the body and embodiment, but also on the whole enterprise called practical theology. We will not be freed from the conundrum of raced bodies on display in our work but we will bear witness to the lived experiences of dismissed raced bodies and the discipline's history of complicity. In the process, we just may transform the scholarship, membership, and practices of the discipline.

Notes

1 "Definition of Conundrum," accessed November 20, 2014, http://www.meni.am-webster.com/dictionary/conundrum.
2 Emilie M. Townes, Introduction to Katie Geneva Cannon and Kristine A Culp, "Appropriation and Reciprocity in the Doing of Womanist Ethics," *The Annual of the Society of Christian Ethics* 13 (1993), 187.
3 Phillis Isabella Sheppard, "Mourning the Loss of Cultural Selfobjects: Black Embodiment and Religious Experience after Trauma," *Practical Theology* I, no. 2 (2008): 233–57; Phillis Isabella Sheppard, *Self,Culture, and Others in Womanist Practical Theology* (London, UK: Palgrave Macmillan, 2011); Bonnie Miller-McLemore, "Embodied

Knowing, Embodied Theology: What Happened to the Body?" *Journal of Pastoral Psychology* 62 (2013): 743–58; Stephanie Crumpton, *A Womanist Pastoral Theology Against Intimate and Cultural Violence* (New York: Palgrave Macmillan, 2013).

4 "For example, Asian Indians were determined by the courts to be non-white in 1909, white in 1910 and 1913, non-white in 1917, white again in 1919 and 1920, but non-white after 1923." Brian K. Obach, "Demonstrating The Social Construction of Race," (1999), http://www.asanet.org/ introtosociology/Documents/TSObacln999.pdf. Also see Noel Ignatiev, *How the Irish Became White* (NY: Routledge, 1995); Ian F. Haney-Lopez, "The Social Construction of Race: Some Observations on Illusion, Fabrication, and Choice," *Harvard Civil Rights-Civil Liberties Law Review* 29, no. 1 (1994), Ruth Frankenberg, *White Women, Race Matters: The Social Construction of Whiteness* (Minneapolis: University of Minnesota Press, 1993).

5 Evelyn L. Parker, "Womanist Theory" in *The Wiley Blackwell Companion to Practical Theology*, ed. Bonnie J. Miller-Mclemore (Oxford: Blackwell Publishing, 2012), accessed August 30, 2015, http://www.blackwellreference.com/subscriber/tocnode.html?id= g9781444330823_chunk_g978144433082320.

6 Joyce McDougall, *Theatre of the Body: A Psychoanalytic Approach to Psychosomatic Illness* (New York: W.W. Norton, 1989) and Janine Chasseguet-Smirgel, *Sexuality and Mind: The Role of the Father and the Mother in the Psyche* (London: Kamac, 1989). See also Chasseguet-Smirgel, *Female Sexuality: New Psychoanalytic Views* (London: Kamac, 1992).

7 Phillis Isabella Sheppard, *Self Culture and Others in Womanist Practical Theology* (New York: Palgrave Macmillan, 2011); Markeva Hill, *Womanism Against Socially-Constructed Matriarchal Images: A Theoretical Model Towards a Therapeutic Goal* (New York: Palgrave Macmillan, 2012); and Stephanie Crumpton, *A Womanist Pastoral Theology Against Intimate and Cultural Violence* (Basingstoke: Palgrave Macmillan, 2014).

8 Sander Gilman, "Black Bodies, White Bodies: Toward an Iconography of Female Sexuality in Late Nineteenth-Century Art, Medicine and Literature," *Critical Inquiry* 12, no.10 (1985), 204–42.

9 James Allen, *Without Sanctuary: Lynching Photography in America* (New Mexico: Twin Palms Publishers, 1999), plate 57. To comprehend my argument, I encourage readers to view the photos.

10 Emmanuel Lartey, "Postcolonial African Practical Theology: Rituals of Remembrance, Cleansing, Healing and Re-Connection" *The Journal of Pastoral Theology* 21, no. 2 (2011): 1–17; 4.

11 Amy Louise Wood, *Lynching and Spectacle: Witnessing Racial Violence in America, 1890–1940* (North Carolina: University of North Carolina Press, 2009), 59–67.

12 Lee H. Butler, "Lynching: A Post-Traumatic Stressor in a Protracted-Traumatic World," *Sacred Spaces: The e-Journal of the American Association of Pastoral Counselors* 4 (2012): 8.

13 Jay-Paul Hinds, "Traces on the Blackboard: The Vestiges of Racism on the African American Psyche," *Pastoral Psychology* 59 (2010), 783–98.

14 Christraud M. Geary, "The Black Female Body, The Postcard and the Archives," in *Black Womanhood: Images, Icons, and Ideologies of the African Body*, ed. Barbara Thompson (Seattle, Washington: University of Washington Press, 2008), 144.

15 Geary, "The Black Female Body," 148.

16 Geary, "The Black Female Body," 158.

17 Darnell L. Moore, "Theorizing the 'Black Body' as a Site of Trauma: Implications for Theologies of Embodiment," *Theology and Sexuality* 15, no. 2 (2009),175–88.

18 Curated by Courtney Bryant (2014), Vanderbilt Divinity School doctoral student in Ethics and Society as part of the "Nightmare on ~~Elm~~ Our Street."

19 Trigger warnings are statements appearing on some syllabi that inform students that they may be affected by the class content. There is considerable debate around their usefulness and their impact on the learning and teaching environment.

20 Laurence J. Kirmayers, "The Body's Insistence on Meaning: Metaphor as Presentation and Representation in Illness Experience" *Medical Anthropology Quarterly* 6, no. 4 (1992), 323.

21 Kinnayers, "The Body's Insistence," 325.

22 Kelly Cogswell and Ana Simo, "Erasing Sakia Who's to Blame?" *The Gully Online Magazine,* 2003, accessed May 3, 2015, https://web.archive.org/web/20130509035706/, http://www. thegully.com/essays/gaymundo/030606_sakia_gunn_murder.html.

23 Will Counts" Photograph, taken September 23, 1957 Indiana University Bloomington Archives Photograph Collection, image number Poo26614 http://webappullib.indiana.edu/archivesphotos/results/item.do?itemId = Poo266I4-&searchId = 1&search ResultIndex = 4.

24 Ayo Abletou Coly, "Housing and Homing the Black Female Body in France: Calixthe Beyala and the Legacy of Sarah Baartman and Josephine Baker," in *Black Womanhood: Images, Icons, and Ideologies of the African Body,* ed. Barbara Thompson (Seattle, WA: University of Washington Press, 2008), 275.

25 Monica Beatriz deMello Patterson, "America's Racial Unconscious: The Invisibility of Whiteness," in *White Reign: Deploying Whiteness in America,* ed. Joe L. Kincheloe, Shirley Steinberg, and Ronald Chennault (New York: St. Martin's Press, 1998).

26 Dana Ford and Josh Levs, "Michael Brown's Mother: This Could be Your Child," *CNN News,* 2014, accessed November 27, 2014, http://www.cnn.com/2014/11/26/justice/ferguson-grand-jury-reaction/.

27 See William T. Cavanaugh, "The Work of the People as Public Work: The Social Significance of the Liturgy," *Institute of Liturgical Studies Occasional Papers,* 2008, accessed May 1, 2015, http://scholar.valpo.edu/cgi/viewcontent.cgi?article=1003&context=ils_papers; Delores S. Williams, "Rituals of Resistance in Womanist Worship," in *Women at Worship: Interpretations of North American Diversity,* ed. Marjorie Procter-Smith and Janet R. Walton (Louisville, KY: Westminster/John Knox Press, 1993), 215–23; and http://www.allsoulscville.com/sites/default/files/web/Liturgy_Drarna%20and%20Work"/42oof%20Worship.pdf, accessed May 2, 2015.

28 Phillis Isabella Sheppard, "Liturgy of Terror;" author's unpublished poem, 2015.

29 Bonnie Miller-McLemore, "Embodied Knowing, Embodied Theology: What Happened to the Body?" *Journal of Pastoral Psychology* 62 (2013), 743

30 "M. Shawn Copeland, "Racism and the Vocation of the Christian Theologian," *Spiritus* 2 (2002): 21.

31 Katie G. Cannon, "Hitting a Straight Lick with a Crooked Stick: The Womanist Dilemma in the Development of a Black Liberation Ethic," *The Annual of the Society of Christian Ethics* 7 (1987), 165.

32 Cannon, "Hitting a Straight Lick," 166.

33 Cannon, "Hitting a Straight Lick,"167.

11

Knowing Through Moving (2016)*
Emmanuel Y. Lartey

Introduction

A senior scholar at Emory University, Emmanuel Y. Lartey's contributions to pastoral and practical theology are immense. His early works, *Pastoral Theology in an Intercultural World* (1987) and *In Living Color: An Intercultural Approach to Pastoral Care and Counseling* (1997), underscore the intercultural context of care, expanding the threefold lexicon for pastoral theology's history as a movement from *classical* to *clinical* to *communal* paradigms. From the beginning, *intercultural* has meant far more than cross-cultural exchange; it depicts a complex polyphonic subjectivity constituted at the intersection of multiple cultures. As someone who grew up in Ghana, traveled to Britain for higher education, and now resides in the United States, he knows this fluidity personally. More than anyone else, Lartey brings a world orientation to the discipline. His latest book, *Postcolonializing God: An African Practical Theology* (2013) builds on this scholarly trajectory, using his unique position to transform the ongoing damage of colonization, reclaiming indigenous African spiritual knowledge, and revealing a conceptualization of divinity that celebrates diversity and contests hegemonies.

In this entry, Lartey knowingly ventures into risky territory. He investigates knowing through the body in religious rituals, dance, drumming, music, and movement in Africa and the African Diaspora, exploring a kind of bodily knowing that does "not fit neatly into Euro-American categories," knowledge marked by Western "dismissiveness" but verified and studied by anthropologists. Lartey has a heart for pastoral care, and so his essay grows out of a deep desire to understand healing. But he moves from a description of healing rituals to their epistemological and ontological implications for theological construction. What do traditional African healers in Ghana and the African diaspora "know and how do they know it?" he asks, and "how is this [knowledge] different from classic Western means of diagnosis and treatment?"

Traditional healers possess a body-centered orientation to discernment that blends repeated kinesthetic action and scientific and religious insight into the world seen and unseen. *Proprioception* is the term for sensate information that requires movement, rhythm, and enactment, also described by anthropologist Katherine Geurts as a "sixth

Original publication details: Emmanuel Y. Lartey, "Knowing Through Moving: African Embodied Epistemologies," pp. 1–23 from *Sensing Sacred*, ed. Jennifer Baldwin (Lanham, Maryland: Rowman and Littlefield, 2016).

sense" or a sense of knowing something without being able to account for how one knows it. Among the people of southeast Ghana, how one carries oneself, how one balances objects on one's head, distinguishes humans from other creatures and even reflects one's moral character. Ways of moving are inextricably tied to ways of thinking, including moral reasoning, and dancing and drumming have the capacity to convey a great deal of knowledge of a variety of sorts, including divine meaning and messages. Lartey encourages practical theologians to seek better hermeneutical means for reading such knowledge.

Suggested Further Reading

- Emmanuel Y. Lartey, *Postcolonializing God: An African Practical Theology* (London: SCM, 2013).
- Abraham Adu Berinyuu, *Pastoral Care to the Sick in Africa: An Approach to Transcultural Pastoral Theology* (Frankfurt: Peter Lang, 1988).
- Aimé Césaire, *Discourse on Colonialism*, trans. Joan Pinkham (New York, Monthly Review Press, 1972).

***

Over the past decade I have been engaged in a study of the spirituality and practices of some African traditional healers located in Ghana and in the African diaspora in the Americas. The questions that have inspired my study are the following: What do they actually do in the quest to bring healing to their clients? What do they know and how do they know it? How do they diagnose or recognize the nature of the illnesses they treat? By what means do they come to a diagnosis? How is this different from classic Western means of diagnosis and treatment? What are their forms of understanding and knowledge? How do they engage their patients in healing? What treatments do they offer and why? How do they know what is wrong and what to do about it? I am interested in the priest-healers' ways of knowing, and basically how they know what they know. I am researching what they know, their means of determining what is worth knowing. I wish to know how they evaluate and come to a judgment of what is needed and then how they use this knowledge. In a word, I have been researching the traditional healer's epistemology. Though there is a fairly extensive literature especially from the field of anthropology in this area, I have sought to give greater priority to the voice of practitioners than that of theorists. This chapter represents a relatively short account of a particular dimension of, a brief reflexive engagement with, and a reflection from a practical theological perspective upon the epistemology of African religious practitioners on the continent of Africa and in the African Diaspora in the Americas.

In traditional African society, though, there are variations on this theme; the healer is also a priest or priestess. Conversely, no one is a priest/ess who is not also a healer. One is considered to be spiritually adept and a "great priest/ess" only if one brings, out of one's spiritual exercises, specific benefits for the living community. Moreover, one attains the honored status of ancestorhood following one's death by virtue of the good one has done for the living community during one's earthy sojourn. This study has brought me to the heart of African religion and spirituality – a central understanding of which is that the well-being of the human person and community is the focus and purpose of spiritual or religious activities. For African religious practitioners, the spiritual and the material are fused. The unseen and the seen realms are related. The natural and the divine are in constant interaction. African religious practitioners' theology, spirituality, discernment, and practice are all of one piece. As a pastoral counselor deeply interested in theological and spiritual practices of care and therapy, I am intrigued at how Divine – human communication is so central and spirituality so essential in African traditional practices of healing and health promotion. As I have listened intensely and participated in the rituals and practices of African religious practitioners, what has been most fascinating for me is that instead of a logo-centric, word-based theory from which is derived particular practices, African priest-healers seem to know through a different means, a means more bodily, more incarnational, and especially more kinesthetic. Their knowledge seemed to be through bodies-in-motion. *Proprioception,* the term used to describe the sensory information that contributes to the sense of position of self and movement, seems to mark the key to human ontology and epistemology in African traditional and diasporan religious practice. I am struck by the centrality of rhythmic bodily movement in their rituals of discernment, diagnosis, and healing. This is the case not only in the continental practice of African Religious Traditions (ARTs) but intriguingly also prominently in the African diaspora in the "New World" of the Americas and the Caribbean. As such it is upon proprioception, especially rhythmic body movement in the practice of African sacred ritual, that I wish to focus in this chapter.

The presence of the divine is signaled by particular forms of expressive movement within the bodies of priests, priestesses, diviners, or on occasion ordinary participants of a ritual. Although I have much familiarity with what anthropologists have long referred to as "possession," or what psychologists have dubbed "trance-states," and have consulted many texts that seek to throw light on this highly observable feature of African religious life, I was drawn to and paid attention to these phenomena because of the closeness of these forms of manifestation to the diagnostic and therapeutic activities of African practitioners of healing. What is of significance for me is how rhythmic bodily movement becomes a means by which the sacred healers come to some knowledge of what is at stake in the rituals of healing.

Anthropologist Kathryn Geurts engaged in ethnographic study among the Anlo-Ewe people of South-East Ghana for twelve years. In her *Culture and the Senses: Bodily Ways of Knowing in an African Community,* she writes of becoming aware of what she describes as a "sixth sense" which the Ewe people appeared to recognize and develop. This "sense" was a way of knowing through and in the body. Whilst trying to capture what she was becoming aware of as a sensing or sense, Geurts came to realize that one discrete lexical term for "the senses" did not seem to exist in the Anlo-Ewe language.[1] Rather, what appeared to be used most frequently by her informants "was the very complicated and polysemous term, *seselelame.*"[2] "*Seselelame*" (which can be translated loosely as "feeling in the body"), Geurts claims, "is best understood in reference to what Thomas Csordas has called 'somatic modes of attention.'"[3] Difficult if not impossible to translate into English, *seselelame,* Geurts continues "is an ideal illustration of a culturally elaborated way in which many Anlo speaking people attend to and read their own bodies while simultaneously orienting themselves to objects, to the environment, and to the bodies of those around them."[4] Geurts comes to understand that *seselelame* refers to various kinds of sensory embodiment that do not fit neatly into Euro-American categories.

> On the one hand, it seems to refer to a specific sense or kind of physical sensation that we might call tingling in the skin (sometimes a symptom of impending illness), but in other instances it is used to describe sexual arousal, heartache, or even passion. In other contexts it refers to a kind of inspiration (to dance or to speak), but it can also be used to describe something akin to intuition (when unsure of exactly how you are coming by some information). Finally, people used it to refer to a generalized (almost synesthetic) *feeling in or through the body,* and it was proposed by some as a possible translation for the English term *sense.*[5]

The Anlo-Ewe term *seselelame,* then, conveys "hearing or feeling within the body, flesh or skin" – a way of experiencing and receiving knowledge through in-the-body sensation.[6] Geurts reports on the basis of her careful and intensive ethnographic investigation that *seselelame* was sometimes used to refer to experiences that were bodily based and that corresponded to the English concept of proprioception. But at other times it seemed akin to "intuition" or even what might be termed "extra-sensory perception." She writes,

> Anlo-speaking people often described sensations for this kind of *seselelame* as uncanny feelings or messages they received that turned out to be a premonition. Examples include *seselelame* as a source of motivation to visit a relative right before he died or as confirming the presence of an ancestor at a specific communal event. A "message" was usually associated with these kinds of *seselelame* experiences, and for that reason people often linked it to the English term for "hearing." They spoke of hearing a message or hearing information not through their ears but throughout their entire being; they somehow "knew something" but could not really account for how they knew it. This kind of *seselelame* was considered deeper and more mysterious than specific bodily sensations and was not necessarily attributed to them.[7]

Agbagbadodo

Another Anlo-Ewe term that Geurts discusses is *Agbagbadodo,* which essentially denotes balancing a load, and a sense of balance in the Anlo-Ewe language.[8] The verb *do agbagba* means "to carry something on the head without touching it with the hands." A second usage of this expression has to do with "a baby's act of raising up on two feet and not falling over," for example, to balance their body on two legs.[9] This skill, acquired in infancy, is so important that to never learn how to do it relegates an individual to the level of an animal – crawling on four legs – and not that of a human being. For the Anlo-Ewe, therefore, *agbagbadodo* (roughly translated as balancing) is an essential feature of their definition of being human. Only humans have this capacity, and it is a means of distinguishing humans from other sentient beings. Now this brings to mind the very obvious and evident oft-depicted view of West African peoples in particular seen balancing objects on top of their heads while walking through a market or down a street; a basket filled with mangoes, a bucket of water, a bundle of firewood, a tray of carefully stacked oranges, etcetera. For the Anlo-Ewe people, standing upright, balancing, being able to balance things on one's head without the use of one's hands whilst walking, are distinguishing skills of the human. Proprioception, therefore, for the Anlo-Ewe people is an ontological and anthropologically defining characteristic.

Azɔlizɔzɔ

The English term *kinesthesia* comes from the Greek words *kinein,* which means "to move," and *aesthesis,* which means "perception." Kinesthesia is therefore etymologically "perception through movement;" in other words, knowledge through movement. This is a commonly understood and discussed phenomenon among dancers. [...] Like dancers, many Anlo-speaking people Geurts found "valued movement and believed that much could be perceived and understood by and about a person through his or her carriage or walk."[10] The Ewe term *zɔ* refers to movement first and foremost and is applied to various forms of movement. Anlo-Ewe speakers associate the term *zɔ* with the phenomena of generalized movement of living bodies, essentially meaning to walk, to travel, to move. Westermann's dictionary of Ewe translates *azɔlizɔzɔ* as "walking, marching or gait." Geurts observes:

> In fact, walking (*azɔlizɔzɔ* or *azɔlinu*) carried such significance that the Anlo-Ewe language contained dozens of ways symbolically essentializing the style or the manner in which a person walks or moves. For instance *zɔ lugulugu* referred to walking as if drunk; walking *kadzakadza* implied the majestic movement of a lion.[11]

Walking is not merely a method of transport or a purely practical thing. It involves movement and gestures that emanate from the whole body. As Geurts learned, there is a *proper* manner for an Anlo woman to walk, for instance. *Azɔlizɔzɔ* is not limited to the propelling action of the legs, but involves choreographic dynamics implicating the whole body. For many Anlo-Ewe a person's character and moral fiber are revealed, embodied, and expressed in his or her walk or mode of comportment. "The term *azɔlime* referred literally to the way or style in which a person moved and behaved, while it also denoted manner or course of life, deportment, nature, and disposition."[12] Geurts's conclusion aptly sums up the matter: "[I]n Anlo epistemological traditions and ontological practices, bodily movements specifically in the form of reified kinds of walks are instrumentally tied to forms of thinking and reasoning, especially about moral character."[13]

Bodily movement then is a vehicle that transmits knowledge concerning humanity. The movement of our bodies conveys ethical and ontological knowledge which can be valuable in all arenas of human life. The African Traditional healers in my research concur with this Anlo-Ewe insight. Many speak very expressively about the "wisdom of the body,"[14] and utilize their knowledge of "body language" in both diagnostic and therapeutic treatment of patients in their care. Africa's sacred healers recognize the somatization of psychic illness in diseased or dysfunctional movement patterns. They prescribe forms of movement, including dance and ritual performance, to correct what has gone awry in the souls and bodies of patients, often to very beneficial effect. In the African Diaspora in the Americas these insights appear in the innovative religious activities evident in the new geographical locations of Africa's peoples.

African Religious Diaspora

Yvonne Daniel, anthropologist, ethnomusicologist, and professor of Dance and African American Studies has for over thirty-five years been studying the religious practices of diasporan Africans in Haiti, Cuba, and Bahia, Brazil. In a well-researched and carefully documented book titled *Dancing Wisdom: Embodied Knowledge in Haitian Vodou, Cuban Yoruba, and Bahian Candomble,* she presents the fruits of persistent participant observation of three faith communities of African origins in the Americas since 1974. She directs researchers and others interested in these religious phenomena to the dance/music practices found in their worship rituals. Daniel declares, "for the communities I study...it is most often the dance/music behavior within ritual behavior that continually reties the worshipping community to its spiritual affinity."[15] Daniel shows how the "divinities of these African American religions receive dance/music offerings within religious rites, and come to dance with the believing community."[16]

Brazil, which demographically is the nation with the largest number of persons of African origins outside of the African continent, is home to the religious tradition known as *Candomblé*, a Yoruba-based religious practice that is also called Nago/Ketu because of the prominence of particular Yoruba peoples within the practice. The term *Candomblé* itself is variously traced to Central Africa as well as Portuguese language and is said to refer both to "ritual drum music" and to "dance in honor of the deities."[...]

Yvonne Daniel correctly directs us to the centrality of dance movement and music in any description or appropriation of African American life, pointing out that dance movement and music interconnect and, while making reference to dimensions of the social life, are pivotal to spirituality and spiritual development in African diasporan cultures.[17] She points out that dance and music performances in the contexts of these religious rituals, far from being engaged in exclusively for their entertainment value, have multiple levels of meaning embedded within them. Says Daniel,

> Patterns of movement and body rhythms are organized and integrated formulaically with specific instrumentation and call-and-response singing. Performance spaces are washed, decorated, and blessed – often with chalked or painted artistic lines or circular configurations that are drawn on objects, on earthen floors, or in the air.[18]

"Dance and music," she continues, "communicate through multiple sensory channels and thereby contain, symbolize, and emit many levels of meaning." Daniel confirms Ajayi's finding that, similar to the Anlo-Ewes (of Ghana and Togo), "to discover meaning in normal communication, Yorubas (of Nigeria) concentrate on keen scrutiny of the body."[19] In her ethnographic studies, Daniel too found that "Yoruba-derived and Fon-derived Americans regularly sense and adjudicate the meanings of the dancing body."[20] Daniel discovers that for the worshippers in the communities she studied, "dance rituals create religious, social, and galactic (of the entire cosmos) harmony."[21]

To my amazement, delight, and enlightenment, Daniel expresses out of the American contexts she has been involved with the very same things I, as well as other researchers such as Marion Kilson and Margaret Field, discovered in my research among Gã and Akan traditional priest/healers in West Africa.[22] Daniel articulates this discovery in words deserving of extensive quotation:

> In the process of dance/music performances in Haitian Vodou, Cuban Yoruba, and Bahian Candomblé, social cohesion results among the living, the ancestors, and the cosmological divinities. Ritual performances are filled with what I call 'social medicine:' power, authority, and community relations are affected, re-arranged, or affirmed; social wounds are healed; each community member is accounted for; and the ritual community continues with strong bonds. The spiritual dimension of performance is connected to the social well-being of individuals and to the solidarity of a social community. Regular, repetitive ceremonial performances function as holistic medicine for community members.[23]

In these religious traditions worshippers generally view ritual dance/music performances as "sacred offerings."[24] The congregation performs the dances until diviners or specialists in expressing and interpreting divine manifestation begin to emerge among the worshipping community. These adepts then lead and intensify the performance, moving the ceremony forward from ritual behavior toward transcendence and transformation. From the perspective of the worshippers, Daniel found that the dance/music performances are presented simultaneously to the human and the communities of the divinities in the hope of transformations that will bring dancing divinities from the spiritual world into the worshipping community. Human dancers at this point dance in sync with the divinities expressing in their bodily movement divine messages.

Daniel pointedly observes that the religious communities she has been studying have encouraged attention to both cognitive (theoretical) and kinesthetic (embodied) knowledge. Because they do not subscribe to Euro-American mind/body dualism, which emphasizes the mental and theoretical over the experiential and kinesthetic, these African American ritual communities do not reject science and theoretical knowledge for experiential knowledge. Instead they incorporate all sorts of knowledge within bodily and ritual practice. In fact some Candomblé priestesses cited by anthropologist Sheila Walker refer to the Candomblé as both a religious system and a science.[25] Afro-Bahian philosopher Edson Nunes da Silva recognizes, discusses, and analyzes the Candomblé as a religious system, "the foundation of which is a complex science of life and nature… some of which is yet unknown to present day science."[26] In her fieldwork, Daniel found that leaders referred to an understanding of the forces of nature and the universe as *orichas, orixās,* or *lwas.* This parallels Yoruba understandings of the divine beings called the *orishas* as being both spiritual entities and forces of nature.

In the religious communities Daniel studied in Haiti, Cuba, and Bahia, regular, routine ceremonial performances have been developed that concentrate heavily on the human body and on what she terms "the suprahuman body." This is how she characterizes the suprahuman body:

> A suprahuman body is the result of spiritual transformation, when the worshipping, believing, and dancing human body is prepared for or overwhelmed by the

arrival of spiritual force. The dancing human body proceeds to unfold spiritual energy, or in believers' understanding, to present or manifest divinities, who are aspects of a Supreme Divinity. Beauty salon operators and truck drivers, as well as journalists and lawyers, are transformed in the ritual setting into suprahuman bodies; they dance beautifully and forcefully in order to give expression to spiritual forces, which then give advice to the community.[27]

Daniel identifies two distinct tendencies in African American ritual dance. In one, there is a reliance on gestures and movement sequences that come from the heritage of a particular ethnic group such as the Fon, Yoruba, Gã, or Kongo-Angola; in the other, the reliance is upon abstract expressions within the dancing body. In both cases ritual performance involves movement vocabulary that is structured. Particular gestures and movement phrases occur with the sounding of specific rhythms and have a specific cultural or religious meaning. For example, in African communities that possess and play "talking drums," dancers and musicians relate stories, parables, and myths from their understanding of the drums in combination with specific movement sequences and their relationship to tonal languages. This is possible because the tones of the talking drums relate to linguistic structures and replicate speech patterns. Yet, as observed by several ethnomusicologists, the alternative practice of abstract or non-codified movement and non-talking, drum-based dance is also part of the African heritage. Both kinds of drumming practices and both kinds of movement sequences can and do lead dancers to convey various aspects of myth, history, and narrative.

Daniel observes that in religious and secular settings dancers and musicians are placed together in "deep, improvisational performance" such as in instrumental jazz music.[28] Jazz dance, for instance, participates in a theme in sound and movement, an overarching series of rhythms, an accumulating series of movements, and changing and projected emotional states, all of which are abstracted and combined to constitute meaning. Similarly, in Haitian Vodou, Cuban Yoruba, and Bahian Candomble, "some gestures and movement sequences signal a literal meaning, but more often the social circumstances of performers have created a deep reliance on the abstracted expressiveness of the dancing body and on non-verbal communication procedures."[29] Meaning registers within visceral responses to kinesthetic and musical affect. Meaning, realizations, and knowledge are thus abstractly embodied.

Daniel recognizes how most of the movement sequences and motifs for the divinities conform to identifiable patterns that are recognizable across the African Diaspora. The dance for and of the deity Ogun is an example of this because it contains both explicit, literal meanings and implied, abstracted meanings that are common in all three ritual communities. In all three sites, the dance's movement patterns denote a fierce male entity that fights as he dances with a sword or machete. With minimal variation, this dance is performed in Haitian Vodou as the dance for the *lwa,* Ogou; in Cuban Yoruba as the dance of the *oricha,* Ogún; and in Bahian Candomblé as the dance of the *orixá,* Ogun. It is also performed in Nigeria as the dance of the orisha, Ogùn, and in Benin as the dance for the vodun, Gu.

[...]Performance elements combine and result in cultural understandings not only about performance and the performer but also about their relationship with the viewer. The whole performance embodies power and protection and urges the Haitian, Cuban, and Bahian worshipper toward courage, strength, and appropriate protective action.

In her interviews and interactions with worshippers in Haiti, Cuba, and Brazil, Daniel learned that as worshippers perform, they sense and learn. As they continue to perform over time, in the process of music making and dance performance, they consult, gain, and express embodied knowledge. It is a dynamic, practical referencing that can mean different things within a lifetime. [...] In particular embodied transformation appears to chiefly mediate three forms of knowledge:

1) Healing of the self
2) Healing of the community
3) Balancing relationships between the cosmos and the ritual community

Daniel realizes that "over time, performers become consciously aware of the knowledge that exists within sacred performance."[30] [...]

> The total wisdom within African American chanting, drumming, and dancing can be viewed as an accumulation and transposition of many different kinds of knowledge. African – derived performance is easily a transposing of philosophy, religion, or belief, as well as natural, technological, and social sciences into the aesthetic and artistic arena of primarily non-verbal, communicative forms. [...][31]

Practical Theological Reflection

In place of the dismissiveness which has so often characterized Western Christian encounters of other, especially African religious practice, I suggest that much is to be gained through respectful dialog with these traditions.[32] It seems to me that in practical Christian theological terms what we are confronted with in the religious observances and everyday practices of Africans on the continent and in the diaspora can be discussed under three main headings, namely, incarnation, hermeneutics, and healing.

Incarnation

Christian doctrine is founded upon an understanding that Jesus, the Christ, was and is the Divine in human flesh, *par excellence.* Pivotal for an appreciation of the life, teaching, and works of Jesus, the Christ is the appropriation of his presence as embodying the Divine. According to the Christian narrative and understanding, all of human life is taken up into the Divine by the life, death, and resurrection of Jesus. And conversely all of the Divine realm is made available to humanity through Jesus, the Christ. Through Jesus all of humanity attains salvation and acceptance within the spiritual realm. The acts and words of Jesus are the very actions and communications of the Divine Creator. This way of thinking concerning the Jewish human person Jesus of Nazareth finds easy and ready acceptance within an African epistemology. The human being can mediate the divine within our bodily presence through close communion with the human Jesus. The Divine can readily communicate with the human, then, through the bodily expression of the human. It behooves us, then, to pay closer attention to the "wisdom of the body" for within it may be contained both that which enhances human flourishing and what the divine may be communicating with the human community.

Hermeneutics

The art of interpretation is characterized in Christian theology through the word "hermeneutics" that etymologically entails an embodiment of the Greek god of communication known as *Hermes.* Hermes is the "messenger" who conveys the words of the gods to humankind. Hermeneutics is the art and science of correctly deciphering and explaining the message of God, especially as contained in the words of Holy Scripture. However, the exclusive location of the messages of God in what is written has rendered Christianity in the West the preserve of the literate, and the art of interpretation a matter of words and titles. What these African religious adepts teach us is that the communication of God may also come to humanity through the bodies of human beings, especially the movements of these bodies under inspiration. As such, hermeneutics has to include the ability to "read" the movements of human bodies as they operate in concert with the impulses and rhythms of the spiritual universe. African religious practitioners affirm that movement, rhythm, and sound may also be divine communication needing to be understood if the whole counsel of God is to be appreciated. Such embodied hermeneutics would seem to follow from any doctrine of incarnation. If the "word became flesh and dwelt among us" (John 1:14), then are we not directed to the flesh (the body) in order to understand the "word." [...] The African insight here invites us to consider that Divine communication to humanity may come in the form of bodily movement. In the dance not only may humans speak to God but more poignantly God may be speaking to the human community. The task of the hermeneutician then becomes interpreting what the Divine communication may actually be in the dance. Such is the art of the "dancers of the gods" in African religious contexts. [...] Inspired by the divine realm they become the embodied and living "word" of the living God available not exclusively to the literate (in particular languages) but to all of humanity.

Healing

The primary message of Jesus the Christ, attested to with word and sign, was one of healing and reconciliation. In fact healing was to be understood as reconciliation with oneself (body-soul-spirit), with others (love of neighbor), and above all with God (salvation). In similar fashion African and African Diasporan ritual as observed especially by Yvonne Daniel is engaged to be a means of healing on all three of these levels. Physical bodily movement is recognized as a necessary means of enhancing physical health. Worship, if it incorporates physical movement on the part of congregants, can thus in itself be a means of community and individual well-being. Through participation in the dance rituals that invite the manifestations of the divine, worshippers may not only receive the benefits of physical movement but also enter into communion with the spiritual realm thus embodying the inspiration of Spirit.

Conclusion

A more respectful engagement with the beliefs, rituals, and practices of African religions may have much to teach us about the nature of the divine (theology), the nature of humanity (anthropology), and the relationship between these, especially in terms of the embodied nature of all dimensions of reality. African religious communities may teach us that much can be known about the Divine through attention to the moving bodies of human persons as these bodies move under inspiration.

Notes

1 Kathryn Linn Geurts, *Culture and the Senses: Bodily Ways of Knowing in an African Community* (Berkeley: University of California Press, 2002), 40.
2 Ibid.
3 Ibid., 41.
4 Ibid.
5 Ibid.
6 Ibid., 52.
7 Ibid., 55.
8 Ibid., 49.
9 Ibid., 49.
10 Ibid., 50.
11 Ibid., 51.
12 Ibid., 51.
13 Ibid., 69.
14 This particular expression, which very well captures the language of the healers I have talked with, comes from Barnaby B. Barratt, *The Emergence of Somatic Psychology and Bodymind Therapy* (New York: Palgrave Macmillan, 2013), 21.
15 Yvonne Daniel, *Dancing Wisdom: Embodied Knowledge in Haitian Vodou, Cuban Yoruba, and Bahian Candomble* (Urbana/Chicago: University of Illinois Press, 2005), 2.
16 Ibid., 1.
17 Ibid., 51.
18 Ibid., 52.
19 Ibid., 53.
20 Ibid.
21 Ibid., 54.
22 See for example, Marion Kilson, *Dancing with the Gods: Essays in Ga Ritual* (New York: University Press of America, 2013), especially chapters 2–5.
23 Daniel, 55.
24 Ibid., 55.
25 Ibid., 58.
26 Ibid.
27 Ibid., 61.
28 Ibid., 62.
29 Ibid., 63.
30 Ibid., 66.
31 Ibid., 93.
32 For a fuller statement and argument of the theological imperative of engagement with African religious cultures see Emmanuel Y. Lartey, *Postcolonializing God: An African Practical Theology* (London: SCM Press, 2013), 124–9.

Section III

Practical Know-How

12

A ChicanaFeminist Epistemology (2002)*

Nancy Pineda-Madrid

Introduction

Nancy Pineda-Madrid, Associate Professor of Theology and Latino/Latina Ministry at Boston College, has long understood her scholarship as standing at the juncture of systematic and practical theology. This orientation rests upon what she calls her "ChicanaFeminist" approach – words purposively merged to capture the multifaceted "gestalt" that shapes her critical consciousness and underscores her contribution.

This essay appears in the first comprehensive anthology of Latina theology, *A Reader in Latina Feminist Theology: Religion and Justice* (2002), compiled at the turn of the twenty-first century. Pineda-Madrid was a doctoral student at Graduate Theological Union at the time, called upon by editors María Pilar Aquino, Daisy Machado, and Jeanette Rodríguez to participate in a volume of first-generation Latina scholars. Even though Pineda-Madrid was working on a dissertation on Our Lady of Guadalupe, she chose, not coincidentally given her practical-systematic interests, to write on epistemology and oppression. Although she does not speak about practical theology per se, she pursues natural curiosities about how we have (mis)understood how we know what we know in theology. She states her argument clearly on the first page: "At its root, oppression…has to do with who controls the creation and validation of knowledge, with *epistemology*; and with the ability to act on that knowledge, with *humanization*." Epistemology is not simply a theoretical problem, therefore; it has consequences for practice, ethics, and human welfare.

As Pineda-Madrid demonstrates in her 2011 book, *Suffering and Salvation in Ciudad Juárez*, salvation is also a deeply practical category pertaining to life and death – in this case, the brutal extermination of girls and women in a precarious border town. Community practices of resistance become religious "texts" for Pineda-Madrid that reveal God's presence in the midst of evil and human travesty. The essay included here raises related themes, showing how idealized and demonized portraits of women as pure or evil follow epistemological binaries between mind and body and reason and

Original publication details: Nancy Pineda-Madrid, "Notes Toward a ChicanaFeminist Epistemology," pp. 241–66 from *A Reader in Latina Feminist Theology: Religion and Justice*, eds. María Pilor Aquino, Daisy Machado, and Jeanette Rodríguez (Austin, TX: University of Texas, 2002). For full citations of the books referenced below, see the Selected Bibliography in Aquino, Machado, and Rodríguez, eds., *A Reader in Latina Feminist Theology*.

emotion that distort our theological reasoning. As she argues in her book, everyday constructs that define, restrict, and control ways of knowing – the "contextual rooted-ness of all knowing" (2011, p. 2) – require redress if we want to hear voices previously silenced in the construction of theology's primary categories. The songs, protests, prayers, and laments of the suffering "often bear particularly insightful theological wis-dom" (6). In other words, Pineda-Madrid's theological concerns are practical through and through, grounded in the particular with implications for broader constructions of knowledge, "a theology in the process of redefining reason itself," as Aquino, Machado, and Rodríguez remark in their introduction. "Our task as Latina scholars is not to give up reason," they say, "but to demonstrate that *how* we think...arises from our plural practices and lived experiences" (2002, pp. xv–xvi, emphasis in original).

Suggested Further Reading

- Nancy Pineda-Madrid, *Suffering and Salvation in Ciudad Juárez* (Minneapolis: Fortress, 2011).
- María Pilar Aquino, *Our Cry for Life: Feminist Theology from Latin America* (Maryknoll, NY: Orbis, 1993).

***

Epistemology,[1] which deals with the origin, nature, and limits of knowing, and with the validity of what constitutes knowledge, plays a preeminent role in Latinas' drive toward full humanity.[2] The very process of creating and validating "knowledge" vitally contrib-utes to the "humanization" of subordinated populations like Latinas. This is so precisely because Latinas, and others, lack the institutional power to re-order the boundaries of what the dominant society defines as knowledge. Even though oppression may be described as racism, sexism, classism, heterosexism, and so forth, or be understood as the cumulative and interconnected effect of several "isms" (which is often the case for Latinas and others), ultimately oppression means being prevented from naming our world and ourselves. At its root, oppression – as both a social and an internalized phenomenon – has to do with who controls the creation and validation of knowledge, with *epistemology;* and with the ability to act on that knowledge, with *humanization.* As theorist Audre Lorde warns, "[I]t is axiomatic that if we do not define ourselves for ourselves, we will be defined by others – for their use and to our detriment."[3]

In recent decades the work of a growing number of theorists, particularly feminist theorists,[4] strongly undermines the idea that knowledge and the process of knowing can be conceptualized ahistorically and acontextually. As a result, the very possibility of a general theory of knowledge is now seriously suspect. What we have commonly referred to as "knowledge," they rightly argue, is bound up in a "structure of inequality which is gendered,"[5] and I would add, bound in multiple ways to a global systemic ine-quality. This insight, among other effects, calls attention to the inherent relationship between epistemology and politics. On the one hand, epistemology must never be reduced to politics; but on the other, any credible epistemology cannot ignore the sociopolitical dimensions of knowledge.

Nonetheless, epistemological commitments, whether implicit or explicit, serve as the rational foundation for all intellectual work and have implications for the pursuit of truth. In striving toward the truth of God, theologians invariably assume an epistemology.

The primary aim of this essay is not to engage in an exhaustive study of the emerging discourse of Chicana feminisms, although this essay does draw on the work of some prominent Chicana theorists; nor is it to detail the multiple and significant connections between such discourse and Latina feminist theologies. Rather, the primary aim of this essay is to offer a prolegomenon toward a possible ChicanaFeminist epistemology *by naming two important "anchoring" themes (la familia and Chicana womanhood)* whose epistemic interpretations matter in Chicanas' drive toward their full humanity.[6] The significance of a Chicana feminist epistemology lies in its ability to provide a theoretical foundation for Latina feminist theologies, which in turn strengthens the force of their assertions.

Why connect an epistemology grounded in *Chicana* feminism to the development of *Latina* feminist theologies? Self-identified Chicanas have written almost all the work used in this essay. Their work as theorists or artists or both deliberately engages Chicana experience. Their work embodies an important and historical field of study thus far not substantially employed by US Latina theologians. Moreover, US Latina theologians hold as one of their central goals the articulation of theology *from* the perspective of women of Latin American ancestry, a large number of whom are Chicanas. Chicana theory has much to contribute to the future of US Latina theologies.

This three-part essay begins by situating the project of a possible ChicanaFeminist epistemology in context. Some preliminary questions are examined: Who is a ChicanaFeminist? Who has a legitimate role in shaping ChicanaFeminist thought? What distinguishes an epistemology as ChicanaFeminist? The second part names the two anchoring themes to be explored and provides an analysis of their significance. In the final part, I briefly explore the contribution which a ChicanaFeminist epistemology can make to Latina feminist theologies.

The Who and What of a ChicanaFeminist Epistemology

Throughout this essay the words "Chicana" and "Feminist" are run together (ChicanaFeminist) to signify the integral reality embodied in this field of discourse.[7] But they are kept separate when they refer to a person or group of people because for some, they are not co-extensive. "ChicanaFeminist" cannot be reduced to simply "a different version of feminist theory," nor to "a different version of race theory." It could be just as easily written "FeministChicana." ChicanaFeminist is a *gestalt* of a particular race and gender consciousness which theorists attempt to capture in ideas and concepts. It typically includes a critical consciousness of class and sexual orientation as well. It cannot simply be understood as a critique or deconstruction of feminist or race theory. It has integrity of its own.

Who is a Chicana feminist? And who has a legitimate role in defining ChicanaFeminist thought? The two extreme positions, one "materialist" and the other "idealist," assist in framing a response to these questions. A materialist position asserts that the life experience that comes with being born a woman of Mexican ancestry makes one a Chicana feminist. Here the deciding factor is biology. Adherents of this position argue that in the United States, most women of Mexican ancestry repeatedly face situations that reinforce the worldview that as a brown person, as a female person, and often as a poor person, she is less than human. Upon reflection, such experiences may provoke a critical awareness of how social structures collude in forming a worldview that deems Chicanas inferior.

At the other end of the spectrum, arguments can be made for the exclusive norm of a critical and political consciousness as determinative of a Chicana feminist. This is the idealist position. On this view, any person who seeks to subvert the hegemonic paradigm, which strives to keep Chicanas subordinate, deserves the title "Chicana feminist." And therefore, such persons, as a result of their ideological commitments, have a legitimate role in shaping ChicanaFeminist thought.

The most compelling response to the questions incorporates elements of both positions. The very origins of the term "Chicana/o" suggest as much. In the 1960s, some US-born people of Mexican descent "recuperated, appropriated and recodified the term Chicano to form a new political class,"[8] one that embodied a critical consciousness aimed at breaking through the hyphenated existence of "Mexican-American" to a more integral identity. Feminist Chicanas assumed significant roles from the outset of the development of this new political class. Contemporary discussions of the term reflect much of its origins. Theorist Norma Alarcón observes:

> Thus, the name Chicana, in the present, is the name of resistance that enables cultural and political points of departure and thinking through the multiple migrations and dislocations of women of "Mexican" descent. The name Chicana is not a name that women (or men) are born to or with, as is often the case with "Mexican," but rather it is consciously and critically assumed. [...][9]

Chicana as a point of "redeparture" foregrounds the importance of a "class/race/gender" critical and political consciousness as well as the life experience of Mexican/indigenous women. While others may contribute to the shaping of ChicanaFeminist thought, the primary responsibility for defining and validating it must rest with those who are Chicanas. A particular authenticity and congruity belongs exclusively to those who not only ascribe to its critical and political consciousness but also materially experience the reality of being a Chicana.[10]

Therefore, Chicana feminist theorists and artists play a unique role when they interpret Chicana experience through writing, activism, art, scholarship, teaching, and intellectual work. This role originates from three sources. First, their day-to-day life experience as Chicanas, according to theologian María Pilar Aquino, gives them a singular view of the world.[11] [...] Second, in cooperation with other Chicanas, Chicana feminist theorists and artists can generate a particular vision that emerges from the dialectic of critical reflection and emancipatory action. [...] Third, through their work Chicana feminist theorists and artists can create the necessary and relatively autonomous space in which an uninhibited discussion of ChicanaFeminism can occur, which in turn can enable the growth of an inner core of authority and confidence in what it means to be a Chicana feminist. The collective work of Norma Alarcón, Cherríe Moraga, Gloria Anzaldúa, and Ana Castillo, to name only a few,[12] exemplifies such an autonomous space. [...] In brief, Chicana feminist theorists and artists play a preeminent role in the creation and validation of knowledge which furthers Chicanas' emancipatory goal.[13]

What, then, distinguishes an epistemology as *ChicanaFeminist*? A brief survey of feminist epistemologies will clarify the need for an explicitly ChicanaFeminist epistemology.

For almost two decades a growing number of feminist theorists from across the academic spectrum have brought to light not only the significance of gender to the production of knowledge but also the inherently political character of validating knowledge-claims.[14] Political scientist Christine Sylvester loosely categorizes feminist epistemologies into three groups. First, *feminist empiricist epistemologies,* which start from "the premise that modern science provides a valuable way of knowing the activities of women in the world and, therefore, [modern science is] a potentially helpful tool for recovering ... [women's] contributions to civilization." These epistemologies judge the scientific approach to knowledge as "contaminated" only by virtue of its "social biases against women." This contamination can be remedied by "incorporating more feminist women and problematiques into research enterprises."[15] But ultimately these epistemologies leave the mechanics and politics of knowledge production largely unchallenged. To put it more colloquially, the rules of the game are not under scrutiny. Only who has a seat at the game table is called into question. The commitments of these epistemologies imply that when "reason" and "rationality" are used well, they ultimately lead everyone to reliable and unbiased knowledge. An effective ChicanaFeminist epistemology would have little in common with empiricist epistemologies because a ChicanaFeminist epistemology would need to call into question the game itself – a much more radical concern than is operative in this group.

Feminist standpoint epistemologies, the second group, begin "from the perspective of women's lives ... because [this perspective] leads to socially constructed claims that are less false – less partial and distorted" – than claims that privileged men can socially construct."[16] In a general sense, a standpoint refers to a group of people who "share socially and politically significant characteristics."[17] Yet feminist standpoint epistemologies face a host of challenges. Women's ways of knowing "may be distorted by patriarchy" and distorted by the racist, classist, and heterosexist biases embedded in the social network of relationships which shape women's lives. As Alarcón argues, if the ideal woman is assumed to be the self-sufficient individual as is the case in much feminist theory, then the "native female's" and "woman of color's" ways of knowing can be greatly marginalized if not summarily excluded.[18] Standpoint epistemologies "can homogenize the diversity of women's experiences in the world" by making "biological difference" the primary difference and therefore the "ultimate foundation of truth."[19] However, some feminist theorists who take these limitations seriously have theorized the idea of "standpoint" so as to reflect the complexity and significant differences in women's lives.[20] Admitting the challenges which surface in the attempt to describe "standpoint," they nonetheless consistently recognize and thereby call attention to, "women as agents of knowledge and theory."[21] In addition, standpoint epistemologies poignantly challenge epistemologies that claim objectivity while articulating the perspectives of only a few elites. They move toward embodying what theorist Cherríe Moraga refers to as "theory in the flesh," namely a theorizing which emerges out of the daily experiences of women rather than one which begins with some faceless, abstract, "generic" woman. But do these epistemologies go far enough?

Postmodern feminist epistemologies, the third and final group, incorporate strands of the skepticism of postmodern thought regarding the "social formation of subjects" with strands of "standpoint feminism." Drawing from postmodern thought, these epistemologies take a critical approach toward the universalizing interpretations of gender, race, social relations, knowledge, and so forth which reside in the notion of the "social formation of subjects." Hence, the serious failures of these universalizing interpretations must be exposed. From standpoint feminism, these epistemologies retain the "politics of self assertion." Within this group, epistemologists tenuously negotiate the intellectual ground between the significance of gender and self assertion, the hallmark of standpoint epistemologies, on the one hand, and the utter inadequacy of any universalizing, coherent explanations which ignore and appropriate difference and particularity – a central insight of postmodern thought – on the other hand.[22]

Broadly speaking, ChicanaFeminist discourse and its explicit and implicit emerging epistemologies belong in this final group.[23] ChicanaFeminist discourse resonates strongly with the politics of self-assertion characteristic of standpoint feminism, and also with the postmodern critique of theory which ignores difference. In the work of Chicana feminist theorists and artists, differences of class, race, and so forth matter *as much as* gender. [...] In short, Chicana consciousness is a multilayered reality.

A specific ChicanaFeminist theory of knowledge is necessary because the primacy of Chicanas' multiple consciousness, distinguished by various asymmetrical relations (e.g., race, class, culture, sexual orientation) does not typically characterize Anglo-feminist epistemologies. While some developed Anglo-feminist epistemologies recognize and explore these differences, in the end they use difference largely for descriptive and illustrative purposes, and therefore not as part of their central analytical work. This is inadequate. Alarcón supports this conclusion, calling it the "common denominator" problem.[24]

[...]

Moreover, a ChicanaFeminist epistemology is necessary because much of Anglo feminist thought proceeds as if becoming a woman can be understood, defined, and clarified fundamentally in "opposition to men." Yet in this country, and many others, race and class as well as gender function as preeminent, organizing principles. A woman becomes a woman not only in opposition to men but also in opposition to other women. The sociopolitical consciousness of being a woman becomes dangerously simplistic, narrow, and distorted when the asymmetrical relations of race, class, and sexual orientation are deemed secondary or irrelevant. Consciousness can be the site of a multi-voiced subjectivity, which means that a woman can come to know her subjectivity through several themes, not merely one. In this schema, it is the experience of several "competing notions for one's allegiance or self-identification" that forms one's subjectivity. Multi-voiced subjectivity requires opting for several themes, a decision which is at once theoretical and political.[25]

It is only through naming and struggling with the dissonance provoked by prevailing but inadequate common-denominator feminisms that Chicanas will begin to glimpse the potential strands for a new ChicanaFeminist epistemology. This essay attempts to catch sight of some of those "potential strands" to examine the evolving, dynamic, and fluid self-understanding of Chicanas and its epistemic, humanizing implications. [...]

Anchoring Themes for a ChicanaFeminist Epistemology

In peering through the multifaceted kaleidoscope of Chicana particularity, how do we discover the material backdrop for Chicanas' particular *standpoint(s)* on their own experience? The term *standpoint(s)*, and not *standpoint* or *standpoints*, best signifies the shared experience yet enormous differences that exist between Chicanas. Chicana identities are and have been "constructed in a crisis of meaning situation."[26] At these crisis moments the very question of how we know and what knowledge is valid for a particular Chicana or for Chicanas collectively becomes of vital significance. Chicanas' drive toward self-understanding in their familial relationships, in their own woman-hood, in their response to claims on their sexual identity and power, and so forth, sur-faces a crisis-of-meaning situation. As theologian David Tracy points out, these crisis moments embody occasions in which our humanity is at stake. Interpretation is a life-long project for any individual in any culture. But only in times of cultural crisis does the question of interpretation itself become central. [...][27] In sum, crisis-of-meaning situa-tions create the space for interpretations that reveal self-understanding even as they embody "knowing." [...]

Moreover, the liberation of Chicanas weighs in the balance of their interpretations. Their interpretations either perpetuate a silencing of and a disconnection from the self, or they forge the development of interior authority and self-trust. When Chicanas tenaciously and critically cling to their own reality by naming themselves and their world, they not only affirm but actualize their humanity. Through this interpretative process, cognitive authority emerges and deepens. However, as stated above, a ChicanaFeminist epistemology will ally itself more closely with postmodern feminist epistemology than with standpoint feminist epistemology. At stake in this choice of alliance is how *difference* is taken into account. Obviously, enormous differences are evident among Chicanas. Not all are poor. Not all experience race in a comparable manner. The same may also be said of Anglo women, but the key distinction here is that for a ChicanaFeminist epistemology, *race* and *class* complement gender as pri-mary categories for analytical work. Chicanas' standpoint(s) reflect(s) not an essen-tialized understanding of experience but a loosely resonant collection of interpretations which link Chicanas together under the umbrella term Chicana. If the term "Chicana" is to have any meaning at all, and it does, there must be some distinguishing factors, patterns, or processes that bring about broad recognition. The necessary challenge is to avoid essentializing the diverse experiences of Chicanas while explicating the meaning of the term "Chicana." The term standpoint(s) signifies this particular challenge.[28]

Various anchoring themes constitute Chicanas' particular standpoint(s). These anchoring themes reflect points of notable tension [...].[29] The notions of *la familia* and *Chicana womanhood*, both anchoring themes, play a potent and pervasive role in shaping the collective Chicana (and Chicano) consciousness. The significance of these two themes lies in their symbolic character, in other words, in their ability to bear such an abundance of meaning that any explication of their meaning is ulti-mately insufficient. Thus, these themes are vital. [...] Chicanas' drive toward an emancipatory self-understanding utterly depends upon how they interpret these themes.

The Unsettled Notion of *La Familia*

The symbol and idea of *la familia* functions in a compelling fashion for both Chicanas and Chicanos. The efficacious power of *la familia* resides in the deeply rooted com-munal, relational self-understanding of Chicanas and Chicanos. Notions of the "self" invariably mean "self in community." Accordingly, the social construct of *la familia* constitutes one of the anchoring themes that Chicanas necessarily interpret in their drive toward self-understanding. *La familia* endures as a potent symbol.[30]

One example of the potency of *la familia* can be observed in the ideological and organizational role which it has played in the Chicano movement. *La familia* emerged as the central organizing symbol around which the movement rallied and forged a deep loyalty among its proponents. The language of *carnalismo* associated with the movement expressed this deep loyalty.[31] A *carnal* is someone who is of one's flesh. *Carnalismo* therefore can loosely be translated to mean a sisterhood or brotherhood. But unlike these rough equivalents in English, *carnal* carries a strong material sensibility. Being a *carnal* or *carnala* means being part of an extended family which affirms your presence within the family and anticipates your loyalty. Patricia Zavella explains that the centrality of *la familia* to the ideology of the Chicano movement served to promote ideas of "unity, strength and struggle within adversity."[32] When conflicts and antagonisms surfaced, loyalty to *la familia* was invoked as a means to suppress discord.

The Chicano movement remains a helpful point of reference because many of the challenges evidenced in the movement continue to influence the contemporary Chicana/o community. What follows are examples illustrating how *la familia* continues to be a symbol of contested meanings and a symbol whose interpretation shapes and reflects Chicana knowing, thereby influencing Chicanas' humanizing quest.

During the Chicano movement, Chicanas opted for differing interpretations of their own humanity – some interpretations silenced and cut off dimensions of Chicana womanhood, signaling a distorted commitment to Chicana humanity, whereas other interpretations signaled an enhanced, open-ended commitment to their humanity. In the former instance, Chicanas held that *la familia* implied a tacit acceptance of male dominance. For these Chicanas ("loyalists"), sexual equality was not among the central priorities of the movement. For them, liberation meant liberation of *la raza* (the Chicano people) as defined by the male leadership. Too much was at stake to consider liberation in more far-reaching terms. As feminist Chicana NietoGomez observes:

> Many loyalists felt that these complaints from women ("feminists") were potentially destructive and could only divide the Chicano movement. If sexual inequalities existed they were an "in-house" problem which could be dealt with later. However, right then, there were more important priorities to attend to, e.g., Vietnam, *La Huelga*, police brutality, etc.[33]

[...]

Thus Chicana humanity [...] was subverted by a traditionally defined vision of *la familia*. In the process, oppressions became hierarchically ranked, with race occupying the apex, and gender and class part of the second or third tier. At first glance, such a position might have appeared attractive because it entailed an assertion of cultural identity and racial pride, one which linked all Chicanas/as together. But for Chicanas who accepted such a ranking, they did so at the price of minimizing a principle dimension of themselves. [...]

But some Chicanas opted for a different path, insisting upon Chicanas' liberation as women. These feminist Chicanas criticized the norm of exclusive male leadership and, as sociologist Alma García explains, found themselves at the center of controversy and accused of being *anti-familia*. The loyalists asserted that these feminist Chicanas had allowed themselves to be influenced by the Anglo women's movement and by the individualism of the Anglo society. In spite of this, feminist Chicanas continued to affirm that self-determination, liberation, and equality for *Chicanas* as well as for Chicanos could not merely be swept under the rug.[34]

[...] The traditional, patriarchal interpretation of *la familia* did not hold these Chicanas captive. In the act of redefining themselves, they began to forge an altered understanding of *la familia.*

These feminist Chicanas contested the patriarchal interpretation of *la familia* not only in public, but also in the private sphere of their home life. In this private sphere, these Chicanas reinterpreted their identities such that their own subjectivity and personhood took on a much greater significance for them.[35] Some sought sweeping changes, while others chose not to reject the traditional female role within the family but to open it up by discarding its constricting features and enhancing its importance. Their knowing of themselves and their world had shifted. No longer did they identify themselves exclusively in terms of the roles they played in relation to the male figures in their lives. They now assumed greater responsibility for their particular personhood.

However, these examples only mention interpretations of *la familia* from within a heterosexually circumscribed universe. This begs the same question: Who interprets *la familia*? Some Chicanas, out of fidelity to their own reality and in their drive toward full humanity, have questioned the short-sided boundaries of this heterosexual universe, a move which has again elicited *anti-familia* accusations. In *The Last Generation,* Moraga strongly criticizes the norms that have traditionally defined and confined *la familia,* keeping it a "culturally correct" *familia.* These traditional norms have excluded and continue to exclude the validity of "female sexuality generally and male homosexuality and lesbian specifically," all of which she argues are relevant today.[36] [...]

[...]In the process of interpreting their experience in a manner which honors the fullness of that experience, Chicana thinkers like Moraga provoke new understandings of *la familia.*

How Chicanas interpret *la familia* matters. Their interpretations of *la familia* signify their knowledge and belief about the self-others-world relationship. In their drive toward self-understanding, do Chicanas swallow in silent acceptance the traditional explanations of who they are in the context of *la familia,* or do they struggle toward fullness in their lives, attempting to make sense of reality as they experience it?

Contested "Models" of Chicana Womanhood

Tracing their origins back to the conquest of Mexico, particular symbols of womanhood continue to play significant roles in shaping the imagination of the Mexican and Chicana/o community. These idealized and demonized versions of womanhood (e.g., Our Lady of Guadalupe, La Malinche, La Llorona) powerfully symbolize the "good" and "evil" of female humanity. Even so, simple or definitive interpretations of these symbols always elude the interpreter. Such interpretations are never secured, nor will they ever be. Nonetheless, the significance of these symbols for Chicanas becomes apparent with the extent to which Chicanas do or do not identify with particular interpretations of these symbols. In this negotiation of identity, Chicanas actualize their self-understanding.

The oppression experienced by Chicanas (e.g., the cumulative effect of racism, classism, sexism, and heterosexism) finds its ideological legitimacy in particular meanings attributed to symbols and powerful myths. [...] More specifically, these symbols, have been and still are used to cloak and sanitize oppressive social relations. [...]

For those who control current sociopolitical systems, the "otherness" of Chicanas is rooted in an epistemology of oppositional dichotomies such as mind/body, reason/emotion, fact/opinion, and so forth. These hierarchically ordered dichotomies create patterns of domination and subordination in which most Chicanas, along with many women of color, "occupy a position" representing the cumulative subordinate half.

[...]

It remains clear that those who effectively define these symbols hold a major instrument of power. The extent to which Chicanas interpret these symbols so as to resist their assigned position of subordination makes a profound difference. Inside this resistance lives a transformed knowledge of the self for Chicanas, and in transforming themselves Chicanas transform the world. When Chicanas take on a self-understanding which furthers their resistance to positions of subordination, then Chicanas claim power over their own lives and actualize the integral value of their humanity.

Two symbols are worthy of particular attention: *la madre pura y sufrida*, symbolized by Our Lady of Guadalupe; and the whore, *la vendida*, symbolized by La Malinche.

La Madre Pura Y Sufrida Symbolized by the Virgin of Guadalupe

Arguably the most influential icon of Chicana womanhood, the Virgin of Guadalupe provokes charged passion around diverging interpretations.[37] [...] Many scholars and artists, but not all, call attention to the apparent connections between the Virgin of Guadalupe and the Virgin Mary. In these discussions her attributes include varying combinations of motherhood, faith, purity, goodness, strength, power, self-abnegation, liberation, and passivity. Others call attention to her association with the mother goddess Tonantzín, one of the Náhuatl deities. This most formidable female goddess had power over the creation and extinction of life and had the capability to act for good or evil. When drawing connections between Guadalupe and Tonantzín, Chicana writers emphasis Guadalupe's more progressive and powerful aspects.

Some Chicanas interpret the Virgin of Guadalupe as the ideal to which they should aspire as wives and mothers. However, this "ideal" often contains an implicit judgment, namely that the value of Chicana womanhood is reflected *exclusively,* or at least ultimately, through the roles of wife and mother. To define the value of Chicana womanhood so narrowly restricts and undermines Chicanas who choose to define their womanhood in other ways. Moreover, some Chicanas uncritically accept the patriarchally defined ideal of "good wife and mother." This ideal, they believe, is symbolized in Guadalupe conflated with the Virgin Mary, which for them upholds a woman who aspires to docility, purity, self-abnegation, obedience, and de-sexualized existence.[38] NietoGomez (as quoted by Alma M. García) critiques the resulting effects of such an interpretation when she writes:

> Some Chicanas are praised as they emulate the sanctified example set by [the Virgin] Mary. The woman par excellence is mother and wife. She is to love and support her husband and to nurture and teach her children. Thus, may she gain fulfillment as a woman. For a Chicana bent upon fulfillment of her personhood, this restricted perspective of her role as a woman is not only inadequate but crippling.[39]

Yet, other writers put forward a contrasting interpretation of Guadalupe, one which honors her strength and power precisely as a mother.

> [...] She is the higher being who can be appealed to on a very personal level ... Many women feel the Virgin has much more power than the "official" ascendancy given to her by the church. [...] In her images in Chicano culture, she stands alone – without her son – and in her dress she wears the ancient symbols of Tonantzín.[40]

Chicanas [...] maintain that Guadalupe can symbolize autonomous and virtuous power, a woman who is not primarily defined by her relationships to men. This interpretation of Guadalupe supports a more expansive ideal of womanhood, one which affirms a self-referential mode of authority. This interpretation de-centers externally imposed, patriarchy-serving interpretations and offers instead a vision of vital Chicana personhood.

In addition to embodying an ideal for wives and mothers, the Virgin of Guadalupe has been used to signify the unattainable goal of *virgin motherhood.* Because Chicanas can never measure up to *virgin motherhood,* some Chicanas interpret this unattainable goal to mean blind endurance, selfless "love," and utter fidelity in the face of the most self-destructive circumstances. For some in such circumstances Guadalupe represents *aguante* (endurance at all cost) and through *aguante,* survival. Yet, other Chicanas in their desire for the fullness of life challenge this crippling interpretation of Guadalupe.

[...]

How Chicanas interpret the Virgin of Guadalupe matters. Whatever interpretation Chicanas hold will invariably function as a measuring stick of Chicana womanhood. Chicanas must criticize interpretations which idealize them as mute and passive and which narrowly define their possible aspirations. But such a critique, while absolutely essential for growth, comes at a price. Criticism of sociopolitically entrenched interpretations brings pain and suffering. It means being misunderstood by those who cling to accepted but detrimental explanations of themselves and their world. Yet only Chicanas who risk much to forge liberative understandings of themselves can hope to transform themselves and their world.

The Whore, *La Vendida*, Symbolized in the Image of La Malinche/Malintzin

Just as the Virgin of Guadalupe has idealized goodness, the indigenous woman Malintzin has been demonized as the evil woman. She was twice betrayed, once by her family when they sold her into slavery, and again at the age of fourteen when she was given away to the Spanish conquistador, Hernán Cortéz. Cortéz took particular interest in Malintzin due to her ability to speak both Nahuatl and Maya, which he used to his advantage during the conquest. As Cortéz's mistress, she bore him a child. Afterward, Cortéz kept their child and married off Malintzin to one of his soldiers. By the age of twenty-four she had died. Over the years Malintzin has been referred to as La Malinche, which has come to mean a traitor. Blamed for the Spanish conquest of Mexico, her title "Malinche" has often been invoked in attempts to control Chicanas' behavior.[41]

Some Chicanas fail to question longstanding interpretations of the myth of Malinche which link the idea of "the traitor" with that of "the whore." This link has served as an omen. Chicanas who too freely traverse the boundaries of cultural sexual norms become traitors or Malinches to their families and their people. As such, this link functions to repress Chicana sexual drives and behavior and acts to suppress the development of Chicana sexual agency. Alarcón rightly insists that "... the male myth of Malintzin is made to see betrayal first of all in her very sexuality, which makes it nearly impossible at any given moment to go beyond the vagina as the supreme site of evil until proven innocent by way of virginity or virtue, the most pawnable commodities around."[42] In this "male myth of Malintzin" woman's behavior is *not* the result of her own decisions, but the result of either her weakness or forces beyond her control. Obviously, such an interpretation paints an immature, passive, and limp portrait of Chicana womanhood.

Revisionist interpretations of La Malinche, like the one put forward by poet Carmen Tafolla, offer a contrasting and hope-filled portrait. In this interpretation, La Malinche acts on her own behalf and that of her people; she is a woman with significant command of her historical and sexual agency. Not only does she act on her own authority, but she sees what neither Cortéz nor Moctezuma can see, the dawning world of *La Raza.* She courageously pursues her vision.[43] [...]

[...]

In Chicanas' drive toward fullness, liberative interpretations of symbols like the Virgin of Guadalupe and La Malinche are important for several reasons. First of all, given the contemporary oral nature of Mexico/Chicano culture, "symbolic icons, figures, or even persons" take on highly significant roles in the transmission and organization of "knowledge, values and beliefs."[44] More to the point, the tenacity and vitality of knowledge, values, and beliefs to a large extent depend upon the effective heuristic use of symbolic icons and figures. Second, these symbolic icons and figures can and do prompt strong emotional responses. Such responses intensify Chicanas' need and drive to understand their experience. Third, these symbolic icons and figures retain broad universal appeal, commanding unrivaled attention, and yet they effect a sense of intimate connection. In other words they enable Chicanas to recognize the transcendent, spiritual nature of their humanity. For these reasons, a liberative interpretation has the powerful effect of enabling Chicanas to know themselves differently and, as a result, to act differently in the world.

Having reflected on two important anchoring themes, I now turn to the final topic of this essay: How is the creation of a ChicanaFeminist epistemology important for a Latina feminist theology?

Of Theological Import

Whenever Latina theologians interpret Christian beliefs or religious symbols (such as the nature of grace and sin, Our Lady of Guadalupe) or investigate the meaning of popular religious practices (*posadas, los reyes magos*) or explain the scriptures or church documents, on each of these occasions their epistemological commitments undergird their theological claims. When theologians interpret Latina religious experience, they also reveal their assumptions about *how Latinas* know *God's revelation.* A theologian's work invariably discloses the theologian's epistemological commitments.[45]

An effective ChicanaFeminist epistemology would allow greater depth and critical insight concerning the nature of the relationship between knowing and liberation. Additionally, it would assist in probing how the knowledge which emerges from an emancipatory interpretation of themes like *la familia* relates to the pursuit of truth in the work of each Latina feminist theologian. What follows are some reflections on the potential contributions an effective ChicanaFeminist epistemology would make to the work of Latina feminist theologians.

First, a ChicanaFeminist epistemology, by examining the nature of the relationship between knowing and liberation, would *contribute to a fuller understanding of what humanization means* and thereby enable Latina feminist theologians to probe more deeply a central concern of their work. The process of developing a mature, valid, and fruitful ChicanaFeminist epistemology would necessitate the creation of a relatively autonomous space, a space in which Chicanas could openly and without restraints explore, deliberate on, and test their own self-understandings. In such a space Chicanas could develop an inner core of cognitive authority based on the self understanding, both individual and collective. [...]

Second, a ChicanaFeminist epistemology would *provide a critical framework* for the work of Latina feminist theologians. As a result of an effective ChicanaFeminist episte-mology, Latina feminist theologians could uncover and analyze the gender, racial, and class hegemonies operative in the work of US Latino theologians in particular and in theology in general. For example, much of US Latino theology draws on and develops insights from the story and symbol of the Virgin of Guadalupe. But what vision of wom-anhood is given legitimacy through the discussion of Guadalupe in the work of US Latino theologians? And how does each theologian account for the varied ways in which this symbol functions in the lives of women, as well as men, in the lives of *mulatos* and *mestizos,* in the lives of the rich and the poor? And how does the social location of the theologian influence what they "know" of this symbol? Much is at stake here. Unarticulated epistemological assumptions often shape how theological debates proceed and where they ultimately settle.

Finally, a ChicanaFeminist epistemology would *provide a theoretical foundation* for a relevant, compelling and in-depth presentation of the Christian faith. Theologians invariably confront two fundamental questions: How do we know what God has com-municated? What is the relationship of religious knowledge to the production of knowl-edge? If we understand "religious knowledge (to be) the product of our interpretative response to our experience, (and) not some absolutely certain grasp of divinely revealed truth,"[46] then what Latinas come to "know" from their experience is fundamental to the very possibility of religious knowledge. By providing a coherent explanation of how Chicanas come to know, a ChicanaFeminist epistemology would allow Latina feminist theologians to demonstrate the significance and value of the Christian faith and tradi-tion in relation to what Latinas "know" of their experience.

Epistemology is presumed and assumed when Latina feminist theologians respond to a number of fundamental questions which reside beyond the bounds of epistemology. [...]

As long as Chicanas and Latinas long for and actively pursue the fullness of their humanity, and as long as Latina feminist theologians hope to advance the liberation of Latinas, the relationship between knowing and liberation must be of paramount con-cern. Placing Chicanas at the center of inquiry creates new paradigms of thought, new epistemologies that humanize. Any ChicanaFeminist epistemology must begin and proceed as an iconoclastic endeavor, breaking down life-consuming visions of Chicana womanhood and drawing forth life-giving visions. Such efforts will assist Chicanas and Latinas as they seek to transform their lives and the world.

Notes

1 Epistemology, the study of knowing, attempts to respond to a wide range of questions: How does knowing occur? What are the grounds of knowing? What are the limitations of knowing? How do we judge the validity and trustworthiness of knowledge? Finally, what is the relationship between knowledge and truth? See Sandra G. Harding, *Whose Science? Whose Knowledge? Thinking From Women's Lives*, 308. I am especially indebted to María Pilar Aquino, Kirk Wegter-McNelly, Mary Lowe, Larry Gordon, and Jane Redmont for generously offering their ideas, recommendations, and insightful critique of various drafts of this work.

2 Throughout this essay I use the term "Latina" for the purpose of signifying women of Latin American ancestry who live in the United States. I use the term "Chicana" to indicate a more specific population, namely women who are of Mexican ancestry and who identify themselves as Chicanas. The term Chicana indicates a particular consciousness. See Norma Alarcón, "Chicana Feminism: In the Tracks of the Native Woman," in *Living Chicana Theory*, ed. Carla Trujillo, 371–82.

3 Audre Lorde, *Sister Outsider: Essays and Speeches*, 45.

4 The following works represent a rather small sample of some of the most important contributions which have been made in the expanding field of feminist epistemology. See *The Second Wave: A Reader in Feminist Theory*, ed. Linda Nicholson; *Knowing the Difference: Feminist Perspectives in Epistemology*, ed. Kathleen Lennon and Margaret Whitford; *Feminist Epistemologies*, ed. Linda Alco and Elizabeth Potter; Harding, *Whose Science?*; Judith P. Butler, *Gender Trouble: Feminism and the Subversion of Identity*; *Feminism/Postmodernism*, ed. Linda Nicholson; *Gender/Body/Knowledge: Feminist Reconstructions of Being and Knowing*, ed. Alison M. Jagger and Susan R. Bardo; *Feminist Thought and the Structure of Knowledge*, ed. Mary McCanney Gergen; Mary Field Belenky and Blythe Clinchy et al., *Women's Ways of Knowing: The Development of Self, Voice, and Mind*; bell hooks, *Feminist Theory from Margin to Center*; Carol Gilligan, *In a Different Voice: Psychological Theory and Women's Development*.

5 Elizabeth Frazer, "Epistemology, Feminist," in *The Oxford Companion to Philosophy*, ed. Ted Honderich, 241.

6 I am indebted to Patricia Hill Collins; her work functioned as a primary interlocutor for this essay. See Patricia Hill Collins, *Black Feminist Thought: Knowledge, Consciousness, and the Politics of Empowerment*.

7 Some works in this emerging field include *Living Chicana Theory*, ed. Carla Trujillo; *Chicana Feminist Thought: The Basic Historical Writings*, ed. Alma García; Tey Diana Rebolledo, *Women Singing in the Snow: A Cultural Analysis of Chicana Literature*; Norma Alarcón, "Traddutora, Traditora: A Paradigmatic Figure of Chicana Feminism," in *Scattered Hegemonies: Postmodernity and Transnational Feminist Practices*, ed. Inderpal Grewal and Caren Kaplan; Ana Castillo, *Massacre of the Dreamers: Essays on Xicanisma*; Cherríe Moraga, *The Last Generation: Prose and Poetry*; *Making Face, Making Soul–Hacienda Caras: Creative and Critical Perspectives by Feminist of Color*, ed. Gloria Anzaldúa; *This Bridge Called My Back: Writings by Radical Women of Color*, ed. Cherríe Moraga and Gloria Anzaldúa; Norma Alarcón, "Chicana's Feminist Literature: A Re-Vision Through Malintzin/or Malintzin: Putting Flesh Back on the Object," in Moraga and Anzaldúa, *This Bridge*, 182–90.

8 Alarcón, "Chicana Feminism," 371.

9 Ibid., 374, 379.
10 Collins, *Black Feminist Thought,* 34.
11 María Pilar Aquino, *Our Cry for Life: Feminist Theology from Latin America,* 38–41. See also the idea of *lo cotidiano* in Ada María Isasi-Díaz, *Mujerista Theology: A Theology for the Twenty-First Century,* 66–73, 131, 134.
12 See note 8.
13 Collins, *Black Feminist Thought,* 20, 32–6; Alarcón, "Chicana Feminism," 380.
14 See note 4.
15 Christine Sylvester, *Feminist Theory and International Relations in a Postmodern Era,* 31–6.
16 Sylvester, *Feminist Theory,* 43.
17 Nancy Hirschmann, *Rethinking Obligation: A Feminist Method for Political Theory,* 167.
18 Norma Alarcón, "The Theoretical Subject(s) of *This Bridge Called My Back* and Anglo-American Feminism," in Anzaldúa, *Making Face, Making Soul,* 357.
19 Sylvester, *Feminist Theory,* 47.
20 Alarcón, "Theoretical Subject(s)"; Hirschmann, *Rethinking Obligation;* Donna Haraway, "Situated Knowledges: The Science Question in Feminism and the Privilege of Partial Perspective," *Feminist Studies* 14, no. 3 (1988): 575–99; Kathy Ferguson, "Interpretation and Genealogy in Feminism," *Signs* 16, no. 2 (1991): 322–39.
21 Sylvester, *Feminist Theory,* 48.
22 Ibid., 52–63.
23 See note 7.
24 Alarcón, "Theoretical Subject(s)," 358–9.
25 Alarcón, "Theoretical Subject(s)," 360–66. Also see María Lugones, "Playfulness, 'World'-Traveling, and Loving Perception," in Anzaldúa, *Making Face, Making Soul,* 390–402.
26 Alarcón, "Theoretical Subject(s)," 359.
27 David Tracy, *Plurality and Ambiguity: Hermeneutics, Religion, Hope,* 8–9.
28 In the field of US Latina/o theology, for a discussion of the dilemma of difference see Isasi-Díaz, *Mujerista Theology,* 66–73; Alejandro García-Rivera, "The Whole and the Love of Difference: Latino Metaphysics as Cosmology," in *From the Heart of Our People: Latino/a Explorations in Catholic Systematic Theology,* ed. Orlando O. Espín and Miguel H. Díaz, 54–83; Alejandro García-Rivera, *The Community of the Beautiful: A Theological Aesthetics.*
29 Alarcón, "Theoretical Subject(s)," 359.
30 In the field of US Latina/o theology, for a discussion of the relational self-understanding of Latinos and Hispanics see Roberto S. Goizueta, *Caminemos con Jesus: Toward a Hispanic/Latino Theology of Accompaniment,* 50. And for a discussion of the notion of *la familia* see Isasi-Díaz, *Mujerista Theology,* 128–47.
31 NietoGomez, "Chicana Feminism," 55; Patricia Zavella, "The Problematic Relationship of Feminism and Chicana Studies," *Women's Studies* 17 (1989), 26; Terry Mason, "Symbolic Strategies for Change: A Discussion of the Chicana Women's Movement," in *Twice a Minority: Mexican-American Women,* ed. Margarita Melville, 105.
32 Zavella, "Problematic Relationship," 26–7.
33 Anna NietoGomez, "La Feminista," in García, *Chicana Feminist Thought,* 89.
34 Alma García, "The Development of Chicana Feminist Discourse 1970–1980," *Gender and Society* 31 no. 2 (1989): 221, 225.

35 García, "The Development of Chicana Feminist Discourse," 219, 224.

36 Moraga, *Last Generation,* 158.

37 See for example Jeanette Rodríguez, *Our Lady of Guadalupe: Faith and Empowerment among Mexican-American Women.*

38 Rebolledo, *Women Singing,* 52–3.

39 García, "The Development of Chicana Feminist Discourse," 222.

40 Rebolledo, *Women Singing,* 53.

41 Tey Diana Rebolledo and Eliana S. Rivero, ed. *Infinite Divisions: An Anthology of Chicana Literature,* 191.

42 Alarcón, "Chicana's Feminist Literature," 183.

43 Carmen Tafolla, "La Malinche," in *Infinite Divisions,* ed. Rebolledo and Rivero, 198–9.

44 Alarcón, "Traddutora, Traditora," 113.

45 Epistemology has been addressed in the work of US Latina theologians. See Aquino, *Our Cry for Life,* 101–2, 109–29; María Pilar Aquino, "Theological Method in US Latino/a Theology: Toward and Intercultural Theology for the Third Millennium," in Orlando Espín and Miguel Díaz, *From the Heart,* 6–48; Isasi-Díaz, *Mujerista Theology,* 59–85. Epistemology has likewise been addressed in the work of US Latino theologians. See García-Rivera, *Community of the Beautiful;* Orlando O. Espín, "Popular Religion as an Epistemology (of Suffering)," in his *The Faith of the People: Theological Reflections on Popular Catholicism,* 156–79; Alejandro García-Rivera, "Creator of the Visible and Invisible: Liberation Theology, Postmodernism and the Spiritual," *Journal of Hispanic/Latino Theology* 3, no. 4 (1996), 35–56; Roberto S. Goizueta, "US Hispanic Popular Catholicism as Theopoetics," in *Hispanic/Latino Theology: Challenge and Promise,* ed. Ada María Isasi-Díaz and Fernando F. Segovia, 261–88; Goizueta, *Caminemos con Jesus.*

46 Thomas E. Hosinski, "Epistemology," in *A New Handbook of Christian Theology,* ed. Donald W. Musser and Joseph L. Price, 153.

13

Black *Phronesis* as Theological Resource (2008)*
Robert L. Smith, Jr

Introduction

In addition to Robert Smith's long tenure as parish minister in Alaska and now at Rubislaw Parish Church in Aberdeen, Scotland, he earned a doctorate in divinity and religious studies from the University of Aberdeen where he also serves as Honorary Researcher. A few years ago, he joined Dale Andrews in editing *Black Practical Theology* (2015), where they experimented with embedding dialogue at the heart of the book's design, risking the complications that arise when three parties – pastors, academic practical theologians, and scholars from others disciplines – are invited into a round-robin conversation on prominent issues in the black community.

Although writing within a Black British context, Smith's remarks are, he emphasizes, "no less pertinent" to non-blacks elsewhere. What he says on "Black *phronesis*" pertains to ways of knowing beyond this specific location. In using this particularity, he opens up more general questions about the nature of theological knowledge. Standard categories of knowledge, exemplified by Aristotle's three types, are themselves shaped by particular social and political contexts, he contends, including biases against certain groups of people, women and slaves in particular. This location does not negate the value of Aristotle's categories, which continue to have meaning and usefulness today. But identifying the hierarchies tied up with the typology forewarns people of its limitations. *Phronesis* takes different forms in different historical and social contexts, a reality that previous definitions among practical theologians have tended to overlook. The wider *telos* for which scholars seek knowledge matters. In particular, he questions whether Don Browning's Kantian imperative of equal regard suffices as an undergirding definition of the aim of Christian practical reason. Within African American communities, one of the highest goods that guides action, God's liberation from evil, the evils of slavery and racism in particular, has significant moral and theological foundations and implications. Practical wisdom in this context aims not just at treating others well but at resisting evil in its more virulent forms. Similar to Dale Andrews, Smith also argues that systematic theology, including black theology, has failed to appreciate the wisdom of religious communities, a resource that practical theologians attempt to explore.

Original publication details: Robert L. Smith, Jr., "Black Phronesis as Theological Resource: Recovering the Practical Wisdom of Black Faith Communities," pp. 174–87 from *Black Theology: An International Journal* 6:2 (2008).

The Wiley Blackwell Reader in Practical Theology, First Edition. Edited by Bonnie J. Miller-McLemore.
© 2019 John Wiley & Sons Ltd. Published 2019 by John Wiley & Sons Ltd.

Suggested Further Reading

- Robert London Smith, *From Strength to Strength: Shaping a Black Practical Theology for the 21st Century* (New York: Peter Lang, 2007).
- Anthony G. Reddie, *Black Theology in Transatlantic Dialogue* (New York: Palgrave, 2002).

***

One of the most pressing concerns facing the Black church and Black theology today is the need to create constructive and relevant responses to the myriad and polyvalent issues of twenty-first-century contemporary culture. Some of these issues, such as racism, poverty and discrimination, have long existed and are among those historical struggles that past generations of Black people have faced for centuries. Others matters, such as those related to the growing phenomenon of globalization, sex and gender bias, and ecological issues, such as impact of global warming and shrinking natural resources, classism in the Black community, and the struggle for justice in an ever-shrinking multi-cultural world, have emerged from today's more contemporary setting. While I am writing as an African American whose experiences and approaches have been largely shaped within that context, the arguments and observations I will make in this article are no less pertinent to the Black British and other settings.

Racism, its psychic and physical violence a reminder of its systematic assault on Black humanity, remains an insipid and smoldering problem. Although some progress has been made, "the problem of the twenty-first century remains the problem of the color line."[1] Unemployment in the Black community remains disproportionally high as does levels of poverty and incarceration, while access to health care and education remains disproportionally low.[2]

Meeting the needs and facing the issues created by these conditions with ever-shrinking resources, both financial and human, is a constant challenge for Black scholars and leaders. [...]

[...]

These issues all impact upon the Black faith community in different and complex ways. What is apparent is that they are placing new demands on the Black church and Black theology as they work to address them. This is the case because, in part, the contemporary context in which the Black church is now located has changed, significantly, from the earlier epochs in which the early Black church was born and began to evolve, and where the re-interpretive and liberationist voice of Black theology was created. What this means, *inter alia*, is that creative new approaches and perspectives are needed, which recognize these changes, and takes them seriously.

Black church leaders and theologians today are asking searching questions regarding the future and place of the Black church and Black theology. Recent works such as *Blow the Trumpet in Zion: Global Vision and Action for the 21st Century Black Church*,[3] *Living Stones in the Household of God: The Legacy and Future of Black Theology*,[4] and *Heart and Head: Black Theology Past, Present and Future*[5] reflect this trend towards refocusing Black theological work in new and exciting ways.

This trajectory in the more recent scholarship in Black theology and religion concerns the need to find a *constructive and relevant Black voice* to speak to the challenges of contemporary society. Importantly, it demands a redirection in methodological approach. Early forms of Black theology and scholarship sought to articulate theology from a Black perspective, giving voice and value to Black experience and expression. Using primarily a systematic approach, Black theology challenged White and Black communities intellectually and emotionally; as it called for immediate attention to the continuing need of liberation for oppressed Black people in America and around the world.[6] What I want to call for is a shift – not away from Black experience as the prime interpretive framework for reimaging and reinterpreting God and Christian faith[7] – but towards a concern for the shaping of alternate modes of Black church *praxis* in ways that take seriously the contemporary contextual realities that currently shape Black experience.

This shift, for which I am calling, reflects, among other things, the recognition that academic Black theology is not the sole bearer of the Black theological tradition.[8] There are new voices and different approaches that can benefit the Black theology project and enhance the work of Black scholars, church leaders and workers. This shift asserts the need to look to different areas and to use different approaches and, in so doing, to discover new and creative theological resources. I want to suggest that the *practical wisdom that has been created and utilized by the Black faith community throughout its history in America* is a valuable theological resource that may have been overlooked. This Black practical wisdom, or *Black phronesis* as I will refer to it in this article, is located in the history and experiences of Blacks in America. It is reflected in the ecclesial organization, faith traditions, religious expression and culture, all of which have helped shape the Black presence in America.

The issues and challenges mentioned earlier provide a new sense of urgency for the arguments, positions and alternatives asserted by those involved in the work of the church and in theological reflection. I want to suggest that the recovery of modes of Black *phronesis* is necessary in order to make available to Black faith communities this valuable theological resource as it seeks to re-imagine and re-invent its empowering and prophetic voice in contemporary society. It is my argument that this theological resource can have significant and constructive impact on the contemporary *praxis* of Black faith communities. The discipline of practical theology, with its focus on the value and importance of human experience as a source of theological inquiry and its multidisciplinary approach, provides the researcher with some compelling methodological frameworks for his or her work. By approaching the theological task from the perspective of human experience, which is located within human situations (the events and issues that shape human experience),[9] space can be created for recognizing and recovering modes of *Black phronesis*.

Developing a Methodological Approach

In coming to develop a theological framework with which to understand the value of *phronesis* as an important theological resource, the methodological approach of Don Browning is suggestive. It provides a sound starting point from which to begin to develop a deliberately Black understanding and nuanced position of *phronesis*. In his book, *A Fundamental Practical Theology*,[10] which emphasizes theological reflection on the practices of the church, in terms of its social context and theological and religious foundations, we find a compelling argument and method for the recovery of what he calls practical wisdom. I want to state very clearly, here, that Browning's method is a sound *starting point* and cannot be applied to the Black context *as is*. Rather, his approach must be engaged with critically, in order to develop a new method which, while taking some direction and insight from Browning, nevertheless, its cues and focus are located in the *Black* community. This approach must continue to use the *Black* experience for its substantive theologizing.

In his work, Browning draws upon the recently reborn practical philosophies, including Aristotelian philosophy, to provide the foundation for his methodological approach. For him, the recently reborn practical philosophies allow for the creation of new concepts in understanding faith communities as communities of memory and practical reason. Browning argues that this practical reason, or *phronesis,* has an overall dynamic, which is the reconstruction of experience, and an outer envelope, which is the fund of inherited traditional narratives and practices that always surrounds practical thinking. Juxtaposed with this outer envelope is an inner core, which he holds to be the reversible reasoning found in the love command that reads, "You shall love your neighbor as yourself" (Matt 19:19) as does the analogous Golden Rule, "In everything do to others as you would have them do to you" (Matt 7:12; Lk 6:31).[11]

However, it is with the way Browning chooses to define and, therefore, use *phronesis* that I must depart from his approach and begin to tease out what a contextually nuanced understanding might be that reflects *Black* experiences and uses *Black* sources. Browning's argument falls short because he uncritically adopts an Aristotelian view of "the highest good" upon which he then constructs a supposedly objective and universal description to underpin his understanding and application of *phronesis*. The context which shaped Aristotle's understanding and use of *phronesis* was the Greek city-state. He was concerned with understanding the kind of action required to achieve the highest of Greek vocations, or the best possible life.[12] This highest good, or *eudaimonia,* was the life of good political leadership and was achieved through *praxis* or *phronesis*. *Phronesis* in this sense is practical wisdom that informs action; in this case action that leads to *eudaimonia*.

In this particular social context, however, *eudaimonia* was only something that could be pursued by males; specifically Greek, free, aristocratic males. Women, slaves, indentured persons, people of color and non-Greeks were excluded from the political process, and hence, from participation in the highest good. Browning fails to address the exclusive nature of Aristotelian *phronesis* as he uses it to develop a theological ethic for his model. As Elaine Graham correctly points out, Browning fails to take into consideration the multiplicity of social morality, the particular expressions of what constitutes virtue by diverse human groups, and the many ways in which human interpretation and activity is manifested.[13]

My position is that *phronesis* does have a place within the work of theological reflection. However, it must be positioned in such a manner that it becomes part of the larger dialectic rather than the foundation that informs the struggle for truth. Such a dialectical approach necessitates the involvement of other disciplines such as history, sociology and cultural criticism, as it critically analyzes and describes the religio-cultural universes, or historical locations, within which Black faith communities and their various modes of *praxis* have been shaped and influenced.

While Browning's main aim is to show that Christian theology is governed by practical interests, my aim is to first show how *phronesis* is contextually located, and why.

This means that its use must be nuanced, such that it reflects the Black community's historical and cultural particularity, and therefore, allows for the development of *Black phronesis.* Secondly, I want to demonstrate that *Black phronesis* is a valuable theological resource and, finally, to call on Black scholars and church leaders to identify and recover this resource for use in their work. These arguments are based on my understanding and development of Black *phronesis;* an understanding that deliberately draws upon Black history, culture, and theology.

To demonstrate the contextual character of *phronesis,* let's return for a moment to Aristotle. We see that he defines *phronesis* in the *Nicomachean Ethics* as,

> ... a true and reasoned state or capacity to act with regard to the things that are good or bad for man.[14]

This is a description of practical reasoning that provides the framework within which a person can decide "What should I do in this situation?" This is an important part of Aristotle's ethical theory, because it involves an understanding of what constitutes the "highest good" for humankind. In fact, he describes *phronesis* as an intellectual virtue, as a state which allows the individual who attains it to be able to ascertain what is good for humankind and then to deliberate about how best to reach that good. To properly understand *phronesis* is to first grasp what constitutes the "highest good" in a given culture.

As mentioned previously, Browning's understanding of the "highest good" is located in his notion of mutual regard or the "Golden Rule," which he uses as the inner core for *phronesis.*[15] With this usage, he has chosen to elevate a Kantian deontological perspective, and subsume the Aristotelian *teleological perspective.* By grounding his ethic in a perspective that relies upon the supposed "universal" rights and duties of human moral obligation, not only does he wrongly presuppose the universality of human culture, but he also deprives his method of the valuable theological perspective of ultimate purpose.

A teleological notion, which understands that all nature reflects the purposes of an imminent final cause, reflects the value of the Christian eschatological perspective, and is a crucial element of Black theological perspective. This understanding is crucial for a Black theological perspective that values *Black phronesis* in its approaches.

The understanding of the "highest good" that I offer, here, locates itself within the universe of Black history, culture, religion and experience. It takes its cues from Black resources, and flows from a Christian teleological perspective, which embraces the overall theme of liberation. This liberation theme's eschatological dimension is built on the *telos* of God's redemptive purposes for humankind and is at the core of Black theology. Gayraud Wilmore examines the nature of history and hope among Christian slaves in America and argues that:

> Christian slaves were an eschatological people who believed that Christ was coming again and that there would be a radical transformation of the world and in relationship between people.[16]

This belief is firmly rooted in their understanding of redemptive and liberative acts of God on their behalf that were gleaned from the reinterpretation of biblical narratives.[17] The beginning point of the slave's liberation from bondage was God and God's purposes for humanity. Therefore, this teleological perspective reflects a liberative paradigm for theology. This liberation theme remains crucial for Black theology.

> Liberation is the theme of Black theology. Christ is the Liberator and the Christian faith promises deliverance to the captives.[18]

To speak of liberation within the context of Black theology is to speak of human struggle in the presence of evil; in this case slavery, violence and racism. It portrays the fact that

> at any given time the desire for liberation is a response to the concrete historical and existential concerns of the oppressed.[19]

What I am presenting here is an understanding of *Black phronesis*, which is practical wisdom that reflects a concern to do or to act in accordance with what should be done by and for Black people, who are in need of liberation from socio-economic, political and spiritual oppression. Ergo, liberation, as an ethical good, becomes the core of *Black eudaimonia*, or the "highest *Black* good." The next concern, then, is to demonstrate how this understanding of *Black phronesis* becomes a valuable theological resource. Within the Black faith community, the sources of ethical understanding that lead to the creation of modes of *Black phronesis* are necessarily drawn from Black culture, history and religious traditions. They are located within Black experience and are shaped by Black reinterpretations of Scripture, Black interpretations of historical events and unfold within the context of human situations reflecting Black behavior and responses. As Anthony Reddie points out, Black theology is concerned with the "reinterpretation of Christian traditions and practices in light of liberationist themes and concepts, which arise out of Black experiences."[20] Therefore, *Black phronesis* becomes a key theological resource. The focus now becomes one of how to develop a means by which to begin to recover these unique modes of *Black phronesis,* and to work to create them. My argument is that this can be accomplished through the critical correlation of African American church *praxis,* Christian tradition, and other sources of knowledge.

The work of critical investigation will help to uncover and recover modes of *phronesis* in their various settings and conditions. Critical investigation seeks to peel back the layers of meaning and value which are inherent in all modes of praxis, but which often remain implicit. By making them explicit, they become open to investigation, and so reveal their hidden meanings. This can be accomplished by asking questions of why we do what we do and what do our actions or praxis really mean?

By delving beyond that which is surface and most readily apparent in our modes of praxis, we can begin to uncover, identify and then recover modes of *Black phronesis.*[21] In this way, *phronesis* becomes a bridge between theory and *praxis* and a useful way forward. It provides an historical and cultural bridge between the past, present and future, by drawing on the Black religio-cultural heritage that informs Black faith communities to "fund" the creation of new forms of *Black phronesis,* which will be available as a resource for the future. This understanding of *Black phronesis,* I am asserting here, is valuable for Black theological work because it grounds *phronesis* historically, culturally and contextually, therefore becoming an important theological resource for Black religious scholars.

Black Faith Response and Black *Phronesis*

The Black church in America has come a long way from its humble beginnings in the darkened hush arbors, hidden away from slave masters late at night and in the violence and oppression of the segregated South. The Black church grew and flourished as it faced many harsh realities from institutionalized slavery to Jim Crow racism and legalized segregation in America; nurturing and healing generations who struggled to survive and make sense of life in America as Black people.[22] Due to such origins, the Black church has established itself as the premier Black institution in America. It maintains that privileged position today, having solidified a unique place within the American historical, cultural and religious landscape.

The Black church's ability to nurture, sustain and effectively speak to the Black condition in America is because of its capacity *to draw upon Black resources from its own community*, which includes its historical legacy, cultural ingenuity and folk and religious traditions. These Black resources allowed the creation of compelling modes of Black faith responses to the prevailing conditions of racism, violence, poverty and exclusion.

[...] My position is that the Black faith response was *praxiological*.[23] It was *praxiological* in the sense that it was created utilizing the resources of the Black community in a manner which held together a critical awareness of the existential realities of their contextual location [...] with their religious and theological beliefs. [...]

[...] As the challenges, issues, and events shifted and changed, the *praxiological* nature of the Black faith community's approach facilitated the creation of new forms of *Black phronesis*, which then became resources themselves, in the struggle for freedom, in all its forms. In other words, these modes of *Black phronesis* reflected the concern to do or act in accordance to what ought to be done within *Black contextual realities*.

[...]

Within contemporary society, there is beginning to emerge a Black thematic milieu that is dominated by themes that are different from those which shaped the reality of earlier generations of Black Americans. [...] The dominant themes of this thematic universe are *capitalism, consumerism* and *racism*, all of which are implicated within the overall phenomenon of *globalization*. As I mentioned earlier, these themes are increasingly shaping the experiences of reality of all Americans. However, the ways in which these themes are interpreted and responded to within the African American community are unique and particular. What is needed then is to make available new theological resources to bring to bear on these issues, and subsequent ones, which will invariably arise. *Black phronesis* is such a theological resource.

Cornel West rightly observes that there appears to be a loss of the sense of meaning in life beyond the accumulation of wealth. This can be seen in the eclipse of hope, as reflected by the nihilistic spirit of the times and witnessed in the breakdown of family and neighborhood bonds, and the cultural denudement of urban residents.[24]

> The result is that we now live lives of what we might call "random nows", of fortuitous and fleeting moments preoccupied with "getting over" – with acquiring pleasure, property and power by any means necessary.[25]

He asserts that the answer to this situation lies in the recovery of our help, hope, and power, out of a sense of self and common history, the re-engagement with the common good, and the development of new leadership. While I agree with this positive, yet general response, I maintain that the answer lies in the ability of the *Black church* to identify and recover modes of *Black phronesis* with which to engage, transform and make relevant its actions as it speaks to the realities of contemporary Black life. What West and others may have failed to appreciate is that within the African American community, the sense of *Black phronesis,* the foundation of which is rooted deeply in Black religious tradition and is expressed through modes of Black church *praxis,* is being attenuated and runs the risk of being completely lost. [...]

[...] Many contemporary Black faith responses [...] appear to be struggling in their ability to create authentic, relevant, and constructive modes of *praxis* with which to struggle against the hopelessness, individualism, materialism and loss of the sense of self that are so prevalent today.

Conclusion

A nuanced understanding of *phronesis* for the African American community is one that flows from a Christian teleological perspective, and is grounded in the historical, cultural and religious particularity of Black Americans, and embraces the theme of liberation. [...] What is required, then, is the recovery of those forms of *Black phronesis* that have sustained the Black community for centuries in America, in order to facilitate the creation of new modes of practical wisdom that are relevant and constructive within the contemporary milieu, just described.

There is new and important work now taking place by some scholars that reflects my call for the recovery and use of *Black phronesis.* While those engaged in this work may not conceive of it in such terms, the direction and results of their work point to the fact that *Black phronesis* does play a vital, if unrecognized, role. For example, Dale Andrews has called for a re-modeling of its historical foundations such that it might locate new ways to close the current chasm between Black religion and Black theology.[26] [...]

[...] In Britain, Anthony Reddie's call for the use of a jazz hermeneutic to re-image Black theology draws on the improvisational nature of jazz music and calls for this creative approach to be included in Black theological work.[27]

[...] His use of the jazz motif, with its improvisational and interpretive approach, draws on various and in some cases, previously hidden modes of *Black phronesis* in the Black community, and in so doing, he facilitates the creation of new modes which can be made available to that community.

What the work of these, and other, Black scholars demonstrates, is that *Black phronesis* is an important theological resource that must not be overlooked. However, it is a resource that, for various reasons, is not now widely available to Black scholars and church practitioners. Making *Black phronesis* deliberately explicit in our theological work is to recognize its value and, importantly, to make it available to those whose work can benefit from this vital resource.

Notes

1 Cornel West, *Race Matters*, 2nd ed. (Boston, MA: Beacon Press, 2001), xiv.
2 Clarence Lusane, *Race in the Global Era: African Americans at the Millennium* (Boston, MA: South End Press, 1997).

3 Linda E. Thomas, ed., *Blow the Trumpet in Zion: Global Vision and Action for the 21st Century Black Church* (Minneapolis, MN: Fortress Press, 2004).

4 Iva E. Carruthers, Frederick Haynes, III, and Jeremiah A. Wright, Jr, eds, *Living Stones in the Household of God: The Legacy and Future of Black Theology* (Minneapolis, MN: Fortress Press, 2005).

5 Dwight N. Hopkins, *Heart and Head: Black Theology Past, Present and Future* (New York: Palgrave, 2002).

6 Hopkins, *Heart and Head.*

7 Anthony G. Reddie, *Black Theology in Transatlantic Dialogue* (New York: Palgrave, 2006).

8 Frederick L. Ware, *Methodologies of Black Theology* (Cleveland, OH: Pilgrim Press, 2002).

9 Robert L. Smith, *From Strength to Strength: Shaping a Black Practical Theology for the 21st Century* (New York: Peter Lang, 2007).

10 Don S. Browning, *A Fundamental Practical Theology: Descriptive and Strategic Proposals* (Minneapolis, MN: Fortress Press, 1996).

11 Browning, *A Fundamental Practical Theology.*

12 Aristotle, *The Nicomachean Ethics,* III 3, 1112b11, trans. David Ross, revised J.L. Ackrill and J.O. Urmson.

13 Elaine L. Graham, *Transforming Practice: Pastoral Theology in an Age of Uncertainty* (Eugene, OR: Wipf and Stock Publishers, 1996).

14 Aristotle, The *Nicomachean Ethics.*

15 Browning, *A Fundamental Practical Theology,* 11.

16 Gayraud Wilmore, *Last Things First* (Philadelphia, PA Westminster Press, 1974) as quoted in James H. Evans, Jr, *We Have Been Believers. An African-American Systematic Theology* (Minneapolis, MN Fortress Press, 1992), 151.

17 Dwight N. Hopkins, *Shoes that Fit Our Feet: Sources for a Constructive Black Theology* (Maryknoll, NY: Orbis Books, 1993).

18 J. Deotis Roberts, *Liberation and Reconciliation: A Black Theology* (Philadelphia, PA Westminster Press, 1971), 11.

19 Evans, Jr, *We Have Been Believers,* 15.

20 Reddie, *Black Theology,* 17.

21 Smith, *From Strength to Strength.*

22 Anne H. Pinn and Anthony B. Pinn, *Fortress Introduction to Black Church History* (Minneapolis, MN: Fortress Press, 2002).

23 This term was borrowed from James Evans. See Evans, Jr, *We Have Been Believers.*

24 West, *Race Matters.*

25 West, *Race Matters,* 10.

26 Dale P. Andrews, *Practical Theology for Black Churches: Bridging Black Theology and African American Folk Religion* (Louisville, KY: Westminster John Knox, 2002).

27 Reddie, *Black Theology.*

14

An Intercultural, De-colonial Epistemic Perspective (2012)*

Michel Elias Andraos

Introduction

When it comes to sustaining a broad world orientation, Michel Andraos matches Emmanuel Lartey in terms of background and conceptualization of practical theology and theological knowledge. His interest in intercultural studies comes from his Middle Eastern origin and educational degrees from countries on three continents – Lebanon, Italy and France, and Canada. His current teaching appointment at Catholic Theological Union (CTU) in Chicago as Associate Professor of Intercultural Theology and Ministry brings him into contact with one of the most diverse student bodies in the Association of Theological Schools and one of the more innovative curricula focused on integration. Although his doctorate is in systematic theology, he sustains significant interest in practical theology as critical to his exploration of political causes and ministerial practices. He pursues scholarship in related areas of critical cultural studies, interreligious dialogue, and research on behalf of indigenous peoples of the Americas. His interreligious interests originate in part out of his own experiences with Levantine Catholic communities – Christians in the eastern Mediterranean countries of Syria, Iraq, Jordan, Palestine, Israel, and Lebanon where Islam and Christianity intermingle in ways that Western Christians have overlooked and misconstrued.

More than one chapter in this final section of twenty-first century practical theology is devoted to pedagogy and that interest surfaces prominently in Andraos's essay. As Thomas Groome made clear in his publications in the 1980s, scholars in religious education can hardly avoid questions of epistemology. Anyone in theological education who has revised curriculum gets caught up in bigger questions about the nature of knowledge and learning. Andraos follows suit with one critical addition: he uses coloniality as his analytic lens, focusing on the epistemic distortions that it continues to spawn within the psyches of teachers and learners long past the years of empire regardless of our place on the Eurocentric hierarchy of knowledge (e.g., knowing as abstract, universal, rational, individual).

Original publication details: Michel Elias Andraos, "Engaging Diversity in Teaching Religion and Theology: An Intercultural, De-colonial Epistemic Perspective," pp. 3–15 from *Teaching Theology and Religion* 15:1 (January 2012).

In discussions on diversity in teaching, colonial difference "is rarely clearly named" or "given the attention it merits," Andraos argues. Even when colonialism is mentioned, insufficient attention is given to practical theological questions about exactly what and how we teach. How do we even see, much less honor, the subaltern knowledges when colonial relations persist and a "coloniality of knowledge" is in the air we breathe? As he shows through a detailed exposition of his own course, "delinking" coloniality and knowledge requires multiple considerations: space for other ways of knowing; a shift from speaking *about* theology to *doing* theology; attention to one's own cultural religious context; maximum diversity in readings; assignments that build confidence and trust; respectful encounter with religions on which people have looked down; committed participation; and room for genuine breakthroughs. Such strategies have the potential to alter conventional ways of doing and knowing theology.

Suggested Further Reading

- Michel Elias Andraos, "Christian Communities of the Middle East: Persecuted Minorities or Indigenous Peoples?" *Concilium* 3 (2017): 77–83.
- Walter D. Mignolo, *Local Histories/Global Designs: Coloniality, Subaltern Knowledges, and Border Thinking* (Princeton, NJ: Princeton University Press, 2000).

***

The West was, and still is, the only geo-historical location that is both part of the classification of the world and the only perspective that has the privilege of possessing dominant categories of thoughts from which and where the rest of the world can be described, classified, understood and "improved."

Walter Mignolo, 2005

Few of us would challenge that in too many of our [theology] classrooms the learning/teaching style privileges the values of Western Enlightenment.

Gary Riebe-Estrella

Overview and Introduction

In recent years, thanks to many new voices of scholars on the cultural "margins," as well as in mainstream academia, the boundaries of the discourse on cultural diversity in relation to teaching and learning and the production of knowledge have expanded in many ways. These voices have resonated also in the institutions of theological higher education and have raised new challenges to the traditional ways of teaching and learning theology and religion, as well as to curricular designs and content. As a result of these new challenges, rethinking the pedagogy of teaching and learning in religion and theology, particularly in racially and culturally diverse classrooms, became the focus of many consultations, research projects, and workshops.[1] Given the growing cultural diversity of students in seminaries and divinity schools in the US today, and the growing awareness of the significance and implications of this diversity, it has become unacceptable – and politically incorrect – in most educational institutions not to take cultural diversity in the classroom seriously. In addition, the growing number of international students at ATS

[Association of Theological Schools] schools, mostly from non-Western countries, adds other dimensions to this diversity and makes the intercultural conversation, particularly in relation to the role of religion, theology, and the churches in colonial history and the questions of theological knowledge and power, more complex, yet necessary.[2] How do we do theological education that takes both the issues of diversity and coloniality seriously in the globalized seminaries and divinity schools of North America? [...]

Building on the arguments developed by Charles Foster on diversity in theological education, Lee, Shields, and Oh, in their article "Theological Education in a Multicultural Environment: Empowerment or Disempowerment?," question many uncritical assumptions faculty in theological schools have regarding preparing students from different cultural and racial backgrounds for academic success and effective ministry in a variety of cultural settings. However, despite the significant effort by educators to deal with these issues, the question of how to create and sustain learning environments that are welcoming and empowering to students of all cultural backgrounds, especially when the classroom includes a significant number of international students, remains open (Lee, Shields, and Oh (2008); see also Charles Foster (2002), cited by Lee et al.). In general, the lenses of race, ethnicity, class, gender, culture, and so forth have often been used as hermeneutical, pedagogical, and sometimes epistemic, critical perspectives on the production and function of knowledge in many disciplines. The lens of colonial difference in the classroom, [...] however, is rarely clearly named and given the attention it merits. From this perspective, there are key questions that need to be addressed concerning the power of Eurocentric educational approaches that highly emphasize reason and individualism. These approaches include both the content and methods of communicating knowledge, which are still dominant in the fields of theology and religion. How do we transcend the Eurocentrism of theological education in order to allow more creativity and explore the epistemic potential of truly intercultural learning in global theological institutions and classrooms? How do we engage diversity taking into consideration the colonial difference in the classroom? How does colonial difference change from a topic of learning to a way of teaching, learning, and production of new knowledge? How do we deal with the colonial difference as an epistemic issue as well as an ethical question of justice in theological education? Is recognizing diversity and teaching postcolonial theories in religion and theology enough? [...]

Theological educator Gary Riebe-Estrella, quoted in the epigraph, argues that the necessary change in this area is much more fundamental and very challenging. Riebe-Estrella notes that

> rarely does this underlying value system [Western Enlightenment] and its historical and cultural contextuality come up for faculty discussion and critique – understandably, though wrongly, so. For it is the value system that produced the educational system in which most faculty have been trained and which has shaped their understanding and practice of education.... To challenge the worldview is not only to introduce change but to threaten the fundamental stability of the educational enterprise. (2009, 23)

The author then raises the key question of "How might we get below the pedagogical waterline to the base of the educational iceberg?" and shares some insights based on his experience of engaging the border between Black and Hispanic theologies [...] (Riebe-Estrella 2009, 23).

Without ignoring the significant work for achieving racial justice in theological education and dealing with diversity, the focus of this essay will primarily be on the critique of the perennial dominant Eurocentric approach to teaching and learning in the classroom. This critique, in my opinion, should be an integral part of the broader analysis of theological education and diversity. The statement by Mignolo about the dominant and contested power of Western perspectives quoted in the epigraph is not a recent discovery. The work of unmasking dominant Eurocentric frameworks of knowledge and their interconnectedness with colonial power in all its forms, past and present, is also not new. Yet, not enough attention has been given so far to this question in the classroom context in relation to both *what* (content and knowledge) and *how* (pedagogy) we teach. Pedagogical awareness, diversifying the readings and voices in our syllabi, intercultural sensitivity activities, and the occasional addition of guest speakers who represent different cultural perspectives on certain areas in religion, theology, and ministry, are all important and common activities. However, the question remains whether these are sufficient for making theological education fundamentally less Eurocentric and truly intercultural.

In the following section, I will present a brief summary of some recent articles that reflect the significant progress made in the area of diversity and theological education. Then, using theoretical frameworks primarily from the field of cultural studies that have been advanced over the past few decades by the writings of several scholars on globalization, modernity/coloniality, and the geopolitics of knowledge, I will describe and discuss how this newly developed theoretical analysis might help us tackle the questions raised above around coloniality, interculturality, and knowledge in the classroom and in theological education in general.

In the last part of this essay, using the example of teaching *Religion in Context*, a required course on religion and culture for all Master of Divinity students at Catholic Theological Union [CTU] that I have regularly taught (or team-taught) for the last ten years, I will describe an instance of re-thinking/re-imagining theological education in light of the insights discussed above. I do not pretend here to propose a finished model of a decolonized educational practice. Rather, [...] the last part describes a modest effort at re-thinking and re-imagining that is still a work in progress. The essay will conclude by summarizing an emerging vision for epistemic decolonization. [...]

Colonial Difference in the Classroom

[...]

What I mean in this essay by colonial difference in the multi-racial, multicultural, international classroom is the dominant consensus, often very subtle and silent, that the different representations and systems of cultural knowledge by authors, students, professors, and so forth do not have the same value. The lack of awareness that this consensus is primarily historically shaped by colonial relations between peoples and cultures, I would argue, is also part of the colonial difference. In other words, the cultural, religious, and theological knowledge represented in the classroom are not equally valued. Using Mignolo's terms, persons who *come from different places*, and *think from different locations*, that is from different worldviews, are not interacting mutually (Mignolo 2007, 490–92). Retrospectively, I can say that in almost all the courses I took as a student in a variety of educational institutions, cultural contexts, and countries, and in the courses I taught, there is a hierarchy of systems and sources of knowledge, with the Western perspectives at the top of the pyramid, that is consistently affirmed in subtle, and sometimes unsubtle ways, as universal. This hierarchical relation shapes students' approach to "academic" knowledge, their relation to other students who come from *different* places, and to professors, the authority figures representing "academic" knowledge. Established over a long period of time between the West and the rest of the world, this situation is in my experience still very powerful and continues to prevail in our theology and religion classrooms today. Sanctioned by a dominant academic cultural consensus, silent and subtle in many ways, this reality strongly permeates all educational relations as I experience them (for example, theological curriculum, syllabi, disciplinary knowledge, as well as power relations in the classroom). This is what I am calling in this essay, broadly using Mignolo's term, the colonial difference in the classroom.

Usually, colonial relations are talked about in political, economic, or military terms. Cultural colonization, however, which involves colonized minds and educational systems (well articulated in the writings of W.E.B. Du Bois, Frantz Fanon on colonization, and Edward Said on Orientalism, culture, and imperialism, among many others before and after them) is a deeper and long lasting form of colonial power. This form of colonial power is more subtle and more difficult to identify, resist, and transform. "In order to uncover the *perverse logic* – that Fanon pointed out – underlying the philosophical conundrum of modernity/coloniality and the political and economic structure of imperialism/colonialism," notes Mignolo, "we must consider how to decolonize the 'mind'… and the 'imaginary'… that is knowledge and being" (Mignolo 2007, 450). In his article "On the Coloniality of Being: Contribution to the Development of a Concept," Nelson Maldonado-Torres elucidates the meaning of coloniality as used by Mignolo and others in relation to knowledge and being in daily life. The author distinguishes this meaning of coloniality from the common understanding of colonialism.

Coloniality, in the words of Maldonado-Torres,

> refers to long-standing patterns of power that emerged as a result of colonialism, but that define culture, labor, intersubjective relations, and knowledge production well beyond the strict limits of colonial administration. Thus, coloniality survives colonialism. It is maintained alive in books, in the criteria of academic performance, in cultural patterns, in common sense, in the self-image of peoples, in aspirations of self, and so many other aspects of our modern experience. In a way, as modern subjects we breathe coloniality all the time and everyday. (2007, 243)

According to Mignolo, even though the notion of decolonizing knowledge has been a topic of discussion in many academic disciplines since the seventies, it was the groundbreaking work of Peruvian sociologist Aníbal Quijano that "explicitly linked coloniality of power in the political and economic spheres with the coloniality of knowledge" (Mignolo 2007, 451; Quijano 2000; see also Quijano 1992). Following this argument, Mignolo asks how we decolonize knowledge. Again, using a concept developed by Quijano, the approach advanced by the author for decolonizing knowledge is described in terms of "Delinking." Delinking, Mignolo explains,

> presupposes to move toward a geo- and body politics of knowledge that on the one hand denounces the pretended universality of a particular ethnicity (body

politics), located in a specific part of the planet (geo-politics), that is, Europe where capitalism accumulated as a consequence of colonialism. De-linking then shall be understood as a de-colonial epistemic shift leading to other-universality, that is, to pluri-versality as a universal project…. [Delinking] leads to de-colonial epistemic shift and brings to the foreground other epistemologies, other principles of knowledge and understanding and, consequently, other economy, other politics, other ethics. "New inter-cultural communication" should be interpreted as new inter-epistemic communication. (2007, 453)

From the perspective of Latin America, notes Mignolo, such a process of decolonizing the pretended universality and constructing new intercultural knowledge, is "understood in the constant double movement of unveiling the geo-political location of theology, secular philosophy and scientific reason and simultaneously affirming the modes and principles of knowledge that have been denied by the rhetoric of Christianization, civilization, progress, development, and market democracy" (2007, 463). Delinking as described above, argues the author, is potentially capable of fracturing the epistemic hegemony of Western *theo and ego-politics of knowledge* and of changing the terms of the conversation (Mignolo 2007, 490).

These analyses and insights, I would argue, are helpful for shedding some light into a deeper understanding of the complex questions around interculturality and theological education, curriculum, pedagogy, and the multi-layered power relations in the classroom. […]

Toward an Intercultural, De-colonial Pedagogical Approach

The example I will use for making my reflection on teaching and learning in the culturally diverse classroom concrete is a course on religion and culture I have been regularly teaching, in one form or another, for the past ten years. In its current design, this required course is part of a newly revised curriculum and its objective is to help M.Div. students understand the cultural context of religion and the relationship between culture, spirituality, religion, religious experience, other religions, and theology. The course emphasizes the importance of understanding these relations as a primary context for the study of theology and the integration of theological knowledge. Because of the diversity of its student body and the school's global focus on mission and ministry, the MDiv curriculum at CTU takes interculturality seriously. In the words of Stephen Bevans, a systematic theologian and leading member of the 2004 curriculum design team, "One cannot really do *Christian* theology today without a sense of rootedness in one's own culture, dialogue with other cultures, and dialogue with the world's religions" (Bevans 2008, 112).[3] The course is one of four foundational courses that cover, in addition to religion and culture, non-conventional introductions to systematic theology, doing ministry, and Christian history. All four courses emphasize interculturality and are designed to complement each other in introducing the above mentioned vision of theological education to students. "The curriculum we developed," notes Bevans, "has at its core four principles: ministerial identity, a focus on *doing* theology rather than just knowing answers, a recognition of the contextual and interreligious nature of ministry and theology, and a knowledge and love of the Christian tradition," principles that are also conssistent with ATS standards for the MDiv program, adds the author (2008, 108). A main emphasis of the foundational courses, as well as of the rest of the curriculum, lies in offering an integrated theological education, that is, an education that helps students make connections between historical and theoretical information, lived reality, and their personal and communal life experience, taking into consideration the complexities of the different perspectives in each of these areas, particularly in the new global context of North America. This set of courses, the type of students, the mandate of the curriculum, and the topics discussed provide an ideal opportunity for experimenting with new creative ways for dealing with the challenges of the dominant Eurocentric approach for the study of religion and theology.

In order to introduce the concept of interculturality as production of new knowledge, and help students make connections between the course and their personal experience, cultural knowledge, and context, one of the first assignments in the early part of the course is asking students to write a short paper on personal religious experience with particular attention to their own cultural context, where they grew up, and where they come from. This is the first movement in the course: connection with lived experience and students' cultural context, and introducing interculturality. This helps students realize that their personal and communal cultural experiences are sources of knowledge that require interpretation. They begin to appreciate the importance of this awareness for the theological knowledge about religion and culture before engaging "classical" theoretical frameworks. Students are normally organized in culturally diverse small working groups where they share their personal reflections and knowledge. Small groups provide an opportunity for learning from one another, which is an essential part of the learning process, and create a space for intercultural knowledge to emerge, evolve, and feed into the class discussion and final reflection papers. After dedicating a number of sessions to examining a variety of theoretical frameworks and historical development of concepts, the second written assignment in the course is to write a short paper that focuses on engaging personal experience with the discussed theoretical categories. This becomes another opportunity in the process of constructing intercultural knowledge.

Given the learning objectives and process of the course, finding textbooks for such a class is unthinkable.[4] The course reader consists of a collection of articles from different cultural perspectives from around the world, which include a variety of interreligious theological views. Including such a wide variety of readings on a wide range of topics in one course, to say the least, is a very challenging task. In this case, the six faculty who have alternated in team-teaching this course over the past years, several of whom are people of color from within and outside the US, have all contributed to the compilation of the course reader. As part of its philosophy, the course is intentional about giving voice to historically oppressed and marginalized communities and peoples, from the US as well as from other parts of the world. This is expressed in both the choice of readings, audiovisual material, and in creating an encouraging and trusting environment for students from such groups to speak in class about their personal and community's experience, if they choose to do so. Listening to these perspectives is key for pointing out the limits of dominant frameworks and is one of the eye-opening moments in the course for advancing intercultural learning.

The focus of the rest of the course is on developing a learning attitude for encountering the religious (and cultural) "other." The main assignment for this part involves a small group visit to and participation in a religious service of another religion, which is not difficult to find in almost any neighborhood in Chicago. The site visit is not an ethnographical "participant observation" exercise; rather, it is intended to be a respectful encounter with a community of faith that has a different religious experience. Group visits culminate in writing a short descriptive (phenomenological) report and giving a half-hour class presentation on the group's reactions and questions after their brief encounter with a religious "other." This is usually an "a-ha" moment in the process. For many students, this could be the first time they step into the "sacred space" of another religion, which for some is like breaking a taboo. It is often the case that students – no matter where they come from – have been exposed in their early Christian education and socialization to a prejudiced theology of other religions. Learning to see the religious dignity and humanity of the other is a first step toward encounter and dialogue. A brief practice of these values during the visit is a liberating experience for most students. They begin to see and analyze their prejudice and this becomes an important first step of a process of interreligious and intercultural learning and transformation. This is new knowledge about the religion of the other. It is another way of learning about other religions that does not have as a starting point a preoccupation, common in dominant theologies of religion among seminary students, with what is a true religion and what is not, who is saved and who is not, who has the fullness of "Truth" and who does not, and who needs the Christian gospel to be saved and who does not.

After the group presentations, a class session is dedicated to discussing the relation to the cultural and religious "other" in students' early religious education and cultural experience. In light of some analytical readings on understanding other religious worlds, students do a critical theological reflection on their formative experience of learning about other religions and cultures. We try to analyze and understand where the prejudiced theology comes from and why it has such a powerful grip on students' minds. Colonial relations of Western Christianity to other world religions and cultures are also discussed from historical and theological perspectives with many examples from around the world. Many students also share their personal stories in this area. In an international, culturally diverse classroom, students have different experiences of living with people from other religions. Many students come from areas in the world where they experienced ethnic and religious conflicts, wars, and violence. Listening to the experience of these students gives the class an opportunity to discuss the question of religion and violence and why the same religions co-exist peacefully in one place and are at war in another.

The last class assignment is writing a final reflection paper that includes a summary of the learning from the course, critical personal reflection engaging some of the reading material, and an articulation of the challenges of the course. In addition to learning basic skills for doing cultural analysis of religion and connecting personal and communal experience to knowledge from the fields of religion and culture, some of the learning outcomes of the course at the personal level include healing and transformation, which are often expressed in students' final class sharing and papers. A new theological vision of intercultural and interreligious dialogue that makes room for the "other" helps students restore the dignity of the religious and cultural other in their consciousness. Since many of our students come from areas in the world where cultural, religious, and ethnic tensions, conflicts, wars, and violence have contributed to shaping their worldview, this new learning experience becomes for some an opportunity for empowerment, healing of their memories, and for re-imagining cultural and religious reconciliation. Reading students final papers is always a deep learning experience for me. I consider it a privilege to be able to read the summary of their new learning, breakthroughs, and transformation, as well as to learn about their challenges, frustrations, resistance, and fears. For me personally, accompanying students during such an intellectual, academic, and personally transformative learning process for a semester is both empowering and challenging because their journey, in many ways, is also my journey.

The philosophy and method of the course consider the students in the classroom as a learning community. Students are invited to be active participants in the learning process and production of new knowledge, and not be passive recipients of knowledge from the professors' banks of information and textbooks. Through intensive small group work, focused class discussions, readings from several perspectives from around the world on the topic, and writing reflection papers, the class opens a space for students to *do* inter-cultural theology, and not only *talk* or *hear* about it. From a de-colonial perspective, awakening and engaging seriously the thinking of students who bring different knowledge from their respective traditions and the experience and wisdom of their peoples and communities is crucial. This way of constructing knowledge shifts the focus from abstract thinking that values individualism and ideas from dominant theoretical frameworks to a way of learning that is rooted in cultural experiences in conversation with multiple theoretical frameworks. It is often the case that students from non-Western cultures feel pressured, in many subtle ways and for a variety of reasons, to use Western academic ideas and frameworks to interpret their own experience and cultural context. This approach, which is very common in theological education, is not conducive to integrated learning, alienates learners from their experience and cultural knowledge, and perpetuates coloniality. On the other hand, when students are respected, given theoretical tools, and a space to explore their experience in a particular course that is relevant to this approach of learning, they develop a positive attitude regarding the wisdom and knowledge of other traditions and peoples, their findings become part of a communal process of constructing new knowledge. As a result, intercultural learning begins to happen and coloniality is challenged. For example, when students from different Asian, Latin American, and African countries bring new knowledge about the interaction between traditional religions, Islam, and Christianity in their home communities and cultures, which is substantially different from the interactions between religions and cultures in the US context, many commonly held notions about relations among religions, civilized and uncivilized cultures, violent and peaceful religions, just to name a few areas, are fundamentally challenged. The new knowledge offers an opportunity for intercultural communication and engaging "border thinking" in the classroom that broadens everybody's perspective. In this sense, such a learning space opens an opportunity for de-coloniality and de-linking from dominant categories and ways of thinking […].

As mentioned above, the concepts of "coloniality" and "de-linking" are much broader and more complex analytical frameworks than the limited scope of this article. And for obvious reasons, achieving an intercultural, de-colonized theological education cannot be done in one course; this has to become the general theoretical orientation of the whole theological curriculum and learning environment, and is a life-long process.

Conclusion

It is only recently in my teaching experience that I have been able to name more clearly the colonial difference and its impact on the dynamics of teaching and learning as well as on knowledge production in the classroom. This new perspective on teaching and learning, which has significantly expanded my view of the elephant in my classroom, constantly challenges me to broaden my analysis and search for new insights on how to address the topic of interculturality in the classroom and the theological curriculum in general. "Coloniality" has become a significant hermeneutical key for understanding the dynamics of colonial difference, particularly from an epistemic perspective in a global theological classroom. In my opinion, this is an urgent conversation for theological education because of its global, intercultural dimensions (see Mignolo 1993 and 1999; Dussel 2002 and 2009). In the words of Dussel, "The struggle for epistemic decoloniality lies, precisely, here: de-linking from the most fundamental belief of modernity: the belief in abstract universals through the entire spectrum from the extreme right to the extreme left" (Mignolo 2007, 500).

The dominant Eurocentric universality claim must continue to be challenged and dismantled in order to make room for other religious and theological traditions to become included as partners in an authentic and mutual intercultural dialogue. Such a dialogue, in Dussel's words, will enable us to understand many aspects unknown to us, aspects that may be better developed in some traditions than in others (2009, 499–500). [...]

What Dussel says about dialogue between the world's philosophical traditions is equally relevant to dialogue among religious and theological traditions. How we bring this dialogue to the level of the theological curriculum, syllabi, pedagogy, and transform colonial power relations of theological knowledge in the seminary classroom will continue to be a main challenge to theological education and educators for a long time.

Notes

1 The following recent articles [...] are [...] an indication of the growing interest in this field of scholarship [...]. Jack A. Hill, Melanie L. Harris, and Hjamil A. Martínez-Vázquez (2009), "Fighting the Elephant in the Room: Ethical Reflections on White Privilege and Other Systems of Advantage in the Teaching of Religion"; Cameron Lee, Candace Shields, and Kristen Oh (2008), "Theological Education in a Multicultural Environment: Empowerment or Disempowerment?"; and Fernando A. Cascante-Gómez (2008), "Advancing Racial/Ethnic Diversity in Theological Education: A Model of Reflection and Action," are only a few examples. All three articles include bibliographies of excellent resources on this topic. Also, a recent issue of *Theological Education*, 45, no. 1, 2009 has a special focus on race and ethnicity and includes an article that describes the 2009–13 CORE initiative in this area. See in particular in the same issue the article by Gary Riebe-Estrella, "Engaging Borders: Lifting up Difference and Unmasking Division," 19–25.

2 In his recent article "Gifts Differing: The Educational Value of Race and Ethnicity," Daniel Aleshire, Executive Director of ATS, argues for including international students when considering racial and ethnic diversity (Aleshire 2009, 4). [...]

3 In this article, Bevans includes an outline of the CTU M.Div. curriculum, which provides a good background for better understanding this section of my essay.

4 Most textbooks on religion, including some of those recently written by open-minded and well- informed scholars, continue to evolve around the work of a few European and Euroamerican male scholars who dominate the conversation, which mostly focuses on

Western academic debates on defining religion. Such perspectives are important partners in the conversation, but they should not continue to constitute the center around which the conversation on religion and culture evolves in the curriculum on religion.

Bibliography

Aleshire, Daniel. 2009. "Gifts Differing: The Educational Value of Race and Ethnicity." *Theological Education* 45, no. 1, 1–18.

Bevans, Stephen. 2008. "DB 4100: The God of Jesus Christ – A Case Study for a Missional Systematic Theology." *Theological Education* 43, no. 2, 107–16.

Cascante-Gómez, Fernando A. 2008. "Advancing Racial/Ethnic Diversity in Theological Education: A Model of Reflection and Action." *Theological Education* 43, no. 2, 21–39.

Dussel, Enrique. 2002. "World-System and 'Trans'-Modernity." *Nepantla: Views from South* 3, no. 2, 221–44.

Dussel, Enrique. 2009. "A New Age in the History of Philosophy: The World Dialogue between Philosophical Traditions." *Philosophy and Social Criticism* 35, no. 5, 499–516.

Foster, Charles. 2002. "Diversity in Theological Education." *Theological Education* 38, no. 2, 15–37.

Lee, Cameron, Shields, Candace, and Oh, Kristen. 2008. "Theological Education in a Multicultural Environment: Empowerment or Disempowerment?" *Theological Education* 43, no. 2, 93–195.

Mignolo, Walter D. 1993. "Colonial and Postcolonial Discourse: Cultural Critique or Academic Colonialism?" In *Latin American Research Review* 28, no. 3, 120–34.

Mignolo, Walter D. 1999. "I am Where I Think: Epistemology and Colonial Difference." In *Journal of Latin American Cultural Studies* 8, no. 2, 235–45.

Mignolo, Walter D. 2000. *Local Histories/Global Designs: Coloniality, Subaltern Knowledges, and Border Thinking*. Princeton, N.J.: Princeton University Press.

Mignolo, Walter D. 2005. *The Idea of Latin America*. Malden, MA: Blackwell Publishing.

Mignolo, Walter D. 2007. "Delinking: the Rhetoric of Modernity, the Logic of Coloniality and the Grammar of De-Coloniality." *Cultural Studies* 21, no. 2–3, 449–513.

Nelson Maldonado-Torres. 2007. "On the Coloniality of Being: Contribution to the Development of a Concept." *Cultural Studies* 1, no. 2–3, 240–70.

Quijano, Aníbal. 1992. "Colonialidad y modernidad/ racionalidad." In *Los conquistados. 1492 y la población indígena de las Américas*, Heraclio Bonilla, ed. Quito: Tercer Mundo-Libri Mundi.

Quijano, Aníbal. 2000. "Coloniality of Power and Eurocentrism in Latin America." *International Sociology* 15, no. 2, 215–232.

Riebe-Estrella, Gary. 2009. "Engaging Borders: Lifting up Difference and Unmasking Division." *Theological Education* 45, no. 1, 19–25.

Shor, Ira, and Freire, Paulo. 1987. *A Pedagogy for Liberation: Dialogues on Transforming Education*. South Hadley, MA: Bergin & Garvey Publishers.

15

Mis-Education: A Recurring Theme? (2017)*

Almeda M. Wright

Introduction

Almeda M. Wright, Assistant Professor of Religious Education at Yale Divinity School (YDS), comes from a long line of prominent educators within the African American community and within practical theology itself. In her recently published book, *The Spiritual Lives of Young African Americans* (2017), she names important mentors: Yolanda Smith – a "pillar of strength even before [Wright] came to YDS" (p. x) – taught at Yale in religious education and practical theology until her untimely death from cancer; Evelyn Parker, one of the first womanist practical theologians, offers what Wright considers the only explicit treatment thus far of the fractured spirituality of African American youths; and, finally, Wright completed her doctoral study at Emory University with Mary Elizabeth Moore in 2010, co-editing a book on youths and religion, and had valuable connections with religious education scholar Anne Wimberly who taught at the Interdenominational Theological Center down the road.

In a word, the scholarly influences are more extensive than the suggested reading at the end of this entry reveals. Included instead are two readings that bear directly upon Wright's argument and, true to the *Reader*'s mission, showcase scholarship that unsettles conventional ways of knowing. Olivia Stokes is the first African American woman to earn a doctorate in religious education; the "epistemic responsibility" that Wright demands for a representative canon makes Stokes's inclusion important. In the 1970s, Stokes promoted contextualized forms of education, pushed students toward cross-cultural experiences, and contested stereotypes of women and African Americans embedded in traditional curriculum. Wright's essay also draws directly upon the work of Carter Woodson who wrote a seminal book in 1933, *Mis-education of the Negro*, that foreshadows contemporary debates. One of the first scholars to study African American history, he argued that education can distort and damage as much as enlighten when it fails to embolden its pupils to claim their rightful place in the production of knowledge, thereby perpetuating economic and political discrimination. Mis-education leads people, in his words quoted

Original publication details: Almeda M. Wright, "Mis-Education, A Recurring Theme? Transforming Black Religious and Theological Education," pp. 66–79 from *Religious Education* 112:1 (2017).

by Wright, to "unconsciously contribute to their own undoing by perpetuating the regime of the oppressor."

Woodson provides the perfect baseline for Wright's argument about the need to ward off mis-education in theological education. Through empirical study, she amplifies Woodson's case for an alternative process that attends more fully to the lived realities of African Americans and people in general. There is a huge problem in a theological education "structured such that the lived realities and practices of people [are] undervalued." Knowledge is "more of a liability than an asset" (abstract, p. 66, non-excerpted version) when it devalues persons and their resources. In response to mis-education that persists despite efforts to overcome it, she suggests strategies that include humanization, reconceptualization of the canon, and reclamation of practical wisdom within religious communities. From her first degree in engineering, Wright brings to her argument an incisive reasoning; from teaching middle school, she gains first-hand insight into the split among young people between an avid personal faith and political engagement; perhaps most important, from her American Baptist roots, she possesses a deep hope that personal religion and social activism can be reunited.

Suggested Further Reading

- Almeda M. Wright, *The Spiritual Lives of Young African Americans* (New York: Oxford University Press, 2017).
- Olivia Pearl Stokes, "Education in the Black Church: Design for Change," *Religious Education* 69:4 (1974), 433–45.
- Carter G. Woodson, *The Mis-Education of the Negro* (Washington, DC: Associated Publishers, 1933).

***

In the *Mis-Education of the Negro* (1933), Carter G. Woodson, a historian, educator, and founder of what has become Black History month, offered a reflective and even self-critical assessment of the educational processes of persons of African descent in the United States. Woodson reflects on history, philosophy, business, and sciences, as well as religious studies and the training of African American clergy. His overall assessment was that of *mis-education*. According to Woodson, in becoming "educated" (at that point in history) the *Negro* had in essence been "taught to despise" his people and culture. He writes:

> The Negro thus educated is a hopeless liability to the race. The difficulty is that the "educated Negro" is compelled to live and move among his own people whom he has been taught to despise ... the "educated Negro" prefers to buy his food from a white grocer because he has been taught that the Negro is not clean ... (Woodson 1933, xix)

Education, which was supposed to be a source of empowerment, came at a cost. Woodson even asserts that it was not a point of pride to boast of the increased numbers of educated persons since emancipation, because "If they are of the wrong kind, the increase in numbers will be a disadvantage rather than an advantage" (xvii). For Woodson, the sign of a good education was not "the mere imparting of information" (xvi). Education was supposed to equip people to face "the ordeal before them" and not "unconsciously contribute to their own undoing ..." (xvii).

Reflecting on Woodson's assessment, has education improved since 1933? Is mis-education a recurring theme? Can education still be a *liability*? And how does mis-education connect with religious education and faith development today? Woodson's assertions about mis-education are disconcerting because there is always the potential for mis-education, broadly and within Black theological and religious education today. And yet, I remain confident that mis-education is not an inevitable recurring trend. Education has the power to be transgressive and an act of freedom. Therefore it is important to explore the history of mis-education *and* how we can rethink Black religious and theological education to fully embody transformative education. In my work, I define *Black Religious and Theological Education* as both

- Education within predominately African American religious communities and
- Education about Black religious traditions in academic and religious settings.

Much can be said about the role of European Americans in the early mis-education of Black people in the United States, the ongoing Eurocentric nature of most of theological education,[1] and the continuing segregation of most American churches. However, following Woodson's gaze, this article looks primarily at the failures of religious education within African American Christian contexts to educate in ways that improve the life circumstances of its practitioners and support their efforts towards freedom and liberation. This does not downplay the ongoing absence of meaningful strategies to respond to racism or the naïve multiculturalism of most religious education (see Moy 2000).

This article, instead, offers another perspective on the ways that racism and religious education intersect in the US context. It attends to the institutionalized and structural racism inherent in the content and pedagogy of theological education, as well as what has been embodied and learned by African Americans by participating in this type of implicitly racist theological education. Therefore, I offer a brief overview of early African American religious education, and point toward key pedagogical strategies that reflect the liberative dimensions and possibility of Black religious and theological education.

History and Practices of Mis-Education

Historically, persons of African descent in the United States have struggled on several fronts with regard to education. Enslaved Africans were often legally restricted from obtaining basic literacy skills and risked life and limb in order to learn to read. Even with the end of slavery; with the waves of Northern missionaries coming to the South to teach literacy and the Bible; with the tremendous growth of the Sunday school movement during the reconstruction and early twentieth-century era; literacy and education among African Americans remained sporadic and an often subversive act (if taken seriously).

African American churches and denominations in the eighteenth and nineteenth centuries made great strides in connecting their spiritual practices with social uplift and literacy education. Richard Allen, the founder of the African Methodist Episcopal church in 1787, organized both a church and a school for the instruction of youth and adults in the faith, reading, and writing. Across each of the historically African American denominations, religious educator Kenneth Hill (2007) notes the intricate connection between the founding of denominations, along with educational ministries, publishing boards, and often institutions of higher learning. For example, the African Methodist Episcopal Zion Sunday School Union began publishing curriculum in 1872. Likewise, the African Methodist Episcopal Church established their publishing house in 1882 in conjunction with the founding of the Sunday School Union. The National Baptist Convention, USA Sunday School Board began publishing curriculum in 1897, the Church of God in Christ in 1912, and the Christian Methodist Episcopal Church began in 1918 (Hill 2007, 21–22). The history of literacy and education among African American churches also includes their support of institutions that were started for Blacks by White, Northern missionaries and denominations.

However, even in the wake of many of these efforts, the interconnection between subversive education and African American Christianity did not remain. By the 1930s Carter G. Woodson notes that all was not well within these independent African American churches. Woodson argues that while the "Negro church is the only institution the race controls," others controlled the education of the Negro (Woodson 1933, 57). Woodson further argued that the primary approach to clergy education was "go to school to memorize certain facts to pass examination for jobs." Afterward the educated clergy paid "little attention to humanity" (56). Woodson offers an example of a minister who, as a result of his education, failed to connect with and acknowledge the religious and social lives of his community:

> The minister had attended a school of theology but had merely memorized words and phrases, which meant little to him and nothing to those who heard his discourse. … The minister had given no attention to the religious background of the Negroes to whom he was trying to preach. He knew nothing of their spiritual endowment and their religious experience as influenced by their traditions and environment in which the religion of the Negro has developed and expressed itself. He did not seem to know anything about their present situation … (66)

Woodson's critique is striking and he does not distinguish between whether the minister had been trained in a program designed for Black ministers or a more Eurocentric institution. In fact, Woodson argues that these differences did not truly matter, because of the way the educational programs had been structured such that the lived realities and practices of people were undervalued – and specifically there was no value ascribed to attending to the beliefs and practices of persons of African descent. Woodson was not alone in offering harsh and direct criticism of the theological and religious education of African Americans. His contemporaries like W.E.B. Du Bois and Nannie Helen Burroughs offered their own criticism of the way that Black clergy engaged with the masses of Black people and often failed to address their concerns (Du Bois 1903; Higginbotham 1994). Similar criticisms of Black religious and theological education persisted throughout the twentieth century. For example, early Black liberation theologian and pastor Albert Cleage wrote of his disappointment with both African American and European Christian publishing during the mid-twentieth century. Cleage (1972) writes:

> It's become impossible for Black people to use Sunday school literature from white publishing houses. Literature from Black publishing houses is just as bad because it is a copy of the same material. Such is the persistence of white authority. When white publishing houses began to put Black pictures in every quarterly just to make it "respectable," this did not change the basic white orientation of the literature (xxxv; see also Wright 2016)

Similarly, Hill (2007) notes a "de-radicalization" of Black religious education during the early twentieth century, with only a small re-orientation during the 1960s and '70s (20; see also Wilmore 1998, 163–95).

However, despite the ongoing disappointment with religious education literature and theological training, implicit in Woodson's critique of theological education is an alternative process of theological education, in which attention to the religious and social lives of African Americans (and to the lived realities of people in general) becomes essential to the effective training of clergy and by extension to the empowerment of churches to participate in the process of "social uplift" and liberation. Woodson was making the claim that you cannot save the people, socially or spiritually, if you do not study and value their lives and their religion.

Mis-Education in Contemporary Black Religious and Theological Education

It is perplexing that Woodson's critique still holds in many churches and schools of theology, some 80 years later. The prevalence of *mis-education* persists despite the efforts of many African American religious educators and womanist practical theologians to push for more cultural inclusion and reform in theological education and churches. In particular, educators such as Olivia Pearl Stokes (1974) and Grant Shockley (1976, see also Foster and Smith 2003), in the wake of the Civil Rights and Black Power movements, developed models of religious education that take seriously the concerns of Black people and perspectives of Black Liberation Theology.

More recent educators have also attempted to incorporate elements from both African and African American history. Anne Wimberly (1994) offers methods of religious education that attend to the practices of enslaved communities to link their cultural heritage, the biblical story, and personal experiences. Likewise, Yolanda Smith (2004) emphasizes the *triple heritage* of African American Christian education through a rich analysis of spirituals and offers models for congregations to attend to culture and religious education. Others, like N. Lynne Westfield (2008), have pushed the conversation further in the religious academy by writing from her experiences of teaching as a Black woman.

Collectively these scholars make a similar, although sometimes implicit, critique to Woodson's. And yet, the nature of mis-education is insidious and pervasive, such that Woodson's critique and these earlier works have not reversed patterns of mis-education within African American religious communities or in the academy. In part, earlier African American religious educators often assumed a natural and full embrace of the tenets of Black Liberation Theology by Black Christian communities (as well as a continued commitment to African American religion and Black Theology in theological and religious education). They were pointing to the areas of hope and possibility within African American Christianity, without directly acknowledging the difficulty many African American clergy and churches faced in attempting to teach or preach Black Liberation Theology (and the difficult task of undoing centuries of mis-education both in seminaries and churches).

At the same time, many African American churches fail to see the importance of training clergy and constructing religious instruction in ways that are attuned to the religious, social, historical, and political lives of an increasingly diverse African American community. Over the past decade I reviewed educational resources (including Sunday school literature and sermons) used in African American churches.[2] My findings parallel the trends noted in previous generations by Woodson, Cleage, and Hill.[3]

While the sample of Sunday school literature and sermons included a rich array of reflections on the work of God within the lives of God's people, there was minimal discussion of liberation, justice, freedom, or other social concerns of African Americans. In four years of Sunday school literature only three of the lessons reviewed offered explicit discussions of race or racism. Beyond the inclusion of images of Black and brown people in the curriculum, there was limited engagement with the current cultural realities of African Americans.[4] The most widely used African American Sunday school literature was primarily silent on discussions of structural or institutional concerns, and there was an overall absence of transgressive theology and pedagogy within the educational resources. This sermon and curriculum sample offer only a small snapshot, but the parallels with larger surveys of educational resources for and in African American Christian religious education remain striking (Hill 2007; Lincoln and Mamiya 1990).

Looking also at mis-education in theological education, I also surveyed a small sample of seminarians and new pastors. The survey participants include African American seminarians and recent graduates who are working in a variety of ministry contexts. Half of the students attended historically Black seminaries, and the remaining attended predominately white, university-affiliated divinity schools and stand-alone denominational seminaries.

They were asked to reflect on their connection with course content, readings, and assignments; on how well the faculty presented and reflected the values and concerns of their communities of origin; and if they felt prepared for ministry in diverse and multicultural contexts. They also reflected on their overall satisfaction with their theological education. Recognizing the limitations of self-reporting and the small sample size of students surveyed ($n = 24$), the data are not generalizable to all African American students in formal theological education. Instead, this preliminary data, particularly the open responses, point to places of further exploration as we consider the ongoing effects of mis-education in Black religious and theological education.

The seminarians and recent graduates, overall, are very to extremely satisfied with their theological education (~66% fall in this range) and feel moderately to completely prepared for their current ministry context (96%). These two are tremendous feats. Also, the majority of the students feel that the readings, assignments, and faculty *sometimes* reflect the values and concerns of their communities and cultures. The students were much less positive here, and there was a significant difference across gender. Women, who were more likely to list additional degrees and theological education (beyond the M.Div.), were not as positive about their sense of connection with the readings, assignments, or faculty members, thus possibly pointing to an overlooked dimension of *mis-education* from Woodson's earlier work. Finally in response to whether their theological education made them feel estranged from their communities of origin, which most closely reflects Woodson's definition of mis-education, the vast majority of respondents strongly disagreed.

[…]

Mis-Education as Chasms

Woodson's definition of mis-education (where one comes to despise one's community and culture in the educational process) for the most part does not explicitly hold today. However, this preliminary research indicates that contemporary mis-education includes elements similar to Woodson's critique, but with different contours and intensity. I posit that the best characterization of mis-education within contemporary Black theological and religious education is that of *chasm*. A chasm represents both a boundary that must be crossed, and a breach, which must be repaired. There are several multilayered and overlapping chasms that contribute to mis-education in Black religious and theological education today. In particular, there are chasms between African American students and the structures and content of theological education and between Black religious academics and African American religious leaders, practitioners, and students. These both intersect with the developing chasms within the African American Christian community and wider society because of increasing pluralism.

Chasms Between African American Students and Theological Education

The chasm between African American students, as well as other students of color and formal structures of theological education begins with the limitations to who has access to theological education. However, it also includes perceived and real disconnections with the content of courses. For example what is included in the course offerings, syllabi and assignments, what counts as knowledge or authoritative sources, the forms of communication which are valued, the context in which learning takes place, the diversity of the student body, and even the type of mentors and role models available to students are all part of this chasm.

The students surveyed above offered an even assessment of whether they felt the faculty, readings, and assignments helped them connect with their communities of origin and feel prepared to do ministry in these areas. This sample also represents 50% who were in a historically Black university context, with significantly more faculty of color.

Even as this article looks primarily at the experiences of mis-education among African Americans, it is important to note that the concerns raised are not unique or limited to the African American community. Postcolonial theory and conversations remind us of similar criticisms raised in response to the educational institutions created under oppression and colonialism around the globe. Without reducing these very diverse contexts and historically situated realities into one experience, there are significant patterns and similarities that arise in different contexts. For example, Linda Tuhiwai Smith (1995) echoes Woodson's critiques as she discusses the colonial educational processes for the Maori people in New Zealand. She argues that part of the colonizing educational project was to estrange, if not erase and devalue, the knowledge and practices of indigenous people – as well as to do research that most often exploited the Maori.

Kwok Pui-lan also affirms the ways that education can be a double-edged sword, as she describes the arduous process of wrestling with the ways one's mind, self-knowledge, and theological imaginations have also been colonized. Kwok Pui-lan (2005) writes that:

> I have been reflecting on my long intellectual journey to "struggle to know." Why is knowing a struggle? It is a struggle because you have to spend years learning what others told you is important to know, before you acquire the credentials and qualifications to say something about yourself. It is a struggle because you have to affirm first that you have something important to say and that your experience counts. (29)

The significance of the chasm between formal theological education and minority communities is not simply a lack of diversity in courses, but the internalization of dominant cultural values and knowledge (at the cost of one's community's) is detrimental to transformative education.

Chasms Between Black Academics and African American Religious Practitioners and Students

In addition to the disconnection between students and formal theological education, there is another equally problematic chasm between Black religious academics and African American religious leaders, practitioners, and students. The survey response of a female student who was appalled that a Black professor would demean students at a historically Black seminary is just one example of this chasm. And while her response describes her unique experiences with one faculty member, hers is not an isolated experience or critique. Her critique was not simply that the faculty member demeaned a student, but that this faculty member appeared "to have forgotten where they came from." This points to larger discussions and ongoing tensions regarding the role of African American scholars as public intellectuals and the interconnection of Black religious scholars and African American churches.

Black religious scholars, from Du Bois and Woodson to James Cone and Delores Williams, have offered rich and ongoing reflections on the religious lives and the communal struggles of African Americans. However, the introduction of disciplines such as Black theology and womanist ethics have often not translated into transformed religious practices within Black churches or communities. The reasons for this lack of translation are numerous. But evidence of this chasm between Black religious scholars and practitioners is in part an indicator of ongoing mis-education.

In part, significant numbers of Black clergy still do not have formal theological training, as such exposure to scholarship about Black and womanist theology may not take place. However, even among the seminary-trained ministers surveyed above, they noted that they were not "applying" all that they learned in seminary in their current ministry contexts. As a practical theologian, the failure of Black religious scholarship to connect with Black churches is particularly problematic. However, it is not easily remedied if Black scholars do not participate in changing the culture of knowledge construction, such that their work can speak both about the lived realities of Black people *and* to Black people.

Dale Andrews (2002) notes the somewhat oxymoronic nature of the field of practical theology – in that for some it does not seem possible that the academic study of theology can be made practical and thus connect with communities of practice. He makes the case that fields such as practical theology have a unique task of bridging the gap between these communities. He notes that often in the African American community many of the conversations in academic guilds have served as scathing critiques of communities of practice without the parallel work of attending to and valuing these communities, or working within communities toward mutual positive reform. Instead, there are numerous questions of whether Black religious scholars can take seriously the lived religious practices of the majority of African Americans.

[...]

Related to the chasm between the Black religious academy and practitioners of Black religion, contemporary mis-education is also characterized by other intra-communal chasms. The plurality of the African American community and identity include intersections of race with gender, class, ethnicity or immigrant status, sexuality, geography, religious affiliation, age, ability, among so many others. Rather than embracing this rich tapestry of experiences and identities, at times this diversity has served to further divide and ostracize members within the community.

Black religious and theological education has at times embraced pedagogy, which does not allow for difference. For example, womanists and others had to push for an expansion of early articulations of Black Liberation Theology beyond a patriarchal, heteronormative paradigm. While this goes far beyond anything that Woodson could have conceived, his challenge to attend to the values and realities of people continues to hold true and serves as correctives to academic and theological gaps, that have also failed to take seriously the religious values and practices of women, youth, queer, transgender, and poor people, among so many others. Similarly, Black religious and theological education has yet to make sense of the religious diversity, and even humanist traditions that are also reflected in the African American religious experience.

Studying Black Religion as Transgressive and Emancipatory Action

Reclaiming the Transgressive Elements of African American Religious Education

Beyond the historical shortcomings there are myriad ways studying Black religion is transgressive and emancipatory action. bell hooks (1994) defines transgressive education as "teaching that enables transgressions – a movement against and beyond boundaries. … It is that movement which makes education the practice of freedom" (12). Thus, how do we promote boundary crossings, how do we repair the chasms, and foster this type of education for all students? My assertion is that Black religious and theological education *can be* transgressive and a practice of freedom for historically oppressed and marginalized communities and for the dominant community. In particular, Black religious and theological education can be a source of affirmation and creative transformation for historically oppressed and marginalized communities. It can also be a source of transformation and challenge to the normative claims about what counts as knowledge and as authoritative for dominant communities. Here, I briefly point to three strategies I deem essential for the work of stopping the cycles of mis-education.

Strategy 1: Humanization and Affirming *Somebodiness*

Womanist theologian Jacquelyn Grant (1989) writes that Christian education and theology must help instill a sense of *somebodiness* in youth. Grant describes the idea of somebodiness as an affirmation of the humanity of Black people, but particularly of youth (69). Writing in the 1980s, Grant borrows the idea of "somebodiness" from the practices of Jesse Jackson during the same period, where he encouraged youth to chant: "I am somebody. I may be poor, but I am somebody." Grant notes that "To be somebody is to be human" – to counter the attempts of oppressors to create races and classes of *nobodies*.[5]

Grant argues that Black Christian theology has to be responsible for overturning notions that Black people, women, youth, among others are not fully human. Similarly, Paulo Freire (2000) begins his seminal work, *Pedagogy of the Oppressed*, outlining the vocation of all people as "humanization" – the process of being and remaining fully human, despite the many attempts to thwart this process (43–44). In his discussion of dialogical and liberative education, Freire affirms the need for any efforts towards liberation and transformation to begin and connect with the individual and their questions. Freire offers "problem-posing" education as a corrective to educational practices which further reify oppressive structures, by depositing narratives and knowledge that continue the mythology that the oppressed are less than human or that humanization is not a viable possibility (79). Furthermore within truly liberative education, Freire argues that there must exist "a profound love for the world and people" and

> faith in [humanity's] power to make and remake, to create and re-create, faith in their vocation to be more fully human (which is not the privilege of the elite, but the birthright of all). … Without this faith in the people, dialogue is a farce which inevitably degenerates into paternalistic manipulation. (90–91)

Freire, with Grant and Woodson, undergirds the idea that in order for Black religious studies and theological education to be transgressive, it must also start with the experiences of the people and must center on and include a love of Black people. Teaching Black religion and participating in Black religious education does more harm than good if our starting assumption is that the religious lives and experiences of Black people are irrelevant or somehow insignificant.

Strategy 2: Canon Building and Epistemic Responsibility

Countering the dehumanizing effects of the larger society on historically oppressed persons is not something that can be taken lightly. The need for humanizing education persists because of the many ways that African Americans and others (including youth, women, etc.) have been and continue to be viewed as less than and somehow inadequate as subjects of rigorous academic study and as producers of knowledge. Therefore, the second strategy entails expanding the "canon," such that teaching Black religion serves as a liberative practice for both African American and non-African American students.

In the various contexts where I have taught, in both rural settings and prestigious institutions, for some of my students my mere embodiment is a jarring experience and daily exercise in cognitive dissonance. Often when I walk in on the first day of class, I feel the myriad double takes required for students of all races and ethnicities and ages to mentally and physically adjust to my presence. I lived the reality so aptly described by N. Lynne Westfield (2008), where she states:

> While it is, indeed many years since desegregation and school integration, for the overwhelming majority of my students, I am, if not the first and only, then one of the few African American women teachers in their lives. (64)

However, beyond having to negotiate the cognitive dissonance created by teaching with/in a Black female body, there is a certain transgressive nature in daring to teach Black religion and womanist, feminist, queer, and postcolonial theologies in required courses. In particular, the inclusion of African American religious traditions (as well as other historically marginalized traditions) as essential and not peripheral or special topics in required courses immediately affirms the value of African Americans and their contributions to American religion. However, carefully teaching African American religion de-centers and deconstructs the power held by dominant communities by directly challenging the myth that there are narrowly defined sources of authority or knowledge. Looking at the work of feminist philosopher Lorraine Code (1995), she writes that:

> the issue is less of doing philosophy "in a different voice" ... than of discerning whose voices have been audible, and whose muffled ...; of showing whose experiences count, and how epistemic authority is established and withheld. (155)

Code reminds us that teaching Black religion in "dominant spaces" does more than add readings to the syllabus, but it should push for all knowledge introduced and created in these spaces to be identified as constructed by particular people in history. Code also reminds us that in teaching and creating scholarship we have to take seriously our *epistemic responsibility*, which she describes as the link between what we know and how we act in community (155).

[...]

Strategy 3: Attending to the Traditions of the Communities

Finally, I return to the core of Woodson's critique that the mis-educated minister knew nothing about the religious experiences and present conditions of the people. In order for Black theological and religious education to become transformative, scholars and clergy must pay attention to what is central within the religious communities and to begin with these central components in our educational efforts (and in our efforts towards transformation). As noted above, the contours of mis-education are shaped in relation to an increased awareness of diversity within the African American community. This diversity in some cases has become barriers to inclusion. And tremendous strides need to be made in terms of fostering dialogue around gender equality, inclusion of same-gender loving persons, and affirmation of the pluralistic religious heritage within African American communities.

However, this process cannot begin by denigrating the traditions and practices of the community. For example, African American Christians, like most Christian communities, rely heavily on the Bible as one source of theology and wisdom. [...] While it is easy to argue that the Bible is not the best resource we have for formulating our sexual ethics or our views on sexuality and homosexuality, etc., this does not eliminate the work of religious educators and theologians from creating methods of inviting people for whom the Bible remains significant into critical conversation with it. [...] Truly transformative religious education has to honor the traditions of the communities and to invite them into the process of knowledge construction – such that we are not simply changing the content of information imparted but the way that learning and knowing take place.

Mis-Education is not the Final Word

[...] While transformation of religious and theological institutions and curriculum will not take place over night, transformation is possible. It becomes a reality when we continuously rethink our overall understanding of the purposes of education as practices of freedom and transgression – such that classrooms and other educational settings becomes the loci for boundary crossing and cross-cultural encounters.

I first embraced the idea of education as a practice of freedom reading bell hooks' 1994 book, *Teaching to Transgress*. In her more recent text, *Teaching Critical Thinking*, hooks (2010) writes that

> Since there has not been a radical transformation of education at its roots, education as the practice of freedom is still a pedagogy only accepted by individuals who elect to concentrate their efforts in this direction ... (27–28)

hooks asserts that systemic changes have not occurred in education (at any level) and that resistance to education as a practice of freedom is rampant both in power structures, in individual educators, and in students who do not see the need for this type of education. At first this statement is disheartening, but in it hooks is also offering an invitation to participate, anew, in this type of education. In truth, it is the invitation offered by Woodson in the early twentieth century and the one that scholars and practitioners who continue to value the transformative nature of religious education must fully consider.

Notes

1 It is important to note the limited treatment of issues of race and racism within the field of religious education. While an assessment of this is beyond the scope of this article, a quick literature search shows that the last *Religious Education* journal issue focused primarily on the contributions of African American Christianity to religious education was in 1974.

2 For a fuller discussion of these research findings see Almeda M. Wright, *The Spiritual Lives of Young African Americans* (Oxford: Oxford University Press, 2017).

3 Many of the original publishing companies established in connection with the Independent Black church movement are still producing literature for churches. However, for this research I used a cross-denominational resource, *Urban Ministries Inc. (UMI)*, as it reflects a higher rate of usage (and copies sold) than the denomination specific publications. Curriculum sample ($n = 104$ lessons over a 3-year span).

4 The sermons ($n = 25$) include a national sample collected from Christian media outlets, such as *Streaming Faith* and *YouTube*. Sermons were analyzed across two time frames within the last decade: 2007–09 and 2014–16. The national sermons were selected based on their popularity based on the "hits" or views each had on social media. Local or smaller church sermons represented a sample of convenience based on the researchers' access to local congregations in two geographic locales.

5 There are echoes in contemporary youth movements such as *Black Lives Matter* to also affirm the worth and *somebodiness* or humanity of Black people in the United States.

References

Andrews, D. 2002. *Practical Theology for Black Churches: Bridging Black Theology and African American Folk Religion*. Louisville, KY: Westminster John Knox.

Cleage, Jr. A. 1972. *Black Christian Nationalism*. Detroit: Luxor Publishers.

Code, L. 1995. *Rhetorical Spaces*. New York: Routledge.

Du Bois, W.E.B. 1903. *The Negro Church*. Eugene, OR: Cascade, 2011.

Foster, C.R., and F. Smith. 2003. *Black Religious Experience: Conversations on Double Consciousness and the Work of Grant Shockley*. Nashville, TN: Abingdon Press.

Freire, P. 2000. *Pedagogy of the Oppressed, 30th Anniversary Edition*. New York: Bloomsbury Academic.

Grant, J. 1989. "A Theological Framework." In *Working with Black Youth: Opportunities for Christian Ministry*, ed. Charles Foster and Grant Shockley, 55–76. Nashville, TN: Abingdon Press.

Higginbotham, E.B. 1994. *Righteous Discontent: The Women's Movement in the Black Baptist Church, 1880–1920*. Cambridge: Harvard University Press.

Hill, K. 2007. *Religious Education in the African American Tradition*. Danvers: Chalice.

hooks, b. 1994. *Teaching to Transgress: Education as the Practice of Freedom*. New York: Routledge.

____. 2010. *Teaching Critical Thinking: Practical Wisdom*. New York: Routledge.

Lincoln, C.E., and L. Mamiya, 1990. *The Black Church in African American Experience*. Raleigh, NC: Duke University Press.

Moy, R.G. 2000. "American Racism: The Null Curriculum in Religious Education." *Religious Education* 95:2, 120– 33. doi: 10.1080/0034408000950202

Pui-Lan, K. 2005. *Postcolonial Imagination and Feminist Theology*. Louisville, KY: Westminster John Knox.

Shockley, G.S. 1976. "Liberation, theology, Black theology and religious education." In *Foundations for Christian Education in an Era of Change*, ed. Marvin J. Taylor. Nashville: Abingdon Press.

Smith, L.T. 1995. *Decolonizing Methodologies: Research and Indigenous People*. London: Zed Books, 2012.

Smith, Y. 2004. *Reclaiming the Spirituals: New Possibilities for African American Christian Education*. Cleveland: Pilgrim Press.

Stokes, O.P. 1974. "Education in the Black Church: Design for Change." *Religious Education* 69:4, 433–45. doi:10.1080/0034408740690406

Westfield, N.L. 2008. *Being Black, Teaching Black: Politics and Pedagogy in Religious Studies*. Nashville, TN: Abingdon Press.

Wilmore, G. 1998. *Black Religion and Black Radicalism, 3rd ed.* Maryknoll, NY: Orbis.

Wimberly, A.S. 1994. *Soul Stories: African American Christian Education*. Nashville, TN: Abingdon Press.

Woodson, C.G. 1933. *The Mis-Education of the Negro*. Chicago: African American Images, 2003.

Wright, Almeda M. 2016. "Image is Everything? The Significance of the Imago Dei in the Development of African- American Youth." In *Albert Cleage, Jr and the Black Madonna and Child*, ed. Jawanza Clark, 171–88. New York: Palgrave McMillan.

16

Ventriloquism and Epistemic Violence (2017)*

Courtney T. Goto

Introduction

Like Wright, Courtney T. Goto writes as a scholar well versed in religious education with a particular focus on power, white supremacy, and the production of practical theological knowledge. Associate Professor of Religious Education at Boston University School of Theology, she also studied at Emory University, and her engagement with practical theology has been propelled by frustration with the discipline's uncritical perpetuation of problematic race politics.

"I invite the reader to notice and be curious," Goto says in the essay, "about any visceral reaction to the connections I am making." If her essay rubs readers the wrong way, in other words, she would register that reaction as a sign of success. Here and in her new thought-provoking book, *Taking on Practical Theology: The Idolization of Context and the Hope of Community* (2018), she knows it will not be easy for readers to see what we do not want to see. Even though she eases into her argument, "telling it slant" to coax readers along, readers should be troubled, she implies, but hopefully not impeded from heeding the deeper message. The aim of her essay and her book is to heighten critical consciousness about our academic proclivity, especially given our desire to represent local knowledge, to assume that we can speak for others in all their particularity, a form of what she and others identify as ventriloquism. The essay is built around Gayatri Spivak's evocative claim about the "epistemic violence" that occurs when the colonizer refuses "to recognize the colonized as knowers." Goto expands the term to include systemic and institutional damage inflicted when those with power and privilege erase the voices and visibility of others, distorting and dismissing their reality and existence. Practical theologians fall prey to this danger, perhaps more than others, because we try to "give voice" to everyday religious experiences. Despite good intentions, a great deal is "lost in translation as the researcher becomes further removed from the lived experiences under investigation."

Even if Goto sometimes risks a reductive reading of the scholars who she portrays, she greatly advances the discussion, underscoring the need for heightened awareness of distorted disciplinary knowledge. She concludes her essay with concrete strategies to

Original publication details: Courtney T. Goto, "Experiencing Oppression: Ventriloquism and Epistemic Violence in Practical Theology," pp. 175–93 from *International Journal of Practical Theology*, 21:2 (2017).

avoid epistemic violence, such as more participatory research, self-reflectivity, and equity in student – professor relationships. She exemplifies the kind of practical wisdom that we will all need to hear each other out. For some, this will mean admitting and addressing mistakes, for others protesting wrongful injury, and for all a kindness and generosity of spirit. On this score and in general, Goto's essay serves as a pivotal final essay for Part I. It does not so much provide closure as incitement and invitation, suggesting the need for more work on how practical theological knowledge is produced and the kind of dispositions that its production requires, especially when the desire is to understand the production of knowledge as grounded in lived experience.

Suggested Further Reading

- Courtney T. Goto, *Taking on Practical Theology: The Idolization of Context and the Hope of Community* (Leiden: Brill, 2018).
- Fumitaka Matsuoka, *Out of Silence: Emerging Themes in Asian American Churches* (Cleveland: Pilgrim Press, 1995).
- Rey Chow, *Writing Diaspora: Tactics of Intervention in Contemporary Cultural Studies* (Bloomington: Indiana University Press, 1993).

***

Truth must be "told slant" as Emily Dickinson says.[1] The whole truth must be revealed but through "explanation kind," says the poet, lest every person be "blinded" by truth too intense or "bright." What I have to say is that truth must be told by taking an indirect route, with small steps, so that it might be taken in more gradually and thoughtfully. In this spirit, I start with a case as practical theologians often do, but "telling it slant" from a cognate field, psychotherapy.

American theorists in psychotherapy and theology Alvin Dueck and Kevin Reimer discuss the implications of Christians providing psychotherapeutic care in a multicultural world.[2] They tell the story of Juanita, who comes from the small village of Santiago de Atitlán in the mountains of Guatemala.[3] She experienced what no human being should be allowed to endure – the disappearance, torture, and murder of her husband. In her village, loved ones were regularly kidnapped by guerrillas, neighbors were mutilated, and people were afraid of sleeping in their own homes. They turned to the church for aid, seeking prayer, comfort, and protection. Juanita is one of the lucky ones who escaped to the United States, but like anyone with her history she suffers from trauma and depression. She has found some measure of comfort in her faith and in belonging to a Pentecostal community.

Dueck and Reimer draw from the experience of Juanita, a real person, and imagine her receiving care in a therapeutic setting, under the care of "Dr. Davidson," a fictitious psychotherapist whom she would be "fortunate" to have – a colleague that many of us might recommend. Davidson is a white, middle-aged man who graduated from an American research university and earns six figures annually.[4] He does what he has been trained to do, that is, to recommend a course of therapy that draws upon democratic models of parenting, cognitive restructuring, and stress management – all of which are standard tools in clinical practice. While Juanita finds the therapist to be a kind man, his suggestions do not ring true with the ways that she knows, thinks about, or describes her life.[5] He speaks to her about stress, parenting, and "inner talk" – language that is entirely foreign to Juanita. While he discusses "spiritual coping strategies," she is waiting for him to talk to her about God in the ways that Pentecostals do.

We might think that Juanita's case is isolated or that her situation is characteristic of a time before cultural sensitivity training, but, sadly, we would be wrong. Rather, Davidson's interaction with Juanita is regrettably typical and emblematic of a powerful, taken-for-granted system of care. Dueck and Reimer argue that Western psychology is not the saving grace that many have assumed. In the midst of trying to do good, practitioners often unwittingly inflict harm. They write, "Rather than recognizing and affirming the client's traditioned sense of healing, the instrumentally trained psychologist unwittingly creates an individual fashioned in the image of Western ideals."[6] In other words, rather than seeing and hearing a client as she is in herself, practitioners see and hear their *representations* of her. In doing so, they are, in effect, constructing a version of themselves. Dueck and Reimer attribute the harm that therapists unknowingly perpetrate in the clinic to a long history of psychology being co-opted for purposes of domination. We often forget the fact that psychological research has been used to make war, interrogate, and torture prisoners, as well as undermine local cultures for political and economic ends.[7] Combine this history with the fact that clinicians and researchers are trained in secular, modern research universities that inculcate students in methods that are thought not only to be "objective" and neutral but also superior – even though they are steeped in implicit, cultural commitments of the dominant group (e. g., in the case of American psychology, that of liberal democracy).[8] Dueck and Reimer argue that too often psychotherapists unwittingly inflict what they term "psychological violence" on people like Juanita.[9]

We might think that nothing could be worse than harming individuals that one is trying to help, but it gets worse. Harm is not only perpetrated on an individual level; it is carried out on a massive scale. Dueck and Reimer demonstrate that Western psychology and all its prejudices have been exported, displacing the wisdom and language of other cultures to explain human experience. In other parts of the world (India, New Zealand, and Turkey, for example) psychology is practiced primarily or exclusively in the Western tradition.[10] Psychologists trained in Western psychology have inflicted epistemic violence on a global scale as an expression of progress and a vehicle of humanitarian aid.

No doubt we can feel outrage at the harm being done in a field that is not our own. Far easier is it to point to the refuse in someone else's backyard than to see what is stashed in the closets of one's home. However, the truth is that practical theologians embody and enact their own version of the violence that Dueck and Reimer observe in psychology and clinical care. I speak about this as epistemic violence.

As I proceed by "telling it slant," I cannot underplay or mute the truth I wish to examine, though it is uncomfortable for me to say and probably discomfiting at times for readers to consider. This essay is divided into five "acts," if you will, since I later claim that all of us are performers or showpeople. In the first act, I address how all human beings (myself included) resist becoming aware of and examining what they would rather not know. In the second, I open up the meaning of epistemic violence by discussing Gayatri Spivak's use of the term and exploring the implications of ignoring or overriding another person's experience or knowledge. Third, I introduce the image of ventriloquism to help illustrate the experience of epistemic violence in practical theology. I call attention to how easy it is to make dummies of others, especially subjects of research. In the fourth act, I outline two approaches in practical theology that demonstrate how often we unknowingly inflict harm by making dummies out of those we intend to serve. For my finale, I conclude with some ideas for taking steps toward practicing a practical theology community that we aspire to be.

The logic of this essay draws from a method that American philosopher William James introduces in his classic text *The Varieties of Religious Experience*.[11] James seeks to understand religion – or more accurately, the *experience* of religion. His starting assumption is that all human beings have religious experiences. His methodological tack is this: rather than examining all cases, James invites us to examine instances of religious experience in "exaggerated form," as he calls it.[12] In other words, by studying those who most acutely register and reflect upon religion, we will understand not simply *their* experience but what is basic to *all* human experience. James' method negotiates the tension between particularity and universality. By inferring from particular cases what is common to all human experiences of religion, his approach might seem to erase the very notion of varieties, that is, the respect for particularities of religious experience. However, if experiences of religion were so unique that they had nothing in common, we would have no sense of the phenomenon of religion. He assumes each case expresses features of what is universal, yet experiences of religion are sufficiently different that they cannot be collapsed and treated as one. James makes the same assumption upon which case study method is based.

In this paper, I seek to understand oppression, or more specifically, the *experience* of oppression. In theorizing oppression, researchers and scholars are accustomed to working with the symbol *oppression*, a symbol that is used to refer a wide range of states and processes of domination. Unfortunately, however, the process of discourse tends to obscure lived experiences of oppression. As a result, the sense of oppression felt from the inside is often lost. I wish to define oppression in a way that builds on previous discussions but also points afresh to what is common within the varieties. I propose a working definition of oppression as *institutionalized, culturally normed, social phenomena in which a dominant group benefits from directly or indirectly (consciously or unconsciously) legislating reality for a minoritized group of people, and in that process diminishing their agency*.[13] Because all of us are members of social groups, and groups stand in power relations with one another, each of us has lived experiences, in different moments and in varying degrees, of participating in or having institutionalized behavior, practices, and assumptions override if not determine one's own or someone else's reality. In this regard, human beings inflict and experience harm that is at once mental, physical, emotional, and spiritual.

Following James, then, [...] I examine how oppression presents itself in "exaggerated form," by exploring Juanita's case and the metaphor of ventriloquism. My remarks are informed by my own experience of epistemic violence both in the academy and in society, including conversations with friends and colleagues of color in the academy who have also suffered epistemic violence. In the spirit of James' work, by studying those who most acutely register and/or reflect upon oppression, we will understand not simply *their* experience but what is in some ways basic to *all* human experience. Juanita's case and the metaphor of ventriloquism shed light on how violence, and epistemic violence in particular, are fundamental to the experience of oppression.[14] Epistemic violence provides a window into something crucial about oppression, though, of course, the latter cannot and should not be reduced to the former. One might say that oppression felt from the inside is violence.

Act I: Say It Isn't So

Because no one welcomes feeling embarrassed, colleagues in practical theology are probably skeptical about the possibility of practical theology being implicated in oppression and violence. I invite the reader to notice and be curious about any visceral reaction to the connections I am making. I would expect colleagues to be wary of aspersions cast upon practical theology, or more accurately, practical theologians. After all, oppression is antithetical to the noble aspirations enshrined in both the academy and faith traditions. However, it is important to recognize that all human beings at times turn a blind eye, do not want to know, and make excuses not to know. Moreover, oppression of many kinds, which is embedded in social institutions and processes, emerges within and is enacted by each of us. We are liable not to observe what we *collectively* tend to ignore.

All of us, that is, those of us who claim practical theology as a disciplinary home, operate according to a powerful set of rules that govern thinking and behavior, rules that are difficult to detect. French philosopher Pierre Bourdieu uses the metaphor of a "game" to illustrate how members of any field – artists, religious practitioners, political actors, and other people who produce cultural goods – pay an "entry fee" to participate, conform to implicit rules, and understand the stakes and internal logic of the game.[15] Every field abides by a *habitus*, "a system of dispositions acquired by implicit or explicit learning," that governs how we operate without anyone setting it up as such.[16] Bourdieu argues that an academic field (sociology in his case) operates like any other field. In the case of the academy, those who dominate the field maintain what he describes as a "monopoly" over the field's social capital; they are vested in keeping the state of power relations as it is.[17] Those with power in the field are implicit guardians of what he calls "*doxa*," which create the "universe of the undiscussed" and therefore are undisputed.[18] *Doxa* are "experiences" of a "quasi-perfect correspondence between the objective order and the subjective principles of organization," which give the impression that the world is as it appears to be.[19] For example, because the earth appears to be flat from an ordinary point of view, for hundreds of years no one questioned the match between what people could see and their idea of flatness. People's resistance to accepting that the earth is round illustrates Bourdieu's observation about the difficulty of bringing what is *doxic* to the arena of public debate. In our case, it is likely that some readers will promptly forget everything I have written because it does not fit the world as they know it. Nonetheless, I write in the role of a heretic, as Bourdieu says, or perhaps in the tradition of prophets, to use more theological language. I am attempting to bring to the fore the experience of oppression in terms of epistemic violence.

Act II – Epistemic Violence

Gayatri Spivak uses the term "epistemic violence" to describe the colonizer's obliteration of subaltern knowledge, as the powerful refuse to recognize the colonized as knowers.[20] Examples of the subaltern, she says, include "men and women among the illiterate peasantry, the tribals, the lowest strata of the urban subproletariat."[21] Spivak is doubtful that those who have been silenced by colonization can be heard or understood by elites who have no analogs (or close enough analogs) in their own experience to help them make accurate sense of what the subaltern have to say. [...] Epistemic violence is more complex than what Spivak describes, occurring in subtle ways in the daily life of the practical theologian. Because she does not provide [a] definition, I offer my own.

Epistemic violence refers to the harm done to an individual when her understanding of her reality is ignored, obscured, and overridden by another person (or persons) who in words and actions redefine(s) that reality. What is so *violent* about epistemic violence is that by replacing the way others represent themselves, we dictate whether and how someone is to be seen or not seen at all, what is real and unreal. If effect, we say to the other, "You are to be seen only in terms of how I see you. Otherwise you are not seen. Otherwise you do not exist." This is violence. The potential for epistemic violence is ever present in practical theology, where we are given institutional authority to interpret and represent the lived experiences of others, as well as the responsibility to shape student experience.

Though interpretation and representation are practices we perform individually; when we act we are in part embodying a *habitus* shaped by institutionalized *doxa*. Therefore, we are disposed to enacting epistemic violence according to larger, pernicious social dynamics. Each of us interprets reality as members of communities of interpretation – communities that have histories of ignorance, prejudice, and oppression. A parallel in everyday life is the practice of microaggressions,[22] as individuals do their daily part in exercising power and privilege, participating in and perpetuating legacies of harm without knowing it. Like microaggressions, epistemic violence tends to express the contours of *doxa*, as people interpret others according to the unexamined habits of the dominant group that is vested in preserving power and privilege. As one can see, epistemic violence perpetrates the greatest injury when it is institutionalized, that is, when the power to ignore, obscure, or override another person's understanding of reality is sanctioned, guided, and protected by structures and processes that maintain privilege.

Act III – Ventriloquists by Training

To illustrate, in a graphic way, the experience of epistemic violence, I proceed once again by "telling it slant," offering a benign if not quirky metaphor – that all of us are trained as ventriloquists.[23] Like all academics, the practical theologian is a performer whose stage is the lecture, the academic journal, the conference, or the book project. In each of these settings, the audience is comprised of colleagues in the field or perhaps scholars from other fields who are conversation partners expecting to be dazzled, engaged, and inspired by what they read or hear.

It is all too easy for the practical theologian to introduce the persons about whom she is writing in her research as a ventriloquist would a dummy. The old-fashioned, wooden dummy takes human form but in miniature – a pet creation of the performer, if you will. Likewise, what the practical theologian presents to colleagues *attempts to portray* the real person, community, or situation that has been researched. However, the representation is a *version* of reality authored by the scholar. At best, the researcher provides glimpses of lived experiences which have been translated into the language of the academy. Some translations are better than others, but much is lost in translation as the researcher becomes further removed from the lived experiences under investigation.

A good ventriloquist performs in such a way as to make the audience forget that the dummy is a dummy. The dummy appears to speak its mind, capable even of making fun of or outwitting the performer. At moments the audience believes that the dummy is a real person – which of course it is not. In practical theology, scholars bring representations of the other to life in the minds of the audience – be it the other whose problems we seek to understand and address or be it the other whom we serve as scholars and representatives of religious communities. A good essay, article, book, lecture, or presentation makes colleagues feel as if we have "met" the people that the author has researched. In fact, the reader may feel as if (s)he has met Juanita.

When we read or listen to a colleague's research, we expect a performance and at some level bear some responsibility for applauding acts of ventriloquism. In our eagerness to learn about the other, we are often complicit in the illusion that the dummy being presented is real. In other words, we are invested in accepting that the practical theologian's version of reality *is* reality, forgetting the fact that it is the performer making the dummy speak. As long as the research method is sound and the rendition of the other seems plausible, we often accept the practical theologian's claim to know "what is going on" and by extension we believe *we* know what is going on.

In practical theology, a common euphemism for ventriloquism is "giving voice" to the other. As John Swinton and Harriet Mowat write, "*Knowledge of the other* occurs when the researcher focuses on a particular individual or group and explores in-depth the ways in which they view and interact with the world...Such a mode of knowledge gives a voice to particular groups...and allows previously hidden life experiences and narratives to come to the fore and develop a public voice."[24] "Giving voice" assumes that the other is more or less voiceless, mute – essentially dumb – and that the practical theologian is in a privileged position to know what the other would say, to speak on the other's behalf, or to allow the other to speak and be heard like never before.

Giving voice to the voiceless might seem like a noble, liberal project. In some cases, if a scholar does not bring a person's case, a community, or a situation to light, other academics would probably not become aware of it. We presume that raising awareness about the implications of our research could benefit those who are misunderstood or ignored. Furthermore, research on diverse people, communities, and situations enriches the field. The problem I am seeking to bring to the fore is that "giving voice" as Swinton and Mowat advocate is an illusion, just as it is in ventriloquism. I would argue that we trust our good intentions and give ourselves too much credit for knowing the other well enough. In our eagerness to share the modicum that we have discovered in our research, we forget that what we present is a domesticated version of the other, created primarily for our use and benefit, even as we hope the research will be of use to the other.[25] Good intentions cover up the *doxa* of practical theology – that which is "unthinkable," as Bourdieu says.

Making a dummy talk enacts epistemic violence, as the performer dictates reality, including how the dummy is perceived, experienced, and known by the audience. The study of others, says postcolonial feminist theorist Trinh Minh-ha, is "mainly a conversation of 'us' with 'us' about 'them,' of the white man with the white man about primitive-native man."[26] Invariably, "them" is silenced,[27] even as we naively believe that we are "giving voice." Dummies have no power to talk back to an audience in their own voice, to correct how they are presented, or to refuse to sit on the knee of the performer. By definition, dummies are dependent on the performer to be seen and heard.[28] The subjects of research have the impossible choice *of being seen and heard as a dummy or not being seen or known at all.*

Act IV – How Easily We Make Dummies of Those We Serve

Psychology

Before moving to scenarios in practical theology, let us return to Juanita and Dr. Davidson, seeing how the therapist unwittingly makes a dummy of the client. Recall that the clinician does not speak what Dueck and Reimer refer to as Juanita's "mother tongue" – a term that encompasses not simply Spanish but even more especially the particular language and practices through which Juanita constructs the world she inhabits. Dueck and Reimer describe a person's "mother tongue" as "local, ethnically freighted, emotionally laden, and capable of poetic nuance."[29] In Juanita's case, in order to receive care, she finds that in conversation she is perpetually forced to abandon her mother tongue and speak in the language that Davidson understands, using words and concepts that *he* recognizes. Davidson speaks what Dueck and Reimer call "trade language," which is "distant, utilitarian, contractual, and general."[30] By ignoring some of what she says and responding only to what approaches what he knows, Davidson subtly but surely teaches Juanita not only to speak and act like a dummy but also to *be* a dummy.

When Davidson presents Juanita's case to his colleagues, he makes her intelligible by using trade language and by making her "speak" in ways that he understood (and by extension, in ways that colleagues will understand). Using words spoken by the real Juanita, Davidson screens, edits, and frames the dummy for his purposes. His audience (we, his colleagues) eagerly take in the performance, satisfied we have glimpsed something real and true about Juanita. We have been duped – not because Davidson has been dishonest, but because he approaches *his creation* as the real Juanita. This is a form of what Bourdieu calls "gentle violence" – the violence that well-intended academics often inflict in their research methods, which they attempt to rationalize.[31]

Practical Theology

Far from being unique to psychology, the practice of making dummies out of the people we are trying to serve is prevalent in practical theology. In a moment I describe two, divergent approaches to practical theology that enact epistemic violence in different ways. The two theorists I have chosen happen to be white and male; however, what I wish to highlight is the power of the field's *doxa*, which implicates all of us. As we apply these approaches to Juanita's case, both provide glimpses of a disturbing pattern of overriding her and/or her community's particular experiences and ways of defining reality.

Imagine that Juanita and her community are the subjects of research and that we are on the research team led by Dutch practical theologian Johannes van der Ven.[32] For decades, van der Ven has been a leading theorist in empirical research, bringing some of the principles and tools of science to practical theology. Van der Ven's method enables him to ask far-reaching questions that would be impossible to answer if he were only studying one community. He provides statistical and qualitative evidence that supports what he finds, coming to conclusions that are not only plausible but also testable and "objective."

Suppose that van der Ven is conducting a study of refugees from Latin America who live in diaspora in Europe and the United States. Juanita's community is but one of a number communities that are participating in our project, which has both qualitative and quantitative phases. First, we submerge ourselves in the life of Juanita's community, developing the theological problem and goal of the project in conversation with her and others. Second, we gather data from observation and reading. Third, we develop a hypothesis about our question. Fourth, we test our hypothesis by conducting interviews and administering a questionnaire. Finally, we interpret the results of the study in terms of the hypothesis. We accomplish these steps simultaneously with multiple communities in the study.[33]

Picture Juanita completing the questionnaire developed under van der Ven's leadership, which contains both closed and open-ended questions. On multiple choice questions, there is no opportunity for Juanita to express her experience in her "mother tongue," that is, language that is most heartfelt, personal, and culturally meaningful. Her response is only registered and understood in our terms derived from trade language. When answering open-ended survey questions (or interview questions), Juanita is in the same position that she was in with Davidson – solely at the mercy of the theorist's power to interpret and represent her. Even if van der Ven recognizes when Juanita responds to his questions in the language of her heart, he is focused on screening the encounter for what is common with encounters with people from other communities. He cannot afford to pay attention to her particularity. His sight is trained on discerning what the aggregate data reveal about his research question.

While van der Ven's research might yield insights that are important to all the communities involved in the study, it also poses risks by inviting ventriloquism and threatening Juanita with institutionalized epistemic violence. Juanita and her cohort would only be re-presented in a version most intelligible and meaningful to van der Ven and his colleagues. In effect, those whom he re-presents would be akin to dummies. If the dummy Juanita that Davidson constructs by working with one person is a shadow of the complex, flesh-and-blood Juanita, one wonders how much less our composite dummy will resemble those it represents, working with hundreds of people, speaking multiple mother tongues and representing diverse cultures. I question the harm that researchers can do inadvertently, with so much particularity and complexity glossed.

Now let us consider a second, notably different approach to practical theology. Imagine that we have joined American practical theologian Richard Osmer, who is leading a team to train leaders of Juanita's congregation to engage in practical theological reflection. Osmer believes that congregational leaders are "interpretative guides," leaders who are in the best position to understand their own situations, having "access to the everyday experiences and problems of ordinary people."[34] His vision is that if properly trained in the methods of practical theology, congregational leaders can be highly effective at discerning, interpreting, and responding to their own problems and challenges, which they know better than anyone else.

If congregational leaders engage in practical theology in their own communities, one might think that ventriloquism can be avoided altogether. There would be no academic stage on which to perform, no scholar to present the findings of research, and no need to represent anyone. Osmer's approach avoids the problem that van der Ven faces in outside researchers interpreting and representing lives they have never experienced. This would seem to be the perfect solution.

Following Osmer's congregational model, we proceed to teach leaders of Juanita's Pentecostal community the four tasks of practical theology – the descriptive-empirical task, the interpretative task, the normative task, and the pragmatic task. We train the leaders of the congregation much like we do our own doctoral students, teaching them how to form a research plan,[35] various methods of research,[36] how to draw on theories to interpret data,[37] how to approach theological normativity,[38] and how to understand organizational change.[39] However, the leaders have not studied at an accredited, elite seminary like the one where Osmer teaches. In fact, in this particular group no one has earned a college degree. When we teach the theology that Osmer uses to explain the tasks of practical theology, they find that his Protestant theology departs in significant ways from their Pentecostal theology.

Training congregational leaders parallels the same well intended, but imperialistic maneuver of exporting Western models of psychology to the rest of the world. If we follow in the spirit of Osmer's approach, we make dummies of ordinary Christians, teaching them to think and speak like academics, using not *their* mother tongue but *our* trade language. In this advanced and more subtle form of ventriloquism, the academic practical theologian need no longer be present if the dummy learns to mimic the scholar. Expecting local leaders to think like academics forecloses appreciation for native, more culturally appropriate ways that Juanita's congregation engages in theological construction and reflection. When experts insist only on teaching trade language, it undermines awareness of and language for local knowledge, much of which is embodied.

Because the real Juanita cannot speak on her behalf or that of her community, I could properly accuse myself of making dummies of them, posing hypothetical situations and encouraging us to anticipate how they would be affected. Indeed, I may have misrepresented her and her community. However, like Dueck and Reimer, I have been careful to remind the reader that my representation of Juanita is fictitious, that is, that the dummy is not the real Juanita. Because practical theologians refer to real people and communities, there is no avoiding representation. If we can become vigilant of our propensity and practices to objectify, misrepresent, and override the other's knowledge, we can find alternative ways – perhaps not avoid but mitigate the problems to which I am drawing attention.

Act V – Implications

In a larger book project, I survey diverse research methods of six theorists, and I could have addressed how each of them engaged in ventriloquism to one degree or another, even where one would least suspect. Unfortunately, ventriloquism is prevalent not only in practical theology but is ubiquitous throughout the academy, having been noted in folklore studies, feminist studies, and postcolonial studies.[40] Bourdieu would say that all of us are implicated in the violence of our respective fields because we all participate in upholding the belief in the value of what is at stake in the field.[41] We all benefit from the social capital of the field, even if it is unevenly distributed among us. The best we can do, he says, is to become critically aware of cultural domination perpetuated by our field and in society.[42]

Because *doxa* is difficult to challenge, it must be approached indirectly, that is "telling it slant," while disturbing people's habits of deflecting or minimizing institutionalized epistemic violence. If I had taken a traditional, straightforward approach to discussing the topic of epistemic violence, I would have presented the problem upfront in a distanced discussion of "it." I would have unwittingly occupied the reader's attention solely with theory and concepts, rather than facilitating an *experience* of ideas, an experience that is, necessarily, decentering. Using the metaphor of ventriloquism, I have attempted to engage the reader in a gradual process of opening up experiences of epistemic violence in which we inevitably participate and in which we are unconsciously complicit. In other words, I have invited us *to make ourselves the subjects of our investigation.* Otherwise, I would have been liable to conform to the very *doxa* that I am attempting to resist and, ideally, to revise.

As I conclude, I wish to highlight practices in research, writing, and teaching that have the potential to temper epistemic violence in practical theology. Because it is so basic to the experience of oppression in general, I do not believe epistemic violence can be eradicated entirely, but I affirm an ethical imperative to mitigate it. In this sense, I disagree with feminist theorists such as Spivak and Judith Butler, who in my judgment hold an unduly pessimistic view of the capacity of human beings to communicate in authentic or life-giving ways. Like Spivak, Butler does not believe that the self can be heard. She argues that the "I" can only narrate her experience in terms of categories that facilitate recognition but are not of her choosing, which puts "I" at a distance from experiences that she is attempting to share.[43] Spivak and Butler appropriately challenge widespread, mistaken assumptions that the oppressed, marginalized person can speak – readily, fully, truly – and can be heard – deeply, and meaningfully. However, in making their cases they forge extreme positions: the oppressed person cannot speak and/or cannot be heard. In doing so, the chasm across difference is insurmountable, empathy between people who will always be strangers is foreclosed, and communication is not simply fraught with misunderstanding – it is by definition futile. What purpose, then, is served by their writings and more, by education more broadly?

I have sought to explain how and why communication between Juanita and Davidson is replete with accidents waiting to happen. But it is not impossible. Rather, the related point I have sought to convey is that in taking seriously some of the problems and limits in their communication, they are in a position to work, constructively, to bridge the chasm, to negotiate difference, to improve empathy and develop increased understanding. While Spivak and Butler may be satisfied with the role of critics, my responsibility as a practical theologian is not only to critique but also to offer hope.

One way to resist utilitarianism and "dummification" in practical theology is through participatory action research (PAR), in which subjects and academics treat one another as co-researchers, investigating and engaging one another in practical theological reflection. PAR is used in many fields, including practical theology, especially by the Action Research Church Society (ARCS) based in Great Britain.[44] PAR destabilizes ventriloquism by enabling local stakeholders to represent themselves. In the ARCS model, "insiders" interpret their own situation and share their findings with academics and vice versa. In some cases, local and academic researchers even co-present their research so that both perspectives are distinct. Elsewhere I discuss my concerns about the ARCS model;[45] however, its emphasis on dialogue represents a positive step toward interrupting ventriloquism and epistemic violence.

A second means of challenging these habitual, oppressive tendencies is to engage in more critical, self-disclosive reflexivity in our writing. While the importance of practicing reflexivity is widely recognized in practical theology, it is rarely done with sufficient depth and vulnerability in presentations or publications. However, failing to reflect publicly on one's power to represent and potential to misrepresent is like the ventriloquist speaking for the dummy without moving his/her lips. In contrast, critically examining and openly reflecting on one's power and privilege to make dummies of one's subject helps us not to get away with ventriloquism. *In other words, one must allow the audience to see one's lips move to dispel the illusion of who is speaking.* One practical theologian who models this self-disclosive reflexivity is American practical theologian, Mary McClintock Fulkerson, as she interrogates her own privilege as a white, able-bodied academic.[46] One could also practice honest, consistent, public reflexivity in terms of class, gender, sexual orientation, and theological tradition. The goal would be to become so expert at troubleshooting our own privilege that we are constantly wary of how we tend to make dummies of those we study in ways consistent with our particular social locations.[47]

Disrupting epistemic violence must not only involve finding alternative means of researching and writing, but it must also include training future practical theologians in ways that do not comply with the field's *doxa* but in fact contribute to altering and revising it. As a third strategy, we need to become regularly alert to ways in which we practice not listening to the mother tongues and lived experiences of our students, to the degree to which we may be substituting what we have valorized. We often train students to think, sound, and act like us. Making students into protégés is a venerable tradition in academia. Students are apprenticed to those who are senior in the field, who ensure the continuity of the field by forming novices in the ways that experts have learned. Too often students, for example international students, bring wisdom about practical theological reflection that is appropriate to their community and culture, yet we focus mainly on giving them the most widely used tools of Western practical theology, expecting them to master using them. Rather than focusing primarily if not solely on giving them trade language with which to examine their context, which we assume is applicable to any context, we could help them to become critical of it. We could devote more energy to helping students to birth their own practical theological sensibilities, the likes of which we instructors may have never before witnessed. We could model a different kind of inquiry by practicing learning with them and from them in the midst of their doing so with us.

Juanita's case, interpreted in conjunction with the metaphor of ventriloquism, helps illumine an "extreme case" of the ubiquitous phenomenon of epistemic violence. In doing so, it provides a means of conveying some of the lived experience of oppression. The fact that oppression is not only pervasive but also horribly destructive should invoke in practical theologians an urgent call to work strenuously and unceasingly to pursue and achieve a profound and robust vision of community, beyond what is characterized in terms of diversity and inclusivity. In the image of God's new creation, we have a vision to which we can aspire, where institutional power has been reigned in so that all may be subjects, that is, so that all may be persons.

Notes

1 Emily Dickinson, "Tell All the Truth but Tell It Slant." *The Poems of Emily Dickinson: Reading Edition* (The Belknap Press of Harvard University Press, 1998), https://www. poetryfoundation. org/poems/56824/tell-all-the-truth-but-tell-it-slant-1263, accessed November 24, 2017.

2   Alvin C. Dueck and Kevin S. Reimer, *A Peaceable Psychology: Christian Therapy in a World of Many Cultures* (Grand Rapids, MI: Brazos Press, 2009).

3   Dueck and Reimer, *Peaceable*, 18–20.

4   Dueck and Reimer, *Peaceable*, 90.

5   Dueck and Reimer, *Peaceable*, 91.

6   Dueck and Reimer, *Peaceable*, 12.

7   Dueck and Reimer, *Peaceable*, 36–50. They cite the role of psychologists in the US government's Project Camelot in the 1960s, as well as in devising interrogation and torture tactics used in Guantánamo and Iraq.

8   Dueck and Reimer, *Peaceable*, 61, 87–95.

9   Dueck and Reimer, *Peaceable*, 72.

10 Dueck and Reimer, *Peaceable*, 49.

11 William James, *The Varieties of Religious Experience* (Mineola, NY: Dover Publications, 2013).

12 James, *Varieties*, 39–45. [...]

13 See Ann E. Cudd, "How to Explain Oppression: Criteria of Adequacy for Normative Explanatory Theories," *Philosophy of the Social Sciences* 35, no. 1 (March, 2005), 23. [...] Marilyn Frye, "Oppression," in *The Politics of Reality: Essays in Feminist Theory* (Trumansburg, NY: Crossing Press, 1983), 1–16; Young, "Five Faces of Oppression."

14 Hussein Bulhan writes about the inextricable relationship of oppression and violence as well as the pervasiveness of violence in everyday life. Hussein Abdilahi Bulhan, *Frantz Fanon and the Psychology of Oppression* (New York: Plenum Press, 1985), 131.

15 Pierre Bourdieu, *Sociology in Question* (London: Sage, 1993), 72–5.

16 Bourdieu, *Sociology*, 76.

17 Bourdieu, *Sociology*, 72–3.

18 Pierre Bourdieu, *Outline of a Theory of Practice*, 18th printing, 2004 ed. (Cambridge, UK New York: Cambridge University Press, 1977), 168.

19 Bourdieu, *Outline*, 164.

20 Gayatri Chakravorty Spivak, "Can the Subaltern Speak?" in *Marxism and the Interpretation of Culture*, ed. Cary Nelson and Lawrence Grossberg, (Urbana, IL: University of Illinois Press, 1988), 280–81.

21 Spivak, "Subaltern," 283.

22 In the 1970s, Chester Pierce coined the term 'microaggressions' to refer to "...subtle, stunning, often automatic, and nonverbal exchanges which are "put-downs" of blacks by offenders." Chester M. Pierce, Jean V. Carew, Diane Piece-Gonzales, Deborah Willis, "An Experiment in Racism: TV Commercials," in *Television and Education*, ed. Chester M. Pierce (Beverly Hills, CA: Sage, 1978), 66. See Derald W. Sue, *Microaggressions in Everyday Life: Race, Gender, and Sexual Orientation* (Hobboken, NJ: Wiley, 2010); Cody J. Sanders and Angela Yarber, *Microaggressions in Ministry: Confronting the Hidden Violence of Everyday Church* (Louisville, KY: Westminster John Knox, 2015).

23 As I note below, the metaphor of ventriloquism has been used in multiple fields, but closest to this discussion is perhaps Mary John's notion of the "ventriloquist's fantasy," referring to the practice of white feminists speaking for so-called "Third World" women. Mary John, *Discrepant Dislocations: Feminism, Theory, and Postcolonial Histories* (Berkeley, CA: University of California Press, 1996), 22.

24 Swinton and Mowat, *Practical Theology and Quantitative Research*, 33; *Emphasis* in the original.

25 Susan Ritchie, "Ventriloquist Folklore: Who Speaks for Representation?" *Western Folklore* 52, no. 2/4 (Apr–Oct, 1993), 367.

26 Trinh is critiquing a view of anthropology as a "conversation of man with man." T. Minh-Ha Trinh, *Woman, Native, Other: Writing Postcoloniality and Feminism* (Bloomington: Indiana University Press, 1989), 65.

27 Trinh, *Woman*, 67.

28 Trinh, *Woman*, 67.

29 Dueck and Reimber, *Peaceable Psychology*, 103.

30 Dueck and Reimer, *A Peaceable Psychology*, 103.

31 Bourdieu, *Sociology*, 3.

32 His seminal work includes Johannes A. van der Ven, *Practical Theology: An Empirical Approach*, trans. Barbara Schultz (Kampen, Netherlands: Kok Pharos, 1993); Johnnes A. van der Ven, *Ecclesiology in Context* (Grand Rapids, MI: W.B. Eerdmans, 1996). His most recent work involves human rights. See Johannes A. van der Ven, *Human Rights Or Religious Rules?* (Leiden; Boston: Brill, 2010).

33 The research process described here reflects van der Ven's discussion of the empirical cycle in Johannes A. van der Ven, *God Reinvented?: A Theological Search in Texts and Tables* (Leiden; Boston: Brill, 1998), 52–6.

34 Richard R. Osmer, *Practical Theology: An Introduction* (Grand Rapids: William B. Eerdmans, 2008), 19.

35 Osmer, *Practical Theology*, 47–9.

36 Osmer, *Practical Theology*, 49–57.

37 Osmer, *Practical Theology*, 113.

38 Osmer, *Practical Theology*, 161.

39 Osmer, *Practical Theology*, 199.

40 Ritchie, "Ventriloquist Folklore"; M. E. Hawkesworth, *Feminist Inquiry: From Political Conviction to Methodological Innovation* (New Brunswick, NJ: Rutgers University Press, 2006); Bonnie McElhinny, "Recontextualizing the American Occupation of the Philippines: Erasure and Ventriloquism in Colonial Discourse Around Men, Medicine, and Infant Mortality," in *Words, Worlds, and Material Girls: Language, Gender, Globalization*, ed. Bonnie S. McElhinny (Berlin: Walter de Gruyter, 2007), 205–36; Diane E. Goldstein, "Rethinking Ventriloquism: Untellability, Chaotic Narratives, Social Justice, and the Choice to Speak for, about, and Without," *Journal of Folklore Research* 49, no. 2 (May–Aug, 2012), 179–98.

41 Bourdieu, *Sociology*, 74.

42 Bourdieu, *Sociology*, 3.

43 Judith Butler, *Giving an Account of Oneself* (New York: Fordham University Press, 2005).

44 See Helen Cameron et al., *Talking about God in Practice: Theological Action Research and Practical Theology* (London: SCM Press, 2010); Clare Watkins, "Developing Ecclesiology as a Non-Correlative Process and Practice through the Theological Action Research Framework of Theology in Four Voices," *Ecclesial Practices* 2, no. 1 (2015), 23–39.

45 I address concerns about the ARCS model in my book, *Taking on Practical Theology: The Idolization of Context and the Hope of Community*.

46 Mary McClintock Fulkerson, *Places of Redemption: Theology for a Worldly Church* (Oxford: Oxford University Press, 2010); Mary McClintock Fulkerson, "Interpreting a Situation: When is "Empirical" also "Theological"?" in *Perspectives on Ecclesiology and Ethnography*, ed. Pete Ward (Grand Rapids, MI: Eerdmans, 2012), 124–44.

47 For an excellent example, see Tom Beaudoin and Katherine Turpin, "White Practical Theology," in *Opening the Field of Practical Theology: An Introduction*, eds. Kathleen A. Cahalan and Gordon S. Mikoski (Lanham, MD: Rowman & Littlefield, 2014), 251–69.

Part II

Twentieth-Century Foreshadowing: Reimaging Theological Knowledge

Section I

1950–1980s: New Claims for Knowledge in Practice

17

Operation-Centered Theology (1958)*

Seward Hiltner

Introduction

Seward Hiltner hardly needs an introduction. He is often heralded as a forerunner of twentieth-century pastoral and practical theology. However, this claim needs qualification: he holds this position in historical accounts that harbor an unexamined bias toward liberal Protestantism and fail to recognize the pivotal influence of figures and sources in other streams of the Christian tradition. Other selections in Part II of this *Reader* make this oversight more apparent (in contrast to the original *Reader* where Hiltner stands alone as the only historical figure). In the late 1950s through the 1970s, Karl Rahner and Juan Luis Segundo also made groundbreaking contributions. Hiltner leads off Part II chronologically but do not mistake sequential order for a ranking.

If Hiltner deserves a special place, it is for the adamancy and success of his mid-twentieth-century fight for pastoral theology as deserving of a rightful place in the academy and for the study of practice as a valid source of theological knowledge. He established the discipline in the two institutions where he taught, the University of Chicago Divinity School (1950–1961) and Princeton Theological Seminary (1961–1980). Later in the book from which the following essay comes, *Preface to Pastoral Theology* (1958), he credits his clinical teacher and founder of clinical education, Anton Boisen, who twenty-five years prior to Hiltner did "more than any other [person] in our century to prepare the soil for a new pastoral theology" (p. 51) by establishing "living human documents" as containing theologically meaningful material. In one of Hiltner's many long footnotes, several of which are retained here because of their importance, he also recognizes Friedrich Schleiermacher as the "one premodern writer who in methodological principle foreshadowed" Hiltner (p. 225, note 23). Even though Hiltner remains oblivious of the Protestant-centric, pastor-centered, and sexist tone of his analysis, he completes what he believes Boisen initiates by detailing a "systematic" portrait of pastoral theology. In his view,

Original publication details: Seward Hiltner "Task," pp. 15–29, and "Notes," pp. 216–24 from *Preface to Pastoral Theology* (New York: Abingdon, 1958).

reflective examination of its unique arena of theological "data" – "practice or func-tions or events" – leads to new "theory" and "new knowledge."

In this entry and later in his book, Hiltner makes clear his preference for *pastoral* rather than *practical* theology, even though scholars in both disciplines have claimed him as a founding figure. Since the "logic-centered" branches (e.g. Bible, history, dogmatic theology) do not have an umbrella discipline over them, why should the "operation-centered" branches? So, instead of a "master discipline" that would rule over all the offices of ministry, he suggests that there are two other "operation-centered" branches, parallel to pastoral theology, focused on "communicating" and "organizing." He also believed that practical theology's history as the area that dis-penses "hints and helps" and applies knowledge gained elsewhere had misled schol-ars into believing it had no theological substance of its own. His own rise to academic power came through pastoral care and had everything to do with the mid-century popularity of modern psychology and its rapid absorption into pastoral counseling.

Suggested Further Reading

- Seward Hiltner, *Theological Dynamics* (Nashville: Abingdon, 1972).
- Anton Boisen, *The Exploration of the Inner World: A Study of Mental Disorder and Religious Experience* (New York: Willett, Clark, 1936).
- Friedrich Schleiermacher, *Brief Outline on the Study of Theology* (revised translations of 1811 and 1830 editions), trans. and notes by Terrence N. Tice (Louisville: Westminster John Knox, 2011).

***

What is pastoral theology? How important is it? To whom?

It is the thesis of this book that pastoral theology is a formal branch of theology resulting from study of Christian shepherding, that it is just as important as biblical or doctrinal or historical theology, and that it is no less the concern of the minister of the local church than of the specialist.

From the days of the Reformation the term "pastoral" has been used in two senses. Beginning with Zwingli's book *The Shepherd*, "pastoral" was used as the functional extension of the noun "pastor."[1] Whatever the pastor or shepherd did was pastoral or shepherding. Functions followed from title. By implication everything done by one called a "pastor" was shepherding. [...]

"Pastoral" was also used in a second sense, which attempted to emphasize the thrust of the original metaphor. The eighteenth and nineteenth centuries spoke of "poimen-ics." This meant the study of shepherding since it came from the Greek word for shepherd, *poimen*, which in turn came from a verb form that meant to feed or to tend the flock. "Poimenics" appeared along with a list of other important functions of minister and church, such as "catechetics," the study of religious instruction; "homiletics," the study of preaching and religious communication; and certain others. [...]

We believe that neither of these ways in which Protestantism has understood shepherding can be fruitful in itself in establishing an adequate pastoral theology. But we believe it of great positive importance that neither of these views within the tradition has pushed out the other. Each view testifies, we believe, to an important aspect of the truth. A normative definition of shepherding can learn from both views. But it will require more than a sum, since the two views appear mutually exclusive. The truth of the first view, in which shepherding was seen as whatever one does who is known as shepherd, is attitudinal. If one is genuinely a pastor, then no act that he performs can avoid having behind it as motivation and as disposition or readiness an attitude of tender and solicitous concern for person or group with whom he is dealing.

The truth of the second view, in which shepherding was associated with one type of event as against other types, is structural or categorical. There are some events, or functions, or operations, in which shepherding is properly the dominant and overriding end. There are other events or types of events in which another immediate end may be dominant.

We are grateful, then, that both ways of looking at Christian shepherding have been retained in the tradition, for each has truth to contribute to a normative conception. But until that conception has actually been stated, using whatever intellectual and spiritual tools are necessary and available, we cannot have a relevant pastoral theology. It is to that task that this entire volume is devoted.

It would be pleasant and gratifying to reader and writer alike if the task of defining first shepherding and then pastoral theology could be carried out on a relatively uncomplicated level, as if the intellectual dimensions of the job were simple and nothing were required except vivid illustrative material. Unfortunately, the facts are otherwise. We must include the truth from both views of shepherding as these have been in our tradition, and that requires us to pay some attention to history. The study of shepherding demands some looking at actual events that involve shepherding, so there must be both an empirical and a contemporary dimension to our study. And since our concern goes beyond the activity of shepherding to a pastoral or shepherding theology, we must pay attention to the content and the method of any valid branch of Christian theology. In these several senses our inquiry must be theoretical, since we seek general and comprehensive principles worthy of the name "pastoral theology."

At the same time this inquiry is immensely practical. Every minister, whatever his specific location, must carry out shepherding. And in carrying out this aspect of ministry, either he has a grasp of fundamental principles or he must operate half blindly. In addition he needs to interpret to his people the meaning of shepherding. The unique place of shepherding in Christianity comes from the way in which our relationship to God and our relationship to our fellow men are regarded as inseparable. This is the basis for the high position held by shepherding in Christian practice, and we believe the understanding or theory of it, then, can occupy no less significant a position in Christian thought and Christian theology.

The Meaning of Shepherding

We propose to consider shepherding as a perspective. The term "perspective" suggests that there is a certain point of view in the subject who is performing the viewing or feeling or helping. [...]

[...]

To view shepherding as a perspective solves in principle the problem of the two kinds of meanings that shepherding has had in Protestantism. From the one view we want to retain the truth that shepherding is in some degree present in everything done by pastor or church. [...]

From the other view of shepherding in Protestantism we wish to keep the truth that shepherding, although much, is not everything, that it is properly dominant when need and readiness so indicate, but that something else may properly be dominant under other conditions. [...]

[...] Is shepherding the same as pastoral care? The answer is No if pastoral care is viewed as one of the so-called "offices" of the ministry, correlative with such other offices as preaching, church administration, religious education, evangelism, or the church's social outreach. The answer is Yes if pastoral care is seen to be involved in some degree in every act of church and minister, and to be dominantly important in some act but not in others.

[...]

But the system of offices is, after all, only one possible way in which to examine what the minister and the church do. Let us look at a specific act or event. Here is a particular minister on a particular Sunday morning preaching a particular sermon to a particular group of people. If we are using the scheme of offices, we simply classify this event as preaching. But some members of the congregation may say the sermon was instructive and mean it literally. To others it brought a solicitous concern easing their burden. Calling this whole event "preaching," therefore, does not deal exhaustively with its meaning and significance. It is simply one useful way of classifying events or functions, but not the sole way and not necessarily the way best calculated to get at basic theory.

[...] Pastoral care *could* be used as we are using the term shepherding, but in that case we should have to be careful not to revert to thinking by way of the offices. For the purposes of our inquiry it has seemed better to return to the ancient metaphor of shepherding rather than attempting to wrest the idea of pastoral care from the typological context in which it is embedded.

The Meaning of Pastoral Theology

Pastoral theology is defined here as that branch or field of theological knowledge and inquiry that brings the shepherding perspective to bear upon all the operation and functions of the church and the minister, and then draws conclusions of a theological order from reflection on these observations.

This means, first, that pastoral theology comes out of inquiry from the shepherding perspective, when the latter is defined as in the previous section. I hold that there are two other perspectives cognate with shepherding, which I call "communicating" and "organizing," which should also lead to branches of theology [...].

Second, the definition asserts that pastoral theology is a branch of theology in the strict sense of the term. It has the same kind of autonomy as any other branch of theology – biblical, doctrinal, historical, ethical, and so on – although all branches are of course interrelated. But pastoral theology is not derivative from the other branches except in the same sense in which all branches derive in part from one another.[2]

Third, the definition implies that pastoral theology is an operation-centered or function-centered branch of theology rather than what we shall call for lack of a better name a logic-centered branch of theology.[3] Within the whole body of divinity what is distinctive about the operation-centered inquiries such as pastoral theology is that their theological conclusions, or theory or basic principles, emerge from reflection primarily on acts or events or functions from a particular perspective. There are other branches of theology, such as biblical theology or doctrinal theology, whose organizing principle is of a different nature. The study of the Bible, or biblical theology, is centered logically around anything that contributes to understanding the meaning, development, and significance of that book and the people and events and experiences lying behind the book. The study of doctrine is organized systematically and logically around the relation of doctrines to one another and their mutually reinforcing capacity to give testimony to the total faith. From these focal concerns each of the logic-centered fields of theology pursues its special investigations, which of course include the questions of practical significance and implication.

The logic-centered fields of theology are so obviously indispensable that they have led unwittingly to a misconception, namely, that any branch of theology must proceed as they do. They find their focuses in something that is overridingly logical and necessary, such as the Bible, the interrelation of doctrines, the development of history, or the meaning of morals. The contention here is that there is another kind of branches of theology, whose focuses are a particular perspective upon operations.[4] We distinguish three such branches, of which pastoral theology is one. A picture of the "body of divinity" is indicated schematically in the table [see the figure below].[5]

Fourth, our definition suggests that pastoral theology is systematic, as any branch of theology must be, but that the principles around which the system is organized are those given by the nature of the shepherding perspective.[6] For instance, doctrinal theology is organized systematically around doctrines and their interrelationship. It uses the common currencies of the faith – such as God, sin, salvation – primarily in terms of the relation of their meaning to one another. Pastoral theology, like any branch of theology, also uses these common currencies of the faith. But it organizes its material according to the data secured from inquiry according to the shepherding perspective. Thus pastoral theology is not a different kind of theology in terms of ultimate content. It is not a competitor of any other branch of theology, but its principle of self-organization is uniquely its own, just as theirs are.[7] [...]

Fifth, our definition of pastoral theology enables us to use a method in relation to it that is consistent with the standards for any critical theological method. How do we approach critical and discriminating inquiry in any branch of theology? We first acknowledge that we do not bring a blank mind, that our whole previous experience with the faith and with the world affects the questions and presuppositions we bring. In so acknowledging, we are in a better position to see what is in the material we are studying. So it is with pastoral theology. We do not come at this with minds wiped blank of experience with the faith. We acknowledge our views and convictions, and thus become more open to what study of this particular kind, namely, reflection on acts viewed from the perspective of shepherding, has to teach us.

[...]

All realms of theological inquiry involve relationship between faith and culture. Sometimes the questions raised in culture – for example, What kind of stability can man have in a world of instability? – can be answered by faith.[8] And at times questions asked within the faith – for example, How can a man avoid simple repetition of actions he deplores? – can have at least partial answers given by the world of culture – perhaps to this question the insights of psychology into our inner ambiguous motivations. Material of tremendous potential significance for the questions of theology is now available in the personality sciences. When pastoral theology studies this material, as it pertains to the perspective of shepherding, it is following not a nontheological or an extratheological method but something that is part of method in every branch of theology. Faith can remain faithful and relevant only when it is in constant and discriminating dialogue with culture.

In concluding this initial discussion of the meaning of pastoral theology, it will be well to note briefly the definitions that are excluded. First, pastoral theology is not merely the practice of anything. The practice or functions or events are examined reflectively and thus lead to theory. Any merely practical study of practice, if it failed to lead to fundamental theory, could not be pastoral theology.

Second, pastoral theology is not merely applied theology. Such a notion implies that principles are acquired through, for example, study of the Bible or of Christian doctrine and that these are applied in one-way fashion to acts and functions. We acknowledge fully that study of Bible and doctrine results in principles that may and must be applied. We assert further, however, that the process moves the other way also, that adequate critical study of events from some significant perspective makes creative contributions to theological understanding. Pastoral theology, like any branch of theology, applies some things learned elsewhere. But it is more than that as well.

Third, pastoral theology is not just pastoral psychology or pastoral sociology under a new name. The data considered may frequently be the same. What pastoral theology insists on is that the knowledge gained from observation and reflection be placed in a theological context. The principal criteria and methods employed are themselves theological. Pastoral psychology deals with insights emerging out of psychological inquiry for any and all aspects of the pastor's work and thought. Pastoral theology deals with the theological theory of the shepherding perspective upon the pastor's acts and functions. There is much overlap; but the two studies are not identical in scope, method, or aim.

Fourth, pastoral theology is not, as it has sometimes been held to be in the past, the theory of all the functions and operations of pastor and church. Such a view has seldom been held to completely, for the theory of preaching was usually excluded from the rubric of pastoral theology. We hold equally that pastoral theology cannot be the theory of all pastoral operations save preaching, for that gives it a kind of "Whatever is left over" definition. We believe attempts to define pastoral theology in this way will lead to either imperialism or amorphousness, as in the past, and we reject both.

Finally, we reject the possible conception of pastoral theology as the link between organized fields of theological study and the acts and functions of minister and church. We reject this for two reasons. On the one hand, it implies that study of operations and functions cannot lead through reflection and systematization to a branch of theology, and we believe it can and must do so. We reject it, on the other hand, because it implicitly defines any branch of theology in terms of what we have called a "logic-centered" point of reference. We must acknowledge the great importance of bringing together the findings from the logic-centered fields with those from the function-focused fields. But we believe this task is the job of all the branches and is not a function that can be performed by any alleged "master discipline."

[...] Some astute theologians in the nineteenth century proposed a branch of theology known as "practical theology," which would in turn have subbranches, of which pastoral theology might be one. There are two senses in which our conception of pastoral theology agrees with the intention behind the formation of practical theology. The first is the implication that the study of operations can and must be theological in character, must somehow lead to theological understanding. The second is that pastoral theology is not the sole branch of theology that can emerge from proper study of the functions of pastor and church.

With other aspects of this nineteenth-century idea of practical theology, we must take issue. We do not believe there is or can be a discipline of "practical theology" or "operational theology" that can be regarded as co-ordinate with biblical theology, doctrinal theology, and historical theology, and seen in the same series. The branches of theology whose focus is operations are *collectively* co-ordinate to the branches of theology whose focus is some logical reference point, such as the Bible. Further, we do not believe there can be a master perspective on acts and operations that would swallow all the others, any more than there can be a master perspective in the logic-centered fields, such that Bible would swallow up doctrine or history or ethics or that doctrine would consume the others.

Pastoral theology, to present the definition in slightly different language, is an operation-focused branch of theology, which begins with theological questions and concludes with theological answers, in the interim examining all acts and operations of pastor and church to the degree that they involve the perspective of Christian shepherding.

Importance of Pastoral Theology

There are five reasons why the study of pastoral theology is important today. The first is the peculiar nature and extent of the need for shepherding in our time. In our country more people belong to churches, both absolutely and proportionately, than at any previous time. Joining the church and professing faith in Jesus Christ do not automatically eliminate personal needs and problems. The churches and ministers now have an opportunity to help many persons to whom previously they would have been denied access.

[...]

A second reason why the study of pastoral theology is important lies in the development of new knowledge, new tools, and new professions that bear upon helping and healing. The new knowledge that is coming from psychology, from psychiatry, from anthropology, and from other sources is not easy to assimilate; but its riches are such that no thoughtful person can set them aside.[9] [...]

There are new problems and opportunities through the rise of new helping professions or through extension of functions among older helping professions such as the medical. [...] But what is the shepherding function of the ordained minister in relation to the shepherding actually being carried out by the social worker, the psychiatrist, the student personnel worker, the clinical psychologist, the leader of group therapy, and all the others?[10] It is not the minister's Christian faith that distinguishes him from them. They too may well be Christians. How does he co-operate with them? Where do their skills extend beyond his and his beyond theirs? These questions and relationships demand continued study and discussion at a basic theoretical level as well as in terms of daily practice. Without a pastoral theology the minister has no theoretical structure to use in trying to answer them but must resort to a kind of practical opportunism. And we must speak not only to the question of the ordained minister as shepherd but also to that of the universal pastorhood of believers when some of those unordained Christian shepherds have skills and knowledge to which the ordained do not profess.

Third, pastoral theological study is important because without it the acts of shepherding, though they be many and mighty, will not illumine our understanding of the faith in the United States. It is clear that there is much shepherding activity within the churches. But it is not always clear that this is based on understood Christian presuppositions and that reflection upon the activities is regarded as something more than the application of psychology or sociology in a purely practical sense.[11] Unless pastoral theology is studied, we lose many of the best opportunities with which God has provided us for deepening and correcting our understanding of the faith and that of those we try to help.

Fourth, the study of pastoral theology is important because of the peculiarly psychological intellectual climate of our time. Harry A. Overstreet has suggested that the language of our century is psychological in a way not true of any previous age.[12] Whether the psychology is good or bad, true or false, it is a mode of thinking in some respects unique to our time. Unless this modern man learns that this psychological language may also be a theological language, he is disposed to relegate theology as irrelevant to his thought and his concerns. There seems to be a growing amount of popular psychological thought that really deals with theological questions but that, by failing to acknowledge accurately the theological context, distorts theology and drives a deeper wedge between a misunderstood theology and an apparently more "comfortable" psychology. These trends should be arrested. Pastoral theology, studying shepherding in the light of theological questions and returning with theological answers, can take full account of psychology but can help prevent the false bifurcation that many now believe to represent the relation of theology and psychology. [...]

Finally, the study of pastoral theology is important in the context of our general theological revival today. The renewed and widespread concern among laymen as well as clergy for a deepened understanding of biblical and doctrinal theology, and sometimes of historical and moral theology, is incomplete unless there is a new depth to pastoral theology. [...]

The general point in this section, the importance of a pastoral theology – and not alone of a pastoral psychology, an applied theology, a pastoral practice, or even a right spirit – is deserving of brief illustration. Let us suppose a psychiatrist or clinical psychologist to be studying "acceptance" as he finds this in his therapeutic work. In many instances he may discover that, precisely at the point where the patient or client comes to feel most deeply that the psychiatrist accepts him, there is where he feels also at the same time most threatened. [...]

From experiences like this the psychiatrist may properly generalize that there are occasions when a new step in development is, while ultimately liberating, temporarily threatening. He may properly conclude that one should be careful about pushing people in even the best directions in view of the threatening potentiality of recoil.

[...]

THE BODY OF DIVINITY

THE ORGANIZATION OF THEOLOGICAL KNOWLEDGE AND STUDY

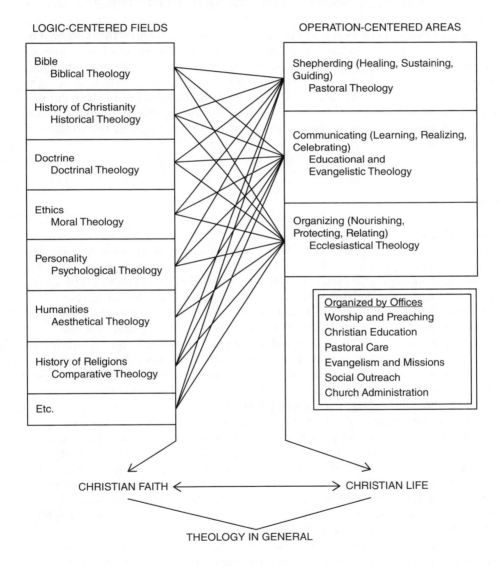

The pastoral theologian, dealing with such data, will carry his questions further. He may well say in this type of situation it would appear that just when love that has long been offered is finally recognized and received as love, at precisely that moment does judgment seem to be felt most terribly. The depth of one's unacceptability is recognized only as this has been accepted by something not of one's own creation.

At this point the pastoral theologian may find his thoughts turning to Paul with special reference to Romans.[13] Paul drives home the point that the law judges and condemns us, and that only by accepting the reality of God's love and his grace through Jesus Christ can we find new life. Presumably a pastoral theologian will see a genuine relationship between Paul's statements and the process the psychiatrist is reporting on. But the pastoral theologian cannot conclude that, having found it in Paul, his work is done, that all he need do thereafter is go about finding other instances of how right Paul was. Perhaps Paul did experience all the complexities and ambiguities that may exist in the relation between love and judgment. But we cannot assume this in advance, even of Paul. Study of the processes of such relationships may augment Paul's understanding, indeed may even help in our understanding of Paul's experience. Paul may be right without being adequate. We can never forget Paul and by implication all traditional theological wisdom. But this can never be a substitute for observing our pastoral experience, generalizing on it theologically, and checking it against the wisdom of the Christian ages.

Notes

1 Huldreich Zwingli, *Der Hirt*, 1524.
2 The word "autonomy" runs some risks of being misunderstood, even when we qualify it at every point by indicating the interrelationship of the several branches of theology. By analogy what I want to say is what Paul Tillich says in using the terms autonomy, heteronomy, and theonomy in a different connection. If the branches of theology were heteronomous, they would be related but in the pattern of a power structure such that some would engulf others. If they were merely autonomous without genuine relationship, they would be anarchic. In the other context Tillich uses the term "theonomy" to indicate the fulfillment of man, man's law, through God, God's law. Autonomy not seen in this context is not true autonomy but anarchy. See Tillich, *Systematic Theology*, University of Chicago Press, 1951, I, 147 ff.

Any branch of theology that regarded itself as the whole of theology would be either anarchic or imperialistic. While it cultivates rightly the subject matter peculiar to its nature, it also pays attention to the subject matter that is common currency for every branch. It aims at precision in what is unique about it, but it also brings its offerings to the common table. If pastoral theology exists and is important, as this volume contends, then it is necessary for its autonomy to be recognized in order that it may not prematurely be the victim of an intellectual or theological heteronomy that would, for example, regard it as merely practical without the ability to make genuinely theological contributions.

3 What I am calling the "logic-centered" fields of theological inquiry are sometimes referred to as the "theological sciences." This term is unsatisfactory, not only because of the specialized way in which the term "sciences" is now used, but also because it implies that no real knowledge is involved unless it is organized in a certain way. We call these fields "logic-centered" to suggest that the key to their distinctive nature lies in a "logical"

organization of subject matter. The logical organization of the subject matter in each field leads, then, to certain consequences which, potentially, enrich the whole.

For instance, biblical scholars now use linguistic analysis, archaeology, paleography, oriental history, and other special methods and disciplines in the pursuit of their inquiry that has the Bible as its logical center. [...]

The point here is not of course to argue the case for the biblical scholar's need to pursue archaeology or oriental history, for he can do that far better himself. It is, rather, by clarifying the nature of the distinctive way in which he organizes his inquiry, to indicate that another way of organizing a branch of theological study may also be both possible and necessary. This point must be made in order to lay claim to the right of pastoral theology to be a theological discipline, even though its principle of organization is function-centered rather than logic-centered. Proper study of functions with resulting systematization of knowledge leads to a body of knowledge and not merely to skill or technique.

4 From the latter part of the nineteenth century until today the principal scheme of organizing theological knowledge that was used in the theological seminaries was fourfold, involving biblical, systematic, historical, and practical theology. The overall error in this plan was the attempt to deal with practical theology, so-called, as if it were co-ordinate with each of the other items. [...] To regard practical theology or any branch of operation focused theology as one of a list of branches that are otherwise logic-centered is to force on a branch like pastoral theology organizational and structural criteria that prevent its making its inherent contribution to the whole body of divinity.

5 The figure attempts to represent the shape of the body of divinity according to the principles already indicated. On one side are the logic-centered fields and on the other the operation-centered areas. Each is shown connected with the other, as interpenetrating, as engaging in two-way communication. The primary point is not to argue for a specific number of fields and areas, but to demonstrate the proper mode of relationship among the fields and areas. If it is objected that this outline lacks unity because it insists on two different ways of organizing theological inquiry, two answers can be given. The first is that all attempts to deal with theological inquiry without making this distinction result either in an antipractical bias or in detheologizing the operational studies. In other words, I did not make the distinction but only discovered it. Second, the kind of unity that is needed for the richest theological inquiry is that which emerges from two-way communication at all points. No single field or area has the responsibility for integration in such a way that any other field can dispense with its integrative obligation. It is simply a fact that this linkage function must be shared or it cannot be performed at all. But that cannot be done by the equivalent of back-slapping, acting as if there were no distinction in the organizing principles of the two types of theological inquiry. And it certainly cannot be done if the fields treat the areas like illegitimate theological children fit only to apply what has been learned elsewhere and incapable of creative theological contribution.

6 [...] In theology the question of system has been complicated because doctrinal theology has often used the term "systematic theology" for itself. Indeed, it is necessary for doctrinal theology to be systematic in order to be intelligible and coherent. But this use, although unintentionally, has sometimes obscured the fact that every theological discipline must be systematic, that is, must bring together into a statement the representation of the relationships actually seen among items of the data, including statement of that about which there is ignorance or unclarity. In other words, any good system is open, even though struggling to represent adequately all the relationships it sees among its data.

[...] The historical theologian organizes his data systematically around a historical center, which he usually interprets as chronological sequence but which may assume other developmental forms. The system of the doctrinal theologian is focused around his logical organizing center of doctrinal relationship and coherence.

[...]

Our special concern is of course the system that is proper to pastoral theology. Around what shall its data be systematized? The answer is that the primary center for its system is its organizing principle, which I have defined as shepherding when shepherding is understood as a perspective present in all pastoral events and dominantly important in some. [...]

This volume divides the shepherding perspective into three aspects: healing, sustaining, and guiding. As an inquiry what pastoral theology is systematic about is the actual process by which shepherding – healing, sustaining, or guiding – is brought about. When this knowledge is put together into a system, although an open one, clarifying the common currency of the faith, we have a systematic pastoral theology. Any demand to pastoral theology that its primary focus of system be something else, such as systematic doctrine or Bible or morals, would be denying its claim to be a branch of theology. [...]

Pastoral theology, then, in summary, needs to be as systematic as any other branch of theology. That which distinguishes the center of its system within the body of divinity is its inquiry after and drawing conclusions from the exercise of the shepherding perspective. In relation to the shepherding disciplines which as disciplines are not theologically oriented, its system is focused around the common currency of the Christian faith. Thus the system of pastoral theology may be called bifocal, depending on whether it is speaking within the body of divinity or in relation to human knowledge in general.

[...] If both tasks are carried out, then pastoral theology becomes an open and inquiring and theologically focused system, enriching the whole body of divinity and having an impact on nontheological disciplines as well as learning from them.

7 [...] So long as it kept its place as practical, deluding itself that it merely applied what had been found out elsewhere, its existence was safe but dull, uncreative, and intellectually dishonest. Now that, at least in the person of this author, it alleges its theological character and an autonomy similar to that of other disciplines, something other than a passive parallelism will have to take place. Perhaps other theologians are so uniformly enlightened that they will rejoice unambiguously at the emergence of this talking sibling. It is more likely that the pastoral theologian will meet some new resistances from within and without the theological fold. This is good; for it means, at last, genuine encounter. An adult may spank a baby, but he does not fight it. Pastoral theology wants to be encountered – accepted as a sibling if possible – but better fight and even lose than to be mentally clothed with diapers.

8 This is the way Paul Tillich puts it in discussing his theological method as one of "correlation." He writes, "The method of correlation explains the contents of the Christian faith through existential questions and theological answers in mutual interdependence." Op. cit., 60. Not everything is yet clear about Tillich's use of the key term "correlation" to describe his theological method. Plainly he intends by it to establish theological relevance; theology does not talk in a corner by itself but speaks to the vital questions men ask. Thus he says to the theologian that culture and life cannot be neglected, and to the ordinary man that faith has a message for him. But to what extent is correlation a two-way method? Tillich apparently solves this problem by indicating that theology deals with matters of ultimate concern and other disciplines with preliminary concerns. But this

does not solve the problem. No one can say in advance when the emerging knowledge or insight is going to be ultimate or only preliminary. Nor does it seem sufficient to say that the sacred may erupt from the profane. Knowledge or insight of the utmost importance to theology may emerge at any time from a discipline that seems far removed from theology, and it hardly seems fair to say that that discipline has no claim to what it has discovered.

We believe that a full two-way street is necessary in order to describe theological method. If we hold that theology is always assimilation of the faith, not just the abstract idea of the faith apart from its reception, then it becomes necessary to say that culture may find answers to questions raised by faith as well as to assert that faith has answers to questions raised by culture. Tillich apparently hesitates to put the matter this way, and there is obvious risk to the ultimate meaning of faith in so putting it. But if psychiatry, for example, enables us to help someone to turn a corner and thence move on into the faith, how can we avoid saying that culture has given the answer to a problem posed by faith – provided we believe that our understanding of faith is never known apart from such actual concrete processes? [...]

9   See my "Bibliography and Reading Guide in Pastoral Psychology," *Pastoral Psychology*, vol. V:50, January, 1955.

10 See my "Psychotherapy and Counseling in Professions Other than the Ministry," *Pastoral Psychology*, vol. VII: 62, March, 1956.

11 Although I must reject certain aspects of the book's content, Albert C. Outler's *Psychotherapy and the Christian Message* (New York: Harper & Bros., 1954) is nevertheless an important call to a consideration of these presuppositions. So is an earlier but in some respects a more deep-reaching book, *Psychotherapy and a Christian View* of *Man* by David E. Roberts (New York: Charles Scribner's Sons, 1950). William E. Hulme in *Counseling and Theology* (Philadelphia: Muhlenberg Press, 1956), also attacks this question but with a tendency to find an answer too quickly in parallelism of psychology and theology.

12 *The Mature Mind* (New York: W.W. Norton & Co., 1949), l.

13 See especially Rom. 3:19–25, 27–8; 4:16–17; 5:1–5; 7:1–6; 8:1–11; 10:5–13.

18

Practical Theology within the Theological Disciplines (1972)*

Karl Rahner

Introduction

Many people regard Karl Rahner as the most influential Catholic theologian of the twentieth century. A German Jesuit, he played an especially significant role in the renewal of the Catholic Church that followed the Second Vatican Council (1962–1965). His view of "everyday things" as imbued with God's mystery played a key role in his endorsement of practical theology as a discipline specifically designed to grasp the movement of God in the world. His understanding of God as the "infinite incomprehensible mystery…present intrinsically in the world" drew deeply on his reinterpretation of Thomas Aquinas freed from a rigid neo-scholasticism bent on defending the Church's pronouncements in modernity.

Although Rahner's primary contributions lie in philosophical and dogmatic theology, his theology was consistently pastoral, shaped by the demands that the church and world place on theology as a whole, and his place in practical theology's history deserves greater recognition. This essay appears in one of the twenty-three English volumes of *Theological Investigations* that collect his papers and was written in 1967 for a study group in Munich on practical theology, approximately a decade after Hiltner's *Preface to Pastoral Theology* (1958). With greater self-consciousness than Hiltner on his Protestant assumptions, Rahner delimits his focus to Catholicism. He also recognizes his own place as an outsider; he is, he admits, a "dogmatician" who has gracefully "strayed into this field."

Although Hiltner and Rahner stood in different traditions and different parts of the world, there is surprising agreement on several fronts. In the essay, Rahner defends practical theology's place in the academy with a unique boldness and clarity of vision, demanding a "right epistemological understanding" of the discipline and "all its consequences." It should not be reduced to the application of truths learned elsewhere. As he argues in an essay on theology and social work, practical theology is a "theological science in its own right, and not simply a 'practical' supplement to the other theological disciplines" (1972, p. 369). Distinct from Hiltner, however, he prefers *practical* theology as the best term because it expands the task beyond people's narrow perception of

Original publication details: Karl Rahner, "Practical Theology within the Totality of Theological Disciplines," pp. 101–14 from *Theological Investigations*, vol. IX, trans. Graham Harrison (New York: Herder and Herder, 1972).

pastoral theology as focused entirely on clerical protocol. Practical theology investigates the church's "actualization" in the world, the "*theoria* which indwells...practice itself." From this perspective, it has a great deal to offer not only to the church but also to other academic areas. In fact, the "actual practice of theology" as a academic and ecclesial discipline is "subject matter" for practical theology's critical analysis.

All told, Rahner's argument for practical theology is unusually forthright. He even speaks to institutional culture, calling for the appointment of university chairs in practical theology, for example. As a scholar with considerable authority, it is unfortunate that his manifesto did not have greater impact, especially in the United States where Catholic universities have been slow to acknowledge practical theology as an area of doctoral study. Rahner's concise definition and his exploration of its primary tasks and relationship to other academic areas remain important to the ongoing establishment of the discipline.

Suggested Further Reading

- Karl Rahner, "The Second Vatican Council's Challenge to Theology," *Theological Investigations*, IX, 3–27 and "Practical Theology and Social Work in the Church," *Theological Investigations* X, 349–70, trans. Graham Harrison (New York: Herder and Herder, 1972).
- Karl Rahner, *Everyday Things*, trans. M. H. Heelan (London: Sheed and Ward, 1965).
- Franz Xaver Arnold, Karl Rahner, Victor Schur, and Leonhard M. Weber, eds., *Handbuch der Pastoraltheologie* (Freiburg: Herder, 1964–6).

***

The question raised in this paper is "What does practical theology expect of the other fields of theological study?" First of all we must define the limits of our discussion of the matter in question. The approach and the situation of modem practical theology among the Protestant churches cannot be described. And as far as practical theology within the Catholic Church is concerned, the author is really more of a dilettante who has strayed into this field by a number of chance occurrences. There may be advantages in this if one regards it as a sign that a dogmatician *can* be interested in practical theology and that, therefore, such an interest can justifiably be expected from him. Seen thus it is perhaps not so untoward that practical theology's demands upon other theological studies should be put forward not by a representative of practical theology but by an "outsider".

Since there is no really clear and generally accepted agreement on the Catholic side as to what practical theology is and should be, and consequently there is amongst us no general consensus as to its relationship with the other departments of theological study and as to what demands it can and must make on the latter, the author has no choice but to say – on his own account and at his own risk – what he himself imagines practical theology to be. Anything which follows as a result of this is subject to the proviso that one *cannot* speak in the name of a *single* Catholic theology. At the same time of course this does not mean that the author's view is simply unique within Catholic theology or claims any patent for its personal originality. In any case we possess a sketch of a practical theology of this kind in the *Handbook of Pastoral Theology*, even if such a composite work naturally reveals many deficiencies, since not all its contributions adequately realise the fundamental conception equally well if at all.[1] H. Schuster gives an account of the history of practical theology's understanding of itself from the Catholic point of view in the first volume of the *Handbook*.[2] The author regards the name "practical theology" as better than our more usual "pastoral theology" because the latter indicates a false constriction of the discipline's field of activity, as we shall mention directly.

I

Practical theology is that theological discipline which is concerned with the Church's self-actualisation here and now – both that which *is* and that which *ought to be*. This it does by means of *theological* illumination of the particular situation in which the Church must realise itself in all its dimensions. We shall now amplify this essential description. For a detailed justification of this we refer to other studies.[3]

The Church is a historical quantity. Without endangering its abiding essence it is true to say that the Church not simply *is*, but must be continually "happening" anew. This "occurrence" of the Church, however, is not simply its being in essence perpetually present in a space-time always external to it, but the historical form of this essence – unique in each instance – to which the Spirit of the Church calls it through its particular and unique historical situation. Because of its Spirit's eschatologically triumphant grace the Church cannot be untrue to the particular "occurrent" form of its self-realisation to such an extent that it simply ceases being the Church of Christ; but that does not alter the fact that the Church has the task of making a commitment to realise this particular historical form in responsibility and freedom, and can therefore also fall far short of it. Consequently the Church must reflect consciously upon the question how the Church's self-actualisation is to take place arising out of and in response to its particular given situation in each instance. Practical theology is the scientific organisation of this reflection.

This practical theology is a unique, independent science, a fundamental one in essence in spite of its reciprocal relationship with other theological disciplines, since its business of scientifically critical and systematic reflection is a unique quantity and its nature is not deducible. For it is reflection orientated towards committal. It follows from a correct evaluation of the relationship between theory and practice; from an appropriate understanding (from the point of view of existential ontology) of the nature of freedom; from a right theology of the intractability of the Holy Spirit as the principle of the Church's history; from a correct understanding of the nature of hope; from all this it follows that the Church's committal to the particular self-realisation to which it is called at any one time cannot adequately be deduced from its *essence*. And so the aim of practical theology – precisely this continually new self-actualisation in committal on the part of the Church – is not the mere consequence of an "essential" theology of the nature of the Church, the Word of God and the kerygma, the nature of the Sacraments, the service of love etc., however possible and necessary this may be. If, in spite of this, this non-deducible factor which inheres in each committal is to be the object of a reflection *sui generis* which sees into the future, seeking what is to be done here and now, extending the horizons of the possible future, trying the spirits which are proclaiming the future, then the process of reflection upon it, scientifically organised, is an independent and primary science and not only an "application" of the results of the essential sciences within theology, whether the latter be systematic or historical. It is true that the decisions of the Church are not really made in practical theology, for that is a matter for the whole Church (and within this totality it is a matter for official authority), even if the theory of practical theology, as actually carried on, is itself one factor in the Church's practice. But in being this kind of theory practical theology is not simply an "essential" science but a quite unique one, a testing of the spirits with a view to the act of committal; it implies a prophetic element – which one may be permitted to call "political" – since it must be aware of the impulse of the Church's Spirit, which is not simply identical with the perpetually valid truth in the Church, but translates the latter into the concrete challenge valid at the particular hour. Practical theology can and must be this, because the *theoria* realised in actuality is also an internal factor of the Church's practice and only remains genuine *theoria* under this presupposition. In a word, it is "theory" and thus science. But it is the *theoria* which indwells the practice itself as an internal factor which is thus not simply identical with the objectifying "essential" sciences, which simply ascertain from a "neutral" position what is the case, or what must always be, or what will surely occur independently of decisions. Consequently it is "critical" towards the Church although it cannot annexe the latter's decisions. It attempts to be of service in continually overcoming the Church's given deficient self-realisation and transcending it in the next new form to which the Church is being called. It exercises a critical function in respect of the other theological disciplines since it is always questioning whether they are adequately making the particular local contribution required of them (and of which they are capable) towards the Church's self-realisation in committal. In spite of this critical aspect practical theology is an essentially ecclesial discipline, since it is not only concerned with the Church in its relation to its activity, but comprehends itself as the factor of reflection which inheres in this activity and is not merely applied to it from outside. As a result it is dependent on everything which constitutes this Church's continuing essence.

Practical theology's subject-matter is everyone and everything in the Church, i.e. all those who participate in the Church's self-realisation, not only those holding office in the Church and in its official care of souls. Consequently its subject-matter is not only the "care of souls" in the more narrow sense, but the totality of that particular action required of all members of the Church at any one time, in so far as this action is a factor in the life of the Church as such.

Everything is its subject-matter; i.e. the Church's self-realisation in *all* its dimensions. From this point of view homiletics, catechetics, the study of mission and welfare work are partial fields within practical theology as such, although this does not eliminate the question of these partial disciplines' technical and practical independence.

II

The task of practical theology as an original science demands a *theological* analysis of the particular present situation in which the Church is to carry out the especial self-realisation appropriate to it at any given moment. In order to be able to perform this analysis of the present by means of scientific reflection and to recognise the Church's situation, practical theology certainly needs sociology, political science, contemporary history etc. To this extent all these sciences are in the nature of ancillary studies for practical theology. However, although the contemporary analysis provided by these profane sciences is necessary and sufficient for its use, it cannot simply draw on it uncritically as though it were already complete and given. Practical theology must itself critically distil this analysis within a theological and ecclesial perspective, a task which cannot be taken over by any other theological discipline. This contemporary analysis does not remain its only task, but it is indispensable. For the committal to the Church's particular relevant self-realisation cannot be unequivocally deduced solely even from a *dogmatic* knowledge of the essence of the Church and the reflex insight into its contemporary situation. Practical theology, on the other hand, can supply – asymptotically at least – the element of reflection and the offer of possible solutions. Beyond the confrontation of the Church's essence with the contemporary situation, practical theology should contain an element of creativity and prophecy and be engaged in critical reflection.

At this point we take the liberty of adding a small observation, even if it is perhaps not absolutely necessary for our subject. Today it is possible to observe that the concrete achievements of science as such are by no means exclusively due to university scientists. Besides universities there is an increasing number of other places of research, institutes, learned societies, etc.; even in public and economic administration itself there are scientific organisations which do not merely apply science but carry out actual research. We cannot here enter into the reasons for this – no doubt inevitable – partial migration of science away from the universities. But it can be questioned whether, as regards practical theology, an analogous process is not to be expected and even thought necessary and desirable. In concrete terms: can today's and tomorrow's practical theology be *merely* a university study sustained by the confidence that its work and its results will to some extent be taken note of benevolently by the "practitioners" in office in the Church, while in general these practitioners still continue in actual fact to live, make decisions and take action in the future on the basis of their own individual experience of life, which has not been subjected to critical reflection? Or would it be desirable, for instance, for the Church's authorities to have something in the nature of a practical theology being studied scientifically alongside them, since they stand in need of it and since much of what is needed from it can only be seen in enough detail as a result of the closest contact with the practice of the Church? University theology, almost as a result of its very nature, lacks this rapport to a large extent. The politician is someone quite different from the student of political thought. But if it is the case today that life is becoming irresistibly subject to science, the student of political thought and the politician must carry on their work in such close collaboration – organisationally too – that the study of politics can no longer be pursued exclusively in the university. Is not the same sort of thing valid for practical theology too? Would it not be fruitful if the university were to train representatives of practical theology who would then continue to work scientifically within the Church's official organs and in direct contact with it and its tasks, exercising an advisory, critical and prompting function on the basis of this work?

III

What does practical theology, understood in this way, expect of the other theological subjects, and what must it demand from them?

Firstly it demands the *recognition of its originality and significance as a theological discipline in its own right*. As far as the other disciplines are concerned that is by no means a readily acceptable view. For the most part the representatives of the other disciplines look on practical theology as a mere hotch-potch of practical consequences which follow automatically from these disciplines. In the Romance countries, for instance, we do not yet have any really serious and distinct discipline of "practical theology" and in this respect the demands of the Second Vatican Council have not yet begun to be met. Or else the representatives of the other disciplines regard practical theology merely as a collection of psychological, didactic, sociological rules of prudence, gained directly from the ordinary practice of the care of souls. No wonder that one's instinctive attitude – not explicitly stated of course – is to make for the most part less imposing demands on the practical theologian's intellectual and scientific competence than in the case of the other theological disciplines. So the first thing required of the other theological studies is a right epistemological understanding of practical theology – with all its consequences. Although we are not able to pursue this matter further here, it implies certain effects as regards the number of and the manner of appointment to professorial chairs, the arrangement of courses, and the provision of the necessary finance, etc.

The *second* demand – still of a general character – is the demand that *the other theological disciplines should recognise the element of practical theology which must be contained within themselves, and that they should cherish it*. The whole of theology is an ecclesial field of study in all its disciplines, precisely because (and in so far as) it exercises its critical function with respect to the Church as well, since this criticism is always immanent in the Church's faith as such. But this also means that all theological disciplines must serve in the Church's self-realisation, and therefore contain within themselves an element of practical theology. As a discipline in its own right it cannot deny the relatedness of the other disciplines to the Church's self-realisation and thus to her faith, her message, her sacramental practice, to the life of the Church, her love issuing in works and her critical service to the world in all its dimensions, although in this respect practical theology always has to act in stimulation and criticism of the other disciplines.

[...] If it carries out itself an analysis of the Church's present situation by means of theological reflection, practical theology does not thereby become engaged in contemporary Church history, simply because this analysis is impossible *without* Church history and particularly contemporary history. However, by criticism and new ways of questioning it will make Church history (as a *theological* and ecclesial science) aware that a Church history studied theologically is not the satisfaction of historical inquisitiveness but the critical implementation of that anamnesis of the Church's past without which she cannot sufficiently take possession of her present, adopting it as the germ of her future. Practical theology will not itself carry on the dialogue with man's profane understanding of existence, as that is a matter for fundamental theology and dogmatics; but it will continually make these disciplines aware that their tasks are not to be fulfilled in the unhistorical and sterile realm of eternally valid truths, but in the historical situation which is ours at any one particular time.

When we said previously that practical theology is concerned with the Church's self-realisation in the continually new given contemporary situation, which it illuminates theologically, that does not mean that it either must or can itself determine the *content* of the Church's selfrealisation in all its dimensions by means of theoretical reflection, but that it is to submit to reflection the tasks of the other disciplines as they touch the Church and arise from the contemporary situation. By means of its own analysis of the present, which is not the business of other theological disciplines, it will carry out a process of reflection which can now no longer be provided in a scientifically responsible and satisfactory manner by these other disciplines. Today they must allow the compass of their tasks, *in so far as* they are set by the Church and her future, to be prescribed by another discipline; by practical theology. To this extent practical theology takes precedence over the other disciplines, although the reverse is the case in other respects, i.e. to the extent that these other theological disciplines, as the essential fundamental alignment, constitute the precondition, perspective and standard for practical theology.

Practical theology challenges the other theological studies to recognize the task which inheres immanently in them, orientated to the practice of the Church; the second demand it makes is that they should apply themselves to this task. Of course that does not mean that practical theology is *only* a sort of formal conscience for the other theological disciplines. For on the one hand it implies, as its subordinate departments, the study of mission, catechetics, homiletics and the study of welfare work. However difficult it is to separate these individual disciplines from those which they presuppose as their foundation, it is in any case immediately apparent that practical theology is not only the critical and formal conscience of the other disciplines. Then there are many concrete factors in the Church's self-realisation (i.e. the whole "organization" of the "care of souls"), which are not considered by any other theological discipline, especially what is "institutional" in the Church's self-realisation, which is not simply coextensive with its right to be so, but far exceeds it. Conversely, what has been said previously does not deny the fact that practical theology can take on in addition subsidiary tasks which in themselves belong to other disciplines but which, under certain circumstances, the latter are not actually dealing with. So far for example there are many questions which Catholic dogmatic ecclesiology has not considered sufficiently, although they are really its province and are of the greatest importance for practical theology. In such a case practical theology can pursue a piece of dogmatic ecclesiology in a subsidiary role. The same thing can happen as regards dogmatic sacramental theology, canon law, moral theology, ecumenical theology, etc.

IV

We shall now try to fill in the details of this fundamental demand as it is addressed to the individual theological disciplines, even if it is unfortunately only possible here to formulate these demands and expectations in a very general and vague way. In addition it must be observed that the epistemological kind of question as to how the theological disciplines are related to each other at a more intimate level, forming the totality of the theology of Christianity and the Church, must be set aside.

1) Firstly, as far as *exegetics* and *biblical theology* are concerned, the question as to how far this discipline itself has the task of actualising the Word of God in scripture and how far it shares it with "systematic theology" is a problem which cannot be solved here. In any case, as Christian theology, which is something other than the mere study of religion, this discipline is in the service of the Church's kerygma and must

make its contribution to the correct and effective proclamation of the "Gospel" in the Church according to scripture. It is a basic conviction of the Christian Faith that this is possible, in spite of – or rather *because of* – the methods of modern scientific exegesis as genuinely practised. An exegesis which does not share this conviction ought to withdraw from theology and become attached to a profane field of religious studies, if it is still thought interesting. Christian exegesis must serve the Church's kerygma; it must not only supply the critical standard but also be of positive assistance. It is precisely practical theology which will have to put this fundamental demand to exegesis, clarifying it and showing its specific application. This does not mean that it interferes thereby in the autonomous field of exegesis, but speaks in the name of the whole of theology, of which exegesis forms one part, receiving its task, its justification and its autonomy from this whole. Here I must admit that I cannot say precisely what practical theology's demands upon exegesis would look like in more specific and concrete terms, nor how it could be executed technically. But to say this is only to touch upon the more general problem of how to overcome the mutual alienation of the sciences and also of the theological disciplines. In my estimation in any case, practical theology ought to ask exegesis and biblical theology to be providing continually (as well as the increasingly detailed studies which tend to become boundless, and which are no longer digestible from the preacher's point of view) the kind of theological literature which the theologian and preacher (who can no longer be an exegetical specialist in the strict sense) finds useful in his work and which keeps him close enough to scholarly exegetical research. [...]

2) As far as practical theology's demands upon *systematic theology* (i.e. chiefly fundamental theology, dogmatics and moral theology) are concerned, it must be said at once that a more intensive dialogue between both disciplines would be desirable, to discuss their different nature. We have already observed that systematic studies continually tend to be quick to misunderstand practical theology as the mere practical consequences of the theses of systematic theology or as a straightforward echo of actual practice.

Furthermore, practical theology must draw the attention of systematic theology to the fact that the latter does not carry on its business in a vacuum, not subject to history and for its own sake, but in the concrete situation of the times and of the Church. It cannot set its own tasks and priorities just as it likes. It seems to me then, that this implies the following consequences for Catholic theology: Catholic systematic theology in universities – together with the historical work which accompanies it – seems to me today still to have too strong a flavour of historicism, too calmly pursuing historical theology detached from the question of proclamation today. It still tends to deal too intensively with peripheral dogmatic questions, to concern itself too little with the central issues involved in a new reflection upon the fundamental assertions of the faith, and (since Vatican II) it is in danger of focusing its whole attention on the Council's explicit theses, which neither were nor could have been the themes laid upon us today. It might very well be one of practical theology's tasks to investigate the strategy and "politics" which lie unexamined and inexplicit behind the study of systematic theology; it would have to initiate an examination of the hidden tendencies and governing images of systematic theology as it is actually practised, from the point of view of a sociology of the Church, including statistical investigations; for the actual practice of theology is one factor in the Church's self-realisation and thus also subject-matter for practical theology. This kind of analysis of what is actually done and not done in the rest of theology could then lead to the question as to what *should* be done and what ought *not* to be done, or at least, not done with such over-emphasis. To my knowledge for instance there is today nowhere a text-book of fundamental or dogmatic theology for the young theological student which presents the subjects wholly in a way which is both good from a didactic point of view and appropriate to the demands of the present situation. And we simply accept this fact without a qualm. Ought not practical theology to protest loudly about this matter? Surely it is part of its real task, if it is to reflect critically and creatively upon the Church's particular self-realisation presented at any one time in all its dimensions (i.e. also in the field of theology)? While maintaining all due respect for the freedom and autonomy of the individual theological disciplines, it is surely part of the dignity of these disciplines that they can accept criticism where they are proceeding against their own aims, at least by default. Surely this kind of admonition cannot today be based merely on an unregulated private experience, but rather it must be established in a very precise and exact manner? But by whom, if not by practical theology?

3) As far as *Church history* is concerned, practical theology will first of all be surprised to find that we – as Catholics – have a greatly underdeveloped theological reflection concerning the real nature of Church history. Consequently the compass of Church history and its relation to the other theological disciplines and to the Church itself in its concrete form remain highly obscure. Of course, as such Church history has to do with the past and not directly with the future; it is not a prophetic oracle, nor is it a drawing-office of creative programmes as to what is to take place in the Church today or tomorrow. But if it is really interested in genuine theological issues and looks into the past from this standpoint, it could recognise – in accordance with its own true nature – much of the past as initiating future possibilities and tasks for the Church. [...] From the point of view of the open questions of the future which practical theology endeavours to uncover, the past could be asked to reveal its own theological mystery, thereby shedding more light on these questions and bringing into view a horizon in which an answer could be sought. If a Christian can only grasp the Old Testament in its deepest essence from the standpoint of the New, why should he not understand the Church's past better from the standpoint of *that* theology which anticipates the Church's future in its *formal* nature and tries, in practical theology, to plan out its more immediate possibilities in concrete terms?

[...] If history (*Geschichte*) is to be the teacher of the present and the future – and to say this is not an unscientific self-alienation of history (*Historie*) – one must know to some extent (including all possible surprises in one's calculations) *what kind* of instruction for the future one expects from history. And on *this* matter surely practical theology could have something to say to Church history, and might expect the study of Church history to take advice from history on these matters? It is unfortunately impossible here to clarify by means of concrete cases what we have said in this very abstract manner. Ultimately the Church's past achievements are only interesting in connection with what lies ahead of her. If the Church historian is imbued with this awareness, he will write Church history which is also of service to practical theology. But not otherwise.

4) The relationship between *canon law* and practical theology is or ought to be very close. First of all practical theology must cherish its independence *vis-à-vis* canon

law. Practical theology is not identical with the sum total of observations concerning the more concrete implementation of canon law. Only a small portion of the life of the Church is accessible to legal ordering. Practical theology ought to defend the remaining sphere of the Church's life which is not subject to legalistic manipulation. That is not as obvious as it sounds, since our Catholic canon law tends to formulate *moral* norms in its own sphere, which on the one hand are not really *legal* norms at all, and on the other hand it tends to manipulate them as if they *were* legal norms. In so far as canon law is not only concerned *de lege condita* (historical, interpreting and casuistic) but is also seeking the correct law which ought to exist and yet does not at present, the *lex condenda*, and in so far as this law of the future is not *only* that law which develops out of the immanent dynamic of the currently valid law, it is the task of practical theology to discover aims and horizons for canon law in respect of this *lex condenda*. Today this can only take place as a result of a scientifically critical and simultaneously theological analysis of the contemporary situation. This, however, cannot be the task of canon law. For it is not a legal matter and at the same time constitutes such a difficult and extensive reality, demanding its own methodology for study, that it cannot be investigated as an appendage by canon law merely because the latter as the science *de lege condenda* happens to need some knowledge of it. Criticism of current law and fundamental exposition of the recommended law are therefore tasks of practical theology and imply as many demands of practical theology upon canon law. The relationship here is similar to that between the study of politics, sociology, etc. on the one hand and jurisprudence on the other. Just as profane jurisprudence must accept observations from these other profane disciplines although they are historically junior to it, the same applies also to canon law in relation to practical theology.

5) Finally something must be said concerning practical theology's demands upon the *study of liturgy*. This question depends to some extent on whether liturgiology is to be understood as a subordinate discipline of practical theology or not. However that may be, modem liturgiology has taken as its object the scientifico-theological reflection of a liturgy yet to be created, and deals no longer primarily with the history and appraisal of existing liturgy. Thereby it has developed a broader and more comprehensive concept of liturgy than was the case previously within a markedly ritualistic and rubricistic understanding of liturgy. As a result, in any case, liturgiology has come into the immediate neighbourhood of practical theology. The question of the *liturgia condenda* is above all a question of practical theology seen from the standpoint of its whole task, or at least one requiring an answer for which practical theology must create the presuppositions. For one can only answer the question as to *how* liturgy ought to be done *today* if one knows what Christians are like as contemporary men, if practical theology approaches its problems with the help of sociology of religion etc. Precisely because liturgiology has now become in actuality quite independent, practical theology as a whole will continually have the task of delivering liturgiology from the dangers of a romantic glorification of the old forms of the liturgy, the danger of an aesthetic view, of a rubricistic legalism and also of the private whim of the connoisseur. It will lead to a liturgy which can really be a liturgy of the People of God here and now.

We cannot discuss here the question of the relationship between practical theology and the profane disciplines which constitute its necessary ancillary studies (like psychology, sociology, etc.). It will be clear too that we have only touched upon the relation of practical theology to those theological disciplines which to a certain extent have a fundamental and normative significance for practical theology. The prime intention of this contribution has been to demonstrate the urgency of the basic task. If we find ourselves only at the beginning of our endeavours and deliberations it may be all the more a health-giving challenge to pursue the matter with more energy and with greater sensitivity. If that were done, even to a small extent, it would be a good beginning.

Notes

1 cf. F.X. Arnold (from vol. III onwards F. Klostermann), K. Rahner, V. Schurr, L.M. Weber (ed.), *Handbuch der Pastoraltheologie. Praktische Theologie der Kirche in ihrer Gegenwart* I (Freiburg, 1964), II/1–2 (Freiburg, 1966); III. [...]
2 cf. the second chapter, "Die Geschichte der Pastoraltheologie", I, 40–92; cf. also F.X. Arnold, "Pastoraltheologische Ansätze in der Pastoral bis zum 18. Jahrhundert", I, 15–39.
3 cf. apart from the contributions of H. Schuster and K. Rahner in the *Handbuch der Pastoraltheologie* (esp. I, pp. 93–114, 117–215, 323–31, 333–43; II/1, 181 ff., 233 ff., 256 ff.; II/2,. 19 ff., 46 ff.) esp. H. Schuster, "Wesen und Aufgabe der Pastoraltheologie," *Concilium* 1 (1965), 165 ff.; K. Rahner, "A Theological Interpretation of the Position of Christians in the Modem World", *Mission and Grace*, vol. I (London, 1963), 3–55. K. Rahner, "The Second Vatican Council's Challenge to Theology", in this volume [i.e. source document],. 3–27; also "On the theological problems entailed in a Pastoral Constitution" and "Practical theology and social work in the Church", *Theological Investigations* X; cf. also F. Klostermann, "Pastoraltheologie heute", *Dienst an der Lehre*, ed. Catholic Theology Faculty of the University of Vienna = *Wiener Beiträge zur Theologie* X (Vienna, 1965), pp. 51–108; F.X. Arnold, "Was ist Pastoraltheologie?", *Wort des Heils as Wort in die Zeit* (Trier, 1961), 296–300; K. Delahaye, "Überlegungen zur Neuorientierung der Pastoraltheologie heute", *Gott in Welt. Festgabe für K. Rahner*, ed. J.B. Metz, W. Kern, A. Darlap, H. Vorgrimler, vol. II (Freiburg, 1964), 206–18.

19

The Hermeneutic Circle as Epistemology (1976)*
Juan Luis Segundo

Introduction

Uruguayan Jesuit priest and internationally renown theologian Juan Luis Segundo was a major figure in founding and developing Latin American liberation theology in the late 1960s and 1970s alongside others such as Gustavo Gutiérrez in Peru and Leonardo Boff in Brazil. The Conference of Latin American Bishops in Medellín, Colombia in 1968 is often heralded as a turning point. Drawing on ideas, such as those of Paulo Freire, spokespersons pushed the Second Vatican Council (1962–65) toward deeper social and political engagement, challenging the gap between rich and poor, adopting a preferential option for the poor, and creating base communities where lay people read and interpreted the Bible for themselves.

The abridged excerpt from the introduction and first chapter of Segundo's *Liberation of Theology* is the one of the few selections in the *Reader* that does not reference practical theology. Nor, in contrast with Hiltner and Rahner, is Segundo concerned with establishing a disciplinary area by that name. Equally notable, although Gutiérrez, Boff, and other Latin American theologians appear in *The Wiley Blackwell Companion to Practical Theology* (2012) index, Segundo does not. So why does his writing appear here?

Latin American liberation theology has had a profound impact on practical theology that prominent figures in the European and North America revitalization of the discipline in the 1980s often ignore. Few of the early scholars credit liberation theology for practical theology's reemergence, an omission tainted by racism and northern imperialism that seems especially troubling today. In fact, there is little written on the connections and divergences between the rise of liberation theology in Latin American Catholic contexts and the appearance of a renewed disciplinary area called *practical theology* in the north in predominantly Protestant universities and seminaries. Inclusion of Segundo here, therefore, allows for greater recognition of key ideas that originated in Latin America and gravitated to (or were misappropriated in) practical theology. More positively stated, there are important parallels and alliances worth noting between

Original publication details: Juan Luis Segundo, "Introduction," pp. 3–6, and "The Hermeneutical Circle," pp. 7–38 from *The Liberation of Theology* (Maryknoll, NY: Orbis Books, 1976).

The Wiley Blackwell Reader in Practical Theology, First Edition. Edited by Bonnie J. Miller-McLemore.
© 2019 John Wiley & Sons Ltd. Published 2019 by John Wiley & Sons Ltd.

practical and liberation theologies, including the commitment to the concrete and particular in the construction of theological knowledge.

Equally significant, however, Segundo made a unique contribution that is especially important to practical theology. The very title of his book makes this clear. By deliberately turning the words *theology* of *liberation* around, he underscores that theology itself, its practice and construction within the university, is under examination. In this reversal, he is not undoing a "theology of liberation," the title of Gutiérrez's 1973 book; rather Segundo is taking the analysis to a deeper level, showing how a liberation theology demands an epistemological and methodological overhaul of theology itself, especially the "erudite theology of textbooks" and the "rarefied atmosphere of academia." His book responds to three concerns about liberation theology's fate. On one hand, its friendship with the poor is seen as dangerous, while on the other hand its terminology is misappropriated by those who claim adherence, yet fail to demonstrate genuine allegiance. Most troubling and relevant to the *Reader*, however, is a third challenge that motivates his book – "academic disdain" for "theology rising out of the urgent problems of real life" as "naïve and uncritical." This problem may be the most virulent because it is so deeply "rooted…by virtue of the mechanisms by which it operates."

Equally significant, Segundo articulates and illustrates through the study of four examples the four movements of a "hermeneutical circle" in which theology emerges within the "here and now." The phrase *hermeneutical circle* has appeared and reappeared in practical theological literature without sufficient attribution to Segundo and his unique emphasis on exposing ideologies at every turn in the circle. In raising up James Cone's 1970 book, *A Black Theology of Liberation*, as the only instance where each step of the circle is successfully negotiated (the others are Harvey Cox, Marx, and Weber), Segundo shows the close connection between Latin American liberation theology in the southern hemisphere and Black theology in the United States.

Suggested Further Reading

- Juan Luis Segundo, *Signs of the Times: Theological Reflections*, ed. Alfred T. Hennelly, trans. Robert R. Barr (Maryknoll, NY: Orbis 1993).
- Karl Mannheim, *Ideology and Utopia: An Introduction to the Sociology of Knowledge* (New York: Harcourt, Brace, and Company, 1936).

***

What will remain of the "theology of liberation" in a few short years? The question may seem to be pessimistic in tone, suggesting that liberation theology was a superficial thing or a passing fad. That is certainly not the case. My question should be approached in a positive and hopeful spirit.

It is my opinion that the "theology of liberation," however well or poorly the name fits, represents a point of no return in Latin America. It is an irreversible thrust in the Christian process of creating a new consciousness and maturity in our faith. Countless Christians have committed themselves to a fresh and radical interpretation of their faith, to a new re-experiencing of it in their real lives. And they have done this not only as isolated individuals but also as influential and sizeable groups within the Church.

While the process is irreversible, it is also broad in scope and varied within itself. Therefore it is not easy to say what the exact content of the theology of liberation is for all the Christians involved in it. Certain basic points, however, are clearly shared by all. They would maintain that the longstanding stress on individual salvation in the next world represents a distortion of Jesus' message. He was concerned with man's full and integral liberation, a process which is already at work in history and which makes use of historical means. They would maintain that the Church does not possess any sort of magical effectiveness where salvation is concerned but rather liberating factors in its faith and its liturgy; that the victory of the Church must be viewed in functional terms rather than quantitative or numerical terms, insofar as the Church's specific and proper means manage to exercise a truly powerful impact on human history. They would also maintain that there are not two separate orders – one being a supernatural order outside history and the other being a natural order inside history; that instead one and the same grace raises human beings to a supernatural level and provides them with the means they need to achieve their true destiny within one and the same historical process.

The situation changes somewhat if we try to predict the future impact of liberation theology on classical theology and on the internal and pastoral structures of the Church, outside of Latin America in particular. Here our optimism must be toned down considerably. Indeed it may give way to diffidence or dismay with regard to the short-term situation. For the *content* of liberation theology is jeopardized by three tendencies which, working separately or together, could destroy it.

The first tendency derives from the fact that ecclesiastical authorities have learned rather quickly that even the minimum content of liberation theology, the mere repetition of the basic declarations that were voiced without any great difficulty at the Medellín Conference, literally constitute a political crime today. They can entail imprisonment and torture for lay people. And though they may not entail exactly the same things for priests and bishops, they threaten to jeopardize something which the latter regard as just as important and critical: i.e., the privileged status of religious activity and even the basic right of its free exercise. Since the Medellín Conference we have witnessed a growing gap between the poor countries and the rich countries, and also an inevitable growth of political awareness in the former. Bit by bit this has led to the replacement of democratic governments, of even the most stable ones, by military dictatorships which can keep discontent under control though they may not be able to control its causes. Liberation theology, even when reduced to its most minimal content, has been singled out by these dictatorships as something as potentially explosive as the existence of Marxist groups and political parties.

The second tendency stems from the fact that ecclesiastical authorities themselves have adopted the terminology of liberation. Gradually this has led to a watering down of its content, so that the language of liberation is emptied of all real meaning. Everyone mouths the words, only to go on as before. Classical Catholic education describes itself as an education in liberation, and even the most extreme right-wing ideology makes frequent use of the idiom of liberation. And so we are confronted with a paradox that is readily comprehensible in ideological terms: on the one hand the authentic theology of liberation is persecuted as subversive; on the other hand its terminology is adopted in watered-down form to front for ideas and attitudes that have no connection whatsoever with truly liberative changes.

The third tendency is more subtle, but no less real and effective. Indeed it may be the most solidly rooted of the three by virtue of the mechanisms by which it operates. From its very inception liberation theology was a theology rising out of the urgent problems of real life. Faced with those problems and deeply influenced by them, it resorted to the traditional means of theologizing: that is, to biblical tradition and to dogmatic tradition. It did this seriously and earnestly, feeling a responsibility towards both the problems of real life and the canons of worldwide theology. But it did this, as it had to, with the means at its disposal. It did not move in a precipitate, hare-brained way to meet some inescapable pragmatic necessity, but it did move forward without the erudite exploration and attention to detail which is evident when a new line of theological thought is introduced into present-day European or North American theology. In affirming certain essential points, moreover, it left aside other points which may have been important in their consequences.

As a result, liberation theology evoked two reactions at the same time. It aroused interest among the noninitiate, but it also clearly evoked a certain amount of academic disdain from the great centers of theological thought around the world. Now the fact is that the everyday theology of Latin America, the theology that is passed on to priests in the seminaries and thus eventually to lay people in universities and churches, continues to be the erudite theology of textbooks. And if this latter theology continues to view liberation theology as a well-intentioned but rather naive and uncritical effort, it is clear that Latin Americans will not be immune to the influence of this outlook.

These three negative tendencies are being felt more and more keenly by Latin American theology. Perhaps it is now time to attack them head on. Gustavo Gutiérrez did that in his book, *A Theology of Liberation*, proving rather convincingly that liberation theology is not provincial or fundamentalist, whatever else one might think about it. Now, however, it may be time to get down to epistemology. By that I mean it may be time to get down to analyzing not so much the content of Latin American theology but rather its methodological approach and its connection with liberation. The fact is that only a study of our method of theologizing vis-à-vis the reality of Latin America, and an agreement on that methodology, can successfully challenge the mechanisms of oppression and the efforts of the oppressor system to expropriate the terminology of liberation.

Perhaps the time has come to go on the offensive even, to frontally attack the third tendency mentioned above. Perhaps we should now challenge theological methodology as it is practiced in the great centers of learning. I am not championing a partisan attack of a nationalistic or regional nature. I am suggesting that we hurl down a challenge that is authentically and constructively theological in nature. Every Latin American knows from personal experience that any struggle or combat of this sort is a rematch of David against Goliath. But that knowledge does not excuse us from the fight. Perhaps subsequent critiques and criticisms of Latin American theology, if they are sufficiently *erudite*, will be forced to begin by justifying themselves. And that in itself could mark the start of a dialogue.

[...]

The Hermeneutic Circle

We cannot start with the chicken and the egg, so let us start with the reality of everyday life and consider whether it is possible to differentiate the attitudes of a liberation theologian from those of some other theologian on that basis.

[...]

For example, a theologian as progressive as Schillebeeckx can arrive at the conclusion that theology can never be ideological – in the Marxist sense of the term – because it is nothing but the application of the divine word to present-day reality. He seems to hold the naive belief that the word of God is applied to human realities inside some antiseptic laboratory that is totally immune to the ideological tendencies and struggles of the present day.

Now a liberation theologian is one who starts from the opposite end. His suspicion is that anything and everything involving ideas, including theology, is intimately bound up with the existing social situation in at least an unconscious way.

Thus the fundamental difference between the traditional academic theologian and the liberation theologian is that the latter feels compelled at every step to combine the disciplines that open up the past with the disciplines that help to explain the present. And he feels this necessity precisely in the task of working out and elaborating theology, that is to say, in the task of interpreting the word of God as it is addressed to us here and now.

[...]

In this book I am going to try to show that an approach which attempts to relate past and present in dealing with the word of God has to have its own special methodology. I shall give this special methodology a pretentious name and call it the *hermeneutic circle*. Here is a preliminary definition of the hermeneutic circle: it is the continuing change in our interpretation of the Bible which is dictated by the continuing changes in our present-day reality, both individual and societal. "Hermeneutic" means "having to do with interpretation." And the circular nature of the interpretation stems from the fact that each new reality obliges us to interpret the word of God afresh, to change reality accordingly, and then to go back and reinterpret the word of God again, and so on.

The term "hermeneutic circle" is used in a strict sense to designate the method used by Bultmann in interpreting the Scriptures, and the New Testament in particular. At first glance it might seem that my use of the term here is less rigorous. But I hope to show, and the reader will be able to judge this, that my "hermeneutic circle" deserves that designation far more strictly than does Bultmann's. But first I must spell out in greater detail what I am referring to in concrete terms.

I think that two preconditions must be met if we are to have a hermeneutic circle in theology. The first precondition is that the questions rising out of the present be rich enough, general enough, and basic enough to force us to change our customary conceptions of life, death, knowledge, society, politics, and the world in general. Only a change of this sort, or at the very least a pervasive suspicion about our ideas and value judgments concerning those things, will enable us to reach the theological level and force theology to come back down to reality and ask itself new and decisive questions.

The second precondition is intimately bound up with the first. If theology somehow assumes that it can respond to the new questions without changing its customary interpretation of the Scriptures, that immediately terminates the hermeneutic circle. Moreover, if our interpretation of Scripture does not change along with the problems, then the latter will go unanswered; or worse, they will receive old, conservative, unserviceable answers.

It is most important to realize that without a hermeneutic circle, in other words, in those instances where the two aforementioned preconditions are not accepted, theology is always a conservative way of thinking and acting. It is so not so much because of its content but because in such a case it lacks any *here-and-now* criteria for judging our real situation. It thus becomes a pretext for approving the existing situation or for disapproving of it because it does not dovetail with guidelines and canons that are even more ancient and outdated.

It is my feeling that the most progressive theology in Latin America is more interested in *being liberative* than in *talking about liberation*. In other words, liberation deals not so much with content as with the method used to theologize in the face of our real-life situation.

In this chapter I shall present four sample attempts at fashioning a hermeneutic circle. But first I think it would be wise for me to reiterate the two preconditions for such a circle. They are: (1) profound and enriching questions and suspicions about our real situation; (2) a new interpretation of the Bible that is equally profound and enriching. These two preconditions mean that there must in turn be four decisive factors in our circle. *Firstly* there is our way of experiencing reality, which leads us to ideological suspicion. *Secondly* there is the application of our ideological suspicion to the whole ideological superstructure in general and to theology in particular. *Thirdly* there comes a new way of experiencing theological reality that leads us to exegetical suspicion, that is, to the suspicion that the prevailing interpretation of the Bible has not taken important pieces of data into account. *Fourthly* we have our new hermeneutic, that is, our new way of interpreting the fountainhead of our faith (i.e., Scripture) with the new elements at our disposal.

The examples chosen in this chapter may or may not be good ones. But if we keep our attention focused on these four factors, I think the examples will be comprehensible and useful. At least that is my hope.

I. First Sample Attempt: Cox and the Secular City

As I just indicated, the circle that I described above in theoretical terms begins with a special or particular way of experiencing and evaluating reality in general. It is a critical way of experiencing, almost by its very definition – at least if it is to be the start of a hermeneutic circle. [...]

Karl Mannheim writes: "An increasing number of concrete cases makes it evident that (a) every formulation of a problem is made possible only by a *previous actual human experience*, which involves such a problem; (b) in selection from the multiplicity of data there is involved an *act of will* on the part of the knower; and (c) forces arising out of living experience are significant in *the direction which treatment of the problem* follows."[1]

Keeping this in mind about the starting point, let us consider our first sample attempt. Many examples could have been chosen, of course, but I have picked the well-known book by Harvey Cox entitled *The Secular City*.[2] His starting point dovetails with Mannheim's description. It presupposes Cox's own personal experience of his secular society, and it also entails a meaningful selection from the multiplicity of data in that society. [...]

One of the subtitles to the book, "A celebration of its liberties and an invitation to its discipline," clearly indicates what Mannheim referred to as "an act of will" on the part of the investigator. Harvey Cox *chooses* to celebrate the liberty of the new pragmatic society and, at the same time, to speak to it of Christianity and its message. Thus, as Mannheim indicated, the author's act of will is significant in determining the way in which the problem will be treated. [...]

That brings us to the second point in our hermeneutic circle: secularization and urbanization provide an ideological basis for interpreting reality – including theological reality – in a new and presumably more correct way. This is clearly suggested by another subtitle in the book: "Secularization and urbanization in theological perspective." According to Cox, in other words, a "celebration" of the secular city's liberties and an "invitation" to its discipline should provide us with meaningful direction in our attempt to deal with theological problems.

[...]

The real challenge posed to the theology of Cox is this: Can the Gospel answer questions that are not even asked by pragmatic man? In other words, can it answer questions in which ultimate concern is not present?

When we see that Cox gives an affirmative answer to these questions, we find ourselves at the third point of our hermeneutic circle. What exactly is the new theological experience that enables us to pose new questions to the Christian sources? Clearly enough the fundamental feature of this experience is the theologian's dialogue with pragmatic man. Dialoguing with him, Cox finds a new light for interpreting many portions of the biblical message. He discovers the possibility for establishing what he himself calls "a viable theology of revolutionary social change."[3] Here we cannot analyze all the rich implications of his new interpretation. The only thing that is of crucial interest to us here is this question: Will this new theology reach pragmatic man?

[...]

Cox has no intention of formulating a new – pragmatic – interpretation of the Bible in order to continue his dialogue with the man of the secular city. The hermeneutic circle is interrupted when it seemed at the point of reaching its (provisional) terminus: i.e., that of providing a new interpretation of Scripture.

Of course *The Secular City* is much more than an interrupted hermeneutic circle. But the latter is our interest here. We are not interested in enumerating all the interesting and fecund points in the book.

Now let us ask another question: Exactly why and where is the circle interrupted? At first glance the latter aspect of the question (where?) seems easy enough to answer. The circle is interrupted at the third point, just before it moves to the fourth point (a new interpretation of the Bible). But if we consider the first part of our question (why?), we arrive at the curious and interesting conclusion that the circle was doomed from the very *first* stage. We now know, albeit *a posteriori*, that Cox never really accepted pragmatic man as he is nor the consumer society as it is. He never really committed himself to them. Thus the "act was will" cited by Mannheim as an essential feature of the starting point was never fully present. And this lack of an enthusiastic base, in my opinion, will prevent Harvey Cox from completing his hermeneutic circle and thus revolutionizing theology in some way. This is true, at least, in the case of his book entitled *The Secular City*.

So let me sum up briefly. A hermeneutic circle in theology always presupposes a profound human commitment, a *partiality* that is consciously accepted – not on the basis of theological criteria, of course, but on the basis of human criteria.[4]

The word "partiality" may cause surprise, since the common assumption is that a scholarly science starts out from a state of total impartiality. That is precisely the pretension of academic theology. But it is very important that we do not make the mistake of accepting this claim as valid. Academic theology may well be unaware of its unconscious partiality, but the very fact that it poses as something impartial is a sign of its conservative partiality from the very start. We must realize that there is no such thing as an autonomous, impartial, academic theology floating free above the realm of human options and biases. However academic it may be, theology is intimately bound up with the psychological, social, or political status quo though it may not be consciously aware of that fact.

II. Second Sample Attempt: Marx and his Critique of Religion

Our first example showed us how the hermeneutic circle can be interrupted in the absence of a clearcut and total commitment vis-à-vis some human alternative. As our second example we shall use an author whose partiality and commitment are beyond any shadow of a doubt, whatever one may think of the man or his work. I refer to Karl Marx.

It is not easy to include Marx among the theologians, of course. He himself would be the first to protest such inclusion. At the same time, however, there can be no doubt about his influence on contemporary theology, particularly on the most imaginative and creative brands of it.[5]

The point of departure for Marx's thinking, and specifically for its relationship with religion, is the choice he made between interpreting the world and changing it. As Marx sees it, we must change the world; and we must do this with the proletariat and for the proletariat.[6]

[...]

[...] Despite countless attempts, however, the revolution did not come and Marx died waiting for it. From the start it would seem that Marx was keenly aware of the delay, felt the need to find some explanation for himself, and sought to find some solid basis for his hopes.

I believe that he found what he was looking for in the notion of *historical materialism*. And with this theory of historical materialism we come to the second stage or point of our hermeneutic circle. We now have a theory that enables us to discover the authentic face of reality in line with our own historical commitment.

For our purposes here we need only say that the theory of historical materialism can be summed up in one sentence from the *Manifesto*: "The ruling ideas of each age have ever been the ideas of its ruling class."[7] [...]

Historical materialism, in other words, teaches us two things: (1) The theoretical and practical superstructure depends unwittingly but in large measure on the economic structure of society. (2) Even though one cannot possibly expect a profound change in the superstructure unless the economic structure is altered, nevertheless ideological changes are not only possible but also decisive if the proletarian class is to become consciously aware of its own true interests and possibilities, if it is to be revolutionary despite its oppressed condition.

[...]

If we take Marx's work as a whole, it seems that we can say without fear of error that Marx never failed to include these two conditions in the revolutionary struggle of the proletariat: (1) economic change in the existing mode of production; (2) the theoretical liberation of human consciousness vis-à-vis the ideologies that conceal and sacralize the existing mode of production that is exploiting the proletariat.

[...]

Now is this distinction designed to tell the proletariat that it should leave aside the *ideological* struggle or rely wholly on the economic process alone? While Marx's work as a whole clearly gives the lie to such an hypothesis, certain passages in his work do seem to point in that direction. In *The German Ideology*, for example, he writes: "Morality, religion, metaphysics, and other ideologies… no longer retain… their appearance of autonomous existence."[8] [...]

[...]

So we find ourselves now at the third stage of the hermeneutic circle. When we view religion under the lens of ideological suspicion, it shows up as two things: (a) as a specific interpretation of Scripture imposed by the ruling classes in order to maintain their exploitation – though this intention may never be made explicit; and (b) as an opportunity for the proletariat to convert religion into their own weapon in the class struggle through a new and more faithful interpretation of the Scriptures.

But what happens at this point in the case of Marx? The circle stops because he goes against his own principles. Instead of examining the specific concrete and historical possibilities of religion and theology, he takes the easy way out of disqualifying religion in general insofar as he views it as an autonomous and ahistorical monolith. In the thought of Marx, religion is not viewed as belonging to an ambiguous superstructure. Instead it is viewed as belonging to a purely spiritual plane or, even worse, as being a merely ideal refutation of historical materialism.

Marx writes: "[...] Religion … is the opium of the people. The *abolition* of religion, as the illusory happiness of men, is a demand for their real happiness."[9] Instead of "abolition," one would expect Marx to have talked about "changing" religion so that it might accentuate and eventually correct the situation being protested against.

Thus the hermeneutic circle of theology is interrupted. To be sure, we could cite various passages from Marx's writings in which his profound intuition spotlights the social influence of such dogmas as that of original sin and individual salvation. Marx, along with Freud and Nietzsche, is regarded by Paul Ricoeur as one of the great masters of "suspicion." But somehow Marx does not seem to have ever entertained the suspicion that ideology could have warped the thinking of the theologians and the interpreters of Scripture so that they ended up unwittingly interpreting it in a sense that served the interests of the ruling classes. Marx does not seem to have shown any interest in trying to find out whether distortion had crept into the Christian message and whether a new interpretation favoring the class struggle of the proletariat might be possible or even necessary.

From our standpoint here, the important thing is to determine at what point the circle was interrupted. At the third point, it might seem. But it might be really interesting and worthwhile to show that it was really interrupted at the second stage, and that Marx's hermeneutic circle was doomed to interruption from there on.

To fully appreciate the significance of the third point or stage in the hermeneutic circle of theology, we must realize that it is a repetition of the first stage in the more restricted area of theology proper. If the first stage assumes a commitment to change the world, the third stage assumes a commitment to change theology. The third stage, in other words, reproduces the three elements that Mannheim spelled out for the first stage: a concrete evaluational experience of theology, an act of the will on the part of the theologian with respect to his theology, and a direction in treating new problems that derives from this act of the will.

Now while Marx made a personal commitment to change the world, he never had a personal experience of theology as a science tied to sources. A philosophy of religion cannot perform the same function as theology, since it does not feel bound to an interpretation of the biblical sources. Moreover, Marx's act of will to abolish religion is not an act of will from within theology itself, an act of will that could signify a change in the way of treating problems theologically. It is rather an abandonment of them.

[...]

[...] The important point is that for some reason or another Marx never managed to carry out the scientific task he had proposed to do: i.e., to infer the specific, spiritualized forms in the superstructure that correspond to the material production relationships. To put it a little better, he never managed to carry out that task at the level of the complex societies existing in his own day and ours, leaving that task for present-day Marxism. [...]

This would seem to suggest, in principle at least, that the more or less developed social sciences should be able to carry through the analysis which Marx foresaw and described and set in motion but which he never carried through on certain decisive levels. In any case Marx's work was such a stimulus for theology that new methods and profound questions in present-day theology are an inheritance from him, even though Marx had rejected theology.

Let me sum up. The purpose of my second example is to make it clear that a general theory about our perception of reality is called upon to be incorporated into theological methodology. For insofar as it discovers a deeper or rich layer of reality, it enriches theology with new questions and obliges it to undertake a new interpretation of its own sources. Even if it did just that and nothing else, any general theory capable of providing a methodology for ideological analysis would deserve to be call liberative; for in doing that, it would keep biblical interpretation moving back and forth between its sources and present-day reality. It would thus free academic theology from its atavism and its ivory tower, toppling the naive self-conception it entertains at present: i.e., that it is a simple, eternal, impartial interpretation, or authorized translation, of the word of God.

III. Third Sample Attempt: Weber on Calvinism and Capitalism

For our third example we shall use a thinker who certainly did make the move from the second to the third[10] stage of the hermeneutic circle. I refer to Max Weber.

Like Marx, Weber was not a theologian. But his work obliged him to engage in theological activity to the point where Weber styled himself an "amateur theologian." He was at least that, and a brilliant one. Let us consider a specific work of his.

In one of his most well-known works, Weber's sociological interest led him to study the principal dogmas of Calvinism in connection with the economic attitudes of Western capitalism, using in the process a methodology whose roots can and must be traced back to Marx's historical materialism.[11]

That statement might sound strange to some ears, for Weber has often been dubbed the *Anti-Marx*. [...] But I do not think that one can maintain any radical opposition between the methodology of Weber and that of Marx. It seems clear that Weber's intention was to complement rather than to correct Marx; or at most to correct an excessive emphasis on the economic structure.

In any case, both Marx and Weber base their sociological analysis on the necessary and inevitable relationship between economic and cultural forms, between structure and superstructure. In his analysis Weber concretely tries to point out the *necessity* and the *possibilities* of carrying forward the analysis of the cultural superstructure of modern society. [...]

[...] In other words, it is as if Marx had carried out his proposal to infer the spiritualized forms that correspond to the mode of production at the start of the capitalist era. [...]

An academic theologian might well be put off by Weber's lack of interest in the fonts of theology. Weber certainly pays little attention to the connection between the dogmas he is examining and the internal logic of the Reformation. He is even less interested in some possible distortion of the biblical message. [...] His only interest is to find the relationship between really existing ideas, wherever they may come from, and attitudes really existing in the realm of ethical and economic praxis. Weber writes: "We are naturally not concerned with the question of what was theoretically and officially taught in the ethical compendia of the time, however much practical significance this may have had... We are interested rather in something entirely different: the influence of those psychological sanctions which, *originating in religious belief* and the practice of religion, gave a direction to practical conduct and held the individual to it."[12]

Thus Max Weber does not take the easy way out of writing off the "earthly core" of religion – as Marx in fact does while censuring that approach. Instead he takes the difficult but scientific path of "inferring the spiritualized forms" that go hand in hand with the real conduct of human beings at that particular paint in the process of material production.

To accomplish this, Weber builds a psychological bridge between economic attitudes and religious. For example, he asserts that it is not just logic that connects the religious superstructure to economic attitudes; many times there is an unexpected psychological connection between the two. [...]

Stressing the psychological relationship between the superstructure and economic attitudes does not mean that Weber is trying to evade the social and political consequences of ideas. On the contrary, psychology enables him to carry out the task that Marx had talked about. In the complex realm of the whole superstructure he is able to infer the "spiritualized forms" which often correspond to economic attitudes. Psychology, in short, is a decisive feature of any modern ideological analysis of a complex social superstructure.

Now when all is said and done, the reader must not forget that the relationship discovered by Weber between Protestant Calvinism and the spirit of Western capitalism has never been proved by any empirical sociology, much less by statistical studies. [...]

[...]But it is not our task here to pass judgment on Weber. We are interested only in examining the methodology he uses to move from a general ideology to the specific analysis of theological ideas.

That brings us to the third point of our hermeneutic circle. We must ask ourselves: What is the real experience of Weber himself vis-à-vis the theological reality which he has just discovered, and which he has seen to be linked with all sorts of human vicissitudes and options such as those connected with the course of capitalism? Does he experience that theological life laid hold of in history as a need for judging Calvinism by its fruits? [...]

Strange as it may seem, none of those questions interests Max Weber: "We are here concerned not with the *evaluation*, but the historical significance of the dogma."[13] Even if this particular religious belief were the cause of an atomic war, in other words, Weber would still not be interested in evaluating it. He would simply be interested in considering its historical significance, its bare results. He expresses the same basic intention a bit more precisely elsewhere in the same book: "In such a study, it may at once be definitely stated, no attempt is made to evaluate the ideas of the Reformation in any sense, whether it concerns their *social* or their *religious* worth."[14]

[...]

To go even further, Weber is quite capable of "impartially" using descriptive phrases such as "extreme inhumanity." In a central passage of the book, he writes: "In its extreme inhumanity this doctrine must above all have had one consequence for the life of a generation which surrendered to its magnificent consistency. That was a feeling of unprecedented inner loneliness of the single individual. In what was for the man of the age of the Reformation the most important thing in life, his eternal salvation, he was forced to follow his path alone to meet a destiny which had been decreed for him from eternity. No one could help him."[15]

Not even when he uses such qualifying phrases and descriptions as these does Weber admit that he is making a value judgment on Calvinism. And he insists on his impartiality explicitly. [...]

At two points Weber does allow himself to challenge the soundness and solidity of Calvin's interpretation of the Bible. But they are only passing observations; they do not represent an evaluational theological commitment. [...]

At first glance such judgments might seem to indicate that Weber is making his first moves from the third to the fourth stage of the hermeneutic circle: in other words, that he is moving towards a new and enriched interpretation of the biblical sources. But that is not the case. Weber is not interested in finding a more authentic and richer theology to liberate people from the anxiety and loneliness which, among other things, are part of the influence of Calvinist theology on their society. For the sake of extending the range of knowledge as far as possible, Weber simply wants to make comparisons between different religious ideas insofar as they exert influence on different economic attitudes. There is no personal commitment involved.

[...]

Right now I think I have made it sufficiently clear to the reader what the last systematic obstacle for any theology committed to human liberation is. It is a certain type of academicism which posits ideological neutrality as the ultimate criterion; which levels down and relativizes all claims to absoluteness and all evaluations of some ideas over others. This is the theological equivalent of another great ideological adversary of liberation: the so-called quest for the *death of ideologies* or their suicide on the altars of scientific and scholarly impartiality.[16]

IV. Fourth Sample Attempt: Cone and *Black Theology of Liberation*

Let us move on to a fourth example. This time the hermeneutic circle will be completed. Remember that this fact in itself is not a sufficient proof of the truth of the theology in question. The hermeneutic circle itself merely proves that a theology is alive, that it is connected up with the vital fountainhead of historical reality. Without the latter source, the other font of divine revelation would remain dry, not because of anything wrong with it but because of our own opaqueness.

The fourth example is provided by James Cone in his book entitled *A Black Theology of Liberation*. Though the language of the book might seem to be a bit demagogic and shocking – all depending on the color of your skin and your thinking perhaps – Cone's book is a much more serious theological effort than many people might think at first glance. In any case it affords us a chance to see and examine all four points in our hermeneutic circle.

Cone's interpretation begins with personal experience and an act of will on the part of the investigator, as Mannheim posited. Now it is obvious that any "act of will" in the limited range of human possibilities comes down to taking a stand for some individual or community over against other individuals and communities. There is no help for it. Every hermeneutic entails conscious or unconscious partisanship. It is partisan in its viewpoint even when it believes itself to be neutral and tries to act that way.

What is noteworthy and important here is the fact that partiality is not in itself inimical to universality. [...] For the universality in mind here has to do with getting down to the deeper human roots that explain attitudes which are truly universal in their value and influence.

Right from the start of Cone's book, a consciously accepted partiality shows up as a positive and decisive element. For him theology is "a rational study of the being of God in the world in light of the existential situation of an oppressed community, relating the forces of liberation to the essence of the gospel, which is Jesus Christ. This means that *its sole reason for existence* is to put into ordered speech the meaning of God's activity in the world, *so that the community of the oppressed will recognize that their inner thrust for liberation is not only consistent with the gospel but is the gospel of Jesus Christ.*"[17]

Thus Cone, not worrying about causing scandal to academic theology, goes on to establish the usefulness of a particular historical community as the criterion for any subsequent theological investigation: "Black Theology will not spend too much time trying to answer the critics *because it is accountable only to the black community.*"[18] The universality that is renounced on the horizontal level is recovered in spades on a deeper level of the human condition – i.e., where it is revealed to us in an oppressed community that is still in need of liberation. In the process of liberation, the one and only truth is the truth of liberation itself as defined by the oppressed in their struggle. [...]

Before moving on to the second stage of the hermeneutic circle, a few comments on this point of departure are very much in order. In seminaries and universities we are used to the idea of considering theology as an academic discipline, as a degree program in the liberal arts. The historical fact is that once upon a time theologizing was a very different sort of activity, a dangerous one in fact. It certainly was not a "liberal art" for men like the prophets and Jesus. They died before their time because of their theologizing, because of their specific way of interpreting the word of God and its implications for the liberation of the oppressed.

Perhaps the reader may now understand more readily why only academic theologians can talk about the "death of God." In the concrete struggle for liberation, the danger is not the death of God but the death of the theologian, his interpreter. The theologian may well lie in the very name of God, who draws a sharp dividing line between the two opposing positions with regard to liberation.

Faced with these two alternatives (that is, theology as an academic profession versus theology as a revolutionary activity), I must confess that I can understand those who refuse to do theology or to have anything to do with it, because they feel it has no meaning or value for the liberation process, much better than I can understand those who practice it as an academic discipline in the security of some chamber immune to the risks of the liberation struggle. We are fortunate that our God takes a stand in history, and our interpretation of his word must follow the same path. Cone is quite right when he refers to theology as a "passionate language."[19]

Arriving at the second stage in our circle, we must find a theory of some general nature which will enable us to unmask the reality of oppression in general, and specifically its repercussions in theology. For oppression usually does not reveal itself in barefaced fashion; it hides and hallows itself behind ideologies that obscure what is really happening in concrete human reality.

One cannot say that Cone is Marxist in his analysis, for he explicitly diverges from Marx on occasion. For example, he states that the basis of exploitation is not an economic difference which forms different social classes but rather the racial difference which is rooted far more deeply in human psychology. At the same time, however, Cone's divergence here is not as alien to historical materialism as it might seem at first glance. Rather it complements or corrects Marx, pointing up a factor which has been, and continues to be, important in the division of labor. What Mannheim says in a general way might be applied to Cone here. The fact is that many of the elements which Marx used in his ideological analysis of the exploitation of the proletariat have become general features of Western culture – more specifically, of the general methodology of the sociology of knowledge. This means that they can and often are used independently of any Marxist or even Socialist commitment.

Cone is certainly aware of ideological mechanisms and takes them into account in his theologizing. For example, he writes "[...] From the very beginning to the present day, American white theological thought has been 'patriotic,' either by defining the theological task *independently of black suffering* (the liberal northern approach) or by defining Christianity as compatible with white racism (the conservative southern approach). In both cases theology becomes *a servant of the state*, and that can only mean death to black people."[20]

The fine edge of Cone's ideological analysis shows up in the fact that he manages to espy the most potent weapon of the adversary in this ideological conflict. That weapon is an ideology claiming to be *color-blind*. In other words, the oppressor constructs an ideological edifice in which the *cause* of the oppressed people's suffering is not even mentioned, much less studied. In this way law, philosophy, and religion join with the mechanism of oppression and become its witting or unwitting accomplices: "That is why American theology discusses sin in the abstract, debating it in relation to *universal man*. In white theology, sin is *a theoretical idea and not a concrete reality*."[21] In other words, "there is no place in Black Theology for a colorless God in a society *where people suffer precisely because of their color*."[22]

Cone therefore calls for a more concrete and realistic sensitivity so that this sort of rationalization will be wiped out in a society where color is a decisive factor. [...]

[...]

It should be evident that Cone arrives at the third stage of the hermeneutic circle with a new experience of theology and with an act of will to place it in the service of the Black community. Thus the new direction to be taken by scriptural interpretation will be dictated by the uncovering of the mechanisms of ideology and by the will to root them out of theology.

In doing the latter, the important thing is not so much not to accept the accustomed answers of theology but rather not to shoulder the accustomed questions of theology. As Cone puts it: "It is clear, therefore, that the most important decisions in theology are made at this juncture. The sources and norm are presuppositions that determine *which questions are to be asked*, as well as the answers that are given."[23] [...] Put another way: "Black theologians must work in such a way as to destroy the corruptive influence of white thought by building theology on the sources and norm that are appropriate to the black community."[24]

If we should ask Cone what he considers "appropriate to the black community," his initial response would be that an oppressed community needs a theology by which to become aware of itself as people "who are in search of new ways of talking about God which will enhance *their understanding of themselves*."[25] If this particular task is to be properly undertaken by theology (rather than by education or politics, for example), then of course there must be a change in the notion of God and his plans: "It is unthinkable that the oppressors could identify with oppressed existence and thus say something relevant about God's liberation of the oppressed. In order to be Christian theology, white theology must cease being white theology and become Black Theology by denying whiteness as a proper form of human existence and affirming blackness as *God's intention for humanity*."[26]

From the theological standpoint it is worth noting that Cone, with only one exception, makes these decisive options regarding the pathway that theology is to take before he comes to treat the sources and norm of an authentic theology specifically. At first glance it might seem that theology is being determined by alien criteria. But since theology is part of the superstructure, the ground must be broken by first rooting up the ideological traps. Hence ideological criteria are logically *prior*, but in no way *alien* to theology.

When Cone begins to list the fonts of theology, he begins by listing the experience, the history, and the culture of Black people rather than Scripture. He fully realizes that this will scandalize academic theology, which has a long tradition of proceeding quite differently. But he is not alone in such an approach, and he can cite Tillich in his favor: "I am not unaware of the danger that in this way [the method of relating theology to culture] the substance of the Christian message may be lost. Nevertheless, this danger must be risked, and once one has realized this, one must proceed in this direction. Dangers are not a reason for avoiding a serious demand."[27]

[...]

On the other hand, if Scripture stands as the unique and unbalanced criterion for theology, then one cannot avoid *literalism* and the consequent ideological justification of oppression. As Cone puts it: "Literalism always means the removal of doubt in religion, and thus enables the believer to justify all kinds of political oppression in the name of God and country. During slavery black people were encouraged to be obedient slaves because it was the will of God."[28] [...]

To avoid the danger signalled by Tillich as well as the danger of literalism, one need only erect his theology on a twofold base or source: "Black people have heard enough about God. What they want to know is what God has to say about the black condition. Or, more importantly, what is he doing about it? What is his relevance in the struggle against the forces of evil which seek to destroy black being? These are the questions which must shape the character of the norm of Black Theology. On the other hand, Black Theology must not overlook the biblical revelation. This means that Black Theology should not devise a norm which ignores the encounter of the black community with the revelation of God. Whatever it says about liberation must be said in the light of the black community's experience of Jesus Christ."[29] In short, "the norm of Black Theology must take seriously two realities, actually two aspects of a single reality: the liberation of black people and the revelation of Jesus Christ."[30]

With this new experience of theological reality, this act of will and its directional impulse, Cone arrives at the fourth stage of the hermeneutic circle: i.e., the new inter-pretation of Scripture based on new and decisive questions. His hermeneutic orienta-tion might be summed up in these words: "If I read the New Testament correctly, the resurrection of Christ means that he is also present today in the midst of all societies effecting his liberation of the oppressed. He is not confined to the first century, and thus our talk of him in the past is important only insofar as it leads us to an *encounter* with him *now*. As a black theologian, I want to know what God's revelation means right now as the black community participates in the struggle for liberation."[31]

It must be stressed once again that the simultaneous presence of past and present in biblical interpretation is an essential hermeneutic principle. The value of this orienta-tion for achieving a richer interpretation of Scripture lies in the fact that one thereby rediscovers a pedagogical principle that presides over the whole process of divine revelation. The fact is that God shows up in a different light when his people find themselves in different historical situations. That does not simply mean that we must take pains to re-create each specific historical context in the past. For if God continually presents himself in a different light, then the truth about him must be different also. The Israelites moving out of Egypt and heading for the promised land received the revelation of God's wrath towards their enemies. That particular revelation has little or nothing to do with the image of God which the gospel message conveys when it urges people to "turn the other cheek," or when Paul urges slaves to obey their masters.

[...]

It may well be difficult for us to appreciate the total novelty and freshness of this principle which is introduced into theological interpretation by Cone. For the fact is that from the viewpoint of orthodoxy one of those images of God must necessarily be false at a given moment. Either the old or the new image has to be false at a given point if God is to continue being *universal*, according to the orthodox viewpoint. Cone's logic forces him to reject this search for universality which seems to be the key to the orthodox interpretation of the Bible. [...]

What is Cone trying to say here? Unless I am mistaken, he is asserting that ortho-doxy possesses no ultimate criterion in itself because being orthodox does not mean possessing the final truth. We only arrive at the latter by orthopraxis. It is the latter that is the ultimate criterion of the former, both in theology and in biblical interpretation. The truth is truth only when it serves as the basis for truly human attitudes. "Doers of the truth" is the formula used by divine revelation to stress the priority of orthopraxis over orthodoxy when it comes to truth and salvation.

Needless to say, there are many hermeneutic dangers in this approach to conceiving and carrying out biblical interpretation, just as there were in the previous stage. But one cannot rule out a particular theological method which is consistent, just because it entails dangers.

[...]

[...] I hope that it is quite clear that the Bible is not the discourse of a universal God to a universal man. Partiality is justified because we must find, and designate as the word of God, that *part* of divine revelation which *today*, in the light of our concrete historical situation, is most useful for the liberation to which God summons us. Other passages of that same divine revelation will help us tomorrow to complete and correct our present course towards freedom. God will keep coming back to speak to us from the very same Bible.

[...]

If we understand and appreciate this circle, then we also will understand and appreciate something that is very important for Latin American theology of liberation. When it is accused of partiality, it can calmly reply that it is partial because it is faithful to Christian tradition rather than to Greek thought. It can also say that those who attack it are even more partisan, though they may not realize it, and tend to muzzle the word of God by trying to make one particular portion of Scripture the word of God not only for certain particular moments and situations but also for all situations and all moments.

Notes

1 Karl Mannheim, *Ideology and Utopia*, Eng. trans. (New York: Harcourt, Brace, Jovanovich, Harvest Book, 1936).

2 Harvey Cox, *The Secular City*, rev. ed. (New York: Macmillan, 1966), 60.

3 Ibid., 95.

4 "[...] There can be no question of a point of departure without prejudice. What is held to be an unprejudiced point of departure turns out to be an 'arbitrary' leap into a certain stream of thought and belief. [...] Any choice of a point of departure in science, philosophy and theology is an a priori choice of a certain view of the world or life... From the very beginning the choice proves that a person has chosen *even the before the choice was mode*" (W.H. van de Pol, *The End of Conventional Christianity*, Eng. trans. (New York: Newman Press, 1967) 191).

5 On the influence of Marxist thought on the creation of a theology of liberation in Latin America, see especially the next two chapters. It must be admitted, however, that there are problems connected with applying the label "Marxist" to a line of thought or a source of influence. First of all, those who identify themselves with Marx and his thinking have a thousand different ways of conceiving and interpreting "Marxist" thought. Aside from that fact, the point is that the great thinkers of history do not replace each other; rather, they complement and enrich each other. Philosophic thought would never be the same after Aristotle as it was before him. In that sense all Westerners who philosophize now are Aristotelians. After Marx, our way of conceiving and posing the problems of society will never be the same again. Whether everything Marx said is accepted or not, and in whatever way one may conceive his "essential" thinking, there can be no doubt that present-day social thought will be "Marxist" to some extent: that is, profoundly indebted to Marx. In that sense Latin American theology is certainly Marxist. I know my remark will be taken out of context, but one cannot go on trying to forestall every partisan or stupid misunderstanding forever.

6 Karl Marx, *Manifesto of the Communist Party*, Eng. trans., Great Books of the Western World 50, (Chicago: Encyclopaedia Britannica, 1952), 419.

7 Ibid., 428.

8 *Karl Marx: Selected Writings in Sociology and Social Philosophy*, Newly translated and ed. T.B. Bottomore (London: Watts, 1956; New York: McGraw-Hill, 1964), 75.

9 *Critique of Hegel's Philosophy of Right*, in *Selected Writings*, 27.

10 The need for a *third* and *fourth* stage in our hermeneutic circle stem from the fact, established at the very start, that we are dealing here with a hermeneutic for *Christian theology*. [...] Now theology, unlike philosophy, does not derive its interpretation of existence from itself but rather from certain written sources. So the hermeneutic circle requires it to propose a new interpretation for those sources if something profound is to change, in line with the basic commitment from which the hermeneutic circle started. [...]

11 Max Weber, *The Protestant Ethic and the Spirit of Capitalism*, Eng. trans. (New York: Charles Scribner's Sons, 1958).

12 Ibid., 97.

13 Ibid., 101.

14 Ibid., 90.

15 Ibid.,. 104.

16 As is well known by now, liberation theology arose as a reaction against the developmentalist theories and models formulated by the United States for Latin America in the decade of the sixties. The developmentalist model was characterized by the fact that it covered over and tried to hide the critical and decisive relationship of dependence versus liberation. [...] To bolster this ideology, the point was often stressed that this modernization process meant that people would have to accept the "death of ideologies" brought about by a scientific and *neutral* technology common to any and every social model. On this point see Gustavo Gutiérrez, *A Theology of Liberation*, Eng. trans. (Maryknoll, NY: Orbis Books, 1973), Chapter II.

17 James H. Cone, *A Black Theology of Liberation* (Philadelphia: Lippincott, 1970),

18 Ibid., 33.

19 Ibid., 45.

20 Ibid., 22.

21 Ibid., 191.

22 Ibid., p. 120.

23 Ibid., 52–3.

24 Ibid., 53.

25 Ibid., 40.

26 Ibid., pp. 32–3.

27 Ibid., 62.

28 Ibid., 68.

29 Ibid., 77. [...]

30 Ibid., 79–80.

31 Ibid., 64; Cone's italics too.

20

Pastoral Theology as Practical Knowledge (1980)*

Rodney J. Hunter

Introduction

Rodney J. Hunter, a student of Hiltner at Princeton in the 1970s and now Professor Emeritus of Pastoral Theology from Emory University, is perhaps best known for his monumental effort coaxing along the first encyclopedic overview of pastoral care as General Editor of *The Dictionary of Pastoral Care and Counseling* (1990). A master of the short essay more than a prolific book writer, his contributions are consistently profound and suggestive. His attention to detail and his pension for methodically thinking questions through to their completion may have limited his productivity. But students and colleagues alike have benefited from his thoughtfulness and can often be heard remarking admirably on the length and depth of his written feedback, whether on papers or institutional deliberations.

On first blush, Hunter's essay appears to be simply an in-house report on a Colloquy in Pastoral Theology held on the Princeton campus in honor of Seward Hiltner on the occasion of his retirement. Hunter does not even use full names, assuming his readers will have the entire journal issue compiled from the Colloquy in their hands and will know the people that he mentions (e.g., William Oglesby, James Lapsley, Clyde Stekel). His focus on *pastoral* rather than *practical* theology also seems confusing in a *Reader* on practical theology. His essay seems narrowly focused on a theology of pastoral care. The gathering and the journal issue do, indeed, mark the end of two decades in which specialized ministries of counseling and chaplaincy and seminary positions in pastoral theology and care had flourished and expanded in the United States.

On further reading, however, it is apparent that Hunter has a bigger agenda in mind, one that he hoped to turn into a book-length exploration if dedication to other tasks had not intervened. Here, in the opening sections, we see the very beginnings of the forging of a discipline. After the first two sections on disciplinary definition, institutional and conceptual respectively, he gets to his more substantive and creative ideas on "pastoral theology as practical knowledge" in the final section. Readers get a clue early on about where he is going, however, when he suggests at the end of the first section that any worthwhile discipline must be about producing knowledge. Pastoral

Original publication details: Rodney J. Hunter, "The Future of Pastoral Theology," pp. 58–69 from *Pastoral Psychology* 29:1 (1980).

theologians need to get to work figuring out exactly the kind of knowledge that they are uniquely equipped to provide. "Only if pastoral theologians learn to see themselves as attempting to create *knowledge* of some kind," he says, "will they be able to lay claim to their field as a serious intellectual discipline." He drops another hint in the second section, pointing out that people have focused on Hiltner's concept of "shepherding" and overlooked his more important effort to grapple with "operation-centered" knowledge.

It is not until the final section, however, that we learn why pastoral theologians and scholars in other disciplines struggle to understand what pastoral theology has to offer. Practical knowledge differs from theoretical knowledge, Hunter argues, making it harder to convey, investigate, contain, systematize, articulate, and enact. His critique cuts both ways, exploring why scholars inside the discipline struggle and why those outside resist. He puts on the table an important question that remains with us: "Precisely what is learned" theologically "through case analysis"?

Suggested Further Reading

- Rodney J. Hunter, "Wisdom and Practical Knowledge in Pastoral Care" (pp. 1325–6) and "Prudence (Moral Theology) (pp. 968–9) in Rodney J. Hunter, ed., *The Dictionary of Pastoral Care and Counseling* (Nashville: Abingdon, 1990).
- James N. Lapsley, *Salvation and Health: The Interlocking Processes of Life* (Philadelphia: Westminster Press, 1972).
- Michael Polanyi, *The Tacit Dimension* (Chicago: University of Chicago Press, 1966).

***

The Question of Pastoral Theology as a Discipline

The Colloquy on Pastoral Theology in Honor of Seward Hiltner had as its broad agenda the task of assessing the present status and future prospects of pastoral theology, understood as a discipline of theoretical and practical research within the larger compass of theological inquiry. Early in the Colloquy's conversations it became clear, however, that in certain important respects the existence as well as the status of this discipline was in question.

While all of the participants – pastors, counselors, and professors alike – viewed what they were doing as pastoral theology in some sense, there was some uncertainty about the meaning of the term itself in relation to practical theology or theology in general other than its simply designating theological reflection done in the situation of, or from the perspective of, ministry. It seemed further significant that only a minority – and a small one at that – of the numerous seminary professors present actually had chosen "pastoral theology" as part of their institutional titles, that there is no professional organization or journal specifically devoted to pastoral theology, and that very little research and publication clearly identifiable as pastoral theology, with consequences for theology as a whole, has so far emerged, as one would reasonably expect of an enterprise conceiving of itself as a theological discipline.

But while there was considerable interest expressed in bringing about more social embodiment for this field, the Colloquy did not pursue this organizational problem in order to concentrate on more fundamental issues concerning the discipline itself.

In broad terms, the question underlying a wide range of discussion topics seemed to be whether the interests and concerns that presently constitute this somewhat diffuse and uncertain field can or need to be brought to greater disciplinary concentration and focus, and if so, what sort of discipline it would be, how it would conceive of its task, and how it would relate to other academic and theological disciplines on one hand and the church's caring ministries and concerns on the other.

In considering this multifaceted problem it may be helpful to review some of the main themes of the Colloquy by imposing retrospectively on its discussions a simple distinction between two ways in which a discipline can be defined and described. Broadly assuming that "discipline" usually refers to any ongoing, corporate inquiry with more or less agreed upon topics of investigation and principles of research, we may distinguish between (1) defining it humanly and descriptively in terms of its social task and function, institutional location, what its practitioners do, and so forth, or, (2) defining it ideally in terms of its intellectual problematic and principles of procedure. In each case, it seems to me, significant questions for the discipline of pastoral theology emerged in this Colloquy.

Social and Institutional Definition of the Discipline

Probably most persons who identify themselves as pastoral theologians, at least in part, think of the discipline in basically personal, social and institutional terms rather than theoretically. In this sense pastoral theology embraces a wide variety of religious, educational and social concerns and functions, generally centered in or near theological education. Thus the Colloquy participants discussed everything from seminary teaching methods and curricula to the pastoral counseling movement and recent trends in church and society, not as incidental to their sense of the field but as somehow basic to it.

Extrapolating a bit, we may say that discussions of this kind among pastoral theologians presuppose an understanding of the discipline in broadly professional terms, as the practice of teaching, guiding, critiquing and developing the church's caring ministries. Professor [William] Oglesby's paper, for instance, with its wide-ranging vision and critique of trends in pastoral care and counseling, and the discussion it triggered in the Colloquy on topics like professionalism, the ministry of the laity, pastoral counseling's cultural bondage, and the role of the pastoral theologian as interpreter of Scripture in relation to the Biblical specialists, may be said to presuppose such a view of the discipline, though Oglesby did not address his presuppostions about the discipline directly.

A similar understanding was represented by Professor Peggy Way in more explicit and emphatic terms. In her view pastoral theologians should address very concrete situations of need and conflict in the church with the primary aim of making practical, consultative contributions to its corporate life and ministry, and especially, it would seem, by developing new methods and strategies for dealing with such situations. Referring to Professor Browning's paper that cites a case study concerning a decision about abortion, for instance, Professor Way remarked that she would be primarily interested in "what would happen if Mary Jones showed up at church," that is, interested in the specific problems and methods of care and guidance present in such a congregation for Mary Jones during and after her decision. Professor Way also made it clear in discussion that she would not limit pastoral theology to personal ministries only, but would see the discipline addressing larger institutional problems of the church as well, specifically ecumenism and other forms of conflict resolution at the corporate level. Clearly, this conception of pastoral theology emphasizes not only its churchly character and confessional commitment but its professional, service orientation as well.

A significantly contrasting view of the social function of pastoral theology was presented by Professor Don Browning. Far more than Way, Browning views pastoral theology as a discipline of moral culture in general, and hence sees it involved in society's larger problem of redefining the human good in a time when the culture as a whole is undergoing profound transitions. The pastoral care and counseling movements have in fact "participated in the triumph of the therapeutic" and have "helped launch a cultural model" of internal, psychological preoccupation as the goal of life. Therefore pastoral theology's self-understanding only in terms of institutional religious concerns is too narrow, both as an interpretation of the actual situation of the discipline and as a thesis about its future identity.

A better interpretation, he suggests, is to see pastoral theology as essentially an ethical discipline functioning within a particular moral tradition but participating more generally in the arena of public moral discussion concerning normative issues of personhood and care in secular society. This means locating the discipline more broadly in the realm of public discourse, primarily the university, and including in its task the pastoral and moral critique of all forms and institutions of personal care, not only those of ministry and the church, together with the normative images of human wellbeing that they embody. In a secular, pluralistic society this also means being able to debate and discuss such issues philosophically, as well as theologically within the community of faith.

The contrast between Browning's conception of the discipline and Way's is obvious though not necessarily contradictory. Browning clearly recognizes the necessary and proper role of pastoral theology within the church and seminary as well as the university, and Way explained that even her extreme emphasis on the religious institutional locus of the discipline was intended ultimately to serve the larger society by promoting the particular identity and integrity of the church. How her position would sponsor this purpose seemed less clear to me, but in any case a basic difference of emphasis and orientation clearly remains between these two conceptions of the social function of pastoral theology, the one emphasizing its professional role and character, the other its academic and cultural function.

While most participants in the Colloquy seemed to favor a mediating position, the issue of pastoral theology's place in the world of secular scholarship and research is, in my judgment, nevertheless an important if somewhat uncomfortable one for this field. Professor [James] Lapsley's observation that pastoral theologians have tended to be too cautious in speaking beyond their immediate constituencies to the public audience seemed well taken, and there were a number of insightful observations by others to the effect that this discipline has unnecessarily intimidated itself in the academic community. On a more positive note Professor Browning stressed the potential significance of pastoral theology in our cultural situation, noting Weber's theory that in every society religious and ethical care-givers perform a crucial and disproportionately influential role in mediating between symbol systems and the society.

However this may be, the question of the relation of pastoral theology to the secular disciplines symbolized by the university is in my view an important question, not because pastoral theologians need to win status and prestige for themselves, and certainly not because the secular disciplines merit unqualified respect for their own intellectual purity and integrity in the bureaucratic politics of the university. It is important because it requires pastoral theology to come to terms with itself as a discipline in quest of knowledge, and not simply as a professional practice – a point that I think has been unnecessarily obscured by its otherwise valuable professional function and service. Only if pastoral theologians learn to see themselves as attempting to create *knowledge* of some kind will they be able to lay claim to their field as a serious intellectual discipline. But this in turn requires that the field come to greater clarity concerning the kind of knowledge it seeks and the importance of this knowledge, a problem related not so much to its theological character, in my judgment, as to its practical nature.

[...]

Theoretical and Methodological Definition of the Discipline

The other way of defining a discipline, in some distinction from its social and institutional locus and function, is to articulate its formal intellectual agenda and operational principles, that is, to formulate it abstractly, theoretically, and perhaps ideally. The problem is essentially to determine what it is trying to learn or discover, and by what means it is trying to do so.

It scarcely needs saying that in this respect Seward Hiltner has been the preeminent American theoretician of the contemporary discipline of pastoral theology as a formal field of theological investigation. In particular, his *Preface to Pastoral Theology* is the classic text of the discipline, which like all classics must be reckoned with positively or negatively in any serious attempt at constructive thinking about the field today. It is therefore not surprising that the more theoretically oriented discussions of the Colloquy tended implicitly and often explicitly to revolve around, and struggle with, Hiltner's definition of the field as "an operation-focused branch of theology, which begins with theological questions and concludes with theological answers, in the interim examining all acts and operations of pastor and church to the degree that they involve the perspective of Christian shepherding" (p. 24).

Though Hiltner's concept of "shepherding" as an organizing perspective in ministry (together with "communicating" and "organizing") has tended to be the aspect of this definition that has attracted the most attention, in my view it is the concept of "operation-centered discipline," in contrast to the "logic-centered" fields like Biblical studies and systematic theology, that is the more crucial and problematic feature of his definition for purposes of establishing pastoral theology as a fundamental discipline. This point was demonstrated, I think, in the Colloquy's efforts to clarify the field's basic intellectual agenda and methodology in response to Professor Browning's views of pastoral care as a form of moral inquiry and pastoral theology as a form of theological ethics, as presented in his Colloquy paper. It may be useful therefore to examine the focal issue of that discussion.

Browning emphasizes the moral nature of all helping and caring endeavors; no counseling or therapy can be morally neutral, though in both religious and secular modes the moral dimensions of the caring process may be relatively inobvious and latent in conscious consideration, or even deliberately bracketed. But the care and counseling ministries of religious institutions and professions, because of their fundamentally normative social purpose and function, ought ordinarily to give primacy to the moral dimensions of human need over dynamic aspects, especially under current conditions of widespread moral confusion and uncertainty. Thus also the theory of these helping ministries – pastoral theology – needs to conceive of itself as an ethical inquiry seeking the nature of the human good through the critical analysis, development, and application of the moral tradition to specific human problems. Browning's pastoral theological method therefore broadly resembles the Roman Catholic tradition of moral theology – a comparison that elicited some theological criticism from various Protestant confessional viewpoints in the Colloquy – though unlike that tradition it incorporates an empirical, pragmatic method of inquiry, and therefore has some real affinity with Hiltner's approach as well.

But there is an important difference between Hiltner and Browning. Browning's major concern, in both pastoral care and its theory, lies in moral construction – the development of the moral tradition and ways of implementing it in particular situations – whereas Hiltner and the Hiltnerians, as Professor Lapsley neatly put it, are more interested in critically analyzing and generalizing from the "actualities and possibilities of situations of ministry." Both positions include moral inquiry and empirical analysis in some form, but the question at issue, said Lapsley, is whether moral inquiry constitutes the "foreground or the background" of pastoral theology's disciplinary agenda.

In practical terms this dispute over priorities appeared most clearly in the relative importance given to the case study in pastoral theological method, and in the way case material is used. For Browning any empirical data, carefully (i.e. scientifically) examined, can contribute to the ethical task of the discipline. But Browning is critical of attempts to focus or confine empirical investigation too narrowly to particular events. Instead he emphasizes the examination of human experience in broad, sociocultural and historical terms, and rejects the existentialist limitation of the meaning of "experience" to immediate consciousness, as sometimes done in clinical pastoral "reflections on experience." Thus the concreteness of the case is in a sense processed through the larger moral tradition in order to yield its fruit, a perspective that tends, I think, to lessen its overall importance and to shift the pastoral theologian's attention somewhat away from descriptive detail and generalization to more abstract and systematic moral reasoning. It also tends to give his method the appearance of deduction from general to particular (i.e., the application of principle to case) though Browning wished to emphasize that his method is not ultimately deductive but empirical and pragmatic.

The Hiltnerians in the Colloquy, on the other hand, viewed this approach with suspicion, feeling that it moved away from what Professor [Clyde] Stekel termed the "truth of the case" and its "truth-telling function" in theology. While pastoral care and theology clearly involve ethical dimensions for the Hiltnerians, it is the "idiosyncratic truth of the case" that makes the distinctively pastoral contribution to theology.

But if "the case is the center of our heritage," as John Patton argued, it nevertheless remains for the Hiltnerian to explain precisely what is learned through case analysis in the shepherding perspective. This question was not considered in depth in the Colloquy, but the debate between Browning and Hiltner and their advocates seemed, at least to me, to point back to this basic question from Hiltner's *Preface*. Then and since Hiltner's own answer to this question has been "theology," meaning that pastoral theology can contribute important insights, distinctions, elaborations, or other enrichments and corrections of general theological understanding by means of its unique angle of vision. The practical exigencies and complexities of ministry, when critically examined, press theology to become more true to human realities and God's ways with the world.

Epistemological questions aside, however, it may be asked whether pastoral theology conceived in this way differs methodologically from other kinds of empirical theology in which acts of ministry do *not* constitute the data for analysis. Is there anything theologically significant about "acts and operations" as such, in their nature as acts and operations? Or are these acts of ministry simply opportune occasions for observing human (and possibly divine) nature in action, as it were – occasions which could be exchanged for nonministerial or nonhelping events? If this is the case, the pastoral or helping act is significant simply for being a concrete instance of human experience, and pastoral theology becomes a particular form of experiential or situational theology generally.

This view of the discipline may be valid and useful but it does not show how the operations of ministry can disclose anything fundamental or theological as operations, and therefore cannot justify the definition of the discipline as operation-centered in any primary sense. A lack of clarity on this point, in my judgment, has made it difficult for Hiltnerians to get a clear fix on what is or may be distinctive about pastoral theology and has therefore left it somewhat uncertain of its calling and struggling to get on with its work as an intellectual discipline. The root problem is not, I think, its empiricism so much as its focus on operations, that is, its intrinsically practical orientation.

Pastoral Theology as Practical Knowledge

In response to this dilemma I would like to suggest that pastoral theology be seen as a form of practical knowledge, and to suggest further that the work of this discipline is in some quandary about itself intellectually because the distinctive character of practical knowledge in relation to other kinds of knowledge has not been clearly enough understood. Whereas descriptive knowledge tells about what is, and normative knowledge tells what ought to be, practical knowledge gives information about how to do things. It is concerned distinctively with methods; and though methods presuppose normative and descriptive knowledge, they are not derived entirely from the knowledge of what is and what ought to be but must be gained pragmatically, and therefore constitute a distinctive kind of knowledge.

Unclarity about this point, I feel, has led pastoral theologians to attempt to establish their discipline theoretically by pointing to real or intended contributions to other kinds of knowledge than their own, usually the logic-centered fields of doctrinal theology and ethics. Without doubting that such contributions may be possible from pastoral studies, it seems to me that such derivative insights are not the first order of business for this discipline. Its primary task is to develop a body of practical theological knowledge of how to care for human beings. My proposal, in other words, is that pastoral theologians reconsider and further develop Seward Hiltner's original insight that pastoral theology is an operation-centered discipline in the shepherding perspective.

It seems likely that the reason this distinction between logic- and operation-centered disciplines has not borne more fruit in the history of the discipline is related to certain intellectual attitudes and prejudices concerning practical knowledge in general in our society. It is perhaps a curious irony that a civilization as pervasively pragmatic as America, which even invents a philosophy of pragmatism, should not have developed a more significant understanding of practical knowledge itself – as distinct from descriptive or normative knowledge discovered pragmatically. Among the cultural elite in our society practical knowledge, which in its advanced technological forms has tremendous economic and political power, nevertheless has little fundamental interest or value. Typically it is regarded as the application of fundamental knowledge to concrete problems rather than being anything fundamental in itself. Its value is derived entirely from the ends it achieves; the means themselves are of little intellectual, philosophic, or religious interest.

But in this our culture itself may be significantly impoverished by its technological narrowing of the meaning of practical knowledge to excessively rational-technical forms of environmental and human manipulation. For practical knowledge in this impoverished sense may in fact be intellectually and morally inferior to descriptive and normative kinds. What is needed, therefore, is an expansion in the meaning of practical knowledge beyond what the advanced industrial world narrowly defines it to be.

The first step is to recognize that what is usually thought of as practical knowledge, whether as everyday as baking cakes or as involved as brain surgery, generally exhibits the same, relatively simple logical structure as a sequence of directions or instructions for accomplishing a specific end. "First you do this, then you do this, then you do that." Complications in this structure arise as contingencies are considered: if the cake fails to rise, if the patient's blood pressure falls, and so on, then one does certain other things. But examples of this kind of practical knowledge seem almost absurdly simple compared to the intricacy and profundity of the knowledge required, say, to raise children well, to guide a process of psychotherapy successfully, to exercise effective political leadership, to preach convincingly, or to live wisely, whatever the concrete situation and norms in each case. Knowledge of this order is also practical, but obviously of immensely greater logical complexity and human significance. One would suppose, of course, that pastoral theology as a form of practical knowledge is more nearly like these very complex varieties than it is like the dominant rational-manipulative technologies of our culture, and therefore closer to the everyday notion of the "wisdom of experience" than to simple technique or know-how.

In this connection it may be noted that this meaning of the word "experience" is considerably broader, and perhaps basically different from the more common existentialist meaning today where it tends to be identified with the moment of consciousness. The phrase "wisdom of experience" instead suggests a form of knowledge that has accrued and matured through a history of practical, contingent events. It may also be noted that the Bible includes a large if somewhat neglected literature of practical knowledge, or wisdom, of this kind, which seems to have moved historically from being simply a collection of astute maxims and proverbs to theological intuitions and speculations of remarkable proportion and importance for later religious tradition.

Another important feature of practical knowledge, in addition to its potential complexity, is precisely its pragmatic character. It cannot be derived entirely from descriptive or normative knowledge, important and inseparable as that is, but must always be learned by trial and error, "through experience." This fact in turn makes for certain difficulties in acquiring and transmitting it, especially in its more complex forms, because what is learned through experience is to a certain extent, and sometimes to a very large extent, specific to particular practitioners or communities of practice. In a certain sense one must be an insider, a practitioner oneself, disciplined by practice, in order to acquire it. Hence its acquisition and development always involve something like practice, apprenticeship, or discipleship. Wisdom is not, like the products of a consumer society, simply there for the taking – though it may be available to all who will devote themselves to the discipline of the search.

Nevertheless, experience and wisdom are not utterly esoteric or incommunicable. To a certain extent one can "show and tell" what one knows about any of these complex learnings, and a tradition of practical knowledge can develop in a community of seekers that can be made available by "precept and example," and even subjected to as much critical examination and mutual regulation as any purely scientific or moral tradition of inquiry. Admittedly the communication of the most complex kinds of practical knowledge in the form of codified instructions tends to take the form of general principles governing complex contingencies of events, rather than simple sequential instructions, and thus requires considerable intuition and interpretation on the part of the one who is learning. Examples include theories of psychotherapy and preaching. Similarly, the transmission of complex practical knowledge by *example* tends to lose its simple character as demonstration to be imitated, to the extent that it is complex, and acquires increasingly the significance of a model of authenticity calling the disciple to his or her own comparable wisdom, as in the advanced teaching of the creative arts in which the student's unique gifts are brought to expression in resonance with, but not strict imitation of the master's. Thus the most complex forms of practical knowledge are in a sense communicated and subjected to the discipline of community practice, even though what one might consider to be the most distinctive and crucial elements of it remain inaccessibly unique to particular practitioners. Nevertheless enough of it can be communicated to make possible traditions and communities of practical knowledge – what in this essay is termed a practical discipline.

A further question, however, is whether *religious* practical knowledge exhibits special features requiring their own investigation in any attempt to construct a discipline of pastoral theology along these lines, that is, as a critical discipline reflecting on religious forms of practical knowledge. At first thought it may not seem so, since religious practice in many ways resembles other kinds of practical knowledge, for instance in having a similar range of complexity, from primitive magical and cultic instructions to activities as complex as preaching and counseling in a secular society.

Nevertheless, certain complications are involved in any practical discipline that attempts to learn how to deal with the limits of human agency itself, as religion presumably does. One might well wonder what sort of wisdom can be gained about how to live at the very boundaries of human experience. "The fear of the Lord is the beginning of wisdom," and could well be also its end, in both the teleological and chronological senses of "end," for can anything at all be learned about these things, that is, about how to live with that which transcends even life and death? The dangers in failing to take these limitations seriously are evident in the temptation of all practical religious knowledge to veer toward magical manipulations of the divine. But the question in fact is more than one of imprudence or abuse, for it asks whether any human practical knowledge of "methods" is not necessarily magical and inappropriate when it presumes to learn, for instance, how to be saved from death and sin, the ultimate practical religious questions, or how to facilitate the salvation of others.

Without adequate elaboration, I wish only to suggest that whatever the answers may be to these questions and the thorny theological issues they raise, it seems to me that the ultimate expression of practical knowledge is probably best conceived in paradoxical terms having to do with self-transformation and transcendence. Practical knowledge of all kinds seeks to influence the world or life in general, but in its more elaborate varieties, as in the knowledge of how to care for others, the unilateral manipulative aspect seems to give way to processes of mutual influence, the end point of which, one might suppose, is some sort of change in the self rather than the self's affecting of change in the world. However, religiously speaking, it has to do not so much with change in the self as with a transcendence of self. For practical religious learning must in some sense entail a learning about how to live with life's transcending limits themselves – moral evil, death, meaninglessness – as destructive of the self yet not ultimate for the self. Thus it involves learning something like how to receive one's existence from God beyond life and death, beyond righteousness and sin, beyond meaning and meaninglessness, and thus how to live transcendently as a child of God. To be sure, this implies that one not only receives grace but in a real sense can practice living in grace, can become experienced in receiving it and paradoxically grow in it, as perhaps the proper and unique form of human participation in life with God. Only here the practical knowledge involved is entirely paradoxical, that is to say, it lives at the very limits of human possibility in the human contradiction of self-transcendence, and finds its fulfillment only eschatologically.

Presumably a pastoral theology conceived along these lines would be concerned with developing practical religious knowledge about caring for others, that is, how to care for others in their concrete contingencies and problems so as to stimulate or enable their life of faith and practical knowledge of God. And presumably it should operate in the very broad dimensions of the meaning of these ideas as roughly indicated here rather than indulging in narrow pietisms. Beyond this it is difficult to trace out in much detail the work of such a discipline. Nevertheless it may be helpful for the present simply to suggest that pastoral theology as a discipline can be eminently practical in character, and that practicality rightly understood can be as profound and significant as descriptive insight into reality or visions of the good, with which in any case it is intimately related. It may also be worth noting, for a discipline with some questions from time to time about its own worth as an intellectual enterprise, that our society probably needs some broadening and deepening of its conceptions of methods of living and even methods of caring and curing. An approach to these practical concerns undertaken with religious seriousness and theological perspective may be precisely what is needed for helping our civilization develop more humanly rich and fulfilling traditions of the art of life, beyond the very superficial moral and religious methodologies that presently prevail.

21

Practical Theology as Critical Praxis Correlation (1987)*

Rebecca S. Chopp

Introduction

Although not among the first generation of twentieth-century US feminist theologians, Rebecca Chopp followed closely on the heels of figures like Rosemary Radford Ruether and Elisabeth Schüssler Fiorenza and is the only woman included in important US anthologies in practical theology from the 1980s. Although not closely aligned with practical theology over the years, her doctoral study at the University of Chicago with David Tracy, the liberationist bent of her scholarship toward practice, and her singularity as a woman invested in theological education led to her identification with the early movement. She completed her study at Chicago in 1983 just as practical theological discussions were heating up, and after teaching there for a few years, she went on to become one of first woman provosts, deans, presidents, and chancellors at several universities.

The following essay appears in an important early book in practical theology edited by Lewis Mudge and James Poling, *Formation and Reflection: The Promise of Practical Theology* (1987), that grew out of seminars addressing the gap between the academy and religious communities, sponsored by the Association of Theological Schools and funded by the Lilly Endowment Inc. Her chapter stands out because it takes on other participants such as Edward Farley, Don Browning, and her own mentor Tracy, asserting that their "liberal-revisionist project" falls short in its obsession with cognitive claims, its resistance to analyzing its own institutional location and practices, and its failure to address the political nature of all theological knowledge. A practical theology aimed at the non-believer rather than the oppressed, she argues, errors on the side of an elitist academy anxious about sustaining intellectual belief in secular society. It also obscures a fuller understanding of *praxis*. *Praxis* refers to more than reflective action and requires analysis of oppressive politics and transformation of systemic suffering at multiple levels.

People today may not find Chopp's essay as innovative as it was when published since its argument has infiltrated today's discussion. However, she was singular at the time in turning to liberationist theories to formulate her critique. She draws on three schools of thought – Latin American liberation theology, German political theology, and feminist theology – all of which informed her dissertation, published in 1986, *The Praxis of*

Original publication details: Rebecca S. Chopp, "Practical Theology and Liberation," pp. 120–38 from *Formation and Reflection: The Promise of Practical Theology*, eds. Lewis S. Mudge and James N. Poling (Philadelphia: Fortress, 1987).

The Wiley Blackwell Reader in Practical Theology, First Edition. Edited by Bonnie J. Miller-McLemore.
© 2019 John Wiley & Sons Ltd. Published 2019 by John Wiley & Sons Ltd.

Suffering: An Interpretation of Political and Latin American Liberation Theologies. Tracy's revised correlational framework of "Christian fact" and "common human experience" comes under considerable fire, a noteworthy confrontation since the method has had such an influence on practical theology. As she argues, there is no such reality as "common human experience," an ideal that belies Tracy's own desire to respect pluralism. And any engagement with the Christian tradition must analysize its "radical, systemic distortion." She does not throw out the idea of correlation; instead she calls for a "critical praxis correlation" that overhauls the basic categories and reframes the *telos* to include more explicitly people that liberal Christianity has "ignored, forgotten, and even oppressed."

Suggested Further Reading

- Rebecca S. Chopp, *The Praxis of Suffering: An Interpretation of Political and Latin American Liberation Theologies* (Maryknoll, NY: Orbis, 1986).
- Gustavo Gutiérrez, *A Theology of Liberation: History, Politics and Salvation*, trans. and ed. Sister Caridad Inda and John Eagleson (Maryknoll, NY: Orbis, 1973).
- Johann Baptist Metz, *Faith in History and Society: Toward a Practical Fundamental Theology*, trans. David Smith (New York: Seabury, 1980).

***

As the introductory essay indicates, most of the articles in this text [Lewis S. Mudge & James N. Poling, ed. *Formation & Reflection: The Promise of Practical Theology*, 1987] creatively reflect on the application of the revised correlation method for practical theology. Such application of the revised correlation method is a necessity, our various authors tell us, because theology is too far from the church, because theology is simply in our heads, because we do not reflect on intentional action, and/ or because practical theology is not foundationally rooted. Together the various diagnoses suggest that the application of the revised correlation method can occur by taking the praxis of Christian witness more seriously and more concretely, and by enriching the play among text, context, and interpreter. But I want to contend that such broad and sweeping claims for the revised method of correlation must be questioned. Does the method of correlation, even when concretely applied in the many levels of discourse, set some limits on problems and possibilities for reflection and theory by its basic presuppositions? Does the method of correlation privilege certain issues and certain experiences as significant while ignoring or marginalizing other issues and other experiences? [...]

[...] With full recognition that the liberal-revisionist project of correlation must be both commended and respected for its theoretical agility as well as for its political support of the continuation of Christianity in modernity, my argument will be that the revised method of correlation and the liberal-revisionist theology to which it is linked is a discursive practice that, [...] while having certain possibilities, also has certain limits. I am not interested in totally dismissing the liberal project, but I do want to suggest that liberalism construes religion and theology in a way that may not be adequate to the present situation. In sum, my argument will be that what Charles Winquist calls the fundamental rootedness of much of contemporary practical theology is the liberal project of Christianity, a project that engineers a basic identity between two abstract referents for interpretation – human experience and Christian tradition – [...] masking the compliancy of Christianity with what Johann Baptist Metz calls bourgeois existence.[1]

Having made this bold claim, I must defend my accusations and also point toward possibilities for a different model of *practical theology*, with emphasis both on practical and theology. To do this I want to take some theologies that are close to liberal-revisionist theology, those being the voices of liberation theologies including Latin American liberation theology, German political theology, and feminist theology. These liberation theologies have all been influenced by the liberal project of identifying Christianity and human freedom, but in this identification all attempt to speak for those people that liberal Christianity has ignored, forgotten, and even oppressed. Hence, there is a double relationship: as voices of victims they oppose, even contradict liberal theology, and as recipients of the tradition they are informed by and in turn transform that liberal project. This type of dialectical relationship has been suggested by Gustavo Gutierrez's distinction between historical praxis and liberating praxis.[2] Historical praxis is the project of modernity as the intentional manipulation and control, characterized by the dual values of rationalism and individualism, over nature, society, and the self. Yet historical praxis, be it in industrial, philosophical, or political revolutions, was successful only because of its dependency on massive contradictions between the "persons" and the "nonpersons" of history. This historical praxis, expressive of humanity's historical nature, is now interrupted by liberating praxis, the activity of the poor to "fashion an entirely different social order."[3] Gutierrez parallels this break-from-within history with a belief that a new form of liberating Christianity emerges out of modern Christianity. [...] Thus, we can bring liberation theologies into conversation with the liberal project only if we realize that we are comparing different models that are at least somewhat incommensurable in that they cannot always be evaluated against each other in a point-by-point fashion. Liberation theologians ask different questions, consider different human experiences and existences, and most of all, experience Christianity in a very different way than liberal theologians are able to conceive of or reflect upon.[4] Yet it is precisely this incommensurability, provided we remember that within each model are representations of real religious experience, that allows us to position the liberal-revisionist method of correlation as a set of discursive practices which are part of modernity's political and ideological history and not, as sometimes claimed, a universal approach to theological reflection.

It is also the case that the critique, both in the sense of understanding the presuppositions and in the sense of uncovering the distortions, of liberal-revisionist theology that I want to delineate could be argued without the aid of liberation theologies. [...] One could, and someone should, use a genealogical argument styled after the works of Michel Foucault to consider the structuring of the correlation method and its *correlation* with power and knowledge in our society, including how it is resisted through daily capillaries of discourse and relations among those without "power" in religious and social institutions. But I want to use liberation theology for the basic reason that besides criticizing the ideological presuppositions and structures of oppression, it also criticizes the intrinsic experiences and piety of Christianity that the method of correlation, liberal-revisionist theology, and modern Christianity both depend and reflect upon. Feminist theology, for instance, questions the religious experiences constituted in the liberal church and disclosed in liberal theology: is there a real experience of God as a generally uninvolved, uncaring, reigning power that secures the superiority of maleness, and shields the tyranny of patriarchalism under the guise of the natural order of creation? [...] Thus liberation theologies, though not the only way to critique the discursive practices of the liberal-revisionist approach to practical theology, enable us to struggle [...] with the way of being religious that the method of correlation presupposes and substantiates.

But is this kind of question not far from being practical? Am I not falling into the very trap, warned of by the essays, of not getting to the real facts or contexts in congregations? [...] This liberal-revisionist response to critiques such as mine reveals two important presuppositions of the revised correlation approach to practical theology: (1) that there is a progression in the hierarchy of order from fundamental through systematic to practical theology, and (2) that the congregation has some privileged primacy for correcting the errors of theologians. Both presuppositions have a great deal to do with the way theology has been structured not merely within the theological education curriculum but within the society, being located in or guaranteed by university centers of theoretical knowledge. This, in turn, is related to the larger modern project of education which inducts persons into our society and into the guilds of professions by separating them off from the actual practice of the craft or service. [...] In dealing with these two presuppositions we can sketch, quickly, the brief outlines of liberal theology and its project to accommodate Christianity to modernity.

Practical theology dates its modern history to the restructuring of the disciplines through the now-famous encyclopedia approach. This history has been carefully documented and I only wish to underscore the fact that "regions" such as preaching, liturgy, and education were relegated to moments of clerical application worked out through systematic theology and undergirded by fundamental theology.[5] This basically deductive approach assumes that the logically important questions arise at the fundamental or foundational level, which, as the cornerstone of liberal theology, assumes that the ability to understand lies in theories that bracket daily practices to arrive at what these theologians call the "essence" of common human experience, an essence that is forthrightly entitled the religious dimension. Once the essence of common human experience is worked out, religion can be explained, at least in principle, to anyone and everyone, so that the tradition can be reinterpreted in light of human existence (since there is a fundamental relation between tradition and existence) and then reapplied to the daily practices of experience. [...]

The second presupposition is the question of turning directly to the congregation as a way to accomplish the "doing" of practical theology. A number of the authors decry the distance between theology and the church. [...] This turn to the congregation raises the question, How did theology ever get separated from the congregation? – a question, as I mentioned before, that has to do with the structure of knowledge in our society and the need for legitimization of theology as a form of knowledge. But that question does not interest me as much as the subtle romanticization of the congregation that this critique entails. I applaud theologians being involved in the congregation, and theology does not make much sense without a relation to religious witness. But theologians will find no gnostic formulas in the congregation; indeed the questions and experiences of most congregations parallel, in a rather frightening way, the questions and experiences of liberal-revisionist theologians. One example will have to suffice, though many could be enumerated. [...] One of the most interesting studies [...] is the book entitled *Building Effective Ministry*, which considers, from a variety of disciplines and approaches, a case study of the Wiltshire United Methodist Church.[6] The quite helpful essays by various consultants share one underlying assumption with the congregations: that religious language, in order to be meaningful or to have meaning, must be translated into secular categories. Theologians will discover no magic formulas, different questions, or naive religious experience in this congregation: indeed, the Wiltshire case is enough to convince anyone that secularized culture, privatized religion, and the crisis of the truth, meaning, and meaningfulness of religious language is the burden not only of modern theologians but also of contemporary congregational participants. The issue, then, is not that theology should be related in closer fashion to the church; this solution tries to reverse the first presupposition about the hierarchical order of theology. Rather, the problem lies on another level, for both the church and theology find it difficult to speak of God in a society whose ideology and politics demand strict adherence to secularistic language and that places experiences such as religion on the margins of public life in the realm of the private. As the voices of liberation theology will soon suggest to us, liberal-revisionist theology and the modern church are manifestations of their culture, twin manifestations that disclose the constitution of Christianity in bourgeois society as individualistic, existentialistic, and private.

Having examined the assumptions behind the question, Will this essay be practical? I want to answer yes, but not in relation to the assumption of the hierarchy of the fundamental-systematic-practical order or the assumption that if theologians paid attention to congregations they would be able to offer a truly practical theology. Rather I contend that the only way to consider practical theology is to look at theology quite practically, in terms of how it reflects and secures a certain form and function of religion in our culture, and how a new theology may well depend upon a quite practical fact: relating a new theological substance to a new theological method that speaks to a new experience and role of Christianity in history. In order to do this, I will, with the aid of some liberation theologians, pose three questions to liberal-revisionist theology and its method of correlation: (1) What is the point of religion for liberal-revisionist theology? (2) What is the nature of the method of correlation? and (3) What are the limits of "praxis" in liberal-revisionist theology?

What is the Point of Religion?

The first question about the limits of the liberal-revisionist project asks of what religion basically consists, or alternatively, what is the primary experience, meaning, message of Christianity? Paul Tillich referred to this in his concept of the material norm of theology, and argued, correctly I think, that each historical age gives rise to a new norm.[7] [...]

The liberal project dedicated itself primarily to the crisis of cognitive claims, the crisis of the possibility of belief. Van Harvey's excellent book *The Historian and the Believer* suggests the seemingly contradictory position of the modern theologian who, on the one hand, must be loyal to the scientific morality of free, critical, autonomous inquiry, and, on the other hand, must remain loyal to the Christian community and its traditional belief structure.[8] Harvey locates the problem as one of morality and knowledge: as a problem of morality the theologian must either choose between or bring together two institutions – one in which authority is given only through autonomous research and arguments based on evidence; the other where authority is given through tradition and based in belief. This moral crisis depends upon a fundamentally episte-mological problem since, in the crisis of cognitive claims, the theologian must attempt to make known through the human subject that which essentially lies beyond the human subject.

The liberal theologians solved or at least pacified their moral crisis by two important strategies: (1) selecting the epistemological issue as the religious question, and (2) reflect-ing, even supporting the continual privatization of religion in the secular world. When liberals could not know God through special privilege, they opted for discerning God in history and, most importantly, discovering God as the referent for the self. Indeed, Schleiermacher, the great father of liberal theology, represents this first strategy quite well. Remember that Schleiermacher took as the religious issue of his day the cognitive crisis of the cultural despisers. To the cultural despisers of religion, Schleiermacher argued that religion was neither knowing nor doing, but "a sense or taste for the infinite," an "intuition and feeling of the infinite."[9] Since the despisers could not know God (and thus their fundamental problem, an epistemological-moral issue) Schleiermacher asked them to look within, to discover certain feelings, and to recognize these feelings as the real seat of religion. Schleiermacher continued this basic strategy in *The Christian Faith*, accepting as the fundamental religious issue the possibility of belief, and responding to this issue by locating religion in the experience of the historical self.[10]

Liberal theology accomplished this alliance between historical knowledge and traditional belief through what revisionist theologians are prone to call a project of accommodation, an uncritical acceptance of the modern project. To be sure, out of liberalism burst neo-orthodoxy which based its origin upon a critique of liberalism's all-too easy acceptance of the dictates and whims of modernity. [...] Revisionist theology, while taking neo-orthodoxy as an important internal critique, is committed to con-tinuing the liberal project, but in a postliberal age. David Tracy's early work, *Blessed Rage for Order*, is the definitive statement of the revisionist project.[11] [...] As Tracy suggests, the goals and loyalties of liberal and revisionist theologies are the same, though the methodological resources and substantive resources are now mutually critical in approach. The problem, at least for our purposes, is that the point of reli-gion, or the religious question, is identical for liberals and revisionists, the question of the nonbeliever or, theologically stated, the question of the crisis of cognitive claims. All other questions – justice, liturgy, discipleship – have to be understood through this modem crisis of secularistic nonbelief.

Gustavo Gutierrez, among other theologians, has been critical of the religious question for modern theology or what he calls progressivist theology, which accepted the limits of the bourgeois nonbeliever as the religious problem that Christianity had to face. For Gutierrez, the difference between progressivist theology and liberation theology can be stated as the difference between basic questions:

> The modern spirit, whose subject frequently is the nonbeliever, questions the faith in a context of the meaning of religion. [...] The questions asked by the "nonperson" and the "nonhuman," by contrast, have to do with the economic, the social and the political. [...][12]

While liberal-revisionist theologians respond to the theoretical challenge of the nonbelievers among the small minority of the world's population who control the wealth and resources in history, liberation theologians respond to the practical challenge of the large majority of global residents who control neither their victimization nor their survival.

Gutierrez also moves us to consider the second strategy of liberal and revisionist theologians, the privatization of religion or what he calls "the role of the church in modern society." [...] The church in the modern world became that institution where this private religious meaning was offered. Metz identifies the function of the church in the bourgeois world as the privatization of religion; Metz argues that as "persons" become defined by production and exchange in the evolutionary logic of modernity, the meaningfulness of life is relegated to the margins of society in the private realms of family, religion, and art.[13]

Among the most trenchant criticisms of the church in the modern world has been that of Jürgen Moltmann's in *The Theology of Hope*. In modernity, Moltmann argues, the church became the *cultus privatus*, where its first function was to be the cult of a new subjectivity.[14] Moltmann argues that both the theology of liberalism and neo-orthodoxy function to secure this privatization, securing ultimate meaning in the realm of the personal. In modern religious experience, freedom becomes largely the project of accepting oneself, and religion becomes that vehicle whereby one says yes to self and God in the private, existential encounter. [...]

As compared to liberal-revisionist theology, the point of religion of liberation theology has to do with emancipation and enlightenment of persons in history and is formulated in a number of different ways: the option for the poor in Latin American liberation theology, the dangerous memory of those who suffer in political theology, and women's experiences in feminist theology. The radical difference of what liberation theology understands as the point of Christianity underlines the importance of dwelling at some length on the question of the point of religion since the substance of any theological model depends, to a great extent, on the issues it addresses and the historical situation in which it lives. The comparison between liberation theology and liberal-revisionist theology allows us to understand that in the liberal project, the point of religion arises out of the crisis of cognitive claims and the question of nonbelievers and becomes intertwined in a church institution which met a person's needs for meaning and ultimacy and in a theology which protected the meaning and ultimacy of the subject through a turn to the limits or depths of private, bourgeois individuals. The method of correlation, the subject of our next question, was born in the liberal-revisionist project to continue Christianity by protecting the individual and securing the individual by privatizing Christianity.

What is the Nature of the Method of Correlation?

Having, with the aid of liberation theologians, understood the point of religion in the liberal-revisionist project, we can move directly to the second question about the nature of the method of correlation. The critical issue here is how tradition and experience are understood, and, second, how the correlation between tradition and experience occurs. The criticisms of liberation theology about the source of experience in liberal-revisionist theology should need only to be identified. Feminist theologians, to take one example, make clear that the experience most often reflected upon is that of white, bourgeois males. Out of reflecting upon this experience, liberal-revisionist theologians arrive at an interpretation of what they call *common* human experience. Note the basic trajectory of liberal-revisionist theology to correlate experience and tradition has been a method to elevate the experience of a certain group of men and make it universal. This is, of course, a classic example of ideology, where the experience of one group of persons is universalized, and even determined as *the* human experience. This epistemic sense of ideology joins, in liberal-revisionist theology, with a functional sense as it legitimizes the social world of the bourgeoisie.[15] The attempt to understand a *common* human experience is epistemically and functionally ideological in the method of correlation, limiting liberal-revisionist theology's ability to deal with questions of historical particularity and difference within a religion as well as between religions. [...]

The other source of theology has been tradition. By this theologians often mean the "classical" texts favored by the educated, male clerics and theologians of the church. Liberal-revisionist theologians increasingly appreciate Hans-Georg Gadamer's philosophical hermeneutics which allows such a tradition to be the possibility for continual engagement with a world, and allows the text to speak to us and not be limited through methods that explain the text in its historical situatedness.[16] One awareness that feminist theology can never avoid is that tradition is a living history of social practices. This means that the concept of tradition has to broaden to include other kinds of historical witnesses than those authorized by ecclesial and theological elites and that tradition must be studied in its historical situatedness and its historical effects. One of the most disturbing implications of feminist theology is the almost complete distortion of the classical tradition in relation to women. What happens when the tradition simply cannot be a source for theological reflection; when the only meanings one can retrieve from it are those of the terrible misogyny that Christianity has conceived, enforced, secured, and policed in regard to women?[17] What if, as some feminist theologians believe, we cannot be "at home" in the tradition? The method of correlation begins by assuming the at-homeness of tradition, and while it may use experience to correct tradition, it cannot, in principle, even entertain the question of radical, systemic distortion.

Though there are other questions of the sources for the method of correlation, we can now move to analyzing just *how* the correlation occurs in this method. As Matthew Lamb has demonstrated, the nature of the correlation in the liberal-revisionist approach is always a theoretical correlation.[18] The limits of this theoretical correlation lie in the dominance, and even the hegemony, of theory over praxis. Liberation theology argues for a practical correlation, which uses theories only as ways to solve problems; in this model theories can be adopted, argued, discarded in relation to the material and not vice versa. The theoretical correlation of liberal-revisionist theology must fit all human experience (which is, after all, supposedly held in common by all) into theories of depth, dimension, limit, or ultimacy. Phenomenology and phenomenological-related hermeneutical theories have been favored by the liberal-revisionist theologians because these theories depend upon bracketing out daily practices, arriving at the essence of a phenomenon, and then approaching the concrete realities. But in opposition to this attempt to give meaning via a theory of the essence of the text and of experience, one can question if meaning is not located rather in the historical practices, in what Terry Eagleton has called, "the changing, practical transactions between individuals."[19]

It is at the point of comparing the method of liberation theologians to the method of liberal-revisionists that I feel the most tension of the incommensurability problems.

Liberation theology is not concerned about the crisis of cognitive claims; so it has no need for a method of theoretical correlation while, on the other hand, it is concerned with the practical crisis of the victims of history and needs a method that can critique and transform situations. Liberation theology in this sense is closer to pragmatic philosophy that begins with a problem arising out of a particular situation than to phenomenological method which begins by abstracting of meanings, giving power to the interpreter to select the "interesting" issues. It does not begin with some predetermined assumption about the essence of common human experience or about the privileged status of tradition; it begins with a need to approach different, varied, complex realities, and a willingness to privilege human emancipation and enlightenment over tradition. Indeed liberation theologies force us to wonder whose tradition the liberal-revisionists want to privilege – is the tradition of Christianity identified with the victors of history or with the prayers and hopes of the victims? Liberation theology opts for a method best called a critical praxis correlation which includes a de-ideologization of scriptures, a pragmatic interpretation of experience, a critical theory of emancipation and enlighten-ment, and a social theory to transform praxis.[20] That is, liberation theologians begin in what they call praxis – the practices of agents and institutions – so that practical theology names the whole rather than one special part; but with this concern of praxis, it is time to turn to our third and final question.

What are the Limits of Praxis in Liberal-Revisionist Theology?

The third question of the method of correlation considers the meaning of praxis, and now the criticisms of liberation theology can be aligned with those of current practical philosophy. These criticisms are three fold: (1) In liberal-revisionist theology the first referent for praxis has to do with the regions of intentional application while in libera-tion theology the first referent of praxis is the broad matrix or web of social systems and structures, social being and doing; (2) Reflection on praxis is aimed at understanding and reconciliation with the underlying order or transcendental norms in liberal-revisionist theology, while reflection on praxis in liberation theology seeks to transform and "remake" history, thus praxis in liberation theology is future-oriented, and in liberal-revisionist theology it is present-oriented; (3) Politics is one region of activity for liberal-revisionist theology while, in liberation theology, the political is the context and condition for all reflection and action. By concentrating on the meaning and use of the popular term "praxis" in liberal-revisionist theology and in liberation theology, we can see again the vast differences in these discursive practices.

As we have already seen, liberalism moves from fundamental to systematic to practical theology, with practical theology being the application of meanings gleaned from the two prior theological realms. This is the reason that practical theology so easily slides over into regions of practice, and the discrete approaches to preaching, religious education, and the like are enumerated. It is also the reason that ethics becomes so important for practical theology in the liberal-revisionist model, for, as Don Browning has effectively demonstrated, if practice is identified with intentional human activity, then practical theology must be focused fundamentally through ethics. The underlying presupposition is that the primary referent for praxis is intentional human activity. It is this intentional activity as the primary referent for praxis that liberation theology challenges. Liberation theologians, in a manner similar to some contemporary philosophers, wonder if praxis is not better understood in a broader sense of the web of social interactions. This web might be traced through three factors: contemporary retrievals of Aristotle and Marx, a theory of structuration combining anthropology and social structure, and attention to unintended consequences and effects. The first factor retrieves Aristotle's location of praxis in the community's continuous determination of its own becoming combined with Marx's notion of praxis involving structural relations and human interests. Here we might place the broad web of praxis not into disparate regions of praxis but in the dynamic, structural, and communal relationality of history.

The second factor concerns the recursive nature of praxis and, similar to social theorists such as Anthony Giddens, seeks to view society as composed neither of intentional individuals nor functional organisms, views that give rise to either the dominance of ethics or of sociology.[21] Giddens's model of structuration attempts to hold together the interdependency of human agency and social systems in what he calls the duality of structure. Liberation theology, like the model of structuration, assumes that human activity and social systems are co-constituted by producing and reproducing each other.[22] This factor pushes liberal-revisionist theology at its separation of the human agency and social systems, its talk of praxis either through individual intentional activity or functional social systems, its refusal to study the recursive nature of praxis and the time-space construction of history within praxis.

The third factor arises out of the first two, this factor considers the unintended effects and consequences in praxis. Activity always occurs in a complex web of relationships, within which activity rarely reaches its conscious goals. [...] One implication of this is to pay less attention, in liberation theologies, to large ethical and political theories *about* power and more attention to the capillaries and daily practices *of* power. Despite theories which talk about equality and justice, for instance, feminists become quite aware that what is really repressive are the hundreds of daily practices such as linguistic etiquette which encourages men to speak the most, media references to women as soft and round, familial relations which now expect women to manage jobs both at home and office. Thus feminists may intend to be equal, and live by promised theories of justice and distribution of power, but the "unintended" consequences of social practices are more repressive than any ethical-political theory could ever intend. In sum, praxis is not first application, formulated as intentional human activity, but, in liberation theology, first the web of relations in which the individual doing and being is enabled and contained.

The second issue of praxis has to do with the purpose of reflection on praxis in liberal-revisionist theology and in liberation theology. This issue was summarized quite well by Nicholas Lobkowicz in referring to the difference between Hegel and Marx, which, for our own purposes, can symbolize the philosophical differences between liberal-revisionist theology and liberation theology. Hegel, says Lobkowicz, understood that the order of the cosmos was disturbed and changing, but thought the only hope was to reconcile the human subject to the universe by helping the subject to understand it. Marx, argued Lobkowicz, "lost all faith in the healing and reconciling power of mere thought" and believed reflection on praxis had to be for transformation and not just acceptance.[23] Liberal-revisionist theology, stemming from what Jon Sobrino has called the first enlightenment, still wants to bring humanity into correlation with the universal order.[24] Its theoretical presuppositions orient its temporality to the present, and its reliance on transcendental arguments accents the universality of its claim. Liberation theology, concerned with the second enlightenment, understands the purpose of all reflection as transformation and thus its temporality is decidedly future-oriented.[25]

The differences in the underlying purpose of reflection accounts for a quite different view of the nature of theology. Both liberalism and liberation theology like to think of their theology as "critical reflection." Gutierrez identifies three tasks for liberation theology as "critical reflection": (1) it is a theory of definite praxis; (2) it is a critique of church and society; and (3) it is the projection of future possibilities related to the present situation.[26] For liberal-revisionist theology, critical reflection [...] means the correlation of meanings, meanings that are already given and at most can apply to individual, intentional action. The limits, as well as the possibilities, of the method of correlation are established by this underlying view of reconciliation to an order or normative view and thus the privileging of balancing or reconciling meanings. Transformation, future, radical conversion can only exist as deferred implications within one particular region of intentional activity.

This differentiation of praxis leads to the third criticism of praxis in liberal-revisionist theology and that is its political intent. Now, liberal-revisionist theologians prefer to talk of politics as one distinct arena of praxis and to contend that only those statements specifically intended to talk of politics are political. But liberation theology, based on its understanding of praxis as the complex web of relations that is primary for all of life, believes that all theology is political. If praxis is understood in this fashion, any theological reflection has some political implications, precisely as it shows new ways of being in the world, new relations of power, interests, knowledge, and so on. Feminist theology has observed over and over how the privatization of certain spheres of life as nonpolitical has had great political implications for women, giving rise to the feminist slogan that the personal is the political. Indeed, the limits of liberal-revisionist theology, as this essay has tried to demonstrate, are really its own political nature and effects, as liberal-revisionist theology reflects and reinforces repressive structures of consciousness and oppressive structures of social practices in the bourgeois world.

Despite revisionist appeals to liberation praxis, the political contradiction, as Gutierrez calls it, is demonstrated in the liberal-revisionist refusal to take the other requirement of critical reflection: the option for the victims of history.[27] This is not because liberal-revisionists refuse to have a subject; quite clearly its subject has been the bourgeois nonbeliever. Jose Miguez Bonino has argued that because of the contextualization of theology in the polis, theology speaks from and for a specific situation, and, Miguez Bonino argues, the goal must be to position and not simply ideologically reflect the interests of the authors of theological reflection.[28] The criticism is threefold: the method of correlation makes political choices under the guise of value-free or common existence, it denies the political import of any but a narrow range of statements, and it refuses to position itself for the oppressed.

We might conclude by suggesting that the very use of the term "praxis" in liberal-revisionist theology – despite the attempts to sound as if a serious conversation is being entertained with liberation theology – disguises yet another attempt to secure the modern project. This is not, I hope, to deny the worthiness of practical theology in the method of correlation. It is to suggest that this method is limited, and in spite of its rhetorics of totality and universalism, is a situated and particular discursive practice that cannot do all things for all persons. It is also to suggest that given our own historical situation of global crisis, the method of correlation may prove too limited to address the religious, human, practical needs of our age. As we deal with issues such as justice, pluralism, and other religions, the task may not be merely to understand, but to transform ourselves and our world. Liberation theology, at least in the judgment of this author, forces us to grapple with historical particularity and differences so that we may work toward a future where we can all live together. This will take theoretical and practical change and transformation, and whereas I do not think liberation theology has all the answers, I do think it addresses the issues of our present period in a way outside the limits and possibilities of liberal-revisionist theology with its revised correlation method.

Notes

1 Johann Baptist Metz analyzes the compliancy of modern Christianity with bourgeois existence in his *Faith in History and Society: Toward a Practical Fundamental Theology*, trans. David Smith (New York: Seabury Press, 1980), and *The Emergent Church: The Future of Christianity in a Post-Bourgeois World*, trans. Peter Mann (New York: Crossroad, 1981).

2 Gustavo Gutierrez, "Faith as Freedom: Solidarity with the Alienated and Confidence in the Future," *Horizons* 2 (Spring 1975) 36–7.

3 Gustavo Gutierrez, "Liberating Praxis and Christian Faith," in *Frontiers of Theology in Latin America*, ed. Rosino Gibellini, trans. John Drury (Maryknoll, NY: Orbis Books, 1974), 8.

4 For one interpretation of the problems of incommensurability, see Richard J. Bernstein, *Beyond Objectivism and Relativism: Science, Hermeneutics, and Praxis* (Philadelphia: University of Pennsylvania Press, 1983), 79–108.

5 The best recent study of the structuring of the theological disciplines is Edward Farley's *Theologia: The Fragmentation and Unity of Theological Education* (Philadelphia: Fortress Press, 1983).

6 Carl S. Dudley, ed., *Building Effective Ministry* (San Francisco: Harper & Row, 1983).

7 Paul Tillich, *Systematic Theology* (Chicago: University of Chicago Press, 1951), 1:48.

8 Van A. Harvey, *The Historian and the Believer: The Morality of Historical Knowledge and Christian Belief* (Philadelphia: Westminster Press, 1966).

9 Friedrich Schleiermacher, *On Religion: Speeches to Its Cultural Despisers*, trans. John Oman, reprint ed. (New York: Harper & Brothers, 1958).

10 Friedrich Schleiermacher, *The Christian Faith*, ed. H.R. Macintosh and R.S. Stewart (Edinburgh: T. & T. Clark, 1948).

11 David Tracy, *Blessed Rage for Order: The New Pluralism in Theology* (New York: Seabury Press, 1979).

12 Gustavo Gutierrez, *The Power of the Poor in History: Selected Writings*, trans. Robert R. Barr (Maryknoll, NY: Orbis Books, 1983), 212–13.

13 Metz, *Faith in History and Society*, 36–39.

14 Jürgen Moltmann, *The Theology of Hope: On the Ground and the Implications of a Christian Eschatology*, trans. James W. Leitch (New York: Harper & Row, 1967), 311–16.

15 For a discussion of epistemic and functional ideologies, see Raymond Geuss, *The Idea of a Critical Theory: Habermas and the Frankfurt School* (Cambridge: Cambridge University Press, 1981), 13–19.

16 Hans-Georg Gadamer, *Truth and Method*, trans. G. Borden and J. Cumming, 2nd ed. (New York: Seabury Press, 1975). For one example of Gadamer's influence on a revisionist theologian who is also influenced by the critical theories implicit in liberation theology, see David Tracy, *The Analogical Imagination: Christian Theology and the Culture of Pluralism* (New York: Crossroad, 1979).

17 A similar concern about the ability of hermeneutical philosophy to deal with radical distortion in tradition occurs in the debate between Gadamer and Jurgen Habermas. Two interesting summaries of this debate are David Hoy, *The Critical Circle: Literature, History, and Philosophical Hermeneutics* (Berkeley and Los Angeles: University of California Press, 1982), 117–28, and Paul Ricoeur, "Hermeneutics and the Critique of Ideology," in *Hermeneutics and the Human Sciences: Essays on Language, Action, and Interpretation*, ed. and trans. John B. Thompson (New York: Cambridge University Press, 1981), 63–100.

18 Matthew Lamb, *Solidarity with Victims: Toward a Theology of Social Transformation* (New York: Crossroad, 1982), 75–6.

19 Terry Eagleton, *Literary Theory: An Introduction* (Minneapolis: University of Minnesota Press, 1983), 24.

20 For an interpretation of the method employed by liberation theologies, see my *The Praxis of Suffering: An Interpretation of Political and Latin American Liberation Theologies* (Maryknoll, NY: Orbis Books, 1986).

21 Anthony Giddens, *Central Problems in Social Theory: Action, Structure and Contradiction in Social Analysis* (Berkeley and Los Angeles: University of California Press, 1983).

22 Anthony Giddens, *The Constitution of Society: Outline of the Theory of Structuration* (Berkeley and Los Angeles: University of California Press, 1984), 374.

23 Nicholas Lobkowicz, *Theory and Practice: History of a Concept from Aristotle to Marx* (Notre Dame, Ind.: University of Notre Dame Press, 1967), 340–41.

24 Jon Sobrino, *The True Church and the Poor*, trans. Matthew J. O'Connell (Maryknoll, NY: Orbis Books, 1984), 12.

25 Ibid., 20.

26 Gustavo Gutierrez, *A Theology of Liberation: History, Politics and Salvation*, trans. and ed. Sister Caridad Inda and John Eagleson (Maryknoll, NY: Orbis Books, 1973), 11–13.

27 Gutierrez, *Power of the Poor*, 200.

28 Jose Miguez Bonino, *Toward a Christian Political Ethics* (Philadelphia: Fortress Press, 1983), 44.

Section II

The 1990s: Redefining Practice, Reimaging Knowledge

22

Reconceiving Practice (1991)*

Craig Dykstra

Introduction

Religious educator and Reformed Presbyterian pastor Craig Dykstra is best known for his long-term leadership at Lilly Endowment, the largest grant-making program in religion in the United States. Educated at Princeton Theological Seminary in the late 1970s, he brought to the Endowment interests in philosophy and education, longstanding commitments to vibrant congregations, and a disciplined faith life. He followed another religious educator Robert Lynn as senior vice president. Lynn had already begun initiatives for religious renewal in a time of church decline (mostly mainline Protestant). Dykstra continued and refined this aim, building programs during his twenty-three year tenure (1989–2012) that aided young persons in faith, fledgling congregations, and beleaguered pastors and faculty.

Although this essay was initially conceived while Dykstra was teaching at Princeton, it marks the fundamental articulation of a long-term vision that guided the agenda and funding of the Endowment under his watch. Its most important innovation is its insight into the nature and dynamics of practice, which initiated a paradigm shift in how people understand the term. His first sentence names the problem: a view of practice bogged down by "harmfully individualistic, technological, ahistorical, and abstract" assumptions. In a kind of phenomenology of practice, he describes step by step how each of these assumptions permeates and distorts theological education and, as deliberately, unpacks the alternative.

Dykstra's reframing of practice as a social and historical activity that evolves over time in communities was greatly aided by the work of virtue ethicist Alasdair MacIntyre, even though Dykstra was never satisfied with MacIntrye's truncated grasp of religious traditions and Christian faith. Although Dykstra does not acknowledge Seward Hiltner's influence, his premise that practices, when properly reconceived, "bear epistemological weight" and "give rise to new knowledge" has obvious similarities to Hiltner's own claim. His use of MacIntrye offers a different kind of criticism of liberal theology than Rebecca Chopp's, one governed by communitarian politics rather than liberationist

Original publication details: Craig Dykstra, "Reconceiving Practice in Theological Inquiry and Education," pp. 35–66 from *Shifting Boundaries: Contextual Approaches to the Structure of Theological Education*, eds. Barbara G. Wheeler and Edward Farley (Louisville: Westminster John Knox, 1991).

principles. Recently, practical theologians Tom Beaudoin and Katherine Turpin show how this orientation renders the narrative- and virtue-based practices approach particularly susceptible to perpetuating an unanalyzed white dominance in the field.

Nonetheless, in many ways Dykstra was ahead of his time. Although his essay is almost three decades old, the narrow view of practice and hence of practical theology that he describes still rules in many places (e.g., scripture, history, and doctrine are still seen as "foundational"; practice is relegated to the "fourth" area). He depends on but also refines Edward Farley's widely recognized historical analysis, *Theologia: The Fragmentation and Unity of Theological Education* (1983). Whereas Farley led people to believe that the major problem in education was the focus on clergy skills, Dykstra shows that the difficulty lies in deeper conceptual impasses around misperceptions about practice itself. His renewed understanding allows us to see academic disciplines as practices themselves that are often dominated by secular, Enlightenment assumptions. Farley's proposal for a return to theology as *habitus* – knowledge of God as a "cognitive disposition of the soul" – is a good example. As Dykstra points out, Farley's conception does not recognize the diverse forms of intelligence required to sustain *habitus* (e.g., bodily, spatial, aesthetic), and his pessimism about congregations prevents him from appreciating communal capacities to enrich it. As with Hiltner, Dykstra uses long discursive end notes to make key arguments that readers should not overlook, including the additional analysis and trenchant critique in very first page-length note.

Suggested Further Reading

- Dorothy C. Bass and Craig Dykstra, eds., *For Life Abundant: Practical Theology, Theological Education, and Christian Ministry* (Grand Rapids: Eerdmans, 2008).
- Edward Farley, *Theologia: The Fragmentation and Unity of Theological Education* (Philadelphia: Fortress, 1983).
- Alasdair MacIntyre, *After Virtue* (Notre Dame: University of Notre Dame Press, 1981).

***

Theology and theological education are burdened by a picture of practice that is harmfully individualistic, technological, ahistorical, and abstract. This current picture, implicit in our imaginations and explicit in our actual ways of doing things, is implicated in many of the problems that communities of faith, theology as a body and activity of thought, and theological education in all its contexts are now struggling to overcome.[1] Unless a revised understanding of practice takes root in our endeavors, these problems will remain unresolved. But there is an alternative to the current picture available to us, one that has potential to reorient our ways of thinking theologically about practice. Then certain dimensions of our understandings and practice of theological education, not only in seminaries and divinity schools but also in congregations, might be improved.

I

What is the current picture? When we imagine practice, we see someone doing something. And when we think of practice in relation to theology and theological education, we see, I would suspect, someone doing something like preaching to a congregation, teaching a class, moderating a meeting, or visiting someone in the hospital. Usually, the person we see doing one of these things in our mind's eye is a clergyperson. This picture, I suggest, is the one that comes first, most naturally, almost automatically into view. This is the picture of practice that much of the church and almost all of theological education takes for granted.

One of the problems with this picture that is quickly picked out and has been much discussed lies in the assumption that the practice is the practice of a clergyperson. The fact that we focus on clergy so readily is evidence of the pervasiveness of what Edward Farley calls "the clerical paradigm," which he says governs theological education in general and practical theology in particular.[2] This is surely a problem, for the many good reasons Farley discusses. But it is not a problem intrinsic to our understanding of practice. Were we to substitute a layperson in our minds (or in the actual situation), the basic problem with our view of practice would not be solved. This is because the emphasis on clergy is only a symptom and manifestation of deeper issues.

Closer to the heart of the problem is the fact that we almost automatically see someone doing something. It is true, of course, that the one doing something (let us call him or her "the practitioner") is often doing it in the presence of others. Indeed, the practitioner is doing it *to* the others, often *for the sake of* the others who are there. But notice the assumptions here. The person doing something to and for others is the one engaged in the practice. The preacher, the teacher, the counselor is the one who is doing the thing we are interested in. The others are objects or recipients of the practice. If we pay any attention at all to what the others are doing, it is in terms of the effects generated in them by the practice of the practitioner. The others are not themselves engaged in the practice. Our assumptive vision of practice is that it is something *individuals* do. This points to what I mean when I say that our current picture of practice is individualistic.

Why does the fact that our picture assumes that practice involves individuals doing something make the picture individualistic? After all, there is no getting away from the fact that practice does involve individuals doing things. True. The problem is not what is included in the picture. The problem lies in where we focus and in what is left out. Our point of focus is the individual actor. What is left out is the larger social and historical context in which individual actions takes places.[3] From the point of view of an alternative understanding of practice that I will be developing, practice is not the activity of a single person. One person's action becomes only insofar as it is participation in the larger practice of a community and a tradition.

The individualism of the current picture is related to another of its features. When we think of practice, we picture the practitioner as someone who knows what he or she is doing, and we expect that person to carry out his or her practice effectively. "Good practice" does not mean just the exercise of routine, mechanical technique. It means knowledgeable, thoughtful action. This is why we invest so heavily in the professional education of practitioners. We want them to know what to do and how to do it, and we insist that they know why as well. We want them to recognize the point of what they are doing and to be aware of the reasons for doing something one way rather than another. They should be able to give explanations of their action in the light of the situations in which they do what they do. We want them, in short, to be guided in their practice by theory.

This is all good, of course. We would not want practitioners *not* knowing what they are doing. It is not desirable that people be stupid and ineffectual in their practice. Rather, the problem lies in what this picture naturally suggests most aids and forms intelligent practice.

In the case of the professional education of ministers, the social sciences have had a fairly considerable role to play – particularly in that part of theological education we call "practical theology." The reason is that these sciences seem to be quite useful in providing the kind of theory (the kinds of reasons and explanations and predictions) that helpfully guide action. The value of other theoretical disciplines, such as biblical studies, history, and systematic theology, in guiding action is more difficult to discern. Usually, in fact, we cannot find ways to think of them in these terms at all. Therefore, these areas of study are relegated to providing the "content" for practice; that is, what is preached and taught. Or we take the tack that these "academic" disciplines shape the practitioners' character; teach them to be better, clearer thinkers; or help them become more discerning in their perceptions and interpretations of the people and situations in which they work – all examples of influencing practice in some indirect way.[4] Even so, making connections between the so-called academic and practical fields seems difficult, not only to students but to teachers and scholars as well.[5]

The problem, again, is with the assumptions behind the current picture. The picture is a technological one. We assume the theory – practice relation to be a form of the science – technology relation. "Practice" means for us "making something happen." Practitioners are not supposed just to be doing something. They are supposed to be doing something to something or someone *in order to gain some desired outcome or result*. The reasons we consider for doing any particular thing are the *effects* it generates. The criterion by which practice is evaluated is whether it produces the effects we expect. That is, the criterion is effectiveness.

When theory and practice are related in this way, the kind of theory that is particularly relevant to practice is theory that helps us understand and trace causal relationships. Under the power of this picture, what we need to know from theory is how things work. When we know that, we can see how best to intervene in their workings and influence the course of events. Theory that can help us do that is highly valued. Theory that cannot do that (or can do so only marginally) is not valuable to practice.

This way of understanding practice not only focuses our attention on issues of cause and effect; it prescinds moral questions. Moral issues are not so much excluded as they are kept hidden or extraneous. This is because moral questions are made extrinsic to cause-and-effect relations, and thus to both theory and practice understood this way. When practice is procedure, its value depends upon its utility. Morality, then, has to do with the value of the results or effects of practice rather than with anything intrinsic to practice itself. Morality and practice have become separate issues in this.

Again, the problem has to do with focus and exclusion. We do not want people to be ineffective. Nor should we deny that there are often causal relations among events that, if we understand them, are important to know about and do something with. The problem is that we easily assume that *all* relations are causal; that practice is fundamentally intervention into a causal network and thus always the purposeful creation of change (especially in other people or in groups and institutions); that the creation of such change is both within our power and the point or purpose of any and every practice; and that the criterion of all practice must be an extrinsic one such as effectiveness. And with these assumptions we are forced to conclude that if we do not know how or do not have the power to intervene in certain causal relations in order to make change, there is nothing to do. Lacking such understanding and ability, we are left with no practice, or, what practice there is, is mere habit or technique with no point. This is what I mean by a technological understanding of practice.

If we conceive of practice technologically, it is likely that our conception will also be ahistorical and abstract in character. When "practice" refers to what someone does to and for someone or something else in order to create change, and if we come to know how to do that by understanding the causal relations involved, our tendency is to focus primarily on *present* circumstances and the possibilities inherent in them. We do, of course, often try to trace what has led up to the present circumstances in order to discern better what the causal relations involved are, but our interest in the past is exhausted by what it can tell us about this. Furthermore, our historical interest is in the history of the current situation, not in the history of practice. Practice is *applied* to a situation – perhaps historically (or better, genetically) understood – but the practice itself is not regarded as part of the situation to be understood historically. Indeed, practice, technologically understood, can have no real history. Practices may be repeated (that is, one may do the same kind of thing in sufficiently similar situations), but each practice is essentially a singular event, beginning and ending upon its intervention into each situation. Practice has no internal history of its own.

In theological schools, the assumed ahistoricism of practice is evident in how little work is done in the various subfields of practical theology on the history of Christian education, homiletics, pastoral care, church administration, and so forth.[6] We see little reason to analyze carefully the continuities and discontinuities of practice in various historical periods, traditions, and cultures. The research of this kind that does exist is marginal to the curriculum largely because its relevance to contemporary practice is so difficult to discern. When it is perceived to be relevant, it is usually as data out of which certain methods and techniques or, more generally, principles and guidelines may be recovered from earlier periods for use today.

The assumption that the value of history is the current usability of technical resources found there is an indication of what I mean by the abstractness of the current picture of practice. What we are after are theoretical principles and guidelines, together with tested methods, approaches, and techniques, which we regard as historically and culturally neutral.[7] We get these principles and methods mainly from contemporary theory-building and experimentation. If we turn to historical documents for help at all, we do so assuming that our task is to abstract the principles and methods from any historical narrative or tradition of which they may be a part. The tradition or context is, intentionally or unintentionally, distilled out. When we have these principles and methods, we may then employ them in our contemporary action. We understand, of course, that situations vary considerably and that our principles, guidelines, methods, and techniques must be applied differently in different situations, but we rely on theory together with direct observation rather than history or tradition to help us do this.

II

This, I suggest, is the picture that currently governs our understanding of practice in theology, in theological education, and to a large extent in the life of the church – particularly in the First World. The point is not that this is the only picture at all operative on the contemporary scene, or that all of its dimensions as articulated here prevail equally in every situation. Correctives to the tendencies we have lifted up do exist in many actual situations as well as in the minds of many thinkers. Various aspects of the current picture and many of its implications and effects have numerous critics. Nevertheless, this remains the dominant picture. It is the one around which most ministers and members of congregations orient church life. It is the one that most faculty in theological seminaries take for granted. It defines for many in the "academic" fields what the "practical" department is concerned with, and few in practical departments really question that definition, even when they chafe under its effects. This picture is the one that so naturally comes to mind for so many that conscious resistance to and articulated criticism of this one is required in order to function on the basis of any other.

Criticism of this picture may take place on two levels. One may criticize its implications and effects, or one may criticize the assumptions implicit in it. Both kinds of criticism are available across a broad literature.[8] But criticism, even if it is thoroughgoing, can take us only so far. What we really need is an alternative. Fortunately, an alternative is being put forward by some of those who have been most involved in the kind of criticism just mentioned. The picture of practice being suggested is quite different from the current picture in each of the aspects we have discussed. Its clearest formulation is provided by Alasdair MacIntyre, who defines a practice as

> any coherent and complex form of socially established cooperative human activity through which goods internal to that form of activity are realized in the course of trying to achieve those standards of excellence which are appropriate to, and partially definitive of, that form of activity, with the result that human powers to achieve excellence, and human conceptions of the ends and goods involved, are systematically extended.[9]

In the picture of practice carried by this definition, we do not first see an individual doing something. Rather, practice is inherently *cooperative*, so the lens broadens to include numbers of people. And these people are not doing things *to* one another so much as they are doing things *with* one another. Though each may be engaged in different specific actions, they are not doing different things. Individual actions interrelate in such a way that they constitute engagement in a common practice.

Jeffrey Stout's favorite example of a practice is baseball.[10] Baseball simply cannot be played alone. It is fundamentally cooperative. If you can't get a team together, you can't play the game. The players are gathered together, however, not in order to do different things *to* each other but to do one thing together – play baseball. Each player does, of course, do many things individually. We might see, for instance, Nolan Ryan pitching and Jose Canseco batting, while others are fielding, stealing bases, or watching from the dugout. Each of them, at a particular time, is doing something distinctive and individual. But at the level of practice, they are all doing the same thing – playing baseball.

Even this formulation may be too limiting, however; for the practice we have just been describing is "playing baseball" rather than "baseball itself." In the practice of baseball itself, Tommy LaSorda managing, Vin Scully and Joe Garagiola doing the play-by-play, and even my sons and I watching games on television and Roger Angell writing about it in *The New Yorker* are all included as well. A practice involves people doing things with one another, and normally at least some part of the time people will be doing what they do in physical proximity to one another. But not everyone engaged in a practice need be physically with others in order to participate.

Practice does not reduce to group activity. On the one hand, you do not have to be in a group to be participating in a practice. Prayer is a practice of the church. People praying by themselves are involved in this practice. Even though they are not at the moment involved in a group activity, they are involved in a "coherent and complex form of socially established cooperative human activity." It is cooperative because we pray, even when praying alone, as participants in the praying of the church. The principle is illustrated by an example MacIntyre uses – portrait painting.[11] Painting is something an individual does, so it is hard to see how this is a cooperative human activity. But the cooperation comes not primarily through persons interacting physically so much as it does through persons engaging in activities that gain their meaning from the *form* that emerges through a complex tradition of interactions among many people sustained over a long period of time. Portrait painting and private prayer are in this way social established forms of human activity, just as baseball is.

Conversely, the mere fact of a group of people doing something together does not mean we necessarily have a practice. Practice is participation in a cooperatively formed pattern of activity that emerges out of a complex tradition of interactions among many people sustained over a long period of time. This is what MacIntyre means when he says that a practice is "socially established." What is socially established is a "form" of human activity. Some cooperative human activities build up, over time, patterns of reciprocal expectations among participants, ways of doing things together by which the cooperative activity is given not only direction but also meaning and significance. The form itself comes to embody the reasons for the practice and the values intrinsic to it. This is why, in order to participate in a practice intelligently, one must become aware of the *history* of the practice.

A practice cannot be abstracted from its past, because the past is embedded in the practice itself. To abstract the practice from its tradition is to reduce the practice to a group activity. An implication of this feature of practices is that a practice cannot be made up, created on the spot by an individual or even a group. Because practices come into existence through a process of interaction among many people over a sustained period of time, individuals can only participate in them; they cannot create them. This does not mean, of course, that new practices never emerge or that established practices do not change. As people participate in practices, they are involved in their ongoing history and may in the process significantly reshape them. Practices may be deepened, enriched, extended, and to various extents be reformed and transformed. Individuals, usually persons profoundly competent in a practice, may have considerable historical effect on its shape and direction.

The "form" of a practice is related to its value. In order for a socially established activity to be a practice, its form must be "coherent" and "complex" enough to generate "goods internal to that form" that may be realized through participation in the practice. Taking long showers, says Stout, is not a practice.[12] As an activity, it lacks the coherence and complexity necessary for generating value internal to the activity itself. It can certainly generate "external goods" (smelling better, feeling more relaxed), but the activity itself cannot simply through our participation in it make us better people or involve us in a kind of life that is itself good. A practice may do this.

MacIntyre uses his example of the practice of portrait painting to make this point. There are two different kinds of goods internal to painting, he says. The first kind is "the excellence of the products, both the excellence in performance by the painters and that of each portrait itself." The second kind is "what the artist discovers within the pursuit of excellence in portrait painting," namely, "the good of a certain kind of life."[13] That is, things of value arise through engagement in the practice itself. Some of these things are products emerging from the practice; others are the effects of the practice on the practicing persons and their communities – including the effects on their minds, imaginations, and spirits.

The goods internal to a practice can be realized, according to MacIntyre, only by participating well in it. These goods "can only be identified and recognized by the experience of participating in the practice in question."[14] Baseball often seems an utter waste of time to those who do not participate in the practice. Only by getting inside the world of baseball, through playing the game, attending to its nuances, do its intrinsic values become evident. And, according to MacIntyre, we come to identify and recognize these goods more clearly and powerfully as we more fully satisfy the standards of excellence "appropriate to and, partially definitive of, that form of activity." Baseball may be played well or badly. It is baseball "at its best" that most clearly reveals the values embedded in it. Furthermore, the criteria revealed and by which a practice is ultimately to be judged are not entirely external criteria. Some of the criteria – indeed, often the most significant criteria – are intrinsic to the practice, criteria that constitute the practice as the practice it is. Moral standards and values are built into practices. Practices themselves bear moral weight.

We must go beyond MacIntyre, however, to make another claim about practices. Practices bear more than moral weight; they also bear epistemological weight. The point here is that in the context of participation in certain practices we come to see more than just the value, the "good" of certain human activities. Beyond that, we may come to awareness of certain *realities* that outside of these practices are beyond our ken. Engagement in certain practices may give rise to new knowledge.

Some of this knowledge may be almost entirely somatic in nature. A fine batter comes to "know" what a ball will do, and his body will "know" what to do to hit it. It is possible that without such somatic knowledge, other forms of cognition for which this is a prerequisite become impossible. Edward Farley reminds us also how "social relationships mediate realities [through] their capacity to effect new powers of perceptiveness" and suggests that "what is true for physical perception carries over, it seems, into the more subtle realms of insight or perceptiveness into various regions of reality; the nuances of poetry, the complex interrelations of a bureaucracy, the shadings of human vocabulary."[15]

But Farley points this out while making a larger, theological point that runs much deeper. He argues that under certain conditions changes in perceptivity may take place that bring more than simply new perspectives on things. Sometimes, new *realities* appear on the horizon to be apprehended, thus generating new knowledge. More specifically, within what Farley calls "the situation of faith" there come into being "states of affairs which at one time had no existence and which now have emerged in the course of history and individual existence."[16] In the situation of faith, these new realities include a new way of life, a new form of existence, which in turn presupposes a transcendent source and ground.

It is important to ask whether participation in certain practices provides physical, social, and even intellectual conditions necessary to knowledge intrinsic to the life of faith.[17] Marianne Sawicki has argued that the New Testament itself makes clear that certain practices are in fact conditions to the possibility of "recognizing the risen Lord." She contends that both Luke-Acts and Matthew posit the insufficiency of their own words and stipulate that "action on behalf of the needy is not an implication of resurrection faith, but a precondition for it. Talk about resurrection is literally meaningless in the absence of such action."[18] The claim is that engagement in the practice of service is a *condition* for the knowledge of a reality absolutely central to faith – the reality of resurrection presence.

III

We have put forward an understanding of practice that is quite different from the standard current picture. Alasdair MacIntyre's discussion of the nature of "practices" as fundamental features of the moral life has provided us a way to move forward. But in order to discern the significance of practice for Christian life, we have needed to move beyond MacIntyre's historical-moral claim to make epistemological-theological suggestions. Once we have reached this level of discussion, it begins to become clear how intrinsic practices are to the life of faith.

In the prevailing picture, practice cannot be intrinsic to or constitutive of a way of life. Practice understood technologically, individualistically, and ahistorically is practice reduced to the merely functional. But things are different with the alternative picture. Our identities as persons are constituted by practices and the knowledge and relationships they mediate. Some of these are so central to who we are that we cannot give them up without our very existence undergoing transformation. Correlatively, communal life is constituted by practices. Communities do not just engage in practices; in a sense, they *are* practices.[19]

Our suggestions obviously raise a host of questions on all fronts. What status do practices so defined really have? Under what conditions do certain practices in fact have power to create new perceptivities and even make accessible to us such realities as are central to the life of faith? What have been the practices by which Christian life in the world has been sustained across the centuries? What have people done, and what has their doing meant? How have their practices taken on different shape and meaning in various historical and cultural contexts? What have people come to see and know and be through participation in these practices? How has that happened? What agencies are involved – both immanent and transcendent – and how? Where are these practices still alive in some form in the contemporary world? What does participation in them involve? What are their consequences and effects? What are the grounds of their possibility?

These questions admit of no easy answers, but there are good reasons to raise them here. First, the prevailing conception of practice fails even to generate such questions. That is a sign of its poverty. Second, to answer such questions we must cross the lines that now divide biblical studies, European church history, Reformed systematic theology, and religious education, to cite a few specific curriculum areas in contemporary theological study, from one another. And clearly, a list of pastoral activities will do us no good.

The identification, study, and pursuit of practices that are central to and constitutive of Christian faith and life are, in my view, among the signal tasks of Christian theological study. This is especially true today, when this task has been singularly neglected. Answers to questions about practices are relatively simple when we are talking about baseball or even portrait painting. But matters become quite complicated when we attend to practices that have histories often going as far back as biblical times and further, practices that have been embodied in various ways in societies and situations around the globe. Moreover, in the context of theological study, we attend to practices of a form of life that claims to bear intimacy with God as well as world-transforming power.

That there would ever be unanimity on what the constitutive practices of Christian life are or at what levels of discourse they ought to be identified is unlikely. But it is best not to strive for common agreement in any case, because some ways of construing practices may serve some specific purposes and occasions better than others. I articulated a series of practices in a previously published essay. The list included such practices as interpreting scripture, worship and prayer, confession and reconciliation, service, witness, social criticism, and the mutual bearing of suffering.[20] Margaret Miles's recent book *Practicing Christianity: Critical Perspectives for an Embodied Spirituality* includes a section on "practices of Christian life." What she means by "practice" is consistent with the meaning we have been discussing here, and our lists overlap. She mentions a number of practices in her introduction and devotes a chapter each to ascetic practices, worship and sacraments, service, and prayer.[21] In these chapters, she poses some of the important questions we have suggested need pursuing.

[...]

The point here is neither to recommend a specific list of practices nor a particular way of identifying and studying them. The point is to call for their recognition and to suggest their centrality in Christian life and, hence, in theological study and theological education. Suppose that practices central to Christian life are conditions under which various kinds and forms of knowledge emerge – knowledge of God, of ourselves, and of the world; knowledge that is not only personal but also public. Suppose that through such practices, the virtues and character and wisdom of the communities and individuals who participate in them are formed. Suppose that through participation in practices of Christian life, the community of faith comes continually to awareness of and participation in the creative and redemptive activity of God in the world. If these suppositions are sustainable, practices deserve a pivotal place in Christian formation, theological study, and theological education.

IV

Edward Farley has suggested that we recover an understanding of theology as habitus.[22] I suggest that what such habitus involves is profound, life-orienting, identity-shaping participation in the constitutive practices of Christian life. If theology is habitus, then it follows that we learn theology (are formed in this habitus) by participation in these practices.

Participation in these practices, certainly participation at any significant level of depth and understanding, must be learned. We need more than just to be included in the practices. We need to come to understand them from the inside and to study and interpret carefully the realities we encounter through engagement in them.

In order to learn them and learn in the context of them, we need others who are competent in these practices to help us: to be our models, mentors, teachers, and partners in practice. We need people who will include us in these practices as they themselves are engaged in them and who will show us how to do what the practices require. We also need them to explain to us what these practices mean, what the reasons, understandings, insights, and values embedded in them are. And we need them to lure us and press us beyond our current understandings of and competence in these practices, to the point where we together may extend and deepen the practices themselves.

[...]

Participation in some of the practices of Christian life can and should occur naturally in the context of everyday life in a community constituted by them. But communities, especially in such culturally and socially fragmented situations as our own, cannot depend entirely upon this for initiating people into these practices and guiding them in them. The situation requires planned and systematic education in these practices. But such education must never be detached from participation in the practices; it cannot be satisfactory simply to describe and analyze them from afar.[23] Nonetheless, education must order this participation in such a way that all the practices are engaged in meaningfully and with understanding at increasingly broader and more complex levels. And that presupposes systematic and comprehensive education in the history and wider reaches of the practices as well as in the interpretation and criticism of the reasons and values embedded in the practices. This is true in the theological education of children and youth as well as in the education of adults.

The range of such education is still more extensive than this, however. None of us live only in communities constituted by such practices as we have articulated, and such practices never exist in a vacuum. We both live and learn in multiple social contexts and institutions, each of which is constituted by a much broader plurality of practices than those on which we have focused. Our wider intellectual, political, social, and occupational lives involve us all in a great variety of practices. And because such contexts naturally infiltrate faith communities, this broad spectrum of practices is internal to congregations, to theological seminaries, and even to convents. We all live our lives in an intersection of many practices.

Theological education must concern itself with the mutual influences that various practices have on each other, as well as whatever complementarity and/or conflict there may be between the goods internal to ecclesial practices and others. Because we are all citizens, for example, we must inquire into the nature, effects, and implications of our simultaneous engagement in practices constitutive of Christian life and those central to public politics. We need to inquire into the continuities and discontinuities between medical practice in our society and practices of care for the ill and the dying that now are and have in the past been characteristic of the church. Various intellectual disciplines (such as physics, literary studies, and psychology) are also practices in the sense we mean. Inquiries into the relations between disciplines (including those that are theological and those that are secular) engage us in similar issues and are thus central to theological study and theological education.

V

The understanding of practice we have been developing has manifold implications for theological inquiry and theological education. The constriction of the range of appropriate participants in theological education will need to be broken. The organization of theological study might well need to change significantly. And in response to both of these alterations, the kind of institutions responsible for theological education might well need to be significantly expanded and the educational processes structured by them considerably enriched.

[...]

Clergy, like all Christians, need to be formed and schooled in the practices of the life of Christian faith. This should not be just beginning when candidates enter a theological seminary or divinity school. Prerequisite to seminary education are not just certain studies in the liberal arts and sciences, but education in ecclesial practices. The theological education of clergy is dependent upon and should be continuous with the theological education these same people receive as lay people.

To presuppose much of an education along these lines may be, under present circumstances, to traffic in an ideal. Seminary or divinity school education is not the first exposure or context of participation people have to any practices of the life of Christian faith; otherwise, they would not be enrolled. But it may well be their first exposure to some of them. And it is likely to be their first opportunity to explore ways in which all of the practices are carried out in contexts beyond those they have personally experienced. Because these practices, understood as practices that take place worldwide and over a long history, are so central to Christian life and community, a key task in clergy education is to insure that all students are exposed to and participate in all of these practices in some context and at some level and become aware of the breadth and depth to which these practices may extend.

The continuity of the theological education of clergy with their previous theological education is premised on the fact that clergy are involved in the same fundamental practices as are all other Christians. But clergy have some responsibilities and roles that not all of us do. They are responsible not only for their own participation in the practices of Christian life. They are uniquely responsible for the participation of whole communities in them. This requires that they organize these practices corporately in a particular situation and insure that the people of that community, young and old, are initiated into them, guided in them, and led in them. It requires them to work to insure that all the practices are learned by everyone in breadth and in depth, in their increasing complexity, and with ever more profound understanding. It requires them to work to insure that the practices happen and that the dangerous proclivities of the institutionalization necessary to sustaining a community in these practices not subvert them.

Because clergy must be teachers of these practices in their own communities, it is essential that they know and understand the histories of these practices and the reasons, insights, values, and forms of judgment borne both by the traditions of which they are a part and by competent and wise contemporary engagement in them. But not only this. [...] Christian teachers are not ultimately teachers of practices; they are teachers of the gospel. The education that clergy are responsible for is education in truth and reality in and through those practices by which truth and reality may be made manifest.

[...]

The present system of curricular fields and departments of seminaries and divinity schools leaves much of this unattended. Under the dominance of the current picture of practice, practical theology attends either to other issues or to a stripped-down form of practice that reduces it to know-how. The other fields disregard practice almost entirely. But we do not have to reform the structure of departments and fields in order to ameliorate this situation considerably. Every field of seminary education currently existing has contributions to make to the understanding and interpretation of every one of these practices – if they become aware that these practices actually permeate their own subject matters and are, to various extents, actually or potentially implicated in the practice of their own disciplines.

In the Bible, for example, we can see all of these practices being carried out – and in a great variety of situations and circumstances. Moreover, the coming of the Bible into its present form is itself the engagement of a people in many of these practices, as the various forms of criticism clearly show. The case is similar with respect to the historical study of any era, dimension, text, or community of the Christian tradition. But historical studies are not the only relevant ones. The practices carry a broad and complex range of theological, ethical, and philosophical assumptions, convictions, insights, and reasonings, all of which are in need of exposure, display, and continuing scrutiny. Here the systematic disciplines come heavily into play. They are essential for helping communities and persons know what they are doing and why as they engage in these practices. They are also essential for the continuing criticism and reform of these practices, the goods internal to them, and the knowledge that they make possible.

This is not to assert that the curriculum of seminary education can or should be exhausted by attention to these practices or that the historical, theological, and philosophical investigation of these practices should define and circumscribe every field. It is more than enough to say that all of these fields and disciplines are relevant and necessary to the kind of systematic investigation and understanding of these practices that clergy require. And all of these fields could be enhanced by recognizing and making explicit this relevance and necessity.

At this point, one might ask, If education in the history and inner workings and meanings of these practices were actually taking place in the Bible, history, and theology departments of a school, and especially if this were done in relation to actual engagement in these practices, would there be anything left for a practical theology department to do? My own response to this question is ambivalent. Ideally, I am inclined to think probably not.

Realistically speaking, however, and short of an entire reformulation of the departmental structure of theological education, attending to the history, inner rationality, and truth of the practices may be enough to ask of the "academic" fields. For the time being at least, disciplined reflection on and engagement in the practices as such may have to fall to those who teach in the departments and curriculum area we now gather under such rubrics as social ethics, church and society, and practical theology. This would provide a context in which the practices and their engagement in the various concrete, contemporary situations and environments in which they are carried out would be *the* focusing subject matter. It would be the responsibility of such fields to articulate these practices, describe them, analyze them, interpret them, evaluate them, and aid in their reformation. It would also be their focal responsibility to help students participate actively in them in actual situations of the kind they do and will face in their roles as clergy.

This is a somewhat more traditional understanding of the function of practical theology departments than I myself am happy with, but even this would call for significant change in the way we currently conceive practical theology and social ethics. Furthermore, I believe that more radical revision of the current curriculum structure is unlikely, and I am sure that we will not get from where we are to where we might someday be in a single leap. Where these functions and issues do not yet permeate the curriculum as a whole, they must not be left unattended. At present, there may be no other choice than to give them to some particular curriculum area.

[...]

MacIntyre has said that "a living tradition...is an historically extended, socially embodied argument," and that the argument is "precisely in part about the goods which constitute that tradition."[24] I would add that it is also about the shape of the practices in the context of which those goods emerge and the truth and reality on which they are grounded and to which they point. If all this is what a living tradition is, then the shape of theological study and the contours of theological education ought to engage deeply the elements that are vital to it. Eminent among these for the Christian tradition are the practices central to its life.

Notes

1 With regard to the theological education of clergy, the main focus has been on problems in "practical theology" as a department of teaching or area of study. Some (particularly professors in other departments) say practical theology is too much oriented to teaching people how to carry out certain procedures in church life (such as managing conflict in a group, organizing budgets, teaching a class, giving a sermon, or counseling with a couple having marital difficulties). Others (particularly recent graduates who don't know how to do these things) plead for more of such teaching, not less. Some regard practical theology as far too untheological and overly dependent upon such nontheological disciplines as psychology and sociology and studies in organizational behavior and communications theory. Others say that practical theology is not disciplined enough by the social sciences, is always picking up what has become popularized and out of date, and thus is trailing years behind and is superficial at that.

The confusion regarding these and many other problems is so great that, according to Edward Farley, "'practical theology' may prove not to be a salvageable term. The term is still in use as a term some seminary faculty members use to locate their teaching in the curriculum of clergy education. As such it functions more as a rubric for self-interpretation and location on the curricular map than a name for a discrete phenomenon. So varied are the approaches and proffered definitions of practical theology in recent literature that it is not even clear what is under discussion." (See "Interpreting Situations: An Inquiry into the Nature of Practical Theology," in *Formation and Reflection: The Promise of Practical Theology*, eds. Lewis S. Mudge and James N. Poling (Philadelphia: Fortress Press, 1987), 1. For a sampling of some of the proposals Farley refers to, including Farley's own, see the various chapters in *Formation and Reflection*; Don S. Browning, ed., *Practical Theology: The Emerging Field in Theology, Church and World*

(San Francisco: Harper & Row, 1983); and the many other articles and books referred to in the bibliographies included in these two works.)

The problems redound not only on practical theology, however. The inadequacy of our current picture of practice also creates problems for other areas of theological study and theological education. When practice means the application of theory to contemporary procedure, biblical studies, history, systematic theology, philosophy, and ethics all become theoretical disciplines in which practice has no intrinsic place. This is a problem not only because of the usual pedagogical complaints heard about such disciplines by those who want from them something immediately usable, but also for reasons intrinsic to the meaning of the disciplines themselves. For when practice is rightly understood, the "academic" disciplines are themselves seen to be practices; it also becomes clear how their subject matter includes practices. Thus, when "practice" is entirely relegated to something called "practical theology," certain features intrinsic to the "academic" theological fields are hidden; they themselves become distorted, fragmented, and overly dependent upon and conformed to university disciplines and their secular, Enlightenment assumptions; and their own point, or telos, as dimensions of theological study is then obscured.

A major problem for congregations, as Farley has pointed out, is that congregations are left without theological study altogether when theological study is identified with "clergy education." (See *Theologia: The Fragmentation and Unity of Theological Education* (Philadelphia: Fortress Press, 1983), chaps. 2 and 7; and esp., *The Fragility of Knowledge: Theological Education in the Church and the University* (Philadelphia: Fortress Press, 1988), chap. 5.) This is a tragic loss. But the answer is not simply to reduplicate clergy education in churches. This is sometimes attempted, but the outcome is almost always the transmission of some of the tips and techniques clergy may have picked up from their own studies of "practice" plus some of the "contents" garnered from their studies in the "academic" fields. And both are watered down and left bereft of the understandings, assumptions, and skills that make theological inquiry sustainable in local church settings. As a result, communities of faith are left with the effluvium of theological study.

The current picture of practice is not, of course, alone responsible for these problems. But it is a major contributing factor that, unless reconceived, will continue to plague communities of faith, theology, and theological education in seminaries and divinity schools.

2   See Farley, *Theologia*, esp. 84–8, 127–35.

3   See Alasdair MacIntyre, *After Virtue* (Notre Dame: University of Notre Dame Press, 1981), chap. 15, on the necessity of a social and narrative-historical account of any action that is to be rendered intelligible.

4   In a few cases, more sophisticated connections are made, so that ways such studies can indeed provide theoretical guidance to practice become more evident. I have in mind here, as an example, Marianne Sawicki, *The Gospel in History* (New York: Paulist Press, 1988). Sawicki both rethinks what practice is (though she does not use this language to talk about what she is doing) and uses revisionist historiographical methods to get at it in the Bible and in the Christian tradition. See also her essays: "Historical Methods and Religious Education," *Religious Education* 82, no. 3 (Summer 1987), 375–89 and "Recognizing the Risen Lord," *Theology Today* 44, no. 4 (January 1988), 441–9. The kind of thing Sawicki does requires, however, that we see the "academic" disciplines as involving practice – both as method and subject matter. And this, in turn, presses toward a different understanding of practice than that contained within the prevailing picture. It leads, I believe, to the kind of alternative I will be suggesting.

5 In view of this, some have simply defined the problem away by substituting the single word "praxis" for the phrase "theory and practice." But "thought-filled practice," which is what many seem to mean by "praxis," is what good practice involves anyway, and the regular appearance of the oddity "theory and praxis" proves that nothing is really solved by a name change.

6 Another indication is the inattention to practice that prevails in most history departments in theological schools. Such departments normally do not give systematic attention to the practices of, say, Christian education, homiletics, pastoral care, and so forth. Nor do they seem to attempt systematic connection between the history they teach and the practices their students are supposedly going to be engaged in after graduation. There are several possible reasons for this. One may be that historians simply do not care about practice. Another may be that they assume that it is taken care of by the people in the practical department. More likely, however, the current picture of practice, which both historians and practical theologians assume, keeps each at some distance from the concerns of the other, giving neither group much to think historically about. [...]

7 See related comments on this point in Farley, *The Fragility of Knowledge*, 10–11: "Empirical method has stunning success in understanding very specific causal relations. When isolated from all correctives, [however,] it loses the concrete reality in its complexity and, with this, the conditions of criticizing itself. Isolated, it tends to become a paradigm of reality itself, but of reality without the social and political contexts of knowledge, reality dispersed into abstract formulas or causal sequences, reality absented from the deposits of the past's wisdom....Praxis isolated becomes situational abstraction."

8 Important sources of this criticism are: Robert N. Bellah, Richard Madsen, William M. Sullivan, Ann Swidler, and Steven M. Tipton, *Habits of the Heart: Individualism and Commitment in American Life* (Berkeley: University of California Press, 1985); Hans-Georg Gadamer, *Truth and Method (New* York: Crossroad, 1975), and *Reason in the Age of Science* (Cambridge: MIT Press, 1981); Stanley Hauerwas, *Vision and Virtue* (Notre Dame: Fides Publishers, 1974), and *The Peaceable Kingdom: A Primer in Christian Ethics* (Notre Dame: University of Notre Dame Press, 1983); Christopher Lasch, "The Communitarian Critique of Liberalism," *Soundings* 69 (1986): 60–76; Alasdair MacIntyre, *Against the Self Images of the Age* (Notre Dame: University of Notre Dame Press, 1978), and *Whose Justice? Which Rationality?* (Notre Dame: University of Notre Dame Press, 1988); Michael Sandel, *Liberalism and the Limits of Justice* (Cambridge: Cambridge University Press, 1982); Thomas L. Shaffer, *Faith and the* Professions (Provo, Utah: Brigham Young University Press, 1987); and Jeffrey Stout, *The Flight from Authority* (Notre Dame: University of Notre Dame Press, 1981), and *Ethics After Babel* (Boston: Beacon Press, 1988). The most important single text, however, is Alasdair MacIntyre's *After Virtue.*

9 MacIntyre, *After Virtue*, 175. MacIntyre's understanding of practice comes in the middle of chap. 14 on "The Nature of the Virtues" and is developed in important ways in the next chapter on "The Virtues, the Unity of a Human Life and the Concept of a Tradition." [...] For a briefer but extremely helpful presentation of MacIntyre's understanding of practice, see Stout, *Ethics After Babel*, chap. 12.

10 See Stout, *Ethics After Babel*, esp. 276, 303.

11 MacIntyre, *After Virtue*, 177.

12 Stout, *Ethics After Babel*, 303.

13 MacIntyre, *After Virtue*, 177.

14 MacIntyre, *After Virtue*, 176.

15 Edward Farley, *Ecclesial Man* (Philadelphia: Fortress Press, 1975), 213.

16 Ibid., 214, 215. See also pp. 215–231 for Farley's argument concerning apprehended "realities-at-hand" and the realities they "appresent" that are not accessible to direct apprehension.

17 In raising this point, we are not suggesting that any practice in and of itself provides *sufficient* conditions. As Farley makes clear, these conditions are many and deeply interrelated. They are comprised in what he calls the "faith-world," the key structures of which are its language, the co-intentionalities of its intersubjectivity, and its experience of the redemptive modification of existence. Lacking the category of "practices," however, Farley is forced to leap from these deep-structural levels to institutions and situations or events without benefit of any mediating form of concrete social structure. His accurate awareness of the dangers to the faith world of institutionalization makes him sometimes pessimistic about the sustainability of the life-world of Christian faith, as well as frustratingly abstract to his readers. The idea of "practices," we would suggest, provides a level of analysis more concrete than "life-worlds," less rigid than institutions, and more sustained and sustainable than situations and events.

18 Sawicki, "Recognizing the Risen Lord," 449.

19 "Practices" names what I believe Lewis S. Mudge tries to lift up. […] (See "Thinking in the Community of Faith: Toward an Ecclesial Hermeneutic," in *Formation and Reflection*, eds. Mudge and Poling, 107, 116–17.) Practices are indeed "networks of signifying action and interaction," and they are not to be identified with institutions. As Stout points out: "[…] Institutions also "typically pose significant moral threats to the social practices they make possible" primarily because "institutions necessarily trade heavily in external goods," and such goods "can compete with and even engulf goods internal to [a] practice" *(Ethics After Babel*, 274).

20 See "No Longer Strangers," *Princeton Seminary Bulletin* 6, no. 3 (November 1985), 188–200. A revised version of this listing plus some discussion of the rationale for it appears in a paper adopted for study by the General Assembly of The Presbyterian Church (USA), which I helped to write. See "Growing in the Life of Christian Faith," *Minutes of the 201st General Assembly* (1989), Part II (Louisville: Office of the Stated Clerk, 1990), 38.087–38.231.

21 Margaret Miles, *Practicing Christianity: Critical Perspectives for an Embodied Spirituality* (New York: Crossroad, 1988), 87–144. […]

22 See Farley, *Theologia*, 31, 35–6, 151–73. With the word *habitus*, Farley is suggesting a meaning of theology that refers to "a state and disposition of the soul which has the character of knowledge." The nature of this knowledge is "*practical*, not theoretical, habit having the primary character of wisdom" (p. 35). Later, in *The Fragility of Knowledge*, Farley defines theology as "the reflectively procured insight and understanding which encounter with a specific religious faith evokes" (p. 64). I prefer his earlier understanding of theology as wisdom, which includes, in my view, not only insight and understanding but also the kind of judgment, skill, commitment, and character that full participation in practices both requires and nurtures.

23 […] Though Farley is right about the need for ordered learning, he seems to restrict it primarily to the analysis and interpretation of the cognitive products of practices. […] Some criticize Farley's approach as being thereby too cognitive in orientation. That is not my problem with him. I believe theological education ought to be very cognitive. The reason, however, is not that our subject matter is the cognitive products of practices, but that cognition is vitally important to and involved in the practices themselves.

Further, we must be careful not to fall into understandings of cognition (and interpretation) that are too limited in scope, as I believe Farley has. Howard Gardner, in *Frames of Mind: The Theory of Multiple Intelligences* (New York: Basic Books, 1985), articulates seven different kinds of intelligence: linguistic, musical, logical-mathematical, spatial, bodily-kinesthetic, and two personal forms (one, the capacity to have access to the shape and range of one's own feeling life, and the other, "the ability to notice and make distinctions among other individuals and, in particular, among their moods, temperaments, motivations, and intentions" (p. 239)). Each of these intelligences is somewhat distinct, according to Gardner, and each involves modes of insight, interpretation, and expression characteristic of it. Farley seems to identify both cognition and interpretation with linguistic and logical-mathematical intelligence, leaving the others completely unattended to. I would argue that *all* these forms of intelligence are involved in theology-habitus and that all of them must be systematically engaged in theological education at every level.

24 MacIntyre, *After Virtue*, 207.

23

Phronesis and the Rebirth of Practical Theology (1991)*

Don S. Browning

Introduction

During the last decade of the twentieth century, Don S. Browning was one of the most influential scholars in practical theology's renewal in the United States and internationally. His wide-ranging intellectual interests supported a more comprehensive definition of practical theology. After studying at the University of Chicago in the 1960s in Hiltner's wake, his career on the faculty there stretched across three doctoral areas: he began in religion and psychological studies; he created a new area for practical theology; and when both of these areas lost institutional support, he gravitated to ethics. His scholarship addressed divergent audiences – pastoral care and theology, religion and the social sciences, ethics, and practical theology. He sought a wide non-Christian public, speaking, for example, with psychiatrists on impact of "psychological man," with therapists about values in counseling, and with lawyers on crises in modern families. His final book proposed a "Christian humanism," which could advocate for the public role of religious traditions and values in contrast to the extremes of both religious fundamentalism and secular atheism.

Occasionally, Browning would remark that many book-length treatments of a subject begin with a good article. Such is the case here. This essay is essentially a trial run on his longer book, *Fundamental Practical Theology* (1991), which came out the same year and had an extended impact on the field, representing for a time the state of the art in the discipline. Some people find the book cumbersome in its cryptic references to major scholars and philosophical theories, and many US pastoral theologians who already disliked his turn to ethics in pastoral care (see Ch. 20 in this volume) believed that his abstractions in this book forfeited the very best insights of a pastoral orientation. Browning's chapter appeared originally in the same collection as Craig Dykstra's essay on reconceiving practices. But by contrast with Dykstra's close examination of a fundamental concept, Browning takes on the entire arrangement of theological education and proposes, in essence, a "theory of the structure of theological studies" comparable to frameworks by the likes of Schleiermacher, Tillich, Schubert Ogden, and David Tracy.

Original publication details: Don S. Browning, "Toward a Fundamental and Strategic Practical Theology," pp. 53–74 from *Practical Theology: International Perspectives*, eds. Friedrich Schweiter and Johannes A. van der Ven (Frankfurt: Peter Lang, 1999). Reprinted from *Shifting Boundaries: Contextual Approaches to the Structure of Theological Education*, 1991.

The Wiley Blackwell Reader in Practical Theology, First Edition. Edited by Bonnie J. Miller-McLemore.
© 2019 John Wiley & Sons Ltd. Published 2019 by John Wiley & Sons Ltd.

This essay comes after Rebecca Chopp's pointed critique of liberal practical theology (see Ch. 21). But Browning does not acknowledge or respond to the problems that she itemizes. In his account of the turn to practice, he only recognizes European philosophers, seeming to confirm Juan Luis Segundo's worry (see Ch. 19) that terms lifted up and redefined by liberation theology, such as *praxis*, will get misused.

Nonetheless, despite these limits, this essay shows where the conversation stood in 1991 and distills key ideas from practical philosophy that have proven helpful in providing a method for doing theology in practice. Here we discover yet another definition of theology as *habitus* – a "practice-theory-practice" movement across four fronts. Understanding this movement and redefinition of theology as "practical through and through" may be most useful pedagogically, as his creative teaching example underscores (see especially the section on CPE where he discusses a pedagogical exercise that he used in class). Students doing ministerial projects and pastors in religious communities have used the submovements that he describes – descriptive, historical, systematic, and strategic – to address problems in ministry. Richard Osmer's *Practical Theology: An Introduction* (2008) is actually a modified rendition of this "fundamental practical theology," breaking down its four parts and showing how ministers might implement them in ministry.

Suggested Further Reading

- Don S. Browning, *Fundamental Practical Theology: Descriptive and Strategic Proposals* (Minneapolis: Fortress, 1991).
- Thomas Groome, *Christian Religious Education* (San Francisco: Harper & Row, 1980).
- Hans-Georg Gadamer, *Truth and Method* (New York: Crossroad, 1982).

***

Recent philosophical currents have taught us much about the practical nature of human knowledge. The hermeneutical philosophy of Gadamer and Ricoeur, the critical theory of Habermas, the ordinary language philosophy of Wittgenstein, Peters, and Winch, the pragmatism of Peirce, James, and Dewey, the neo-pragmatism of Bernstein and Rorty, and the philosophy of science of Thomas Kuhn all in different ways argue for the priority of practical interests in the formation of our cognitive and moral worlds.[1] Historical reason and practical reason, under the impact of Heidegger and Gadamer, are now seen by many as intimately related, if not identical. If these views are correct, the way we view the past as largely shaped by our present concerns as indeed the way that we deal with the present involves a reconstruction of the past.

These intellectual currents are influencing theological education and the way we envision the structure and movement of theology. This is especially true in the writings on theological education that have come from the pen of Edward Farley. The concern with the historicity of knowledge and the importance of the interpretation of situations for the integrity of theological education have been quite prominent in his writings.[2] The heightened prominence of practical knowledge can also be seen in the proposals of Joseph Hough and John Cobb to make "practical theological thinking" and "practical theology" the center of their reform of theological education.[3]

In addition to this appreciation for the practical in these systematic attempts to reformulate theological education, there is additional scattered evidence of the rebirth of the practical in theological education. New efforts to redefine practical theology can be found in Germany, Holland, England, Canada, and Latin America, as well as the United States.[4] These more recent formulations greatly enlarge the province of practical theology. Rather than envisioning practical theology as primarily theological reflection on the tasks of the ordained minister or the leadership of the church, as was the view of Schleiermacher,[5] these newer trends define practical theology as critical theological reflection on the church's ministry to the world.[6] In the United States, two volumes of essays[7] plus several books dealing explicitly with the reconceptualization of practical theology by Browning, Fowler, Gerkin, Groome, Schreiter, Winquist, Miller and Poling, and McCann and Strain all point to the breadth and vigor of this renewed interest in practical theology.[8]

In spite of this new interest in the practical in recent reconceptualizations of theological education and in practical theology, it is my conviction that the radical implications of the turn to "practical philosophy" have still not been comprehended fully in theological education circles. It seems not to be understood that, if this philosophical turn is taken seriously, all humanistic studies, including theological studies, are practical and historical through and through. In this view, all theology becomes practical theology; historical theology, systematic theology, and what I will call "strategic" practical theology become moments within a more inclusive fundamental practical theology. Furthermore, since much of the turn to practical philosophy is presently characterized by an emphasis on dialogue and conversation, I will define fundamental practical theology as *critical reflection on the church's dialogue with Christian sources and other communities with the aim of guiding its action toward social and individual transformation.*

The Rebirth of Practical Theology

I use the phrase "practical philosophy" to refer to a loosely associated group of philosophical positions that emphasize the importance of practical wisdom or *phronesis* in contrast to the modem fascination with *theoria* (theoretical knowledge and thinking) or *techne* (technical knowledge and thinking). Since the Enlightenment, the modern experiment increasingly has been dedicated to the improvement of human life through the increase of objective scientific knowledge that is then applied to the technical solution of human problems. The modern university has built itself on the idea of increasing our cognitive grasp of the universe. Issues pertaining to the goals of human action are generally reduced to the technical solution of perceived problems. The goals of action increasingly are held to be self-evident, thought to be a matter of individual choice, or taken over uncritically from the surrounding culture. The rebirth of practical philosophy is designed to question the dominance of theoretical and technical reason, to secure in the university a stronger role for practical reason, to demonstrate that critical reflection about the goals of human action is both possible and necessary, and that, as a matter of fact, practical reason does indeed function in much wider areas of human life than we realize – even, in fact, in the social and natural sciences. Furthermore, the rise of the practical philosophies, especially as influenced by Gadamer, has brought into closer relation historical thinking, hermeneutics, and practical reason or ethics.

These features of the practical philosophies can best be illustrated by examining certain aspects of the thought of Hans-Georg Gadamer. Many of Gadamer's interpreters have overlooked the strong relation he believes to exist between understanding and what Aristotle called practical wisdom or *phronesis*. He writes, "if we relate Aristotle's description of the ethical phenomenon and especially of the virtue of moral knowledge to our own investigation, we find that Aristotle's analysis is in fact a kind of model of the problems of hermeneutics."[9] Gadamer makes this point in discussing the role of application in both his view of understanding and Aristotle's concept of *phronesis*. The hermeneutic process aimed at the understanding of a classic text is, for Gadamer, like a moral conversation when moral is understood in the broadest sense. The hermeneutical conversation is like Aristotle's concept of practical wisdom because neither applies abstract universals to concrete situations. In both hermeneutical conversation and moral judgment, concern with application is there from the beginning.

Hence, understanding or interpretation, whether in law, history, or theology, has for Gadamer from the outset a broadly moral concern with application. As Gadamer writes, "application is neither a subsequent nor a merely occasional part of the phenomenon of understanding, but co-determines it as a whole from the beginning."[10] Understanding is a kind of moral conversation with a text or historic witness shaped throughout by practical concerns about application that emerge from our current situation.

Hence, more than we sometimes have acknowledged, hermeneutics is a broadly moral conversation with a tradition's classic religio-cultural monuments in which concern with practical application shapes from the beginning the questions that we bring to these monuments. When seen from this perspective, understanding and *phronesis* as practical wisdom interpenetrate and overlap. Richard Bernstein astutely makes this observation when he writes that it is a central thesis of Gadamer's *Truth and Method* (1975) that understanding, interpretation, and application are not distinct but intimately related. Bernstein writes,

> They are internally related; every act of understanding involves interpretation, and all interpretation involves application. It is Aristotle's analysis of *phronesis* that, according to Gadamer, enables us to understand the distinctive way in which application is an essential moment of the hermeneutical experience.[11]

Rather than application to practice being an act that follows understanding, concern with practice, in subtle ways we often overlook, guides the hermeneutic process from the beginning. Gadamer's hermeneutic theory clearly breaks down the theory-to-practice (text-to-application) model of humanistic learning. By analogy, it undercuts this model in theological studies as well. The model it implies is more nearly a radical practice-theory-practice model of understanding which gives the entire theological enterprise a thoroughly practical cast.

The practical nature of the hermeneutical process is even more interesting and complicated when considered from the perspective of Gadamer's theory of "effective history." Gadamer develops the idea that the events of the past shape present historical consciousness. As Gadamer writes, there is a "fusion of the whole of the past with the present."[12] This suggests that when we interpret the classic religious texts of the past, we do not confront them as totally separate and alien entities, even if we consider ourselves unbelievers. Rather, these texts are already part of the believer and unbeliever before they begin their interpretation. Through our cultural heritage these monuments of culture shape the fore-concepts and prejudices that make up the practical questions that we bring to our efforts to interpret the monuments themselves. The understanding process, finally, is depicted by Gadamer as a fusion of horizons between the practical questions and fore-concepts that we bring to our classic texts and the meaning and horizon of these texts and the questions they put to us.[13]

Gadamerian hermeneutic theory has profound implications for the reconceptualization of the full range of university studies. Not only does it have implications for the reenvisionment of the purposes of philosophy, the social sciences, and theology, but Richard Bernstein and Richard Rorty, with different degrees of debt to Gadamer, have carried hermeneutic theory into the philosophy of the natural sciences.[14] Earlier Thomas Kuhn's own variety of hermeneutic theory helped first alert us to the tradition-laden and historically situated nature of the natural sciences.[15] These contemporary movements all have undercut foundationalist preoccupations with objectivity and have helped us understand how *all Geisteswissenschaften,* and perhaps the *Naturwissenschaften* as well, can best be understood as dialectical movements from theory-laden practice to theory and back to a new theory-laden practice.

A Preliminary Sketch of the Structure of Theological Studies

So far I have not argued that Gadamer's hermeneutical theory is a correct model for the humanities. Nor have I argued that his view of hermeneutics is more sound than the subjective and idealistic models of hermeneutics of Schleiermacher and Dilthey. My goal has been to present an interpretation of Gadamer that emphasizes a point that is often lost, i.e., that there is an intimate relation in his thought between the hermeneutical process and practical wisdom or *phronesis.* Hence, my argument is addressed to those already attracted by the conversational model of hermeneutics. Guided by his view of the practical nature of understanding and the hermeneutic task, I would like to propose a theory of the structure of theological studies.

I recommend that we conceive of theology as primarily fundamental practical theology that contains within it the four submovements of descriptive theology, historical theology, systematic theology, and what I call *strategic* practical theology. This view differs from several well-known proposals for the organization of theology. For instance, it differs somewhat from Schleiermacher's organization of theology into philosophical theology, historical theology, and practical theology.[16] Although Schleiermacher saw practical theology as the teleological goal and "crown" of theology, his view of theology still had a theory-to-practice structure; he understood theology as a movement from philosophical and historical theology to application in practical theology.[17] It is true that this structure is somewhat mitigated by the fact that Schleiermacher understood the whole of theology as a "positive" science in contrast to a "pure" or theoretical science. By positive science, Schleiermacher meant "an assemblage of scientific elements which belong together not because they form a constituent part of the organization of the sciences, as though by some necessity arising out of the notion of science itself, but only insofar as they are requisite for carrying out a practical task."[18] Such a view of theology clearly emphasizes the practical, conditioned, and historically located nature of all theology and goes far toward making all of theology a basically practical task. Nonetheless, Schleiermacher saw theology as moving from historical knowledge to practical application and, in addition, had little idea about how the practices of the contemporary church play back into the way we bring our questions to the historical sources.

My proposal also can be distinguished from other current understandings of the structure of theology. Paul Tillich divided theology into historical theology, systematic theology, and practical theology.[19] In the end, this too was a theory-topractice model even though Tillich granted that practical theology has a role in formulating the questions that systematic theology answers.[20] Regardless of this minor admission, the weight of his perspective clearly emphasized the theory – practice dichotomy. In his systematic theology he wrote,

> It is the technical point of view that distinguishes practical from theoretical theology. As occurs in every cognitive approach to reality, a bifurcation between pure and applied knowledge takes place in theology.[21]

This statement is softened somewhat by the fact that Tillich saw the entire theological task as an existential enterprise, but even here "meaning" rather than the reconstruction of practice was the central thrust of his existential view of theology.

Both Schubert Ogden and David Tracy give heightened visibility to practical theology in their respective proposals for the organization of theology. Ogden indicates in a number of ways that he believes that practical theology is the application to practice of the truth of norms discovered by historical and systematic theology. He proposes a division of theology into historical, systematic, and practical. He gives a strongly cognitive definition of theology proper (systematic theology) as the task of "understanding the meaning of the Christian witness and assessing its truth…." And he believes that theology as critical reflection on the truth of the Christian faith should be distinguished from what he calls "witness".[22]

A Revised Correlational Fundamental Practical Theology

My proposal takes its point of departure from the revisionist view of theology found in the work of my colleague David Tracy. But whereas Tracy divides theology into fundamental theology, systematic theology, and practical theology, I reverse his pattern by proposing a revised correlational fundamental practical theology that has within it the subspecialties of descriptive, historical theology, systematic theology, and strategic practical theology.

The strength of Tracy's proposal is that it is a revised or critical correlational approach to theology. Its weakness is that his vision of fundamental theology is concerned primarily with the conditions for cognitive and metaphysical verification. The principle criteria for the verification of the truth of fundamental theological claims are thought by Tracy to be "transcendental."[23] Although even in his fundamental theology Tracy builds significantly on the hermeneutical theory of Gadamer and Ricoeur, he seems not to acknowledge that it is a fundamental practical theology that philosophical hermeneutics suggests rather than a fundamental theology concerned primarily with questions of cognitive and transcendental verification.[24]

However, the strength of Tracy's view of theology is easily applicable to a fundamental practical theology. But because of Tracy's revisionist correlational commitments, it would be a critical correlational fundamental practical theology. Fundamental theology, according to Tracy, determines the conditions for the possibility of the theological enterprise. If the conditions are strongly influenced by the close association between hermeneutics and *phronesis* as I outlined above, then fundamental theology determines the conditions for the possibility of a theology that would be seen first of all as an enterprise that deals with the normative and critical grounds of our religious *praxis.* Questions of the truth of Christian belief and conviction would be addressed as issues that are derivative of issues pertaining to practice.

Tracy's revised correlational theology is a *critical* correlational program. The meaning of this can be stated with reference to his understanding of Tillich's correlational approach to theology. Tillich believed that theology is correlation of existential questions that emerge from cultural experience with answers from the Christian message.[25] Tracy's revised or critical correlational method goes beyond Tillich in envisioning theology as a mutually critical dialogue between the Christian message and contemporary cultural experience. Christian theology becomes a critical dialogue between the questions and the answers of the Christian faith and the questions and answers of cultural experience. In fact, according to Tracy, the Christian theologian is obliged to have this critical conversation in principle with "all other 'answers.'"[26]

When Tracy applies the revised correlational model to practical theology, the following definition emerges: "...practical theology is the mutually critical correlation of the interpreted theory and praxis of the Christian faith with the interpreted theory and praxis of the contemporary situation."[27] I propose that this excellent definition of practical theology be extended to become the definition of a fundamental practical theology. Furthermore, this fundamental practical theology should be the most inclusive definition of theology, making descriptive, historical, systematic, and strategic practical theology submoments within the larger framework.

This view insists that the description of situated and theory-laden religious and cultural practices is the first movement of both theology and theological education. That is why I suggest that we call this first movement descriptive theology. Questions of the following kind guide this moment of theological reflection: What, within a particular arena of practice, are we actually doing? What reasons, ideals, and symbols do we use to interpret what we are doing? What do we consider to be the sources of authority and legitimation for what we do? The description of these practices engenders questions about what we really should be doing and about the accuracy and consistency of our use of our preferred sources of authority and legitimation. For those who claim to be Christians, this process inevitably leads to a fresh confrontation with the normative texts and monuments of the Christian faith – the source of the norms of practice. Historical theology becomes the heart of the hermeneutical process, but it is now understood as a matter of putting the questions emerging from theory-laden practice to the central texts and monuments of the Christian faith.

This is the second movement within theology and theological education. The question that guides historical theology is, what do the normative texts that are already a part of our effective history "really" imply for our praxis when they are confronted as carefully and honestly as possible? This is the place where the traditional disciplines of biblical studies, church history, and the history of Christian thought are to be located. But in this scheme, these disciplines and all of their technical literary-historical, textual, and social scientific explanatory interests would be understood as basically practical hermeneutical enterprises. Their technical, explanatory, and *distancing* maneuvers would be temporary procedures designed to gain clarity within a larger hermeneutic effort to achieve understanding about our praxis and the theory behind it.[28]

The third movement is the turn to systematic theology. Systematic theology, when seen from the perspective of Gadamer's hermeneutics, is the fusion of horizons between the vision implicit in contemporary practices and the vision entailed in the practices of the normative Christian texts. This process of fusion between the present and the past is much different from a simple application of the past to the present. Systematic theology tries to gain as comprehensive a view of the present as possible. It tries to examine large encompassing themes about our present practices and the theory and vision latent in them. The systematic character of this moment of theology comes from the effort to investigate general themes of the Gospel that respond to the most generic questions that characterize the situation of the present. This may entail questions which emerge out of the theory-laden practices of such general trends as modernity, liberal democracy, or technical rationality. There is a role for systematic theology within a fundamental practical theology, but it is a submoment or specific movement within a larger practical framework.

Two fundamental questions guide systematic theology. The first is what new horizon of meaning is fused when the questions coming from our present practice are brought to the central Christian witness? The second is, what reasons can be advanced to support the validity claims of the new horizon of meaning that comes from the fusion of present and past? This last question points to the additional obligation of systematic theology to introduce a critical and philosophical component into the theological process. There is, for instance, a role for transcendental judgments in critically testing the metaphysical claims of the Christian faith. But even more practical claims of the Christian faith need to be tested philosophically. And in the order of things suggested here, transcendental questions are the last rather than the first validity claims to be defended. This is true because many areas of collaboration between Christians and non-Christians are frequently developed without the resolution of transcendental claims. Furthermore, many reflective Christians themselves justify their faith on primarily practical grounds even though they are quite unclear about the validity of its metaphysical claims. [...]

My emphasis on the importance to hermeneutics of defending validity claims implicit in these new horizons places me in some tension with Gadamer. Habermas and Bernstein have severely criticized Gadamer for being a traditionalist and for having no method to test the adequacy of the horizons that emerge out of the hermeneutic conversations between the questions of the present and the witness of the classic texts and monuments.[29] To develop the general criteria for testing the practical validity claims of the Christian faith is the task of theological ethics. Theological ethics in turn should be seen as a dimension of systematic theology. This, in fact, is the way it generally has been conceived in the history of the Protestant encyclopedia.[30] [...]

And finally, the fourth movement of theology and of theological education is what I am calling *strategic practical theology*. I have chosen the word strategic to distinguish this form of practical theology from fundamental practical theology which is, I am proposing, the most inclusive term for the theological task. There are four basic questions of strategic practical theology. First, how do we understand this concrete situation in which we must act? (The concern with the concrete features of situations in contrast to their general features is what distinguishes strategic practical theology from systematic theology.) Second, what should be our praxis in this concrete situation? Third, what means, strategies, and rhetorics should we use in this situation? And fourth, how do we critically defend the norms of our *praxis* in this concrete situation? By *praxis*, I do not just mean ethical practice in any narrow sense of that word, although I certainly mean that in part. *Praxis* here refers to all the realms of strategic practical theology—ethical, educational, homiletic, liturgic, and poimenic (care). For all these areas questions of norms, rhetorics, and strategies are relevant. At the same time, the ethical component does have a unique relevance to all of these realms. But in this fourth moment, ethics has to do with the concrete situations rather than the general features of situations typical of the ethical interests of systematic theology. The range of questions that guide strategic practical theology helps us to understand the complexity of both this moment of theology and this aspect of theological education. This is the place of theology where the interpretation of present situations comes together with both the hermeneutical process and our final critical efforts to advance justifications for the relative adequacy of the new horizons of meaning that hermeneutics has brought into existence. It is indeed the crown, as Schleiermacher said, of the theological task. But strategic practical theology is no longer the application to practice of the theoretical yield of Bible, church history and systematic theology as it was in the old Protestant quadrivium. Concern with questions of practice and application, as Gadamer has argued, has been persent from the beginning. Strategic practical theology is more the culmination of an inquiry that has been practical throughout than it is the application of theory to the specifics of *praxis*.

The traditional fields associated with practical theology will still be present. These might include liturgics, homiletics, education, and care. But in keeping with the move to go beyond yet include the clerical paradigm, strategic practical theology is concerned with areas of *praxis* that relate to the church's activity in the world as well as its ministries within its own walls. Therefore a practical theology of care is not just *pastoral* care; it has to do with the church's strategy to create and influence the structures of care in society, most of which are allegedly secular. The same is true with education; it entails not only concern with the religious education of the faithful but with the goals and purposes of all education in modem societies. This view also would include liturgics and homiletics. They would not only be concerned with the church's internal worship and preaching; they also would be concerned with the public liturgics and public rhetoric in both the church and the rest of society. As I indicated above, theological ethics as concerned with the concrete contexts of action would be an abiding concern touching all of these traditional regions of practical theology.

[...] Let me conclude this section on strategic practical theology by pointing to how this moment of theology plays back on the entire hermeneutic circle. [...] The practices that emerge from the judgments of strategic practical theology will themselves soon engender new questions that start the hermeneutical circle again. Within the flux and turns of history our present practices only seem secure for a period before they meet a crisis and pose new questions that take us through the hermeneutical circle once again.

Implications for the Movements of Theological Education

The reader will notice that I have spoken simultaneously about the *structure* and *movements* of both *theology* and *theological education*. If one is somewhat convinced by this suggested outline for the structure of theology, what would it imply for the rhythm and movements of theological education? It implies that theological education would be organized around four movements: 1) descriptive theology understood as a thick description of present religious and cultural practices (and the theories – symbols, myths, ethics – that ground them), 2) historical theology (guided by questions that emerge from movement one), 3) systematic theology (a search for generic features of the Christian message in relation to generic features of the present situation), and 4) strategic practical theology (studies about the norms and strategies of the concrete practices of the church – first for the laity in the world and then for clergy as leaders of both the mission and cultic life of the church). One can imagine these movements being organized serially over a period of three or four years. One can also imagine them being taught simultaneously in a spiral built around successive exercises in the description and normative address of practice-theory-practice situations. But whether they are organized serially or taught simultaneously is less important than that they be recognized as moments of the total fundamental practical theological task. The main point is that both faculty and students would need to understand and agree that something like these four movements constitute the practical *habitus* of theological education and approach their studies with some variations of this practical hermeneutical model in mind.[31]

In this view of things, the distinction between university theological education and seminary education for clergy would be modest; all would be the same for both settings except that seminary education for the professional clergy would give additional attention to descriptions of the practices of ordained ministers and work in its strategic practical theology on the specific leadership practices of ordained ministers. The fact that strategic practical theology serves the church would not mean that it, in principle, would have no place in the university. Just as law, business, and social work educate in the university the leadership of these institutions, the university can as well, as it does in Europe, Great Britain, and Canada, provide for critical theological studies relevant to the education of the leadership of those religious institutions that have been central to the life of that society. This is a point that Schleiermacher saw well and argued for in his own view of theology as a positive science.

Fundamental Practical Theology and the CPE Model

Possibly the most novel aspect of my proposal is the suggestion to incorporate into the movements of theological education some of the purposes of clinical pastoral education (CPE). Although I have criticized CPE, there are important insights to be gained from this model. The clinical pastoral education method goes back to Anton Boisen's suggestion that ministers should learn to study the "human document" as well as the literary text.[32] This developed into a widely popular supplement to ministerial education. Ministry students would spend a 10–12 week period ministering under the guidance of an accredited supervisor to the patients of a general or mental hospital. Although the patient as human document was the main focus or reflection early in the movement, gradually the person of the ministerial student and his or her relation to the patient became the center of attention. The methodology of the CPE movement varies from center to center and frequently degenerates into subjectivism and specialization. Too frequently the interior perceptions and psychological history of the student are central. Also, visions and models of ministry often are restricted to the specialized functions of the modern hospital. This leaves students with narrow understandings of ministry to bring back into the life or the congregation and other nonmedical contexts.

In spite of these criticisms, most students have felt they received something from the CPE experience that was present in few places in theological education. I suggest that the CPE model actually hit upon a rather unsystematic practical hermeneutical model and gained its power from its rough approximation of the early part of the four movements of theological education outlined above. Its strength lay in the fact that it enacted rather well the first movement – the descriptions of present theory-laden practices. [...] Its main weakness can be found in the unsteady and uncareful progression that the CPE methodology took through the last three steps of the practical hermeneutical process – the movements through historical and systematic theology to strategic practical theology. [...]

But in spite of these shortcomings, the CPE model has planted a seed that now needs to be carefully nurtured by a far more adequate practical hermeneutical model. In addition, the insights of the CPE model need to be moved out of the medical setting and into theological studies in the university and seminary. This can happen if we understand the full implications of beginning the hermeneutical circle with a careful and multidimensional description of present practices, both religious and secular and both individual and corporate.

This can be done if one broadens the revised correlational model presented by Tracy. For Tracy, a theology operates on a genuinely revised correlational model if, as he says in his book on fundamental theology, it critically correlates its investigation into the two sources of theology. The two sources are, for him, "Christian Texts and Common Human Experience and Language".[33] As we already have seen, when this formulation is transferred to the arena of *praxis*, practical theology becomes "the mutually critical correlation of the interpreted theory and praxis of the Christian fact and the interpreted theory and praxis of the contemporary situation."[34] Although one pole of the correlative task actually involves "interpretations" of common experience, Tracy, in effect, elects common *cultural* experience and practices as one of the poles of the correlative process.

In order to make contact between Tracy's revised correlational model and the CPE approach, one needs to refine Tracy's concept of "common human experience" and his more practical reformulation of it into "interpreted theory and praxis of the contemporary situation." Evelyn and James Whitehead in their *Method in Ministry* recommend differentiating Tracy's "'common human experience'...into two separable poles of reflection."[35] The Whiteheads divide common experience into "personal" experience and the "corporate" experience of the community. Transferred to the arena of *praxis* this division would entail 1) personal interpretations of the practices (religious and secular) of individual agents, 2) interpretations of the practices of their communities and institutions, and 3) interpretations of religiocultural self-interpretations, symbols, and narratives. CPE has its power, I believe, because it permits personal interpretations of individual practices into its systematic reflections. [...] The power of CPE does not derive from its concern with general or common experience but from its concern with interpretations of "my experience and practice" and "my community's experience and practice." I propose that something like the full range of the description of experience and practices (from the personal, to the person's immediate communities, and then to broader religiocultural symbols and stories) be more systematically included in the first movement of theological education in any of its settings.

This first movement, of course, would not be an end in itself; to stop the theological educational process with the first step would be subjectivism. But if this first movement is used to refine the questions (the practical prejudices of Gadamer's hermeneutics) that lead back to historical theology, systematic theology, and then finally to the complexities of strategic practical theology, then the spirit and impulse of CPE can have a healthy influence indeed on theological education in all contexts, both the university as well as the seminary that is dedicated to the education of ordained ministers.

Various disciplines can help describe the theory-laden practices of concrete people in their specific communities within the context of larger cultural symbols and narratives. Clearly psychology and psychoanalysis can uncover aspects of the interpreted practices of individuals. However, these psychological disciplines should not function as natural sciences exhaustively explaining individual subjective experience. Rather, they should function more as hermeneutic disciplines that permit a unique retrospective glance at the developmental history of the interpretations that the individual brings to his or her social and religious practices.[36] [...]

Furthermore, [...] sociology can function similarly to uncover the unconscious or suppressed interpretations and practices for the communities of the theological student. Also, as Habermas has suggested, psychoanalysis and Marxist social thought can constitute a kind of critical theory uncovering systematic distortions in the communicative practices of individual theological students and their communities.[37] These disciplines, within the context of historical and systematic theology, can also help uncover ideological distortion s within the normative religious texts. Furthermore, psychoanalysis and sociology can be used to uncover the depth or "archeology", to use a phrase of Paul Ricoeur's, of broader cultural trends as Freud, Weber, Rieff, and many others have shown.[38] [...]

Yet the description of situated individual, communal, and general cultural practices is never accomplished by the social sciences alone. These practices are also interpreted by the ideals and norms implicit in the theory of these practices. And, insofar as the practices gain their norms from Christian sources, these meanings too play back on them and constitute one perspective on their interpretation. But this raises the question, does the practice in question *really* conform to Christian norms? Is the practice humanly authentic when measured from the perspective of Christian meanings? Such questions move the theological student backward through the practical hermeneutical circle that I described above. [...]

I will conclude this section with a brief illustration of what this approach to theological education might mean, not so much for the details of a theological curriculum, but for a teaching ethos that might permeate the entire process of theological education. After completing an early draft of this essay, I wondered what its point of view might mean for teaching an introductory course in practical theology. In addition to assigning a variety of theoretical readings, I made an assignment for a writing project that necessitated the students making use of these four movements. I did this by asking them to choose a contemporary issue in religious life in our society that was also of vital importance to them. It was to be an issue so vital that it served as a basic motivation behind their interest in theological education. In order to aid them in their thick description of the issue they chose (the first movement of a fundamental practical theology), I held a long evening meeting when each of the nine students of this small class told the history of their interest in the issue. One student chose the tension between new age religion and Christianity. Another chose the way psychiatry relates to the religion of its patients. Another was interested in the status and theological understanding of the newly emerging profession of lay ministers in the Catholic Church. Another student chose homosexuality. Another chose the phenomenon of community organizations and the way various churches are using them as extensions of their public ministry. In each case, the student had a significant history of existential concern with their chosen issues. Their initial task was to describe this history at several levels – their personal involvements and motivations, the institutional context of the issue as they saw it, and the religiocultural meanings that surrounded the issue, especially as they experienced them.

This first step of what we are calling descriptive theology was to be carried over into a major paper to be written for the course. But the paper was actually to center on an interview the student was to have with another person who was, in some way, dealing with the student's chosen issue. The students were to begin the paper with a thick description of their own practices and attitudes as they related to their respective issues. More specifically, each student was to record her or his preunderstanding of the issue. For instance, the student who was concerned with homosexuality recorded his own prejudgments about it. The student concerned about the relation of new age religion to Christianity recorded his preunderstanding of that issue. But then, they were to describe, as best they could, the personal, institutional, and religiocultural situation of the interviewee as this related to the selected issue. The student interested in new age religion interviewed a manager of a new age bookstore. The student interested in psychiatry's handling of religion interviewed a psychiatrist. The student interested in cults interviewed an acquaintance who had converted to Jehovah Witness. The student interested in homosexuality interviewed a gay graduate student. Their papers summarized these interviews and provided thick descriptions of the situation of both the student and the person being interviewed.

Questions about practice (about what good practice would really be) emerged from these thick descriptions of both interviewer and interviewee. This led to the second movement, i.e., historical theology. In the midst of this limited project, however, this movement was addressed by asking the student to present the argument of two serious books that could serve as guides to the Christian witness on the issue they were investigating. The point, here, was to investigate the historical sources from the angle of vision of the student's description of contemporary practices, the theories implicit within them, and the questions that they pose. The student investigating homosexuality, for instance, took Helmut Thielicke's *The Ethics of Sex* (1956) and James Nelson's *Embodiment* (1978).

The next task, which captured some of the features of systematic theology, was to not only lay out the general themes of these guides to the classic Christian sources but to begin a critical dialogue between these guides in an attempt to determine their relative adequacy. In the case of some projects, this task of isolating basic general themes and beginning the process of critically testing their adequacy was enriched by analytic insights from moral philosophy. The task, here, was to give the student an introductory exercise in making critical judgments about the relative adequacy of different interpretive theological perspectives and advancing reasons as to why one view might be better than another. This, of course, is a large task that involves much more than either I can discuss here or the student could adequately address within the context of an introductory course. Nonetheless, they were introduced to the task of critically testing theological arguments.

The fourth movement, however, gave the project its distinctively practical cast and made it a unique assignment in comparison to their other theological studies. Here the task was to write the conclusion of their paper for their interviewee rather than for me the professor. They were to attempt to communicate their preferred position on the issue at hand to the person they had interviewed. They were to communicate this position with sensitivity to the views and situation of [their interviewee] as well as their own situation and preunderstandings of the issue. The student was to look for identities, nonidentitites, and analogies between their preferred view and the situated views of their interviewee. The student also was to advance critical reasons for the more adequate position but do so in such a way as to make contact with the situation and preunderstandings of the person they had interviewed. In most cases, the student actually went back to their interviewee and shared their paper with them. Hence, the entire project was a dialogue between the students and their subject around an issue which the classics of the Christian faith also in some fashion address. In virtually all cases, the student reported a change – sometimes quite revolutionary – between their initial preunderstanding and their understanding of the issue at the conclusion of their dialogue. Because they were sensitive to the changes in themselves, they were also more sensitive to the changes that this dialogue invoked in their subjects – changes that were sometimes modest and sometimes profound.

Space does not permit a full commentary on this project. I will add only this: I explained to the students that not all classes in their theological education should be structured in this manner. But I suggested that they might better keep track of the various twists and turns of their theological education if they saw it in its entirety as entailing various deeper investigations of each of these four movements, often considered more discretely and deeply than was the case in this rather large practical synthetic assignment. Theological education should provide an opportunity to both see and practice this process as a whole as well as delve deeply into the various movements and submovements considered both relatively discretely but also, once again, in relation to the entire fundamental practical theological task.

Further Comparisons

There are several recent proposals pertaining to the structure of theology that have influenced or are similar to the view presented here. The proposal to make the capacity for "practical theological thinking" the goal of theology and the central task of theological education in Hough's and Cobb's *Christian Identity and Theological Education* (1985) is extremely appealing [...].[39] Yet in many ways their excellent proposals are still caught in a theory-to-practice model; their justifiable concern with Christian identity still leads them to move from historical theology to practical theology, almost leaving out systematic theology altogether.[40] [...] I am deeply impressed with Charles Wood's definition of theology in *Vision and Discernment* (1985) as "critical inquiry into the validity of the Christian witness."[41] [...] But Wood comes dangerously close to a theory-to-practice model in his organization of the structure of theology into the five subdisciplines of historical theology, philosophical theology, practical theology, systematic theology, and moral theology.[42][...]

Finally, my concept of fundamental practical theology is close to Johann Baptist Metz's concept of "practical fundamental theology."[43] But there are important differences as well. [...] Descriptive theology would seek for a more concrete description of a variety of specific situations. [...] In addition, Metz's view of theology is more thoroughly confessional than my view. Although a revised correlational practical theology starts in a confessional mode, it is willing to engage in a critical conversation with all other interpretations of human existence. Furthermore, it is willing to meet validity claims which the discourse situation might place upon it.

Habermas and Fundamental Practical Theology

Introducing the phrase "validity claims", and the need for a fundamental practical theology to support the claims it makes, introduces the critical theory project of Jürgen Habermas. One need not be tied to Habermas's particular version of these validity claims (for instance his division of them into "comprehensibility, truth, rightness, and truthfulness") to appreciate his insistence that communicative competence entails a willingness to advance reasons for our actions.[44] This is certainly an obligation that a revised correlational fundamental theology must be willing to assume. [...] Bernstein's counsel is [...] appropriate when he writes the following with reference to Gadamer's avoidance of the question of validation.

> I have argued Gadamer is really committed to a communicative understanding of truth, believing that "claims to truth" always implicitly demand argumentation to warrant them, but he has failed to make this view fully explicit.... For although all claims to truth are fallible and open to criticism, they still require validation – validation that can be realized only through offering the best reasons and arguments that can be given in support of them – reasons and arguments that are themselves embedded in the practices that have been developed in the course of history. We never escape from the obligation of seeking to validate claims to truth through argumentation and opening ourselves to the criticism of others.[45]

In my own work, I differentiate the validity claims of a fundamental practical theology into five types. [...] I argue that these five validity claims reflect the five dimensions of all forms of practical thinking whether they be explicitly religious or avowedly secular. I call these dimensions 1) the visional or metaphorical dimension (which inevitably raises metaphysical validity claims), 2) the obligational dimension (which raises normative ethical claims), 3) the tendency-need dimension (which raises claims about the fundamental needs of human nature and the kinds of nonmoral goods that meet them), 4) the contextual dimension (claims about the social-systemic and ecological integrity of situations), and 5) the rule-role dimension (claims about what should be our most concrete behaviors and actions).[46] In fact, I use these five dimensions (I sometimes call them levels) both to describe the theory-laden practices of contemporary situations and to guide the description of the thickness of the Christian witness. Hence, the model is useful to guide description and interpretation at both poles of the revised correlational conversation – the pole of contemporary experience and the pole of the central Christian message.

There is no room here to amplify and justify this division of the validity claims that a fundamental practical theology should address. My goal, rather, is to assert that a revised correlational practical theology must be willing to support its implicit validity claims if it is to take part in the discourse of a free society aimed at shaping the common good. Here I agree with Bernstein. The arguments that a critical practical theology advances cannot be foundational arguments assuring absolute authority. But its arguments can have the status of good reasons which, although not absolutely certain, can advance discourse about the action we should take.

The critical testing of a fundamental practical theology must come at a variety of points in the hermeneutical circle. [...]

But it is important to note that when this structure of theology is translated into the rhythms of theological education, one would still begin theology with a thick description of contemporary practices (personal, institutional, and religiocultural) and then only gradually move back to historical theology. One would then move through a systematic consideration of the themes of the faith (considered from the perspective of the questions engendered by present practice), to an ideology critique of these themes and the critical examination of the validity claims of the faith, and finally to the critical and strategic consideration of proposals for the alteration of our present practices. The task of supporting the validity claims of the faith is difficult and challenging but important. Yet it is not the first order of business in theological education. To understand our own present practices in their various situations and the questions these practices evoke – this is the first task of theological education. How these moments might be organized into a course of study in different situations – the seminary, the graduate department of religion, or even the church – would doubtless vary to some extent. But if the position outlined above has some plausibility, these differences would be more matters of degree and matters of emphasis rather than matters of categorical distinction.

Notes

1 The list of books pointing toward this turn to practical philosophy is extensive Representative titles following the order of the names in the text are as follows. Hans-Georg Gadamer. *Truth and Method* (New York: Crossroad, 1982); Paul Ricoeur, *Freud and Philosophy* (New Haven: Yale University Press, 1970); Jurgen Habermas, *Knowledge and Human Interests* (Boston: Beacon Press, 1971); Peter Winch, *The Idea of a Social Science and Its Relation to Philosophy* (London: Routledge and Kegan Paul, 1958); R.S. Peters, *The Concept of Motivation* (London: Routledge and Kegan Paul, 1958); Richard Bernstein, *Praxis and Action* (Philadelphia: University of Pennsylvania Press, 1971) and *Beyond Objectivism and Relativism* (Philadelphia: University of Pennsylvania Press, 1983); Richard Rorty, *Philosophy and The mirror of Nature* (Princeton, NJ; Princeton University Press, 1979); Thomas Kuhn, *The Structure of Scientific Revolutions* (Chicago: University of Chicago Press, 1970).

2 Edward Farley, *Theologia* (Philadelphia: Fortress Press, 1983) and *The Fragility of Knowledge* (Philadelphia: Fortress Press, 1988).

3 Joseph Hough and John Cobb, *Christian Identity and Theological Education* (Chico, CA: Scholars Press, 1985), 81–94.

4 Examples for the various countries are: Germany, Dietrich Rössler, *Grundriss der Praktischen Theologie* (Berlin: Walter de Gruyter, 1986), N. Mette, *Theorie der Praxis* (Düsseldorf, 1978); Holland, J.A. van der Ven, "Practical Theology: from Applied to Empirical Theology", *Journal of Empirical Theology* I:1 (1988), 7–28, and J. Firet, *Dynamics in Pastoring* (Grand Rapids, MI: Eerdmans, 1987); England, Paul Ballard (ed.), *Foundations of Pastoral Studies and Practical Theology* (Cardiff: Faculty of Theology, 1986); Canada, M. Viau, *Introduction aux etudes pastorales* (Montreal, 1987); Uruguay, J.L. Segundo, *Liberation of Theology* (New York: Orbis Books, 1976).

5 Friedrich Schleiermacher, *Brief Outline on the Study of Theology* (Richmond, VA: John Knox Press, 1970), 92.

6 An excellent statement of this approach can be found in the early article by Alasdair Campbell, "Is Practical Theology Possible?" *Scottish Journal of Theology*, V:25 (1972), 217–227.

7 The two volumes of essays are Don Browning (ed.), *Practical Theology* (San Francisco: Harper and Row, 1983), and Lewis Mudge and James Poling, *Formation and Reflection* (Philadelphia: Fortress Press, 1987).

8 The book-length studies are Don Browning, *Religious Ethics and Pastoral Care* (Philadelphia: Fortress Press, 1983); James Fowler, *Faith Development and Pastoral Care* (Philadelphia: Fortress Press, 1987); Charles Gerkin, *Widening the Horizons* (Philadelphia: Westminster Press, 1986); Thomas Groome, *Christian Religious Education* (San Francisco: Harper and Row, 1980); Robert Schreiter, *Constructing Local Theologies*, (Maryknoll, NY: Orbis Books, 1985); Charles Winquist, *Practical Hermeneutics* (Chico, CA: Scholars Press, 1980); James Poling and Donald Miller *Foundations for a Practical Theology of Ministry* (Nashville: Abingdon Press, 1985); Dennis McCann and Charles Strain, *Polity and Praxis* (New York: Winston, 1986).

9 Gadamer, *Truth and Method*, 289.

10 Ibid.

11 Bernstein, *Beyond Objectivism and Relativism*, 38.

12 Gadamer, *Truth and Method*, 273.

13 Ibid., 273–4, 337–41.

14 Bernstein, *Beyond Objectivism and Relativism*, 173–4; Rorty, *Philosophy and the Mirror of Nature*, 192–209.

15 Kuhn, *The Structure of Scientific Revolutions*, 41–53.

16 Schleiermacher, *Brief Outline of the Study of Theology*, 25–27; John Burkhart, "Schleiermacher's Vision for Theology," *Practical Theology*, 42–60.

17 Schleiermacher, *Brief Outline*,. 91–126.

18 Ibid., 19.

19 Paul Tillich, *Systematic Theology I* (Chicago: University of Chicago Press, 1951), 29.

20 Ibid., 33.

21 Ibid.

22 For discussions of Ogden's view of the organization of theology, see his *On Theology* (San Francisco: Harper and Row, 1986), 7–16 and "The Concept of a Theology of Liberation: Must a Christian Theology Today Be So Conceived?", *The Challenge of Liberation Theology: A First World Response*, Brian Mahan and Dale Richesin (eds.) (Maryknoll, NY: Orbis Books, 1981). To be fair to Ogden he does say that theology as a

whole should be conceived as practical "in a broad sense." But if this is so, Ogden should come up with a different flow to the structure of theology and also come to understand the importance of questions coming from practice as animating the theological task.

23 David Tracy, *Blessed Rage for Order* (Minneapolis: The Winston-Seabury Press, 1975), 52–56.

24 Ibid., 49–52.

25 Tillich, *Systematic Theology I*, 36.

26 Tracy, *Blessed Rage for Order*, 46.

27 David Tracy, "The Foundations of Practical Theology," *Practical Theology*, 76.

28 Tracy, *Blessed Rage for Order*, 75–6; Paul Ricoeur, *Hermeneutics and the Human Sciences*, (Cambridge: Cambridge University Press, 1981), 149–64.

29 Bernstein, *Beyond Absolutism and Relativism*, 42–4; Jürgen Habermas, *Knowledge and Human Interests* (Boston: Beacon Press, 1971), 301–17 and *Communication and Evolution of Society* (Boston: Beacon Press, 1979), 201–3.

30 Wolfhart Pannenberg, *Theology and the Philosophy of Science* (Philadelphia: Westminster Press, 1976), 410.

31 Farley, *Theologia*, 35.

32 Allison Stokes, *Ministry after Freud* (New York: Pilgrim Press, 1985), 51–62.

33 Tracy, *Blessed Rage for Order*, 43.

34 Tracy in *Practical Theology*, 76. For an adaptation of Tracy's model to a practical theology of care, see My "Mapping the Terrain of Pastoral Theology: Toward a Practical Theology of Care", *Pastoral Psychology*, 36:1 (Fall 1987), 20.

35 James & Evelyn Whitehead, *Method in Ministry* (New York: Seabury Press, 1980), 12.

36 This is the basic meaning of Paul Ricoeur's view that psychoanalysis helps us uncover the "archeology of the subject". See his *Freud and Philosophy* (New Haven: Yale University Press, 1970), 419–58.

37 Habermas, *Knowledge and Human Interests*, 274–300.

38 For the best review of how both psychoanalysis and Weberian sociology can be used to uncover cultural trends, see Philip Rieff: *Freud: The Mind of the Moralist* (New York: Doubleday & Co., 1961) and *Triumph of the Therapeutic* (New York: Harper and Row, 1966).

39 Hough and Cobb, *Christian Identity and Theological Education*, 104. For my positive response to their proposals, see Don Browning, "Globalization and the Task of Theological Education", *Theological Education*, 23:1 (Autumn 1986), 43–59.

40 Hough and Cobb, *Christian Identity and Theological Education*, 29–30.

41 Charles Wood, *Vision and Discernment* (Atlanta, GA: Scholars Press, 1985), 20.

42 Ibid., 39–55.

43 Johann Baptist Metz, *Faith in History and Society* (New York: The Seabury Press, 1980), 5–8.

44 Habermas, *Communication and the Evolution of Society, 58 and Theory of Communicative Action I*, (Boston: Beacon Press, 1981), 325–9.

45 Bernstein, *Beyond Absolutism and Relativism*, 68.

46 Browning, *Religious Ethics and Pastoral Care* (Philadelphia: Fortress Press, 1983), 53–71 and "Practical Theology and Political Theology," *Theology Today* 42 (April 1985), 207–12.

24

Learning from Our Sisters in the Trenches (1997)*

Teresa L. Fry Brown

Introduction

Like Segundo but two decades later, Teresa L. Fry Brown does not reference practical theology and has no need to do so. For also like Segundo, her horizons are broader. Her agenda as an accomplished womanist scholar in preaching is clear: Black women's survival. For, she must answer the question asked by women beyond academe: what use is the liberating agenda of womanism or disciplinary machinations if you cannot even breathe or make ends meet?

That Brown takes this question seriously and tries to answer it in both theoretical and pragmatic terms makes her essay of interest for the *Reader*. As she sees it, womanist theology is only a means to a more significant end goal, that of "avoiding asphyxiation." "Academe teaches how to learn. Life experience teaches us how to survive." Because black women's lives have been under threat for centuries, this distinction is crucial. Defying the stultifying conventions of male-dominated pulpits and white-dominated universities, Brown herself has survived and thrived despite political impediments, and a mainstay of her work is ensuring that other black women do also. As the first black woman to earn tenure at Candler School of Theology at Emory University where she has taught since 1994 and now holds a premier chair in homiletics, she teaches in an area where women face the greatest opposition and might wield the most influence – the pulpit.

A speech pathologist prior to doctoral study and an ordained minister in the African Methodist Episcopal Church, Brown understands intuitively the value of knowledge gained through practice, the impact of embodiment (e.g., breathing and speaking), and the power of religious communities. She insists that her academic peers take the "ordinary," "vernacular," "day-to-day, in the trenches" more seriously. In the essay, she tries to bridge the dissonance between womanist academics and lay women within and beyond the church, which include women who may not grasp the technicalities of scholarly discourse but have paved the road for womanist developments through their everyday roles as mothers, churchwomen, and leaders.

Original publication details: Teresa L. Fry Brown, "Avoiding Asphyxiation: A Womanist Perspective on Intrapersonal and Interpersonal Transformation," pp. 72–94 from *Embracing the Spirit: Womanist Perspectives on Hope, Salvation, and Transformation*, ed. Emilie M. Townes (Maryknoll, NY: Orbis, 1997).

The Wiley Blackwell Reader in Practical Theology, First Edition. Edited by Bonnie J. Miller-McLemore.
© 2019 John Wiley & Sons Ltd. Published 2019 by John Wiley & Sons Ltd.

Brown examines conversion and transformation in women's lives through empirical exploration, although she engages in the latter in a way that differs from conventional qualitative study. She proposes a multi-faceted model developed through her ministry, all designed to support change in black women's lives, that ranges from engaging women in their own ethnographic and historical investigation of family elders and black women leaders to intergenerational family education to consciousness raising meetings and clergy support groups. In contrast to some of the preceding chapters, this chapter is incredibly grounded. In short, Brown attempts to forge a way where few have trod before her.

Suggested Further Reading

- Teresa L. Fry Brown, *Weary Throats and New Songs: Black Women Proclaiming God's Word* (Nashville: Abingdon, 2003).
- Delores Williams, *Sisters in the Wilderness: Womanist God-Talk* (Maryknoll, NY: Orbis, 1993).
- Anna Julia Cooper, *A Voice from the South by a Black Woman of the South* (Xenia, OH: Aldine Printing House, 1892).

***

We need women who are so sure of their own social footing that they need not fear leaning to lend a hand to a fallen or falling sister.
Anna Julia Cooper, educator, 1892[1]

This quotation is as true today as it was more than one hundred years ago when Sister Cooper outlined her vision for the empowerment of African American women. Based on my personal experience, I believe that the person most likely to understand the needs and goals of Black women is another Black woman. Over the past ten years, I have learned about womanist theology and ethics and attended conferences at every opportunity to listen to sisters talk about their perspectives on womanist thought. In the beginning these experiences invigorated me, and I could not wait to get back home and discuss them with other African American women. As I pulled together study sessions, seminars, and sermons for African American women at the church I served, I proclaimed the liberating power of being a womanist. To my dismay, I was met with curious looks, head shaking, and tongue-in-cheek comments and "Child, that's what happens when they go to seminary. At least she ain't trying to be a feminist." I thought I had a precious gift for my church sisters, yet I was met with closed hands and heads. My academic elitism was showing. I had learned womanist language but forgot to translate it into the language of my sisters. I knew something and assumed other women needed to know it. Then I began to analyze why my sisters were seemingly slow to accept this "new" body of information and why they did not want to be associated with being a "womanist." Through informal inquiry and formal discussion groups, I was told, "You keep talking about finding your own voice; we can't even breathe!" Transformation was not the primary consideration for these women – staying alive, gasping for air, making ends meet, raising children were.

In fifteen years as a speech/language pathologist, I taught people how to breathe deeply, effectively use their voices, articulate speech, and communicate with clarity. Although they may have entered therapy with speech problems, after a designated number of sessions I could see the change in their behavior, because others slowly understood who they were and what they needed to say. Even being able to take air into the lungs without coughing or sputtering, and breathing out without pain or misdirected air and sounds were measures of success.

As African American women, we have learned to breathe on stolen air, silently so that no one could detect our presence. We have attempted to inhale and then exhale to set our vocal folds in motion, only to stop because we were told we were too loud or that it was not time for us to speak. Some of us learned to breathe through someone else, like babies breathing through their mothers' umbilical connections. We were often tethered to a man or another power source who regulated where and when we could activate our respiratory system. Others of us found the strength to breathe on our own, only to be stifled because we found the air too heavy or polluted by barriers, acidic reactions, or pillows of doubt suffocating even gasps for air. During my thirteen years in ministry, Black women have related to me how difficult sustaining their breath flow is – whether in the home, church, community, office, or street; regardless of age, education, religion, income, size, or shape. Most understand the need for individual change, engagement of systemic evil, conversion from individual sins, strengthening their reserve, standing on the edge, and challenging oppression, but they need a discipline to articulate their beliefs, and vehicles to transform themselves and to aid their sisters and brothers in community transformation.

The central thesis of this essay is that in order for womanist thought to survive as a viable transformative agent in the lives of African American women, womanist scholars must develop methods of sharing womanist perspectives with our sisters who are not ensconced in the academy or as seminary-trained clergy. Additionally, the essay will provide a practical model for sharing womanist thought with "ordinary" African American women, families, churches, and community organizations. The model will focus on the transformative power of individual and small group discussions of African American women's social, theological, occupational, psychological, and health concerns; ethnographic studies of family members and friends who may have possessed womanist characteristics; and composition of womanist sermons and liturgical study groups. It will also review and discuss African American women's literature to avoid asphyxiation.

"Sister, Help Me Find the Oxygen"

Audre Lorde, in *Sister Outsider*, speaks of the danger of "tyrannies of silence"; of our needs to transform the silent spaces into action and for each person to establish her own voice; and of our individual responsibility to help ourselves and each other.[2] It is crucial for Black women to devise tools or ways to correct or obliterate oppressive systems, instruments that are innovative and consider or meet the needs and abilities of the entire community. In her provocative essay "The Master's Tools Will Never Dismantle the Master's House," Lorde challenges us with our responsibility for individual and collective transformation:

> Those of us who stand outside the circle of this society's definition of acceptable women; those of us who have been forged in the crucibles of differences – those of us who are poor, who are lesbians, who are Black, who are older – know that *survival is not an academic skill.*[3]

Academe teaches how to learn. Life experience teaches us how to survive. Sisters in the academy must remember those sisters who model survival every day and who stopped long enough to teach us how to act and live longer and better than they. Even in the presence of what we in the academy may classify as deference to men and "the man," these women find ways to insure that we can live and do more than they themselves will ever achieve in terms of education or income. Are womanist scholars in danger of "selective amnesia"? Wasn't womanist thought generated by analysis of the lives of "ordinary women" striving to be more than what others said they could become or could achieve? Higher education provided a technique for us to name their struggle in "acceptable academese," but their lives enable us to survive by naming our ability to "be the best you can" and "don't let nobody turn you around."

Lorde continues. Black women's implementation strategies particular to their culture and belief systems are essential to lasting, effective transformation. Billie Holiday sang "God Bless the Child That's Got His [Her] Own," and Lorde seems to say, "No one can save us but us" with our own specific, culturally devised methods:

> It is learning how to stand alone, unpopular and sometimes reviled, and how to make common cause with those others identified as outside the structures in order to define and seek a world in which we can all flourish. It is learning how to take our differences and make them strengths. *For the master's tools will never dismantle the master's house.*[4]

We must be cognizant and inform our sisters that beginning any procedure toward social change is seldom popular. They will lose the support of friends and garner insults from enemies. Others will label and define them derogatorily. Whenever one steps out of a prescribed role, pain will follow. But after the initial pain, a sense of relief similar to the cessation of a bad cold will follow, and one can breathe freely – often for the first time in life. Freedom is contagious. If one is selfless enough to risk showing another how to seek empowerment, how to take deep cleansing breaths rather than pant, both are strengthened.

Our sisters are suffocating every day. They cannot find the air to begin to speak. It is caught in their lungs, in their throat just below the vocal folds. They feel it when fear wells up as they try to cry out for help. It comes when they face the supervisor who harasses them or objectifies them. They are asking for our help, and we dare not ignore them, even when we no longer understand what it is like to be a laywoman in a male-dominated denomination. We stand in the academy because those who stay at home urged some of us to continue the struggle because they did not have the energy to speak. They need to be "sistered" into individual transformation and social change. "Sistering" can be accomplished only if there are no value judgments based on age, belief, sexual orientation, economic standing, education, family status, geography, occupation, or any other artificial barrier we seem to erect to establish "we–they" paradigms.

Womanist scholars are still in process, still defining themselves, still broadening the idea. We need information from laywomen to deepen the richness of the discipline. We will become a fad unless womanist thought receives a constant infusion of reality and social relevance. Before one can accept, one must know what one is required to accept. There needs to be an explanation of the womanist definitions in "sisterspeak," or the vernacular of the day-to-day, in-the-trenches, ordinary sisters who provide supporting information and who are potential procreators of womanist beliefs.

[...]

Furthermore, womanist scholars must become more than special guest lecturers, token program participants, photo opportunities, or preachers at academic or women's conferences with brief, theoretically profound insights into the lives of Black women, or we will asphyxiate also. We must avoid the situations of the early civil rights workers who came to register persons to vote and then left them to deal with the entrenched, dangerous power and social structures alone. We must remember our inextricable link to our sisters and use "sisterspeak" – the articulated as well as the more often unspoken language of Black women – to share the empowering vision of womanist thought. When we see our sisters, we must remember whence we came and who broke down the doors that allow us to sit in book-lined offices and complain about the disparity in the system. We must use the voices we have found to articulate the needs of our sisters. When we are in conversation with our sisters, we must not speak at, over, under, or to them. We must speak *with* them and *hear* what they are saying, rather than assume that we know. Our social location has changed and our worldview is at a slightly different slant as privileged Black women in the academy. But we can be relevant, authentic bridges for our sisters who yearn to stop the madness and be free.

Black feminist Patricia Hill Collins's groundbreaking work *Black Feminist Thought* proposes that the key role of African American intellectuals is to ask the right questions, listen, hear, see, and fully accept Black women as they share "taken-for-granted knowledge" about their lives.[5] We must analyze the social location, worldview, belief system, and resource availability of each sister we directly influence. We need to stick around, build discussion groups, go one-on-one with our sisters, discuss the "whys" and "hows" of womanist perspectives, and provide continual support as they seek their own empowerment, their own air space. We must remember that it has been ten short years since womanists began the process of avoiding asphyxiation, the struggle to breathe on our own. Womanists are still learning how to articulate disappointments, needs, ideas, and definitions. Womanists are currently finding ways to assist our brothers to accept the fact that we are equally created humans. Womanists are at different levels, depending on how long they have been in the academy or in ministry, or have lived. [...] In the conversion process, we are all at different levels. In like fashion, we must remain cognizant of the multiplicity of levels of acceptance and engagement of womanist principles by sisters in the academy and in communities.

"A Change, a Change Has Come Over Me"

> *For one thing we can teach each other the differences in our experiences rather than struggling all the time to say, "It's the same." We can ask each other, "What's different about us?"*
>
> Alice Childress, playwright[6]

Sociologist S.N. Eisenstadt's classic study on social change sets forth fundamental elements of transformation.[7] All humans seek some form of transformation. We each face the same general types of problems. The direction, level, conditions, degree, time, specialization, or differentiation of problems is variable. The relative strength and composition of the collective determine the amount and type of change. "Innovating elites" are change agents. They are able to offer vision and solutions to the problems. These change agents, however, must be aware of the readiness for change, possible rejection of or resistance to the proposed solution, and absence of resources.

[...]

The crucial point is to establish why change is necessary and what one is doing to be transformed. Transformation is relative and takes place at different paces for different people. In 1831, Maria Stewart wrote, "Sue for your rights and privileges. Know the reason you cannot attain them. Weary them with your importunities. You can but die if you make the attempt; and we shall certainly die if you do not."[8] The old saying is that "the more things change the more they remain the same." Maria Stewart advocated going to any length, even death, to change circumstances. One must decide for oneself how much one is willing to give up, to sacrifice for freedom. No one can determine that for us. Part of the rhetoric that separates womanist scholars and laywomen is that misappropriation of what it means to give up a part of one's life for the current liberation movement focus. Because a sister in the trenches is reluctant to give up her current life situation even if judged oppressive by the enlightened scholar does not mean that that sister does not want to be changed. Think of how long it took for those of us in our thirties or forties to accept our calls to preach with all the attendant baggage or to complete doctoral studies with all the political games? Did we begin the processes understanding the sacrifice and with eagerness to be beaten up by the system? In most cases we connected with a stronger sister, or at least a sister who was like-minded, who would say to us, "I got your back," and we believed her. Did every sister in the academy who started out touting a "womanist pedagogy" end up with the same fervor, or have some stepped away or back into the old self? Change means discomfort, and some of us are not strong enough to weather the storm alone or even with hundreds of others. As we demand change in systems and expect change in the lives of our sisters, we need to ask ourselves who is with that sister when she has to stand alone before her family, her ministerial board of examiners, her tenure committee, her dissertation defense committee, her pastor, or even her sisters who think that womanist thought is a fad that will pass as soon as its proponents are tired.

Learning from Our Sisters in the Trenches

Over the past thirteen years of ordained ministry, I have worked with social, civic, religious, and educational women's groups, attempting to develop a practical model for Black women's intrapersonal and interpersonal transformation and empowerment. My grandmother and other women in my life had begun the process and continued to support and encourage me. However, I still needed more information to sustain me as a Black woman seeking to serve the church and survive the academy. Through insightful lectures and motivating conversations with Katie Cannon, Jacquelyn Grant, and Cheryl Townsend Gilkes, I began to understand the genesis of womanist perspectives and the potential for personal growth and sharing with others. In recognition of the need for a new discipline to sustain my sisters in ministry and the church as we struggled to breathe freely in an aftershave-filled pulpit, I was led to initiate a practical model for Black women's transformation from a womanist perspective.

The components of this model were conceived, developed, modified, recorded, implemented, and eventually duplicated in other churches and cities. Any process of transformation must follow similar steps and honing in order for the program, concept, or idea to be effective and enduring. Change, whether individual or collective, does not come overnight.

This model was generated over the period of 1988–1994 with a core group of forty African American women, beginning at Shorter Community African Methodist Episcopal Church in Denver, Colorado. Membership and participants ranged from approximately five hundred to six hundred African American women from various organizations, individual interest groups, and churches in Denver. Sisters Working Encouraging Empowering Together (SWEET) was formed as a network for intentionally sharing womanist perspectives and undergirding Black women's efforts for spiritual and social liberation. SWEET was formed at a time when African American women were separated, fragmented, distrustful, defamatory, and competitive.

Membership was opened to any African American woman or woman of color who needed an opportunity for spiritual and social renewal, healing, sustenance, empowerment, and cooperation. There was also a group of about thirty African American men who regularly supported the group and attended seminars on relationships and community activities. The members ranged in age from five to seventy-eight years. Educational levels were from grade school to professional schools. Women were married, single, divorced, and widowed. They were heterosexual, lesbian, and bisexual.

The sisters were Baptist, Methodist, Catholic, Pentecostal, Muslim, Church of God in Christ, Episcopalian, and unchurched. Some had been incarcerated or on the way to jail, or knew someone there. There were Deltas, Alphas, Zetas, Sigmas, and Links sitting alongside Granny, MaDear, Mama, Big Momma, and Auntie. Each woman, whatever her status or station in life, brought similar concerns to the group. They felt stagnant, hemmed in, pushed down, limited and wanted to do more than survive. They each wanted to know how to really sing, "My soul looks back and wonders how I got over."

We began to develop annual seminars, inclusive sermons, intensive women-centered Bible studies, monthly workshops, relationship-building exercises, small group discussions, potluck dinners, informal and formal luncheons, community action projects, intergenerational mentoring groups, individual and group counseling sessions, guest speakers and in-group speakers, panel discussions, role-playing, ethnographies, health support groups, and African American women's literature study and discussion groups. Alice Walker's definition of *womanist* was used as the point of departure for each discussion. We targeted one section of the definition at each meeting to begin to share womanist perspectives with the group.[9]

Pedagogically, the model is deliberately inductive, teaching women to think for themselves and form their own paradigms while receiving support from and giving support to other women in the process of transformation. The viability of the model rests in each person being empowered to deconstruct oppressive paradigms, reconstruct liberating ones, and activate models that are most conducive to intrapersonal and interpersonal transformation. Conversations flowed from the requests of the sisters present. The coordinator was responsible for guiding discussions on particular issues. Delegation of leadership was the rule of the day. Everyone had a chance to lead, and all were encouraged to try new things and test their skills. Initially, meetings were held weekly, and, depending on agenda items, either on bimonthly or monthly Saturday mornings or Friday nights thereafter. Agreed meeting length was one and one half hours. If the discussion lasted longer, those who needed to leave did, and others remained until they felt the discussion was exhausted.

We began SWEET with one ground rule – "We will respect our sister's space, speech, issues, voice, pain, and sensitivities." There were no value judgments. Instead we replaced judgment with "I love you like you are," "I don't agree, but you have a right to your opinion," or "We're going to make it in spite of ourselves." We ran all meetings on a consensus basis. There was a coordinator but no elected officers. No dues were collected; each gave as she could whenever there was a need. We defined ourselves as a spiritual, universal sisterhood with no walls, barriers, or exclusions.

We pledged to "sister" each other into wholeness using "sisterspeak" – informal, no-pretense, at-home, dangling-participles, double-negative, tell it-like-it-is, intense-body-language speech. There was no need to impress each other with credentials so we called everyone Sister —, Girlfriend, or by first names, with the exceptions of our respected elder sisters, whom we called Mother — or Miss —.[10] The "mothers" of the group were the spiritual anchors of the group. Their presence added a sense of authenticity to the belief in the possibility of change. The model of their courageous living, sense of humor, and deep-seated faith helped us to continue to build when detractors – male and female – said there was no need for another women's group.

We treated teens and children with the same respect as others. They met in individual, age-appropriate groups or with the adults, depending on the subject matter of the day. While disagreements arose, especially over sensitive issues, everyone had to be heard. One sister would facilitate the discussion but could step out of the role and yield leadership to another person when she needed to contribute her thoughts.

Meetings began with sharing praise reports and requests for support. Women were not pressured to be a member of a church, but there was an understanding that the group was spiritually based. Each sister determined and articulated her own sense of spirituality. African American spirituality is the conscious awareness of God, self, and others in the total response to Black life and culture. It is an expressive style, a mode of contemplating God, a prayer life, and that which nourishes, strengthens, and sustains the whole person.[11] We coupled prayer, testimony, tears, laughter, or silence with embracing each other.

Sisters passed on their ideas of how to survive and thrive to each other and to younger women, and listened respectfully to the othermothers in the group. One opening exercise might be, "Who was the woman in your life who had the greatest impact on who you are today and why?" or "Where were you ten years ago, and how have you changed?" As each woman spoke, she also received affirmation of her situation or overcoming through a similar story repeated by another sister and embryonic sustenance from one who would become a sister.

The buds of extended families began when the discussion opened with, "What kind of sister are you?" "Who is your sister?" or "Do you need a sister?" Reassessment of the role of women in churches, ministry, or private quests for spirituality was initiated with questions such as, "Who is God?" "Who/what does your God look like?" "How do you name God?" or even, "Why do you go to church?" or "What is the most difficult part of attending church?" This usually evoked extensive discussion and usually reassessment of sisters' roles and responsibilities in churches or faith settings. This provided an opportunity to air opinions, to grieve the oppression relative to their experiences in churches, and to strategize ways to move the church structure to become more inclusive of women and to help other women identify church-centered discrimination and role stigmatization.

The majority of women had never questioned what women were required to wear or do, what positions in the church were traditionally assigned to women, what positions were closed to them, the language of sermons and songs that excluded women, and the instances when women were described as evil or weak by men and by some women in churches. We were at different levels of faith and different places in transformation. Old tapes [...] take a long time to wear out for some sisters. These discussions were generally initiated because the coordinator and four other members were pursuing ordained ministry, and questions were constantly presented regarding how we came to "decide to go against the men."

Releasing the Power Within

SWEET ventured into many areas based on the needs and desires of the membership and community. Through trial and error, components were added and subtracted. I will describe eight of the major components. One of the most powerful small group projects for understanding and cultivating womanist perspectives such as valuing self and gaining a sense of empowerment was ethnographies. Within the first part of Walker's definition of *womanist* is the phrase "wanting to know more and in greater depth than is considered 'good' for one." The ethnography activity required women to discover more about themselves by getting to know about where they came from and what family persons – grandmothers and othermothers – gave birth to them. We asked that each sister call, write, or visit the oldest living female family member and ask her about her life. Each woman chose her own questions based on what she wanted to know about spiritual, professional, familial, personal, or political aspects of the woman's life. [...]
   [...]
   Initially, some were hesitant to undertake the project but covenanted to do the best they could. Some were amazed at what the relative would not talk about, such as deaths, births, family members, or religion. Others unearthed a treasure right under their nose. One woman was inspired to finally answer a call to preach. She had been discouraged by several brothers and sisters but then discovered that there had already been two women in her family who had been preachers. [...]

A second component was a self-empowerment/living history project. It was a review of the lives of contemporary African American women leaders in various fields and in history who had exemplified the behavior or social consciousness necessary for intrapersonal transformation. The section of Walker's *womanist* definition focal to this exercise was "appreciates and prefers women's culture, women's emotional flexibility, and women's strength." Each member selected a biography or autobiography, then agreed to form a study group with six other women and report back to the larger group answering the same type of questions used in the ethnographic exercise. The lives of Anna Julia Cooper, Fannie Lou Hamer, Mary McLeod Bethune, Ella Baker, Jo Anne Robinson, Maria Stewart, Daisy Bates, Nannie Helen Burroughs, Jarena Lee, Amanda Berry Smith,

Leontyne Kelly, Shirley Chisholm, and Barbara Jordan were a few of the women selected, along with any other woman who caught a sister's interest. Finally, the lives of the older relative/friend, the extraordinary woman, and the SWEET sisters were compared and contrasted in terms of location, situation, coping mechanisms, prejudices, and goals as a source of transformation. [...]

[...] Robert Staples argues that the assimilation of dominant society values has had a significant impact on the Black family. Since 1960, there has been a quest among Blacks for personal freedom and job mobility. Other cultural values have supplanted traditional child rearing in the name of "fitting in."[12] The African family value system incorporated respect, responsibility, restraint, reverence, and reciprocity.[13] [...]

A third component of SWEET was the "Back to the Kitchen Table" program. It was held on Saturday mornings for six-week sessions. Families discussed ways of reinstituting these values and other biblically based ways of being in community. Activities such as crafts, films, music, exercise, and Bible study were cultivated around a sit-down pot-luck breakfast. Each week a different family grouping was responsible for the food. The average attendance on Saturday mornings was seventy-five.

[...]These extended family breakfasts served two purposes – to share food and to share information. [...] Issues of sexuality, parenting, domestic violence, suicide, education, relationship building, health, and job preparedness were discussed with SWEET members using their expertise, invited guests, and films. Family was defined as blood relatives, relatives by marriage, friends, or "fictive" kin.[14] No one was left out because of marital status. Teens often volunteered to care for younger children so sisters and brothers could converse about particular topics without distraction.

[...]

We instituted the fourth component to fill a major void in the lives of most SWEET members. Many were professional women who had little contact with other African American women during the week and felt "in this mess all by myself." Due to Denver's demographics and the dispersement of the African American population, the majority of women saw each other at church or at some social setting but had not intentionally sought out friendships with other African American women. We started sister-to-sister mentoring with an occupational/talent mentoring program accomplished through "talent sheets." Members wrote down their profession, a talent they wished to share, what they wanted to learn or needed help with, and a pledge to commit one hour per week. The sheets were placed on a board, and they selected the person whom they could either learn from or teach for that commitment period. They could change every two weeks to another person.

[...]

The SWEET experience and model compel me to push Alice Walker's definition of *womanist* in a more theocentric direction. I would add "believes in Somebody bigger than you and me" or "possesses a radical faith in a higher power" to the established *womanist* definition as the basis for a fifth SWEET component. Churched and unchurched Black women carry deep-seated spiritual beliefs. Through conversations, counseling sessions, interviews, and analysis of women's roles in worship services, I have concluded that the majority of Black women are "recovering" Christians. They have a love/hate relationship with the church and with their own spirituality. They love God but strive to recover from the addictive nature of church-related oppression. It is difficult for some to stay away from church, even when they know that they might be carried away battered and bruised. [...]

[...] Bible studies or sacred text studies led by womanists, or any religiously oriented seminars are crucial vehicles for planting seeds of change. Women appear to be more open in these settings, because they may have been excluded or beaten up in the regular worship service.[...]

[...]Bible studies may include assignments wherein the sisters trace family trees, locate women in the text, study the origin of the household codes, imagine the lives of women in the biblical world and compare and contrast them to contemporary situations, or provide a reinterpretation of the text that is inclusive of all class members.

Lyrics in traditional and contemporary gospel music are also rich topics for dialogue on womanist theology and ethics. In the 1950s and 1960s, Black women wrote, arranged, sang, directed, and recorded gospel music, in many cases as an alternative ministry to preaching.[15] We asked that sisters bring in their favorite song with research on the songwriter's life. Questions ranged from, "What do you think she was thinking about when she wrote the song?" to, "What did you learn about her belief in God?" to, "Why do you identify with this song?" [...]

[...]

Finally, in terms of spirituality, women in SWEET were encouraged to ask the church hierarchy questions about the role of women in the church. We paired those who feared male authority with a sister who could "stand boldly before the throne." The number of sisters who feared the pastor or the "leaders" was staggering. These same women ran businesses, supervised hundreds, taught school, raised children alone, yet felt out of place talking to men in the church. Through lengthy discussion, the group began to hash out the reasons for the fear and possibilities for resolution. The deification of the pastor and the "sanctity of the pulpit" as the place where God dwelled and only preachers (men) could stand because God was a man, were addressed through the belief in "the priesthood of all believers." [...]

[...] Faced too long with charges that women are to "keep silent in church," that they "defile the pulpit," or that they should "speak" rather than "preach," some women formed an auxiliary group called Sisters in the Spirit in 1992. This composed a sixth component. The members of this group were SWEET members who were also women in ministry. This became a support group for a group often labeled as "audacious and courageous." The sisters met at different homes for informal Saturday late lunches to laugh, cry, commiserate about the status of women in ministry, discuss sermon styles and plans, develop ways to cope with and confront those brothers who denied them access to ministry, and just to listen to music or sing. [...]

[...]

Self-concept, competition with other women, starving oneself to try to look like the cover girls in *Vogue* or *Essence*, stagnant jobs, continuing unhealthy relationships, worshiping like a marionette, and failure to obtain timely medical examinations were at the top of the list when SWEET members first met. "Loving and Caring for Yourself" was a seventh component of the SWEET model. Seminars and support groups such as the Hysterectomy Group, the Breast Cancer Survivors Group, the Divorcée Group, the New Christian Group, the Single Mothers Group, and the Workout Group were all subsections of the larger sisterhood. Members of the sisterhood were the "experts" for seminars. Using our own people was an assent to their abilities. We each realized that we often overlook the people right before us. This also provided additional insight into who our sisters were.

[...]

Group members accomplished hearing voices of African American women through literary study groups, leading to an eighth component that permeated the entire paradigm. Although the women were generally well read, many had not read women's literature. Self-concept, competition with other women, adverse relationships with men, feelings of inadequacy, being shut out of corporate promotions, day-to-day battles with racism, classism, or sexism, fear of failure, and a thirst for deeper spiritual presence in their lives compelled the women to seek answers through literature. Literary groups selected books from a reading list, and several different groups read books and compared the content, identified the characters, analyzed the characters' lives, their relationships with men and women, and their methods of change. In the literary groups, the womanist definition was used as a tool of analysis. The women in the groups decided for themselves if the protagonists were womanists or not. [...] Regardless of the component addressed, the voices of Black women in fiction, nonfiction, biography, medicine, education, finance, health, or relationship books or films were the center points of the discussion.

[...]

Womanist scholars have a wealth of knowledge just around the corner of the academy – perhaps in sisters who are walking around emptying trash cans. [...] If womanists seek to avoid both being esoteric and holding meetings to impress ourselves with the profundity of our perspectives, then we must sit at the feet of our elders. We must also hear the inquiries of our little sisters whose zeal for life must not be snuffed out early in their careers. We must attend to the self-conceptions of Black girls whose self-image begins to change around age eleven. Often they begin to hate their appearance, hate their skin color, hate their hair, hate their bodies, and hate their inability to have a boyfriend before puberty begins to turn their hormones upside down. Consider for just a moment where they get the idea that they are ugly and worthless or that they need to change their appearance surgically or artificially. Womanists need to extend the dialogue from grade school to those sisters entering the academy. The conversation on womanist definition and perspectives must extend also to the nursing homes so that valuable pearls of wisdom are not lost on the lips of our mothers. We have to talk with our sisters who are not middle class, who are not well educated, who live where we might feel uncomfortable walking. If womanists seek to be a breath of fresh air in the academy, they must exhale the stale air of academic discourse from time to time and "sisterspeak."

Once we implement a continuing process of 'sistering' each other, then we will be in a position to help sisters in the 'real world' avoid asphyxiation. [...] When we remember that 'we are our sisters' keepers' and that we must dialogue with our brothers too, womanists will begin steps toward lasting viability.

Notes

1 Anna Julia Cooper, *A Voice* from *the South by a Colored Woman from the South* (Xenia, Ohio: Aldine Printing House, 1892), 32–3.
2 Audre Lorde, *Sister Outsider* (Trumansburg, NY: The Crossing Press, 1984), 40–112.
3 Ibid., 112.
4 Ibid.

5 Patricia Hill Collins, *Black Feminist Thought: Knowledge, Consciousness, and the Politics of Empowerment* (New York: Routledge, 1990), 30, 98.

6 Quoted in Diane J. Johnson, ed., *Proud Sisters: The Wisdom and Wit of African American Women* (White Plains, NY: Peter Pauper Press, 1995), 51.

7 S.N. Eisenstadt, "Social Change, Differentiation, and Evolution," *American Sociological Review* 29:3 (1964), 375–86.

8 Quoted in Marilyn Richardson, ed., *Maria W. Stewart, America's First Black Woman Political Writer* (Bloomington: Indiana University Press, 1987), 38.

9 Alice Walker, *In Search of Our Mothers" Gardens: Womanist Prose* (San Diego: Harcourt, Brace, Jovanovich, 1983), xi–xxii. Subsequent references to Walker's definition of *womanist* are also from this source.

10 See Cheryl Townsend Gilkes, "Role of Church and Community Mothers: Ambivalent American Sexism or Fragmented Familyhood?" *Journal of Feminist Studies in Religion* 2 (Spring 1986): 41–59. Gilkes argues the importance of elder women as the guardians of the oral tradition and cultural mores. She writes that churched and unchurched Black women tell of the purpose, meaning, and importance of sociocultural events and serve as the connective tissue of the community and culture.

11 See Celestine Cepress, ed., *Sister Thea Bowman, Shooting Star* (Winona, Minnesota: Saint Mary's Press), 17–125.

12 Robert Staples, "The Family," in *The Black Family: Essays and Studies*, 3rd ed. (Belmont, Calif.: Wadsworth Publishing, 1986), 145–8.

13 See Wallace C. Smith, *The Church in the Life of the Black Family* (Valley Forge: Judson Press, 1985), 13–42.

14 Fictive kin are those persons who are not related by either blood or marriage but function in the understood capacity of a brother, sister, mother, father, or other family member. Fictive kin are evident in most African American church "families" and in instances where one's blood relatives are living in other parts of the country.

15 See J. Wendell Mapson, *The Ministry of Music in the Black Church* (Valley Forge: Judson Press, 1984).

25

Wisdom and the Fear of Knowing (1997)*

Mary Elizabeth Mullino Moore

Introduction

Mary Elizabeth Mullino Moore was among the first few women at the forefront of practical theology's rebirth in the United States in the 1980s and 1990s. Distinct from Rebecca Chopp, however, she joined women internationally, such as Riet Bons-Storm and Denise Achermann, in the effort to further practical theology as a discipline. An ordained United Methodist deacon, she was the first woman president of the US Association of Practical Theology and the International Academy of Practical Theology and the first woman co-editor of the prestigious *International Journal of Practical Theology*. After more than two decades of teaching religious education at Claremont School of Theology and Emory University, she now serves as Dean of the School of Theology at Boston University.

In this essay, Moore reveals several unique aspects of a practical theological approach to knowing in general and "faith knowing" in particular. Most immediately noticeable, she begins with evocative case material, grounded in gender and race politics and emotions, capturing the personal and political nature of knowing. Written as the twentieth century closes, she draws on two events that rocked national sensibilities – the O.J. Simpson trial in 1995 and the Re-Imagining Conference in 1993. While the former remains in nearly everyone's consciousness, the latter is often unknown or forgotten but is no less telling. Whereas the trial revealed a deep divide between whites and blacks over racist injustice in the US legal and police system, the conference sent the Christian world into a panic when more than 2000 people, primarily women, gathered from 49 states and 27 countries to promote gender equality in religious life. Both controversies reflect issues of race, gender, and sexuality that continue to unsettle religious and cultural life today. In the furor that ensued after both events, our "very ways of knowing" were under duress, Moore argues. When women sought to change images for the divine, for example, and claim symbols like milk and honey as evocative of Christian faith, they made explicit the power of liturgy over everyday theological knowing that most theologians had largely ignored.

Original publication details: Mary Elizabeth Moore, "Wisdom, Sophia, and the Fear of Knowing," pp. 227–43 from *Religious Education* 92:2 (Spring 1997).

Moore uncovers primal intrapsychic impulses that often lie beyond our consciousness and control. "Faith knowing" is dynamic, responsive, disruptive, and relational and includes practices such as silence and prayer even if these lack conventional intellectual validity. Most interesting, however, she connects knowledge to fear. She shows how religious knowledge disrupts and reveals "what is real in the world" and hence inevitably evokes fear of God, others, and ourselves, giving new meaning to biblical understandings of fear of God as the "beginning of wisdom" described in Proverbs 9.10 and Psalm 111.10.

Suggested Further Reading

- Mary Elizabeth Moore, *Teaching From the Heart: Theology and Education Method* (Minneapolis: Fortress, 1991).
- Thomas Groome, *Sharing Faith: A Comprehensive Approach to Religious Education and Pastoral Ministry* (San Francisco: Harper, 1991).
- Rebecca S. Chopp, *Saving Work: Feminist Practices of Theological Education* (Louisville: Westminster John Knox, 1995).

***

The focus of this essay is wisdom. [...] Wisdom is that force continually emerging from below the surface of daily living to confront us with its persistence and power to disrupt [...] and to help us see what is real in the world. Understood in this way, one can understand why wisdom inevitably evokes fear.

The purpose of this essay is threefold: (1) to explore the fear of knowing; (2) to explore the meaning of wisdom as questing to know; and, (3) to propose possibilities for education that meet people in the midst of their fears and inspire people in their questing. While each purpose can only be addressed briefly, the focus on all three may help us understand and respond to the pressing issues confronting religious people in the closing years of the twentieth century.

Exploring Issues of Fear

In order to explore the fear of knowing, we will analyze two case studies to identify critical issues revealed by them. Each story is partial, but each is part of an intricate web of relationships and larger realities; thus, exploring the cases can illuminate the issues of fear that rage in our society and in our religious communities.[1]

Sophia and the Fear of Knowing

The Re-Imagining Conference of November 1993 may have been the most incendiary event in United States Protestant circles in this decade. The planning led by a group of women in the church and theological education culminated when more than 2000 people (mostly women) gathered in Minneapolis, Minnesota, to celebrate the Ecumenical Decade of the Church in Solidarity with Women, an emphasis of the World Council of Churches of Christ. The newspapers and magazines of most Protestant denominations covered the conference, and a fiery furor arose in regard to three particular events – references to *Sophia* [Greek for Wisdom], a comment by Delores Williams that we do not need "folks hanging on crosses and blood dripping... we just need to listen to the God within," and the closing ritual of milk and honey.

All three events evoked strong feelings, public outcries, reprimands within denominational staff who had attended the conference on denominational budgets, position statements by church institutions (with two opposing statements emerging from Princeton Theological Seminary), study committees of episcopal leaders (such as the United Methodist Council of Bishops), and so forth. The Re-Imagining Conference continues to be a major symbol for many in Protestant denominations. Letters to the editors still flow, along with letters to denominational officials; denominational staff seek to avoid controversial language (especially *Sophia)* and controversial issues; and impassioned responses still echo through denominational newspapers, local churches, and judicatory bodies.

Reflecting on this story as a case study, one can identify at least three kinds of fear that have charged the atmosphere of mainline Protestantism in the aftermath of Re-Imagining: the fear of knowing God, the fear of questioning dominant metaphors and constructs of God, and the fear of liturgies of inclusion. To these fears we now turn our attention.

The Fear of Knowing God. The fear of knowing God is surfaced by the outrage regarding *Sophia* in the Re-Imagining Conference. Conference participants received a *Sophia* blessing as they entered the convocation: "Bless *Sophia*, dream the vision, share the wisdom dwelling within." The emphasis was on relating with *Sophia* – namely, Wisdom – as echoed in the biblical heritage of Proverbs: "Does not wisdom [*Sophia*] call, and does not understanding raise her voice?" (Proverbs 8:1, NRSV) The attention of this [chapter] is not to interpret the biblical texts or analyze the meaning of *Sophia*, though that is an important task. The purpose here is to interpret the *responses* to recent events when such texts have been called upon and, further, to reflect on the epistemological issues raised by those responses.

Note that the blessing used in the Re-Imagining Conference not only addresses *Sophia*, but also emphasizes the vision ("dream the vision") and wisdom that dwells within. Both imply transcending principles, one from the future and one from within. Both imply mystery – that which is sensed but not fully known. And both imply presence and accessibility. One part of the blessing calls upon imagining, or envisioning, as a way of knowing, and the other, upon intuition, or listening to the voices within. Perhaps these very ways of knowing are called into question by the furor following the Re Imagining Conference.

The very term "Re-Imagining" similarly connotes an active interaction with God via images that are constantly being re-experienced, re-visited, re-constructed, and re-imagined. The implication is clear that neither God nor God's people are static, that the relationship is an active one, that God's presence permeates the creation and draws us toward new visions, that God is known more through experience than dogma, that God cannot be controlled by our definitions, and that God is known in relationship. The fear of knowing God, then, is a fear of experiencing God, of not being able to define and control God, and of relating with God. In short, it is a fear of being open to the future and the deepest impulses within ourselves.

The description of the Re-Imagining case and ensuing cases indicates a very deep issue, one echoed by Elizabeth Johnson when she says:

> [T]he symbol of God functions as the primary symbol of the whole religious system, the ultimate point of reference for understanding experience, life, and the world. Hence the way in which a faith community shapes language about God implicitly represents what it takes to be the highest good, the profoundest truth, the most appealing beauty. Such speaking, in turn, powerfully molds the corporate identity of the community and directs its praxis (1994, 4)

The language people use for God is at the very heart of their worldview and ethical frameworks. The fear of knowing God is, thus, tied to the fear of transformation – transformation of our religious system, worldview, ethical practice, and identity. Why, then, are we surprised when we see evidence of fear in knowing God?

The Fear of Questioning Dominant Metaphors and Constructs of God. Strong responses were expressed after the Re-Imagining Conference to one short sentence made by Delores Williams regarding the cross and blood of Jesus. This reveals how deep are our metaphors and constructs of God. Her comments were actually buried in a much larger discussion, but neither her formal remarks nor the details of the discussion have been quoted in the reporting. Instead, reporters and their readers seem much more interested in Williams' questioning of the central symbols than the contextual matrix of her remarks.

The strength of feeling evoked by her comments should not be surprising. If symbols of God carry the power described above, they are connected to a web of meaning that is critical to our human understanding of, and response to, the world. To be confronted by alternative symbols is extremely threatening, and to be invited to explore other webs of meaning – namely, other contexts of meaning-making – can be overwhelming. Delores Williams' controversial comment about Jesus' cross and blood, for example, was said in a web of communication regarding the destructiveness of a theology that centers on sacrifice and death, especially when that theology is used to encourage self-sacrifice among women, even to accept abuse as a sacrificial act. The full matrix of this discussion was not reported. Perhaps its particular web of meaning is too threatening?

As we recognize the intense resistance to changing God-images and the continued pervasiveness of male images, we also recognize that changing metaphors and constructs is an act of what Rebecca Chopp calls emancipatory transformation (1989, 7). Changing images is never cosmetic. We are faced with transformed views of God, and also with transformed views of the world and our relationships to it. The reverberations of the Re-Imagining Conference reveal a profound fear of such transformation, a fear revealed in the statement of a United Methodist Bishop who called *Sophia* theology the "worst heresy in 1,500 years of Christianity" (Keller 1994).

The stakes are high. Elizabeth Johnson makes this point in her observation that that language of God in female images simultaneously disrupts literal interpretations of male images and their dominance in theological discourse. Further, female language of God functions socially to "question prevailing structures of patriarchy" and "give rise to a different vision of community" (Johnson 1994, 6). The fact that such changes evoke fear should be no surprise.

The Fear of Liturgies of Inclusion. Perhaps more surprising is the controversy that erupted around liturgies in the Re-Imagining Conference. The closing liturgy of milk and honey tapped into deep imagery – namely, the milk and honey of the promised land (thus connecting Christianity with Judaism) and the milk that flows from women's bodies as they nurse (thus connecting Christian celebration with women's bodiliness). As a closing worship, some also saw it as a distorted Eucharist. In fact, this was not intended to be a service of Eucharist in the first place, but rather to be a service of celebration for the riches of God's creation and the promises of God for abundance.

Within the Christian tradition, the Eucharist – which is a sacrament of thanksgiving and a symbol of unity in Christ – has actually been one of the most divisive practices of the church. For instance, some churches practice the Eucharist without welcoming other Christians to partake; some churches practice the Eucharist in ways that other Christians do not feel able to partake; and many churches practice the Eucharist in ways that communicate exclusion to people outside the Christian church. The purpose of the Re-Imagining Conference was not to negate Eucharist, but to practice a ritual of inclusivity – inclusive of all persons and inclusive of the fruits of the earth.

The fear of inclusion had already been accentuated in the Conference when a speaker invited lesbian and bisexual women to join her on stage. When many did so, the audience responded with a standing ovation. While the invitation and the spontaneous ovation were intended as acts of inclusion, they were interpreted by many outside the Conference as a celebration of homosexuality. This reaction is similar to other controversies in recent years when rituals of inclusion (usually women's rituals) have been widely discussed and shunned as inappropriate in many Christian seminaries. Thomas Oden, one public critic, has inspired a movement to eliminate such "heretical" acts and teachings (1995, 140–61). The very fire in the controversy reveals the threat embodied in liturgies of inclusion. While many may see these liturgies as embracing more of the human family, others see them as excluding orthodoxy. The questions remain, and so does the fear.

The Fear of Communal Power. After the Re-Imagining Conference, some of its planners lost their jobs, some have been ostracized in their denominations, and some have been asked, "Has it gone away yet?" As one planner was told, the problem was that 2000 women were gathered in a powerful conference planned by and for women. Perhaps the vastness of the conference and the power of the women's community evoked a fear of communal knowing or a fear of communal power.

Politics and the Fear of Knowing Ourselves

Let us turn now to a second case of the fear of knowing.

> On the third day of October, 1995, at 10:00 a.m. Pacific time, the verdict was read in the trial of O.J. Simpson. The actual reading was framed by two statements. The last instruction by Judge Lance Ito was that the jurors had requested not to be interviewed by the Prosecution, Defense, or media after the verdict was read. Then, following the "Not Guilty" verdict, the Judge thanked the jurors and suggested that they freely draw boundaries for themselves as representatives of the media pursue them. He further asked the media to be respectful, but he said to the jurors that he could not promise them that they would not be pressured.

This public event was shaped by the technology and habits of the contemporary media. Behind this obvious fact is the hunger of US people for high profile people (cultural icons) and high profile situations (cultural events). In this case, high profile people – namely, O.J. Simpson, Nicole Brown Simpson, Ron Goldman, the lawyers, Mark Fuhrman, and Judge

Ito – served an important social function. They became the focal point of our national (and even international) energies, including our energetic hero-worship, love of violence, fear of violence, rage, passion for justice, fear of injustice, suspicions based in race or gender, and distrust of power and money. The furies raging inside us could be simplified and personified in the key characters. Thus, these figures could become symbols of that massive, unthinkable, and unknowable energy within the psyches of a nation.

Not only were these figures cultural icons, but also the events themselves – namely, the murder, the trial, and the verdict – were cultural events. They riveted our attention, distracting it from the war in Bosnia, the visit of the Pope to New York, and countless other events in the nation and world. National and local news broadcasts were given almost entirely to this one story. Only after the verdict was read was attention turned to the culture itself. Countless interviews were conducted, focusing largely on African-American men and white women. Extensive polls were conducted and analyzed by race. The differences between African-American and European-American responses were enormous. More than 70% of the African-Americans polled agreed with the jury's verdict of not guilty, and many of those thought that Simpson had been framed by the Los Angeles Police Department. More than 60% of the European-Americans disagreed with the verdict, and many of those thought that Simpson was judged not guilty because of a majority black jury (Decker 1995, A36).

Suddenly the cultural event and the cultural icons were doing what icons are expected to do, opening a window into reality. Through the window, deep passions were surfaced: racial prejudices, fears, stereotypes, and hatreds; competition between issues of gender and race; fears of spousal abuse and fears of ignoring spousal abuse; and deep distrust of power systems and of people different from oneself. The country's story was laid bare – if for only a moment.

One of the most revealing aspects of this case is the subjectivity of the public, who were shaped by multiple histories, fears, and hopes. Here I am not speaking about the subjectivity of lawyers or jurors, whose internal motivations cannot be fully known. I am speaking about the subjectivity of the general public, whose passionate cries of joy and disappointment communicate a great deal about knowing. What people knew and the ethical judgments they made were shaped by political realities and by their social locations within historical and political contexts.

As a white woman who has heard too many stories of domestic violence in my lifetime, I was convinced that Simpson was guilty. I was disappointed in the verdict. But as a white Southern woman, I was able to say to myself within two or three minutes after the verdict that in US history too many African-Americans have been convicted for crimes they did not do and too many European-Americans have been released for crimes they did do. In reflecting on my responses, I had to admit to myself something that I did *not* want to know, namely, that my knowing is trapped in my white woman's body. Not only is knowing a political activity, but also my knowing is political, and so is everyone else's.

Wisdom as Questing to know God and the World

The purpose of this section of the essay is to explore *the meaning of wisdom as questing to know God and the world in a deep and responsive way*. Wisdom is questing for intimate relationship. Such a view echoes Sharon Warner's idea that knowing is an intra-experiential affair that is dynamic and grows out of experience. Warner further identifies faith knowing as knowing "deep truth," which, like all knowing, arises from experience and forms one's identity (1993, 2, 12). What, then, is experience? Experience can be understood simply as living in relationships and participating actively with God and the world; thus, experience is the fabric out of which wisdom is made.

As I consider the case studies analyzed above, I am aware that the cases themselves – and the fears they arouse – are evidence that questing takes place as people live in the messy middle of relationships. The cases are probably evidence also that people are trying to avoid the demands of questing, for wisdom has to do both with knowing deeply and with responding to that which is known. Here is where the correspondence with the work of Thomas Groome becomes most clear.

When Groome speaks about conation, he identifies it with wisdom. He defines conation as the holistic knowing of "agent-subjects-in-relationship," that is, the totality of knowing that weaves together theoretical consciousness with desire and the will to act (1991, 26–32) [...].

On the surface, the understanding of knowing that is presented in this essay seems to be the same as that of Groome [...] and it is very similar. The differences are probably three: that the view of wisdom presented here is an active questing (more verb than noun); that knowing is understood as formed of internal as well as external relationships; and, that the view itself is embedded in social analysis. I use the term "probably" in identifying differences, for they are differences of degree more than of kind. Certainly, Groome's understanding of conation is an active process, and he does consider how our personal and communal stories intertwine. Also, his pedagogical method begins with social analysis; in other words, to 1) name/express "present praxis," and 2) to reflect critically on present action.

What is most significant here, however, is the emphasis placed by Groome on wisdom and its significance for human action. On this matter, his view and mine flow together into a larger river where attention can be focused on the power of wisdom and the urgency of questing. To this we now turn, giving particular attention to two movements of wisdom: questing to know God and questing for ourselves and the world.

Questing to Know God

One clear movement of wisdom is the yearning to know God, a seemingly primal yearning among people living in theistic religious cultures. In analyzing the case study of the Re-Imagining Conference, some clear implications for knowing God were identified: that views of God are deep in human psyches; that God is known through experience and relationship; that God cannot be controlled by definitions; and, that religious understandings of God are inextricably bound with the entirety of religious and ethical systems.

In its most primal form, the yearning to know God is not the yearning to know about God, or to define the nature or qualities of God. The yearning is rather to be in relation to God. And the experience of being in relation is accompanied by another yearning, that is, the yearning to express and respond to that experience Such a yearning leads to actions in the world and to language, dance, painting, and music, but it is never fully embodied in these human expressions. It is always beyond.

To speak about yearning to know God sounds quite idealistic, but it actually takes many forms. When David Wolpe, a Conservative Rabbi, faced the sudden illness of his mother after a stroke, he was stunned. He described his response:

> I prayed for the recovery of my mother, but with very mixed emotions. Part of me felt that it was like treating God like the Doctor in the Sky. The philosopher Martin Buber cautions us not to treat God as an "it," as a celestial dispensary of gifts, as a Being whose purpose is to grant wishes, however urgent. I was not seeking relationship, closeness, intimacy with God. All the things I preached as a Rabbi slipped from my grasp. I was a consumer, a desperate consumer of the goods God is said to harbor – health, magic, miracle. I wanted my mother cured. Yet I did not believe that God worked that way. Still I prayed (1992, 21–2)

In this moment David Wolpe was faced with two realities regarding the human yearning for relationship with God. He was aware that the more profound yearning is for closeness and intimacy, but yearning for God can also take the form of desperation. Wolpe judged his own yearning inadequate in this moment, but he reported, "Still I prayed."

Perhaps prayer is the most profound symbol of the yearning to know God. Wolpe pointed out that "the ultimate aim of prayer, at most times, is not to ask, nor to be answered. The aim of prayer is to pray" (153). What arises from prayer is the opportunity "to express oneself, to seek understanding, to bring forth out of the inchoate and jumbled bits of the self an expression of what is real, and what is true" (ibid., 153–4). This view of prayer again reveals how intimately tied are the yearning to know God and the yearning to know oneself.

Yearning to know God is not expressed only in direct discourse with God, but also in discourse with other people about God and the world. No sharp distinction should be made between discourse with God and discourse about God, for our language about God is a strong influence on our relationship with God. Certainly the strong feelings toward the Re-Imagining Conference reveal that. Discourse about God and the world takes many forms – for instance, narrative, dogmatic, conceptual, metaphorical, visual, musical, and kinesthetic. In these many forms, the discourse can function to reinforce existing worldviews and social or ecclesial structures, or it can function to subvert and, perhaps, to reframe the same.

In this regard, Rebecca Chopp's call for a "discourse of emancipatory transformation" is critical (1989, 21–4). She insists that one of the greatest needs of our day is "to speak to and of what we love, and what, in a world of destruction and death, we know as beautiful" (24). We need to be engaged in discourse about what really matters – namely, what is good, just, and beautiful. Our ability to know God will actually be nurtured, formed, and re-formed as we engage in talk that matters – in other words, in discourse that contributes to emancipating and transforming the world. In short, our discourses *with* God and our discourses *about* God go together and affect one another. The questing to know God includes both.

Questing for Ourselves and the World

A second movement of wisdom is questing for ourselves and the world – namely, questing to understand and respond to ourselves and to the human and ecological contexts in which we live. Epistemological issues are both philosophical and theological, and they are inevitably complex; but the grounding of these issues is very important. Thus, one cannot deal adequately with theories of knowing without considering the contextual reality of those who know. The case of the Simpson verdict reveals starkly that the knowing of the general public is shaped by the different contextual realities in which people live.

To speak in this way is to join with Rebecca Chopp in seeking a contextual critical method for religious education. In rethinking Christian theological education, she examines three factors: the subjects of theological education, the larger cultural movements and changes, and the symbolic patterns of Christian practice (1995, 12–15). These insights are appropriate also to religious education. [...] To design religious education without consideration of these contextual factors is to avoid knowing ourselves.

For Chopp, the contextual critical method is necessary in knowing God, and also in knowing the world and oneself. This emphasis is the heritage of feminism, and it demands critique of every concept and theory, including one's own. The racist heritage of white feminism further underscores the urgency of self-critique and social analysis. It also underscores a necessity for the many colors of feminism, womanism, mujerista theology, and the necessity of theologies formed by women and men in all corners of the world. To know the world is to know more than one's own experience, but to know a world of vast and richly diverse experience.

Education and Wisdom

What is the role of religious education when wisdom is controversial and filled with fear? What is the role when central symbols are being questioned in the name of emancipatory transformation, but alternative symbols are being scorned and the fear of these alternatives is near panic? [...]

If education is to support and enhance knowing, then educators will need in some way to engage people in experiencing, exploring, deconstructing, and reconstructing symbols. And if knowing is relational, then the starting point for engaging symbols will be those very symbols that emerge as people relate with God and the world.

Educating as Questing to Know and Respond to God

If questing for God is questing for relationship, then an urgent educational goal is to inspire and support people in relating with God. The yearning to know God lies deep in the human psyche and is central to religious education, at least in theistic religious traditions. David Kelsey, in writing about Christian theological education, identified the purpose as understanding God more truly (1992). Expanding the boundaries of his definition, he stated that the heart of religious education could be understood as a quest to know and respond to God. And at its heart, this quest is a search to be in relationship with God.

One educational task is to quest for God through a rhythm of expressive action and silence. Human expression – namely, speaking, laughing, crying, and acting – is the way by which we embody and make public our experience of God and the world. It is also the way we communicate our experiences with others. And silence is the way by which we listen for God, listen to the rhythms of the earth and sky and sea, and listen to our own heartbeat.

Wolpe affirms something similar by appealing to the dynamics of speech and silence. He reaches into his Jewish tradition to affirm that "speech and silence together form the path that leads to the presence of God" (Wolpe 1992, xiii). Though his own accent is on speech, he acknowledges that silence is "the background from which speech arises and to which it returns" (7). It is not simply an empty background, however; it is a way of knowing. In Wolpe's view, silence is that which abides "after we exhaust ourselves in words" (7).

Human expression includes more than speech, but we can focus first on speaking, for that act is rooted so deeply in Jewish, Christian, and Muslim traditions. Wolpe [...] describes a practice in some traditional Jewish communities in which children enter *cheder*, or religious school, with the experience of facing a chart of letters covered with honey. The children are asked to lick the honey from the letters, thus learning that "learning is sweet, and the very letters of the words carry the sweetness." Wolpe concluded, "Study is so sweet because it is wresting meaning from the world" (147). [...]

I propose, however, that speech is too narrow to become the sole focus of human expressive acts. The acts of caring for children, visiting elders in the community, administering a church council, registering a political protest, planting vegetables, recycling resources, dancing, making music, and creating visual arts only begin to name the human expressions that will come forward. The expressions are limitless. But education, if it is to be a questing to know and respond to God, will need to invite people into silence and into all modes of human expression, encouraging people to enter deeply into the quietness and encouraging them to speak words and perform actions that express the deepest truths of their experience.

Another urgent educational task is to face daring questions and to address these questions to God and to one another (as Chopp proposes in emancipatory discourse). Certainly, the Re-Imagining Conference has become a central symbol in the quest to know God, and it is filled with daring questions. The symbol has quite different meanings from community to community, but engage the symbol we must. Robert Olmstead said just this to his United Methodist congregation:

> It is healthy for us to debate whether the Spirit of truth was moving at the Re-Imagining conference. I think it is sad and discouraging that so many men seem threatened when women see God (find God, experience God) in feminine imagery. What is the place for this feminine Wisdom which has been with God since the beginning? Well, she has crashed the theological party. And I am happy to welcome her! (1995, 8–9)

Olmstead's sermon was followed by spontaneous applause. Perhaps the applause itself says something about the yearning people carry to know God and to face controversial questions with open inquiry and vigorous courage.

Such a yearning to know God is not limited to people who applaud Olmstead's sermon. It is also represented in people who engage the symbol of the Re-Imagining Conference with disdain, and who interpret the symbol as cause for protest rather than applause. What is most urgent is that people be encouraged to: engage such a symbol; explore its meanings, including its historical and contextual (political, economic, and ecclesial) meanings; and recognize their engagement as an act of questing to know God.

Education as Seeking to Know Ourselves and the World

Wisdom has to do with questing for ourselves, namely, questing to understand and respond to ourselves and the human and ecological contexts in which we live. This leads to yet another educational *goal of encouraging people to know themselves and to relate with the world around them with depth and integrity*. It has to do with knowing the land, waters, plants, and animals with which we live. It has to do with coming to know the multivalent social reality: the people with whom we work and play, the people in our cities and towns, the people in our religious communities past and present, and the social structures in which we participate. It has to do with knowing our own bodies, with their rhythms; it has to do with knowing our passions, hopes, and fears.

The literature on multicultural education is particularly helpful as regards social context, for it is filled with reminders to listen to the sounds of unique people and diverse cultures. Peter McLaren says that we need a "critical multiculturalism" (as opposed to conservative, liberal, or left-liberal multiculturalism). He urges that we "take up the issue of 'difference' in ways that don't replay the monocultural essentialism of the 'centrisms' – Anglocentrism, Eurocentrism, phallocentrism, androcentrism, and the like" (1994, 57).

By recognizing difference, we can listen more acutely to the dreams and intuitions inside ourselves, and the dreams and intuitions of our neighbors. By recognizing difference, we are more likely to listen to ourselves and others without imposing invisible requirements that everyone fit prescribed categories. By recognizing difference, we are more likely to attend to the silent partners of the earth – namely, the plants, animals, and soil.

Difference is not the last word, however, for we also need to attend to acts of solidarity. If education is seeking to know ourselves and the world, then education includes responding. McLaren speaks about this as "alliance-building" (1994, 57). In other words, solidarity cannot simply be distant appreciation or interest in exotic differences, but it needs to be a genuine understanding, appreciation, and standing with others. For religious communities, this means genuine engagement with diverse peoples within the community, in other religious communities, and in the public forum; it also means joining together to act on issues of common concern. This is what it means to know ourselves and the world: to know the rich colors and textures of life, to respond with awe and respect, and to do justice for the well-being of all God's creation.

Conclusion: Education as Searching Together for What We do not Know

This discussion about wisdom ends with an admonition for us to be real with God and others. [...]

[...]

To this end, education needs to help people explore below the surface, to go ever deeper into questions. [...]

[...] We have circled back to the idea of wisdom as questing to know God and the world in a deep and responsive way. This view of knowing is relational; it has to do with sensitivity toward that which is known and imagination toward the unknown.

The accumulation of facts or the mastery of skills are only important if they nourish relationships. In a relational view of knowing and a relational approach to education, one inevitably meets that which one does not know. A person or community is laid bare to discover yet again what is not known, to be disrupted (sometimes uncomfortably), and to be inspired once again to continue the journey, to continue the quest. [...]

Note

1 The original version of this paper included two more fears: the fear rooted in not finding answers and the fear that originates in what we do not know.

References

Chopp, Rebecca S. 1989. *The Power to Speak Feminism, Language, God*. New York: Crossroad.

_____ 1995. *Saving Work. Feminist practices of theological education*. Louisville, KY: Westminster/John Knox.

Decker, Cathleen. 1995. "Most in County Disagree with Simpson Verdicts." *Los Angeles Times*, 8 October 1995 Al, A36–7.

Groome, Thomas H. 1991. *Sharing Faith. A Comprehensive Approach to Religious Education and Pastoral Ministry – The Way of Shared Praxis*. San Francisco: Harper.

Johnson, Elizabeth A. 1994. *She Who is The Mystery of God in Feminist Theological Discourse*. New York: Crossroad.

Keller, Catherine. 1994. "Inventing the Goddess. A study of Ecclesial Backlash," *The Christian Century* 6 April.

Kelsey, David H. 1992. *To Understand God Truly. What's Theological About a Theological School*. Louisville, KY: Westminster/John Knox.

McLaren, Peter. 1994. "White Terror and Oppositional Agency. Towards a Critical Multiculturalism." *Multiculturalism: A Critical Reader*, ed. David Theo Goldberg. Cambridge, MA: Basil Blackwell 45–74.

Oden, Thomas C. 1995. *Requiem. A Lament in Three Movements*. Nashville: Abingdon.

Olmstead, Robert. 1995. *Sophia crashes the Trinity*. Sermon preached at First United Methodist Church, Palo Alto, CA, 11 June, 8–9.

Warner, Sharon Ruth. 1993. *Knowing as an Intra-Experiential Affair. Toward an Epistemology of Religious Formation*. PhD dissertation, School of Theology at Claremont, California.

Wolpe, David J. 1992. *In Speech and in Silence. The Jewish Quest for God*. New York: Henry Holt and Company.

26

Words Made Flesh (1999)*

Elaine Graham

Introduction

In Stephen Pattison's forward to Elaine Graham's collection *Words Made Flesh: Writings in Pastoral and Practical Theology* (2009), he crowns Graham "dean of British practical theologians" (p. v), mentioning among her many achievements her work as founding chair of the British and Irish Association for Practical Theology. Her entrance into practical theology began through the social sciences and participation in Britain's Student Christian Movement and university chaplaincy. She was appointed to a chair in practical theology at Manchester University in 1998 after completing doctoral studies ten year earlier, the first woman and layperson in Britain to hold such a post. She currently holds a chair at University of Chester where she is also Canon Professor of Chester Cathedral. The title *Words Made Flesh* "says it all" (p. x), she remarks in her introduction to the book, capturing her conviction about the intermingling of sacred and secular in the everyday. In her work, she searches the "'vernacular' of ordinary life" (p. x) for the transcendent, seeking a theology interwoven within practice.

The following essay post-dates by a few years Graham's influential book *Transforming Practice: Pastoral Theology in an Age of Uncertainty* (1996) and carries forward its agenda. She defines practical theology as a performative discipline that "excavates" practice and adheres to norms of *orthopraxis* rather than right belief. If theology is "enacted and embodied in Christian practice" (p. 3), as she argues in *Transforming Practice*, then practical theology must become a kind of "*critical phenomenology*" devoted to "excavating" the "norms which inhabit pastoral *praxis*" (p. 140). Although she begins the essay below by using *pastoral* and *practical* interchangeably, similar to her usage in her book, we can see the early stages of her growing sense that *practical* best describes the broader horizon of the study of practice and *pastoral* the more interpersonal dimensions of care. She uses pastoral care as an instance of a practice most proximate to the emergence of theology on the ground. Caring for sick and dying bodies is where we find a "practice to match the theory" and "new patterns of relationship" that go beyond simply talking

Original publication details: Elaine Graham, "Words Made Flesh: Women, Embodiment and Practical Theology," pp. 109–21 from *Feminist Theology* 21 (1999).

conceptually about ways to think about the divine. If such practices genuinely inform and transform theology, then theology can gain "new impetus" by heeding developments in practical theology. Practical theology is designed to "bring bodies into speech" in illness, disability, and other sites of bodily duress (e.g., gender, race, sexuality, age, and economy). Bodily knowledge is not just of epistemological weight but also of moral consequence. The "'ultimate epistemological issue is justice itself.'"

The reverse ordering of essays in the *Reader*, beginning with twenty-first century writings in Part I and placing twentieth-century material in Part II, puts this essay last in the book. But, as is true for *Transforming Practice* (1996) more generally, this essay serves as a powerful turning point, written in 1999 as one century ends and the next opens, pushing practical theology to fresh places. Therefore, her essay changes the *Reader* from a linear document, read from start to finish, into a circle, leading naturally back to where the *Reader* starts with an investigation of theology through place, bodies, and practical know-how.

Suggested Further Reading

- Elaine L. Graham, *Making the Difference: Gender, Personhood and Theology* (London: Mowbray, 1995).
- Elaine L. Graham, *Transforming Practice: Pastoral Theology in an Age of Uncertainty* (London: Mowbray, 1996).
- Nancy L. Eiseland, *The Disabled God: Toward a Liberatory Theology of Disability* (Nashville: Abingdon, 1994).

***

In this article, I want to contribute to the development of what the North American theologian James Nelson has termed "Body Theology".[1] Feminist theology has famously characterized the dualism of classical Christianity – and in particular, its valuing of the spiritual over the material – as one of the fundamental aspects of the denigration and subordination of women.[2] One of the corollaries of this is the ambivalence, to say the least, exhibited by the Christian tradition towards the facts of human embodiment. However, in what follows, I wish to argue two things: first, that critical attention to the experience of embodiment is a necessary, if problematic, aspect of women's passage from subordination to selfhood; and secondly, that an exploration of the pastoral, ethical and theological dimensions of embodiment might point us towards a new model of "Body Theology" from a practical theological perspective. I will propose that embodiment is more than an "issue" exciting our compassion; rather, it points us to the performative, incarnational nature of all theology. I want to argue that bodily *practice* is the agent and the vehicle of divine disclosure; and the faithful practices of the Body of Christ are "sacraments" of suffering and redemption. Feminist theology is finding new impetus, I believe, from its encounter with practical or pastoral theology. [...]

In recent years, feminist writers have broken new ground in the discipline of pastoral or practical theology.[3] New insights are bringing distinctively feminist perspectives to bear on the area of women giving and receiving pastoral care.[4] Feminist practical theologians are seeking to address issues of gender and power in the churches; and to correct the androcentric nature of pastoral care. The central concern has been to expose systems of patriarchal theory and practice that create and justify a world in which women are ignored or misunderstood and to call attention to "...a gap between the promise of redemption and liberation on the one hand, and on the other the reality of subtle or brutal marginalization and exploitation of women going on inside and outside the churches".[5] [...] But alongside the critical task there is a reconstructive project too: a more adequate theological language and appropriate models of pastoral care through which women can articulate a more credible and liberative account of their lives, relationships and spiritual aspirations.

Feminist practical theology is not simply committed to challenging the status quo, but also to finding forms of healing and empowerment for women: a practice to match the theory. It is this insistence that care cannot be conducted without critical and rigorous analysis, that practice and theology are inseparable, that distinguishes such work. These pioneers of a feminist practical theology, a discipline both critical and reconstructive, offer hope for the renewal of the Christian community, a renewal characterized by new patterns of relationship as well as new apprehensions of the divine.

[...]

This quest for authoritative spaces from which women can speak for themselves is reflected in many works in feminist practical theology.[6] [...] Yet while I concur with the importance of such a project, I cannot simply assume that once women start telling their stories they will instantly shed the false illusions of patriarchal accounts and emerge, free of oppression, as the tellers of completely authentic, totally self-actualized narratives. The transition from silence to speech is never easy.

One example of the problems feminist-inspired theory and practice has encountered in attempting to articulate a more "genuine" account of women's lives may be seen in relation to the issue of embodiment. In the drive for women's self-definition the nature of embodied subjectivity has proved difficult and controversial. Patriarchal representations [...] portray women as misbegotten and abnormal males, inhabiting a lesser sphere of nature and emotion, in contrast to men who occupy the superior world of culture, reason and transcendence.[7] With such a dualistic characterization, however, goes a further association: of women equated with the body and men with the mind. Women are thus denigrated and excluded from the cultural domain by virtue of their links with the non-rational, capricious and profane body.

Feminist theory and politics have therefore inherited an ambivalence towards the body. "Liberal" feminists prefer to reclaim women's rationality and intellectual equality with men, regarding embodiment as a barrier to emancipation. Simone de Beauvoir is a famous example of such a perspective, arguing that femininity is so associated with body, sex and finitude that if women are to aspire to autonomy they must transcend their bodiliness.[8]

Other feminists seeking to ground a claim for women's distinctive or oppositional experience within bodily difference have been derided as "essentialists" uncritically valorizing a fixed biological foundation for gender difference, merely reversing but not abolishing the determinism of patriarchal gender dualism. [...] But there are signs of new approaches to embodiment. Francophone traditions of "writing the body", which were initially interpreted as essentialist by Anglo-American feminists, have now been reappraised as constituting not a collapse into the discourse of biological determinism, but a new way of configuring the relationship between bodily representation and identity.[9] [...] Women reclaim the right to exercise their own "imaginations" in speaking, acting and writing the body; and the authoritative nature of this process lies in its ability to envision and make possible a more wholesome human community:

> The epistemic authority of such experiences lies not in their ontological foundations in some absolute truth, but in their possible moral status: namely, to what extent do such experiences sustain, advance, enhance, or extend a socionatural environment conducive to perpetuating further human creativity itself? In short, the ultimate epistemological issue is justice itself.[10]

I have argued so far that [...] a feminist practical theology needs to seek ways of bringing bodies into speech, both in the ways it reconstructs practical caring and reconfigures our images of the divine. Practical theology will need to start by listening to people's experiences of embodiment, especially those places where appearance and reality seem out of step. The stories of giving and receiving care – which are always *embodied* stories – are the ideal vantage-point from which to begin. Those who give and receive pastoral care are confronting all the time [with] dilemmas of illness, sexuality, poverty, disability and ageing. And the pastoral encounter itself is always necessarily and variously embodied: the touch, be it informal or as a ritual of anointing or healing; or the reassurance of eye contact, the one-to-one conversation.

So practical theology begins with embodied experience in its practice of care; but its theology is never disembodied, either. It seems to me that practical theology is well-placed to affirm the centrality to Christian life of Word and sacrament as a concrete, tangible expression of the divine-human encounter. After all, at the heart of the Christian faith is the mystery of the incarnation: of God sharing human life in the form of the person of Jesus. [...] A practical theology that tells stories of embodiment can really examine what it might mean for God to be revealed in a human *body*, broken and suffering, whose resurrection proclaims that Love is stronger than death.

[...]

Where's the Body?

We may wish to regard our bodies as the most intimate and transparent repository of information about ourselves, but the ambivalence within feminism shows that bodies are never innocent of social construction or unmarked by the dynamics of power and difference. Bodies are therefore both the agents and objects of culture, "both location and artefact of human imagination...",[11] creative imagining subjects and socially constructed products. [...] Formerly subordinate groups, defined and constrained by patriarchal constructions, have sought to find new, more empowering ways of talking about themselves as bodily agents as well as objects. Black, gay and lesbian, subaltern or postcolonial, feminist or disabled political movements and critical theories have provided such space: but those who speak from the vantage-point of such subject-positions often still find themselves defined in opposition to a hegemonic and unexamined norm of white, able-bodied, first-world straight masculinity which is never itself required to own up to its own embodied nature. What would it mean for men to "write their bodies"? There is an urgent need for dominant, privileged groups to become critical about their own racial, sexual and gender identity, and begin to make it possible for everyone to think from the Body; or else bodily experience is restricted to a property of those speaking from a position of "difference", which in practice means the abnormal, problematic, victimized body. It is therefore essential that embodiment is affirmed as a common human trait, even though our experiences may be diverse and characterized by inequality of representation, access to resources and self-determination.

[...]

In seeking more nuanced and constructive ways of bearing witness to human embodiment, therefore, I look for clues [...] in social theory and cultural studies which makes a shift from the formal analysis of "the Body" to the more narrational and phenomenological emphasis on "our bodies".[12]

A constant theme in this literature is the sense in which, far from being mute and agnostic,[13] bodies offer us epiphanies of meaning, which, whilst locating us firmly in space and time, also take us beyond mere flesh and blood to confront and reveal deeper threads. Consistently such accounts focus on the disclosive nature of pain and suffering; the power of illness to take us beyond the limits of taken-for-grantedness, out to the margins of existence.

Some writers attribute this to the disruptive nature of pain or illness. Leder argues that phenomenologically the "normally" functioning body is self-effacing: most bodily activities, such as digestion and muscle functioning, occur at such an automatic and unconscious level that we are hardly aware of their taking place.[14] The usual task of bodily movement is actually to take us beyond our material existence, into a world of communication and creation: a kind of self-transcendence which Leder terms the "ecstatic".[15] But pain renders our customary disregard for bodily functioning problematic:

> [...]No event more radically and inescapably reminds us of our bodily presence. Yet at the same time pain effects a certain alienation... The painful body is often experienced as something foreign to the self.[16]

So this rupture of pain brings uncertainty and disorientation, halting us in our tracks, silencing our usual bodily fluency. Yet the very strangeness of such bodily dissonance compels us to explore its contours more thoroughly; because however strange and unsettling, however unrecognizable and distorted the world of pain may be, it invites us beyond the margins of taken-for-granted existence into new, uncharted territory.

Other sources develop this revelatory theme of dissonant bodies, arguing for the inherently moral nature of such bodily testimonies. The locatedness and specificity of the body in pain, and its journey to the edges of existence, constitutes an ethical imperative to counter the relativism of postmodern theory in the form of the cry of suffering:

> Ultimately there would be no ethics of the body, but rather all ethics would take the body as its fundamental point of departure... The reason is simple: only bodies suffer. Only by a studied concentration on the body can we bear adequate witness to this suffering. Only an ethics or a social science which witnesses suffering is worthy of our energies or attention.[17]

However, I wonder whether the narrative disclosure of suffering bodies might not also be echoed by other kinds of bodies-in-extremis. I say this, mindful of my earlier point about a practical theological hermeneutics of the body needing to eschew accounts of bodily experience which assume that only "abnormal" bodies are real. [...] This reminds us that we are all prone to cyclical fluctuations of bodily well-being and that any kind of demarcation – most especially an ontological distinction – between able/disabled actually polarizes and distorts lived experience.

[...] Stories of bodily experience that transgress boundaries and unsettle taken-for-granted categories literally bring us to our senses, bringing us face-to-face with the artifice of even the most intimate aspects of our world. We realize how the abstract forces of economic, religious, cultural and political power may also be written on our bodies; how the texture of embodiment renders tangible the texts of social construction.[18] As well as stories of suffering bodies, therefore, I would wish to privilege other narratives that challenge ideas of bodily naturalism, fixity or uniform ability. Such bodily ambivalence and dislocation affords opportunities to review the way in which the underlying values of our culture are enacted and embodied, through the eyes and voices of those whose bodily integrity or identity has been discounted or denied by the hegemonic mainstream.

So bodies offer a "vantage-point" from which the complexity of human nature, as creator and creation of culture, can be experienced and analyzed. Bodies are the bearers of important narratives, some of which unsettle superficial or entrenched understandings; and such unexpected stories excite compassion and serve as the foundation for new moral narratives of hope and obligation.

But in focusing on the disclosive potential of such narratives of exclusion and ambivalence, we are also invited to encounter the theological dimensions of such a commitment. To what extent can narratives of embodiment act as disclosures of divine reality and activity; bodies as incarnating theological truth-claims?

One case-study may help to illustrate how a practical theology of embodiment enables us to appreciate the complexity of bodily experience as well as suggesting ways in which the creative potential of bodies might be brought to life. [...]

The significance of Nancy Eiseland's book, *The Disabled God* is limited if we pigeon-hole it into a special category of "theology of disability".[19] In fact, Eiseland avoids the objectification of disability as an "issue" of interest only to those directly affected, or else merely requiring the compassion and concern of the able-bodied. Instead, Eiseland transforms a "theology of disability" into a practical theology of embodiment, in which all bodies – albeit diverse and heterogeneous – become sources of experiential and theological disclosure.

[...]

Bodies as "Sacraments" of the Divine

The theological significance of the broken body is firmly privileged in Eiseland's practical theology. She illustrates how disabled lives might be a revelation of Christ-like ministry in today's church and world. In the bodies of those living with chronic illness and disabilities, we glimpse the suffering but transfigured incarnation of the Almighty: the scandal of the divine embodied in a finite, broken human body – "God in a sip-puff wheelchair". Eiseland embraces a theology of the Cross from the vantage-point of bodies rendered problematic by exclusive definitions of physical normality and integrity, and turns such judgments on their head. The disabled God is at work in the broken bodies of the faithful; not all-powerful, nor helpless, but a survivor, interdependent with others in mutual care.[20]

[…] Eiseland does not content herself with merely stating this theology as a matter of disembodied principle, or with a call for a change of attitudes. She takes her argument into the realm of Christian pastoral *practice*, and discusses in particular how the enacted and performative realms of liturgy and ritual might themselves be embodiments of her theology of disability. So the emphasis is on how faithful (and corporate) practice might enable people of faith to relate and enact stories of suffering and redemption. Eiseland focuses upon the Eucharist as a sacramental act that rehearses and incarnates the drama of a body crucified and resurrected. The corporate communion of the eucharistic body of Christ is the visible sign of a practice of resistance to exclusive and foreclosive understandings of personhood, opening our horizons to a more generous apprehension of the nature of God. The Eucharist, for Eiseland, incarnates (in liturgical practice) the "disabled God" in whom the signs of suffering and impairment are shown not as weakness or failure but as strength and solidarity.[21]

I have thus been arguing that the task of the practical theologian is to examine how (embodied) pastoral practices constitute a "Christian" (or faithful) identity – an identity which, of course, is always already performative. We thus begin with bodily experience, in the narratives of our bodies;[22] but we end, too, with bodily practices and sacraments as the incarnations of the divine in our midst. […]

A practical theology of the body/our bodies is therefore never merely the statement of principles; more the cultivation of the *habitus* of the body[23] whereby the words of suffering and redemption may become flesh. If theological values have any substance, they will exist in primary form as bodily practices – clinical, liturgical, kerygmatic, prophetic – and only derivatively as doctrines and concepts. Practical theology essentially gives voice to the "body language" of the Christian faith.

[…]

Practical theologians, whatever their context, are seeking to make sense of the values that underpin faithful and purposeful practices of care. It is in humanity's flawed and faltering attempts to realize the values of unconditional love, healing and liberation that the divine is ultimately revealed. So it is precisely in the dynamics and practices of human care that Christians embody their truth-claims.[24] Bodily practices are sacraments of the divine at work in human relationships; and the vocation of the Body of Christ is thus, as Melanie May has put it, to "become the flesh of our words".[25]

Notes

1 J.B. Nelson, *Body Theology* (Louisville, KY: Westminster/John Knox Press, 1992).

2 Rosemary Ruether, *Sexism and God-Talk* (Boston: Beacon Press, 1983).

3 For the purposes of this discussion, I shall be using these terms interchangeably.

4 See D. Ackermann and R. Bons-Storm (eds.), *Liberating Faith Practices: Feminist Practical Theologies in Context* (Leuven: Peeters, 1998), for a recent collection of feminist perspectives from Europe, South Africa, North America and Australasia.

5 R. Bons-Storm, *The Incredible Woman: Listening to Women's Silences in Pastoral Care and Counseling* (Nashville: Abingdon Press, 1996), 15.

6　See E.L. Graham and M. Halsey (eds.), *Life-Cycles: Women and Pastoral Care* (London: SPCK, 1993); J.S. Moessner (ed.), *Through the Eyes of Women: Insights for Pastoral Care* (Philadelphia: Westminster/John Knox Press, 1996); B. Miller- MacLemore, *Also a Mother: Work and Family as Theological Dilemma* (Nashville: Abingdon Press, 1994).

7　See E.L. Graham, *Making the Difference: Gender, Personhood and Theology* (London: Mowbray, 1995), esp. chap. 1; and G. Lloyd, *The Man of Reason: "Male" and "Female" in Western Philosophy* (London: Methuen, 1984).

8　S. de Beauvoir, *The Second Sex* (London: Picador, 1979).

9　R. Braidotti, "The Politics of Ontological Difference", in T. Brennan (ed.), *Between Feminism and Psychoanalysis* (London: Routledge, 1989), 89–105.

10　P.M. Cooey, *Religious Imagination and the Body* (New York: Oxford University Press, 1994), 116.

11　Cooey, *Religious Imagination and the Body*, p. 7.

12　Graham, *Making the Difference*, pp. 128–9.

13　A play on words: incapable of giving knowledge, but with undertones of agnosticism.

14　Drew Leder, *The Absent Body* (Chicago: University of Chicago Press, 1990), chap. 2.

15　Leder, *The Absent Body*, chapter 1.

16　*The Absent Body*, p. 76.

17　Arthur Frank, "For a Sociology of the Body: an Analytical Review", in M. Featherstone, M. Hepworth and B.S. Turner (eds.), *The Body: Social Process and Cultural Theory* (London: Sage, 1991), 95–96, my emphasis. […]

18　David Schenck, "The Texture of Embodiment: Foundation for Medical Ethics", *Human Studies* 9 (1989), 43–54.

19　N.L. Eiseland, *The Disabled God: Toward a Liberatory Theology of Disability* (Nashville: Abingdon Press, 1994), chap. 1.

20　*The Disabled God*, p. 103.

21　*The Disabled God*, p. 114.

22　Might this involve a new understanding of the "living human document" of Clinical Pastoral Education? See Evans B. Holifield, *A History of Pastoral Care in America* (Nashville: Abingdon Press, 1983), 244–7.

23　Edward Farley, *Theologia: The Fragmentation and Unity of Theological Education* (Philadelphia: Fortress Press, 1983) advances a *habitus* model of practical theology as the discipline which cultivates faithful *praxis*.

24　See E.L. Graham, *Transforming Practice: Pastoral Theology in an Age of Uncertainty* (London: Mowbray, 1996).

25　Melanie A. May, *A Body Knows: A Theopoetics of Death and Resurrection* (New York: Continuum, 1995), 88.

Index

Page references to Figures are followed by the letter 'f', while references to Tables are followed by the letter 't'. References to Notes are indicated by the page number followed by 'n' and the Note number.

a

Acevedo, Labor Gómez   76n8
Achermann, Denise   363, 381n4
Acosta, José de   7–8
Action Research Church Society (ARCS),
     UK   233, 236n45
Adams, Júlio Cézar   13, 17n59
Adorno, Theodor W.   123
Advent   84
Affirmative Action/Equal Employment
     Opportunity (AA/EEO)
     employers   130
Africa
  Anlo-Ewe language   159–161
  bodily knowledge   157
  Candomblé   162
  religious diaspora   157–159,
     162–165, 166
  traditional healers   157–159, 161, 165
African American communities   5, 97
  see also Black churches; Black religion;
     Black theology
  bodily proprieties   99
  chasm between religious practitioners
     and Black academics   216–217
  chasm between students and theological
     education   215–216
  clergy   210, 214
  folk traditions, religious   23–28, 33
African Methodist Episcopal Church   212

African Methodist Episcopal Zion Sunday
     School Union   212
African Religious Traditions (ARTs)   159
agbagbadodo (balancing)   160–161
Agren, David   89n16
Alarcón, Norma   174, 175, 184n2, 184n8,
     185n18, 185n20
Alegría, Ricardo E   76n2
All Lives Matter movement   154
Allen, James   146
  Without Sanctuary   155n9
Allen, Richard   212
alopecia areata   149–150
alterity   109–112
alternative consciousness   25–26, 31, 34
Althaus-Reid, Marcella   105
  Indecent Theology   128
Alves, Rubero   107
American Academy of Religion (AAR)
     5, 8
Ammerman, Nancy   80
Anderson, Victor   23
Andraos, Michel Elias   197–207
Andrews, Dale P.   x, 23–36, 79, 194, 217
  Black Practical Theology   12, 16n54,
     24, 187
  Practical Theology for Black Churches
     23, 195n26
animism   69
Anlo-Ewe language   159–161

The Wiley Blackwell Reader in Practical Theology, First Edition. Edited by Bonnie J. Miller-McLemore.
© 2019 John Wiley & Sons Ltd. Published 2019 by John Wiley & Sons Ltd.